Welfare Economics
Volume III

The International Library of Critical Writings in Economics

Series Editor: Mark Blaug

Professor Emeritus, University of London, UK
Professor Emeritus, University of Buckingham, UK
Visiting Professor, University of Amsterdam, The Netherlands

This series is an essential reference source for students, researchers and lecturers in economics. It presents by theme a selection of the most important articles across the entire spectrum of economics. Each volume has been prepared by a leading specialist who has written an authoritative introduction to the literature included.

A full list of published and future titles in this series is printed at the end of this volume.

Wherever possible, the articles in these volumes have been reproduced as originally published using facsimile reproduction, inclusive of footnotes and pagination to facilitate ease of reference.

For a list of all Edward Elgar published titles visit our site on the World Wide Web at http://www.e-elgar.co.uk

Welfare Economics Volume III

Edited by

William J. Baumol

Director
CV Starr Center for Applied Economics, New York University, USA

and

Charles A. Wilson

Professor of Economics
New York University, USA

THE INTERNATIONAL LIBRARY OF CRITICAL WRITINGS IN ECONOMICS

An Elgar Reference Collection
Cheltenham, UK • Northampton, MA, USA

Published by
Edward Elgar Publishing Limited
Glensanda House
Montpellier Parade
Cheltenham
Glos GL50 1UA
UK

Edward Elgar Publishing, Inc.
136 West Street, Suite 202
Northampton
Massachusetts 01060
USA

A catalogue record for this book is available from the British Library.

Library of Congress Cataloging in Publication Data

Welfare economics / edited by William J. Baumol and Charles A. Wilson.
p. cm. — (International library of critical writings in economics ; 126)
Includes bibliographical references and index.
1. Welfare economics. I. Wilson, Charles A., 1948- II. Baumol, William J. III. Series.

HB99.3 .W432 2001
330.15'56—dc21 00–066239

ISBN 1 85278 200 5 (3 volume set)

Printed and bound in Great Britain by MPG Books Ltd, Bodmin, Cornwall

Contents

Acknowledgements

The editors and publishers wish to thank the authors and the following publishers who have kindly given permission for the use of copyright material.

Academic Press, Inc. for article: M. Boiteux (1971), 'On the Management of Public Monopolies Subject to Budgetary Constraints', *Journal of Economic Theory*, **3** (3), September, 219–40.

American Economic Association for articles: Harvey Averch and Leland L. Johnson (1962), 'Behavior of the Firm Under Regulatory Constraint', *American Economic Review*, **LII** (5), December, 1052–69; William J. Baumol and David F. Bradford (1970), 'Optimal Departures From Marginal Cost Pricing', *American Economic Review*, **LX**, 265–83; Peter A. Diamond and James A. Mirrlees (1971), 'Optimal Taxation and Public Production I: Production Efficiency', *American Economic Review*, **LXI** (1), March, 8–27; Peter A. Diamond and James A. Mirrlees (1971), 'Optimal Taxation and Public Production II: Tax Rules', *American Economic Review*, **LXI** (3, Part I), June, 261–78; William J. Baumol (1972), 'On Taxation and the Control of Externalities', *American Economic Review*, **LXII** (3), June, 307–22.

Blackwell Publishers Ltd for articles: F.P. Ramsey (1927), 'A Contribution to the Theory of Taxation', *Economic Journal*, **XXXVII** (145), March, 47–61; J.E. Meade (1952), 'External Economies and Diseconomies in a Competitive Situation', *Economic Journal*, **LXII** (245), March, 54–67; James M. Buchanan and Wm. Craig Stubblebine (1962), 'Externality', *Economica*, **XXIX** (113–116), New Series, November, 371–84.

Elsevier Science Ltd for articles: J.A. Ordover and R.D. Willig (1979), 'The Role of Information in Designing Social Policy Towards Externalities', *Journal of Public Economics*, **12** (3), December, 271–99; Jean-Jacques Laffont and Jean Tirole (1990), 'The Regulation of Multiproduct Firms – Part I: Theory' and 'The Regulation of Multiproduct Firms – Part II: Applications to Competitive Environments and Policy Analysis', *Journal of Public Economics*, **43**, 1–66.

Harvard Law Review Association for article: Phillip Areeda and Donald F. Turner (1975), 'Predatory Pricing and Related Practices Under Section 2 of the Sherman Act', *Harvard Law Review*, **88** (4), February, 697–733.

Her Majesty's Stationery Office for article: Stephen C. Littlechild (1983), *Regulation of British Telecommunications' Profitability*, February, 1–42.

Journal of Law and Economics, University of Chicago Law School for articles: R.H. Coase (1960), 'The Problem of Social Cost', *Journal of Law and Economics*, **III**, October, 1–44; Harold Demsetz (1968), 'Why Regulate Utilities?', *Journal of Law and Economics*, **XI**, April,

55–65; William J. Baumol (1996), 'Predation and the Logic of the Average Variable Cost Test', *Journal of Law and Economics*, **XXXIX** (1), April, 49–72.

Macmillan Press Ltd for excerpt: A.C. Pigou, M.A. (1952), excerpt from 'Divergences Between Marginal Social Net Product and Marginal Private Net Product', in *The Economics of Welfare*, Fourth Edition, Part II, Chapter IX, Paragraph 10, 183–8.

The Eli Broad Graduate School of Management, Michigan State University for excerpt: Robert D. Willig (1979), 'The Theory of Network Access Pricing', in Harry M. Trebing (ed.), *Issues in Public Utility Regulation*, 109–52.

MIT Press Books for excerpt: Alfred E. Kahn (1989), 'The Traditional Issues in the Pricing of Public Utility Services', in *The Economics of Regulation: Principles and Institutions*, Volume I, Chapter 2, 20–57.

MIT Press Journals for article: Dennis W. Carlton and Glenn C. Loury (1980), 'The Limitations of Pigouvian Taxes as a Long-Run Remedy for Externalities', *Quarterly Journal of Economics*, **XCV** (3), November, 559–66.

Oxford University Press for article: William J. Baumol and Robert D. Willig (1986), 'Contestability: Developments Since the Book', *Oxford Economic Papers*, **38**, Supplement, New Series, November, 9–36.

Public Utilities Reports, Inc. for article: William J. Baumol (1982), 'Productivity Incentive Clauses and Rate Adjustment for Inflation', *Public Utilities Fortnightly*, **110** (2), July, 11–18.

RAND for article: Ingo Vogelsang and Jörg Finsinger (1979), 'A Regulatory Adjustment Process for Optimal Pricing by Multiproduct Monopoly Firms', *Bell Journal of Economics*, **10** (1), Spring, 157–71.

Review of Economic Studies Ltd for article: Martin L. Weitzman (1974), 'Prices *vs.* Quantities', *Review of Economic Studies*, **XLI** (4), No. 128, October, 477–91.

Yale Law Journal Company and Fred B. Rothman & Company for article: Janusz A. Ordover and Robert D. Willig (1981), 'An Economic Definition of Predation: Pricing and Product Innovation', *Yale Law Journal*, **91** (1), November, 8–53.

Yale Journal on Regulation for article: William J. Baumol (1999), 'Having Your Cake: How to Preserve Universal-Service Cross Subsidies While Facilitating Competitive Entry', *Yale Journal on Regulation*, **16** (1), Winter, 1–17.

Every effort has been made to trace all the copyright holders but if any have been inadvertently overlooked the publishers will be pleased to make the necessary arrangement at the first opportunity.

In addition the publishers wish to thank the Library of the London School of Economics and Political Science, the Marshall Library of Economics, Cambridge University and the Library of Indiana University at Bloomington, USA for their assistance in obtaining these articles.

Part I
Externalities and Pigouvian Taxation

[1]

Excerpt from A.C. Pigou, M.A. (1952), 'Divergences Between Marginal Social Net Product and Marginal Private Net Product', in *The Economics of Welfare*

§ 10. I now turn to the second class of divergence between social and private net product which was distinguished in § 3. Here the essence of the matter is that one person A, in the course of rendering some service, for which payment is made, to a second person B, incidentally also renders services or disservices to other persons (not producers of like services), of such a sort that payment cannot be exacted from the benefited parties or compensation enforced on behalf of the injured parties. If we were to be pedantically loyal to the definition of the national dividend given in Chapter III. of Part I., it would be necessary to distinguish further between industries in which the uncompensated benefit or burden respectively is and is not one that can be readily brought into relation with the measuring rod of money. This distinction, however, would be of formal rather than of real importance, and would obscure rather than illuminate the main issues. I shall, therefore, in the examples I am about to give, deliberately pass it over.

Among these examples we may set out first a number of instances in which marginal private net product falls short of marginal social net product, because incidental services are performed to third parties from whom it is technically difficult to exact payment. Thus, as Sidgwick observes, "it may easily happen that the benefits of a well-placed lighthouse must be largely enjoyed by ships on which no toll could be conveniently levied."[1] Again, uncompensated services are rendered when resources are invested in private parks in cities; for these, even though the public is not admitted to them, improve the air of the neighbourhood. The same thing is true—though here allowance should be made for a detriment elsewhere—of resources invested in roads and tramways that increase the value of the adjoining land—except, indeed, where a special betterment rate, corresponding to the improvements they enjoy, is levied on the owners of this land. It is true, in like manner, of resources devoted to afforestation, since the beneficial effect on climate often extends beyond the borders of the estates owned by the person responsible for the forest. It is true also of resources invested in lamps erected at the doors of private houses, for these necessarily throw light also on the streets.[2] It is true of resources devoted to the prevention of smoke from factory chimneys:[3] for this smoke in large towns inflicts a heavy uncharged loss on the community, in injury to buildings and vegetables, expenses for washing clothes and cleaning rooms, expenses for the provision of extra artificial light, and in many other ways.[4] Lastly and

[1] *Principles of Political Economy*, p. 406.

[2] Cf. Smart, *Studies in Economics*, p. 314.

[3] It has been said that in London, owing to the smoke, there is only 12 per cent as much sunlight as is astronomically possible, and that one fog in five is directly caused by smoke alone, while all the fogs are befouled and prolonged by it (J. W. Graham, *The Destruction of Daylight*, pp. 6 and 24). It would seem that mere ignorance and inertia prevent the adoption of smoke-preventing appliances in many instances where, through the addition they would make to the efficiency of fuel, they would be directly profitable to the users. The general interest, however, requires that these devices should be employed beyond the point at which they "pay." There seems no doubt that, by means of mechanical stokers, hot-air blasts and other arrangements, factory chimneys can be made practically smokeless. Noxious fumes from alkali works are suppressed by the law more vigorously than smoke (*ibid.* p. 126).

[4] Thus the Interim Report of the Departmental Committee on smoke and Noxious Vapours Abatement 1920 contains the following passages:

"17. *Actual economic loss Due to Coal Smoke.*—It is impossible to arrive at any complete and exact statistical statement of the amount of damage occasioned to the whole community by smoke. We may, however, quote the following investigations.

"A report on an exhaustive investigation conducted by an expert Committee

most important of all, it is true of resources devoted alike to the fundamental problems of scientific research, out of which, in unexpected ways, discoveries of high practical utility often grow, and also to the perfecting of inventions and improvements in industrial processes. These latter are often of such a nature that they can neither be patented nor kept secret, and, therefore, the whole of the extra reward, which they at first bring to their inventor, is very quickly transferred from him to the general public in the form of reduced prices. The patent laws aim, in effect, at bringing marginal private net product and marginal social net product more closely together. By offering the prospect of reward for certain types of invention they do not, indeed, appreciably stimulate inventive activity, which is, for the most part, spontaneous, but they do direct it into channels of general usefulness.[1]

Corresponding to the above investments in which marginal private net product falls short of marginal social net product, there are a number of others, in which, owing to the technical difficulty of enforcing compensation for incidental disservices, marginal private net product is greater than marginal social net product. Thus, incidental uncharged disservices are rendered to third parties when the game-preserving activities of one occupier involve the overrunning of a neighbouring occupier's land by rabbits—unless, indeed, the two occupiers stand in the relation of landlord and tenant, so that compensation is given in an adjustment of the rent. They are rendered, again, when the owner of a site in a residential quarter of a city builds a factory there and so destroys a great

of engineers, architects, and scientists in 1912 in Pittsburgh, U.S.A., estimated the cost of the smoke nuisance to Pittsburgh at approximately £4 per head of the population per annum.

"18. A valuable investigation was made in 1918 by the Manchester Air Pollution Advisory Board into the comparative cost of household washing in Manchester—a smoky town—as compared with Harrogate—a clean town. The investigator obtained 100 properly comparable statements for Manchester and Harrogate respectively as to the cost of the weekly washing in working-class houses. These showed an extra cost in Manchester of 7½d. a week per household for fuel and washing material. The total loss for the whole city, taking the extra cost of fuel and washing materials alone, disregarding the extra labour involved, and assuming no greater loss for middle-class than for working-class households (a considerable under-statement), works out at over £290,000 a year for a population of three quarters of a million."

[1] Cf. Taussig, *Inventors and Money Makers*, p. 51.

part of the amenities of the neighbouring sites; or, in a less degree, when he uses his site in such a way as to spoil the lighting of the houses opposite:[1] or when he invests resources in erecting buildings in a crowded centre, which, by contracting the air space and the playing-room of the neighbourhood, tend to injure the health and efficiency of the families living there. Yet again, third parties—this time the public in general—suffer incidental uncharged disservices from resources invested in the running of motor cars that wear out the surface of the roads. The case is similar—the conditions of public taste being assumed—with resources devoted to the production and sale of intoxicants. To enable the social net product to be inferred from the private net product of the marginal pound invested in this form of production, the investment should, as Mr. Bernard Shaw observes, be debited with the extra costs in policemen and prisons which it indirectly makes necessary.[2] Exactly similar considerations hold good in some measure of foreign investment in general. For, if foreigners can obtain some of the exports they need from us by selling promises, they will not have to send so many goods; which implies that the ratio of interchange between our exports and our imports will become slightly less favourable to us. For certain sorts of foreign investments more serious reactions come into account. Thus, when the indirect effect of an increment of investment made abroad, or of the diplomatic manœuvres employed in securing the concession for it, is an actual war or preparations to guard against war, the cost of these things ought to be deducted from any interest that the increment yields before its net contribution to the national dividend is calculated. When this is done, the marginal social net product even of investments, which, as may often happen in countries where highly profitable openings are still unworked and hard bargains can be driven with corrupt officials, yield a very high return to the investors, may easily turn out to be negative. Yet

[1] In Germany the town-planning schemes of most cities render anti-social action of this kind impossible; but in America individual site-owners appear to be entirely free, and in England to be largely free, to do what they will with their land. (Cf. Howe, *European Cities at Work*, pp. 46, 95 and 346.)

[2] *The Common Sense of Municipal Trading*, pp. 19-20.

again, when the investment consists in a loan to a foreign government and makes it possible for that government to engage in a war which otherwise would not have taken place, the indirect loss which Englishmen in general suffer, in consequence of the world impoverishment caused by the war, should be debited against the interest which English financiers receive. Here, too, the marginal social net product may well be negative. Perhaps, however, the crowning illustration of this order of excess of private over social net product is afforded by the work done by women in factories, particularly during the periods immediately preceding and succeeding confinement; for there can be no doubt that this work often carries with it, besides the earnings of the women themselves, grave injury to the health of their children.[1] The reality of this evil is not disproved by the low, even negative, correlation which sometimes is found to exist between the factory work of mothers and the rate of infantile mortality. For in districts where women's work of this kind prevails there is presumably—and this is the cause of the women's work—great poverty. This poverty, which is obviously injurious to children's health, is likely, other things being equal, to be greater than elsewhere in families where the mother declines factory work, and it may be that the evil of the extra poverty is greater than that of the factory work.[2] This consideration explains the statistical facts that are known. They, therefore, militate in no way against the view that, *other things equal*, the factory work of mothers is injurious. All that they tend to show is that prohibition of such work should be accompanied

[1] Cf. Hutchins, *Economic Journal*, 1908, p. 227.

[2] Cf. Newsholme, *Second Report on Infant and Child Mortality* [Cd. 6909], p. 56. Similar considerations to the above hold good of night work by boys. The *Departmental Committee on Night Employment* did not, indeed, obtain any strong evidence that this work injures the boys' health. But they found that it reacts injuriously on their efficiency in another way, *i.e.* by practically precluding them from going on with their education in continuation classes and so forth. The *theory* of our factory laws appears to be that boys between 14 and 18 should only be permitted to work at night upon continuous processes of such a kind that great loss would result if they did not do so. The *practice* of these laws, however, permits them to be employed at night on unnecessary non-continuous processes which are carried out in the same factory as continuous processes. Consequently, the Committee recommend that in future "such permits should be granted in terms of processes, and not of premises, factories, or parts of factories without reference to processes" ([Cd. 6503], p. 17).

by relief to those families whom the prohibition renders necessitous.[1]

[1] Cf. *Annual Report of the Local Government Board*, 1909–10, p. 57. The suggestion that the injurious consequences of the factory work of mothers can be done away with, if the factory worker gets some unmarried woman to look after her home in factory hours, is mistaken, because it ignores the fact that a woman's work has a special personal value in respect of her own children. In Birmingham this fact seems to be recognised, for, after a little experience of the bad results of putting their children out to "mind," married women are apt, it was said before the war, to leave the factory and take to home work. (Cf. Cadbury, *Women's Work*, p. 175.)

[2]

EXTERNAL ECONOMIES AND DISECONOMIES IN A COMPETITIVE SITUATION [1]

I. The Scope of the Paper

The purpose of this note is to distinguish between certain types of external economies and diseconomies which are connected with marginal adjustments in purely competitive situations. We shall not be dealing with divergences between private and social interests due to monopolistic or monopsonistic situations, nor with any of the problems which arise from indivisibilities such as the lumpiness of investment in particular forms, nor with any questions about large structural changes such as whether a particular industry should exist at all or not. We shall be concerned only with small adjustments to existing competitive situations.

II. The Competitive Situation with no External Economies or Diseconomies

Let us consider two industries. These " industries " may or may not in fact produce identically the same product and so in reality constitute a single industry. That is immaterial to our general theory. But we assume that within each " industry " there are a large number of independent competing firms, so that to each individual entrepreneur the price of the product and of the factors is given. In the absence of any external economies or diseconomies, each entrepreneur will hire each factor up to the point at which the additional product of the factor multiplied by its price is equal to the price of the factor. Moreover, there will be constant returns to scale. If every factor in either of our two industries were increased by 10%, including the number of entrepreneurs, then the product also would be increased by 10%.

Let us write x_1 and x_2 for the products of industry 1 and industry 2 respectively. We assume that there are two factors, l and c, or labour and capital, employed in both industries, so that $l_1 + l_2 = l$ and $c_1 + c_2 = c$. We will write $\bar{x}_1$, $\bar{l}_1$, $\bar{c}_1$, etc., for the market prices of the products and factors; and $X_1 = x_1\bar{x}_1$, $L_1 = l_1\bar{l}_1$, $C_1 = c_1\bar{c}_1$, etc., for the total value of the output of

[1] This note has arisen, out of a consideration of the problems of the economic development of under-developed territories, in the preparation of Volume II of my *Theory of International Economic Policy* for the Royal Institute of International Affairs.

x_1 or for the total income earned by l_1, etc. Finally, we shall write $\bar{L}_1$, $\bar{C}_1$, etc., for the amounts which the factors would have to be paid if they received the value of their marginal social net products. In our model capital is always the hiring factor, and its reward is, therefore, always equal in each industry to the total output of that industry minus the wages paid to labour in that industry, so that $C_1 = X_1 - L_1$ and $C_2 = X_2 - L_2$.

In the case in which there are no divergences between private and social net products we can write

$$\left.\begin{aligned} x_1 &= H_1(l_1, c_1) \\ x_2 &= H_2(l_2, c_2) \end{aligned}\right\} \quad . \quad . \quad . \quad . \quad . \quad . \quad (1)$$

where H_1 and H_2 are homogeneous functions of the first degree, expressing the fact that there are constant returns to scale in both industries. Now

$$x_1 = \frac{\partial x_1}{\partial l_1} l_1 + \frac{\partial x_1}{\partial c_1} c_1$$

or

$$1 = \frac{l_1}{x_1} \frac{\partial x_1}{\partial l_1} + \frac{c_1}{x_1} \cdot \frac{\partial x_1}{\partial c_1}$$

We shall write $\epsilon^{x_1}_{l_1}$ for $\frac{l_1}{x_1} \cdot \frac{\partial x_1}{\partial l_1}$ and so on, so that we have

$$\epsilon^{x_1}_{l_1} + \epsilon^{x_1}_{c_1} = \epsilon^{x_2}_{l_2} + \epsilon^{x_2}_{c_2} = 1 \quad . \quad . \quad . \quad . \quad . \quad (2)$$

These expressions describe the fact that if, for example, a 10% increase in labour alone causes a 3% increase in output, then a 10% increase in capital alone must cause a 7% increase in output, because a 10% increase in both factors will cause a 10% increase in output.

In this situation l_1 will be paid a money wage (L_1) equal to $\frac{\partial x_1}{\partial l_1} l_1 \bar{x}_1$ or $\epsilon^{x_1}_{l_1} X_1$, and this will also be equal to the value of its marginal social net product. Capital in industry 1 will receive $X_1 - L_1$ which from equation (2) equals $\epsilon^{x_1}_{c_1} X_1$, which is also equal to the value of capital's marginal social net product, so that in this case we have

$$\begin{aligned} L_1 &= \bar{L}_1 = \epsilon^{x_1}_{l_1} X_1 & \qquad L_2 &= \bar{L}_2 = \epsilon^{x_2}_{l_2} X_2 \\ C_1 &= \bar{C}_1 = \epsilon^{x_1}_{c_1} X_1 & \qquad C_2 &= \bar{C}_2 = \epsilon^{x_2}_{l_2} X_2 \end{aligned}$$

Moreover, since $\epsilon^{x_1}_{l_1} = \frac{L_1}{X_1}$, we can measure $\epsilon^{x_1}_{l_1}$ from the proportion of the total product in industry, which goes to labour. And similarly for the measurement of $\epsilon^{x_1}_{c_1}$, $\epsilon^{x_2}_{l_2}$ and $\epsilon^{x_2}_{c_2}$.

III. Two Types of External Economy and Diseconomy

Such is the simplest competitive model. We intend now to consider cases where what is done in one industry reacts upon the conditions of production in the other industry in some way other than through the possible effect upon the prices of the product or of the factors in that other industry. All such reactions we shall describe as constituting external economies or diseconomies, because the individual entrepreneur in the first industry will take account of the effect of his actions only upon what happens inside the first industry (the internal effect), but will leave out of account the effect of his actions upon the output of the second industry, in which it may improve production (an external economy) or diminish production (an external diseconomy).

But the purpose of this note is to distinguish between two types of such external economies or diseconomies. The first type we shall call "unpaid factors of production," and the second the "creation of atmosphere." The essential difference between these two types of external economy or diseconomy is that in the first case there are still constant returns to scale for society as a whole, though not for the individual industry, whereas in the second case there are still constant returns to scale for each individual industry but not for society as a whole.

IV. Unpaid Factors

Suppose that in a given region there is a certain amount of apple-growing and a certain amount of bee-keeping and that the bees feed on the apple-blossom. If the apple-farmers apply 10% more labour, land and capital to apple-farming they will increase the output of apples by 10%; but they will also provide more food for the bees. On the other hand, the bee-keepers will not increase the output of honey by 10% by increasing the amount of land, labour and capital applied to bee-keeping by 10% unless at the same time the apple-farmers also increase their output and so the food of the bees by 10%. Thus there are constant returns to scale for both industries taken together: if the amount of labour and of capital employed both in apple-farming and bee-keeping are doubled, the output of both apples and honey will be doubled. But if the amount of labour and capital are doubled in bee-keeping alone, the output of honey will be less than doubled; whereas, if the amounts of labour and capital in apple-farming are doubled, the output of apples will be doubled and, in addition, some contribution will be made to the output of honey.

We call this a case of an unpaid factor, because the situation is due simply and solely to the fact that the apple-farmer cannot charge the bee-keeper for the bees' food, which the former produces for the latter. If social-accounting institutions were such that this charge could be made, then every factor would, as in other competitive situations, earn the value of its marginal social net product. But as it is, the apple-farmer provides to the bee-keeper some of his factors free of charge. The apple-farmer is paid less than the value of his marginal social net product, and the bee-keeper receives more than the value of his marginal social net product.

This situation is shown if industry 1 represents bee-keeping and industry 2 apple-farming and if we replace equations (1) and (2) with

$$\left.\begin{aligned} x_1 &= H_1(l_1, c_1, x_2) \\ x_2 &= H_2(l_2, c_2) \\ \text{so that} \quad \epsilon^{x_1}_{l_1} + \epsilon^{x_1}_{c_1} + \epsilon^{x_1}_{x_2} &= \epsilon^{x_2}_{l_2} + \epsilon^{x_2}_{c_2} = 1 \end{aligned}\right\} \quad . \quad . \quad . \quad (4)$$

In this case l_1 will be paid the value of its marginal social net product, and we have $L_1 = \bar{L}_1 = \epsilon^{x_1}_{l_1} X_1$. c_1 will be paid $X_1 - L_1$ or $\epsilon^{x_1}_{c_1} X_1 + \epsilon^{x_1}_{x_2} X_2$; but $\epsilon^{x_1}_{c_1} X_1$ is the value of c_1's marginal social net product, so that we have $C_1 = \bar{C}_1 + \epsilon^{x_1}_{c_1} X_1$. In other words, c_1 will have to have its earnings taxed at an *ad valorem* rate of $\frac{X_1}{C_1}\epsilon^{x_1}_{x_2}$ in order to be paid a net reward equal to the value of its marginal social net product.

But, on the other hand, l_2 and c_2 will be paid just so much less than the value of their marginal social net products.

$$\begin{aligned} \bar{L}_2 &= l_2 \left(\bar{x}_2 \frac{\partial x_2}{\partial l_2} + \bar{x}_1 \frac{\partial x_1}{\partial x_2} \cdot \frac{\partial x_2}{\partial l_2}\right) \\ &= \epsilon^{x_2}_{l_2} X_2 \left(1 + \frac{X_1}{X_2} \epsilon^{x_1}_{x_2}\right) \end{aligned}$$

But l_2 will receive only $\epsilon^{x_2}_{l_2} X_2$, so that $\bar{L}_2 = L_2 \left(1 + \frac{X_1}{X_2} \epsilon^{x_1}_{x_2}\right)$ and the wages of labour in apple-farming will need to be subsidised at an *ad valorem* rate of $\frac{X_1}{X_2}\epsilon^{x_1}_{x_2}$ in order to equate rewards to the value of the factor's marginal social net product. Similarly, $\bar{C}_2 = C_2 (1 + \frac{X_1}{X_2} \epsilon^{x_1}_{x_2})$, and the same *ad valorem* rate of subsidy should be paid to the earnings of capital in apple-farming. Since

$C_2 + L_2 = X_2$, the total tax revenue of $X_1\epsilon^{x_1}_{x_2}$ raised on C_1 will be equal to the two subsidies of $C_2 \frac{X_1}{X_2} \epsilon^{x_1}_{x_2}$ and $L_2 \frac{X_1}{X_2} \epsilon^{x_1}_{x_2}$.[1] In order to discover the appropriate rates of tax and subsidy the essential factor which will need to be estimated is $\epsilon^{x_1}_{x_2}$, the percentage effect on the output of honey which a 1% increase in the output of apples would exercise.

Now the relationship which we have just examined might be a reciprocal one. While the apples may provide the food of the bees, the bees may fertilise the apples.[2] Once again we may have constant returns to scale for society as a whole; a 10% increase in all factors in both industries would cause a 10% increase in the output of both products. In this case instead of equations (4) we should have

$$\left.\begin{aligned} x_1 &= H_1(l_1, c_1, x_2) \\ x_2 &= H_2(l_2, c_2, x_1) \\ \epsilon^{x_1}_{l_1} + \epsilon^{x_1}_{c_1} + \epsilon^{x_1}_{x_2} &= \epsilon^{x_2}_{l_2} + \epsilon^{x_2}_{c_2} + \epsilon^{x_2}_{x_1} = 1 \end{aligned}\right\} \quad . \quad . \quad (5)$$

By a process similar to that adopted in the previous case we can obtain formulæ to show what subsidies and taxes must be imposed in order to equate each factor's income in each industry to the value of its marginal social net product.

We can obtain the actual rewards of the factors in exactly the same way as in the previous example. Labour in industry 1 will obtain a wage equal to the value of its marginal private net product or $\bar{x}_1 \frac{\partial x_1}{\partial l_1}$, so that $L_1 = \epsilon^{x_1}_{l_1} X_1$. Capital in industry 1 will receive the remainder, or $X_1 - L_1$, so that from equations (5) $C_1 = X_1(\epsilon^{x_1}_{c_1} + \epsilon^{x_1}_{x_2})$. Similarly, $L_2 = \epsilon^{x_2}_{l_2} X_2$ and $C_2 = X_2(\epsilon^{x_2}_{c_2} + \epsilon^{x_2}_{x_1})$.

To obtain expressions for the value of each factor's marginal social net product we have now to allow for the repercussions of each industry upon the other. Thus the value of the marginal social net product of labour in apple-farming includes not only the increased output of apples directly produced but also the increased output of honey caused by this increase in apple-output plus the further increase in apple-output due to this increase in honey-output plus the still further increase in honey-output due to this

[1] In this case it would, of course, have exactly the same effect if the subsidy were paid not on the wages of labour and profits of capital in apple-farming but at the same *ad valorem* rate on the value of the apple-output, X_2.

[2] If the bees had a bad effect upon the apples, then we should have an external diseconomy, which may be regarded as an unpaid negative factor of production. The bee-keepers, in addition to getting the bee-food free of charge, are also not charged for some damage which they do to the apple-farmers. In what follows $\epsilon^{x_2}_{x_1}$ would be < 0, so that $\epsilon^{x_2}_{l_2} + \epsilon^{x_2}_{c_2} > 1$.

increase in apple-output and so on in an infinite progression. The final result can be obtained in the following manner. Differentiating the main equations in equations (5), we have

$$dx_1 = \frac{\partial x_1}{\partial l_1} dl_1 + \frac{\partial x_1}{\partial c_1} dc_1 + \frac{\partial x_1}{\partial x_2} dx_2$$

$$dx_2 = \frac{\partial x_2}{\partial l_2} dl_2 + \frac{\partial x_2}{\partial c_2} dc_2 + \frac{\partial x_2}{\partial x_1} dx_1$$

If we keep c_1, l_2 and c_2 constant ($dc_1 = dl_2 = dc_2 = 0$) but allow l_1 to vary ($dl_1 \neq 0$), dx_1 and dx_2 will give the marginal social net products of l_1 in the two commodities. We obtain

$$\frac{dx_1}{dl_1} = \frac{\dfrac{\partial x_1}{\partial l_1}}{1 - \dfrac{\partial x_1}{\partial x_2} \cdot \dfrac{\partial x_2}{\partial x_1}} \quad \text{and} \quad \frac{dx_2}{dl_1} = \frac{\dfrac{\partial x_2}{\partial x_1} \cdot \dfrac{\partial x_1}{\partial l_1}}{1 - \dfrac{\partial x_1}{\partial x_2} \cdot \dfrac{\partial x_2}{\partial x_1}}$$

But

$$\bar{L}_1 = l_1 \bar{x}_1 \frac{dx_1}{dl_1} + l_1 \bar{x}_2 \frac{dx_2}{dl_1}$$

$$= l_1 \frac{\partial x_1}{\partial l_1} \frac{\bar{x}_1 + \bar{x}_2 \dfrac{\partial x_2}{\partial x_1}}{1 - \dfrac{\partial x_1}{\partial x_2} \cdot \dfrac{\partial x_2}{\partial x_1}}$$

$$= L_1 \frac{1 + \dfrac{X_2}{X_1} \cdot \epsilon^{x_2}_{x_1}}{1 - \epsilon^{x_1}_{x_2} \epsilon^{x_2}_{x_1}}$$

Similarly, we get the following expressions for the values of the marginal social net products of the other factors.

$$\bar{L}_2 = L_2 \frac{1 + \dfrac{X_1}{X_2} \epsilon^{x_1}_{x_2}}{1 - \epsilon^{x_1}_{x_2} \epsilon^{x_2}_{x_1}}$$

$$\bar{C}_1 = \epsilon^{x_1}_{c_1} X_1 \frac{1 + \dfrac{X_2}{X_1} \epsilon^{x_2}_{x_1}}{1 - \epsilon^{x_1}_{x_2} \epsilon^{x_2}_{x_1}} = (C_1 - \epsilon^{x_1}_{x_2} X_1) \frac{1 + \dfrac{X_2}{X_1} \epsilon^{x_2}_{x_1}}{1 - \epsilon^{x_1}_{x_2} \epsilon^{x_2}_{x_1}}$$

$$\bar{C}_2 = (C_2 - \epsilon^{x_2}_{x_1} X_2) \frac{1 + \dfrac{X_1}{X_2} \epsilon^{x_1}_{x_2}}{1 - \epsilon^{x_1}_{x_2} \epsilon^{x_2}_{x_1}}$$

On these expressions we can make the following three comments:

First, remembering that $L_1 + C_1 = X_1$ and $L_2 + C_2 = X_2$, we can see from the above expressions that $\bar{L}_1 + \bar{L}_2 + \bar{C}_1 + \bar{C}_2 = X_1 + X_2$. In other words, if the factors were all paid rewards equal to the value of their marginal social net products, this would absorb the whole of the product, neither more nor less. This is due, of course, to the essential constant-returns nature of the production functions at equations (5), from which it can be seen that if l_1, l_2, c_1 and c_2 were to increase by 10%, then the production conditions would be satisfied if both outputs also increased by 10%. In other words, we are still dealing with a pure unpaid-factor case; there is no adding-up problem for society; every factor can be given a reward equal to the value of its marginal social net product if the revenue from the taxes levied on those which ought to be taxed is used to subsidise the earnings of those which ought to be subsidised.

Secondly, $\bar{L}_1$, $\bar{L}_2$, $\bar{C}_1$ and $\bar{C}_2$ are all seen to be positive finite quantities, provided that $\epsilon^{x_1}_{x_2}\epsilon^{x_2}_{x_1} < 1$. From the last of equations (5) it can be seen that $\epsilon^{x_1}_{x_2}$ and $\epsilon^{x_2}_{x_1}$ are both < 1; it requires a 10% increase of land, labour and apple-blossom to increase the output of honey by 10%, so that a 10% increase in the supply of apple-blossom alone will increase the output of honey by less than 10%. But $\epsilon^{x_1}_{x_2}$ and $\epsilon^{x_2}_{x_1}$ are both positive, since we are dealing with external economies and not diseconomies. It follows, therefore, that $0 < \epsilon^{x_1}_{x_2}\epsilon^{x_2}_{x_1} < 1$, so that $\bar{L}_1$, $\bar{L}_2$, $\bar{C}_1$ and $\bar{C}_2$ are all positive finite quantities. It is because $\epsilon^{x_1}_{x_2}$ and $\epsilon^{x_2}_{x_1}$ are both positive fractions that the infinite progression of an increase in apple-output causing an increase in honey-output, causing an increase in apple-output and so on, adds up only to a finite sum. For example, if both $\epsilon^{x_1}_{x_2}$ and $\epsilon^{x_2}_{x_1}$ are one-half, a 10% increase in apple-output causes a 5% increase in honey-output, but this 5% increase in honey-output causes only a $2\frac{1}{2}$% increase in apple-output; which causes only a $1\frac{1}{4}$% increase in honey-output and so on in a diminishing geometric progression.

Thirdly, from the above expressions for L_1 and $\bar{L}_1$, we obtain

$$\frac{\bar{L}_1 - L_1}{L_1} = \frac{\frac{X_2}{X_1}\epsilon^{x_2}_{x_1} + \epsilon^{x_1}_{x_2}\epsilon^{x_2}_{x_1}}{1 - \epsilon^{x_2}_{x_1}\epsilon^{x_1}_{x_2}}$$

which shows the *ad valorem* rate of subsidy which must be paid to l_1 to bring its earnings up to the value of its marginal social net product. We can obtain a similar expression for the rates of tax levyable upon C_1.

$$\frac{C_1 - \bar{C}_1}{C_1} = \frac{\epsilon^{x_1}_{x_2}\frac{X_1}{C_1} - \frac{X_2}{X_1}\epsilon^{x_2}_{x_1} + \frac{X_2 - C_1}{C_1}\epsilon^{x_1}_{x_2}\epsilon^{x_2}_{x_1}}{1 - \epsilon^{x_1}_{x_2}\epsilon^{x_2}_{x_1}}$$

Corresponding expressions for $\frac{\bar{L}_2 - L_2}{L_2}$ and $\frac{C_2 - \bar{C}_2}{C_2}$ can be obtained by interchanging the subscripts 1 and 2. It can be seen from adding $C_1 - \bar{C}_1$ and $C_2 - \bar{C}_2$ that there will be a positive tax revenue raised from capital as a whole. But either $C_1 - \bar{C}_1$

or $C_2 - \overline{C}_2$ might be negative, *i.e.*, a subsidy might be payable on the earnings of capital in one of the two industries as well as upon the earnings of labour in both of the industries. For example, $C_2 - \overline{C}_2$ would be < 0 if $\epsilon^{x_1}_{x_2}$ were very large relatively to $\epsilon^{x_2}_{x_1}$. This would mean, for example, that the production of honey (industry 1) did very little to help the production of apples (industry 2), while the production of apples did much to help the production of bees. Capitalists in apple-farming should be subsidised because the unpaid benefits which they confer upon the bee-keepers more than outweigh the unpaid benefits which they receive from labour and capital employed in bee-keeping. Indeed, all the results obtained from equations (4) can be obtained from the expressions derived from equations (5) by writing $\epsilon^{x_2}_{x} = 0$.

V. The Creation of Atmosphere

A distinction must be drawn between a "factor of production" and a physical or social "atmosphere" affecting production. We may take the rainfall in a district as a typical example of atmosphere. The rainfall may be deficient in the sense that a higher rainfall would increase the farmers' output, but nevertheless what rainfall there is will be available to all farms in the district regardless of their number. Thus if in the district in question the amount of land, labour and capital devoted to, say, wheat-farming were to be increased by 10%, the output of wheat would also be increased by 10% even if the rainfall were to remain constant. This is quite different from the case of a factor of production for which no payment is made; in our previous example, a 10% increase in the output of apples (and so in the supply of apple-blossom) would be necessary, in addition to a 10% increase in the amount of land, labour and capital devoted to bee-keeping, if the output of honey is to be increased by 10%. In these examples, rainfall is an "atmosphere" for wheat-farming; but the output of apples is an "unpaid factor of production" for bee-keeping.

The distinction should now be clear. Both a factor of production and an atmosphere are conditions which affect the output of a certain industry. But the atmosphere is a fixed condition of production which remains unchanged for all producers in the industry in question without anyone else doing anything about it, however large or small—within limits—is the scale of operations of the industry. On the other hand, the factor of production is an aid to production which is fixed in amount, and which is therefore available on a smaller scale to each producer in the industry if the number of producers increases, unless someone does something to increase the total supply of the factor.

The external economies which we have examined in the last section are concerned with factors of production for which the individual producer pays nothing. We must turn now to external economies and diseconomies which are due to the fact that the activities of one group of producers may provide an atmosphere which is favourable or unfavourable to the activities of another group of producers. For example, suppose that afforestation schemes in one locality increase the rainfall in that district and that this is favourable to the production of wheat in that district. In this case the production of timber creates an atmosphere favourable to the production of wheat.

In these cases there is an adding-up problem for society as a whole. There may be constant returns to the factors of production employed in either industry alone. That is to say, a 10% increase in the amounts of land, labour and capital employed in producing wheat might, in any given atmosphere, result in a 10% increase in the output of wheat. And a 10% increase in the amount of land, labour and capital employed in producing timber might, apart from its effect in changing the atmosphere for wheat-farmers, cause a 10% increase in the output of timber. It follows that a 10% increase in the amount of land, labour and capital employed both in the timber industry and in wheat-farming will increase the output of timber by 10% and the output of wheat by more than 10% (because of the improvement in the atmosphere for wheat producers). To society as a whole there are now increasing returns to scale; to pay every factor a reward equal to the value of its marginal social net product will account for more than the total output of the two industries; revenue will have to be raised from outside sources by general taxation if subsidies are to be paid on a scale to bring every factor's reward up to the value of its marginal social net product.

We can express this sort of situation by the following equations:

$$\left.\begin{aligned} x_1 &= H_1(l_1, c_1)A_1(x_2) \\ x_2 &= H_2(l_2, c_2) \end{aligned}\right\} \quad . \quad . \quad . \quad (6)$$

where once more

$$\epsilon^{x_1}_{l_1} + \epsilon^{x_1}_{c_1} = \epsilon^{x_2}_{l_2} + \epsilon^{x_2}_{c_2} = 1.\ ^1$$

[1] Since $l_1 \frac{\partial H_1}{\partial l_1} = \frac{l_1}{H_1 A_1} \cdot \frac{A_1 \partial H_1}{\partial l_1} H_1 = \frac{l_1}{x_1} \cdot \frac{\partial x_1}{\partial l_1} H_1 = \epsilon^{x_1}_{l_1} H_1$, we have $H_1 = \epsilon^{x_1}_{l_1} H_1 + \epsilon^{x_1}_{c_1} H_1$, so that $1 = \epsilon^{x_1}_{l_1} + \epsilon^{x_1}_{c_1}$.

$x_2 = H_2(l_2, c_2)$ is the ordinary competitive constant-returns production function for the timber industry. There is the same type of production function for the wheat industry; but in this case the output due to the use of labour and land ($H_1[c_1, l_1]$) is subject to an atmosphere (A_1). If the atmosphere is favourable then $H_1(l_1, c_1)$ is multiplied up by a large factor to give the actual output (x_1). In the case which we are examining the atmosphere for the wheat industry (A_1) is made to depend upon the output of the timber industry ($A_1 = A_1[x_2]$).

The atmosphere factor (A_1) is thus subject to the following conditions. $A_1(0) = 1$, *i.e.*, we define our terms in such a way that $H_1(l_1, c_1)$ is equal to what the output of wheat would be if there were no timber output. A_1 is always >0, *i.e.*, there cannot be so powerful an external diseconomy that the output of the industry affected becomes negative. When $A_1(x_2) > 1$, then there is an average external economy, *i.e.*, the output of wheat is greater than it would have been had there been a zero output of timber instead of a positive output (x_2); and similarly, when $A_1(x_2) < 1$, there is an average external diseconomy. When $A_1'(x_2)$ is >0, then there is a marginal external economy, *i.e.*, the output of wheat would be improved by a further increase in the output of timber; and when $A_1'(x_2)$ is <0, there is a marginal external diseconomy.

The actual rewards of the factors of production are easily seen to be $L_1 = \epsilon^{x_1}_{l_1} X_1$, $C_1 = X_1 - L_1 = \epsilon^{x_1}_{c_1} X_1, L_2 = \epsilon^{x_2}_{l_2} X_2$ and $C_2 = X_2 - L_2 = \epsilon^{x_2}_{c_2} X_2$. In the case of the factors employed in wheat-farming (industry 1) there will be no divergence between the reward paid and the value of the marginal social net product; and $L_1 = \bar{L}_1$ and $C_1 = \bar{C}_1$.

But the rewards actually paid to the factors of production in the timber industry (industry 2) will be lower than the value of their marginal social net products because they will not be paid for the favourable atmosphere which they create for wheat farmers. Thus

$$\bar{L}_2 = \epsilon^{x_2}_{l_2} X_2 + l_2 \bar{x}_1 \frac{\partial x_1}{\partial x_2} \cdot \frac{\partial x_2}{\partial l_2}$$
$$= L_2 \left(1 + \frac{X_1}{X_2} \cdot \epsilon^{x_1}_{x_2}\right)$$

where $\epsilon^{x_1}_{x_2} = \frac{x_2}{x_1} \cdot \frac{\partial x_1}{\partial x_2}$ or $\frac{x_2}{A_1} \cdot \frac{\partial A_1}{\partial x_2}$, the percentage increase in the output of wheat which would be brought about by a 1% increase in the output of timber through the improvement in the atmosphere for wheat production. And similarly, it can be shown that $\bar{C}_2 = C\left(1 + \frac{X_1}{X_2}\epsilon^{x_1}_{x_2}\right)$. In other words, the earnings of both l_2 and c_2 or, alternatively, the price of the product x_2 must be subsidised from general revenue at the *ad valorem* rate of $\frac{X_1}{X_2}\epsilon^{x_1}_{x_2}$ if all factors are to receive rewards equal to the value of their marginal social net products.

As in the case of unpaid factors, these reactions of one industry upon the other may be reciprocal. Industry 1 may create a favourable or unfavourable atmosphere for industry 2, as well as industry 2 for industry 1. In this case we have

$$\left.\begin{aligned} x_1 &= H_1(l_1, c_1)A_1(x_2) \\ x_2 &= H_2(l_2, c_2)A_2(x_1) \\ \text{where} \qquad & \\ \epsilon^{x_1}_{l_1} + \epsilon^{x_1}_{c_1} &= \epsilon^{x_2}_{l_2} + \epsilon^{x_2}_{c_2} = 1 \end{aligned}\right\} \quad . \quad . \quad . \quad (7)$$

Here again $L_1 = \epsilon^{x_1}_{l_1}X_1$, $C_1 = X_1 - L_1 = \epsilon^{x_1}_{c_1}X_1$, $L_2 = \epsilon^{x_2}_{l_2}X_2$ and $C_2 = X_2 - L_2 = \epsilon^{x_2}_{c_2}X_2$.

But when we come to consider the marginal social net product, we have to take into account the infinite chain of action and reaction of the one industry upon the other, as in the case of apple-growing and bee-keeping examined above. The marginal social net product of l_1, for example, is obtained by differentiating the first two of equations (7), keeping l_2, c_1 and c_2 all constant. We obtain

$$\frac{dx_1}{dl_1} = \frac{\epsilon^{x_1}_{l_1} \cdot \frac{x_1}{l_1}}{1 - \epsilon^{x_1}_{x_2}\epsilon^{x_2}_{x_1}} \qquad \text{and} \qquad \frac{dx_2}{dl_1} = \frac{\epsilon^{x_1}_{l_1}\epsilon^{x_2}_{x_1} \cdot \frac{x_2}{l_1}}{1 - \epsilon^{x_1}_{x_2}\epsilon^{x_2}_{x_1}}$$

Now $\bar{L}_1 = l_1\bar{x}_1\frac{dx_1}{dl_1} + l_1\bar{x}_2\frac{dx_2}{dl_1}$, so that $\frac{\bar{L}_1}{L_1} = \dfrac{1 + \frac{X_2}{X_1}\epsilon^{x_2}_{x_1}}{1 - \epsilon^{x_1}_{x_2}\epsilon^{x_2}_{x_1}}$

Similarly, we can show that $\frac{\bar{C}_1}{C_1} = \frac{\bar{L}_1}{L}$ and that

$$\frac{\bar{L}_2}{L_2} = \frac{\bar{C}_2}{C_2} = \frac{1 + \frac{X_1}{X_2}\epsilon^{x_1}_{x_2}}{1 - \epsilon^{x_1}_{x_2}\epsilon^{x_2}_{x_1}}$$

In other words, in order that each factor should obtain a reward equal to the value of its marginal social net product both labour and capital in industry 1, or alternatively, the price of the product of industry 1, should be subsidised at the *ad valorem* rate of $\epsilon_{x_1}^{x_2} \dfrac{\dfrac{X_2}{X_1} + \epsilon_{x_2}^{x_1}}{1 - \epsilon_{x_2}^{x_1}\epsilon_{x_1}^{x_2}}$; and similarly, in industry 2 a rate of subsidy of $\epsilon_{x_2}^{x_1} \dfrac{\dfrac{X_1}{X_2} + \epsilon_{x_1}^{x_2}}{1 - \epsilon_{x_2}^{x_1}\epsilon_{x_1}^{x_2}}$ should be paid.

So far throughout this note we have assumed that in all external economies or diseconomies, whether of the unpaid-factor or of the atmosphere-creating kind, it is the *output* of one industry which affects production in the other. But this is, of course, not necessarily the case. It may be the employment of one *factor* in one industry which confers an indirect benefit or the reverse upon producers in the other industry.[1] Moreover, in the case in which atmosphere is created, the output of industry 2 may create an atmosphere for industry 1 which increases the efficiency of a particular *factor* in industry 1 rather than the general level of *output*.[2] Or the employment of a particular *factor* in industry 2 might create conditions which improved the efficiency of a particular factor in industry 1.[3] And any combination of these indirect effects of industry 2 upon industry 1 might be combined with any other combination of such effects of industry 1 on industry 2. Clearly, we cannot consider in detail all the very many possibilities.

But consider the following particular case :

$$\left.\begin{aligned} x_1 &= H_1(\lambda_1, c_1) \\ x_2 &= H_2(\lambda_2, c_2) \\ \lambda_1 &= l_1 A(l) \\ \lambda_2 &= l_2 A(l) \\ l &= l_1 + l_2 \end{aligned}\right\} \quad . \quad . \quad . \quad . \quad . \quad (8)$$

where l_1 = the number of workers employed in industry 1 and λ_1 = the equivalent number of workers of an efficiency which an individual worker would have if the total labour force were very small ($l \to 0$, so that $A \to 1$.)

This is the case where the total labour force in the two industries (l) affects the general efficiency of labour. We may suppose that, up to a certain point, a growth in the absolute size

[1] In this case we should have equations of the type of $x_1 = H_1(l_1, c_1, l_2)$ in the case of unpaid factors, and of the type of $x_1 = H_1(l_1, c_1)A_1(l_2)$ in the case of atmosphere-creation.

[2] In this case the equations would be of the type $x_1 = H_1\{l_1 A_1(x_2), c_1\}$.

[3] For example, $x_1 = H_1\{l_1 A(c_2), c_1\}$.

of the labour force employed in these two industries causes a general atmosphere favourable to the efficiency of labour by enabling workers to communicate to each other a certain know-how about, and interest in, the mechanical processes which are common to the two industries.

Now the individual employer in any one firm in either industry will regard A as being unaffected by his own actions, because the indirect effect which an increase in the number of workers employed by him alone will have upon the general efficiency of his own labour will be a negligible quantity. He will go on taking on labour of any given level of efficiency until the wage paid to a unit of labour is equal to the price paid for its marginal product at that level of efficiency. In other words,

$$L_1 = \lambda_1 \bar{x}_1 \frac{\partial x_1}{\partial \lambda_1} = \epsilon^{x_1}_{\lambda_1} X_1$$

The reward paid to c_1 will be $C_1 = X_1 - L_1 = \epsilon^{x_1}_{c_1} X_1$. Similarly, $L_2 = \epsilon^{x_2}_{\lambda_2} X_2$ and $C_2 = \epsilon^{x_2}_{c_2} X_2$.

In this case $\bar{C}_1 = \epsilon^{x_1}_{c_1} X_1$ and $\bar{C}_2 = \epsilon^{x_2}_{c_2} X_2$ because there are no external economies or diseconomies involved in decisions to apply more capital in either industry, so that $C_1 = \bar{C}_1$ and $C_2 = \bar{C}_2$.

But in evaluating the value of the marginal social net product of labour we have to take into account the effect which the employment of more labour by one particular employer may have upon the efficiency of labour for all other employers in industry 1 and for all other employers in industry 2. The value of the marginal social net product exceeds the wage which will be offered for it by these two sums, so that

$$\bar{L}_1 = L_1 + l_1 \bar{x}_1 \frac{\partial x_1}{\partial \lambda_1} \cdot \frac{\partial \lambda_1}{\partial l} \cdot \frac{\partial l}{\partial l_1} + l_1 \bar{x}_2 \frac{\partial x_2}{\partial \lambda_2} \cdot \frac{\partial \lambda_2}{\partial l} \cdot \frac{\partial l}{\partial l_1}.$$

Since $\dfrac{\partial l}{\partial l_1} = 1$, $\dfrac{\partial \lambda_1}{\partial l} = \dfrac{\lambda_1}{A} \cdot \dfrac{\partial A}{\partial l}$, and $\dfrac{\partial \lambda_2}{\partial l} = \dfrac{\lambda_2}{A} \cdot \dfrac{\partial A}{\partial l}$,

we have $\bar{L}_1 = L_1 + (L_1 + L_2) \dfrac{l_1}{l} \epsilon^A_l$, where $\epsilon^A_l = \dfrac{l}{A} \cdot \dfrac{dA}{dl}$.

Similarly, $\bar{L}_2 = L_2 + (L_1 + L_2) \dfrac{l_2}{l} \epsilon^A_l$. Now if the wage-rate is the same in both industries so that $\dfrac{l_1}{l} = \dfrac{L_1}{L_1 + L_2}$ and $\dfrac{l_2}{l} = \dfrac{L_2}{L_1 + L_2}$, we have $\dfrac{\bar{L}_1}{L_1} = \dfrac{\bar{L}_2}{L_2} = 1 + \epsilon^A_l$. The employment of labour in both industries must be subsidised at the *ad valorem* rate of ϵ^A_l, if rewards are to be raised to the value of marginal social net products.

VI. Conclusion

It is not claimed that this division of external economies and diseconomies into unpaid factors and the creation of atmosphere is logically complete. External economies exist whenever we have production functions of the form

$$x_1 = F_1(l_1, c_1, l_2, c_2, x_2)$$
$$x_2 = F_2(l_2, c_2, l_1, c_1, x_1)$$

where F_1 and F_2 are not necessarily homogeneous of the first degree. But it is claimed that it may clarify thought on different types of external economy and diseconomy to distinguish thus between: (1) those cases in which there are constant returns for society, but not necessarily constant returns in each industry to the factors which each industry employs and pays for, and (2) those cases in which there are constant returns in each industry to those factors which it controls and pays for, but in which there are not constant returns for the two industries taken together, the scale of operations being important in the one industry because of the atmosphere which it creates for the other. One of the most important conclusions to be drawn is that in the case of type (1)—the unpaid-factor case—there is no adding-up problem for society as a whole; in order to pay every factor a reward equal to the value of its marginal social net product some factors must be taxed and others subsidised, and the revenue from the appropriate taxes will just finance the expenditure upon the appropriate subsidies. But in the case of the creation of atmosphere (type (2)) the subsidies (or taxes) required to promote (or discourage) the creation of favourable (or unfavourable) atmosphere are net additions to (or subtractions from) society's general fiscal burden. But, in fact, of course, external economies or diseconomies may not fall into either of these precise divisions and may contain features of both of them.

J. E. Meade

London School of Economics.

[3]

The Journal of

LAW & ECONOMICS

VOLUME III OCTOBER 1960

THE PROBLEM OF SOCIAL COST

R. H. COASE
University of Virginia

I. The Problem To Be Examined[1]

This paper is concerned with those actions of business firms which have harmful effects on others. The standard example is that of a factory the smoke from which has harmful effects on those occupying neighbouring properties. The economic analysis of such a situation has usually proceeded in terms of a divergence between the private and social product of the factory, in which economists have largely followed the treatment of Pigou in *The Economics of Welfare*. The conclusions to which this kind of analysis seems to have led most economists is that it would be desirable to make the owner of the factory liable for the damage caused to those injured by the smoke, or alternatively, to place a tax on the factory owner varying with the amount of smoke produced and equivalent in money terms to the damage it would cause, or finally, to exclude the factory from residential districts (and presumably from other

[1] This article, although concerned with a technical problem of economic analysis, arose out of the study of the Political Economy of Broadcasting which I am now conducting. The argument of the present article was implicit in a previous article dealing with the problem of allocating radio and television frequencies (The Federal Communications Commission, 2 J. Law & Econ. [1959]) but comments which I have received seemed to suggest that it would be desirable to deal with the question in a more explicit way and without reference to the original problem for the solution of which the analysis was developed.

areas in which the emission of smoke would have harmful effects on others). It is my contention that the suggested courses of action are inappropriate, in that they lead to results which are not necessarily, or even usually, desirable.

II. The Reciprocal Nature of the Problem

The traditional approach has tended to obscure the nature of the choice that has to be made. The question is commonly thought of as one in which A inflicts harm on B and what has to be decided is: how should we restrain A? But this is wrong. We are dealing with a problem of a reciprocal nature. To avoid the harm to B would inflict harm on A. The real question that has to be decided is: should A be allowed to harm B or should B be allowed to harm A? The problem is to avoid the more serious harm. I instanced in my previous article[2] the case of a confectioner the noise and vibrations from whose machinery disturbed a doctor in his work. To avoid harming the doctor would inflict harm on the confectioner. The problem posed by this case was essentially whether it was worth while, as a result of restricting the methods of production which could be used by the confectioner, to secure more doctoring at the cost of a reduced supply of confectionery products. Another example is afforded by the problem of straying cattle which destroy crops on neighbouring land. If it is inevitable that some cattle will stray, an increase in the supply of meat can only be obtained at the expense of a decrease in the supply of crops. The nature of the choice is clear: meat or crops. What answer should be given is, of course, not clear unless we know the value of what is obtained as well as the value of what is sacrificed to obtain it. To give another example, Professor George J. Stigler instances the contamination of a stream.[3] If we assume that the harmful effect of the pollution is that it kills the fish, the question to be decided is: is the value of the fish lost greater or less than the value of the product which the contamination of the stream makes possible. It goes almost without saying that this problem has to be looked at in total *and* at the margin.

III. The Pricing System with Liability for Damage

I propose to start my analysis by examining a case in which most economists would presumably agree that the problem would be solved in a completely satisfactory manner: when the damaging business has to pay for all damage caused *and* the pricing system works smoothly (strictly this means that the operation of a pricing system is without cost).

A good example of the problem under discussion is afforded by the case of straying cattle which destroy crops growing on neighbouring land. Let us suppose that a farmer and a cattle-raiser are operating on neighbouring proper-

[2] Coase, The Federal Communications Commission, 2 J. Law & Econ. 26–27 (1959).

[3] G. J. Stigler, The Theory of Price 105 (1952).

ties. Let us further suppose that, without any fencing between the properties, an increase in the size of the cattle-raiser's herd increases the total damage to the farmer's crops. What happens to the marginal damage as the size of the herd increases is another matter. This depends on whether the cattle tend to follow one another or to roam side by side, on whether they tend to be more or less restless as the size of the herd increases and on other similar factors. For my immediate purpose, it is immaterial what assumption is made about marginal damage as the size of the herd increases.

To simplify the argument, I propose to use an arithmetical example. I shall assume that the annual cost of fencing the farmer's property is $9 and that the price of the crop is $1 per ton. Also, I assume that the relation between the number of cattle in the herd and the annual crop loss is as follows:

Number in Herd (Steers)	Annual Crop Loss (Tons)	Crop Loss per Additional Steer (Tons)
1	1	1
2	3	2
3	6	3
4	10	4

Given that the cattle-raiser is liable for the damage caused, the additional annual cost imposed on the cattle-raiser if he increased his herd from, say, 2 to 3 steers is $3 and in deciding on the size of the herd, he will take this into account along with his other costs. That is, he will not increase the size of the herd unless the value of the additional meat produced (assuming that the cattle-raiser slaughters the cattle), is greater than the additional costs that this will entail, including the value of the additional crops destroyed. Of course, if, by the employment of dogs, herdsmen, aeroplanes, mobile radio and other means, the amount of damage can be reduced, these means will be adopted when their cost is less than the value of the crop which they prevent being lost. Given that the annual cost of fencing is $9, the cattle-raiser who wished to have a herd with 4 steers or more would pay for fencing to be erected and maintained, assuming that other means of attaining the same end would not do so more cheaply. When the fence is erected, the marginal cost due to the liability for damage becomes zero, except to the extent that an increase in the size of the herd necessitates a stronger and therefore more expensive fence because more steers are liable to lean against it at the same time. But, of course, it may be cheaper for the cattle-raiser not to fence and to pay for the damaged crops, as in my arithmetical example, with 3 or fewer steers.

It might be thought that the fact that the cattle-raiser would pay for all crops damaged would lead the farmer to increase his planting if a cattle-raiser came to occupy the neighbouring property. But this is not so. If the crop was previously sold in conditions of perfect competition, marginal cost was equal to price for the amount of planting undertaken and any expansion would have reduced the profits of the farmer. In the new situation, the existence of crop damage would mean that the farmer would sell less on the open market but his receipts for a given production would remain the same, since the cattle-raiser would pay the market price for any crop damaged. Of course, if cattle-raising commonly involved the destruction of crops, the coming into existence of a cattle-raising industry might raise the price of the crops involved and farmers would then extend their planting. But I wish to confine my attention to the individual farmer.

I have said that the occupation of a neighbouring property by a cattle-raiser would not cause the amount of production, or perhaps more exactly the amount of planting, by the farmer to increase. In fact, if the cattle-raising has any effect, it will be to decrease the amount of planting. The reason for this is that, for any given tract of land, if the value of the crop damaged is so great that the receipts from the sale of the undamaged crop are less than the total costs of cultivating that tract of land, it will be profitable for the farmer and the cattle-raiser to make a bargain whereby that tract of land is left uncultivated. This can be made clear by means of an arithmetical example. Assume initially that the value of the crop obtained from cultivating a given tract of land is $12 and that the cost incurred in cultivating this tract of land is $10, the net gain from cultivating the land being $2. I assume for purposes of simplicity that the farmer owns the land. Now assume that the cattle-raiser starts operations on the neighbouring property and that the value of the crops damaged is $1. In this case $11 is obtained by the farmer from sale on the market and $1 is obtained from the cattle-raiser for damage suffered and the net gain remains $2. Now suppose that the cattle-raiser finds it profitable to increase the size of his herd, even though the amount of damage rises to $3; which means that the value of the additional meat production is greater than the additional costs, including the additional $2 payment for damage. But the total payment for damage is now $3. The net gain to the farmer from cultivating the land is still $2. The cattle-raiser would be better off if the farmer would agree not to cultivate his land for any payment less than $3. The farmer would be agreeable to not cultivating the land for any payment greater than $2. There is clearly room for a mutually satisfactory bargain which would lead to the abandonment of cultivation.[4] But the same argument applies not only to the whole tract cultivated by the farmer but also to any

[4] The argument in the text has proceeded on the assumption that the alternative to cultivation of the crop is abandonment of cultivation altogether. But this need not be so. There may be crops which are less liable to damage by cattle but which would not be as profitable as the crop grown in the absence of damage. Thus, if the cultivation of a new crop would yield a return to the farmer of $1 instead of $2, and the size of the herd which would cause $3 damage with the old crop would cause $1 damage with the new crop, it would be profitable to the cattle-raiser to pay any sum less than $2 to induce the farmer

subdivision of it. Suppose, for example, that the cattle have a well-defined route, say, to a brook or to a shady area. In these circumstances, the amount of damage to the crop along the route may well be great and if so, it could be that the farmer and the cattle-raiser would find it profitable to make a bargain whereby the farmer would agree not to cultivate this strip of land.

But this raises a further possibility. Suppose that there is such a well-defined route. Suppose further that the value of the crop that would be obtained by cultivating this strip of land is $10 but that the cost of cultivation is $11. In the absence of the cattle-raiser, the land would not be cultivated. However, given the presence of the cattle-raiser, it could well be that if the strip was cultivated, the whole crop would be destroyed by the cattle. In which case, the cattle-raiser would be forced to pay $10 to the farmer. It is true that the farmer would lose $1. But the cattle-raiser would lose $10. Clearly this is a situation which is not likely to last indefinitely since neither party would want this to happen. The aim of the farmer would be to induce the cattle-raiser to make a payment in return for an agreement to leave this land uncultivated. The farmer would not be able to obtain a payment greater than the cost of fencing off this piece of land nor so high as to lead the cattle-raiser to abandon the use of the neighbouring property. What payment would in fact be made would depend on the shrewdness of the farmer and the cattle-raiser as bargainers. But as the payment would not be so high as to cause the cattle-raiser to abandon this location and as it would not vary with the size of the herd, such an agreement would not affect the allocation of resources but would merely alter the distribution of income and wealth as between the cattle-raiser and the farmer.

I think it is clear that if the cattle-raiser is liable for damage caused and the pricing system works smoothly, the reduction in the value of production elsewhere will be taken into account in computing the additional cost involved in increasing the size of the herd. This cost will be weighed against the value of the additional meat production and, given perfect competition in the cattle industry, the allocation of resources in cattle-raising will be optimal. What needs to be emphasized is that the fall in the value of production elsewhere which would be taken into account in the costs of the cattle-raiser may well be less than the damage which the cattle would cause to the crops in the ordinary course of events. This is because it is possible, as a result of market transactions, to discontinue cultivation of the land. This is desirable in all

---

to change his crop (since this would reduce damage liability from $3 to $1) and it would be profitable for the farmer to do so if the amount received was more than $1 (the reduction in his return caused by switching crops). In fact, there would be room for a mutually satisfactory bargain in all cases in which a change of crop would reduce the amount of damage by more than it reduces the value of the crop (excluding damage)—in all cases, that is, in which a change in the crop cultivated would lead to an increase in the value of production.

cases in which the damage that the cattle would cause, and for which the cattle-raiser would be willing to pay, exceeds the amount which the farmer would pay for use of the land. In conditions of perfect competition, the amount which the farmer would pay for the use of the land is equal to the difference between the value of the total production when the factors are employed on this land and the value of the additional product yielded in their next best use (which would be what the farmer would have to pay for the factors). If damage exceeds the amount the farmer would pay for the use of the land, the value of the additional product of the factors employed elsewhere would exceed the value of the total product in this use after damage is taken into account. It follows that it would be desirable to abandon cultivation of the land and to release the factors employed for production elsewhere. A procedure which merely provided for payment for damage to the crop caused by the cattle but which did not allow for the possibility of cultivation being discontinued would result in too small an employment of factors of production in cattle-raising and too large an employment of factors in cultivation of the crop. But given the possibility of market transactions, a situation in which damage to crops exceeded the rent of the land would not endure. Whether the cattle-raiser pays the farmer to leave the land uncultivated or himself rents the land by paying the land-owner an amount slightly greater than the farmer would pay (if the farmer was himself renting the land), the final result would be the same and would maximise the value of production. Even when the farmer is induced to plant crops which it would not be profitable to cultivate for sale on the market, this will be a purely short-term phenomenon and may be expected to lead to an agreement under which the planting will cease. The cattle-raiser will remain in that location and the marginal cost of meat production will be the same as before, thus having no long-run effect on the allocation of resources.

IV. The Pricing System with No Liability for Damage

I now turn to the case in which, although the pricing system is assumed to work smoothly (that is, costlessly), the damaging business is not liable for any of the damage which it causes. This business does not have to make a payment to those damaged by its actions. I propose to show that the allocation of resources will be the same in this case as it was when the damaging business was liable for damage caused. As I showed in the previous case that the allocation of resources was optimal, it will not be necessary to repeat this part of the argument.

I return to the case of the farmer and the cattle-raiser. The farmer would suffer increased damage to his crop as the size of the herd increased. Suppose that the size of the cattle-raiser's herd is 3 steers (and that this is the size of the herd that would be maintained if crop damage was not taken into account). Then the farmer would be willing to pay up to $3 if the cattle-raiser would reduce his herd to 2 steers, up to $5 if the herd were reduced to 1 steer and would pay up to $6 if cattle-raising was abandoned. The cattle-raiser would therefore receive $3 from the farmer if he kept 2 steers instead of 3. This $3 foregone is therefore part of the cost incurred in keeping the third steer. Whether the $3 is a payment which the cattle-raiser has to make if he adds the third steer to his herd (which it would be if the cattle-raiser was liable to the farmer for damage caused to the crop) or whether it is a sum of money which he would have received if he did not keep a third steer (which it would be if the cattle-raiser was not liable to the farmer for damage caused to the crop) does not affect the final result. In both cases $3 is part of the cost of adding a third steer, to be included along with the other costs. If the increase in the value of production in cattle-raising through increasing the size of the herd from 2 to 3 is greater than the additional costs that have to be incurred (including the $3 damage to crops), the size of the herd will be increased. Otherwise, it will not. The size of the herd will be the same whether the cattle-raiser is liable for damage caused to the crop or not.

It may be argued that the assumed starting point—a herd of 3 steers—was arbitrary. And this is true. But the farmer would not wish to pay to avoid crop damage which the cattle-raiser would not be able to cause. For example, the maximum annual payment which the farmer could be induced to pay could not exceed $9, the annual cost of fencing. And the farmer would only be willing to pay this sum if it did not reduce his earnings to a level that would cause him to abandon cultivation of this particular tract of land. Furthermore, the farmer would only be willing to pay this amount if he believed that, in the absence of any payment by him, the size of the herd maintained by the cattle raiser would be 4 or more steers. Let us assume that this is the case. Then the farmer would be willing to pay up to $3 if the cattle raiser would reduce his herd to 3 steers, up to $6 if the herd were reduced to 2 steers, up to $8 if one steer only were kept and up to $9 if cattle-raising were abandoned. It will be noticed that the change in the starting point has not altered the amount which would accrue to the cattle-raiser if he reduced the size of his herd by any given amount. It is still true that the cattle-raiser could receive an additional $3 from the farmer if he agreed to reduce his herd from 3 steers to 2 and that the $3 represents the value of the crop that would be destroyed by adding the third steer to the herd. Although a different belief on the part of the farmer (whether justified or not) about the size of the herd that the cattle-raiser would maintain in the absence of payments from him may affect the total payment he can be induced to pay, it is not true that this different belief would have any effect on the size of the herd that the cattle-raiser will actually keep. This will be the same as it would be if the cattle-raiser had to pay for damage caused by his cattle, since a receipt foregone of a given amount is the equivalent of a payment of the same amount.

It might be thought that it would pay the cattle-raiser to increase his herd above the size that he would wish to maintain once a bargain had been made, in order to induce the farmer to make a larger total payment. And this may be true. It is similar in nature to the action of the farmer (when the cattle-raiser was liable for damage) in cultivating land on which, as a result of an agreement with the cattle-raiser, planting would subsequently be abandoned (including land which would not be cultivated at all in the absence of cattle-raising). But such manoeuvres are preliminaries to an agreement and do not affect the long-run equilibrium position, which is the same whether or not the cattle-raiser is held responsible for the crop damage brought about by his cattle.

It is necessary to know whether the damaging business is liable or not for damage caused since without the establishment of this initial delimitation of rights there can be no market transactions to transfer and recombine them. But the ultimate result (which maximises the value of production) is independent of the legal position if the pricing system is assumed to work without cost.

V. The Problem Illustrated Anew

The harmful effects of the activities of a business can assume a wide variety of forms. An early English case concerned a building which, by obstructing currents of air, hindered the operation of a windmill.[5] A recent case in Florida concerned a building which cast a shadow on the cabana, swimming pool and sunbathing areas of a neighbouring hotel.[6] The problem of straying cattle and the damaging of crops which was the subject of detailed examination in the two preceding sections, although it may have appeared to be rather a special case, is in fact but one example of a problem which arises in many different guises. To clarify the nature of my argument and to demonstrate its general applicability, I propose to illustrate it anew by reference to four actual cases.

Let us first reconsider the case of *Sturges v. Bridgman*[7] which I used as an illustration of the general problem in my article on "The Federal Communications Commission." In this case, a confectioner (in Wigmore Street) used two mortars and pestles in connection with his business (one had been in operation in the same position for more than 60 years and the other for more than 26 years). A doctor then came to occupy neighbouring premises (in Wimpole Street). The confectioner's machinery caused the doctor no harm until, eight years after he had first occupied the premises, he built a consulting room at the end of his garden right against the confectioner's kitchen. It was then found that the noise and vibration caused by the confectioner's machin-

[5] See Gale on Easements 237–39 (13th ed. M. Bowles 1959).

[6] See Fontainebleu Hotel Corp. v. Forty-Five Twenty-Five, Inc., 114 So. 2d 357 (1959).

[7] 11 Ch. D. 852 (1879).

ery made it difficult for the doctor to use his new consulting room. "In particular . . . the noise prevented him from examining his patients by auscultation[8] for diseases of the chest. He also found it impossible to engage with effect in any occupation which required thought and attention." The doctor therefore brought a legal action to force the confectioner to stop using his machinery. The courts had little difficulty in granting the doctor the injunction he sought. "Individual cases of hardship may occur in the strict carrying out of the principle upon which we found our judgment, but the negation of the principle would lead even more to individual hardship, and would at the same time produce a prejudicial effect upon the development of land for residential purposes."

The court's decision established that the doctor had the right to prevent the confectioner from using his machinery. But, of course, it would have been possible to modify the arrangements envisaged in the legal ruling by means of a bargain between the parties. The doctor would have been willing to waive his right and allow the machinery to continue in operation if the confectioner would have paid him a sum of money which was greater than the loss of income which he would suffer from having to move to a more costly or less convenient location or from having to curtail his activities at this location or, as was suggested as a possibility, from having to build a separate wall which would deaden the noise and vibration. The confectioner would have been willing to do this if the amount he would have to pay the doctor was less than the fall in income he would suffer if he had to change his mode of operation at this location, abandon his operation or move his confectionery business to some other location. The solution of the problem depends essentially on whether the continued use of the machinery adds more to the confectioner's income than it subtracts from the doctor's.[9] But now consider the situation if the confectioner had won the case. The confectioner would then have had the right to continue operating his noise and vibration-generating machinery without having to pay anything to the doctor. The boot would have been on the other foot: the doctor would have had to pay the confectioner to induce him to stop using the machinery. If the doctor's income would have fallen more through continuance of the use of this machinery than it added to the income of the confectioner, there would clearly be room for a bargain whereby the doctor paid the confectioner to stop using the machinery. That is to say, the circumstances in which it would not pay the confectioner to continue to use the machinery and to compensate the doctor for the losses that this would bring (if the doctor had the right to prevent the confectioner's using his

[8] Auscultation is the act of listening by ear or stethoscope in order to judge by sound the condition of the body.

[9] Note that what is taken into account is the change in income after allowing for alterations in methods of production, location, character of product, etc.

machinery) would be those in which it would be in the interest of the doctor to make a payment to the confectioner which would induce him to discontinue the use of the machinery (if the confectioner had the right to operate the machinery). The basic conditions are exactly the same in this case as they were in the example of the cattle which destroyed crops. With costless market transactions, the decision of the courts concerning liability for damage would be without effect on the allocation of resources. It was of course the view of the judges that they were affecting the working of the economic system—and in a desirable direction. Any other decision would have had "a prejudicial effect upon the development of land for residential purposes," an argument which was elaborated by examining the example of a forge operating on a barren moor, which was later developed for residual purposes. The judges' view that they were settling how the land was to be used would be true only in the case in which the costs of carrying out the necessary market transactions exceeded the gain which might be achieved by any rearrangement of rights. And it would be desirable to preserve the areas (Wimpole Street or the moor) for residential or professional use (by giving non-industrial users the right to stop the noise, vibration, smoke, etc., by injunction) only if the value of the additional residential facilities obtained was greater than the value of cakes or iron lost. But of this the judges seem to have been unaware.

Another example of the same problem is furnished by the case of *Cooke v. Forbes*.[10] One process in the weaving of cocoa-nut fibre matting was to immerse it in bleaching liquids after which it was hung out to dry. Fumes from a manufacturer of sulphate of ammonia had the effect of turning the matting from a bright to a dull and blackish colour. The reason for this was that the bleaching liquid contained chloride of tin, which, when affected by sulphuretted hydrogen, is turned to a darker colour. An injunction was sought to stop the manufacturer from emitting the fumes. The lawyers for the defendant argued that if the plaintiff "were not to use . . . a particular bleaching liquid, their fibre would not be affected; that their process is unusual, not according to the custom of the trade, and even damaging to their own fabrics." The judge commented: ". . . it appears to me quite plain that a person has a right to carry on upon his own property a manufacturing process in which he uses chloride of tin, or any sort of metallic dye, and that his neighbour is not at liberty to pour in gas which will interfere with his manufacture. If it can be traced to the neighbour, then, I apprehend, clearly he will have a right to come here and ask for relief." But in view of the fact that the damage was accidental and occasional, that careful precautions were taken and that there was no exceptional risk, an injunction was refused, leaving the plaintiff to bring an action for damages if he wished. What the subsequent developments

[10] L. R. 5 Eq. 166 (1867–1868).

were I do not know. But it is clear that the situation is essentially the same as that found in *Sturges v. Bridgman,* except that the cocoa-nut fibre matting manufacturer could not secure an injunction but would have to seek damages from the sulphate of ammonia manufacturer. The economic analysis of the situation is exactly the same as with the cattle which destroyed crops. To avoid the damage, the sulphate of ammonia manufacturer could increase his precautions or move to another location. Either course would presumably increase his costs. Alternatively he could pay for the damage. This he would do if the payments for damage were less than the additional costs that would have to be incurred to avoid the damage. The payments for damage would then become part of the cost of production of sulphate of ammonia. Of course, if, as was suggested in the legal proceedings, the amount of damage could be eliminated by changing the bleaching agent (which would presumably increase the costs of the matting manufacturer) and if the additional cost was less than the damage that would otherwise occur, it should be possible for the two manufacturers to make a mutually satisfactory bargain whereby the new bleaching agent was used. Had the court decided against the matting manufacturer, as a consequence of which he would have had to suffer the damage without compensation, the allocation of resources would not have been affected. It would pay the matting manufacturer to change his bleaching agent if the additional cost involved was less than the reduction in damage. And since the matting manufacturer would be willing to pay the sulphate of ammonia manufacturer an amount up to his loss of income (the increase in costs or the damage suffered) if he would cease his activities, this loss of income would remain a cost of production for the manufacturer of sulphate of ammonia. This case is indeed analytically exactly the same as the cattle example.

Bryant v. Lefever[11] raised the problem of the smoke nuisance in a novel form. The plaintiff and the defendants were occupiers of adjoining houses, which were of about the same height.

> Before 1876 the plaintiff was able to light a fire in any room of his house without the chimneys smoking; the two houses had remained in the same condition some thirty or forty years. In 1876 the defendants took down their house, and began to rebuild it. They carried up a wall by the side of the plaintiff's chimneys much beyond its original height, and stacked timber on the roof of their house, and thereby caused the plaintiff's chimneys to smoke whenever he lighted fires.

The reason, of course, why the chimneys smoked was that the erection of the wall and the stacking of the timber prevented the free circulation of air. In a trial before a jury, the plaintiff was awarded damages of £40. The case then went to the Court of Appeals where the judgment was reversed. Bramwell, L.J., argued:

[11] 4 C.P.D. 172 (1878–1879).

> . . . it is said, and the jury have found, that the defendants have done that which caused a nuisance to the plaintiff's house. We think there is no evidence of this. No doubt there is a nuisance, but it is not of the defendant's causing. They have done nothing in causing the nuisance. Their house and their timber are harmless enough. It is the plaintiff who causes the nuisance by lighting a coal fire in a place the chimney of which is placed so near the defendants' wall, that the smoke does not escape, but comes into the house. Let the plaintiff cease to light his fire, let him move his chimney, let him carry it higher, and there would be no nuisance. Who then, causes it? It would be very clear that the plaintiff did, if he had built his house or chimney after the defendants had put up the timber on theirs, and it is really the same though he did so before the timber was there. But (what is in truth the same answer), if the defendants cause the nuisance, they have a right to do so. If the plaintiff has not the right to the passage of air, except subject to the defendants' right to build or put timber on their house, then his right is subject to their right, and though a nuisance follows from the exercise of their right, they are not liable.

And Cotton, L.J., said:

> Here it is found that the erection of the defendants' wall has sensibly and materially interfered with the comfort of human existence in the plaintiff's house, and it is said this is a nuisance for which the defendants are liable. Ordinarily this is so, but the defendants have done so, not by sending on to the plaintiff's property any smoke or noxious vapour, but by interrupting the egress of smoke from the plaintiff's house in a way to which . . . the plaintiff has no legal right. The plaintiff creates the smoke, which interferes with his comfort. Unless he has . . . a right to get rid of this in a particular way which has been interfered with by the defendants, he cannot sue the defendants, because the smoke made by himself, for which he has not provided any effectual means of escape, causes him annoyance. It is as if a man tried to get rid of liquid filth arising on his own land by a drain into his neighbour's land. Until a right had been acquired by user, the neighbour might stop the drain without incurring liability by so doing. No doubt great inconvenience would be caused to the owner of the property on which the liquid filth arises. But the act of his neighbour would be a lawful act, and he would not be liable for the consequences attributable to the fact that the man had accumulated filth without providing any effectual means of getting rid of it.

I do not propose to show that any subsequent modification of the situation, as a result of bargains between the parties (conditioned by the cost of stacking the timber elsewhere, the cost of extending the chimney higher, etc.), would have exactly the same result whatever decision the courts had come to since this point has already been adequately dealt with in the discussion of the cattle example and the two previous cases. What I shall discuss is the argument of the judges in the Court of Appeals that the smoke nuisance was not caused by the man who erected the wall but by the man who lit the fires. The novelty of the situation is that the smoke nuisance was suffered by the man who lit the fires and not by some third person. The question is not a trivial one since it lies at the heart of the problem under discussion. Who caused the smoke nuisance? The answer seems fairly clear. The smoke nuisance was caused both by the man who built the wall *and* by the man who lit the fires. Given the fires, there would have been no smoke nuisance without the wall; given the wall, there would have been no smoke nuisance without the fires. Eliminate the wall *or* the fires and the smoke nuisance would disappear. On the marginal principle it is clear that *both* were responsible and *both* should be forced to include the loss of amenity due to the smoke as a cost in deciding whether to continue the activity which gives rise to the smoke. And given the possibility of market transactions, this is what would in fact happen. Although the wall-builder was not liable legally for the nuisance, as the man with the smoking chimneys would presumably be willing to pay a sum equal to the monetary worth to him of eliminating the smoke, this sum would therefore become for the wall-builder, a cost of continuing to have the high wall with the timber stacked on the roof.

The judges' contention that it was the man who lit the fires who alone caused the smoke nuisance is true only if we assume that the wall is the given factor. This is what the judges did by deciding that the man who erected the higher wall had a legal right to do so. The case would have been even more interesting if the smoke from the chimneys had injured the timber. Then it would have been the wall-builder who suffered the damage. The case would then have closely paralleled *Sturges v. Bridgman* and there can be little doubt that the man who lit the fires would have been liable for the ensuing damage to the timber, in spite of the fact that no damage had occurred until the high wall was built by the man who owned the timber.

Judges have to decide on legal liability but this should not confuse economists about the nature of the economic problem involved. In the case of the cattle and the crops, it is true that there would be no crop damage without the cattle. It is equally true that there would be no crop damage without the crops. The doctor's work would not have been disturbed if the confectioner had not worked his machinery; but the machinery would have disturbed no one if the doctor had not set up his consulting room in that particular place. The matting was blackened by the fumes from the sulphate of ammonia manufacturer; but no damage would have occurred if the matting manufacturer had not chosen to hang out his matting in a particular place and to use a particular bleaching agent. If we are to discuss the problem in terms of causation, both parties cause the damage. If we are to attain an optimum allocation of resources, it is therefore desirable that both parties should take the harmful effect (the nuisance) into account in deciding on their course of action. It is one of the beauties of a smoothly operating pricing system that, as has already been explained, the fall in the value of production due to the harmful effect would be a cost for both parties.

Bass v. Gregory[12] will serve as an excellent final illustration of the problem. The plaintiffs were the owners and tenant of a public house called the Jolly Anglers. The defendant was the owner of some cottages and a yard adjoining the Jolly Anglers. Under the public house was a cellar excavated in the rock. From the cellar, a hole or shaft had been cut into an old well situated in the defendant's yard. The well therefore became the ventilating shaft for the cellar. The cellar "had been used for a particular purpose in the process of brewing, which, without ventilation, could not be carried on." The cause of the action was that the defendant removed a grating from the mouth of the well, "so as to stop or prevent the free passage of air from [the] cellar upwards through the well. . . ." What caused the defendant to take this step is not clear from the report of the case. Perhaps "the air . . . impregnated by the brewing operations" which "passed up the well and out into the open air" was offensive to him. At any rate, he preferred to have the well in his yard stopped up. The court had first to determine whether the owners of the public house could have a legal right to a current of air. If they were to have such a right, this case would have to be distinguished from *Bryant v. Lefever* (already considered). This, however, presented no difficulty. In this case, the current of air was confined to "a strictly defined channel." In the case of *Bryant v. Lefever,* what was involved was "the general current of air common to all mankind." The judge therefore held that the owners of the public house could have the right to a current of air whereas the owner of the private house in *Bryant v. Lefever* could not. An economist might be tempted to add "but the air moved all the same." However, all that had been decided at this stage of the argument was that there could be a legal right, not that the owners of the public house possessed it. But evidence showed that the shaft from the cellar to the well had existed for over forty years and that the use of the well as a ventilating shaft must have been known to the owners of the yard since the air, when it emerged, smelt of the brewing operations. The judge therefore held that the public house had such a right by the "doctrine of lost grant." This doctrine states "that if a legal right is proved to have existed and been exercised for a number of years the law ought to presume that it had a legal origin."[13] So the owner of the cottages and yard had to unstop the well and endure the smell.

[12] 25 Q.B.D. 481 (1890).

[13] It may be asked why a lost grant could not also be presumed in the case of the confectioner who had operated one mortar for more than 60 years. The answer is that until the doctor built the consulting room at the end of his garden there was no nuisance. So the nuisance had not continued for many years. It is true that the confectioner in his affidavit referred to "an invalid lady who occupied the house upon one occasion, about thirty years before" who "requested him if possible to discontinue the use of the mortars before eight o'clock in the morning" and that there was some evidence that the garden wall had been subjected to vibration. But the court had little difficulty in disposing of this line of argument: ". . . this vibration, even if it existed at all, was so slight, and the com-

The reasoning employed by the courts in determining legal rights will often seem strange to an economist because many of the factors on which the decision turns are, to an economist, irrelevant. Because of this, situations which are, from an economic point of view, identical will be treated quite differently by the courts. The economic problem in all cases of harmful effects is how to maximise the value of production. In the case of *Bass v. Gregory* fresh air was drawn in through the well which facilitated the production of beer but foul air was expelled through the well which made life in the adjoining houses less pleasant. The economic problem was to decide which to choose: a lower cost of beer and worsened amenities in adjoining houses or a higher cost of beer and improved amenities. In deciding this question, the "doctrine of lost grant" is about as relevant as the colour of the judge's eyes. But it has to be remembered that the immediate question faced by the courts is *not* what shall be done by whom *but* who has the legal right to do what. It is always possible to modify by transactions on the market the initial legal delimitation of rights. And, of course, if such market transactions are costless, such a rearrangement of rights will always take place if it would lead to an increase in the value of production.

VI. The Cost of Market Transactions Taken into Account

The argument has proceeded up to this point on the assumption (explicit in Sections III and IV and tacit in Section V) that there were no costs involved in carrying out market transactions. This is, of course, a very unrealistic assumption. In order to carry out a market transaction it is necessary to discover who it is that one wishes to deal with, to inform people that one wishes to deal and on what terms, to conduct negotiations leading up to a bargain, to draw up the contract, to undertake the inspection needed to make sure that the terms of the contract are being observed, and so on. These operations are often extremely costly, sufficiently costly at any rate to prevent many transactions that would be carried out in a world in which the pricing system worked without cost.

In earlier sections, when dealing with the problem of the rearrangement of legal rights through the market, it was argued that such a rearrangement would be made through the market whenever this would lead to an increase in the value of production. But this assumed costless market transactions. Once the costs of carrying out market transactions are taken into account it is clear that such a rearrangement of rights will only be undertaken when the increase in the value of production consequent upon the rearrangement

plaint, if it can be called a complaint, of the invalid lady . . . was of so trifling a character, that . . . the Defendant's acts would not have given rise to any proceeding either at law or in equity" (11 Ch.D. 863). That is, the confectioner had not committed a nuisance until the doctor built his consulting room.

is greater than the costs which would be involved in bringing it about. When it is less, the granting of an injunction (or the knowledge that it would be granted) or the liability to pay damages may result in an activity being discontinued (or may prevent its being started) which would be undertaken if market transactions were costless. In these conditions the initial delimitation of legal rights does have an effect on the efficiency with which the economic system operates. One arrangement of rights may bring about a greater value of production than any other. But unless this is the arrangement of rights established by the legal system, the costs of reaching the same result by altering and combining rights through the market may be so great that this optimal arrangement of rights, and the greater value of production which it would bring, may never be achieved. The part played by economic considerations in the process of delimiting legal rights will be discussed in the next section. In this section, I will take the initial delimitation of rights and the costs of carrying out market transactions as given.

It is clear that an alternative form of economic organisation which could achieve the same result at less cost than would be incurred by using the market would enable the value of production to be raised. As I explained many years ago, the firm represents such an alternative to organising production through market transactions.[14] Within the firm individual bargains between the various cooperating factors of production are eliminated and for a market transaction is substituted an administrative decision. The rearrangement of production then takes place without the need for bargains between the owners of the factors of production. A landowner who has control of a large tract of land may devote his land to various uses taking into account the effect that the interrelations of the various activities will have on the net return of the land, thus rendering unnecessary bargains between those undertaking the various activities. Owners of a large building or of several adjoining properties in a given area may act in much the same way. In effect, using our earlier terminology, the firm would acquire the legal rights of all the parties and the rearrangement of activities would not follow on a rearrangement of rights by contract, but as a result of an administrative decision as to how the rights should be used.

It does not, of course, follow that the administrative costs of organising a transaction through a firm are inevitably less than the costs of the market transactions which are superseded. But where contracts are peculiarly difficult to draw up and an attempt to describe what the parties have agreed to do or not to do (e.g. the amount and kind of a smell or noise that they may make or will not make) would necessitate a lengthy and highly involved document, and, where, as is probable, a long-term contract would be desir-

[14] See Coase, The Nature of the Firm, 4 Economica, New Series, 386 (1937). Reprinted in Readings in Price Theory, 331 (1952).

able;[15] it would be hardly surprising if the emergence of a firm or the extension of the activities of an existing firm was not the solution adopted on many occasions to deal with the problem of harmful effects. This solution would be adopted whenever the administrative costs of the firm were less than the costs of the market transactions that it supersedes and the gains which would result from the rearrangement of activities greater than the firm's costs of organising them. I do not need to examine in great detail the character of this solution since I have explained what is involved in my earlier article.

But the firm is not the only possible answer to this problem. The administrative costs of organising transactions within the firm may also be high, and particularly so when many diverse activities are brought within the control of a single organisation. In the standard case of a smoke nuisance, which may affect a vast number of people engaged in a wide variety of activities, the administrative costs might well be so high as to make any attempt to deal with the problem within the confines of a single firm impossible. An alternative solution is direct Government regulation. Instead of instituting a legal system of rights which can be modified by transactions on the market, the government may impose regulations which state what people must or must not do and which have to be obeyed. Thus, the government (by statute or perhaps more likely through an administrative agency) may, to deal with the problem of smoke nuisance, decree that certain methods of production should or should not be used (e.g. that smoke preventing devices should be installed or that coal or oil should not be burned) or may confine certain types of business to certain districts (zoning regulations).

The government is, in a sense, a super-firm (but of a very special kind) since it is able to influence the use of factors of production by administrative decision. But the ordinary firm is subject to checks in its operations because of the competition of other firms, which might administer the same activities at lower cost and also because there is always the alternative of market transactions as against organisation within the firm if the administrative costs become too great. The government is able, if it wishes, to avoid the market altogether, which a firm can never do. The firm has to make market agreements with the owners of the factors of production that it uses. Just as the government can conscript or seize property, so it can decree that factors of production should only be used in such-and-such a way. Such authoritarian methods save a lot of trouble (for those doing the organising). Furthermore, the government has at its disposal the police and the other law enforcement agencies to make sure that its regulations are carried out.

It is clear that the government has powers which might enable it to get some things done at a lower cost than could a private organisation (or at any

[15] For reasons explained in my earlier article, see Readings in Price Theory, n. 14 at 337.

rate one without special governmental powers). But the governmental administrative machine is not itself costless. It can, in fact, on occasion be extremely costly. Furthermore, there is no reason to suppose that the restrictive and zoning regulations, made by a fallible administration subject to political pressures and operating without any competitive check, will necessarily always be those which increase the efficiency with which the economic system operates. Furthermore, such general regulations which must apply to a wide variety of cases will be enforced in some cases in which they are clearly inappropriate. From these considerations it follows that direct governmental regulation will not necessarily give better results than leaving the problem to be solved by the market or the firm. But equally there is no reason why, on occasion, such governmental administrative regulation should not lead to an improvement in economic efficiency. This would seem particularly likely when, as is normally the case with the smoke nuisance, a large number of people are involved and in which therefore the costs of handling the problem through the market or the firm may be high.

There is, of course, a further alternative, which is to do nothing about the problem at all. And given that the costs involved in solving the problem by regulations issued by the governmental administrative machine will often be heavy (particularly if the costs are interpreted to include all the consequences which follow from the Government engaging in this kind of activity), it will no doubt be commonly the case that the gain which would come from regulating the actions which give rise to the harmful effects will be less than the costs involved in Government regulation.

The discussion of the problem of harmful effects in this section (when the costs of market transactions are taken into account) is extremely inadequate. But at least it has made clear that the problem is one of choosing the appropriate social arrangement for dealing with the harmful effects. All solutions have costs and there is no reason to suppose that government regulation is called for simply because the problem is not well handled by the market or the firm. Satisfactory views on policy can only come from a patient study of how, in practice, the market, firms and governments handle the problem of harmful effects. Economists need to study the work of the broker in bringing parties together, the effectiveness of restrictive covenants, the problems of the large-scale real-estate development company, the operation of Government zoning and other regulating activities. It is my belief that economists, and policy-makers generally, have tended to over-estimate the advantages which come from governmental regulation. But this belief, even if justified, does not do more than suggest that government regulation should be curtailed. It does not tell us where the boundary line should be drawn. This, it seems to me, has to come from a detailed investigation of the actual results of handling the problem in different ways. But it would be unfortunate if this investigation were undertaken with the aid of a faulty economic analysis. The aim of this article is to indicate what the economic approach to the problem should be.

VII. The Legal Delimitation of Rights and the Economic Problem

The discussion in Section V not only served to illustrate the argument but also afforded a glimpse at the legal approach to the problem of harmful effects. The cases considered were all English but a similar selection of American cases could easily be made and the character of the reasoning would have been the same. Of course, if market transactions were costless, all that matters (questions of equity apart) is that the rights of the various parties should be well-defined and the results of legal actions easy to forecast. But as we have seen, the situation is quite different when market transactions are so costly as to make it difficult to change the arrangement of rights established by the law. In such cases, the courts directly influence economic activity. It would therefore seem desirable that the courts should understand the economic consequences of their decisions and should, insofar as this is possible without creating too much uncertainty about the legal position itself, take these consequences into account when making their decisions. Even when it is possible to change the legal delimitation of rights through market transactions, it is obviously desirable to reduce the need for such transactions and thus reduce the employment of resources in carrying them out.

A thorough examination of the presuppositions of the courts in trying such cases would be of great interest but I have not been able to attempt it. Nevertheless it is clear from a cursory study that the courts have often recognized the economic implications of their decisions and are aware (as many economists are not) of the reciprocal nature of the problem. Furthermore, from time to time, they take these economic implications into account, along with other factors, in arriving at their decisions. The American writers on this subject refer to the question in a more explicit fashion than do the British. Thus, to quote Prosser on Torts, a person may

> make use of his own property or . . . conduct his own affairs at the expense of some harm to his neighbors. He may operate a factory whose noise and smoke cause some discomfort to others, so long as he keeps within reasonable bounds. It is only when his conduct is unreasonable, ***in the light of its utility and the harm which results*** [italics added], that it becomes a nuisance. . . . . As it was said in an ancient case in regard to candle-making in a town, "Le utility del chose excusera le noisomeness del stink."
>
> The world must have factories, smelters, oil refineries, noisy machinery and blasting, even at the expense of some inconvenience to those in the vicinity and the

plaintiff may be required to accept some not unreasonable discomfort for the general good.[16]

The standard British writers do not state as explicitly as this that a comparison between the utility and harm produced is an element in deciding whether a harmful effect should be considered a nuisance. But similar views, if less strongly expressed, are to be found.[17] The doctrine that the harmful effect must be substantial before the court will act is, no doubt, in part a reflection of the fact that there will almost always be some gain to offset the harm. And in the reports of individual cases, it is clear that the judges have had in mind what would be lost as well as what would be gained in deciding whether to grant an injunction or award damages. Thus, in refusing to prevent the destruction of a prospect by a new building, the judge stated:

> I know no general rule of common law, which . . . says, that building so as to stop another's prospect is a nuisance. Was that the case, there could be no great towns; and I must grant injunctions to all the new buildings in this town. . . .[18]

In *Webb v. Bird*[19] it was decided that it was not a nuisance to build a schoolhouse so near a windmill as to obstruct currents of air and hinder the working of the mill. An early case seems to have been decided in an opposite direction. Gale commented:

> In old maps of London a row of windmills appears on the heights to the north of London. Probably in the time of King James it was thought an alarming circumstance, as affecting the supply of food to the city, that anyone should build so near them as to take the wind out from their sails.[20]

In one of the cases discussed in section V, *Sturges v. Bridgman*, it seems clear that the judges were thinking of the economic consequences of alternative decisions. To the argument that if the principle that they seemed to be following

[16] See W. L. Prosser, The Law of Torts 398–99, 412 (2d ed. 1955). The quotation about the ancient case concerning candle-making is taken from Sir James Fitzjames Stephen, A General View of the Criminal Law of England 106 (1890). Sir James Stephen gives no reference. He perhaps had in mind *Rex. v. Ronkett,* included in Seavey, Keeton and Thurston, Cases on Torts 604 (1950). A similar view to that expressed by Prosser is to be found in F. V. Harper and F. James, The Law of Torts 67–74 (1956); Restatement, Torts §§826, 827 and 828.

[17] See Winfield on Torts 541–48 (6th ed. T. E. Lewis 1954); Salmond on the Law of Torts 181–90 (12th ed. R.F.V. Heuston 1957); H. Street, The Law of Torts 221–29 (1959).

[18] Attorney General v. Doughty, 2 Ves. Sen. 453, 28 Eng. Rep. 290 (Ch. 1752). Compare in this connection the statement of an American judge, quoted in Prosser, op. cit. supra n. 16 at 413 n. 54: "Without smoke, Pittsburgh would have remained a very pretty village," Musmanno, J., in Versailles Borough v. McKeesport Coal & Coke Co., 1935, 83 Pitts. Leg. J. 379, 385.

[19] 10 C.B. (N.S.) 268, 142 Eng. Rep. 445 (1861); 13 C.B. (N.S.) 841, 143 Eng. Rep. 332 (1863).

[20] See Gale on Easements 238, n. 6 (13th ed. M. Bowles 1959).

were carried out to its logical consequences, it would result in the most serious practical inconveniences, for a man might go—say into the midst of the tanneries of *Bermondsey*, or into any other locality devoted to any particular trade or manufacture of a noisy or unsavoury character, and by building a private residence upon a vacant piece of land put a stop to such trade or manufacture altogether,

the judges answered that

whether anything is a nuisance or not is a question to be determined, not merely by an abstract consideration of the thing itself, but in reference to its circumstances; What would be a nuisance in *Belgrave Square* would not necessarily be so in *Bermondsey;* and where a locality is devoted to a particular trade or manufacture carried on by the traders or manufacturers in a particular and established manner not constituting a public nuisance, Judges and juries would be justified in finding, and may be trusted to find, that the trade or manufacture so carried on in that locality is not a private or actionable wrong.[21]

That the character of the neighborhood is relevant in deciding whether something is, or is not, a nuisance, is definitely established.

He who dislikes the noise of traffic must not set up his abode in the heart of a great city. He who loves peace and quiet must not live in a locality devoted to the business of making boilers or steamships.[22]

What has emerged has been described as "planning and zoning by the judiciary."[23] Of course there are sometimes considerable difficulties in applying the criteria.[24]

An interesting example of the problem is found in *Adams v. Ursell*[25] in which a fried fish shop in a predominantly working-class district was set up near houses of "a much better character." England without fish-and-chips is a contradiction in terms and the case was clearly one of high importance. The judge commented:

It was urged that an injunction would cause great hardship to the defendant and to the poor people who get food at his shop. The answer to that is that it does not follow that the defendant cannot carry on his business in another more suitable place somewhere in the neighbourhood. It by no means follows that because a fried fish shop is a nuisance in one place it is a nuisance in another.

In fact, the injunction which restrained Mr. Ursell from running his shop did not even extend to the whole street. So he was presumably able to move to other premises near houses of "a much worse character," the inhabitants

[21] 11 Ch.D. 865 (1879).

[22] Salmond on the Law of Torts 182 (12th ed. R.F.V. Heuston 1957).

[23] C. M. Haar, Land-Use Planning, A Casebook on the Use, Misuse, and Re-use of Urban Land 95 (1959).

[24] See, for example, Rushmer v. Polsue and Alfieri, Ltd. [1906] 1 Ch. 234, which deals with the case of a house in a quiet situation in a noisy district.

[25] [1913] 1 Ch. 269.

of which would no doubt consider the availability of fish-and-chips to outweigh the pervading odour and "fog or mist" so graphically described by the plaintiff. Had there been no other "more suitable place in the neighbourhood," the case would have been more difficult and the decision might have been different. What would "the poor people" have had for food? No English judge would have said: "Let them eat cake."

The courts do not always refer very clearly to the economic problem posed by the cases brought before them but it seems probable that in the interpretation of words and phrases like "reasonable" or "common or ordinary use" there is some recognition, perhaps largely unconscious and certainly not very explicit, of the economic aspects of the questions at issue. A good example of this would seem to be the judgment in the Court of Appeals in *Andreae v. Selfridge and Company Ltd.*[26] In this case, a hotel (in Wigmore Street) was situated on part of an island site. The remainder of the site was acquired by Selfridges which demolished the existing buildings in order to erect another in their place. The hotel suffered a loss of custom in consequence of the noise and dust caused by the demolition. The owner of the hotel brought an action against Selfridges for damages. In the lower court, the hotel was awarded £4,500 damages. The case was then taken on appeal.

The judge who had found for the hotel proprietor in the lower court said:

> I cannot regard what the defendants did on the site of the first operation as having been commonly done in the ordinary use and occupation of land or houses. It is neither usual nor common, in this country, for people to excavate a site to a depth of 60 feet and then to erect upon that site a steel framework and fasten the steel frames together with rivets. . . . Nor is it, I think, a common or ordinary use of land, in this country, to act as the defendants did when they were dealing with the site of their second operation—namely, to demolish all the houses that they had to demolish, five or six of them I think, if not more, and to use for the purpose of demolishing them pneumatic hammers.

Sir Wilfred Greene, M.R., speaking for the Court of Appeals, first noted

> that when one is dealing with temporary operations, such as demolition and re-building, everybody has to put up with a certain amount of discomfort, because operations of that kind cannot be carried on at all without a certain amount of noise and a certain amount of dust. Therefore, the rule with regard to interference must be read subject to this qualification. . . .

He then referred to the previous judgment:

> With great respect to the learned judge, I take the view that he has not approached this matter from the correct angle. It seems to me that it is not possible to say . . . that the type of demolition, excavation and construction in which the defendant company was engaged in the course of these operations was of such an abnormal and unusual nature as to prevent the qualification to which I have referred coming

[26] [1938] 1 Ch. 1.

into operation. It seems to me that, when the rule speaks of the common or ordinary use of land, it does not mean that the methods of using land and building on it are in some way to be stabilised for ever. As time goes on new inventions or new methods enable land to be more profitably used, either by digging down into the earth or by mounting up into the skies. Whether, from other points of view, that is a matter which is desirable for humanity is neither here nor there; but it is part of the normal use of land, to make use upon your land, in the matter of construction, of what particular type and what particular depth of foundations and particular height of building may be reasonable, in the circumstances, and in view of the developments of the day. . . . Guests at hotels are very easily upset. People coming to this hotel, who were accustomed to a quiet outlook at the back, coming back and finding demolition and building going on, may very well have taken the view that the particular merit of this hotel no longer existed. That would be a misfortune for the plaintiff; but assuming that there was nothing wrong in the defendant company's works, assuming the defendant company was carrying on the demolition and its building, productive of noise though it might be, with all reasonable skill, and taking all reasonable precautions not to cause annoyance to its neighbors, then the planitiff might lose all her clients in the hotel because they have lost the amenities of an open and quiet place behind, but she would have no cause of complaint. . . . [But those] who say that their interference with the comfort of their neighbors is justified because their operations are normal and usual and conducted with proper care and skill are under a specific duty . . . to use that reasonable and proper care and skill. It is not a correct attitude to take to say: 'We will go on and do what we like until somebody complains!' . . . Their duty is to take proper precautions and to see that the nuisance is reduced to a minimum. It is no answer for them to say: 'But this would mean that we should have to do the work more slowly than we would like to do it, or it would involve putting us to some extra expense.' All these questions are matters of common sense and degree, and quite clearly it would be unreasonable to expect people to conduct their work so slowly or so expensively, for the purpose of preventing a transient inconvenience, that the cost and trouble would be prohibitive. . . . In this case, the defendant company's attitude seems to have been to go on until somebody complained, and, further, that its desire to hurry its work and conduct it according to its own ideas and its own convenience was to prevail if there was a real conflict between it and the comfort of its neighbors. That . . . is not carrying out the obligation of using reasonable care and skill. . . . The effect comes to this . . . the plaintiff suffered an actionable nuisance; . . . she is entitled, not to a nominal sum, but to a substantial sum, based upon those principles . . . but in arriving at the sum . . . I have discounted any loss of custom . . . which might be due to the general loss of amenities owing to what was going on at the back. . . .

The upshot was that the damages awarded were reduced from £4,500 to £1,000.

The discussion in this section has, up to this point, been concerned with court decisions arising out of the common law relating to nuisance. Delimitation of rights in this area also comes about because of statutory enactments. Most economists would appear to assume that the aim of governmental action in this field is to extend the scope of the law of nuisance by designating as nuisances activities which would not be recognized as such by the common law. And there can be no doubt that some statutes, for example, the Public Health Acts, have had this effect. But not all Government enactments are of this kind. The effect of much of the legislation in this area is to protect businesses from the claims of those they have harmed by their actions. There is a long list of legalized nuisances.

The position has been summarized in *Halsbury's Laws of England* as follows:

> Where the legislature directs that a thing shall in all events be done or authorises certain works at a particular place for a specific purposes or grants powers with the intention that they shall be exercised, although leaving some discretion as to the mode of exercise, no action will lie at common law for nuisance or damage which is the inevitable result of carrying out the statutory powers so conferred. This is so whether the act causing the damage is authorised for public purposes or private profit. Acts done under powers granted by persons to whom Parliament has delegated authority to grant such powers, for example, under provisional orders of the Board of Trade, are regarded as having been done under statutory authority. In the absence of negligence it seems that a body exercising statutory powers will not be liable to an action merely because it might, by acting in a different way, have minimised an injury.

Instances are next given of freedom from liability for acts authorized:

> An action has been held not to be against a body exercising its statutory powers without negligence in respect of the flooding of land by water escaping from watercourses, from water pipes, from drains, or from a canal; the escape of fumes from sewers; the escape of sewage: the subsidence of a road over a sewer; vibration or noise caused by a railway; fires caused by authorised acts; the pollution of a stream where statutory requirements to use the best known method of purifying before discharging the effluent have been satisfied; interference with a telephone or telegraph system by an elctric tramway; the insertion of poles for tramways in the subsoil; annoyance caused by things reasonably necessary for the excavation of authorised works; accidental damage caused by the placing of a grating in a roadway; the escape of tar acid; or interference with the access of a frontager by a street shelter or safety railings on the edge of a pavement.[27]

The legal position in the United States would seem to be essentially the same as in England, except that the power of the legislatures to authorize what would otherwise be nuisances under the common law, at least without giving compensation to the person harmed, is somewhat more limited, as it is subject to constitutional restrictions.[28] Nonetheless, the power is there and cases more or less identical with the English cases can be found. The

[27] See 30 Halsbury, Law of England 690–91 (3d ed. 1960), Article on Public Authorities and Public Officers.

[28] See Prosser, op. cit. supra n. 16 at 421; Harper and James, op. cit. supra n. 16 at 86–87.

question has arisen in an acute form in connection with airports and the operation of aeroplanes. The case of *Delta Air Corporation v. Kersey, Kersey v. City of Atlanta*[29] is a good example. Mr. Kersey bought land and built a house on it. Some years later the City of Atlanta constructed an airport on land immediately adjoining that of Mr. Kersey. It was explained that his property was "a quiet, peaceful and proper location for a home before the airport was built, but dust, noises and low flying of airplanes caused by the operation of the airport have rendered his property unsuitable as a home," a state of affairs which was described in the report of the case with a wealth of distressing detail. The judge first referred to an earlier case, *Thrasher v. City of Atlanta*[30] in which it was noted that the City of Atlanta had been expressly authorized to operate an airport.

> By this franchise aviation was recognised as a lawful business and also as an enterprise affected with a public interest . . . all persons using [the airport] in the manner contemplated by law are within the protection and immunity of the franchise granted by the municipality. An airport is not a nuisance per se, although it might become such from the manner of its construction or operation.

Since aviation was a lawful business affected with a public interest and the construction of the airport was autorized by statute, the judge next referred to *Georgia Railroad and Banking Co. v. Maddox*[31] in which it was said:

> Where a railroad terminal yard is located and its construction authorized, under statutory powers, if it be constructed and operated in a proper manner, it cannot be adjudged a nuisance. Accordingly, injuries and inconveniences to persons residing near such a yard, from noises of locomotives, rumbling of cars, vibrations produced thereby, and smoke, cinders, soot and the like, which result from the ordinary and necessary, therefore proper, use and operation of such a yard, are not nuisances, but are the necessary concomitants of the franchise granted.

In view of this, the judge decided that the noise and dust complained of by Mr. Kersey "may be deemed to be incidental to the proper operation of an airport, and as such they cannot be said to constitute a nuisance." But the complaint against low flying was different:

> . . . can it be said that flights . . . at such a low height [25 to 50 feet above Mr. Kersey's house] as to be imminently dangerous to . . . life and health . . . are a necessary concomitant of an airport? We do not think this question can be answered in the affirmative. No reason appears why the city could not obtain lands of an area [sufficiently large] . . . as not to require such low flights. . . . For the sake of public convenience adjoining-property owners must suffer such inconvenience from noise and dust as result from the usual and proper operation of an airport, but their private rights are entitled to preference in the eyes of the law where the inconvenience is not one demanded by a properly constructed and operated airport.

[29] Supreme Court of Georgia. 193 Ga. 862, 20 S.E. 2d 245 (1942).

[30] 178 Ga. 514, 173 S.E. 817 (1934).

[31] 116 Ga. 64, 42 S.E. 315 (1902).

Of course this assumed that the City of Atlanta could prevent the low flying and continue to operate the airport. The judge therefore added:

From all that appears, the conditions causing the low flying may be remedied; but if on the trial it should appear that it is indispensable to the public interest that the airport should continue to be operated in its present condition, it may be said that the petitioner should be denied injunctive relief.

In the course of another aviation case, *Smith v. New England Aircraft Co.*,[32] the court surveyed the law in the United States regarding the legalizing of nuisances and it is apparent that, in the broad, it is very similar to that found in England:

It is the proper function of the legislative department of government in the exercise of the police power to consider the problems and risks that arise from the use of new inventions and endeavor to adjust private rights and harmonize conflicting interests by comprehensive statutes for the public welfare. . . . There are . . . analogies where the invasion of the airspace over underlying land by noise, smoke, vibration, dust and disagreeable odors, having been authorized by the legislative department of government and not being in effect a condemnation of the property although in some measure depreciating its market value, must be borne by the landowner without compensation or remedy. Legislative sanction makes that lawful which otherwise might be a nuisance. Examples of this are damages to adjacent land arising from smoke, vibration and noise in the operation of a railroad . . . ; the noise of ringing factory bells . . . ; the abatement of nuisances . . . ; the erection of steam engines and furnaces . . . ; unpleasant odors connected with sewers, oil refining and storage of naphtha. . . .

Most economists seem to be unaware of all this. When they are prevented from sleeping at night by the roar of jet planes overhead (publicly authorized and perhaps publicly operated), are unable to think (or rest) in the day because of the noise and vibration from passing trains (publicly authorized and perhaps publicly operated), find it difficult to breathe because of the odour from a local sewage farm (publicly authorized and perhaps publicly operated) and are unable to escape because their driveways are blocked by a road obstruction (without any doubt, publicly devised), their nerves frayed and mental balance disturbed, they proceed to declaim about the disadvantages of private enterprise and the need for Government regulation.

While most economists seem to be under a misapprehension concerning the character of the situation with which they are dealing, it is also the case that the activities which they would like to see stopped or curtailed may well be socially justified. It is all a question of weighing up the gains that would accrue from eliminating these harmful effects against the gains that accrue from allowing them to continue. Of course, it is likely that an extension of Government economic activity will often lead to this protection against

[32] 270 Mass. 511, 523, 170 N.E. 385, 390 (1930).

action for nuisance being pushed further than is desirable. For one thing, the Government is likely to look with a benevolent eye on enterprises which it is itself promoting. For another, it is possible to describe the committing of a nuisance by public enterprise in a much more pleasant way than when the same thing is done by private enterprise. In the words of Lord Justice Sir Alfred Denning:

> . . . the significance of the social revolution of today is that, whereas in the past the balance was much too heavily in favor of the rights of property and freedom of contract, Parliament has repeatedly intervened so as to give the public good its proper place.[33]

There can be little doubt that the Welfare State is likely to bring an extension of that immunity from liability for damage, which economists have been in the habit of condemning (although they have tended to assume that this immunity was a sign of too little Government intervention in the economic system). For example, in Britain, the powers of local authorities are regarded as being either absolute or conditional. In the first category, the local authority has no discretion in exercising the power conferred on it. "The absolute power may be said to cover all the necessary consequences of its direct operation even if such consequences amount to nuisance." On the other hand, a conditional power may only be exercised in such a way that the consequences do not constitute a nuisance.

> It is the intention of the legislature which determines whether a power is absolute or conditional. . . . [As] there is the possibility that the social policy of the legislature may change from time to time, a power which in one era would be construed as being conditional, might in another era be interpreted as being absolute in order to further the policy of the Welfare State. This point is one which should be borne in mind when considering some of the older cases upon this aspect of the law of nuisance.[34]

It would seem desirable to summarize the burden of this long section. The problem which we face in dealing with actions which have harmful effects is not simply one of restraining those responsible for them. What has to be decided is whether the gain from preventing the harm is greater than the loss which would be suffered elsewhere as a result of stopping the action which produces the harm. In a world in which there are costs of rearranging the rights established by the legal system, the courts, in cases relating to nuisance, are, in effect, making a decision on the economic problem and determining how resources are to be employed. It was argued that the courts are conscious of this and that they often make, although not always in a very explicit fashion, a comparison between what would be gained and what lost by preventing

[33] See Sir Alfred Denning, Freedom Under the Law 71 (1949).

[34] M. B. Cairns, The Law of Tort in Local Government 28–32 (1954).

actions which have harmful effects. But the delimitation of rights is also the result of statutory enactments. Here we also find evidence of an appreciation of the reciprocal nature of the problem. While statutory enactments add to the list of nuisances, action is also taken to legalize what would otherwise be nuisances under the common law. The kind of situation which economists are prone to consider as requiring corrective Government action is, in fact, often the result of Government action. Such action is not necessarily unwise. But there is a real danger that extensive Government intervention in the economic system may lead to the protection of those responsible for harmful effects being carried too far.

VIII. Pigou's Treatment in "The Economics of Welfare"

The fountainhead for the modern economic analysis of the problem discussed in this article is Pigou's *Economics of Welfare* and, in particular, that section of Part II which deals with divergences between social and private net products which come about because

> one person A, in the course of rendering some service, for which payment is made, to a second person B, incidentally also renders services or disservices to other persons (not producers of like services), of such a sort that payment cannot be exacted from the benefited parties or compensation enforced on behalf of the injured parties.[35]

Pigou tells us that his aim in Part II of *The Economics of Welfare* is

> to ascertain how far the free play of self-interest, acting under the existing legal system, tends to distribute the country's resources in the way most favorable to the production of a large national dividend, and how far it is feasible for State action to improve upon 'natural' tendencies.[36]

To judge from the first part of this statement, Pigou's purpose is to discover whether any improvements could be made in the existing arrangements which determine the use of resources. Since Pigou's conclusion is that improvements could be made, one might have expected him to continue by saying that he proposed to set out the changes required to bring them about. Instead, Pigou adds a phrase which contrasts "natural" tendencies with State action, which seems in some sense to equate the present arrangements with "natural" tendencies and to imply that what is required to bring about these improvements is State action (if feasible). That this is more or less Pigou's position is evident from Chapter I of Part II.[37] Pigou starts by referring to "optimistic

[35] A. C. Pigou, The Economics of Welfare 183 (4th ed. 1932). My references will all be to the fourth edition but the argument and examples examined in this article remained substantially unchanged from the first edition in 1920 to the fourth in 1932. A large part (but not all) of this analysis had appeared previously in Wealth and Welfare (1912).

[36] *Id.* at xii.

[37] *Id.* at 127–30.

followers of the classical economists"[38] who have argued that the value of production would be maximised if the Government refrained from any interference in the economic system and the economic arrangements were those which came about "naturally." Pigou goes on to say that if self-interest does promote economic welfare, it is because human institutions have been devised to make it so. (This part of Pigou's argument, which he develops with the aid of a quotation from Cannan, seems to me to be essentially correct.) Pigou concludes:

> But even in the most advanced States there are failures and imperfections. . . . there are many obstacles that prevent a community's resources from being distributed . . . in the most efficient way. The study of these constitutes our present problem. . . . its purposes is essentially practical. It seeks to bring into clearer light some of the ways in which it now is, or eventually may become, feasible for governments to control the play of economic forces in such wise as to promote the economic welfare, and through that, the total welfare, of their citizens as a whole.[39]

Pigou's underlying thought would appear to be: Some have argued that no State action is needed. But the system has performed as well as it has because of State action. Nonetheless, there are still imperfections. What additional State action is required?

If this is a correct summary of Pigou's position, its inadequacy can be demonstrated by examining the first example he gives of a divergence between private and social products.

> It might happen . . . that costs are thrown upon people not directly concerned, through, say, uncompensated damage done to surrounding woods by sparks from railway engines. All such effects must be included—some of them will be positive, others negative elements—in reckoning up the social net product of the marginal increment of any volume of resources turned into any use or place.[40]

The example used by Pigou refers to a real situation. In Britain, a railway does not normally have to compensate those who suffer damage by fire caused by sparks from an engine. Taken in conjunction with what he says in Chapter 9 of Part II, I take Pigou's policy recommendations to be, first, that there should be State action to correct this "natural" situation and, second, that the railways should be forced to compensate those whose woods are burnt. If this is a correct interpretation of Pigou's position, I would argue that the first recommendation is based on a misapprehension of the facts and that the second is not necessarily desirable.

[38] In Wealth and Welfare, Pigou attributes the "optimism" to Adam Smith himself and not to his followers. He there refers to the "highly optimistic theory of Adam Smith that the national dividend, in given circumstances of demand and supply, tends 'naturally' to a maximum" (p. 104).

[39] Pigou, op. cit. supra n. 35 at 129–30.

[40] *Id.* at 134.

Let us consider the legal position. Under the heading "Sparks from engines," we find the following in Halsbury's Laws of England:

> If railway undertakers use steam engines on their railway without express statutory authority to do so, they are liable, irrespective of any negligence on their part, for fires caused by sparks from engines. Railway undertakers are, however, generally given statutory authority to use steam engines on their railway; accordingly, if an engine is constructed with the precautions which science suggests against fire and is used without negligence, they are not responsible at common law for any damage which may be done by sparks. . . . In the construction of an engine the undertaker is bound to use all the discoveries which science has put within its reach in order to avoid doing harm, provided they are such as it is reasonable to require the company to adopt, having proper regard to the likelihood of the damage and to the cost and convenience of the remedy; but it is not negligence on the part of an undertaker if it refuses to use an apparatus the efficiency of which is open to bona fide doubt.

To this general rule, there is a statutory exception arising from the Railway (Fires) Act, 1905, as amended in 1923. This concerns agricultural land or agricultural crops.

> In such a case the fact that the engine was used under statutory powers does not affect the liability of the company in an action for the damage. . . . These provisions, however, only apply where the claim for damage . . . does not exceed £ 200, [£ 100 in the 1905 Act] and where written notice of the occurrence of the fire and the intention to claim has been sent to the company within seven days of the occurrence of the damage and particulars of the damage in writing showing the amount of the claim in money not exceeding £200 have been sent to the company within twenty-one days.

Agricultural land does not include moorland or buildings and agricultural crops do not include those led away or stacked.[41] I have not made a close study of the parliamentary history of this statutory exception, but to judge from debates in the House of Commons in 1922 and 1923, this exception was probably designed to help the smallholder.[42]

Let us return to Pigou's example of uncompensated damage to surrounding woods caused by sparks from railway engines. This is presumably intended to show how it is possible "for State action to improve on 'natural' tendencies." If we treat Pigou's example as referring to the position before 1905, or as being an arbitrary example (in that he might just as well have written "surrounding buildings" instead of "surrounding woods"), then it is clear that the reason why compensation was not paid must have been that the railway had statutory authority to run steam engines (which relieved it of liability for fires caused by sparks). That this was the legal position was

[41] See 31 Halsbury, Laws of England 474–75 (3d ed. 1960), Article on Railways and Canals, from which this summary of the legal position, and all quotations, are taken.

[42] See 152 H.C. Deb. 2622–63 (1922); 161 H.C. Deb. 2935–55 (1923).

established in 1860, in a case, oddly enough, which concerned the burning of surrounding woods by a railway,[43] and the law on this point has not been changed (apart from the one exception) by a century of railway legislation, including nationalisation. If we treat Pigou's example of "uncompensated damage done to surrounding woods by sparks from railway engines" literally, and assume that it refers to the period after 1905, then it is clear that the reason why compensation was not paid must have been that the damage was more than £100 (in the first edition of *The Economics of Welfare*) or more than £200 (in later editions) or that the owner of the wood failed to notify the railway in writing within seven days of the fire or did not send particulars of the damage, in writing, within twenty-one days. In the real world, Pigou's example could only exist as a result of a deliberate choice of the legislature. It is not, of course, easy to imagine the construction of a railway in a state of nature. The nearest one can get to this is presumably a railway which uses steam engines "without express statutory authority." However, in this case the railway would be obliged to compensate those whose woods it burnt down. That is to say, compensation would be paid in the absence of Government action. The only circumstances in which compensation would not be paid would be those in which there had been Government action. It is strange that Pigou, who clearly thought it desirable that compensation should be paid, should have chosen this particular example to demonstrate how it is possible "for State action to improve on 'natural' tendencies."

Pigou seems to have had a faulty view of the facts of the situation. But it also seems likely that he was mistaken in his economic analysis. It is not necessarily desirable that the railway should be required to compensate those who suffer damage by fires caused by railway engines. I need not show here that, if the railway could make a bargain with everyone having property adjoining the railway line and there were no costs involved in making such bargains, it would not matter whether the railway was liable for damage caused by fires or not. This question has been treated at length in earlier sections. The problem is whether it would be desirable to make the railway liable in conditions in which it is too expensive for such bargains to be made. Pigou clearly thought it was desirable to force the railway to pay compensation and it is easy to see the kind of argument that would have led him to this conclusion. Suppose a railway is considering whether to run an additional train or to increase the speed of an existing train or to install spark-preventing devices on its engines. If the railway were not liable for fire damage, then, when making these decisions, it would not take into account as a cost the increase in damage resulting from the additional train or the faster train or the failure to install spark-preventing devices. This is the source of the di-

[43] Vaughan v. Taff Vale Railway Co., 3 H. and N. 743 (Ex. 1858) and 5 H. and N. 679 (Ex. 1860).

vergence between private and social net products. It results in the railway performing acts which will lower the value of total production—and which it would not do if it were liable for the damage. This can be shown by means of an arithmetical example.

Consider a railway, which is *not* liable for damage by fires caused by sparks from its engines, which runs two trains per day on a certain line. Suppose that running one train per day would enable the railway to perform services worth $150 per annum and running two trains a day would enable the railway to perform services worth $250 per annum. Suppose further that the cost of running one train is $50 per annum and two trains $100 per annum. Assuming perfect competition, the cost equals the fall in the value of production elsewhere due to the employment of additional factors of production by the railway. Clearly the railway would find it profitable to run two trains per day. But suppose that running one train per day would destroy by fire crops worth (on an average over the year) $60 and two trains a day would result in the destruction of crops worth $120. In these circumstances running one train per day would raise the value of total production but the running of a second train would reduce the value of total production. The second train would enable additional railway services worth $100 per annum to be performed. But the fall in the value of production elsewhere would be $110 per annum; $50 as a result of the employment of additional factors of production and $60 as a result of the destruction of crops. Since it would be better if the second train were not run and since it would not run if the railway were liable for damage caused to crops, the conclusion that the railway should be made liable for the damage seems irresistable. Undoubtedly it is this kind of reasoning which underlies the Pigovian position.

The conclusion that it would be better if the second train did not run is correct. The conclusion that it is desirable that the railway should be made liable for the damage it causes is wrong. Let us change our assumption concerning the rule of liability. Suppose that the railway is liable for damage from fires caused by sparks from the engine. A farmer on lands adjoining the railway is then in the position that, if his crop is destroyed by fires caused by the railway, he will receive the market price from the railway; but if his crop is not damaged, he will receive the market price by sale. It therefore becomes a matter of indifference to him whether his crop is damaged by fire or not. The position is very different when the railway is *not* liable. Any crop destruction through railway-caused fires would then reduce the receipts of the farmer. He would therefore take out of cultivation any land for which the damage is likely to be greater than the net return of the land (for reasons explained at length in Section III). A change from a regime in which the railway is *not* liable for damage to one in which it *is* liable is likely therefore to lead to an increase in the amount of cultivation on lands adjoining the railway. It will also, of course, lead to an increase in the amount of crop destruction due to railway-caused fires.

Let us return to our arithmetical example. Assume that, with the changed rule of liability, there is a doubling in the amount of crop destruction due to railway-caused fires. With one train per day, crops worth $120 would be destroyed each year and two trains per day would lead to the destruction of crops worth $240. We saw previously that it would not be profitable to run the second train if the railway had to pay $60 per annum as compensation for damage. With damage at $120 per annum the loss from running the second train would be $60 greater. But now let us consider the first train. The value of the transport services furnished by the first train is $150. The cost of running the train is $50. The amount that the railway would have to pay out as compensation for damage is $120. It follows that it would not be profitable to run any trains. With the figures in our example we reach the following result: if the railway is not liable for fire-damage, two trains per day would be run; if the railway is liable for fire-damage, it would cease operations altogether. Does this mean that it is better that there should be no railway? This question can be resolved by considering what would happen to the value of total production if it were decided to exempt the railway from liability for fire-damage, thus bringing it into operation (with two trains per day).

The operation of the railway would enable transport services worth $250 to be performed. It would also mean the employment of factors of production which would reduce the value of production elsewhere by $100. Furthermore it would mean the destruction of crops worth $120. The coming of the railway will also have led to the abandonment of cultivation of some land. Since we know that, had this land been cultivated, the value of the crops destroyed by fire would have been $120, and since it is unlikely that the total crop on this land would have been destroyed, it seems reasonable to suppose that the value of the crop yield on this land would have been higher than this. Assume it would have been $160. But the abandonment of cultivation would have released factors of production for employment elsewhere. All we know is that the amount by which the value of production elsewhere will increase will be less than $160. Suppose that it is $150. Then the gain from operating the railway would be $250 (the value of the transport services) minus $100 (the cost of the factors of production) minus $120 (the value of crops destroyed by fire) minus $160 (the fall in the value of crop production due to the abandonment of cultivation) plus $150 (the value of production elsewhere of the released factors of production). Overall, operating the railway will increase the value of total production by $20. With these figures it is clear that it is better that the railway should not be liable for the damage it causes, thus enabling it to operate profitably. Of course, by altering the figures, it could be shown that there are other cases in which it would be desirable that the railway should be liable for the damage it causes. It is enough for my purpose to show that, from an economic point of view, a situation in which there is "uncompensated damage done to surrounding woods by sparks from railway engines" is not necessarily undesirable. Whether it is desirable or not depends on the particular circumstances.

How is it that the Pigovian analysis seems to give the wrong answer? The reason is that Pigou does not seem to have noticed that his analysis is dealing with an entirely different question. The analysis as such is correct. But it is quite illegitimate for Pigou to draw the particular conclusion he does. The question at issue is not whether it is desirable to run an additional train or a faster train or to install smoke-preventing devices; the question at issue is whether it is desirable to have a system in which the railway has to compensate those who suffer damage from the fires which it causes or one in which the railway does not have to compensate them. When an economist is comparing alternative social arrangements, the proper procedure is to compare the total social product yielded by these different arrangements. The comparison of private and social products is neither here nor there. A simple example will demonstrate this. Imagine a town in which there are traffic lights. A motorist approaches an intersection and stops because the light is red. There are no cars approaching the intersection on the other street. If the motorist ignored the red signal, no accident would occur and the total product would increase because the motorist would arrive earlier at his destination. Why does he not do this? The reason is that if he ignored the light he would be fined. The private product from crossing the street is less than the social product. Should we conclude from this that the total product would be greater if there were no fines for failing to obey traffic signals? The Pigovian analysis shows us that it is possible to conceive of better worlds than the one in which we live. But the problem is to devise practical arrangements which will correct defects in one part of the system without causing more serious harm in other parts.

I have examined in considerable detail one example of a divergence between private and social products and I do not propose to make any further examination of Pigou's analytical system. But the main discussion of the problem considered in this article is to be found in that part of Chapter 9 in Part II which deals with Pigou's second class of divergence and it is of interest to see how Pigou develops his argument. Pigou's own description of this second class of divergence was quoted at the beginning of this section. Pigou distinguishes between the case in which a person renders services for which he receives no payment and the case in which a person renders disservices and compensation is not given to the injured parties. Our main attention has, of course, centred on this second case. It is therefore rather astonishing to find, as was pointed out to me by Professor Francesco Forte, that the problem of the smoking chimney—the "stock instance"[44] or "classroom example"[45] of the second case—is used by Pigou as an example of the first case (services rendered without payment) and is never mentioned, at any rate explicitly, in connection with the second case.[46] Pigou points out that factory owners who devote resources to preventing their chimneys from smoking render services for which they receive no payment. The implication, in the light of Pigou's discussion later in the chapter, is that a factory owner with a smokey chimney should be given a bounty to induce him to install smoke-preventing devices. Most modern economists would suggest that the owner of the factory with the smokey chimney should be taxed. It seems a pity that economists (apart from Professor Forte) do not seem to have noticed this feature of Pigou's treatment since a realisation that the problem could be tackled in either of these two ways would probably have led to an explicit recognition of its reciprocal nature.

In discussing the second case (disservices without compensation to those damaged), Pigou says that they are rendered "when the owner of a site in a residential quarter of a city builds a factory there and so destroys a great part of the amenities of neighbouring sites; or, in a less degree, when he uses his site in such a way as to spoil the lighting of the house opposite; or when he invests resources in erecting buildings in a crowded centre, which by contracting the air-space and the playing room of the neighbourhood, tend to injure the health and efficiency of the families living there."[47] Pigou is, of course, quite right to describe such actions as "uncharged disservices." But he is wrong when he describes these actions as "anti-social."[48] They may or may not be. It is necessary to weigh the harm against the good that will result. Nothing could be more "anti-social" than to oppose any action which causes any harm to anyone.

The example with which Pigou opens his discussion of "uncharged disservices" is not, as I have indicated, the case of the smokey chimney but the case of the overrunning rabbits: ". . . incidental uncharged disservices are rendered to third parties when the game-preserving activities of one occupier involve the overrunning of a neighbouring occupier's land by rabbits. . . ." This example is of extraordinary interest, not so much because the economic

[44] Sir Dennis Robertson, I Lectures on Economic Principles 162 (1957).

[45] E. J. Mishan, The Meaning of Efficiency in Economics, 189 The Bankers' Magazine 482 (June 1960).

[46] Pigou, op. cit. supra n. 35 at 184.

[47] *Id.* at 185–86.

[48] *Id.* at 186 n.1. For similar unqualified statements see Pigou's lecture "Some Aspects of the Housing Problem" in B. S. Rowntree and A. C. Pigou, Lectures on Housing, in 18 Manchester Univ. Lectures (1914).

analysis of the case is essentially any different from that of the other examples, but because of the peculiarities of the legal position and the light it throws on the part which economics can play in what is apparently the purely legal question of the delimitation of rights.

The problem of legal liability for the actions of rabbits is part of the general subject of liability for animals.[49] I will, although with reluctance, confine my discussion to rabbits. The early cases relating to rabbits concerned the relations between the lord of the manor and commoners, since, from the thirteenth century on, it became usual for the lord of the manor to stock the commons with conies (rabbits), both for the sake of the meat and the fur. But in 1597, in *Boulston*'s case, an action was brought by one landowner against a neighbouring landowner, alleging that the defendant had made coney-burrows and that the conies had increased and had destroyed the plaintiff's corn. The action failed for the reason that

> . . . so soon as the coneys come on his neighbor's land he may kill them, for they are ferae naturae, and he who makes the coney-boroughs has no property in them, and he shall not be punished for the damage which the coneys do in which he has no property, and which the other may lawfully kill.[50]

As *Boulston*'s case has been treated as binding—Bray, J., in 1919, said that he was not aware that *Boulston*'s case has ever been overruled or questioned[51]—Pigou's rabbit example undoubtedly represented the legal position at the time *The Economics of Welfare* was written.[52] And in this case, it is not far from the truth to say that the state of affairs which Pigou describes came about because of an absence of Government action (at any rate in the form of statutory enactments) and was the result of "natural" tendencies.

Nonetheless, *Boulston*'s case is something of a legal curiousity and Professor Williams makes no secret of his distaste for this decision:

[49] See G. L. Williams, Liability for Animals—An Account of the Development and Present Law of Tortious Liability for Animals, Distress Damage Feasant and the Duty to Fence, in Great Britain, Northern Ireland and the Common Law Dominions (1939). Part Four, "The Action of Nuisance, in Relation to Liability for Animals," 236–62, is especially relevant to our discussion. The problem of liability for rabbits is discussed in this part, 238–47. I do not know how far the common law in the United State regarding liability for animals has diverged from that in Britain. In some Western States of the United States, the English common law regarding the duty to fence has not been followed, in part because "the considerable amount of open, uncleared land made it a matter of public policy to allow cattle to run at large" (Williams, *op. cit. supra* 227). This affords a good example of how a different set of circumstances may make it economically desirable to change the legal rule regarding the delimitation of rights.

[50] 5 Coke (Vol. 3) 104 b. 77 Eng. Rep., 216, 217.

[51] See Stearn v. Prentice Bros. Ltd., (1919) 1 K.B., 395, 397.

[52] I have not looked into recent cases. The legal position has also been modified by statutory enactments.

The conception of liability in nuisance as being based upon ownership is the result, apparently, of a confusion with the action of cattle-trespass, and runs counter both to principle and to the medieval authorities on the escape of water, smoke and filth. . . . The prerequisite of any satisfactory treatment of the subject is the final abandonment of the pernicious doctrine in *Boulston*'s case. . . . Once *Boulston*'s case disappears, the way will be clear for a rational restatement of the whole subject, on lines that will harmonize with the principles prevailing in the rest of the law of nuisance.[53]

The judges in *Boulston's* case were, of course, aware that their view of the matter depended on distinguishing this case from one involving nuisance:

This cause is not like to the cases put, on the other side, of erecting a lime-kiln, dye-house, or the like; for there the annoyance is by the act of the parties who make them; but it is not so here, for the conies of themselves went into the plaintiff's land, and he might take them when they came upon his land, and make profit of them.[54]

Professor Williams comments:

Once more the atavistic idea is emerging that the animals are guilty and not the landowner. It is not, of course, a satisfactory principle to introduce into a modern law of nuisance. If A. erects a house or plants a tree so that the rain runs or drips from it on to B.'s land, this is A.'s act for which he is liable; but if A. introduces rabbits into his land so that they escape from it into B.'s, this is the act of the rabbits for which A. is not liable—such is the specious distinction resulting from *Boulston*'s case.[55]

It has to be admitted that the decision in *Boulston*'s case seems a little odd. A man may be liable for damage caused by smoke or unpleasant smells, without it being necessary to determine whether he owns the smoke or the smell. And the rule in *Boulston's* case has not always been followed in cases dealing with other animals. For example, in *Bland v. Yates,*[56] it was decided that an injunction could be granted to prevent someone from keeping an *unusual and excessive* collection of manure in which flies bred and which infested a neighbour's house. The question of who owned the flies was not raised. An economist would not wish to object because legal reasoning sometimes appears a little odd. But there is a sound economic reason for supporting Professor Williams' view that the problem of liability for animals (and particularly rabbits) should be brought within the ordinary law of nuisance. The reason is not that the man who harbours rabbits is solely responsible for the damage; the man whose crops are eaten is equally responsible. And given that the costs of market transactions make a rearrange-

[53] Williams, op. cit. supra n. 49 at 242, 258.

[54] Boulston v. Hardy, Cro. Eliz., 547, 548, 77 Eng. Rep. 216.

[55] Williams, op. cit. supra n. 49 at 243.

[56] 58 Sol.J. 612 (1913–1914).

ment of rights impossible, unless we know the particular circumstances, we cannot say whether it is desirable or not to make the man who harbours rabbits responsible for the damage committed by the rabbits on neighbouring properties. The objection to the rule in *Boulston*'s case is that, under it, the harbourer of rabbits can *never* be liable. It fixes the rule of liability at one pole: and this is as undesirable, from an economic point of view, as fixing the rule at the other pole and making the harbourer of rabbits always liable. But, as we saw in Section VII, the law of nuisance, as it is in fact handled by the courts, is flexible and allows for a comparison of the utility of an act with the harm it produces. As Professor Williams says: "The whole law of nuisance is an attempt to reconcile and compromise between conflicting interests. . . ."[57] To bring the problem of rabbits within the ordinary law of nuisance would not mean *inevitably* making the harbourer of rabbits liable for damage committed by the rabbits. This is not to say that the sole task of the courts in such cases is to make a comparison between the harm and the utility of an act. Nor is it to be expected that the courts will always decide correctly after making such a comparison. But unless the courts act very foolishly, the ordinary law of nuisance would seem likely to give economically more satisfactory results than adopting a rigid rule. Pigou's case of the overrunning rabbits affords an excellent example of how problems of law and economics are interrelated, even though the correct policy to follow would seem to be different from that envisioned by Pigou.

Pigou allows one exception to his conclusion that there is a divergence between private and social products in the rabbit example. He adds: ". . . unless . . . the two occupiers stand in the relation of landlord and tenant, so that compensation is given in an adjustment of the rent."[58] This qualification is rather surprising since Pigou's first class of divergence is largely concerned with the difficulties of drawing up satisfactory contracts between landlords and tenants. In fact, all the recent cases on the problem of rabbits cited by Professor Williams involved disputes between landlords and tenants concerning sporting rights.[59] Pigou seems to make a distinction between the case in which no contract is possible (the second class) and that in which the contract is unsatisfactory (the first class). Thus he says that the second class of divergences between private and social net product

> cannot, like divergences due to tenancy laws, be mitigated by a modification of the contractual relation between any two contracting parties, because the divergence arises out of a service or disservice rendered to persons other than the contracting parties.[60]

[57] Williams, op. cit. supra n. 49 at 259.

[58] Pigou, op. cit. supra n. 35 at 185.

[59] Williams, op. cit. supra n. 49 at 244–47.

[60] Pigou, op. cit. supra n. 35 at 192.

But the reason why some activities are not the subject of contracts is exactly the same as the reason why some contracts are commonly unsatisfactory—it would cost too much to put the matter right. Indeed, the two cases are really the same since the contracts are unsatisfactory because they do not cover certain activities. The exact bearing of the discussion of the first class of divergence on Pigou's main argument is difficult to discover. He shows that in some circumstances contractual relations between landlord and tenant may result in a divergence between private and social products.[61] But he also goes on to show that Government-enforced compensation schemes and rent-controls will also produce divergences.[62] Furthermore, he shows that, when the Government is in a similar position to a private landlord, e.g. when granting a franchise to a public utility, exactly the same difficulties arise as when private individuals are involved.[63] The discussion is interesting but I have been unable to discover what general conclusions about economic policy, if any, Pigou expects us to draw from it.

Indeed, Pigou's treatment of the problems considered in this article is extremely elusive and the discussion of his views raises almost insuperable difficulties of interpretation. Consequently it is impossible to be sure that one has understood what Pigou really meant. Nevertheless, it is difficult to resist the conclusion, extroardinary though this may be in an economist of Pigou's stature, that the main source of this obscurity is that Pigou had not thought his position through.

IX. The Pigovian Tradition

It is strange that a doctrine as faulty as that developed by Pigou should have been so influential, although part of its success has probably been due to the lack of clarity in the exposition. Not being clear, it was never clearly wrong. Curiously enough, this obscurity in the source has not prevented the emergence of a fairly well-defined oral tradition. What economists think they learn from Pigou, and what they tell their students, which I term the Pigovian tradition, is reasonably clear. I propose to show the inadequacy of this Pigovian tradition by demonstrating that both the analysis and the policy conclusions which it supports are incorrect.

I do not propose to justify my view as to the prevailing opinion by copious references to the literature. I do this partly because the treatment in the literature is usually so fragmentary, often involving little more than a reference to Pigou plus some explanatory comment, that detailed examination would be inappropriate. But the main reason for this lack of reference is that the doctrine, although based on Pigou, must have been largely the product of an oral tradition. Certainly economists with whom I have discussed these problems have shown a unanimity of opinion which is quite

[61] *Id.* 174–75. [62] *Id.* 177–83. [63] *Id.* 175–77.

remarkable considering the meagre treatment accorded this subject in the literature. No doubt there are some economists who do not share the usual view but they must represent a small minority of the profession.

The approach to the problems under discussion is through an examination of the value of physical production. The private product is the value of the additional product resulting from a particular activity of a business. The social product equals the private product minus the fall in the value of production elsewhere for which no compensation is paid by the business. Thus, if 10 units of a factor (and no other factors) are used by a business to make a certain product with a value of $105; and the owner of this factor is not compensated for their use, which he is unable to prevent; and these 10 units of the factor would yield products in their best alternative use worth $100; then, the social product is $105 minus $100 or $5. If the business now pays for one unit of the factor and its price equals the value of its marginal product, then the social product rises to $15. If two units are paid for, the social product rises to $25 and so on until it reaches $105 when all units of the factor are paid for. It is not difficult to see why economists have so readily accepted this rather odd procedure. The analysis focusses on the individual business decision and since the use of certain resources is not allowed for in costs, receipts are reduced by the same amount. But, of course, this means that the value of the social product has no social significance whatsoever. It seems to me preferable to use the opportunity cost concept and to approach these problems by comparing the value of the product yielded by factors in alternative uses or by alternative arrangements. The main advantage of a pricing system is that it leads to the employment of factors in places where the value of the product yielded is greatest and does so at less cost than alternative systems (I leave aside that a pricing system also eases the problem of the redistribution of income). But if through some God-given natural harmony factors flowed to the places where the value of the product yielded was greatest without any use of the pricing system and consequently there was no compensation, I would find it a source of surprise rather than a cause for dismay.

The definition of the social product is queer but this does not mean that the conclusions for policy drawn from the analysis are necessarily wrong. However, there are bound to be dangers in an approach which diverts attention from the basic issues and there can be little doubt that it has been responsible for some of the errors in current doctrine. The belief that it is desirable that the business which causes harmful effects should be forced to compensate those who suffer damage (which was exhaustively discussed in section VIII in connection with Pigou's railway sparks example) is undoubtedly the result of not comparing the total product obtainable with alternative social arrangements.

The same fault is to be found in proposals for solving the problem of harmful effects by the use of taxes or bounties. Pigou lays considerable stress on this solution although he is, as usual, lacking in detail and qualified in his support.[64] Modern economists tend to think exclusively in terms of taxes and in a very precise way. The tax should be equal to the damage done and should therefore vary with the amount of the harmful effect. As it is not proposed that the proceeds of the tax should be paid to those suffering the damage, this solution is not the same as that which would force a business to pay compensation to those damaged by its actions, although economists generally do not seem to have noticed this and tend to treat the two solutions as being identical.

Assume that a factory which emits smoke is set up in a district previously free from smoke pollution, causing damage valued at $100 per annum. Assume that the taxation solution is adopted and that the factory owner is taxed $100 per annum as long as the factory emits the smoke. Assume further that a smoke-preventing device costing $90 per annum to run is available. In these circumstances, the smoke-preventing device would be installed. Damage of $100 would have been avoided at an expenditure of $90 and the factory-owner would be better off by $10 per annum. Yet the position achieved may not be optimal. Suppose that those who suffer the damage could avoid it by moving to other locations or by taking various precautions which would cost them, or be equivalent to a loss in income of, $40 per annum. Then there would be a gain in the value of production of $50 if the factory continued to emit its smoke and those now in the district moved elesewhere or made other adjustments to avoid the damage. If the factory owner is to be made to pay a tax equal to the damage caused, it would clearly be desirable to institute a double tax system and to make residents of the district pay an amount equal to the additional cost incurred by the factory owner (or the consumers of his products) in order to avoid the damage. In these conditions, people would not stay in the district or would take other measures to prevent the damage from occurring, when the costs of doing so were less than the costs that would be incurred by the producer to reduce the damage (the producer's object, of course, being not so much to reduce the damage as to reduce the tax payments). A tax system which was confined to a tax on the producer for damage caused would tend to lead to unduly high costs being incurred for the prevention of damage. Of course this could be avoided if it were possible to base the tax, not on the damage caused, but on the fall in the value of production (in its widest sense) resulting from the emission of smoke. But to do so would require a detailed knowledge of individual preferences and I am unable to imagine how the data needed for such a taxation system could be assembled. Indeed,

[64] *Id.* 192–4, 381 and Public Finance 94–100 (3d ed. 1947).

the proposal to solve the smoke-pollution and similar problems by the use of taxes bristles with difficulties: the problem of calculation, the difference between average and marginal damage, the interrelations between the damage suffered on different properties, etc. But it is unnecessary to examine these problems here. It is enough for my purpose to show that, even if the tax is exactly adjusted to equal the damage that would be done to neighboring properties as a result of the emission of each additional puff of smoke, the tax would not necessarily bring about optimal conditions. An increase in the number of people living or of business operating in the vicinity of the smoke-emitting factory will increase the amount of harm produced by a given emission of smoke. The tax that would be imposed would therefore increase with an increase in the number of those in the vicinity. This will tend to lead to a decrease in the value of production of the factors employed by the factory, either because a reduction in production due to the tax will result in factors being used elsewhere in ways which are less valuable, or because factors will be diverted to produce means for reducing the amount of smoke emitted. But people deciding to establish themselves in the vicinity of the factory will not take into account this fall in the value of production which results from their presence. This failure to take into account costs imposed on others is comparable to the action of a factory-owner in not taking into account the harm resulting from his emission of smoke. Without the tax, there may be too much smoke and too few people in the vicinity of the factory; but with the tax there may be too little smoke and too many people in the vicinity of the factory. There is no reason to suppose that one of these results is necessarily preferable.

I need not devote much space to discussing the similar error involved in the suggestion that smoke producing factories should, by means of zoning regulations, be removed from the districts in which the smoke causes harmful effects. When the change in the location of the factory results in a reduction in production, this obviously needs to be taken into account and weighed against the harm which would result from the factory remaining in that location. The aim of such regulation should not be to eliminate smoke pollution but rather to secure the optimum amount of smoke pollution, this being the amount which will maximise the value of production.

X. A Change of Approach

It is my belief that the failure of economists to reach correct conclusions about the treatment of harmful effects cannot be ascribed simply to a few slips in analysis. It stems from basic defects in the current approach to problems of welfare economics. What is needed is a change of approach.

Analysis in terms of divergencies between private and social products concentrates attention on particular deficiencies in the system and tends to nourish the belief that any measure which will remove the deficiency is necessarily desirable. It diverts attention from those other changes in the system which are inevitably associated with the corrective measure, changes which may well produce more harm than the original deficiency. In the preceding sections of this article, we have seen many examples of this. But it is not necessary to approach the problem in this way. Economists who study problems of the firm habitually use an opportunity cost approach and compare the receipts obtained from a given combination of factors with alternative business arrangements. It would seem desirable to use a similar approach when dealing with questions of economic policy and to compare the total product yielded by alternative social arrangements. In this article, the analysis has been confined, as is usual in this part of economics, to comparisons of the value of production, as measured by the market. But it is, of course, desirable that the choice between different social arrangements for the solution of economic problems should be carried out in broader terms than this and that the total effect of these arrangements in all spheres of life should be taken into account. As Frank H. Knight has so often emphasized, problems of welfare economics must ultimately dissolve into a study of aesthetics and morals.

A second feature of the usual treatment of the problems discussed in this article is that the analysis proceeds in terms of a comparison between a state of laissez faire and some kind of ideal world. This approach inevitably leads to a looseness of thought since the nature of the alternatives being compared is never clear. In a state of laissez faire, is there a monetary, a legal or a political system and if so, what are they? In an ideal world, would there be a monetary, a legal or a political system and if so, what would they be? The answers to all these questions are shrouded in mystery and every man is free to draw whatever conclusions he likes. Actually very little analysis is required to show that an ideal world is better than a state of laissez faire, unless the definitions of a state of laissez faire and an ideal world happen to be the same. But the whole discussion is largely irrelevant for questions of economic policy since whatever we may have in mind as our ideal world, it is clear that we have not yet discovered how to get to it from where we are. A better approach would seem to be to start our analysis with a situation approximating that which actually exists, to examine the effects of a proposed policy change and to attempt to decide whether the new situation would be, in total, better or worse than the original one. In this way, conclusions for policy would have some relevance to the actual situation.

A final reason for the failure to develop a theory adequate to handle the problem of harmful effects stems from a faulty concept of a factor of production. This is usually thought of as a physical entity which the businessman acquires and uses (an acre of land, a ton of fertiliser) instead of as a right to perform certain (physical) actions. We may speak of a person owning land and using it as a factor of production but what the land-owner in fact possesses is the right to carry out a circumscribed list of actions. The rights of a land-owner are not unlimited. It is not even always possible for him to remove the land to another place, for instance, by quarrying it. And although it may be possible for him to exclude some people from using "his" land, this may not be true of others. For example, some people may have the right to cross the land. Furthermore, it may or may not be possible to erect certain types of buildings or to grow certain crops or to use particular drainage systems on the land. This does not come about simply because of Government regulation. It would be equally true under the common law. In fact it would be true under any system of law. A system in which the rights of individuals were unlimited would be one in which there were no rights to acquire.

If factors of production are thought of as rights, it becomes easier to understand that the right to do something which has a harmful effect (such as the creation of smoke, noise, smells, etc.) is also a factor of production. Just as we may use a piece of land in such a way as to prevent someone else from crossing it, or parking his car, or building his house upon it, so we may use it in such a way as to deny him a view or quiet or unpolluted air. The cost of exercising a right (of using a factor of production) is always the loss which is suffered elsewhere in consequence of the exercise of that right—the inability to cross land, to park a car, to build a house, to enjoy a view, to have peace and quiet or to breathe clean air.

It would clearly be desirable if the only actions performed were those in which what was gained was worth more than what was lost. But in choosing between social arrangements within the context of which individual decisions are made, we have to bear in mind that a change in the existing system which will lead to an improvement in some decisions may well lead to a worsening of others. Furthermore we have to take into account the costs involved in operating the various social arrangements (whether it be the working of a market or of a government department), as well as the costs involved in moving to a new system. In devising and choosing between social arrangements we should have regard for the total effect. This, above all, is the change in approach which I am advocating.

[4]

Externality

By JAMES M. BUCHANAN and WM. CRAIG STUBBLEBINE

Externality has been, and is, central to the neo-classical critique of market organisation. In its various forms—external economies and diseconomies, divergencies between marginal social and marginal private cost or product, spillover and neighbourhood effects, collective or public goods—externality dominates theoretical welfare economics, and, in one sense, the theory of economic policy generally. Despite this importance and emphasis, rigorous definitions of the concept itself are not readily available in the literature. As Scitovosky has noted, " definitions of external economies are few and unsatisfactory ".[1] The following seems typical:

> External effects exist in consumption whenever the shape or position of a man's indifference curve depends on the consumption of other men. [External effects] are present whenever a firm's production function depends in some way on the amounts of the inputs or outputs of another firm.[2]

It seems clear that operational and usable definitions are required.

In this paper, we propose to clarify the notion of externality by defining it rigorously and precisely. When this is done, several important, and often overlooked, conceptual distinctions follow more or less automatically. Specifically, we shall distinguish marginal and infra-marginal externalities, potentially relevant and irrelevant externalities, and Pareto-relevant and Pareto-irrelevant externalities. These distinctions are formally developed in Section I. As we shall demonstrate, the term, " externality ", as generally used by economists, corresponds only to our definition of Pareto-relevant externality. There follows, in Section II, an illustration of the basic points described in terms of a simple descriptive example. In Section III, some of the implications of our approach are discussed.

It is useful to limit the scope of the analysis at the outset. Much of the discussion in the literature has been concerned with the distinction between *technological* and *pecuniary* external effects. We do not propose to enter this discussion since it is not relevant for our purposes. We note only that, if desired, the whole analysis can be taken to apply only to technological externalities. Secondly, we shall find no cause for discussing production and consumption externalities separately. Essentially the same analysis applies in either case. In what follows, " firms " may be substituted for " individuals " and " production functions "

[1] Tibor Scitovosky, " Two Concepts of External Economies ", *Journal of Political Economy*, vol. LXII (1954), p. 143.

[2] J. de V. Graaf, *Theoretical Welfare Economics*, Cambridge, 1957, p. 43 and p. 18.

for " utility functions " without modifying the central conclusions. For expositional simplicity only, we limit the explicit discussion to consumption externalities.

I

We define an external effect, *an externality*, to be present when,

(1) $u^A = u^A(X_1, X_2, \ldots, X_m, Y_1)$.

This states that the utility of an individual, A, is dependent upon the "activities", $(X_1, X_2, \ldots, X_m)$, that are exclusively under his own control or authority, but also upon another single activity, Y_1, which is, by definition, under the control of a second individual, B, who is presumed to be a member of the same social group. We define an *activity* here as any distinguishable human action that may be measured, such as eating bread, drinking milk, spewing smoke into the air, dumping litter on the highways, giving to the poor, etc. Note that A's utility may, and will in the normal case, depend on other activities of B in addition to Y_1, and also upon the activities of other parties. That is, A's utility function may, in more general terms, include such variables as $(Y_2, Y_3, \ldots, Y_m; Z_1, Z_2, \ldots, Z_m)$. For analytical simplicity, however, we shall confine our attention to the effects of one particular activity, Y_1, as it affects the utility of A.

We assume that A will behave so as to maximise utility in the ordinary way, subject to the externally determined values for Y_1, and that he will modify the values for the X's, as Y_1 changes, so as to maintain a state of " equilibrium ".

A marginal externality exists when,

(2) $u^A_{Y_1} \neq 0$.

Here, small u's are employed to represent the " partial derivatives " of the utility function of the individual designated by the super-script with respect to the variables designated by the subscript. Hence, $u^A_{Y_1} = \partial u^A / \partial Y_1$, assuming that the variation in Y_1 is evaluated with respect to a set of " equilibrium " values for the X's, adjusted to the given value for Y_1.

An infra-marginal externality holds at those points where,

(3) $u^A_{Y_1} = 0$,

and (1) holds.

These classifications can be broken down into economies and diseconomies: a marginal external economy existing when,

(2A) $u^A_{Y_1} > 0$,

that is, a small change in the activity undertaken by B will change the utility of A in the same direction; a marginal external diseconomy existing when,

(2B) $u^A_{Y_1} < 0$.

An infra-marginal external economy exists when for any given set of values for $(X_1, X_2, \ldots, X_m)$, say, $(C_1, C_2, \ldots, C_m)$,

$$\text{(3A)} \quad u^A_{Y_1} = 0, \text{ and } \int_0^{Y_1} u^A_{Y_1}\, d_{Y_1} > 0.$$

This condition states that, while incremental changes in the extent of B's activity, Y_1, have no effect on A's utility, the total effect of B's action has increased A's utility. An infra-marginal diseconomy exists when (1) holds, and, for any given set of values for $(X_1, X_2, \ldots, X_m)$, say, $(C_1, C_2, \ldots, C_m)$, then,

$$\text{(3B)} \quad u^A_{Y_1} = 0, \text{ and } \int_0^{Y_1} u^A_{Y_1}\, d_{Y_1} < 0.$$

Thus, small changes in B's activity do not change A's level of satisfaction, but the total effect of B's undertaking the activity in question is harmful to A.

We are able to classify the effects of B's action, or potential action, on A's utility by evaluating the " partial derivative " of A's utility function with respect to Y_1 over all possible values for Y_1. In order to introduce the further distinctions between *relevant* and *irrelevant* externalities, however, it is necessary to go beyond consideration of A's utility function. Whether or not a relevant externality exists depends upon the extent to which the activity involving the externality is carried out by the person empowered to take action, to make decisions. Since we wish to consider a single externality in isolation, we shall assume that B's utility function includes only variables (activities) that are within his control, including Y_1. Hence, B's utility function takes the form,

$$\text{(4)} \quad u^B = u^B(Y_1, Y_2, \ldots, Y_m).$$

Necessary conditions for utility maximisation by B are,

$$\text{(5)} \quad u^B_{Y_1}/u^B_{Y_j} = f^B_{Y_1}/f^B_{Y_j},$$

where Y_j is used to designate the activity of B in consuming or utilising some numeraire commodity or service which is, by hypothesis, available on equal terms to A. The right-hand term represents the marginal rate of substitution in " production " or " exchange " confronted by B, the party taking action on Y_1, his production function being defined as,

$$\text{(6)} \quad f^B = f^B(Y_1, Y_2, \ldots, Y_m),$$

where inputs are included as activities along with outputs. In other words, the right-hand term represents the marginal cost of the activity, Y_1, to B. The equilibrium values for the Y_i's will be designated as $\bar{Y}_i$'s.

An externality is defined as *potentially relevant* when the activity, to the extent that it is actually performed, generates *any* desire on the part of the externally benefited (damaged) party (A) to modify the behaviour of the party empowered to take action (B) through trade, persuasion, compromise, agreement, convention, collective action, etc. An externality which, to the extent that it is performed, exerts no such influence is defined as *irrelevant*. Note that, so long as (1) holds, an externality remains; utility functions remain interdependent.

A potentially relevant marginal externality exists when,

$$(7) \quad u^A_{Y_1}\Big|_{Y_1=\bar{Y}_1} \neq 0.$$

This is a potentially relevant marginal external economy when (7) is greater than zero, a diseconomy when (7) is less than zero. In either case, *A* is motivated, by *B*'s performance of the activity, to make some effort to modify this performance, to increase the resources devoted to the activity when (7) is positive, to decrease the quantity of resources devoted to the activity when (7) is negative.

Infra-marginal externalities are, by definition, irrelevant for small changes in the scope of *B*'s activity, Y_1. However, when large or discrete changes are considered, *A* is motivated to change *B*'s behaviour with respect to Y_1 in all cases *except* that for which,

$$(8) \quad u^A_{Y_1}\Big|_{Y_1=\bar{Y}_1} = 0, \text{ and}$$

$$u^A\,(C_1, C_2, \ldots, C_m, \bar{Y}_1) \geqq u^A\,(C_1, C_2, \ldots, C_m, Y_1), \text{ for all } Y_1 \neq \bar{Y}_1.$$

When (8) holds, *A* has achieved an absolute maximum of utility with respect to changes over Y_1, given any set of values for the *X*'s. In more prosaic terms, *A* is satiated with respect to Y_1.[1] In all other cases, where infra-marginal external economies or diseconomies exist, *A* will have some desire to modify *B*'s performance; the externality is potentially relevant. Whether or not this motivation will lead *A* to seek an expansion or contraction in the extent of *B*'s performance of the activity will depend on the location of the infra-marginal region relative to the absolute maximum for any given values of the *X*'s.[2]

Pareto relevance and irrelevance may now be introduced. The existence of a simple desire to modify the behaviour of another, defined as potential relevance, need not imply the ability to implement this desire. An externality is defined to be Pareto-relevant when the extent of the activity may be modified in such a way that the externally affected party, *A*, can be made better off without the acting party, *B*, being made worse off. That is to say, " gains from trade " characterise the Pareto-relevant externality, trade that takes the form of some change in the activity of *B* as his part of the bargain.

[1] Note that, $u^A_{Y_1}\Big|_{Y_1=\bar{Y}_1} = 0$, is a necessary, but not a sufficient, condition for irrelevance.

[2] In this analysis of the relevance of externalities, we have assumed that *B* will act in such a manner as to maximise his own utility subject to the constraints within which he must operate. If, for any reason, *B* does not attain the equilibrium position defined in (5) above, the classification of his activity for *A* may, of course, be modified. A potentially relevant externality may become irrelevant and *vice versa*.

A marginal externality is Pareto-relevant when[1]

(9) $(-)\ u^A_{Y_1}/u^A_{X_j} > [u^B_{Y_1}/u^B_{Y_j} - f^B_{Y_1}/f^B_{Y_j}]_{Y_1=\bar{Y}_1}$ and when $u^A_{Y_1}/u^A_{X_j} < 0$, and $u^A_{Y_1}/u^A_{X_j} > (-)\ [u^B_{Y_1}/u^B_{Y_j} - f^B_{Y_1}/f^B_{Y_j}]_{Y_1=\bar{Y}_1}$ when $u^A_{Y_1}/u^A_{X_j} > 0$.

In (9), X_j and Y_j are used to designate, respectively, the activities of A and B in consuming or in utilising some numeraire commodity or service that, by hypothesis, is available on identical terms to each of them. As is indicated by the transposition of signs in (9), the conditions for Pareto relevance differ as between external diseconomies and economies. This is because the " direction " of change desired by A on the part of B is different in the two cases. In stating the conditions for Pareto relevance under ordinary two-person trade, this point is of no significance since trade in one good flows only in one direction. Hence, absolute values can be used.

The condition, (9), states that A's marginal rate of substitution between the activity, Y_1, and the numeraire activity must be greater than the " net " marginal rate of substitution between the activity and the numeraire activity for B. Otherwise, " gains from trade " would not exist between A and B.

Note, however, that when B has achieved utility-maximising equilibrium,

(10) $u^B_{Y_1}/u^B_{Y_j} = f^B_{Y_1}/f^B_{Y_j}$.

That is to say, the marginal rate of substitution in consumption or utilisation is equated to the marginal rate of substitution in production or exchange, i.e., to marginal cost. When (10) holds, the terms in the brackets in (9) mutually cancel. Thus, potentially relevant marginal externalities are also Pareto-relevant when B is in utility-maximising equilibrium. Some trade is possible.

Pareto equilibrium is defined to be present when,

(11) $(-)u^A_{Y_1}/u^A_{X_j} = [u^B_{Y_1}/u^B_{Y_j} - f^B_{Y_1}/f^B_{Y_j}]$, and when $u^A_{Y_1}/u^A_{X_j} < 0$, and $u^A_{Y_1}/u^A_{X_j} = (-)[u^B_{Y_1}/u^B_{Y_j} - f^B_{Y_1}/f^B_{Y_j}]$ when $u^A_{Y_1}/u^A_{X_j} > 0$.

Condition (11) demonstrates that marginal externalities may continue to exist, even in Pareto equilibrium, as here defined. This point may be shown by reference to the special case in which the activity in question may be undertaken at zero costs. Here Pareto equilibrium is attained when the marginal rates of substitution in consumption or utilisation for the two persons are precisely offsetting, that is, where their interests are strictly opposed, and *not* where the left-hand term vanishes.

What vanishes in Pareto equilibrium are the Pareto-relevant externalities. It seems clear that, normally, economists have been referring only to what we have here called Pareto-relevant externalities when

[1] We are indebted to Mr. M. McManus of the University of Birmingham for pointing out to us an error in an earlier formulation of this and the following similar conditions.

they have, implicitly or explicitly, stated that external effects are not present when a position on the Pareto optimality surface is attained.[1]

For completeness, we must also consider those potentially relevant infra-marginal externalities. Refer to the discussion of these as summarised in (8) above. The question is now to determine whether or not, A, the externally affected party, can reach some mutually satisfactory agreement with B, the acting party, that will involve some discrete (non-marginal) change in the scope of the activity, Y_1. If, over some range, any range, of the activity, which we shall designate by $\triangle Y_1$, the rate of substitution between Y_1 and X_j for A exceeds the " net " rate of substitution for B, the externality is Pareto-relevant. The associated changes in the utilisation of the numeraire commodity must be equal for the two parties. Thus, for external economies, we have

(12) $$\frac{\triangle u^A}{\triangle Y_1} \Big/ \frac{\triangle u^A}{\triangle X_j} > (-)\left[\frac{\triangle u^B}{\triangle Y_1} \Big/ \frac{\triangle u^B}{\triangle Y_j} - \frac{\triangle f^B}{\triangle Y_1} \Big/ \frac{\triangle f^B}{\triangle Y_j}\right]_{Y_1=\bar{Y}_1},$$ and the

same with the sign in parenthesis transposed for external diseconomies. The difference to be noted between (12) and (9) is that, with infra-marginal externalities, potential relevance need not imply Pareto relevance. The bracketed terms in (12) need not sum to zero when B is in his private utility-maximising equilibrium.

We have remained in a two-person world, with one person affected by the single activity of a second. However, the analysis can readily be modified to incorporate the effects of this activity on a multi-person group. That is to say, B's activity, Y_1, may be allowed to affect several parties simultaneously, several A's, so to speak. In each case, the activity can then be evaluated in terms of its effects on the utility of each person. Nothing in the construction need be changed. The only stage in the analysis requiring modification explicitly to take account of the possibilities of multi-person groups being externally affected is that which involves the condition for Pareto relevance and Pareto equilibrium.

For a multi-person group ($A_1, A_2, \ldots, A_n$), any one or all of whom may be externally affected by the activity, Y_1, of the single person, B, the condition for Pareto relevance is,

(9A) $$(-)\sum_{i=1}^{n} u_{Y_1}^{A_i}/u_{X_j}^{A_i} > [u_{Y_1}^{B}/u_{Y_j}^{B} - f_{Y_1}^{B}/f_{Y_j}^{B}]_{Y_1=\bar{Y}_1} \text{ when } u_{Y_1}^{A_i}/u_{X_j}^{A_i} < 0, \text{ and,}$$

$$\sum_{i=1}^{n} u_{Y_1}^{A_i}/u_{X_j}^{A_i} > (-)[u_{Y_1}^{B}/u_{Y_j}^{B} - f_{Y_1}^{B}/f_{Y_j}^{B}]_{Y_1=\bar{Y}_1} \text{ when } u_{Y_1}^{A_i}/u_{X_j}^{A_i} > 0.$$

That is, the summed marginal rates of substitution over the members of the externally affected group exceed the offsetting " net " marginal evaluation of the activity by B. Again, in private equilibrium for B,

[1] This applies to the authors of this paper. For recent discussion of external effects when we have clearly intended only what we here designate as Pareto-relevant, see James M. Buchanan, " Politics, Policy, and the Pigovian Margins ", *Economica*, vol. XXVIX (1962), pp. 17–28, and, also, James M. Buchanan and Gordon Tullock, *The Calculus of Consent*, Ann Arbor, 1962.

marginal externalities are Pareto-relevant, provided that we neglect the important element involved in the costs of organising group decisions. In the real world, these costs of organising group decisions (together with uncertainty and ignorance) will prevent realisation of some " gains from trade "—just as they do in organised markets. This is as true for two-person groups as it is for larger groups. But this does not invalidate the point that potential " gains from trade " are available. The condition for Pareto equilibrium and for the infra-marginal case summarised in (11) and (12) for the two-person model can readily be modified to allow for the externally affected multi-person group.

II

The distinctions developed formally in Section I may be illustrated diagrammatically and discussed in terms of a simple descriptive example. Consider two persons, *A* and *B*, who own adjoining units of residential property. Within limits to be noted, each person values privacy, which may be measured quantitatively in terms of a single criterion, the height of a fence that can be constructed along the common boundary line. We shall assume that *B*'s desire for privacy holds over rather wide limits. His utility increases with the height of the fence up to a reasonably high level. Up to a certain minimum height, *A*'s utility also is increased as the fence is made higher. Once this minimum height is attained, however, *A*'s desire for privacy is assumed to be fully satiated. Thus, over a second range, *A*'s total utility does not change with a change in the height of the fence. However, beyond a certain limit, *A*'s view of a mountain behind *B*'s property is progressively obscured as the fence goes higher. Over this third range, therefore, *A*'s utility is reduced as the fence is constructed to higher levels. Finally, *A* will once again become wholly indifferent to marginal changes in the fence's height when his view is totally blocked out.

We specify that *B* possesses the sole authority, the only legal right, to construct the fence between the two properties.

The preference patterns for *A* and for *B* are shown in Figure 1, which is drawn in the form of an Edgeworth-like box diagram. Note, however, that the origin for *B* is shown at the upper left rather than the upper right corner of the diagram as in the more normal usage. This modification is necessary here because only the numeraire good, measured along the ordinate, is strictly divisible between *A* and *B*. Both must adjust to the same height of fence, that is, to the same level of the activity creating the externality.

As described above, the indifference contours for *A* take the general shape shown by the curves *aa*, *a'a'*, while those for *B* assume the shapes, *bb*, *b'b'*. Note that these contours reflect the relative evaluations, for *A* and *B*, between money and the activity, Y_1. Since the costs of undertaking the activity, for *B*, are not incorporated in the diagram, the " contract locus " that might be derived from tangency points will have little relevance except in the special case where the activity can be undertaken at zero costs.

Figure 2 depicts the marginal evaluation curves for *A* and *B*, as derived from the preference fields shown in Figure 1, along with some incorporation of costs. These curves are derived as follows: Assume

Figure 1

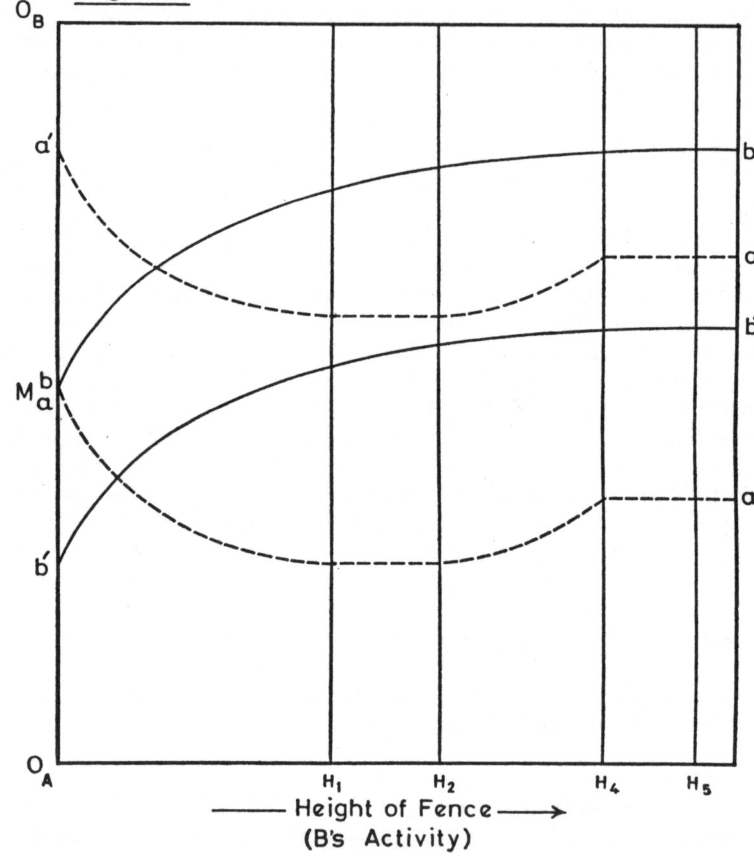

an initial distribution of " money " between *A* and *B*, say, that shown at *M* on Figure 1. The marginal evaluation of the activity for *A* is then derived by plotting the negatives (i.e., the mirror image) of the slopes of successive indifference curves attained by *A* as *B* is assumed to increase the height of the fence from zero. These values remain positive for a range, become zero over a second range, become negative for a third, and, finally, return to zero again.[1]

[1] For an early use of marginal evaluation curves, see J. R. Hicks, " The Four Consumer's Surpluses ", *Review of Economic Studies*, vol. XI (1943), pp. 31–41.

B's curves of marginal evaluation are measured downward from the upper horizontal axis or base line, for reasons that will become apparent. The derivation of *B*'s marginal evaluation curve is somewhat more complex than that for *A*. This is because *B*, who is the person authorised to undertake the action, in this case the building of the fence, must also bear the full costs. Thus, as *B* increases the scope of the activity, his real income, measured in terms of his remaining goods and services, is reduced. This change in the amount of remaining goods and

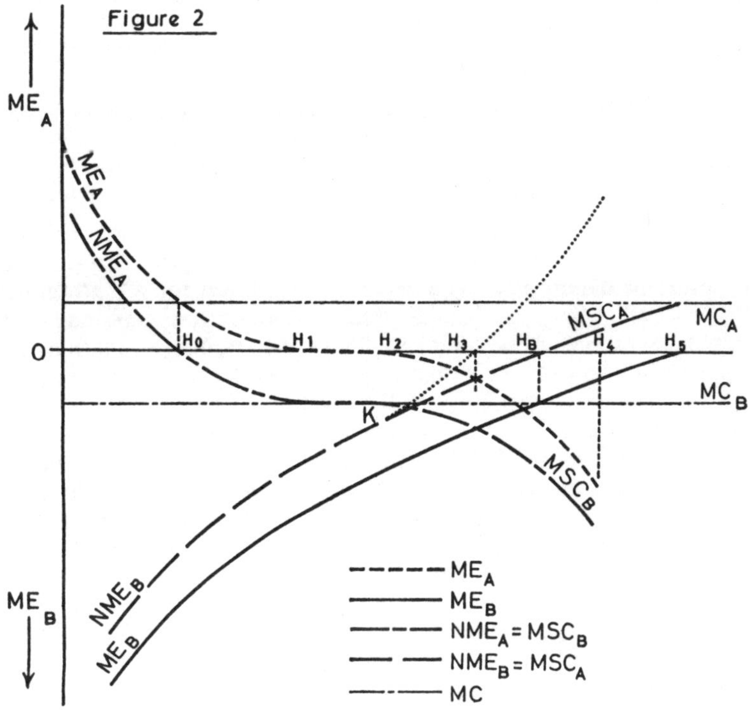

services will, of course, affect his marginal evaluation of the activity in question. Thus, the marginal cost of building the fence will determine, to some degree, the marginal evaluation of the fence. This necessary interdependence between marginal evaluation and marginal cost complicates the use of simple diagrammatic models in finding or locating a solution. It need not, however, deter us from presenting the solution diagrammatically, if we postulate that the marginal evaluation curve, as drawn, is based on a single presumed cost relationship. This done, we may plot *B*'s marginal evaluation of the activity from the negatives of the slopes of his indifference contours attained as he constructs the fence to higher and higher levels. *B*'s marginal evaluation, shown in Figure 2, remains positive throughout the range to the point H_5, where it becomes zero.

The distinctions noted in Section I are easily related to the construction in Figure 2. To *A*, the party externally affected, *B*'s potential activity in constructing the fence can be assessed independently of any prediction of *B*'s actual behaviour. Thus, the activity of *B* would,

(1) exert marginal external economies which are potentially relevant over the range OH_1;

(2) exert infra-marginal external economies over the range H_1H_2, which are clearly irrelevant since no change in *B*'s behaviour with respect to the extent of the activity would increase *A*'s utility;

(3) exert marginal external diseconomies over the range H_2H_4 which are potentially relevant to *A*; and,

(4) exert infra-marginal external economies or diseconomies beyond H_4, the direction of the effect being dependent on the ratio between the total utility derived from privacy and the total reduction in utility derived from the obstructed view. In any case, the externality is potentially relevant.

To determine Pareto relevance, the extent of *B*'s predicted performance must be determined. The necessary condition for *B*'s attainment of " private " utility-maximising equilibrium is that marginal costs, which he must incur, be equal to his own marginal evaluation. For simplicity in Figure 2, we assume that marginal costs are constant, as shown by the curve, *MC*. Thus, *B*'s position of equilibrium is shown at H_B, within the range of marginal external diseconomies for *A*. Here the externality imposed by *B*'s behaviour is clearly Pareto-relevant: *A* can surely work out some means of compensating *B* in exchange for *B*'s agreement to reduce the scope of the activity—in this example, to reduce the height of the fence between the two properties. Diagrammatically, the position of Pareto equilibrium is shown at H_3 where the marginal evaluation of *A* is equal in absolute value, but negatively, to the " net " marginal evaluation of *B*, drawn as the curve NME_B. Only in this position are the conditions specified in (11), above, satisfied.[1]

III

Aside from the general classification of externalities that is developed, the approach here allows certain implications to be drawn, implications that have not, perhaps, been sufficiently recognised by some welfare economists.

The analysis makes it quite clear that externalities, external effects, may remain even in full Pareto equilibrium. That is to say, a position

[1] This diagrammatic analysis is necessarily oversimplified in the sense that the Pareto equilibrium position is represented as a unique point. Over the range between the " private " equilibrium for *B* and the point of Pareto equilibrium, the sort of bargains struck between *A* and *B* will affect the marginal evaluation curves of both individuals within this range. Thus, the more accurate analysis would suggest a " contract locus " of equilibrium points. At Pareto equilibrium, however, the condition shown in the diagrammatic presentation holds, and the demonstration of this fact rather than the location of the solution is the aim of this diagrammatics.

may be classified as Pareto-optimal or efficient despite the fact that, at the marginal, the activity of one individual externally affects the utility of another individual. Figure 2 demonstrates this point clearly. Pareto equilibrium is attained at H_3, yet B is imposing marginal external diseconomies on A.

This point has significant policy implications for it suggests that the observation of external effects, taken alone, cannot provide a basis for judgment concerning the desirability of some modification in an existing state of affairs. There is not a *prima facie* case for intervention in all cases where an externality is observed to exist.[1] The internal benefits from carrying out the activity, net of costs, may be greater than the external damage that is imposed on other parties.

In full Pareto equilibrium, of course, these internal benefits, measured in terms of some numeraire good, net of costs, must be just equal, at the margin, to the external damage that is imposed on other parties. This equilibrium will always be characterised by the strict opposition of interests of the two parties, one of which may be a multi-person group.

In the general case, we may say that, at full Pareto equilibrium, the presence of a marginal external diseconomy implies an offsetting marginal *internal* economy, whereas the presence of a marginal external economy implies an offsetting marginal *internal* diseconomy. In " private " equilibrium, as opposed to Pareto equilibrium, these net internal economies and diseconomies would, of course, be eliminated by the utility-maximising acting party. In Pareto equilibrium, these remain because the acting party is being compensated for " suffering " internal economies and diseconomies, that is, divergencies between " private " marginal costs and benefits, *measured in the absence of compensation.*

As a second point, it is useful to relate the whole analysis here to the more familiar Pigovian discussion concerning the divergence between marginal social cost (product) and marginal private cost (product). By saying that such a divergence exists, we are, in the terms of this paper, saying that a marginal externality exists. The Pigovian terminology tends to be misleading, however, in that it deals with the acting party to the exclusion of the externally affected party. It fails to take into account the fact that there are always two parties involved in a single externality relationship.[2] As we have suggested, a marginal externality is Pareto-relevant except in the position of Pareto equilibrium; gains from trade can arise. But there must be two parties to any trading arrangement. The externally affected party must compensate the acting party for modifying his behaviour. The Pigovian terminology, through its concentration on the decision-making of the acting party alone, tends to obscure the two-sidedness of the bargain that must be made.

[1] Cf. Paul A. Samuelson, *Foundations of Economic Analysis*, Cambridge, Mass., 1948, p. 208, for a discussion of the views of various writers.

[2] This criticism of the Pigovian analysis has recently been developed by R. H. Coase; see his " The Problem of Social Cost ", *Journal of Law and Economics*, vol. III (1960), pp. 1–44.

To illustrate this point, assume that A, the externally affected party in our model, successfully secures, through the auspices of the " state ", the levy of a marginal tax on B's performance of the activity, Y_1. Assume further that A is able to secure this change without cost to himself. The tax will increase the marginal cost of performing the activity for B, and, hence, will reduce the extent of the activity attained in B's " private " equilibrium. Let us now presume that this marginal tax is levied " correctly " on the basis of a Pigovian calculus; the rate of tax at the margin is made equal to the negative marginal evaluation of the activity to A. Under these modified conditions, the effective marginal cost, as confronted by B, may be shown by the curve designated as MSC_B in Figure 2. A new " private " equilibrium for B is shown at the quantity, H_3, the same level designated as Pareto equilibrium in our earlier discussion, if we neglect the disturbing interdependence between marginal evaluation and marginal costs. Attention solely to the decision calculus of B here would suggest, perhaps, that this position remains Pareto-optimal under these revised circumstances, and that it continues to qualify as a position of Pareto equilibrium. There is no divergence between marginal private cost and marginal social cost in the usual sense. However, the position, if attained in this manner, is clearly neither one of Pareto optimality, nor one that may be classified as Pareto equilibrium.

In this new " private " equilibrium for B,

(13) $u^B_{Y_1}/u^B_{Y_j} = f^B_{Y_1}/f^B_{Y_j} - u^A_{Y_1}/u^A_{X_j}$,

where $u^A_{Y_1}/u^A_{X_j}$ represents the marginal tax imposed on B as he performs the activity, Y_1. Recall the necessary condition for Pareto relevance defined in (9) above, which can now be modified to read,

(9B) $(-)\, u^A_{Y_1}/u^A_{X_j} > [u^B_{Y_1}/u^B_{Y_j} - f^B_{Y_1}/f^B_{Y_j} + u^A_{Y_1}/u^A_{X_j}]_{Y_1=\bar{\bar{Y}}_1}$, when $u^A_{Y_1}/u^A_{X_j} < 0$,

and $u^A_{Y_1}/u^A_{X_j} > (-)[u^B_{Y_1}/u^B_{Y_j} - f^B_{Y_1}/f^B_{Y_j} + u^A_{Y_1}/u^A_{X_j}]_{Y_1=\bar{\bar{Y}}_1}$, when $u^A_{Y_1}/u^A_{X_j} > 0$.

In (9B), $\bar{\bar{Y}}_1$ represents the " private " equilibrium value for Y_1, determined by B, after the ideal Pigovian tax is imposed. As before, the bracketed terms represent the " net " marginal evaluation of the activity for the acting party, B, and these sum to zero when equilibrium is reached. So long as the left-hand term in the inequality remains non-zero, a Pareto-relevant marginal externality remains, despite the fact that the full " Pigovian solution " is attained.

The apparent paradox here is not difficult to explain. Since, as postulated, A is not incurring any cost in securing the change in B's behaviour, and, since there remains, by hypothesis, a marginal diseconomy, further " trade " can be worked out between the two parties. Specifically, Pareto equilibrium is reached when,

(11A) $(-) u^A_{Y_1}/u^A_{X_j} = [u^B_{Y_1}/u^B_{Y_j} - f^B_{Y_1}/f^B_{Y_j} + u^A_{Y_1}/u^A_{X_j}]$ when $u^A_{Y_1}/u^A_{X_j} < 0$, and

$u^A_{Y_1}/u^A_{X_j} = (-)[u^B_{Y_1}/u^B_{Y_j} - f^B_{Y_1}/f^B_{Y_j} + u^A_{Y_1}/u^A_{X_j}]$ when $u^A_{Y_1}/u^A_{X_j} > 0$.

Diagrammatically, this point may be made with reference to Figure 2. If a unilaterally imposed tax, corresponding to the marginal evaluation of *A*, is placed on *B*'s performance of the activity, the new position of Pareto equilibrium may be shown by first subtracting the new marginal cost curve, drawn as MSC_B, from *B*'s marginal evaluation curve. Where this new " net " marginal evaluation curve, shown as the dotted curve between points H_3 and *K*, cuts the marginal evaluation curve for *A*, a new position of Pareto equilibrium falling between H_2 and H_3 is located, neglecting the qualifying point discussed in Footnote 1, page 380.

The important implication to be drawn is that full Pareto equilibrium can never be attained via the imposition of unilaterally imposed taxes and subsidies until all marginal externalities are eliminated. If a tax-subsidy method, rather than " trade ", is to be introduced, it should involve bi-lateral taxes (subsidies). Not only must *B*'s behaviour be modified so as to insure that he will take the costs externally imposed on *A* into account, but *A*'s behaviour must be modified so as to insure that he will take the costs " internally " imposed on *B* into account. In such a double tax-subsidy scheme, the necessary Pareto conditions would be readily satisfied.[1]

In summary, Pareto equilibrium in the case of marginal externalities cannot be attained so long as marginal externalities remain, until and unless those benefiting from changes are required to pay some " price " for securing the benefits.

A third point worthy of brief note is that our analysis allows the whole treatment of externalities to encompass the consideration of purely collective goods. As students of public finance theory will have recognised, the Pareto equilibrium solution discussed in this paper is similar, indeed is identical, with that which was presented by Paul Samuelson in his theory of public expenditures.[2] The summed marginal rates of substitution (marginal evaluation) must be equal to marginal costs. Note, however, that marginal costs may include the negative marginal evaluation of other parties, if viewed in one way. Note, also, that there is nothing in the analysis which suggests its limitations to purely collective goods or even to goods that are characterised by significant externalities in their use.

Our analysis also lends itself to the more explicit point developed in Coase's recent paper.[3] He argues that the same " solution " will tend to emerge out of any externality relationship, regardless of the structure of property rights, provided only that the market process works smoothly. Strictly speaking, Coase's analysis is applicable only to inter-firm externality relationships, and the identical solution emerges only because firms adjust to prices that are competitively determined. In our terms of reference, this identity of solution cannot apply because of the incomparability of utility functions. It remains true, however,

[1] Although developed in rather different terminology, this seems to be closely in accord with Coase's analysis. Cf. R. H. Coase, *loc. cit.*

[2] Paul A. Samuelson, " The Pure Theory of Public Expenditure ", *Review of Economics and Statistics*, vol. XXXVI (1954), pp. 386–9.

[3] R. H. Coase, *loc. cit.*

that the basic characteristics of the Pareto equilibrium position remain unchanged regardless of the authority undertaking the action. This point can be readily demonstrated, again with reference to Figure 2. Let us assume that Figure 2 is now redrawn on the basis of a different legal relationship in which *A* now possesses full authority to construct the fence, whereas *B* can no longer take any action in this respect. *A* will, under these conditions, " privately " construct a fence only to the height H_0, where the activity clearly exerts a Pareto-relevant marginal external economy on *B*. Pareto equilibrium will be reached, as before, at H_3, determined, in this case, by the intersection of the " net " marginal evaluation curve for *A* (which is identical to the previously defined marginal social cost curve, *MSC*, when *B* is the acting party) and the marginal evaluation curve for *B*.[1] Note that, in this model, *A* will allow himself to suffer an internal marginal diseconomy, at equilibrium, provided that he is compensated by *B*, who continues, in Pareto equilibrium, to enjoy a marginal *external* economy.

Throughout this paper, we have deliberately chosen to introduce and to discuss only a single externality. Much of the confusion in the literature seems to have arisen because two or more externalities have been handled simultaneously. The standard example is that in which the output of one firm affects the production function of the second firm while, at the same time, the output of the second firm affects the production function of the first. Clearly, there are two externalities to be analysed in such cases. In many instances, these can be treated as separate and handled independently. In other situations, this step cannot be taken and additional tools become necessary.[2]

University of Virginia.

[1] The H_3 position, in this presumably redrawn figure, should not be precisely compared with the same position in the other model. We are using here the same diagram for two models, and, especially over wide ranges, the dependence of the marginal evaluation curves on income effects cannot be left out of account.

[2] For a treatment of the dual externality problem that clearly shows the important difference between the separable and the non-separable cases, see Otto Davis and Andrew Whinston, " Externalities, Welfare, and the Theory of Games ", *Journal of Political Economy*, vol. LXX (1962), pp. 241–62. As the title suggests, Davis and Whinston utilise the tools of game theory for the inseparable case.

[5]

On Taxation and the Control of Externalities

By WILLIAM J. BAUMOL*

It is ironic that just at the moment when the Pigouvian tradition has some hope of acceptance in application it should find itself under a cloud in the theoretical literature. James Buchanan has argued that its recommended taxes and subsidies may even increase resource misallocation in the presence of monopoly. Otto Davis and Andrew Whinston (1962) have, in effect, raised doubts about its applicability in the presence of oligopoly. And Ronald Coase has asserted that the tradition has not selected the correct taxation principle for the elimination of externalities, and may not even have chosen the right individuals to tax or to subsidize. In this paper I will suggest that these authors have led the discussion in our profession to focus on the wrong difficulties. In doing so they have, albeit inadvertently, drawn attention away from some of the most important limitations of the Pigouvian prescription as an instrument of policy and from consideration of the means that might prove effective in practice.

The main purpose of the paper is to show that, taken on its own grounds, the conclusions of the Pigouvian tradition are, in fact, impeccable. Despite the various criticisms that have been raised against it in the large numbers case, which is of primary importance in reality and to which Pigou's analysis directs itself, his tax-subsidy programs are generally those required for an optimal allocation of resources. Moreover, I will attempt to show that where an externality is (like the usual pollution problem) of the public goods variety, neither compensation to nor taxation of those who are affected by it is compatible with optimal resource allocation. Pigouvian taxes (subsidies) upon the generator of the externality are all that is required.

However, as is well known, the Pigouvian proposals suffer from a number of serious shortcomings as operational criteria when one seeks to implement them precisely as they emerge from the theory. I therefore discuss a modified approach that recommends itself more for its promise of effectiveness, than its theoretical nicety. It consists of two basic steps: the setting of standards, more or less arbitrarily, of levels of pollution, congestion and the like, that are considered to be tolerable, and the design of taxes and effluent charges whose rates are shown by experience to be sufficient to achieve the selected standards of acceptability. Such a system of charges will, at least in principle, effect any preselected reduction in,

* Professor of economics, Princeton University and New York University. I would like to express my gratitude to the National Science Foundation whose assistance helped materially in the completion of the paper and to my colleagues James Litvack, Wallace Oates, and David Bradford, to my students Mark Gaudry and Bryan Boulier, and to Peter Bohm, James Buchanan, Ronald Coase, Karl-Göran Mäler, Herbert Mohring, and Ralph Turvey who have given me many very helpful suggestions, and saved me from a number of serious errors. Mohring and J. Hayden Boyd have written an extremely illuminating paper dealing, among other relevant matters, with the portions of the Coase-Buchanan-Turvey arguments in the case where the polluters and their victims "can and do negotiate." Since the present paper concerns itself only with the "relevant" large numbers case where there is no negotiation, it deliberately makes no attempt to consider the interesting negotiation case examined so helpfully by Mohring and Boyd.

say, the pollution content of our rivers, at minimum cost to society. It automatically achieves an efficient allocation of the required reduction in emissions among the offending firms *even if they are neither pure competitors nor profit maximizers*. Thus, a persuasive case can be made for the use of taxes and subsidies to control externalities, even if they will not produce an optimal allocation of resources in the complex world of reality.

I. The Coase Argument in the Case Without Negotiation

Recommendations designed for the competitive case can clearly run into difficulties in the presence of monopolistic elements. Buchanan reminds us that, if a polluting monopolistic industry already restricts the outputs of its products below their competitive levels, the imposition of an effluent charge to restrict output still further is hardly likely to be appropriate. And Davis and Whinston (1962) show for the case of externalities under oligopoly that it is rather difficult to come up with an ideal set of taxes since in the small numbers case just about anything is possible by way of pricing and output levels. However, these arguments have little direct bearing on the Pigouvian analysis because it is couched entirely in terms of pure competition (on this see Stanislaw Wellicz' illuminating discussion), which, in view of the large numbers involved in virtually all of the externalities problems that worry us today, is entirely apropos.

Coase's arguments, buttressed by impressive legal erudition, are less easily dealt with. He offers us a number of illuminating observations, among them the interesting point (see his Section IV) that (in the relatively unimportant cases) where only a small number of decision makers is involved, a process of voluntary bargaining and side payments among those concerned by an externality may produce an optimal allocation of resources, even in the absence of liability for damage. This implies that where small numbers are involved, the imposition of a "corrective" Pigouvian tax may be too much of a good thing—it can produce a misallocation rather than eliminating it.

Coase suggests, however, that even in cases where there is no negotiation among the parties affected by an externality the Pigouvian taxes and subsidies may be the wrong remedy—that they may only modify the character of the misallocation of resources. Coase's central argument appears to be the following: Every social cost is inherently reciprocal in nature. The nearby residents who breathe smoke spewn by a factory must share with the management of the factory the responsibility for the resulting social cost. True, if the factory were closed up the social cost would disappear. But the same holds for its neighbors—were they to move away no one would suffer smoke nuisance. Put another way, just as the smoke emitted by the factory imposes at least a psychic cost on its neighbors, the latter's insistence on the installation of purification devices or a reduction in the pollution-producing activity imposes a cost on the factory.

This position, though at first glance very odd (the murder victim too, is then always an accessory to the crime), grows more persuasive as one considers it further. Coase does not raise the issue as a matter of distributive justice. Rather, he suggests, because of the reciprocal structure of the externality, the traditional taxes and subsidies are likely to lead to a misallocation of resources.[1] If it is socially less costly to

[1] Thus Coase starts out with

. . . the case of a confectioner, the noise and vibrations from whose machinery disturbed a doctor in his work. To avoid harming the doctor would inflict harm on [be costly to] the confectioner. The problem posed by this case was essentially whether it was worthwhile, as a

remove the neighbors from the vicinity of the factory than to reduce the quantity of pollutants emitted by the plant (taking into account the location preferences of the current residents), surely the former is the course of action which is more desirable socially.

In that case, should not a tax sometimes be levied, at least in part on those who choose to live near the factory rather than upon the factory owners?[2] Otherwise might not too many persons be induced to move near the factory thus, incidentally, increasing the magnitude of the Pigouvian tax since the social damage caused by the smoke must then rise correspondingly?

A simple model shows readily that, properly stated, the prescription of the Pigouvian tradition is (at least formally) correct. An appropriately chosen tax, levied only on the factory (without payment of compensation to local residents) is precisely what is needed for optimal resource allocation under pure competition. No tax on nearby residents is required or, taken in real terms, is even compatible with optimal resource allocation. Thus the obvious and apparently common interpretation of the Coase position is simply invalid. We will see, however, that the issue Coase himself intended to raise was rather more subtle and his conclusions are not necessarily at variance with the Pigouvian prescription as I interpret it.

II. Analysis: Should the Victims of Externalities be Taxed or Compensated?

To formalize the argument we construct an elementary general equilibrium model designed to represent in most explicit form the conditions envisioned in the Coase argument, departing from it only by an assumption of universal perfect competition, including thereby the critical stipulation that costs of negotiated and voluntary control of externalities are prohibitive. In addition, we adopt the simplifying premises that there is only one scarce resource, labor, and that the externality (smoke) only affects the cost of production of neighboring laundries, rather than causing disutility for consumers. It is easy to show (see for example, fn. 5) that neither of these simplifications, nor the assumption that there are only four activities, affects the substance of the discussion. We utilize the following notation: Let

x_1, x_2, x_3, and x_4 be the outputs of the economy's four activities, I, II, III, and IV

R be the total supply of the labor resource available

x_5 be the unused quantity of labor (which is assumed to be utilized as leisure)

result of restricting the methods of production which could be used by the confectioner, to secure more doctoring at the cost of a reduced supply of confectionery products. [Section II, p. 2]

[2] If the factory owner is to be made to pay a tax equal to the damage caused, it would clearly be desirable to institute a double tax system and to make residents of the district pay an amount equal to the additional cost incurred by the factory owner (or the consumers of his products) in order to avoid the damage. [Coase, Section IX, p. 41] An even stronger statement on this subject occurs in Buchanan and Stubblebine (Section III):

> . . . full Pareto equilibrium can *never* be attained via the imposition of unilaterally imposed taxes and subsidies until all marginal externalities are eliminated. If a tax subsidy method, rather than 'trade,' is to be introduced, it should involve bi-lateral taxes (subsidies). Not only must *B*'s behavior be modified so as to insure that he will take the costs externally imposed on *A* into account, but *A*'s behavior must be modified so as to insure that he will take the costs 'internally' imposed on *B* into account. [italics added]

However, in a recent letter Buchanan commented:

> In my own thinking . . . I did not ever think of this sort of [double] tax at all, and it would have surely seemed bizarre to me to suggest that taxes be levied on both the factory and the laundries. What we were proposing was the Wicksellian public-goods approach. Suppose that existing property rights allow the factory to put out the smoke . . . There is a public goods problem here; the residents get together, impose a tax on *themselves* to subsidize the factory to install the smoke prevention device.

x_{ij} be the quantity of x_i consumed by individual j ($i=1, \ldots, 5$) ($j=1, \ldots, m$)

p_1, p_2, p_3, p_4, and p_5 be the prices of the four outputs and leisure

$u_j(x_{1j}, \ldots, x_{5j})$ be the utility function of individual j, and

$c_1(x_1)$, $c_2(x_1, x_2)$, $c_3(x_3)$ and $c_4(x_4)$ be the respective total labor cost functions for our four outputs

Here x_1 is an output whose production imposes external costs on the manufacture of x_2 (say, industry II is the oft-cited laundry industry whose costs are increased by I's smoke). To permit the full range of Coase's alternatives (moving of the factory's neighbors and elimination of smoke by the factory), each of these two products is taken to have a perfect substitute. The substitute for x_1 is x_3 whose production yields no externalities, but whose cost is different (presumably higher) than that of x_1. We may think of commodity III as identical with I, but produced in a factory equipped with smoke elimination equipment. Similarly, industry IV is taken to offer the same output as II but its operations have been relocated (at a cost) in order to avoid the effects of the externalities.[3] Thus, by changing the ratio between x_2 and x_4 the model can relocate as much of the laundry output as is desired.

All prices are expressed in terms of hours of labor so that, identically,

$$p_5 = 1 \tag{1}$$

[3] Since product III is a perfect substitute for product I and product IV is a perfect substitute for product II, the utility function for individual j can be written as $u_j(x_{1j}+x_{3j}, x_{2j}+x_{4j}, x_{5j})$. This is, of course, a special case of the more general utility function utilized in the text, and as the reader can verify, the conclusions are totally unaffected by the use of the particular form of the utility function just described.

Pareto optimality then requires maximization of the utility of any arbitrarily chosen individual, say m, subject to the requirement that there be no loss in utility to any of the $m-1$ other persons, i.e., given any feasible level for these other persons' utility. Thus the problem is[4] to maximize

$$u_m(x_{1m}, \ldots, x_{5m})$$

subject to

$$u_j(x_{1j}, \ldots, x_{5j}) = k_j \text{ (constant)} \qquad (j = 1, 2, \ldots, m-1)$$

$$\sum_{j=1}^{m} x_{ij} = x_i \qquad (i = 1, \ldots, 5)$$

and the labor requirement (production function) constraint

$$c_1(x_1) + c_2(x_1, x_2) + c_3(x_3) + c_4(x_4) + x_5 = R$$

We immediately obtain our Lagrangian

$$\begin{aligned} L = & \sum_{j=1}^{m} \lambda_j[u_j(x_{1j}, \cdots, x_{5j}) - k_j] \\ & + \sum_i \nu_i(x_i - \sum_j x_{ij}) \\ & + \mu[R - c_1(x_1) - c_2(x_1, x_2) \\ & - c_3(x_3) - c_4(x_4) - x_5] \end{aligned} \tag{2}$$

where we may take $\lambda_m = 1$, $k_m = 0$.

We use the notation u_{ji} to represent $\partial u_j/\partial x_{ij}$ and c_{ik} to represent $\partial c_i/\partial x_k$ (or dc_i/dx_k, where appropriate).

Then, differentiating in turn with respect to the x_{ij} and the x_i we obtain the first-order conditions

$$\partial L/\partial x_{ij} = \lambda_j u_{ji} - \nu_i = 0 \quad (i = 1, \ldots, 5) \quad (j = 1, \ldots, m)$$

$$\partial L/\partial x_1 = -\mu(c_{11} + c_{21}) + \nu_1 = 0$$

$$\partial L/\partial x_i = -\mu c_{ii} + \nu_i = 0 \quad (i = 2, 3, 4)$$

$$\partial L/\partial x_5 = -\mu + \nu_5 = 0$$

[4] For a more sophisticated variant of this model, using the techniques of non-linear programming, see Robert Meyer.

Now, from consumer equilibrium analysis, we know that for any two commodities, a and b, and any two prices, p_a and p_b, we have $p_a/p_b = u_{ja}/u_{jb}$ $(j=1, \cdots, m)$ or $\omega_j p_i = u_{ji}$ for all i and some ω_j.

Hence, $\lambda_j u_{ji} = \lambda_j \omega_j p_i$, so that writing $s_j = \lambda_j \omega_j$ the first of our first-order conditions becomes $\nu_i = s_j p_i$ for all individuals, j. Consequently the value of s_j must equal the same number, $s = \nu_i / p_i$ for every individual, and that first equation of the first-order conditions now becomes simply $\nu_i = s p_i$ for all i. Substituting this expression for ν_i into the other first-order conditions, we obtain

$$\begin{aligned} sp_1 &= \mu(c_{11} + c_{21}) \\ sp_i &= \mu c_{ii} \qquad (i = 2, 3, 4) \\ sp_5 &= s = \mu \quad \text{since } p_5 = 1 \text{ [by (1)]} \end{aligned} \tag{3}$$

By (3) we may then divide through the preceding conditions by $s = \mu$, and they therefore reduce just to[5]

$$\begin{aligned} p_1 &= c_{11} + c_{21} \\ p_2 &= c_{22} \\ p_3 &= c_{33} \\ p_4 &= c_{44} \\ p_5 &= 1 \end{aligned} \tag{4}$$

In other words, the optimal price for the externality-generating product is equal to the (Pareto optimal) level of its entire social[6] marginal cost, $c_{11} + c_{21}$, while the optimal price for any item, i, which generates no externalities is simply its marginal private cost, c_{ii}. To obtain these prices in our world of pure competition, one need merely levy an excise tax on item I equal to c_{21} (labor hours) dollars per unit, just as the Pigouvian tradition requires. Assuming the appropriate concavity-convexity conditions hold, this will automatically satisfy the necessary and sufficient conditions for the Pareto optimal output levels.[7] In the competitive case, where negotiation is impractical, that is all there is to the matter. The generalization to the case of n outputs, each of them imposing externalities on a number of the others, is immediate.

It is important to observe that, *the solution calls for neither taxes upon x_2, the neighboring laundry output, nor compensation to that industry* for the damage it suffers.

One way to look at the reason is that our model (and the pollution model in general) refers to the important case of *public* externalities. The laundry whose output is

[5] The analysis can also take account of constraints on the availability of land at the relevant locations, which give rise to rents that equalize costs at all locations actually utilized. If S_a and S_b represent the availability of land near and away from the factory, respectively, presumably we would add to the labor constraint in the model the two additional land-use constraints $g_a(x_1, x_2, x_3 + s_a = S_a$ and $g_b(x_4) + s_b = S_b$, with the quantities of unused land, s_a and s_b perhaps entering the utility functions. It then follows, just as before, that the equilibrium conditions are now $p_1 = c_{11} + c_{21} + p_a g_{a1}$; $p_2 = c_{22} + p_a g_{a2}$; $p_3 = c_{33} + p_a g_{a3}$; $p_4 = c_{44} + p_b g_{b4}$; $p_5 = 1$; $p_a = \rho_a/\mu$; $p_b = \rho_b/\mu$; where ρ_a and ρ_b are the Lagrange multipliers for the new constraints and p_a and p_b are the (labor) prices of land at the two locations. Our previous conclusions are, thus, totally unaffected. Only the smoke producer's product sells for more than its marginal private cost of labor plus land.

[6] The social cost is not c_{21} alone but is the sum of the private and the external costs together (see the illuminating terminological discussion by D. W. Pearce and Stanley Sturmey). Note that the tax, implicitly, is a tax on *smoke* not a tax on x_1, the output of the smoke producing industry. For if s is the quantity of smoke and t the unit tax we may write $t = c_{21} = (\partial c_2/\partial s)(ds/dx_1)$ and obviously the firm can reduce its tax rate by decreasing the second of these terms, the smokiness of its product. This point has been emphasized by Charles Plott, who showed that a fixed tax per unit of x_1 might even conceivably increase s, if s were an inferior input.

[7] Moreover, measured in real terms this is the only tax arrangement that satisfies the optimality requirements, neglecting the possibility of a lump sum tax or subsidy which does not affect the marginal conditions. F. Trenery Dolbear has shown that it is generally not possible to find an optimal tax rate that compensates fully those who suffer the effects of the externality. Since no compensation is paid to industry II, the solution that is derived here does not run into Dolbear's problem. We also do not run into the problem of a multiplicity of solutions corresponding to the various points on Dolbear's contract curve because we are dealing with a world of pure competition with a given initial distribution.

damaged by smoky air does not, by an increase in its own output, make the air cleaner or dirtier for others. As with all public goods, an increase in one user's consumption does not reduce the available supply to others.[8] Hence, the appropriate price (compensation) to a user of a public good (victim of a public externality) is *zero* except, of course, for lump sum payments. Thus, perhaps, rather than saying there is no price that will yield an optimal quantity of a public good (externality), it may be more illuminating to say that a double price is required: a nonzero price (tax) to the supplier of the good, and a zero price to the consumer. Of course, no ordinary price can do this job, but a Pigouvian tax, without compensation to those affected by an externality, can indeed do the trick.

III. What Prevents an Excessive Influx of Neighbors?

When only smoke emission is taxed, with the tax level based on the magnitude of x_2, nearby laundry output, what will prevent too many laundries from moving near the smoky factory? The answer is that, when the tax on the externality producer is set properly, the externalities themselves keep down the size of the nearby population. Moreover, the level of the tax will control both the magnitude of smoke emission and thereby (indirectly), the size of the nearby population. A high tax rate will discourage smoke and hence encourage migration into the neighborhood. A low tax rate will encourage smoke and, hence, drive residents away. A tax on smoke alone is all that is needed to control the magnitudes of *both* variables. That is why, as shown by the mathematics of the preceding section, just a tax on the smoke producer is sufficient to produce an optimal allocation of resources among all the activities in our model.[9]

A diagram may help to make the point clearer. Figure 1 shows the response of our two industries' outputs to a change in the tax rate on the polluting industry, I. We see that as the tax rate varies, industry I's output response follows the curve RR'. Thus, if the tax level is t, the output of industry I will be x_{1t}. But, because of the externalities, the output of industry II, in turn, reacts to the output of I. This relationship is described by reaction curve PP'. With $x_1=x_{1t}$ we see that $x_2=x_{2t}$.

The tax rate on II can vary all the way from $t=0$, yielding output combination (x_{10}, x_{20}), to a prohibitive tax rate, t_p, that drives I out of business altogether, so that $x_1=0$ and $x_2=x_{2p}$. Obviously, the ratio x_1/x_2 then decreases monotonically as the tax rate increases and, assuming continuity, there will be some intermediate tax rate at which the two activities will be in balance. The tax will keep x_1 in check while the external cost imposed by x_1 on industry II will keep x_2 to the right relative level. There is no need for a separate tax on II to achieve this goal.

[8] In his discussion of these matters Coase seems at one point to skate awfully close to an error analogous to the confusion between pecuniary and technological externalities. He writes (section IX):

> The tax that would be imposed would . . . increase with an increase in the number of those in the vicinity . . . But people deciding to establish themselves in the vicinity of the factory will not take into account [the resulting] fall in the value of production which results from their presence. This failure to take into account costs imposed on others is comparable to the action of a factory-owner in not taking account the harm resulting from his emission of smoke. [p. 42]

This is analogous to the argument that where the supply curve of labor is rising an increase in output by firm A must produce externalities, by raising B's labor costs. But, of course, this merely represents a transfer from B to his workers and is not a real net cost to society. For that reason, as is well known, pecuniary externalities do *not* lead to resource misallocation. Like a price change, the variation in taxes constitutes a pecuniary externality. Both have real consequences but they are merely "movements along" the production and utility functions, i.e., any given vector of inputs will be able to produce the same outputs as before the change in tax rates, and any vector of output levels will still be able to yield the same utility levels.

[9] See the Appendix for a discussion of an argument by Buchanan and Stubblebine which is related to Coase's.

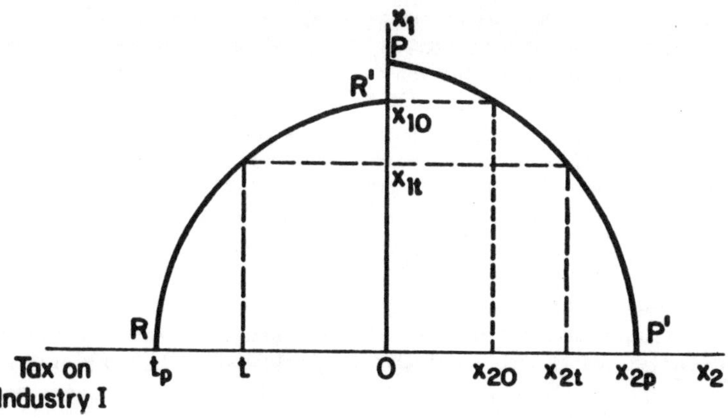

FIGURE 1

In order for this arrangement to work it is clearly necessary that the laundries *not* be compensated (at the margin) for the smoke damage they suffer. If they received in compensation an amount which varied with the magnitude of the smoke damage, that externality would not restrict the level of laundry activity near the factory. If the laundry operators' smoke costs were offset by damage compensation payments, obviously they would lose the economic incentive to eschew the vicinity of the smoky factory[10] and then Coase's tax on laundries would indeed be required to keep them away. But then the tax would be needed only to sop up the compensation payments which should never have been given in the first place.

IV. Multiple Local Maxima in the Coase Model

Coase's discussion is, however, right in pointing out the possibility that the economy may make the wrong choice between smoke elimination and laundry relocation: however the source of the problem, a multiplicity of local maxima, does not emerge clearly. Coase writes:

> Assume that a factory which emits smoke is set up in a district previously free from smoke pollution, causing damage valued at $100 per annum. Assume that the taxation solution is adopted and that the factory owner is taxed $100 per annum as long as the factory emits the smoke. Assume further that a smoke-preventing device costing $90 per annum to run is available. In these circumstances, the smoke-preventing device would be installed.
>
> . . . Yet the position achieved may not be optimal. Suppose that those who suffer the damage could avoid it by moving to other locations or by taking various precautions which would cost them, or be equivalent to a loss in income of, $40 per annum. Then there would be a gain in the value of production of $50 if the factory continued to emit its smoke and those now in the district moved elsewhere or made other adjustments to avoid the damage. [Section IX]

One curious feature of this example is its assumption that while smoke damage is $100, the cost of moving to other locations is only $40. Under these circumstances one

[10] Of course, as smoke cost increases in the neighborhood of the factory, rents will fall to some extent and serve as partial compensation to the laundries. However, this does not change the analysis fundamentally. It is analogous to the case of rise in the price of an input which, as is well known, will tend to reduce the output of competitive firms, even though prices of other complementary inputs fall as a result. As the discussion of footnote 5 shows, explicit consideration of the price of land does not change the character of the solution.

may well wonder why people living near the factory do not just move elsewhere on their own initiative. Moreover, this may not simply be a matter of the numbers he happens to have chosen. The problem arises whenever the cost of moving away from the factory is less than the cost of elimination of the smoke, which in turn is less than the cost of the smoke damage, as the logic of Coase's example requires.

It is perhaps more important to recognize that the example presents us with a choice between (at least) two local optima. As will be argued later, a multiplicity of maxima is generally rendered more likely by the presence of externalities so that this issue is not a pecularity of Coase's illustrations. The first of the two local optima in Coase's example (call it solution *A*) involves zero smoke emission and a full complement of residents near the factory. In the second optimum (solution *B*) no one remains in residence next to the factory and there is no restriction in smoke emission by the plant. Assuming that the (undesirable) initial position is the only other possibility, as Coase seems to suggest, which of these two will in fact be the global optimum depends on the cost of moving everyone away (m dollars) and the cost of elimination of the smoke (s dollars).

Assume with Coase that the initial cost of smoke damage is $100, that $s<100$, but that $s<m$ so that it is cheaper to eliminate the smoke than to move the factory's neighbors. In this case, *A* is obviously the optimal solution. Since inhabitants surround the plant, and smoke emission, by assumption, cannot be changed by small amounts, the incremental social damage of an increase in smoke emission is $100. Thus the correct Pigouvian tax is $100 and, since $s<100$, with such a tax it will pay the factory to do the right thing by society—to install the smoke eliminator.

Now assume instead that $m<s<100$ (it is cheaper to move people than to stop the smoke). This time *B* is the optimal solution, and since under *B* no one lives near the factory, the incremental cost of smoke is clearly zero. Therefore the proper Pigouvian tax is zero, a value that induces the factory to continue smoking, and its neighbors will find it advantageous (since $100>m$) to exit (coughing) from the area. Thus the zero Pigouvian tax value automatically satisfies the requirements of solution *B* when *B* is optimal just as the $100 Pigouvian tax leads to solution *A* when *A* is optimal.

Of course, if *B* happens to be the true global optimum and society mistakenly imposes the $100 Pigouvian tax appropriate for (local) optimum *A*, the economy may well end up with the inferior equilibrium *A*. This is the usual difficulty one encounters whenever there is a multiplicity of maxima, a problem that Pigou so clearly recognized (pp. 140, 224).

V. Departures from the Optimum and Adjustments in the Tax

If there is a departure from the optimal solution, for whatever reason, the value of the Pigouvian tax need not change. If, for example, *B* is the global optimum so that the optimal tax is zero, that tax need not be increased if a few (misguided) individuals choose to move back near the factory so that additional smoke now incurs (say) $50 in damage. *At the optimal solution* the marginal cost of smoke is zero, and the equilibrium Pigouvian tax remains zero—it does not increase to $50.

Here we have arrived at the issue which, I now understand, was really Coase's main point in the portion of his article we are considering. He writes in a letter:

> . . . Let us assume your optimum tax is imposed. Now suppose that *A* establishes himself near the plant which produces the damaging emissions and thus

increases the amount of damage. Would your tax increase? My guess is that it would not (certainly if your tax system is right it should not). The tax system I was attacking was one which would in these circumstances, automatically lead to an increase in the tax as the damage increased.

This point is, surely, quite different from the issue he is usually interpreted to have raised (see the quotations in fn. 1, above, which suggest how the "usual interpretation" arose). It is, however, not inconsistent with the optimal solution derived in the previous section nor is it inconsistent with what I take to be the Pigouvian tradition.

But even on this issue Coase's strictures are not necessarily valid. Suppose that a regulator, having no way of calculating the *optimal* values of the Pigouvian tax is, however, able to determine the value of any marginal social damage at any point in time. *Faut de mieux* he therefore sets a tax rate equal to *current* marginal social damage on the smoke producer. This causes him to reduce his smoke, and so brings more laundries into the neighborhood. The tax is then readjusted to equal the new (higher) value of damage per puff of smoke, more laundries move in, and so on. Will this process of trial and error adjustments of the tax level, always setting it equal to current marginal smoke damage, converge to the optimum of Section II? That is, will the sequence of tax values converge to the optimal Pigouvian tax level, and will resource allocation approach optimality? That now seems to be Coase's main question.

Obviously, such a learning process always involves wastes and irreversabilities, just like the process of convergence of competitive prices to their equilibrium values in the absence of externalities. But if we follow the usual practice of assuming away these costs, one can show that the process may be expected to converge to the optimum, provided the equilibrium is unique and stable. That is, there is then nothing inherently different about gradually moving taxes and prices towards their equilibrium here, and the process of adjustment toward competitive equilibrium when there are no externalities.

Specifically, letting s_t represent the tax per unit on commodity 1 at time t, and G_i be the *i*th adjustment function we may set

$$dx_{1t}/dt = G_1[p_{1t} - s_t - c_{11}(x_{1t})]$$

$$(5) \quad dx_{2t}/dt = G_2[p_{2t} - c_{22}(x_{1t}, x_{2t})]$$

$$dx_{it}/dt = G_i[p_{it} - c_{ii}(x_{it})] \qquad (i = 3, 4)$$

$$(6) s_t = c_{21}(x_{1t}, x_{2t}) \qquad p_{it} = f_i(x_{1t}, \ldots, x_{5t})$$

and where, as usual, we take

$$(7) \qquad G_i(0) = 0$$

$$(8) \qquad G_i' > 0$$

Going back to Section II, when optimality conditions (4) hold, we see by substituting them into (5) that all $dx_{it}/dt = 0$, i.e., (4) is indeed an equilibrium position for the dynamic system (5)–(8). Furthermore, any solution that does not satisfy (4) must involve at least one nonzero argument in the adjustment functions (5), and so no solution that fails to satisfy (4) can be an equilibrium.

It follows that if the dynamic system (5)–(8) is stable, and the solution to (4) is unique, the process with taxes set equal to *current* marginal damage and imposed *only on the polluter* will converge toward the optimum. One does not need to have calculated the optimal tax values from the beginning and stick to them.

The reason this process of simultaneous learning and adjustment does not work in Coase's example is that it involves (at least) two local maxima, as we have already noted. And in such a case, obviously, the adjustment mechanism may well take us to the wrong maximum. Unfortunately, as we will see presently, in the presence of externalities, a multiplicity of maxima is all too likely to be with us.

VI. Implementation Problems

Despite the validity in principle of the tax-subsidy approach of the Pigouvian tradition, in practice it suffers from serious difficulties. For we do not know how to estimate the magnitudes of the social costs, the data needed to implement the Pigouvian tax-subsidy proposals. For example, a very substantial portion of the cost of pollution is psychic; and even if we knew how to evaluate the psychic cost to some one individual we seem to have little hope of dealing with effects so widely diffused through the population.[11]

This would not necessarily be very serious if one could hope to learn by experience. One might try any plausible set of taxes and subsidies and then attempt, by a set of trial and error steps, to approach the desired magnitudes. Unfortunately, convergence toward the desired solution by an iterative procedure of this sort requires some sort of measure of the improvement (if any) that has been achieved at each step so that the next trial step can be adjusted accordingly. But we do not know the socially optimal composition of outputs, so we simply have no way of judging whether a given change in the trial tax values will even have moved matters in the right direction.

[11] For an excellent discussion of some of the work done in trying to implement Pigouvian taxes in practice, see Allen Kneese and Blair Bower, esp. ch. 6 and 8. The difficulty of determining the magnitude of the Pigouvian tax-subsidy level is one of Coase's major points, one that seems often to be overlooked in discussions of his paper. Thus Coase writes in a letter, "The view I expressed in my article was not that such an optimum tax system (levied solely on the damage producing firm) was inconceivable but that I could not see how the data on which it would have to be based could be assembled." An interesting approach to application for the small numbers case that is based on the decomposition principle of mathematical programming is presented by Davis and Whinston (1966).

These difficulties are compounded by another characteristic of externalities which has already been mentioned—the likelihood that in the presence of externalities there will be a multiplicity of local maxima (see Richard Portes, D. A. Starrett, and Baumol). Consequently, even if an iterative process were possible it might only drive us toward a local maximum, and may thus fail to take advantage of the really significant opportunities to improve economic welfare.

A simple model in the spirit of that of Section II can be used to show that the presence of "strong" externalities can be expected to produce a violation of the convexity conditions in whose absence one normally finds a multiplicity of local optima.

Let us assume (to permit the use of a two-dimensional diagram) that there exist only the first two of our four activities (the smoky output, x_1, and nearby laundry, x_2), and that their respective cost functions are, as before, $c_1(x_1)$ and $c_2(x_1, x_2)$. As a result, the equation of the production possibility locus is

$$c_1(x_1) + c_2(x_1, x_2) = R$$

For convenience let us use k as a parameter measuring the strength of the (marginal) externality.[12] Assume first that there are diminishing returns (increasing costs) in the production of the two outputs, and that there are no marginal external effects so that $k=0$. (At the margin industry I's output produces no smoke or smoke is harmless to industry II.) In that case it is easy to show that the production possibility locus must satisfy $dx_2^2/dx_1^2 < 0$, i.e., that the locus must assume the general shape AC_0B in Figure 2 with the concavity property required by the second-order conditions.

Now, suppose that the activity of in-

[12] E.g., k may be interpreted as $\partial^2 c_2/\partial x_1 \partial x_2$, i.e., the additional marginal resources cost of output 2 resulting from a unit increase in output 1.

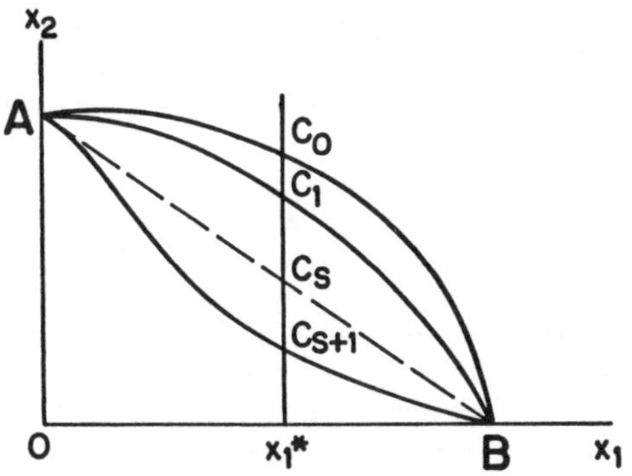

FIGURE 2

dustry I does produce some external damage ($k>0$). What happens to the production possibility locus? First I will argue that neither of its end points, A or B, will normally be affected. At point B, laundry output, x_2, is zero. Hence, no matter how much smoke is produced, there is no laundry output to be damaged. Point B is therefore invariant with the magnitude of k. Similarly, at A, the smoke creating output is zero. Consequently, no matter how smoky the process of producing output II may be (no matter how large the value of k) the total smoke emitted will be (output x_1) · (smoke per unit of output) = 0, since the first of these factors is zero. Thus the position of point A remains invariant with the magnitude of k.

The effect on intermediate points such as C_0 on the locus is quite different. As k increases it takes increasing quantities of resources to produce a given volume of laundry. Thus, with any fixed value of x_1, say x_1^*, as k increases, the quantity of laundry that can be turned out with a given quantity of resources, R, must decline. Point C_0 will be pushed down to some lower point, C_1. With a still greater value of k it will be lowered still further. As smoke damage increases without limit it will take larger and larger quantities of resources to turn out a given quantity of laundry and eventually we approach a limit point γ on the horizontal axis, at which it is no longer possible to produce clean clothes with any finite quantity of resources.

Now draw in straight line segment AB whose position does not vary with k since neither A nor B does. It is clear that as k increases we will eventually come to some point C_s beyond which all remaining points in the sequence C_{s+1}, C_{s+2}, . . . lie below AB. Beyond this point, obviously, the second-order conditions must be violated, as the production possibility curve approaches the axes, AOB.

Thus we see that the presence of sufficiently strong detrimental externalities will generally produce a violation of the second-order conditions. Only in the presence of insignificant externalities can one have any degree of confidence that the convexity conditions will hold.[13]

It is easy to offer an intuitive reason indicating how the presence of externalities increases the likelihood of a multiplicity of maxima, a reason that suggests that the problem is very real and potentially very serious in practice. Where a particular activity reduces the efficiency of another it becomes plausible that the optimal level of that activity, at least at some particular locations, is zero. If there are one hundred possible locations for the plants of a smoke-producing industry the worst possible solution might be to place some plants in each candidate location. *Any* solution leaving at least some combination of smoke-free areas may be preferable, and may well constitute a local maximum.

To make the point more concretely, suppose we are dealing with an island separated by a ridge of mountains that pre-

[13] The analysis can be extended to the case of n activities and externalities that enter utility as well as production functions. The analysis here confines itself to externalities producing inefficiencies on the production side following a suggestion of Jacob Marschak that the argument is more persuasive if framed in these terms.

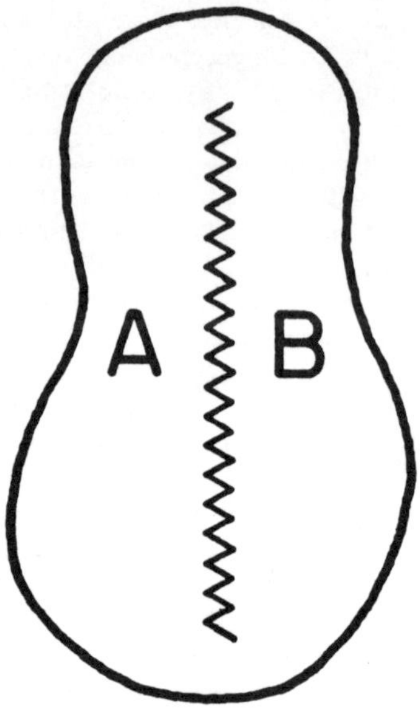

FIGURE 3

vent smoke from going from one side to the other (Figure 3). Let S_a and S_b be the volume of smoke-producing activity located on the two respective sides of the island, and let P_a and P_b be the corresponding number of residents living there. Let $S_a+S_b=S$ and $P_a+P_b=P$. Then, if the social cost of the smoke is great enough, there will obviously be at least two local optima: ($P_a=P$, $P_b=0$, $S_a=0$, $S_b=S$) and ($P_a=0$, $P_b=P$, $S_a=S$, $S_b=0$). For either of these arrangements keeps the smoke and the people apart. This does not mean, of course, that the two solutions are equally desirable. If *A* offers great scenic attractions while *B* is closer to raw materials we may expect the former of the two local maxima to be preferable. We cannot preclude the possibility of a third (interior) maximum, for once there is some industrial activity on each of the two sides of the island there may be some least cost distribution of people and industrial activity. But we see that we may well expect to encounter *at least* two local maxima. With more separated locations and more sources of externalities the number of combinations of zero-valued variables that constitute local maxima may well grow astronomically.

The presence of a number of local maxima clearly means that an "improvement" may merely represent a move toward some minor peak in the social welfare function and it can, therefore, impose serious opportunity losses on society. All in all, we are left with little reason for confidence in the applicability of the Pigouvian approach, literally interpreted. We do not know how to calculate the required taxes and subsidies and we do not know how to approximate them by trial and error.

VII. An Alternative Approach—Adjustment of Taxes to Achieve Acceptable Externality Levels

There is an alternative approach to the matter that seems perfectly natural. On issues as important as those we are discussing, given the limited information at our disposal, it is perfectly reasonable to act on the basis of a set of minimum standards of acceptability. If, say, we treat the sulphur content of the atmosphere as one of the outputs of the economic system, it is not unreasonable to select some maximal level of this pollutant that is considered satisfactory and to seek to determine a tax on the offending inputs or outputs capable of achieving the chosen standard. This is precisely the approach employed in the formulation of stabilization policy, where it is decided that an employment rate exceeding *w* percent and a rate of inflation exceeding *v* percent per year are simply unacceptable, and fiscal and monetary measures are then designed accordingly.[14]

[14] As this discussion indicates, I join Wellicz in refusing to abandon externalities policy entirely to Little's "administrative decisions" (p. 184) or to Ralph Turvey's "applied economist" (p. 313). For further discus-

The advantages (as well as the limitations) of this approach are clear—unlike the Pigouvian procedure, it promises to be operational because it requires far less information for its implementation. Moreover, it utilizes global measures and avoids direct controls with all of their heavy administrative costs and their distortions of consumer choice and inefficiencies. It does not use the police and the courts as the prime instrument to achieve the desired modification of the outputs of the economy. Its effects are long lasting, not depending on the vigor of an enforcement agency, which all too often proves to be highly transitory. Unlike most other measures that have been proposed in the area it need not add to the mounting financial burdens of the state and local governments. Finally, it can be shown that, unlike any system of direct controls, it promises, at least in principle, to achieve decreases in pollution or other types of damage to the environment at minimum cost to society.[15]

One can expect an acceptability criterion procedure to be operational because policy makers think quite naturally in terms of minimum acceptability standards, and while it is no doubt an exaggeration to say that they can arrive at them easily, there are all sorts of precedents indicating that such standards can be decided upon in practice.

Though we are unlikely to be able to determine in advance precisely a set of tax values that will achieve the desired output standards, the output level achieved by a given tax arrangement is readily observed and, at least in principle, it is possible to learn by trial and error, continuing the direction of change of any tax modifications that turn out to bring outputs closer to their target levels. Since the procedure is a satisficing rather than a maximizing approach the possibility of a multiplicity of maxima is not relevant.

That is to say, one generally expects a considerable number of solutions to satisfy a particular set of acceptability conditions (various resource allocation patterns may be able to achieve a given set of reductions in pollution levels) *whether or not the second-order conditions are satisfied.* If several of these do so, then the essence of the satisficing approach is that one simply utilizes the first of the acceptable solutions that is discovered. One gives up any attempt to achieve any standard of optimality (other than minimization of cost[16] for a given degree of protection of the environment) and rests content with *any* solution that happens to satisfy the standards that have been selected.

sion see Baumol and Wallace Oates. For an earlier proposal that is very similar in spirit, see John H. Dales, ch. 6.

[15] This proposition has been suggested elsewhere (see, for example, Kneese and Bower, chs. 5 and 7; Larry Ruff, p. 79), and will be fairly obvious to anyone familiar with the analysis of the allocative effects of price changes and their efficiency properties. Specifically, suppose it is desired to reduce the pollution content of a river by k percent. Obviously a k percent reduction in the number of gallons emitted by each of the plants discharging wastes into the river will generally not be the desired solution. The theorem in question then asserts the following:

Given the production of any desired vector of final outputs by the plants along the river, a tax per gallon of effluent sufficient to reduce the overall pollution content of the river to the desired level will automatically achieve this decrease at minimum total cost to all plants combined.

The proof of the theorem is a straightforward exercise in constrained maximization (see Baumol and Oates). It works, of course, because the lower the marginal cost of reduction in pollution outflows of a particular plant, the larger the reductions it will pay it to undertake to avoid the corresponding tax payment.

What is surprising about the proposition, if anything, is that, unlike many results in welfare analysis, it does not require the firms along the river, or any other firms, to be perfect competitors, nor does it have to assume that they maximize profits rather than share of market or growth or some other target variable. All it requires is that the firms wish to produce whatever output they select at minimum cost to themselves.

[16] Of course it is conceivable that there may be more than one local *cost* minimum. In that case an effluent charge that yields an acceptable pollution level may not yield the global cost minimum. This may be something that practical policy simply has no way of avoiding.

Thus, the acceptability criterion approach does not dispose of the difficulties involved in finding a true optimum—rather it sweeps those difficulties under the rug. Even with pollution reduced to acceptable levels, there will remain the possibility that the (undiscovered) global optimum offers us a world far better than what we have managed to achieve—if only we knew how to attain it. But if we permit ourselves to be paralyzed by councils of perfection we may have still greater cause for regret.

It may be that with time we can learn to improve the workings of a set of standards of acceptability. If, say, it turns out to be unexpectedly cheap to attain the initial pollution standards, it may be reasonable to tighten the standards on the presumption that marginal costs will not yet have equalled the marginal social benefits. Successive modifications in the criteria based on experience and revaluation may produce results that on the whole are not too bad.

If firms are put on notice that the acceptability standards may well be modified in the future this may lead them to construct what George Stigler describes as more flexible plants,—plants which are designed to keep down the cost of response to changes in standards. Of course, flexibility itself is not costless. However, it may be precisely what is appropriate for a society which is only beginning to learn how to grapple with its environmental problems.

Appendix

Buchanan, Stubblebine and Taxation of Both Parties to an Externality

Buchanan and Stubblebine have raised objections to the Pigouvian solution similar to those offered by Coase (see fn. 2, above). Much of their discussion deals with the case where voluntary negotiation in the presence of externalities will lead automatically to a Pareto optimum. As already admitted, in this case a Pigouvian tax will only cause trouble. However, the authors also appear to offer an argument against the Pigouvian tax for the case in which negotiation is absent.

Their argument, if I understand it correctly, is that after industry I adjusts to a Pigouvian tax on its output, for that industry the marginal yield of an increase in x_1 is zero. However, for industry II, at the point γ the marginal yield of x_1 is $c_{21}<0$. There must, consequently, be potential gains from trade between the two industries. They state:

> So long as $[(\partial c_2/\partial x_1)/(\partial c_2/\partial x_2)]$ remains nonzero, a Pareto-relevant marginal externality remains, despite the fact that the full 'Pigouvian solution' is attained. The apparent paradox here is not difficult to explain. Since, as postulated, [II] is not incurring any cost in securing the change in [I's] behavior, and since there remains, by hypothesis, a marginal diseconomy, further 'trade' can be worked out between the two parties. . . . The important implication to be drawn is that full Pareto equilibrium can never be attained via the imposition of unilaterally imposed taxes and subsidies . . .
> [Section III, pp. 382–83]

No doubt this is true—in a competitive situation two interrelated industries can generally increase their joint profits ("gain from trade") by collusion at the expense of the general public. In the case under discussion, if the output of x_1 is reduced it is true that industry I will lose nothing and industry II will gain c_{21}. However, society as a whole will experience no net gain.

Since the analysis deals exclusively with resource *allocation* we must assume that the labor released by the reduced value of x_1 will be employed elsewhere to produce more of some other output or more leisure. Consequently, the goods or services represented by the t units in taxes must be redistributed to the general public either by remission of another tax, increased provision of government services or some other means.

We may now evaluate the consequences of a unit increase in the output of x_1 on the entire society by summing up the direct effects on each of the three groups immediately

	Industry I	Industry II	Consumers	General Public
Incremental gain or revenue	p		$u_1=c_{11}+t$	$t=c_{21}$
Incremental cost	$(c_{11}+t)=(c_{11}+c_{21})$	c_{21}	p	

concerned: industry I, industry II, consumers, and the consequences of the tax receipts for the general public (which encompasses all consumers and producers, including those already mentioned). These are shown in the table above Adding up the incremental gains and revenues we see that the net social gain is zero, precisely as optimality requires. There is only a redistribution from industry II to the general public.

In a recent letter Buchanan comments:

> As for the nonoptimality of a unilaterally imposed tax, the problem here is that income effects enter to make the benefit-receiving side change behavior so that still further adjustments would be necessary . . . Our point was that this new position would not be one of full equilibrium if income effects enter. The laundries would now find that they secure the benefits of cleaner air without cost to themselves. Presumably this would make them do more laundry. This change in behavior would in turn change the apparent optimal solution. Admittedly, the imposed solution qualifies as Pareto-optimal if further trading is prohibited. And here Pareto-equilibrium does take on a different meaning from Pareto-optimal. Gains-from-trade exist, as you agree and, once these take place, we are not in an optimal solution.

In this paper I deal with the case where trading fails to take place not because it is prohibited, but because (as seems characteristic of our most important externalities problems in reality) large numbers make trading virtually impossible to arrange (where have we seen automobile drivers pay one another to cut down their exhaust?). Moreover, one must distinguish between the role of Buchanan's income effect and that of "further trading." Of course, further trading can destroy the optimality of the results achieved by a Pigouvian tax. For, as just argued, in that case the two affected groups gain by exploiting the community. On the other hand, the "income effect"—the influx of laundries near the factory as clean air becomes cheaper is precisely the reason a tax on the smoke producer alone can lead *everyone* to behave Pareto optimally (see Section III).

REFERENCES

W. J. Baumol, "External Economies and Second-order Optimality Conditions," *Amer. Econ. Rev.*, June 1964, *54*, 358–72.

——— **and W. E. Oates,** "The Use of Standards and Pricing for Protection of the Environment," *Swedish J. Econ.*, Mar. 1971, *73*, 42–54.

J. M. Buchanan, "External Diseconomies, Corrective Taxes and Market Structure," *Amer. Econ. Rev.*, Mar. 1969, *59*, 174–7.

——— **and W. C. Stubblebine,** "Externality," *Economica*, Nov. 1962, *29*, 371–84.

R. H. Coase, "The Problem of Social Cost," *J. Law Econ.*, Oct. 1960, *3*, 1–44.

J. H. Dales, *Pollution, Property, and Prices*, Toronto 1968.

O. A. Davis and A. Whinston, "Externalities, Welfare and the Theory of Games," *J. Polit. Econ.*, June 1962, *70*, 241–62.

——— **and** ———, "On Externalities, Information, and the Government-Assisted Invisible Hand," *Economica*, Aug. 1966, *33*, 303–18.

F. T. Dolbear, Jr. "On the Theory of Optimum Externality," *Amer. Econ. Rev.*, Mar. 1967, *57*, 90–103.

A. V. Kneese and B. T. Bower, *Managing Water Quality: Economics, Technology, Institutions*, Baltimore 1968.

I. M. D. Little, *A Critique of Welfare Economics*, 2d ed., New York 1957.

H. Mohring and J. H. Boyd, "Analyzing 'Externalities': 'Direct Interaction' vs. 'Asset

Utilization' Frameworks," *Economica*, forthcoming.

R. A. Meyer, Jr., "Externalities as Commodities," *Amer. Econ. Rev.*, Sept. 1971, *61*, 736–40.

D. W. Pearce and G. S. Sturmey, "Private and Social Costs and Benefits: A New Terminology," *Econ. J.*, Mar. 1966, *76*, 152–57.

A. C. Pigou, *The Economics of Welfare*, 4th ed., London, 1932.

C. R. Plott, "Externalities and Corrective Taxes," *Economica*, Feb. 1966, *33*, 84–7.

R. D. Portes, "The Search for Efficiency in the Presence of Externalities," forthcoming.

L. E. Ruff, "The Economic Common Sense of Pollution," *Publ. Interest*, spring 1970, *19*, 69–85.

D. A. Starrett, "Fundamental Non-Convexities in the Theory of Externalities," Harvard 1971, unpublished.

G. J. Stigler, "Production and Distribution in the Short Run," *J. Polit. Econ.*, June 1939, *47*, 305–27.

R. Turvey, "On Divergences Between Social Cost and Private Cost," *Economica*, Aug. 1963, *30*, 309–13.

S. Wellicz, "On External Economies and the Government-Assisted Invisible Hand," *Economica*, Nov. 1964, *31*, 345–62.

[6]

Prices *vs.* Quantities [1,2]

MARTIN L. WEITZMAN
Massachusetts Institute of Technology

I. INTRODUCTION

The setting for the problem under consideration is a large economic organization or system which in some cases is best thought of as the entire economy. Within this large economic organization resources are allocated by some combination of commands and prices (the exact mixture is inessential) or even by some other unspecified mechanism. The following question arises. For one particular isolated economic variable that needs to be regulated,[3] what is the best way to implement control for the benefit of the organization as a whole? Is it better to directly administer the activity under scrutiny or to fix transfer prices and rely on self-interested profit or utility maximization to achieve the same ends in decentralized fashion? This issue is taken as the prototype problem of central control which is studied in the present paper. There are a great many specific examples which fit nicely into such a framework. One of current interest is the question of whether it would be better to control certain forms of pollution by setting emission standards or by charging the appropriate pollution taxes.

When quantities are employed as planning instruments, the basic operating rules from the centre take the form of quotas, targets, or commands to produce a certain level of output. With prices as instruments, the rules specify either explicitly or implicitly that profits are to be maximized at the given parametric prices. Now a basic theme of resource allocation theory emphasizes the close connection between these two modes of control. No matter how one type of planning instrument is fixed, there is always a corresponding way to set the other which achieves the same result when implemented.[4] From a strictly theoretical point of view there is really nothing to recommend one mode of control over the other. This notwithstanding, I think it is a fair generalization to say that the average economist in the Western marginalist tradition has at least a vague preference toward indirect control by prices, just as the typical non-economist leans toward the direct regulation of quantities.

That a person not versed in economics should think primarily in terms of direct controls is probably due to the fact that he does not comprehend the full subtlety and strength of the invisible hand argument. The economist's attitude is somewhat more puzzling. Understanding that prices can be used as a powerful and flexible instrument for rationally allocating resources and that in fact a market economy automatically regulates itself in this manner is very different from being under the impression that such indirect controls are generally preferable for the kind of problem considered in this paper. Certainly a careful reading of economic theory yields little to support such a universal proposition.

1 *First version received August* 1973; *final version accepted January* 1974 (*Eds*.).

2 Many people have made helpful comments about a previous version of this paper. I would like especially to thank P. A. Diamond and H. E. Scarf for their valuable suggestions. The National Science Foundation helped support my research.

3 Outside the scope of this paper is the issue of *why* it is felt that the given economic activity must be regulated. There may be a variety of reasons, ranging all the way from political considerations to one form or another of market failure.

4 Given the usual convexity assumptions. Without convexity it may not be possible to find a price which will support certain output levels. In this connection it should be mentioned that non-convexities (especially increasing returns) are sometimes responsible for regulation in the first place.

Many economists point with favour to the fact that if prices are the planning instrument then profit maximization automatically guarantees total output will be efficiently produced, as if this result were of any more than secondary interest unless the prices (and hence total output) are optimal to begin with.[1] Sometimes it is maintained that prices are desirable planning instruments because the stimulus to obtain a profit maximizing output is built right in if producers are rewarded in proportion to profits. There is of course just as much motivation, e.g. to minimize costs at specified output levels so long as at least some fraction of production expenditures is borne by producers. With both modes of control there is clearly an incentive for self-interested producers to systematically distort information about hypothetical output and cost possibilities in the pre-implementation planning phase. Conversely, there is no real way to disguise the true facts in the implementation stage so long as actual outputs (in the case of price instruments) and true operating costs (in the case of quantity instruments) can be accurately monitored. For the one case the centre must ascertain *ceteris paribus* output changes as prices are varied, for the other price changes as outputs are altered.

A reason often cited for the theoretical superiority of prices as planning instruments is that their use allegedly economizes on information. The main thing to note here is that generally speaking it is neither easier nor harder to name the right prices than the right quantities because in principle exactly the *same* information is needed to correctly specify either. It is true that in a situation with many independent producers of an identical commodity, only a single uniform price has to be named by the centre, whereas in a command mode separate quantities must be specified for each producer. If such an observation has meaningful implications, it can only be within the artificial milieu of an iterative *tâtonnement* type of " planning game " which is played over and over again approaching an optimal solution in the limit as the number of steps becomes large. Even in this context the fact that there are less " message units " involved in each communication from the centre is a pretty thin reed on which to hang claims for the informational superiority of the price system. It seems to me that a careful examination of the mechanics of successive approximation planning shows that there is no principal informational difference between iteratively finding an optimum by having the centre name prices while the firms respond with quantities, or by having the centre assign quantities while the firm reveals costs or marginal costs.[2]

If there were really some basic intrinsic advantage to a system which employed prices as planning instruments, we would expect to observe many organizations operating with this mode of control, especially among multi-divisional business firms in a competitive

[1] An extreme example may help make this point clear. Suppose that fulfilment of an important emergency rescue operation demands a certain number of airplane flights. It would be inefficient to just order airline companies or branches of the military to supply a certain number of the needed aircraft because marginal (opportunity) costs would almost certainly vary all over the place. Nevertheless, such an approach would undoubtedly be preferable to the efficient procedure of naming a price for plane services. Under profit maximization, overall output would be uncertain, with too few planes spelling disaster and too many being superfluous.

[2] The " message unit " case for the informational superiority of the price system is analogous to the blanket statement that it is better to use dual algorithms for solving a programming problem whenever the number of primal variables exceeds the number of dual multipliers. Certainly for the superior large step decomposition type algorithms which on every iteration go right after what are presently believed to be the best instrument values on the basis of all currently available information, such a general statement has no basis. With myopic gradient methods it is true that on each round the centre infinitesimally and effortlessly adjusts exactly the number of instruments it controls, be they prices or quantities. But who can say *how many* infinitesimally small adjustments will be needed? Gradient algorithms are known to be a bad description of iterative planning procedures, among other reasons because they have inadmissably poor convergence properties. If the step size is chosen too small, convergence takes forever. If it is chosen too large, there is no convergence. As soon as a finite step size is selected on a given iteration to reflect a desire for quick convergence, the " message unit " case for prices evaporates. Calculating the *correct* price change puts the centre right back into the large step decomposition framework where on each round the problem of finding the best iterative prices is formally identical to the problem of finding the best iterative quantities. For discussion of these and various other aspects of iterative planning, see the articles of Heal [4], Malinvaud [5], Marglin [7], Weitzman [9].

environment. Yet the allocation of resources within private companies (not to mention governmental or non-profit organizations) is almost never controlled by setting administered transfer prices on commodities and letting self-interested profit maximization do the rest.[1] The price system as an allocator of internal resources does not itself pass the market test.[2]

Of course, all this is not to deny that in any *particular* setting there may be important *practical* reasons for favouring either prices or quantities as planning instruments. These reasons might involve ideological, political, legal, social, historical, administrative, motivational, informational, monitoring, enforcing, or other considerations.[3] But there is little of what might be called a system-free character.

In studying such a controversial subject, the only fair way to begin must be with the tenet that there is no *basic* or *universal* rationale for having a general predisposition toward one control mode or the other. If this principle is accepted, it becomes an issue of some interest to abstract away all " other " considerations in order to develop strictly " economic " criteria by which the comparative performance of price and quantity planning instruments might be objectively evaluated. Even on an abstract level, it would be useful to know how to identify a situation where employing one mode is relatively advantageous, other things being equal.

II. THE MODEL

We start with a highly simplified prototype planning problem. Amount q of a certain commodity can be produced at cost $C(q)$, yielding benefits $B(q)$.[4] The word " commodity " is used in an abstract sense and really could pertain to just about any kind of good from pure water to military aircraft. Solely for the sake of preserving a unified notation, we follow the standard convention that goods are desirable. This means that rather than talking about air pollution, for example, we instead deal with its negative—clean air.

Later we treat more complicated cases, but for the time being it is assumed that in effect there is just one producer of the commodity and no ambiguity in the notion of a cost curve. Benefits are measured in terms of money equivalents so that the benefit function can be viewed as the reflection of an indifference curve showing the trade-off between amounts of uncommitted extra funds and output levels of the given commodity. It is assumed that $B''(q)<0$, $C''(q)>0$, $B'(0)>C'(0)$, and $B'(q)<C'(q)$ for q sufficiently large.

1 Strictly speaking, this conclusion is not really justified because there may be important externalities or increasing returns within an organization (they may even constitute its *raison d'être*). Nevertheless, the almost universal absence of internal transfer pricing within private firms strikes me as a rather startling contradiction with the often alleged superiority of indirect controls.

2 About a decade ago, Ford and GM performed a few administrative trials of a limited sort with some decentralization schemes based on internal transfer prices. The experiments were subsequently discontinued in favour of a return to more traditional planning methods. See Whinston [10].

3 As one example, if it happens to be the case that it is difficult or expensive to monitor output on a continuous scale but relatively cheap to perform a pass-fail litmus type test on whether a given output level has been attained or not, the price mode may be greatly disadvantaged from the start. The pollution by open-pit mining operations of nearby waterways presents a case in point. It would be difficult or impossible to record how much pollutant is seeping into the ground, whereas it is a comparatively straightforward task to enforce the adoption of one or another level of anti-pollution technology. Another realistic consideration arises when we ask who determines the standards under each mode. For example, if an agency of the executive branch is empowered to regulate prices but the legislature is in charge of setting quantities, that by itself may be important in determining which mode is better for controlling pollution. The price mode would have greater flexibility, but might carry with it more danger of caving in to special interest groups. As yet another realistic consideration, equity arguments are sometimes put forward in favour of price (the supposed " justice " of a uniform price to all) or quantity (equal sharing of a deficit commodity) control modes.

4 It might be thought that an equivalent approach would be to work with demand and supply curves, identifying the consumers' (producers') surplus area under the demand (supply) curve as benefits (costs) or, equivalently, the demand (supply) curve as the marginal benefit (cost) function. The trouble with this approach is that it tends to give the misleading impression that the market left to itself could solve the problem, obscuring the fact that some key element of the standard competitive supply and demand story is felt to be missing in the first place.

The planning problem is to find that value q^* of q which maximizes

$$B(q)-C(q).$$

The solution must satisfy

$$B'(q^*) = C'(q^*).$$

With

$$p^* \equiv B'(q^*) = C'(q^*),$$

it makes no difference whether the planners announce the optimal price p^* and have the producers maximize profits

$$p^*q-C(q)$$

or whether the centre merely orders the production of q^* at least cost. In an environment of complete knowledge and perfect certainty there is a formal identity between the use of prices and quantities as planning instruments.

If there is any advantage to employing price or quantity control modes, therefore, it must be due to inadequate information or uncertainty. Of course it is natural enough for planners to be unsure about the precise specification of cost and benefit functions since even those most likely to know can hardly possess an exact account.

Suppose, then, that the centre perceives the cost function only as an estimate or approximation. The stochastic relation linking q to C is taken to be of the form

$$C(q, \theta),$$

where θ is a disturbance term or random variable, unobserved and unknown at the present time. While the determination of θ could involve elements of genuine randomness,[1] it is probably more appropriate to think primarily in terms of an information gap.

Even the engineers most closely associated with production would be unable to say beforehand precisely what is the cheapest way of generating various hypothetical output levels. How much murkier still must be the centre's *ex ante* conception of costs, especially in a fast moving world where knowledge of particular circumstances of time and place may be required. True, the degree of fuzziness could be reduced by research and experimentation but it could never be truly eliminated because new sources of uncertainty are arising all the time.[2]

Were a particular output level really ordered in all seriousness, a cost-minimizing firm could eventually grope its way toward the cheapest way of producing it by actually testing out the relevant technological alternatives. Or, if an output price were in fact named, a profit maximizing production level could ultimately be found by trial and error. But this is far from having the cost function as a whole knowable *a priori.*

While the planners may be somewhat better acquainted with the benefit function, it too is presumably discernable only tolerably well, say as

$$B(q, \eta)$$

with η a random variable. The connection between q and B is stochastic either because benefits may be imperfectly known at the present time or because authentic randomness may play a role. Since the unknown factors connecting q with B are likely to be quite different from those linking q to C, it is assumed that the random variables θ and η are independently distributed.

As a possible specific example of the present formulation, consider the problem of air pollution. The variable q could be the cleanliness of air being emitted by a certain type of source. Costs as a function of q might not be known beyond doubt because the technology, quantified by θ, is uncertain. At a given level of q the benefits may be unsure since they depend among other things on the weather, measured by η.

1 Like day-to-day fluctuations.
2 For an amplification of some of these points, see Hayek [3].

Now an *ideal* instrument of central control would be a contingency message whose instructions depend on which state of the world is revealed by θ and η. The ideal *ex ante* quantity signal $q^*(\theta, \eta)$ and price signal $p^*(\theta, \eta)$ are in the form of an entire schedule, functions of θ and η satisfying

$$B_1(q^*(\theta, \eta), \eta) = C_1(q^*(\theta, \eta), \theta) = p^*(\theta, \eta).$$

By employing either ideal signal, the *ex ante* uncertainty has in effect been eliminated *ex post* and we are right back to the case where there is no theoretical difference between price and quantity control modes.

It should be readily apparent that it is infeasible for the centre to transmit an entire schedule of ideal prices or quantities. A contingency message is a complicated, specialized contract which is expensive to draw up and hard to understand. The random variables are difficult to quantify. A problem of differentiated information or even of moral hazard may be involved since the exact value of θ will frequently be known only by the producer.[1] Even for the simplest case of just *one* firm, information from different sources must be processed, combined, and evaluated. By the time an ideal schedule was completed, another would be needed because meanwhile changes would have occurred.

In this paper the realistic issue of central control under uncertainty is considered to be the " second best " problem of finding for each producer the single price or quantity message which optimally regulates his actions. This is also the best way to focus sharply and directly on the essential difference between prices and quantities as planning instruments.

The issue of prices *vs.* quantities has to be a " second best " problem by its very nature simply because there is no good *a priori* reason for limiting attention to just these two particular signals. Even if stochastic contingency messages were eliminated on *ad hoc* grounds as being too complicated, there would still be no legitimate justification for not considering, say, an entire expected benefits schedule, or a " kinked " benefit function in the form of a two-tiered price system, or something else. The reason we specialize to price and quantity signals is that these are two *simple* messages, easily comprehended, traditionally employed, and frequently contrasted.[2]

The optimal quantity instrument under uncertainty is that target output $\hat{q}$ which maximizes expected benefits minus expected costs, so that

$$E[B(\hat{q}, \eta)-C(\hat{q}, \theta)] = \max_q E[B(q, \eta)-C(q, \theta)],$$

where $E[.]$ is the expected value operator. The solution $\hat{q}$ must satisfy the first order condition

$$E[B_1(\hat{q}, \eta)] = E[C_1(\hat{q}, \theta]. \qquad ...(1)$$

When a price instrument p is announced, production will eventually be adjusted to the output level

$$q = h(p, \theta)$$

which maximizes profits given p and θ. Such a condition is expressed as

$$ph(p, \theta)-C(h(p, \theta), \theta) = \max_q pq-C(q, \theta),$$

implying

$$C_1(h(p, \theta), \theta) = p. \qquad ...(2)$$

[1] So that it may be inappropriate, for example, to tell him to produce less if costs are high unless a very sophisticated incentive scheme goes along with such a message. For an elaboration of some of these points see Arrow [1], pp. 321-322.

[2] There are real costs associated with using more complicated signals. At least implicitly, we are assuming that the magnitude of such costs is sufficiently large to make it uneconomical to consider messages other than prices or quantities. It would be nice to incorporate these costs explicitly into the model, but this is hard to do in any meaningful way.

If the planners are rational, they will choose that price instrument $\tilde{p}$ which maximizes the expected difference between benefits and costs given the reaction function $h(p, \theta)$:

$$E[B(h(\tilde{p}, \theta), \eta)-C(h(\tilde{p}, \theta), \theta)] = \max_{p} E[B(h(p, \theta), \eta)-C(h(p, \theta), \theta)].$$

The solution $\tilde{p}$ must obey the first order equation

$$E[B_1(h(\tilde{p}, \theta), \eta) . h_1(\tilde{p}, \theta)] = E[C_1(h(\tilde{p}, \theta), \theta) . h_1(\tilde{p}, \theta)],$$

which can be rewritten as

$$\tilde{p} = \frac{E[B_1(h(\tilde{p}, \theta), \eta) . h_1(\tilde{p}, \theta)]}{E[h_1(\tilde{p}, \theta)]}. \quad ...(3)$$

Corresponding to the optimal *ex ante* price $\tilde{p}$ is the *ex post* profit maximizing output $\tilde{q}$ expressed as a function of θ,

$$\tilde{q}(\theta) \equiv h(\tilde{p}, \theta). \quad ...(4)$$

In the presence of uncertainty, price and quantity instruments transmit central control in quite different ways. It is important to note that by choosing a specific mode for implementing an intended policy, the planners are at least temporarily locking themselves into certain consequences. The values of η and θ are at first unknown and only gradually, if at all, become recognized through their effects. After the quantity $\hat{q}$ is prescribed, producers will continue to generate that assigned level of output for some time even though in all likelihood

$$B_1(\hat{q}, \eta) \neq C_1(\hat{q}, \theta).$$

In the price mode on the other hand, $\tilde{q}(\theta)$ will be produced where except with negligible probability

$$B_1(\tilde{q}(\theta), \eta) \neq C_1(\tilde{q}(\theta), \theta).$$

Thus neither instrument yields an optimum *ex post*. The relevant question is which one comes closer under what circumstances.[1]

In an infinitely flexible control environment where the planners can continually adjust instruments to reflect current understanding of a fluid situation and producers instantaneously respond, the above considerations are irrelevant and the choice of control mode should be made to depend on other factors. Similar comments apply to a timeless *tâtonnement* milieu where iterations are costless, recontracting takes place after each round, and in effect nothing real is presumed to happen until all the uncertainty has been eliminated and an equilibrium is approached. In any less hypothetical world the consequences of an order given in a particular control mode have to be lived with for at least the time until revisions are made, and real losses will be incurred by selecting the wrong communication medium.

Note that the question usually asked whether it is better to control prices or quantities for *finding* a plan is conceptually distinct from the issue treated in this paper of which mode is superior for *implementing* a plan. The latter way of posing the problem strikes me as more relevant for most actual planning contexts—either because there is no significant informational difference between the two modes in the first place, or because a step in the *tâtonnement* planning game cannot meaningfully occur unless it is really implemented, or because no matter how many iterations have been carried out over time there are always spontaneously arising changes which damp out the significance of knowing past history. In the framework adopted here, the planners are at the decision node where as much information as is feasible to gather has already been obtained by one means or another and an operational plan must be decided on the basis of the available current knowledge.

[1] We remark in passing that the issue of whether it is better to stabilize uncertain demand and supply functions by pegging prices or quantities can also be put in the form of the problem analysed in this paper if benefits are associated with the consumers' surplus area under the demand curve and costs with the producers' surplus area under the supply curve.

III. PRICES *vs.* QUANTITIES

It is natural to define the *comparative advantage of prices over quantities* as

$$\Delta \equiv E[(B(\tilde{q}(\theta), \eta) - C(\tilde{q}(\theta), \theta)) - (B(\hat{q}, \eta) - C(\hat{q}, \theta))]. \qquad ...(5)$$

The loss function implicit in the definition of Δ is the expected difference in gains obtained under the two modes of control. Naturally there is no real distinction between working with Δ or with $-\Delta$ (the comparative advantage of quantities over prices).

The coefficient Δ is intended to be a measure of *comparative* or *relative* advantage only. It goes without saying that making a decision to use price or quantity control modes in a specific instance is more complicated than just consulting Δ. There are also going to be a host of practical considerations formally outside the scope of the present model. Although such external factors render Δ of limited value when isolated by itself, they do not necessarily diminish its conceptual significance. On the contrary, having an objective criterion of the *ceteris paribus* advantage of a control mode is very important because conceptually it can serve as a benchmark against which the cost of " non-economic " ingredients might be measured in reaching a final judgment about whether it would be better to employ prices or quantities as planning instruments in a given situation.

As it stands, the formulation of cost and benefit functions is so general that it hinders us from cleanly dissecting equation (5). To see clearly what Δ depends on we have to put more structure on the problem. It is possible to be somewhat less restrictive than we are going to be, but only at the great expense of clarity.

In what follows, the amount of uncertainty in marginal cost is taken as sufficiently small to justify a second order approximation of cost and benefit functions within the range of $\tilde{q}(\theta)$ as it varies around $\hat{q}$.[1] Let the symbol " $\underline{\circ}$ " denote an " accurate local approximation " in the sense of deriving from the assumption that cost and benefit functions are of the following quadratic form within an appropriate neighbourhood of $q = \hat{q}$:

$$C(q, \theta) \underline{\circ} a(\theta) + (C' + \alpha(\theta))(q - \hat{q}) + \frac{C''}{2}(q - \hat{q})^2 \qquad ...(6)$$

$$B(q, \eta) \underline{\circ} b(\eta) + (B' + \beta(\eta))(q - \hat{q}) + \frac{B''}{2}(q - \hat{q})^2. \qquad ...(7)$$

In the above equations $a(\theta)$, $\alpha(\theta)$, $b(\eta)$, $\beta(\eta)$ are stochastic functions and C', C'', B', B'' are fixed coefficients.

Without loss of generality, $\alpha(\theta)$ and $\beta(\eta)$ are standardized in (6), (7) so that their expected values are zero:

$$E[\alpha(\theta)] = E[\beta(\eta)] = 0. \qquad ...(8)$$

Since θ and η are independently distributed,

$$E[\alpha(\theta) . \beta(\eta)] = 0. \qquad ...(9)$$

Note that the stochastic functions

$$a(\theta) \underline{\circ} C(\hat{q}, \theta)$$

$$b(\eta) \underline{\circ} B(\hat{q}, \eta)$$

translate different values of θ and η into pure vertical shifts of the cost and benefit curves.

Differentiating (6) and (7) with respect to q,

$$C_1(q, \theta) \underline{\circ} (C' + \alpha(\theta)) + C'' . (q - \hat{q}) \qquad ...(10)$$

$$B_1(q, \eta) \underline{\circ} (B' + \beta(\eta)) + B'' . (q - \hat{q}). \qquad ...(11)$$

1 Such an approximation can be rigorously defended along the lines developed by Samuelson [8].

Employing the above equations and (8), the following interpretations are available for the fixed coefficients of (6), (7):

$$C' \cong E[C_1(\hat{q}, \theta)]$$

$$B' \cong E[B_1(\hat{q}, \eta)]$$

$$C'' \cong C_{11}(q, \theta)$$

$$B'' \cong B_{11}(q, \eta).$$

From (1),

$$B' = C'. \qquad \text{...(12)}$$

It is apparent from (8) and (10) that stochastic changes in $\alpha(\theta)$ represent pure unbiased shifts of the marginal cost function. The variance of $\alpha(\theta)$ is precisely the mean square error in marginal cost

$$\sigma^2 \equiv E[(C_1(q, \theta) - E[C_1(q, \theta)])^2] \cong E[\alpha(\theta)^2]. \qquad \text{...(13)}$$

Analogous comments hold for the marginal benefit function (11) where we have

$$E[(B_1(q, \eta) - E[B_1(q, \eta)])^2] = E[\beta(\eta)^2].$$

From (10) and (2),

$$h(p, \theta) \cong \hat{q} + \frac{p - C' - \alpha(\theta)}{C''} \qquad \text{...(14)}$$

implying

$$h_1(p, \theta) \cong \frac{1}{C''}. \qquad \text{...(15)}$$

Substituting from (15) into (3) and cancelling out C'' yields

$$\tilde{p} \cong E[B_1(h(\tilde{p}, \theta), \eta)]. \qquad \text{...(16)}$$

Replacing q in (11) by the expression for $h(\tilde{p}, \theta)$ from (14) and plugging into (16), the following equation is obtained after using (8)

$$\tilde{p} \cong B' + \frac{B''}{C''}(\tilde{p} - C'). \qquad \text{...(17)}$$

From (12) and the condition $B'' < 0 < C''$, (17) implies

$$\tilde{p} \cong C'. \qquad \text{...(18)}$$

Combining (4), (14), and (18),

$$\tilde{q}(\theta) \cong \hat{q} - \frac{\alpha(\theta)}{C''}. \qquad \text{...(19)}$$

Now alternately substitute $q = \hat{q}$ and $q = \tilde{q}(\theta)$ from (19) into (6) and (7). Then plugging the resulting values of (6), (7) into (5), using (8), (9), and collecting terms,

$$\Delta \cong \frac{\sigma^2 B''}{2C''^2} + \frac{\sigma^2}{2C''}. \qquad \text{...(20)}$$

Expression (20) is the fundamental result of this paper.[1] The next section is devoted to examining it in detail.

[1] In the supply and demand context B'' is the slope of the (linear) demand curve, C'' is the slope of the (linear) supply curve, and σ^2 is the variance of vertical shifts in the supply curve.

IV. ANALYSING THE COEFFICIENT OF COMPARATIVE ADVANTAGE

Note that the uncertainty in benefits does not appear in (20).[1] To a second-order approximation it affects price and quantity modes *equally* adversely. On the other hand, Δ depends linearly on the mean square error in marginal cost. The *ceteris paribus* effect of increasing σ^2 is to magnify the expected loss from employing the planning instrument with comparative disadvantage. Conversely, as σ^2 shrinks to zero we move closer to the perfect certainty case where in theory the two control modes perform equally satisfactorily.

Clearly Δ depends critically on the curvature of cost and benefit functions around the optimal output level. The first thing to note is that the sign of Δ simply equals the sign of $C''+B''$. When the sum of the " other " considerations nets out to a zero bias toward either control mode, quantities are the preferred planning instrument if and only if benefits have more curvature than costs.

Normally we would want to know the magnitude of Δ and what it depends on, as well as the sign. To strengthen our intuitive feeling for the meaning of formula (20), we turn first to some extreme cases where there is a strong comparative advantage to one control mode over the other. In this connection it is important to bear in mind that when we talk about " large " or " small " values of B'', C'', or σ^2, we are only speaking in a relative sense. The absolute measure of any variable appearing in (20) does not really mean much alone since it is arbitrarily pegged by selecting the units in which output is reckoned.

The coefficient Δ is negative and large as either the benefit function is more sharply curved or the cost function is closer to being linear. Using a price control mode in such situations could have detrimental consequences. When marginal costs are nearly flat, the smallest miscalculation or change results in either much more or much less than the desired quantity. On the other hand, if benefits are almost kinked at the optimum level of output, there is a high degree of risk aversion and the centre cannot afford being even slightly off the mark. In both cases the quantity mode scores a lot of points because a high premium is put on the rigid output controllability which only it can provide under uncertainty.

From (20), the price mode looks relatively more attractive when the benefit function is closer to being linear. In such a situation it would be foolish to name quantities. Since the marginal social benefit is approximately constant in some range, a superior policy is to name it as a price and let the producers find the optimal output level themselves, after eliminating the uncertainty from costs.

At a point where the cost function is highly curved, Δ becomes nearly zero. If marginal costs are very steeply rising around the optimum, as with fixed capacity, there is not much difference between controlling by price or quantity instruments because the resulting output will be almost the same with either mode. In such a situation, as with the case $\sigma^2 = 0$, " non-economic " factors should play the decisive role in determining which system of control to impose.

It is difficult to refrain from noticing that although there are plenty of instances where

[1] This is because the *expected* benefit function (see equation (7)) does not depend on the variance of marginal benefits so long as costs and benefits are independently distributed. If they are *not*, so that

$$\sigma_{bc}^2 \equiv E[\{C_1(q,\theta)-E[C_1(q,\theta)]\}.\{B_1(q,\eta)-E[B_1(q,\eta)]\}] = E[\alpha(\theta).\beta(\eta)] \neq 0,$$

(20) must be replaced by: $\Delta \cong \frac{\sigma^2 B''}{2C''^2} + \frac{1}{2C''}(\sigma^2 - 2\sigma_{bc}^2)$. The sole effect of having costs and benefits correlated with each other is embodied in the term σ_{bc}^2. When marginal costs are positively correlated with marginal benefits, the *ceteris paribus* comparative advantage of the quantity mode is increased. If prices are used as a control mode, the producer will tend to cut back output for high marginal costs. But with σ_{bc}^2 positive, this is the very same time that marginal benefits tend to be high, so that a cutback may not really be in order. In such situations the quantity mode has better properties as a stabilizer, other things being equal. The story is the other way around when σ_{bc}^2 is negative. In that case high marginal costs are associated with low marginal benefits, so that the price mode (which decreases output for high marginal costs) tends to be a better mode of control other things being equal.

the price mode has a good solid comparative advantage (because $-B''$ is small), in some sense it looks as if prices can be a *disastrous* choice of instrument far more often than quantities can. Using (20), $\Delta \to -\infty$ if either $B'' \to -\infty$ or $C'' \to 0$ (or both). The only way $\Delta \to +\infty$ is under the thin set of circumstances where simultaneously $C'' \to 0$, $B'' \to 0$, and $C'' > -B''$. In a world where C'' and B'' are themselves imperfectly known it seems hard to avoid the impression that there will be many circumstances where the more conservative quantity mode will be preferred by planners because it is better for avoiding very bad planning mistakes.[1]

Having seen how C'' and B'' play an essential role in determining Δ, it may be useful to check out a few of the principal situations where we might expect to encounter cost and benefit functions of one curvature or another. We start with costs.

Contemporary economic theory has tended to blur the distinction between the traditional marginalist way of treating production theory with smoothly differentiable production functions and the activity analysis approach with its limited number of alternative production processes. For many theoretical purposes convexity of the underlying technology is really the fundamental property.

However, there are very different implications for the efficacy of price and quantity control modes between a situation described by classically smooth Marshallian cost curves and one characterized by piecewise linear cost functions with a limited number of kinks. In the latter case, the quantity mode tends to have a relative advantage since $\Delta = -\infty$ on the flats and $\Delta = 0$ at the elbows. Of course it is impossible to use a price to control an output at all unless some hidden fixed factors take the flatness out of the average cost curve. Even then, Δ will be positive only if there are enough alternative techniques available to make the cost function have more (finite difference) curvature than the benefit function in the neighbourhood of an optimal policy.

What determines the benefit function for a commodity is contingent in the first place on whether the commodity is a final or intermediate good. The benefit of a final good is essentially the utility which arises out of consuming the good. It could be highly curved at the optimum output level if tastes happen to be kinked at certain critical points. The amount of pollution which makes a river just unfit for swimming could be a point where the marginal benefits of an extra unit of output change very rapidly. Another might be the level of defence which just neutralizes an opponent's offence or the level of offence which just overcomes a given defence. There are many examples which arise in emergencies or natural calamities. Our intuitive feeling, which is confirmed by the formal analysis, is that it doesn't pay to " fool around " with prices in such situations.

For intermediate goods, the shape of the benefit function will depend among other things on the degree of substitutability in use of this commodity with other resources available in the production organization and upon the possibilities for importing this

[1] This idea could be formalized as follows. Consider two generalizations of formulae (6) and (7):

$$C(q, \theta) \cong a(\theta)+(C'+\alpha(\theta))(q-\hat{q})+\frac{C''}{2f(\theta)}(q-\hat{q})^2$$

$$B(q, \eta) \cong b(\eta)+(B'+\beta(\eta))(q-\hat{q})+\frac{B''g(\eta)}{2}(q-\hat{q})^2.$$

The only difference with (6), (7) is that now $1/C_{11}(q, \theta)$ and $B_{11}(q, \eta)$ are allowed to be uncertain. The change in the profit maximizing output response per unit price change is now stochastic, $h_1(p, \theta) = f(\theta)/C''$. Without loss of generality we set

$$E[f(\theta)] = E[g(\eta)] = 1.$$

Note that increasing the variance of f (g) is a mean preserving spread of C_{11} (B_{11}). Suppose for simplicity that f and α are independent of each other. Then we can derive the appropriate generalization of (20) as

$$\Delta \cong \frac{B''\sigma^2(1+\delta^2)}{2C''^2}+\frac{\sigma^2}{2C''},$$

where $\delta^2 \equiv E[\{f(\theta)-E[f(\theta)]\}^2]$ is the variance of $f(\theta)$. The above formula can be interpreted as saying that other things being equal, greater uncertainty in $1/C_{11}(q, \theta)$ increases the comparative advantage of the quantity mode.

commodity from outside the organization. These things in turn are very much dependent on the planning time horizon. In the long run the benefit function probably becomes flatter because more possibilities for substitution are available, including perhaps importing. Take for example the most extreme degree of complete " openness " where any amount of the commodity can be instantaneously and effortlessly bought (and sold) outside the production organization at a fixed price. The relevant benefit function is of course just a straight line whose slope is the outside price.

There is, it seems to me, a rather fundamental reason to believe that quantities are better signals for situations demanding a high degree of coordination. A classical example would be the short run production planning of intermediate industrial materials. Within a large production organization, be it the General Motors Corporation or the Soviet industrial sector as a whole, the need for balancing the output of any intermediate commodity whose production is relatively specialized to this organization and which cannot be effortlessly and instantaneously imported from or exported to a perfectly competitive outside world puts a kink in the benefit function. If it turns out that production of ball bearings of a certain specialized kind (plus reserves) falls short of anticipated internal consumption, far more than the value of the unproduced bearings can be lost. Factors of production and materials that were destined to be combined with the ball bearings and with commodities containing them in higher stages of production must stand idle and are prevented from adding value all along the line. If on the other hand more bearings are produced than were contemplated being consumed, the excess cannot be used immediately and will only go into storage to lose implicit interest over time. Such short run rigidity is essentially due to the limited substitutability, fixed coefficients nature of a technology based on machinery.[1] Other things being equal, the asymmetry between the effects of overproducing and underproducing are more pronounced the further removed from final use is the commodity and the more difficult it is to substitute alternative slack resources or to quickly replenish supplies by emergency imports. The resulting strong curvature in benefits around the planned consumption levels of intermediate materials tends to create a very high comparative advantage for quantity instruments. If this is combined with a cost function that is nearly linear in the relevant range, the advantage of the quantity mode is doubly compounded.[2]

V. MANY PRODUCTION UNITS

Consider the same model previously developed except that now instead of being a single good, $q = (q_1, \ldots, q_n)$ is an n-vector of commodites. The various components of q might represent physically distinct commodities or they could denote amounts of the same commodity produced by different production units. Benefits are $B(q, \eta)$ and the cost of producing the ith good is $c^i(q_i, \theta_i)$. As before, for each i the two random variables η and θ_i are distributed independently of each other.

Suppose the issue of control is phrased as choosing either the quantities $\{\hat{q}_i\}$ which maximize

$$E\left[B(q, \eta) - \sum_1^n c^i(q_i, \theta_i)\right],$$

1 The existence of buffer stocks changes the point at which the kink occurs, but does not remove it. For a more detailed treatment of this entire topic, see Manove [6].

2 Note that in the context of an autarchic planned economy, such pessimistic conclusions about the feasibility of using Lange-Lerner price signals to control short run output do not carry over to, say, agriculture. The argument just given for a kinked benefit function would not at all pertain to a food crop, which goes more or less directly into final demand. In addition, the cost function for producing a given agricultural commodity ought to be much closer to the classical smooth variety than to the linear programming type with just a few kinks.

or the prices $\{\tilde{p}_i\}$ which maximize

$$E[B(h(p, \theta), \eta) - \Sigma c^i(h_i(p_i, \theta_i), \theta_i)],$$

where $\{h_i(p_i, \theta_i)\}$ are defined analogously to (2).

Naturally the coefficient of comparative advantage is now defined as

$$\Delta_n \equiv E\left[\left\{B\left(\tilde{q}(\theta), \eta\right) - \sum_1^n c^i(\tilde{q}_i(\theta_i), \theta_i)\right\} - \left\{B(\hat{q}, \eta) - \sum_1^n c^i(\hat{q}_i, \theta_i)\right\}\right].$$

Assuming locally quadratic costs and benefits, it is a straightforward generalization of what was done in Section III to derive the analogue of expression (20),

$$\Delta_n \cong \sum_{i=1}^n \sum_{j=1}^n \frac{B_{ij}\sigma_{ij}^2}{2c_{11}^i c_{11}^j} + \sum_{i=1}^n \frac{\sigma_{ii}^2}{2c_{11}^i}, \qquad \text{...(21)}$$

where

$$\sigma_{ij}^2 \cong E[\{c_1^i(q_i, \theta_i) - E[c_1^i(q_i, \theta_i)]\}\{c_1^j(q_j, \theta_j) - E[c_1^j(q_j, \theta_j)]\}]. \qquad \text{...(22)}$$

To correct for the pure effect of n on Δ_n, it is more suitable to work with the transformed cost functions

$$C^i(x_i, \theta_i) \equiv nc^i(x_i/n, \theta_i). \qquad \text{...(23)}$$

The meaning of C^i is most readily interpreted for the situation where n different units are producing the same commodity or a close substitute with similar cost functions. Then C^i is what total costs would be as a function of total output if each production unit were an identical replica of the ith unit. When " other things being equal " n is changed, it is more appropriate to think of C^i being held constant rather than c^i.

With C^i defined by (23), we have

$$C_1^i = c_1^i \qquad \text{...(24)}$$

$$C_{11}^i = \frac{c_{11}^i}{n}. \qquad \text{...(25)}$$

Relation (24) means that in the quadratic case the coefficients of the marginal cost variance-covariance matrix for the $\{C_1^i\}$ are the same as those given by (22) for the $\{c_1^i\}$. Substituting (25) into (21),

$$\Delta_n \cong \frac{1}{n^2} \sum_{i=1}^n \sum_{j=1}^n \frac{B_{ij}\sigma_{ij}^2}{2C_{11}^i C_{11}^j} + \frac{1}{n} \sum_{i=1}^n \frac{\sigma_{ii}^2}{2C_{11}^i}. \qquad \text{...(26)}$$

The above formula shows that in effect the original expression for Δ holds *on the average* for Δ_n when there is more than one producer. Naturally the generalization (26) is more complicated, but the interpretation of it is basically similar to the diagnosis of (20) which was just given in the previous section.

There is, however, a fundamental distinction between having one and many producers which is concealed in formula (26). With some degree of independence among the distributions of individual marginal costs, less weight will be put on the first summation term of (26). Other things being equal, in situations with more rather than fewer independent units producing outputs which substitute for each other in yielding benefits, there is a correspondingly greater relative advantage to the price mode of control. Although this point has general validity, it can be most transparently seen in the special regularized case of one good being produced by many micro-units with symmetrical cost functions. In such a case

$$B_{ij} = B'' \qquad \text{...(27.i)}$$

$$C_{11} = C'' \qquad \text{...(27.ii)}$$

$$\sigma_{ii}^2 = \sigma^2 \quad \text{...(27.iii)}$$

$$\sigma_{ij}^2 = \rho\sigma^2, \quad i \neq j, \quad -1 \leqq \rho \leqq 1. \quad \text{...(27.iv)}$$

The coefficient ρ is a measure of the correlation between marginal costs of separate production units. If all units are pretty much alike and are using a similar technology, ρ is likely to be close to unity. If the cost functions of different units are more or less independent of each other, ρ should be nearly zero. While in theory the correlation coefficient can vary between plus and minus unity, for most situations of practical interest the marginal costs of two different production units will have a non-negative cross correlation.

Using (27), (26) can be rewritten as

$$\Delta_n \cong \rho\left(\frac{B''\sigma^2}{2C''^2} + \frac{\sigma^2}{2C''}\right) + (1-\rho)\left(\frac{1}{n}\frac{B''\sigma^2}{2C''^2} + \frac{\sigma^2}{2C''}\right). \quad \text{...(28)}$$

If the marginal costs of each identical micro-unit are perfectly correlated with each other so that $\rho = 1$, it is as if there is but a single producer and we are exactly back to the original formula (20). With $n > 1$, as ρ decreases, Δ_n goes up. A *ceteris paribus* move from dependent toward independent costs increases the comparative advantage of prices, an effect which is more pronounced as the number of production units is larger. If there are three distinctly different types of sulphur dioxide emitters with independent technologies instead of one large pollution source yielding the same aggregate effect, a relatively stronger case exists for using prices to regulate output.

When it is desired to control different units producing an identical commodity by setting prices, only a single price need be named as an instrument. The price mode therefore possesses the *ceteris paribus* advantage that output is being produced efficiently *ex post*. With prices as instruments

$$c_1^i(\tilde{q}_i, \theta_i) = c_1^j(\tilde{q}_j, \theta_j) = \tilde{p},$$

whereas with quantities

$$c_1^i(\hat{q}_i, \theta_i) \neq c_1^j(\hat{q}_j, \theta_j)$$

except on a set of negligible probability.

Using prices thus enables the centre to automatically screen out the high cost producers, encouraging them to produce less and the low cost units more. This predominance in efficiency makes the comparative advantage of the price mode go up as the number of independent production units becomes larger, other things being equal. The precise statement of such a proposition would depend on exactly what was held equal as n was increased—the variance of *individual* costs or the overall variance of *total* costs. For simplicity consider the case of completely independent marginal costs, $\rho = 0$. Then (28) becomes

$$\Delta_n \cong \frac{1}{n}\frac{B''\sigma^2(n)}{2C''^2} + \frac{\sigma^2(n)}{2C''}, \quad \text{...(29)}$$

where $\sigma^2(n)$ is implicitly some (given) function of n. If the " other thing " being equal is the constant variance of marginal costs for each individual producing unit, then $\sigma^2(n) \equiv \sigma^2$. If the variance of total costs is held constant as n varies, $\sigma^2(n) \equiv n\sigma^2$. Either way Δ_n in (29) increases monotonically with n and eventually becomes positive.

It is important to note that such *ceteris paribus* efficiency advantages of the price mode as we have been considering for large n are by no means enough to guarantee that Δ_n will be positive in a particular situation for any *given* n. True, what aggregate output is forthcoming under the price mode will be produced at least total cost. But it might be the wrong overall output level to start with. If the $\{-B_{ij}\}$ are sufficiently large or the $\{C_{11}^i\}$ sufficiently small, it may be advantageous to enjoy greater control over total output by setting individual quotas, even after taking account (as our formula for Δ_n does) of the losses incurred by the *ex post* productive inefficiency of such a procedure.[1]

Returning to the general case with which this section began, we note that the basic difference between benefits and costs becomes somewhat more transparent in the n commodity vector formulation. Only the centre knows benefits. Even if it could be done it would not help to transmit $B(.)$ to individual production units because benefits are typically a non-separable function of *all* the units' outputs, whereas a particular unit has control only over its *own* output. In any well formulated mode of decentralized control, the objective function to be maximized by a given unit must depend in some well-defined way on *its* decisions alone. For the purposes of our formulation B need not be a benefit and the $\{c^i\}$ need not be costs in the usual sense, although in many contexts this is the most natural interpretation. The crucial distinction is that B is in principle knowable only by the centre, whereas c^i is best known by firm i.[2]

When uncertainties in individual costs are unrelated so that the random variables θ_i and θ_j are independently distributed, the decision to use a price or quantity instrument to control q_i alone is decentralizable. Suppose it has already been resolved by one means or another whether to use price or quantity instruments to control q_j for each $j \neq i$. To a quadratic approximation, the comparative advantage of prices over quantities for commodity i is

$$\Delta^i \cong \frac{\sigma_{ii}^2 B_{ii}}{2c_{11}^{i^2}} + \frac{\sigma_{ii}^2}{2c_{11}^i}, \qquad \ldots(30)$$

which is exactly the formula (20) for this particular case.

In some situations, " mixed " price-quantity modes may give the best results. As a specific example, suppose that q_1 is the catch of a certain fish from a large lake and q_2 from a small but prolific pond. Let q_1 be produced with relatively flat average costs but q_2 have a cost function which is curved at the optimum somewhat more than the benefit function. The optimal policy according to (30) will be to name a quota for q_1 and a price for q_2.

REFERENCES

[1] Arrow, K. J. " Research in Management Controls: A Critical Synthesis ", pp. 317-327, in Bonini, Jaedicke and Wagner (eds.), *Management Controls* (New York: McGraw-Hill, 1964).

[2] Dales, J. H. *Pollution, Property and Prices* (Toronto: University of Toronto Press, 1968).

1 An even better procedure from a theoretical point of view in the case where an identical output is produced by many firms would be to fix *total* output by command and subdivide it by a price mechanism. This kind of solution is proposed by Dales [2] who would set up a market in " pollution rights ", the fixed supply of which is regulated by the government. In effect, such an approach aggregates the individual cost functions, and we are right back to a single cost function. Note that a basic question would still remain: is it better to fix the total amount by a quantity or price control mode?

2 An interesting application of the ideas of this section is provided by the problem of choosing a control mode for best distributing a deficit commodity in fixed supply (say gasoline). In this case what we have been calling an individual cost function, $c^i(q_i, \theta_i)$, would really be the negative of a user's benefit function (as measured by the area under his demand curve). Our B function (of total demand) would just reflect the opportunity loss of having a surplus or shortage of the implied amount when only a fixed supply is available. All the considerations of this section would apply in determining the coefficient of comparative advantage. Accurately characterizing the B function seems especially difficult in the present context. If the commodity can be bought from or sold to the outside world, the B function would just embody the terms of this opportunity (in particular, it would be flat if any amount of the commodity could be bought or sold at some fixed price). Under autonomy, the shape of the B function would depend on what is done in a surplus or deficit situation. With a surplus (from naming too high a price), it would depend on the value to future allocation possibilities of the excess supply, relative to what welfare was lost at the present

[3] Hayek, F. A. " The Use of Knowledge in Society ", *American Economic Review*, **35**, 4 (September 1945), pp. 519-530.

[4] Heal, G. " Planning Without Prices ", *Review of Economic Studies*, **36** (1969), pp. 347-362.

[5] Malinvaud, E. " Decentralized Procedures for Planning ", ch. 7 in Malinvaud (ed.), *Activity Analysis in the Theory of Growth and Planning* (New York: Macmillan, 1967).

[6] Manove, M. " Non-Price Rationing of Intermediate Goods in Centrally Planned Economies ", *Econometrica*, **41** (September 1973), pp. 829-852.

[7] Marglin, S. " Information in Price and Command Systems of Planning ", in Margolis (ed.), *Conference on the Analysis of the Public Sector* (Biarritz, 1966), pp. 54-76.

[8] Samuelson, P. A. " The Fundamental Approximation Theorem of Portfolio Analysis in Terms of Means, Variances and Higher Moments ", *Review of Economic Studies*, **37** (October 1970), pp. 537-542.

[9] Weitzman, M. " Iterative Multilevel Planning with Production Targets ", *Econometrica*, **38**, 1 (January 1970), pp. 50-65.

[10] Whinston, A. " Price Guides in Decentralized Institutions ", Ph.D. thesis, Carnegie Institute of Technology, 1962.

time from having demand less than supply. With a deficit (from naming too low a price), the loss of welfare hinges on how shortages are actually distributed among consumers. If shortages result in some people doing completely without the product, the overall welfare losses may be very great and $| B'' |$ could be large. If there is some inherent reason to believe that shortages will automatically be evenly distributed, then $| B'' |$ may not be so big. In addition to redistribution losses, there will always be waiting time losses in a shortage. Finally, note that if the amount of the fixed supply is known, a superior policy to naming prices or quantities is to distribute ration tickets (instead of quantities), allowing them to be resold at a competitively determined market price.

[7]

Journal of Public Economics 12 (1979) 271–299. © North-Holland Publishing Company

THE ROLE OF INFORMATION IN DESIGNING SOCIAL POLICY TOWARDS EXTERNALITIES

J.A. ORDOVER*

New York University, New York, NY 10003, USA

R.D. WILLIG*

Princeton University, Princeton, NJ 08540, USA

Received July 1978, revised version received July 1979

1. Introduction

This paper analyzes the externality problem afresh, taking explicit account of the information structure. The analysis is conducted from the viewpoint of agents who are affected by externalities but who are imperfectly informed about the parties who generate them. Information collection is costly, and the amount gathered is determined endogeneously to avoid prior specification of either perfect or no personalized information.[1]

The result of this approach is a new class of abstract allocation mechanisms that outperform those previously studied, when information is costly, and that model many extant social programs. The presented mechanisms combine an impersonal market price with programs to allocate the good to selected groups of consumers. Each program offers a special price to all applying agents who are validated to possess certain characteristics or to

*J.A. Ordover's research has been partially supported by a grant to New York University from the Division of Science Information of the National Science Foundation and by a grant from the Sloan Foundation. R.D. Willig's research was undertaken while he was a member of the technical staff at Bell Laboratories. We would like to think the two referees of the *Journal* for their helpful and insightful comments.

[1]It is well known that with perfect information, the government can utilize perfect price discrimination, see Pigou (1932), or complete internalization to effect a Pareto optimal allocation in the presence of externalities. Further, as Coase (1960) demonstrated, with perfect information and costless transactions, Pareto optimality can also be achieved without government intervention if property rights are clearly assigned. However, because of the costliness of the personalized information required for these classical solutions to the externality problem, much attention has been devoted to the design of governmental tax and subsidy schemes which can partially correct for externalities without the need for any personalized information, see Diamond (1973), Baumol and Oats (1975), Roberts and Spence (1974).

exhibit the requisite signals.[2] Almost any signal that is costless to verify can be gainfully utilized to improve the allocation. However, it may not be desirable to screen on a costly signal. Yet, information costs can be reduced by self-selection to such an extent that price discrimination can be regarded as a viable instrument of social policy. The necessary incentives for self-selection can be provided by suitable application fees which discourage unqualified agents from the costly screening phases of the programs. In fact, existing social programs (e.g. Medicaid, R&D grants, and scholarship funds) do contain the key elements of price discrimination and self-selection.

Most of the paper is devoted to analysis of the socially optimal allocation mechanism under the assumption that the component programs are designed and implemented by an idealized government. Such centralization may, in fact, be the only feasible approach when the effects of the externalities are diffuse and when interpersonal transactions costs are high. Otherwise, however, given the delineation of property rights, an Agent for those affected by the externalities would have the incentive and ability to implement the programs that combine self-selection and price discrimination. We use the socially optimal set of government run allocative mechanisms as a benchmark for the evaluation of the programs that would be optimal for the private Agent. We find that for some information structures, the private and publically optimal allocations are identical, as would be suggested by the Coase Theorem. For other structures, however, this equivalence fails to hold.

We work with the simplest possible model. There is a particular discrete activity which each agent either does or does not perform and which requires a single input with no other uses. This input has a constant marginal cost of production, c. Every agent is characterized by his private benefit, or reservation price, B, for the activity (or its input) and by the total external impact, E (in money units), from his performing the activity. The values of B and E corresponding to each agent are assumed to be exogenous and independent of the allocative events endogenous to the model.

Consumption of the input good, or alternatively, performance of the activity, results in externalities. We restrict attention to the case of positive externalities and assume that for each agent both B and E are nonnegative. The normative framework chosen does not distinguish among costs and benefits that accrue to different individuals and to the government.

We assume that the continuous joint distribution of B and E in the population of agents, $h(B,E)$, is freely available information. Agents themselves know their own B's and will sometimes be assumed to know their own

[2] Akerlof (1978) explored taxation and transfer programs that are keyed to such costlessly observable yet imperfectly revealing signals. Shavell (1978) also analyzes costless and noisey signals in a principal-agent context.

E's and other identifying characteristics as well. We make the usual assumption that self-knowledge of B is available through introspection. However, self-knowledge of E may require announced standards for the evaluation of self-observed qualitative characteristics. However, the characteristics of individuals cannot be identified by others without costly screening, testing, and sorting processes.

In section 2, we consider the benchmark case in which the government develops no personalized information. Here, the government can only set a single, nondiscriminatory, market price for the input good, and we analyze its welfare optimal level. (We call this the pure price subsidy case.) We show that this scheme generally leads to a poor allocation. The basic reason is that a market price, p, can only sort agents by means of their reservation prices into a half-space set of buyers with $B \geqq p$, whereas the agents whose consumptions are socially desirable form the set with $B+E \geqq c$.

In section 3 we develop the theme that society need not confine itself to the instrument of a single market price. Instead, it can break the bounds of the pure price subsidy scheme by utilizing a carefully controlled amount of personalized information to achieve a limited degree of price discrimination. Optimally chosen special prices offered to self-selecting subgroups of agents balance allocative gains against information costs. These programs allocate the good to some agents whose consumptions bring them only small private benefits but which yield large beneficial externalities.

In section 4, we study an allocation mechanism which implements perfect price discrimination, over an optimally chosen subset of the population, by validating self-selected agents' B's and E's. The program is called conditional perfect price discrimination (abbreviated to cppd). We show that no matter how costly it is to discover an agent's B and E, it is always socially advantageous to append a program of cppd to any other allocative scheme. Moreover, we prove that when information is costly, a program of conditional perfect price discrimination, together with an optimized market price below marginal cost, strictly outperforms classical perfect price discrimination.

Maintaining the presence of cppd, in section 5 we study the desirability and market price effects of utilizing other arbitrarily specified signals to sort the population into groups facing distinct prices. We show that as the costs of personalized information drop from infinity to zero, the optimal market price rises from the pure subsidy case level up to marginal cost.

In section 6 we see that specializing the analysis to signals which reveal agents' E's generates a program of conditional perfect internalization. This mechanism is allocatively superior to conditional perfect price discrimination, but it may incur significantly greater information costs. We prove that when information is costly, a properly chosen mixture of conditional perfect internalization and conditional perfect price discrimination, together with a subsidized market price, strictly outperforms a complete program of classical internalization.

Section 7 analyzes the behavior of an individual agent who acts as if he were the sole recipient of the externalities, given that all are entitled by the legal system not to perform the activity. Assuming that the agent faces the same information structure and costs as did the government in the earlier sections, we show that the decentralized allocation is socially optimal if the private benefits of all consumers can be costlessly revealed. However, if it is costly to ascertain the private benefits of consumers with B's near c, then the decentralized allocation systematically deviates from the socially optimal one, and the Coase Theorem fails to generalize.

By way of conclusion, section 8 reviews the information structures of the allocation mechanisms introduced in the previous sections, recapitulates the crucial informational assumptions, and begins the discussion of the consequences of relaxing them.

2. Pure price subsidy

In a pure price subsidy scheme the only instrument used by the government (or center) to effect the allocation of the input is its price. An agent purchases the input and performs the activity if and only if his reservation price is not less than the impersonal market price. Each agent who performs the activity adds his $B+E$ to social welfare; the social cost is the constant marginal cost, c, of the input. Thus, at price p, the money measure of the net social welfare resulting from the allocation of the good is

$$W=\int_p^\infty \int_0^\infty (B+E-c)h(B,E)\,\mathrm{d}E\,\mathrm{d}B. \tag{1}$$

This implies

$$\frac{\partial W}{\partial p}=-\int_0^\infty (p+E-c)h(p,E)\,\mathrm{d}E=[c-p-m(E|p)]\int_0^\infty h(p,E)\,\mathrm{d}E, \tag{2}$$

where $m(E|B)$ is the average externality from the consumptions of the agents with reservation price B.

We assume throughout that $h(B,E)>0$ over the relevant region. Then, the first order condition for an interior ($p>0$) optimal choice of price is

$$p+m(E|p)=c. \tag{3}$$

Eq. (3) says that the interior optimal price is below marginal cost by an amount equal to the average externality from those agents for whom $B=p$. These agents are the marginal buyers of the input and it is their E's that would be lost to society if the price were marginally raised.

Another way to view (3) is to consider as a function of B, $B+m(E|B)$. This is the average gross social value of the consumption of the input by all agents with reservation price B. The first order optimality condition is that *at* $B=p^*$ *(the optimal price),* $B+m(E|B)=c$, *or in words, marginal cost equals the average social benefit from the marginal buyers.* Fig. 1 pictures a $B+m(E|B)$ function and shows that p^* may be found at its intersection with the horizontal at c.

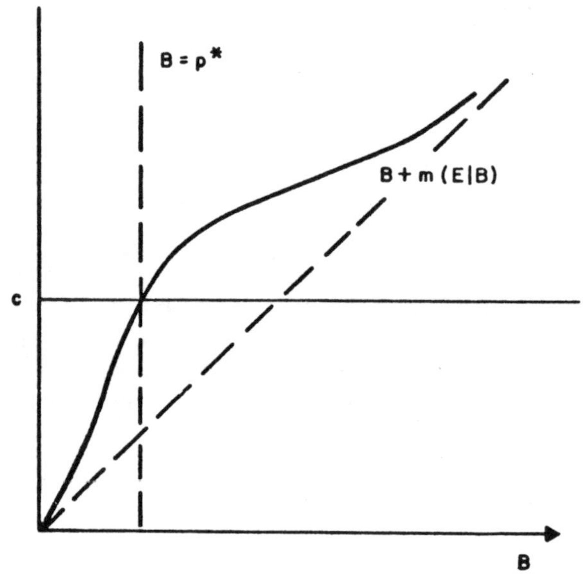

Fig. 1

The second order conditions ($\partial^2 W/\partial p^2 < 0$) for a p satisfying (3) to be optimal is that

$$d[B+m(E|B)]/dB > 0 \quad \text{at} \quad B=p. \tag{4}$$

Thus, p^* *can only be an interior optimum if the average gross social value function is increasing at that point.* Since the buyers are those with $B>p$, (3) and (4) together say that the average social benefit exceeds marginal cost for the first infra-marginal buyers, and inversely for the first infra-marginal non-buyers.

Conditions (3) and (4) are necessary only for an interior solution to the maximization of (1). The extremes of a zero price, or an ineffective price above all reservation prices cannot be ruled out a priori. For example, if the average gross social benefit function were everywhere above the marginal cost line ($B+m(E|B)>c$, for all B), then $p^*=0$ would be indicated. (Perhaps the argument for free public education is of this nature.)

The market price should exclude all consumption if $B+m(E|B)<c$ for all B with positive weight in h. On the other hand, p^* should be effective if $B+m(E|B)>c$ for the largest B's in the population. In particular, since we are restricting outselves to activities with nonnegative E's, p^* should be effective and not above c if there are any agents with $B\geq c$. If there were no such agents, it would suffice to set $p=c$ for p^* to be ineffective and to exclude all consumption. Thus, we need never consider market prices above c.

The optimal market price will generally fail to perfectly allocate the input, for two fundamental reasons. First, the agents with a particular B will usually have diverse E's, some below and some above the average, $m(E|B)$. This variance will lead to misallocation, even with an interior optimal price p^* (satisfying (3) and (4)) which equates marginal cost to marginal average social benefit. In fig. 2, the horizontally shaded region contains the (E,B) points of agents who will purchase the good because their B's exceed p^*, despite the fact that their purchases are socially injurious since $B+E<c$. The vertically shaded set represents agents who will not buy, since $B<p^*$, despite

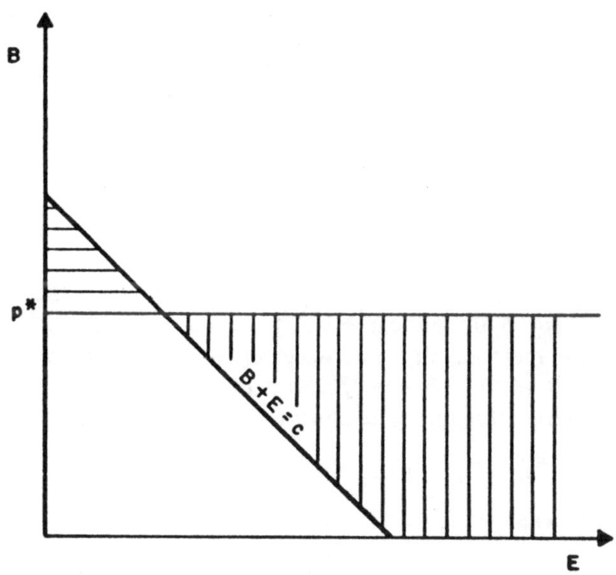

Fig. 2

the social desirability ($B+E>c$) of their purchase. These misallocations are an unavoidable consequence of the fact that while the social desirability of consumption depends on $B+E$, a price system can only sort agents on the basis of their B's.

Second, a market price can only sort agents into the groups with $B \geqq p$ (buyers) and $B<p$ (non-buyers). While this would be the appropriate dichotomization if the $B+m(E|B)$ function were monotone increasing in B, it becomes a serious limitation otherwise. If the gross average social value curve crosses the horizontal at c more than once, then any market price must misallocate the good (in either direction) with respect to an entire group of agents with the same B. If the $B+m(E|B)$ function is decreasing over the population's B's, and crosses the horizontal at c, (4) shows that the only candidates for optimality are a zero price and an ineffectively large price. Either one would misallocate the good to all those agents with B's in an entire interval. These welfare losses would occur even if there were no variance in the distribution of the E's of the agents with each B. The realistic presence of such variance compounds the misallocation with the effect discussed above.

For example, it may be argued that in the sphere of health care, $B+m(E|B)$ is relatively high for the poor and for the rich, while B, the reservation price, is positively correlated with income. These features would yield a U-shaped $B+m(E|B)$ function. Then, the only candidates for optimality would be a zero price which would permit inefficient consumption by groups with $B+m(E|B)<c$, and a price satisfying (3) and (4). Although this price would eliminate inefficient use, it would also prevent the poor from purchasing socially desirable medical services.

To circumvent the misallocations caused by the rigidity of the pure price subsidy allocation scheme, society offers inputs to externality producing activities at special low rates (perhaps zero), through a variety of programs, to a variety of groups, while a regular market price is maintained for everyone else. For example, in the sphere of health care, Medicaid, Medicare, venereal disease treatment centers and drug treatment clinics are programs which offer special prices to selected groups: the poor, the aged, and the specially afflicted. Such allocative programs screen agents for signals indicative of their membership in a subset of the population with a distinctive distribution of B and E. Then, a special price which is optimal for this subset can be presented to the agents exhibiting the proper signals.

3. Screening mechanisms and self-selection

Let us suppose that the government knows not only the distribution $h(B,E)$ in the whole population, but that it also knows the distribution

$h^{\alpha}(B,E)$ in the subpopulation of agents who exhibit the characteristics α which we assume is left unaltered. If the government could costlessly identify those agents with α, then the overall allocation would surely be (weakly) improved by using the signal α to dichotomize the population into groups facing different market prices for the good. Each group-specific price could be set optimally with (1)–(4) separately applied to the group's distribution $h-h^{\alpha}\equiv h^{\bar{\alpha}}$ and to h^{α}.

Generally, though, it is costly to verify that an agent has the characteristic α and it is not clear that these costs won't outweigh the welfare gains from the price discrimination. It is not necessary, however, to test the characteristics of all agents.

The center can induce agents to self-select into the screening program on the basis of their own known characteristics. The government can require a small fee from those applying for the α-test (or force people to incur a transactions cost), and announce that only those who are validated to exhibit α will receive a special price. Then, assuming that people believe both the announcement and the accuracy of the testing procedure, only agents who do actually have the characteristic α will apply for the test. Further, among the agents with α, only those who find the special price attractive enough to induce purchase will have the incentive to enter the program. These agents are assumed to be tested, so as to assure the credibility of the program. (This assumption is discussed in section 8.)

Given that agents are to be offered the special price p_{α} if they select themselves into the α testing program, the social welfare function is

$$W=\int_{p}^{\infty}\int_{0}^{\infty}(B+E-c)h^{\bar{\alpha}}(B,E)\,\mathrm{d}E\,\mathrm{d}B$$

$$+\int_{p_{\alpha}}^{\infty}\int_{0}^{\infty}(B+E-c-s)h^{\alpha}(B,E)\,\mathrm{d}E\,\mathrm{d}B. \tag{5}$$

Here, s is the cost of validating α and, due to the self-selection, it is only incurred for the agents with characteristic α who have $B\geqq p_{\alpha}$. Of course, the testing program would attract no one if $p_{\alpha}>p$, and (5) must be optimized subject to that constraint. Note, however, that if the constraint were binding, p_{α}^{*} would equal p^{*}, society would gain nothing from the sorting procedure, information costs would be borne needlessly, and the α testing program would be wasteful.

Then, assuming that the α-test is desirable, the $p_{\alpha}\leqq p$ constraint is not binding, and the first order conditions for interior optimal prices are (analogous to (3)):

$$p+m^{\bar{\alpha}}(E|p)=c, \tag{6}$$

and

$$p_\alpha + m^\alpha(E|p_\alpha) = c + s. \tag{7}$$

Here, $m^{\bar{\alpha}}(E|p)$ is the mean E among the agents in the group without characteristic α who have reservation price p, and $m^\alpha(E|p_\alpha)$ is the mean E in the α group of those with $B = p_\alpha$. (7) shows that in the α-group, the average gross social benefit of the marginal buyers must equal marginal production cost plus the marginal information cost. Eliminating buyers by raising p_α saves both production costs, and the costs of validating the α signals of those agents.

Intuitively, an α-testing program would be worthwhile if most agents with α were socially desirable consumers ($B + E > c + s$) and if most wouldn't have been consuming without the costly α-test ($B < p^*$). Fig. 3 pictures a subset of the population which meets these criteria. Further, worthwhile screening programs must be based on truly informative signals, i.e. those characteristic of population subsets with genuinely distinctive distributions of B and E. In particular, if α is an uninformative signal, then $h^\alpha(B, E) = kh(B, E)$ and $m^\alpha(E|B) = m^{\bar{\alpha}}(E|B)$. Examination of (5) reveals that in this case at the unconstrained welfare maximum, $p_\alpha > p$. This result follows:

Proposition. *If $h^\alpha(B, E)$ is proportional to $h(B, E)$, then screening on α is undesirable.*

Many social programs can be usefully viewed as realizations of the abstract mechanism developed here. For example, special student subscription rates for technical journals may result from viewing the group of agents with the easily verified signal 'student' as being located in E, B space much like the subset α in fig. 3.

The Medicaid program offers a discriminatory price for health care to 'welfare recipients'. The government may view this group as having low B's and high E's, on average, thus meeting our criteria for special treatment. Furthermore, (7) would stipulate an optimal group-specific price close to 0.

People with the signal 'venereal disease symptoms' may be viewed as having both extremely high spillover benefits from treatment and a wide range of reservation prices. Then, the existence of free treatment centers into which those with the publicized symptoms can self-select is consistent with the theory developed in section 2. There it was shown that the optimal price is zero if the gross average social value is everywhere above the relevant marginal cost.

The efficient allocation of people among such social programs can be hampered by adverse selection. In general, there will be a large set of signals α_i that can be used to sort out population subgroups, each with a different

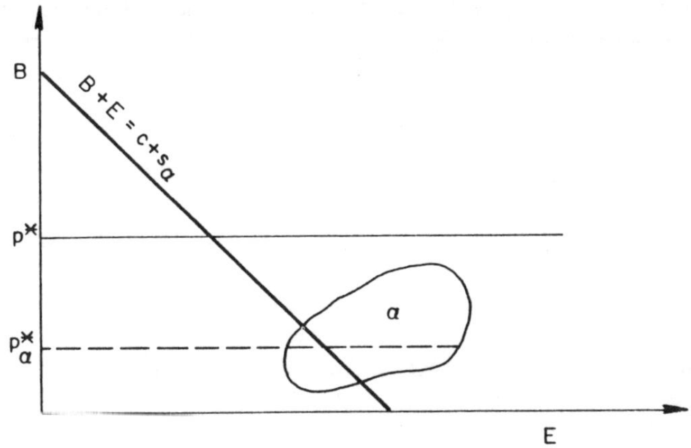

Fig. 3

testing cost s_i. The center is faced with the problem of choosing the best set of sorting signals, as well as the best corresponding group-specific prices. When many signals are utilized to sort the population, agents who can qualify for more than one special price will select themselves into the program offering the lowest one. From the social point of view, this will be adverse selection if the screening cost of the chosen program is not the smallest of the screening costs of the programs available to the agent. In view of this effect, in addition to the combinatorics of the problem, little more can be usefully said, in general, about the optimal choice of signals with which to sort the population. In the next section, however, we treat an important special case in which there is no adverse selection.

4. Conditional perfect price discrimination

In this section we show that irrespective of the signals that are used to sort agents into groups offered special prices, it will always (weakly) increase social welfare to offer, in addition, a program of conditional perfect price discrimination. This program screens self-selected agents for the social desirability of their consumptions with costly tests which reveal both their B's and their E's. These agents are then offered personalized prices just below their reservation prices.

Elements of such an allocative mechanism can be found in the dispensation of health care by some public-minded hospitals and clinics which examine patients who present themselves, treat those who are diagnosed to need care, and offer a sliding fee schedule based on ability to pay. These organizations screen B's with means tests and only offer special subsidized prices to patients who demonstrably cannot afford care at the regular market price. Further, they screen agents' E's by means of medical diagnoses, and refuse to offer special prices to patients, no matter how poor, whose medical needs are not serious enough by common standards. Prospective patients who are aware of these standards will only present themselves to the facilities if they think that they will qualify for special treatment. This process of self-selection keeps manageable the medical and financial screening chores of the hospitals and clinics.

We model conditional perfect price discrimination (henceforth cppd) by assuming that agents know both their own E's and their own B's,[3] and that these can both be validated at a cost of t per agent. The cppd program entails a government announcement that for a small fee, an agent may apply for a special price which will be just below his measured B. The government will test the agent's E and B, and if and only if they meet the announced standards that $E+B\geqq c+t$ will the application fee be returned and the special price offered.

The cppd program has the optimal structure among mechanisms that permit the government to both ascertain the private and external benefits of chosen agents and to price discriminate among them. This optimality property of cppd rests on all the elements of the mechanism. The announcement of the standards together with the application fee assures that only those agents who meet the standards will in fact cause society to incur the screening cost t. Hence, within cppd, the screening cost is added to the production cost, c, to form the full marginal social cost of providing an agent with the input. As a result, $E+B\geqq c+t$ is the first-best standard for allocating the input within the program. The stipulation that an agent's personalized price be set just below his B is required to forestall adverse selection. Otherwise, some agents might prefer cppd to some other allocative program with a small screening cost.[4]

These same arguments establish the fact that agents will only participate in the cppd program if they would not otherwise purchase the good, and if their purchase through cppd would yield greater social benefits than costs. Thus we conclude:

Theorem 1. Under our assumptions, it is (always weakly and sometimes strictly) socially desirable to append a program of conditional perfect price discrimination to any other allocative mechanism.

[3]Some effects of dropping this assumption are discussed in the concluding section.

[4]In theorem 3 below we show that it is never socially optimal to implement an allocation scheme that incurs a screening cost greater than t.

It is instructive to compare cppd to the classical program of complete perfect price discrimination. Under this mechanism, all agents are tested, and those with $B+E \geqq c$ are given the good at or below their reservation prices. Of course, the Pigovian rule $B+E \geqq c$ is optimal given that all information has been collected and the information costs of t per agent are sunk. Yet, cppd improves on the resulting allocation by utilizing self-selection to optimize the extent of information collection. Additional reduction in total information costs can be obtained by market sale of the input at a price $p = c$. In fact, the optimal level of p with cppd in place is below the marginal cost of production c. This holds because dropping p just below c saves t for each of the agents who is induced to leave the cppd program, and because new buyers who are, on average, socially desirable are attracted to the market.

This is the reasoning that underlies:

Theorem 2. If $t>0$, cppd with an optimal market price that is below c, strictly outperforms complete perfect price discrimination.

By the same reasoning, if the α_i are desirable signals with which to sort the population, then classical price discrimination can be further improved upon when information is costly. Due to theorem 1, we shall maintain the assumption of the existence of a cppd program and turn to the questions of the desirability of sorting programs and their effects on the optimal market price.

5. General screening: Its desirability and its impact on market price

With cppd, a market price p, and special prices $p_i<p$ for agents with signals α_i, the welfare function is

$$W=\int_p^\infty \int_0^\infty (B+E-c)g(B,E)\,\mathrm{d}E\,\mathrm{d}B+\sum_{i=1}^{m}\int_{p_i}^\infty \int_0^\infty (B+E-c-s_i)h^{\alpha_i}(B,E)\,\mathrm{d}E\,\mathrm{d}B$$

$$+\int_0^p \int_{\max(c+t-B,0)}^\infty (B+E-c-t)g(B,E)\,\mathrm{d}E\,\mathrm{d}B. \tag{8}$$

Here, $g(B,E)$ is the distribution function of agents not buying at any of the special prices p_i, and $h^{\alpha_i}(B,E)$ is the distribution of agents buying at p_i.[5] We consider the welfare impact of establishing another special price, p_{m+1}, for agents with another characteristic α_{m+1}. Since agents with α_{m+1} may also

[5]If there are agents with more than one of the screened characteristics, h^{α_i} will depend on the special prices offered, although not on the market price.

have some of the other characteristics α_i, the total impact is generally difficult to gauge. Thus, we deal with a series of special cases which clarify the allocative issues.

Suppose that the set of agents with α_{m+1} (henceforth denoted A_{m+1}) has empty intersections with the sets of agents buying at the special prices p_i, at the market price p, and through the cppd program. Then, the desirability of screening on α_{m+1} can be judged irrespective of the other programs. In this case, p_{m+1} should be set optimally in the same manner as was the pure subsidy price in section 2. However, here, the relevant population group is A_{m+1}, the pertinent distribution is $h^{\alpha_{m+1}}(B,E)$, and the associated social marginal cost is $c+s_{m+1}$. The definitive test of the desirability of this α_{m+1} program is whether the optimal p_{m+1} is effective; whether it is below the largest reservation price of the agents in A_{m+1}.

To begin the process of removing the simplifying assumptions, let some agents with the α_{m+1} signal be potential participants in cppd. The allocations of the good to these agents will not be affected by the new program, but those with $B>p_{m+1}$ will have the incentive to purchase via the α_{m+1} scheme instead of through cppd. If $s_{m+1}>t$, then this will be adverse selection, and, in this case, all agents who are desirable consumers through the α_{m+1} track ($B+E\geqq c+s_{m+1}$) would otherwise have been purchasing through the less socially costly cppd. This is the essence of the argument[6] which establishes:

Theorem 3. It is never desirable to sort agents by means of a signal more costly to validate than B and E.

If, instead, $s_{m+1}<t$, as we assume henceforth, then information costs are saved by the α_{m+1} program. Taking this to the extreme, if $A_{m+1}\subset\{a|B(a)+E(a)\geqq c+s_{m+1}\}$, where a denotes an agent and $B(a)$ and $E(a)$ his B and E, then the new mechanism improves the allocation, economizes on information costs and is unambiguously desirable. More generally, if the group $A_{m+1}-\{a|B(a)+E(a)\geqq c+t\}$, viewed as having the marginal cost $c+s_{m+1}$, has an effective optimal pure subsidy price,[7] then it is desirable to screen the group A_{m+1} for the signal α_{m+1}.

Complicating matters further, let some agents with α_{m+1} have B's greater than the market price. With an operational α_{m+1} program, $p_{m+1}<p$, and so these agents will choose the α_{m+1} track, incurring new information costs while leaving their consumption decisions unchanged. Such adverse selection makes the new program less desirable than it would otherwise be. Now the

[6]It is somewhat more detailed, but still valid, if A_{m+1} intersects the sets of agents participating in other allocative programs.

[7]Note that this is not the optimal value for p_{m+1}, into whose calculation goes the additional effect of the savings in information costs due to the movement of agents from the cppd into the α_{m+1} program.

allocative gains and the information cost savings relative to cppd must be balanced against these extra information costs. Similarly, when A_{m+1} intersects other A_i's, although no new effects on the allocation of the good arise, information costs are affected by agents' choices among the tracks open to them. The α_{m+1} program is more or less desirable as s_{m+1} is below or above the information costs of other programs with participating groups which intersect A_{m+1}.

In general, the desirability of a screening program depends on the level of p, and obversely, the presence of a program affects the optimal p. Having already considered the former effect, we now study the effect on p^* of adding the α_{m+1} track, holding constant the existence of the other α_i programs.

Working from (8), we see

$$\frac{\partial W}{\partial p} = -\int_{0}^{\max(c+t-p,0)} (p+E-c)g(p,E)\,\mathrm{d}E - (t)\int_{\max(c+t-p,0)}^{\infty} g(p,E)\,\mathrm{d}E. \tag{9}$$

Assuming an interior optimum ($p^*>0$ and effective), at p^*, $\partial W/\partial p=0$ and $\partial^2 W/\partial p^2<0$. In the spirit of standard comparative statics, if the addition of the α_{m+1} program increases the $\partial W/\partial p$ function, then it follows (if $\partial^2 W/\partial p^2 <0$ in the relevant range) that p^* increases.

If $A_{m+1} \cap \{a|B(a)=p\}=\Phi$, where p is optimal without the α_{m+1} program, then nothing in (9) is altered by the addition of the new program. Otherwise, (9) changes due to the decrease in the $g(p,E)$ function. If most of the agents in A_{m+1} who have $B=p$ (the marginal buyers at the market price) are socially desirable consumers ($B+E>c$), then the decrease in $g(p,E)$ from the addition of the α_{m+1} track increases $\partial W/\partial p$, and hence increases p^*.

As pictured in fig. 4, the benefit of raising p is the extension of the vertically shaded region of agents whose consumptions are socially undesirable and who are, indeed, not consuming. One cost of raising p is the extension of the diagonally shaded region of agents. who are desirable consumers but who are excluded by both the market price and by cppd (this cost and the aforementioned benefits are captured in the first term of (9)). The other cost is the extension of the expensive cppd program (horizontally shaded region) into the area of agents who would otherwise have been buying at the market price (this is the second term of (9)). The addition of the α_{m+1} program insulates the agents in A_{m+1} from the effects of changing p. As drawn, the new track removes none of the benefits of a price increase, while it diminishes the costs. Thus, here, the addition of the α_{m+1} mechanism raises the optimal market price. For it to lower p^*, A_{m+1} would have to be concentrated (at $B=p^*$) inside the $B+E=c$ line, among agents whose consumptions are undesirable. Because this would also tend to make the α_{m+1} program an undesirable addition, we conclude that:[8]

Proposition. *The addition of socially desirable screening programs tends to increase the optimal market price towards marginal cost.*

In the same vein, but more formally, we establish that:

Theorem 4. *With positive information costs, as the costs of cppd fall to zero, the optimal market price rises to marginal cost.*

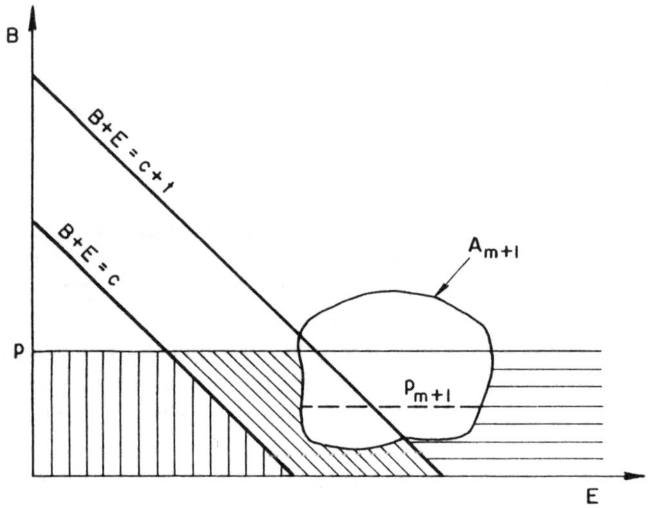

Fig. 4

Obversely:

Theorem 5. *As all information costs increase without bound, the optimal market price falls to the optimal pure subsidy price.*

Briefly, the rationale behind these results is that when screening is impossible, or very costly, the full task of correcting the allocation for the externalities falls to the market price. While the market mechanism incurs no information costs, it can only sort the population coarsely into sets of the

[8]Theorems formally demonstrating this tendency for a particular class of screening programs appear in the Appendix to Ordover and Willig (1976).

form $\{a|B(a)\geqq p\}$ and $\{a|B(a)<p\}$. Unless the distributions of E conditional on B have no variance and have an increasing $B+m(E|B)$, dichotomizations of this form result in relatively poor allocations. Since the market price has to be held down to permit the consumption of high E agents, many low E agents purchase the good as well. Screening on selected signals allows the population to be more finely sorted. As personalized information costs drop, groups of high E agents can be identified and offered special prices. This removes part of the allocative burden from the market price and permits it to rise to exclude undesirable consumption. In the limit, as information costs fall to zero, all externalities can be corrected with full knowledge. Then, and only then, the market price loses all trace of subsidy and becomes equal to production marginal cost.

6. Conditional perfect internalization

In this section, we specialize the analysis to signals which perfectly reveal agents' E's. Such signals are, of course, necessary for the implementation of the classical scheme designed to correct externalities through internalization of spillover effects.

Suppose then that on a self-selection basis, an E verification test is offered to those with E's of some prespecified value. The cost of this test, e, is less than t, the cost of identifying both B and E. Denote by $p(E)$ the special price offered to the agents whose E's are validated by this test. Then, the social benefit, net of testing costs, which accrues from these agents is

$$W(E)=\int_{p(E)}^{\infty}(B+E-c-e)h(B,E)\,\mathrm{d}B. \tag{10}$$

For this E, the optimal price $p(E)$ becomes

$$p^*(E)=\begin{cases}(c+e)-E & \text{if} \quad E<c+e,\\ 0 & \text{if} \quad E\geqq c+e.\end{cases} \tag{11}$$

Eq. (11) is a special case of the optimal price rule developed earlier and is analogous to eq. (7) with the modification that negative prices are replaced, with no welfare loss, by a zero price. Indeed, for a group of agents all having a given E, the gross average social value function is simply $B+m(E|B)=B+E$.

We shall show that selling the input at $p^*(E)$ is equivalent to achieving the perfect internalization which Coase, among others, recommends as the solution to the externality problem. Consider an agent with the requisite particular value of E. Since the government requires deposit of a testing fee which is refundable only upon purchase at the special price, the agent refrains from testing unless his $B \geqq p^*(E) = \max[0, c+e-E]$. If his B exceeds the input price, the agent will test, purchase the input, and will be left with a net surplus of

$$0 \leqq B - p^*(E) = \begin{cases} B+E-(c+e) & \text{if} \quad E < c+e \\ B & \text{if} \quad E \geqq c+e. \end{cases} \tag{12}$$

This process of self-selection yields a perfect allocation, relative to the information cost e. If $E \geqq c+e$, then, of course, all agents in the group are socially desirable consumers, and the consequent zero special price achieves the correct outcome. Otherwise, the buyers are those with $B \geqq c+e-E$, precisely the agents whose gross social benefits of purchase exceed the true social marginal costs.

The classical internalization program also yields a perfect allocation, relative to its information structure. The government, assumed to know each agent's E, offers a subsidy payment of his E to any agent who will buy the input at a price equal to social marginal cost. This is equivalent to each agent being offered a personalized price of (marginal cost)$-E$, exactly the content of (11).

However, when information is costly to obtain, we shall soon see that it is not socially advantageous to offer all agents E-tests and the special prices in (11). Instead, this option will be optimally made available to only a proper subset of agents, conditional on the size of their E's. Hence, we label this allocative program conditional perfect internalization (abbreviated to cpi).

With some agents excluded from cpi, there will be a market price, below c, set optimally for its effect on the allocation of the good to them. Thus, with imperfect information, the classic version of internalization is suboptimal both because it relies on a marginal cost market price and because of its informational requirements. Far better, with costly information, is conditional perfect internalization, due to its personalized prices, self-selection, and optimally selected set of potential participants.

Indeed, the government uses elements of cpi to allocate funds to various R&D projects. The anticipated *private* benefits of some of these projects may be prohibitively costly or impossible for the government to estimate, thus rendering cppd ineffective. Nevertheless, cpi may be effectively implemented because the expected spillover benefits can be feasibly estimated via familiar appraisals of research proposals, facilities, and staff.

The $p^*(E) = 0$ portion of the optimal cpi price schedule can be identified with cost-plus R&D grants. Eq. (11) indicates that cost-plus financing should only be rationally offered when the expected unappropriable part of the social benefit is, by itself, large enough to cover the total cost. If, however, E

$<c+e$, (11) stipulates that the R&D project be supported with a flat-fee grant. The optimal fee implied by (14), $E+$[cost of inputs at market prices] $-(c+e)$, leaves part of the project costs to be defrayed from private benefits.

Let us consider the allocative and informational consequences, as illustrated in fig. 5, of introducing cpi for the particular level of E denoted E^1. Because $t>e$, every agent with that E who is eligible to participate in cppd can achieve a larger surplus from the cpi program, will switch, and thereby save society $t-e$ in screening costs. (These agents lie on the line segment LM

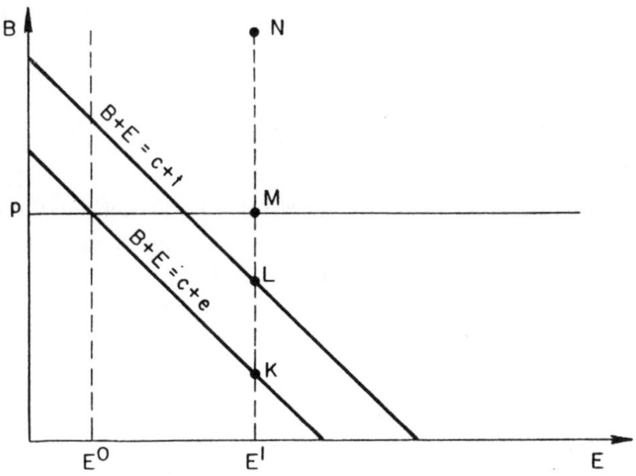

Fig. 5

in fig. 5.) Moreover, those agents with $t+c>B+E\geqq e+c$ (line segment KL) will now purchase the good and thereby increase social welfare. The undesirable countervailing effect of cpi is that agents (on line segment MN) who are given the option to purchase the input at $p(E)<p$ will leave the impersonal market – if their $B\geqq p$ – and will offer themselves for testing, at a social cost of e per agent, without a concomitant improvement in the input's allocation.

It can be seen in fig. 5 that for $E\leqq c+e-p$ (below E^0), the special price $p(E)\geqq p$, and consequently cpi is ineffective for small values of E. Furthermore, for E close to and above E^0, the information costs of implementing cpi exceed the allocative benefits. Consequently, for these values of E it is not desirable to offer cpi and so, in our framework, the classical mechanism which offers internalization to all is strictly suboptimal.

Theorem 6. With costly information, conditional perfect internalization, offered to an appropriate proper subset of agents, combined with a program of cppd and a subsidized market price, strictly dominates complete perfect internalization.

7. Decentralization

In the preceding sections, we approached the problem of allocation of resources with externalities from the vantage point of a benevolent government or center. Whereas the allocative mechanisms relied upon consumer sovereignity, the center itself was posited to play an essential role in them. The center was assumed to design the screening programs and the subsidized market price optimally for the standard *social* objective function. Indeed the center appears to be the appropriate locus for policy towards externalities whose effects are diffuse.

However, our analysis would have remained unchanged were the external effects concentrated on one agent. Yet, in such a case, in the absence of transactions and information costs, Coasian analysis indicates that government intervention is unnecessary. With clear assignment of property rights, self-interested individuals' own actions would effect the socially optimal resource allocation.

In this section, we analyze the behavior of an individual Agent who acts as if he were the sole recipient of the externalities generated by others' actions. The allocation of property rights is such that all are entitled not to perform the activity. We maintain the analytic structure utilized in the earlier sections; assume that the Agent and the center face the same information costs, and find that with arbitrarily small information costs, the decentralized allocation systematically deviates from the socially optimal one.

Within our framework, the Agent can implement all the allocative mechanisms previously analyzed. He can successfully offer the input in the impersonal market at any price below c. (Of course, no one would buy from him at a price above the competitive level of c.) Further, like the center, he can offer a special price to any self-selecting agent who is validated to possess the requisite signal. Moreover, the Agent always finds it desirable to append a cppd program to any other allocative mechanisms he implements.

From a participant in cppd the Agent gains E at a screening cost of t, and a transfer cost of $c-B$. The net gain is $E+B-c-t$, which is guaranteed to be nonnegative by the construction of the program.

Now, maintaining the existence of cppd, let us consider the Agent's incentive to screen on the signals $\alpha_1, \ldots, \alpha_m$ and his determination of the corresponding special prices $p_1, \ldots, p_m$ together with the market price, p. Assuming that $p_1 < p$ (so that screening on α_i is effective), the Agent's private benefit for feasible $p \leqq c$ is,

$$\Pi=\int_{p}^{\infty}\int_{0}^{\infty}(E+p-c)g(B,E)\,\mathrm{d}E\,\mathrm{d}B$$

$$+\sum_{i}\int_{p_i}^{\infty}\int_{0}^{\infty}(E+p_i-c-s_i)h^{\alpha_i}(B,E)\,\mathrm{d}E\,\mathrm{d}B$$

$$+\int_{0}^{p}\int_{\max(0,c+t-B)}^{\infty}(E+B-c-t)g(B,E)\,\mathrm{d}E\,\mathrm{d}B, \qquad (13)$$

where $g(B,E)$ is the distribution of agents not buying at any of the special prices, p_i.

Eq. (13) reflects the assumption that the Agent receives as a private benefit the E corresponding to each consumer of the good. The Agent pays a subsidy of $c-p$ for each unit purchased in the impersonal market, and incurs a net cost of $c+s_i-p_i$ on sales to those with signal α_i. The difference in the contribution made by each consumer to social welfare (in eq. (5)) and to Π is $B-p$, or $B-p_i$, depending on where he buys. This difference is the consumer's net benefit (surplus) which is a legitimate part of social welfare, but which is of no concern to the Agent.

The structural deviation between social welfare and the Agent's private benefit tends to cause the prices that are optimal for the former to be lower than those optimal for the latter.

Theorem 7. Suppose that p^*, the welfare optimal market price, is less than c, and that the welfare and privately optimal sets of screening programs are the same. Then $\hat{p}$, the privately optimal market price, is greater than p^*. Similarly, $\hat{p}_j>p_j^*$, if no consumer with characteristic α_j is eligible for another special price.

The intuitive explanation of this theorem is that the Agent, unlike the center, views as a loss the price dependent subsidies of $c-p$ and $c-p_j$ given to the consumers. Consequently, the Agent is more reluctant than is the center to lower any price.

The hypothesis of theorem 7 that $p^*<c$ is needed because, otherwise, p^* and $\hat{p}$ would both equal c due to the fact that $\hat{p}$ cannot exceed c. In fact, it can be seen that $\hat{p}=c$ if information costs are small.

Theorem 8. There exists $\hat{t}>0$ such that for $t\leqq\hat{t}$, the Π maximal market price is c.

The result says that while the social optimum requires a subsidized market price whenever there are *any* screening costs, under decentralization, for some range of information costs, all subsidizations will be effected through special screening programs.

In fact, it is easy to see that if $t=0$, the Agent's objective, Π, is maximized by sole reliance on cppd. Of course, in this case, the resulting allocation is socially optimal and decentralization obviates government intervention. Unexpectedly, the result does not hinge on the costless availability of *all* information.

The following theorems show that in the present framework, it is the availability of information about consumers' private benefits that is critical for the social efficacy of decentralization. This is surprising because, in the model considered here, any deviations between the social and private optima arise from the externalities, and thus one would expect that only costless information about them would allow the two optima to coincide. However, this surprise stems from a confounding of two distinct comparisons. In general, information costs cause the social optimum to deviate from the one that would be realized if information were free. Moreover, information costs may cause a divergence between the social optimum and the decentralized allocation. Our results in section 6 indicate that it is costless information about consumers' externalities that is required to close the former gap while the results below show that it is costless information about consumers' private benefits that is required to close the latter one.

Theorem 9 (Coase). In the present framework, if it is costless to ascertain the private benefit, B, of each consumer, then the allocations that are optimal for the Agent and for social welfare coincide.

To prove the theorem, note that the Agent has incentive to use the costless information that reveals each consumer's B in order to extract the maximal feasible price, B, from each subsidized buyer of the input. Consequently, both the center and the Agent receive the same benefit, net of information costs, from the provision of the input to each consumer, namely $B+E-c$. Thus, whatever complex of screening mechanisms is optimal for W it is also optimal for Π.

However, we show in the Appendix that the social efficiency of decentralization generally fails to hold when information is costly. Nevertheless, it should be noted that this and our other results may depend critically on the particular assignment of property rights inherent in our model.

Theorem 10.[9] *Decentralization is socially suboptimal if it is costly to discover the private benefits of all consumers whose B's are close to and below c.*

[9]More formally, if there exists an $\varepsilon>0$ such that it is costly to validate all signals which perfectly reveal the private benefits of all consumers with $c-\varepsilon \leqq B \leqq c$, then the Π and W optimal allocations differ.

8. The information structure

In this section we discuss some of the effects of relaxing our assumptions on the information structures of the allocation mechanisms discussed throughout the paper.

In our model, agents must believe in the precise accuracy of the tests, because otherwise, the self-selection processes become imperfect. To assure the credibility of the mechanisms, we have restricted ourselves to those that do, indeed, fully carry out the promised plan. This restriction may rule out some socially advantageous possibilities. For example, costly verification of an α signal is completely unnecessary, given that agents perfectly select themselves into the α-testing program believing that they will be so tested. Perhaps a less costly placebo test should be sometimes substituted for the true test.

Another possibility is randomly administering the true test and fining (with a prior announcement) those agents who are discovered to have misrepresented possession of the requisite characteristics. Under the assumption of perfectly accurate tests, a severe enough penalty could dissuade all cheating, even with a small probability of test administration. If, however, the tests are perceived to be subject to error, or if agents are uncertain about their own characteristics, then such a system would also dissuade from participation some of the agents who do have the desired signal.

Further, people have incentives to attempt to manipulate the tests if they believe that it is possible. For example, a participant in cppd will gain from a downward misrepresentation of his private benefit, as long as his test scores satisfy $B+E \geqq c+t$. Of course, this is also true in the classical price discrimination schemes, and one can appeal to cheat-proof tests to resolve the problem.

For our mechanisms to be effective, there must be no 'black market' for the resale of the good by those who buy it at special prices. An agent with a private benefit below the market price would prefer resale to consumption. But resale would deny society the external benefits from that agent's consumption, and would vitiate the allocative program. (The possibility of resale would also frustrate the classical price discrimination mechanism.) Such a black market could not exist if the good were, by nature, nontransferable (such as personalized educational tuition vouchers). It might also be prevented by requiring evidence of the good's use from agents who purchased at a special price.[10]

Nonetheless, with no black market and with credibly accurate cheat-proof tests, our mechanisms do not deny, and in fact, they rely upon the strength

[10]However, the experience of the food stamp program shows the difficulty in enforcing rules against such resale.

of individuals' selfish incentives. Agents are only asked to behave rationally and consistently with their own welfare.

There is an interesting obverse class of allocative programs which we reject because they are not compatible with individual rationality. These test agents for undesirability of consumption, reward them for refraining from the activity, and distribute the good freely to the remaining desirable consumers. Although in some cases such a program might economize on screening costs, it leaves strong incentives for circumvention. We view as prohibitively high the costs of preventing the undesirable consumers from using inputs which are freely available to others. In contrast, we view as reasonably small the costs of barring the black market transactions which would threaten to ruin our self-selection schemes.

In fact, these costs would be zero if the programs were effected ex post, after the activity had been undertaken. Ex post, the government would be observing the realized values of B and E and using them to compute the optimal personal subsidies. Here, since the subsidies are irrevocably tied to the actual performance of the activity, rather than to the promise of its performance, any black market possibilities disappear.

Ex post versions of the mechanisms, heretofore assumed to be ex ante, can be easily constructed. The government announces, before all purchasing decisions, that sometime later, after the completion of the activity, testing and transfer programs will be implemented. These programs are to have the same structure as the ex ante ones, except that wherever personalized prices were offered in the ex ante mechanisms, transfers will be made in the ex post schemes. The transfers will be set equal to the difference between the market price and the special personalized price of the ex ante mechanism, and will be only given to those who have performed the activity. In this scenario, agents are assumed to correctly anticipate their later subsidies and to make their purchasing decisions accordingly. Again, to assure the credibility of ongoing programs, all promises of government actions must be fulfilled. Then, other things equal, the allocations and information costs resulting from the ex post mechanisms are identical to those of the ex ante versions.

However, it seems likely that the parameters and the effectivenesses of the two classes of programs would differ. It is plausible that more informative signals are available for ex post than for ex ante screening. (For example, ex ante R&D subsidy decisions can only be based on such signals as the perceived quality of research staffs while, ex post, the quality of the research itself becomes an available signal.) Both this effect and the more easily solved resale problem argue for the adoption of ex post programs. On the other hand, the allocation resulting from such a program may be distorted by capital market imperfections. Agents with low B's and high E's who anticipate large subsidies after completing the activity may find it costly or impossible to obtain the funds needed for purchase before their B's and E's are officially verified. Of course, it is the consumptions of this very category of agents which the mechanisms were designed to assure. For example, consider the ineffectiveness of an ex post program of college scholarships. Potential students having high ability but few funds would find it little easier to borrow tuition with such a program than without it.

The most striking difference between the ex ante and ex post mechanisms lies in their basic information structures. If agents are uncertain about their own signals before being screened and completing the activity, then they cannot correctly forecast their subsidies forthcoming from either program. However, the costs to the agent of misjudging his signal are substantially different in the two cases. In the ex ante scheme, the agent can, at worst, lose the testing fee if the test disqualifies him from the special price. But in the ex post version, the agents who would not buy without a subsidy risk the testing fee plus the difference between the market price and their B. To induce the participation of such desirable agents, the market price may have to be lower than would otherwise be optimal, causing misallocations that could be avoided under an ex ante program.

In general, imprecise self-knowledge as well as noisy tests impair the power of self-selection and discriminatory pricing. In our model, based on self-knowledgeable agents and accurate cheat-proof screening procedures, we have constructed and studied self-selection allocation mechanisms designed to optimize the allocation of a good with externalities, in the face of costly information. We think that the simplicity of our assumptions has enabled new analytic insights which, we hope, may contribute to the design of better social programs.

Appendix

Theorem 1

Suppose that signals $\alpha_1,\ldots,\alpha_m$ are being used to sort the population into groups facing prices $p_1,\ldots,p_m$, and that the remaining agents face the market price p. We add to this scenario a program that offers a price just below B to those who pay a refundable application fee and whose measured values of B and E meet the announced standards. The index function $\phi(B,E)$ embodies the announced standards, such that $\phi(B,E)=1$ if an agent with these values of B and E qualifies, and $\phi(B,E)=0$ otherwise. By its construction, the program will attract almost no one (in the measure theoretic sense) who was formerly buying at one of the prices $p,p_1,\ldots,p_m$, $(B\geqq p_i)$. Thus, the increment to W from the new scheme is

$$\Delta W=\int_0^p\int_0^\infty \phi(B,E)[B+E-c-t]g(B,E)\,\mathrm{d}E\,\mathrm{d}B, \tag{A1}$$

where

$$g(B,E) \equiv h(B,E) - \sum_{\substack{1 \leqq i \leqq m \\ B \geqq p_i}} h^{\alpha_i}(B,E) \geqq 0,$$

the distribution function of agents who are not buying at any of the special prices $p_1, \ldots, p_m$.

To find the optimal standards for the program, consider the first variation in ΔW due to changing $\phi(B,E)$ from 0 to 1. This is:

$$\delta(\Delta W) = [B+E-c-t]g(B,E), \quad \text{for} \quad B<p.$$

Hence, optimality requires that $\phi(B,E)=1$ iff $B+E \geqq c+t$. As such, (A1) shows that $\Delta W \geqq 0$, and that $\Delta W > 0$ if the set of agents with $B+E>c+t$ who are not buying at $p, p_1, \ldots, p_m$ has positive measure. Q.E.D.

Theorem 2

The argument in the text established that cppd with a market price is not inferior to complete perfect price discrimination. It remains to show that welfare is improved by dropping p below c. Consider social welfare with cppd and no α screening as a function of market price:

$$W = \int_p^\infty \int_0^\infty (B+E-c)h(B,E)\,\mathrm{d}E\,\mathrm{d}B + \int_0^p \int_{\max(c+t-B,0)}^\infty (B+E-c-t)h(B,E)\,\mathrm{d}E\,\mathrm{d}B,$$

$$\partial W/\partial p = -\int_0^{\max(c+t-p,0)} (p+E-c)h(p,E)\,\mathrm{d}E - t \int_{\max(c+t-p,0)}^\infty h(p,E)\,\mathrm{d}E.$$

For $p \geqq c$, $\partial W/\partial p < 0$, as long as $t>0$. Thus, the optimal price is below c.

Q.E.D.

Theorem 4

Consider the impact on p^* from the implementation of cppd, given the tracks α_i. Without cppd, $\partial W/\partial p = -\int_0^\infty (p+E-c)g(p,E)\,\mathrm{d}E$, and

$$\left(\frac{\partial W}{\partial p}\right)_{\text{cppd}} - \left(\frac{\partial W}{\partial p}\right)_{\substack{\text{no} \\ \text{cppd}}} = \int_{\max(c+t-p,0)}^\infty (p+E-c-t)g(p,E)\,\mathrm{d}E \geqq 0.$$

Thus, assuming $\partial^2 W/\partial p^2 < 0$ in the relevant range, the addition of the socially desirable cppd program raises the optimal market price.

Performing ordinary comparative statics, but holding constant the existence of the α_i programs, we see that

$$\frac{\partial^2 W}{\partial p \partial t} = - \int_{\max(c+t-p,0)}^{\infty} g(p,E)\,\mathrm{d}E < 0,$$

and that $\partial p^*/\partial t < 0$. Thus, as the costs of cppd diminish and more agents (those not purchasing through other programs for whom $B+E \geqq c+t$) are screened for their B's and E's, the optimal market price increases. Of course, (9) shows that as long as $t>0$, $\partial W/\partial p \leqq 0$ for $p \geqq c$, so $p^* \leqq c$. If $t=0$, since any market price below c can mar the perfect allocation from complete costless price discrimination, p should be set at or above c. Q.E.D.

Theorem 5

As the information costs s_i increase, the desirability of screening on α_i, diminishes. When $c+s_i > B+m^{\alpha_i}(E|B)$, for all B represented with positive measure in A_i, we know from (8) that the α_i program is socially undesirable. If the $B+m^{\alpha_i}(E|B)$ functions are all bounded above on their relevant domains, then there are information costs s_i big enough to make all the α_i programs undesirable.

With no α_i programs, $g(p,E)$ is replaced by $h(p,E)$ in (9) and we have

$$\partial W/\partial p = - \int_{0}^{\max(c+t-p,0)} (p+E-c)h(p,E)\,\mathrm{d}E$$

$$- (t) \int_{\max(c+t-p,0)}^{\infty} h(p,E)\,\mathrm{d}E. \tag{A2}$$

We show that (A2) approaches (2), $\partial W/\partial p$ without cppd, in the limit as $t \to \infty$, for each relevant $p\,(p \leqq c)$, given that $m(E|p) < \infty$. Clearly, the first term of (A2) approaches (2) for any fixed p. By Cauchy's Condition, $m(E|p) < \infty$ implies $\lim_{t\to\infty} \int_t^{\infty} Eh(p,E)\,\mathrm{d}E = 0$ for any fixed p. Then, with $p \leqq c$,

$$\int_t^{\infty} Eh(p,E)\,\mathrm{d}E \geqq \int_t^{\infty} (t)h(p,E)\,\mathrm{d}E \geqq \int_{t+c-p}^{\infty} (t)h(p,E)\,\mathrm{d}E \geqq 0,$$

and it follows that $\lim_{t\to\infty}(t)\int_{c+t-p}^{\infty} h(p,E)\,\mathrm{d}E = 0$.

Thus, as $t \to \infty$, the behavior of W with respect to p (in the relevant region) with cppd becomes identical to that in the pure price subsidy program. The proof is completed by putting this together with the result, $\partial p^*/\partial t < 0$, that was used in proving theorem 4, and with the observation above about sufficiently large costs of screening the α_i's. Q.E.D.

Theorem 6

For $E \geqq c+e-p$, with an extant program of cppd, the change in social welfare that results from the extension of cpi to a particular value of E is given by this first variation

$$\delta W = \int_{c+t-E}^{p} (t-e)h(E,B)\,\mathrm{d}B - \int_{p}^{\infty} eh(E,B)\,\mathrm{d}B + \int_{p(E)}^{c+t-E} (B+E-c-e)h(E,B)\,\mathrm{d}B.$$

If the first variation is positive (negative), cpi is socially advantageous (disadvantageous) for this particular E. As E approaches $c+e-p$ from above, both the first and third terms go to zero, while the second term remains bounded away from and below zero. Q.E.D.

Theorem 7

Differentiation of (13) yields

$$\frac{\partial \Pi}{\partial p} = \int_{\max(c+t-p,0)}^{\infty} (E+p-c-t)g(p,E)\,\mathrm{d}E - \int_{0}^{\infty} (E+p-c)g(p,E)\,\mathrm{d}E + \int_{p}^{\infty}\int_{0}^{\infty} g(B,E)\,\mathrm{d}E\,\mathrm{d}B, \tag{A3}$$

$$\frac{\partial \Pi}{\partial p_j} = -\int_{0}^{\infty} (E+p_j-c-s_j)h^{\alpha j}(B,E)\mathrm{d}E\mathrm{d}B, + \int_{p_j}^{\infty}\int_{0}^{\infty} h^{\alpha j}(B,E)\mathrm{d}E\mathrm{d}B, \tag{A4}$$

where (A4) is calculated for a program that does not draw consumers from other special programs or cppd. Comparison of (A3) and (A4) with the derivatives of (8) reveals that when calculated at the same points and given that the same $g(B,E)$ functions are relevant,

$$\partial\Pi/\partial p > \partial W/\partial p \quad \text{and} \quad \partial\Pi/\partial p_j > \partial W/\partial p_j. \tag{A5}$$

Because both Π and W are additively separable functions of p and p_j, it suffices to examine each price separately. Let p^* and $\hat{p}$ maximize W and Π respectively. By assumption, $p^* < c$. At p^*, $0 = \partial W/\partial p < \partial\Pi/\partial p$, by (A5). Thus (A5) implies that $\hat{p} \neq p^*$ and that $\Pi - W$ is an increasing function of p. Suppose $\hat{p} < p^*$. By definition, $\Pi(\hat{p}) > \Pi(p^*)$ and $W(\hat{p}) < W(p^*)$. Thus, $\Pi(\hat{p}) - W(\hat{p}) > \Pi(p^*) - W(p^*)$, which is a contradiction. The same argument applies to p_j. Differentiation shows that (A5) also holds for α programs that draw consumers from cppd. Q.E.D.

Theorem 8

Eq. (A3) shows that at $p=c$, $\partial\Pi/\partial p$ is above and bounded away from 0 as t goes to 0. Further, because all second derivatives of Π with respect to p and t are bounded, there exist ε and $\bar{t}$ such that $\partial\Pi/\partial p$ is positive for $0\leqq t<\bar{t}$ and $c-\varepsilon<p\leqq c$. For $t=0$, $\hat{p}=c$, and so, by continuity of $\hat{p}$ as a function of t, there is some t^* such that $c\geqq p>c-\varepsilon$ for $0\leqq t<t^*$. Let $\hat{t}=\min(\bar{t},t^*)$. For $0\leqq t<\hat{t}$, $c\geqq\hat{p}>c-\varepsilon$ and, were $p<c$, $\partial\Pi/\partial p>0$ would contradict optimality. Q.E.D.

Theorem 10

It suffices to show that the collection and features of the allocative mechanisms that are Π optimal do not coincide with those that are optimal for W. We prove this by deriving a contradiction from the assumption that for Π and W maximization, the market price, the existence of cppd, and the α programs and their special prices are all the same. The argument considers several cases. Suppose, first, that $p^*<c$. Theorem 7 immediately implies that $\hat{p}>p^*$, which is the requisite contradiction.

Suppose, instead, that $p^*=c$. Then, evaluated at $p=c$, $\partial W/\partial p\geqq 0$. Eq. (9) implies that, then, $\int_0^\infty g(c,E)\,\mathrm{d}E=0$. Thus, almost all consumers with $B=p^*=c$ obtain the input in α programs which screen on, say, $\alpha_1,\ldots,\alpha_k$. Assume that $s_i>0$ for $i=1,\ldots,k$. Then, $p_i^*<p^*$, $i=1,\ldots,k$, for the programs to be desirable. Consequently, there would exist a reduction in the market price that would increase W because the savings in information costs would outweigh any concomitant misallocation. This contradicts the assumption that $s_i>0$, $i=1,\ldots,k$. So, let $s_1=0$. Thus, by the hypothesis of the theorem, α_1 cannot reveal the private benefits, B, of any consumers. It follows that the α_1 program cannot be perfectly discriminatory and that there must be an effective special price, $p_1^*<p^*=c$. Finally, by the arguments underlying theorem 7, $\hat{p}_1$ cannot equal p_1^*. This is the needed contradiction. Q.E.D.

References

Akerlof, G.A., 1978, The economics of 'tagging', American Economic Review 68, 8–19.

Baumol, W.J. and W. Oates, 1975, The theory of environmental policy (Prentice Hall, Englewood Cliffs).

Coase, R.H., 1960, The problem of social cost, Journal of Law and Economics 3, 1–44.

Diamond, P.A., 1973, Consumption externalities and imperfect corrective pricing, The Bell Journal of Economics 4, 526–538.

Ordover, J.A. and R.D. Willig, 1976, The role of information in designing social policy towards externalities, Bell Laboratories Economic Discussion Paper #64, Holmdel.

Pigou, A.C., 1932, The economics of welfare, 4th Ed. (Macmillan, London).

Polinsky, A.M. and S. Shavell, 1978, The optimal tradeoff between the probability and magnitude of fines, Harvard Institute for Economic Research Working Paper, Harvard University.

Roberts, M.J. and A.M. Spence, 1976, Effluent charges and licenses under uncertainty, Journal of Public Economics 5, 193–208.

Shavell, S., 1979, Risk sharing and incentives in the principal and agent relationship, The Bell Journal of Economics 10, 55–73.

Weiss, A. and J.L. Guasch, On self-selection strategies, American Economic Review, forthcoming.

[8]

THE LIMITATIONS OF PIGOUVIAN TAXES AS A LONG-RUN REMEDY FOR EXTERNALITIES*

DENNIS W. CARLTON AND GLENN C. LOURY

I. INTRODUCTION

A central problem of economic policy is to assure efficiency of the competitive process when externalities are present. One traditional method of dealing with an externality is the imposition of a Pigouvian tax (per unit tax) on the externality-generating activity [Pigou, 1927, and Baumol, 1972]. This paper shows that contrary to widely held beliefs use of such a tax will not in general lead to an efficient allocation of resources in the long run. The source of the inefficiency of the tax is really quite simple. A per unit tax uniformly raises a firm's average cost curve, and therefore leads the firm in the long run to minimize average cost at the same output as in the pre-tax situation. In general, however, the output that is socially optimal in the presence of externalities is not the output that minimizes the firm's average production costs.[1] However, if one supplements the Pigouvian tax with a lump sum tax-subsidy scheme for participating firms, then a socially efficient allocation can be achieved.

II. THE MODEL

We present a simple partial-equilibrium model to illustrate our arguments. Imagine a competitive industry consisting of identical firms producing a homogeneous product. Each firm incurs production costs $C(q)$ when producing q units of output. Production in this industry also imposes additional damages on society due to some external effect. We assume these external damages resulting from in-

* This work was initiated while both authors were visiting the Economics group at Bell Laboratories. We thank John Panzar, A. Mitchell Polinsky, and an anonymous referee for helpful comments.

1. An example can illustrate this point simply. Suppose that steel is produced with a technology that generates a U-shaped average cost (AC) curve with the min AC point at output q^*. Suppose that steel production causes pollution damage. This pollution damage need not be constant per unit of steel produced by the firm. For example, starting up the steel furnace may generate pollution damage that is independent of output, in which case average pollution damage per ton of steel produced could fall initially, or alternatively the amount of smoke emitted per ton may depend on how many tons of steel the firm is producing. The minimum average pollution damage per unit of steel output will not in general occur at the output q^* which minimizes average production costs. In this case, Pigouvian taxation alone cannot achieve efficiency.

The Quarterly Journal of Economics, November 1980 0033-5533/80/0095-0559$01.00

dustry production may be written as $D(n,q)$, where n is the number of firms in the industry and q is the output of each firm. Thus, we restrict ourselves to symmetric behavior by active firms, and implicitly assume that external damages are invariant with respect to changes in firms' employment of factors of production that keep output constant. Average production costs $C(q)/q$ are taken to be U-shaped with the minimum average production cost occurring at scale q_s. $P(Q)$ represents the industry's inverse demand function, where $Q = nq$ is total industry output. We assume that the efficient scale of firm production is "small" relative to the size of the market, so that the indivisibility of firms may be neglected and the number of firms n can be taken to be a continuous variable. Finally, we assume interior solutions to all maximum problems.

The welfare criterion is the usual sum of consumer plus producer surplus.[2] The short run is defined as a situation in which the number of firms n is fixed.[3] A Pigouvian tax t is a charge to each firm of $\$t$ for each unit of output produced.

A short-run competitive equilibrium with Pigouvian tax t and number of firms n is a price-quantity pair (p,q) such that supply equals demand and price equals private marginal costs. Using the definition of the inverse demand curve, we can summarize these two conditions by the single condition,

$$P(nq) = C'(q) + t. \tag{1}$$

A short-run social optimum with number of firms n is a price-quantity pair (p,q), which maximizes social welfare. If we again use the inverse demand curve to define p, we can completely characterize the optimal q as the solution to

$$\max_{q \geq 0} \int_0^{nq} P(s)ds - nC(q) - D(n,q).$$

Hence q satisfies the first-order condition,

$$nP(nq) = nC'(q) + \frac{\partial D}{\partial q}(n,q),$$

2. The results of this section are unchanged if instead of using a surplus criterion to measure social welfare, we use a Bergsonian social welfare function. Also, the results are unchanged if the problem is reformulated as one in which the number and output of firms of one industry affect the cost curves of other competitive industries.

3. We assume that in the short run, all n identical firms operate. A rising marginal cost curve guarantees this condition, provided that any output is produced at all. See Polinsky [1977] for a discussion of the short-run effects of taxation when firms differ in their production technology.

or

$$P(nq) = C'(q) + \frac{1}{n}\frac{\partial D}{\partial q}(n,q). \tag{2}$$

The following result provides a frequently used justification for the use of Pigouvian taxation.

THEOREM 1. For the appropriately chosen tax t, the short-run competitive equilibrium coincides with the short-run social optimum.

Proof. It is necessary to show that if q^* satisfies (2), it also satisfies (1) for the appropriately chosen t. Suppose that q^* solves (2) and define $t = (1/n)(\partial D/\partial q)(n,q^*)$. Then, it follows immediately from (2) that q^* also satisfies (1).

Q.E.D.

In the long run, entry or exit may occur, so the number of firms n is free to vary. A long-run competitive equilibrium with tax t (LRCE) consists of a price-quantity-number of firms triple such that supply equals demand, price equals private marginal cost, and profits equal zero. Again using the definition of the inverse demand curve, we can completely characterize a LRCE by

$$P(nq) = C'(q) + t, \tag{3}$$

and

$$qP(nq) = C(q) + tq. \tag{4}$$

A long-run social optimum (LRSO) is a price-quantity-number of firms triple that maximizes social welfare. Using the definition of the inverse demand curve, we can completely characterize a LRSO by the q,n that solve

$$\max_{\substack{q\geq 0\\ n\geq 0}} \int_0^{nq} P(s)ds - nC(q) - D(n,q).$$

The first-order conditions are

$$nP(nq) = nC'(q) + \frac{\partial D}{\partial q}(n,q)$$

or

$$P(nq) = C'(q) + \frac{1}{n}\frac{\partial D}{\partial q}(n,q), \tag{5}$$

and

$$qP(nq) = C(q) + \frac{\partial D}{\partial n}(n,q). \tag{6}$$

Theorem 1 asserts that any short-run social optimum may be attained as a short-run competitive equilibrium with the appropriately chosen Pigouvian tax rate. However, as competitive entry occurs, the tax rate must be adjusted to maintain short-run optimality. That this adjustment process need not result in a long-run social optimum is illustrated by the following result.

THEOREM 2. In general there exists no Pigouvian tax rate t such that the long-run competitive equilibrium (LRCE) coincides with the long-run social optimum (LRSO).

Proof. It is necessary to show that if t is the Pigouvian tax, then if n^*, q^* satisfy (5) and (6) (i.e., n^*, q^* are a LRSO), they will not also satisfy (3) and (4) (i.e., n^*, q^* are not a LRCE). First, notice that if t does not equate social to marginal cost, then it is obvious that (3) cannot be satisfied by q^*, n^*. To complete the proof, we must show that if t is chosen to equate social to marginal cost, then (4) will not be satisfied by n^*, q^*.

Suppose that q^*, n^* satisfy (5) and (6) and let the Pigouvian tax $t^* = (1/n^*)(\partial D/\partial q)\,(n^*,q^*)$. For such a t^*, it is clear from (5) that (n^*,q^*) will also satisfy (3). However, for such a (t^*,n^*), q^* will not in general satisfy (4). To see this, rewrite (6) as

$$q^*P(n^*q^*) = C(q^*) + t^*q^* - t^*q^* + \frac{\partial D}{\partial n}(n^*,q^*),$$

or

$$q^*P(n^*q^*) = C(q^*) + t^*q^* + q^*\left[\frac{1}{q^*}\frac{\partial D}{\partial n}(n^*,q^*) - t^*\right], \tag{7}$$

or

$$q^*P(n^*q^*) = C(q^*) + t^*q^* + F^*,$$

where

$$F^* = q^*\left(\frac{1}{q^*}\frac{\partial D}{\partial n}(n^*,q^*) - t^*\right),$$

or using the definition of t^*,

$$F^* = q^*\left[\frac{1}{q^*}\frac{\partial D}{\partial n}(n^*,q^*) - \frac{1}{n^*}\frac{\partial D}{\partial q}(n^*,q^*)\right]. \tag{8}$$

It is immediately obvious from (7) that t^*, n^*, q^* will satisfy (4) iff $F^* = 0$. But there is no reason why F^* should always equal 0 (e.g., if $D(n,q) = nq^{1/2}$, then $F^* > 0$ for any $q > 0$).

Q.E.D.

The reasons for this failure of a pure Pigouvian tax instrument can be explained intuitively as follows. There are essentially two quantities, number of firms and scale of each firm, which the government is trying to control with just one instrument, the Pigouvian tax. In the short run the structure of the industry (n) is fixed and individual firm output is the only matter of concern. This last quantity can be completely controlled by a Pigouvian tax, which shifts marginal private costs so that they coincide with the marginal social costs at the socially optimal level of industry (and individual firm) production. In the long run, however, the industry structure is flexible and should be adjusted optimally along with individual firms' output. Yet the number of firms and the output of each firm cannot in general be varied independently in the long-run competitive equilibrium with just a Pigouvian tax. This is because the tax shifts the firm's average cost curve upward in a parallel manner. Minimum average tax-inclusive cost always occurs at q_s,[4] regardless of the tax rate t. By varying t, the government affects the number of firms but not their scale in the long run.

Only in the special case where, for any given industry output, externality damage is *independent* of individual firm scale (as occurs when constant returns to scale characterize the externality generation) will q_s be the optimal scale of the firm in the long-run social optimum. In such a case, the scale of an individual firm has no effect on externality damages, and the optimal scale is determined solely by production considerations. In this very special case, Pigouvian taxes can lead to the long-run social optimum.[5] The following theorem illustrates this point.

THEOREM 3. If for any given industry output, externality damages are independent of individual firm output so that $D(n,q) = \overline{D}(nq)$, then with appropriate Pigouvian taxation the long-run competitive equilibrium (LRCE) coincides with the long-run social optimum (LRSO).[6]

4. Recall that q_s is the output at which average production cost is minimized.

5. The intuition underlying this result should be clear. If for any industry output, externality damages are independent of firm scale, then only production cost considerations influence optimal firm scale. Competition takes these production considerations into account. Hence the tax need regulate only the number of firms, since competition takes care of optimal scale. One instrument can regulate one variable perfectly.

6. This result also appears in Schultze and D'Arge [1974].

Proof. Suppose that n^*,q^* are a LRSO and therefore satisfy (5) and (6). If $D(n,q) = \overline{D}(nq)$, then from (8) it is obvious that $F^* = 0$, and hence it follows from (7) that if $t^* = (1/n^*)(\partial D/\partial q)\,(n^*,q^*)$, then n^*, q^*, and t^* will satisfy (4), and it follows from (5) that they satisfy (3). Hence (n^*,q^*) represents a LRCE.

Q.E.D.

If the government can levy a lump sum entry tax-subsidy on active firms in the industry along with the Pigouvian tax, then the long-run social optimum can be attained. Define a long-run competitive equilibrium with Pigouvian tax t and lump sum tax F as the triple (p,q,n), which satisfies supply equals demand, price equals marginal cost, and profits equal zero. Using the inverse demand curve, we can write these conditions as

$$P(nq) = C'(q) + t, \tag{9}$$

and

$$qP(nq) = C(q) + tq + F. \tag{10}$$

We can now prove the following.

THEOREM 4. There is always a tax policy (t,F) such that the long-run competitive equilibrium (LRCE) coincides with the long-run social optimum (LRSO).

Proof. It is necessary to show that if q^*,n^* are a LRSO and hence satisfy (5) and (6), then there is a t^* and F^* such that q^*,n^* are a LRCE and hence satisfy (9) and (10).

Choose $t^* = (1/n^*)(\partial D/\partial q)\,(n^*,q^*)$ and define F^* as in (8). It is obvious from (5) that (9) is satisfied. It follows immediately from (7) that (10) is satisfied. Hence q^*,n^* represent a LRCE.

Q.E.D.

This simple result confirms intuition and assures that a Pigouvian tax supplemented by a lump sum tax can restore full optimality. The optimal lump sum F^* can be either negative, zero, or positive. However, as long as damages depend positively on output, the total tax payment $(F^* + t^*q^*)$ will always be positive. The optimal lump sum tax F^* will be positive (negative) when average pollution damage is falling (rising) at the optimal firm output.[7] Moreover, when payment of a lump sum subsidy is indicated $(F^* < 0)$, it can be effected

7. The proof of these results is available on request.

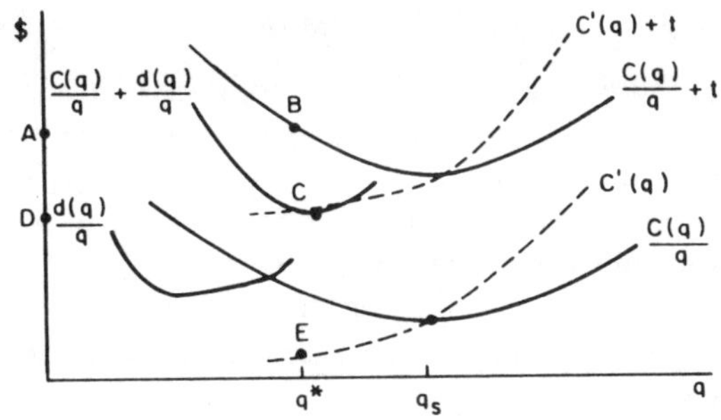

FIGURE I

by exempting the firm from payment of the Pigouvian tax on a certain amount (— F^*/t^*) of its output.[8]

IV. A Special Case

The case $D(n,q) = nd(q)$, in which the damage cost from the externality is additive across firms, is of particular interest because of its simplicity. Here the social cost function for the firm is simply $C(q) + d(q)$. The socially efficient solution requires that firms should pay a lump sum tax if the average damage function is falling at the optimal output level ($d'(q^*) > d(q^*)/q^*$). For the case where $d(q) = q^\alpha$, $\alpha > 0$, a lump sum tax or subsidy is required as α is less or greater than one. When $\alpha > 1$, the optimal lump sum subsidy can be determined without further knowledge of demand or technology. For this damage function, the optimal subsidy is equivalent to a tax exemption of $1 - 1/\alpha$ of a firm's output.

Figure I illustrates the determination of the optimal tax rate and subsidy for the case where $d(q)/q$ is rising at the social optimum. As the figure suggests, only if $d(q)/q$ is constant or else just happens to achieve a minimum at the same point as $C(q)/q$, can a simple Pigouvian tax guarantee a long-run social optimum. Here q^* is the socially optimal scale, while q_s is the scale that would prevail under simple Pigouvian taxation. The optimal subsidy is $ABCD$ and the optimal tax is CE.

8. Proof available on request. Notice that this way of distributing the subsidy completely avoids the problem often mentioned with regard to subsidies, that firms will simply collect the subsidy and produce zero output. Since it can be shown in general that total tax payments are always positive, this method of distributing subsidies can always be used. Moreover, if the exemption is interpreted as the property right allocation of the firm to pollute, it follows that only one assignment of property rights will be efficient.

V. Summary

This paper has argued that Pigouvian taxes alone cannot be expected to correct the most common forms of externalities in the long run. Pigouvian taxes alone are incapable of providing firms in long-run equilibrium with an incentive to operate at a scale of plant other than the one that minimizes average private cost. It is only by using lump sum subsidy or entry fees that a policy maker could guarantee that both marginal production incentives *and* incentives for entry into the industry are efficient.

University of Chicago
University of Michigan

References

Baumol, William, "On Taxation and the Control of Externalities," *American Economic Review,* LXII (1972), 307–32.
Pigou, A. C., *The Economics of Welfare,* 4th ed. (London: 1960).
Polinsky, A. M., "Notes on the Symmetry of Taxes and Subsidies in Pollution Control," Harvard Institute of Economic Research, 1977.
Schultze, W., and R. D'Arge, "The Coase Proposition, Information Constraints and Long Run Equilibrium," *American Economic Review,* LXIV (Sept. 1974), 763–72.

Part II
Ramsey Pricing

[9]

A CONTRIBUTION TO THE THEORY OF TAXATION

THE problem I propose to tackle is this: a given revenue is to be raised by proportionate taxes on some or all uses of income, the taxes on different uses being possibly at different rates; how should these rates be adjusted in order that the decrement of utility may be a minimum? I propose to neglect altogether questions of distribution and considerations arising from the differences in the marginal utility of money to different people; and I shall deal only with a purely competitive system with no foreign trade. Further I shall suppose that, in Professor Pigou's terminology, private and social net products are always equal or have been made so by State interference not included in the taxation we are considering. I thus exclude the case discussed in Marshall's *Principles* in which a bounty on increasing-return commodities is advisable. Nevertheless we shall find that the obvious solution that there should be no differentiation is entirely erroneous.

The effect of taxation is to transfer income in the first place from individuals to the State and then, in part, back again to rentiers and pensioners. These transfers will slightly alter the demand schedules in a way depending on the incidence of the taxes and the manner of their expenditure. I neglect these alterations;[1] and I also suppose that "a given revenue" means a given money revenue, "money" being so adjusted that its marginal utility is constant.

This problem was suggested to me by Professor Pigou, to whom I am also indebted for help and encouragement in its solution.

In the first part I deal with the perfectly general utility function and establish a result which is valid for a sufficiently small revenue, and takes a peculiarly simple form if we can treat the revenue as an infinitesimal. I prove, in fact, that in raising an infinitesimal revenue by proportionate taxes on given commodities the taxes should be such as to diminish in the same proportion the production of each commodity taxed.

In the second part I assume that the utility function is quadratic, which means roughly that the supply and demand

[1] The outline of a more general treatment is given in the Appendix.

curves are straight lines, but does not exclude the most general possibilities of joint supply and joint demand. With this assumption we can show that the rule given above for an infinitesimal revenue is valid for any revenue which can be raised at all.

In the third part I give certain important special cases of these general theorems; and in part four indicate certain practical applications.

PART I

(1) I suppose there to be altogether n commodities on which incomes are spent and denote the quantities of them which are produced in a unit of time by $x_1, x_2 \ldots x_n$. Some of these commodities may be identical, save for the place or manner of their production or consumption; *e.g.*, we can regard sugar used in tea as a different commodity from sugar used in coffee, and corn grown in Norfolk as different from that grown in Suffolk. In order to avoid double reckoning we suppose that these commodities are all either consumed or saved; *e.g.*, we include household coal, but not industrial coal except in so far as an increase in the stock of industrial coal is a form of saving, so that this rate of *increase* can form one of our quantities x. The quantities $x_1, x_2 \ldots$ can be measured in any convenient different units.

(2) We denote by $u = F(x_1 \ldots x_n)$ the *net* utility of producing and consuming (or saving) these quantities of commodities. This is usually regarded as the difference of two functions, one of which represents the utility of consuming, the other the disutility of producing. But so to regard it is to make an unnecessary assumption of independence between consumption and production; to assume, for instance, that the utility of a hot bath is the same whether one does or does not work in a coal mine. This assumption we do not require to make.

(3) If there is no taxation stable equilibrium will occur for values of the x's which make u a maximum. Let us call these values $\bar{x}_1, \bar{x}_2 \ldots \bar{x}_n$ or collectively the point P. Then at P we have

$$\frac{\partial u}{\partial x_r} = 0 \qquad r = 1, \ldots n.$$

$$d^2u = \Sigma\Sigma \frac{\partial^2 u}{\partial x_r \partial x_s} dx_r dx_s \text{ is a negative definite form.}$$

Suppose now taxes are levied on the different commodities

at the rates $\lambda_1, \lambda_2 \ldots \lambda_n$ per unit in money whose marginal utility is unity. Then the new equilibrium is determined by

$$\frac{\partial u}{\partial x_r} = \lambda_r{}^1 \qquad r = 1, \ldots n \quad . \quad . \quad . \quad . \quad (1)$$

In virtue of these equations we can regard the λ's as functions of the x's, which vanish at P, and satisfy identically

$$\frac{\partial \lambda_r}{\partial x_s} = \frac{\partial \lambda_s}{\partial x_r}\left(= \frac{\partial^2 u}{\partial x_r \partial x_s}\right) \quad . \quad . \quad . \quad . \quad (2)$$

Also the revenue $R = \Sigma\lambda_r x_r$.

We shall always suppose R to be positive, but there is no *a priori* reason why some of the λ's should not be negative; they will then, of course, represent bounties.

(4) Our first problem is this: given R, how should the λ's be chosen in order that the values of the x's given by equations (1) shall make u a maximum.

I.e., u is to be a maximum subject to $\Sigma\lambda_r x_r = R \left(\text{where } \lambda_r \text{ is } \frac{\partial u}{\partial x_r}\right)$.

We must have

$$0 = du = \Sigma\lambda_r dx_r \text{ for any values of } dx_r$$

subject to

$$0 = dR = \Sigma\lambda_r dx_r + \sum_r\sum_s x_s \frac{\partial \lambda_s}{\partial x_r} dx_r,$$

and so we have

$$\frac{\lambda_1}{\sum_s x_s \frac{\partial \lambda_s}{\partial x_1}} = \frac{\lambda_2}{\sum_s x_s \frac{\partial \lambda_s}{\partial x_2}} = \quad = \quad = \frac{\lambda_n}{\sum_s x_s \frac{\partial \lambda_s}{\partial x_n}} \quad . \quad . \quad (3)$$

$$= \frac{R}{\Sigma\Sigma \frac{\partial \lambda_s}{\partial x} x_r x_s} = -\theta \text{ (say)}.$$

(5) These equations determine values of the x's which are critical for u, and it remains to discuss the possibility of a plurality of solutions and to determine conditions under which they give a true maximum. We shall show that if R is small enough they will have a unique solution $x_1, x_2 \ldots x_n$, which tends to $\bar{x}_1, \bar{x}_2 \ldots \bar{x}_n$ as $R \to 0$, and that this solution will make u a true maximum.

[1] *E.g.*, if $u = u_1 - u_2$ (consumers' utility — producers' disutility)
$\frac{\partial u}{\partial x_r} = \frac{\partial u_1}{\partial x_r} - \frac{\partial u_2}{\partial x_r}$ = demand price of rth commodity — supply price = tax.

For, since $d^2u = \Sigma\Sigma \frac{\partial \lambda_r}{\partial x_s} dx_r dx_s$ is negative definite at P, $(-)^n \frac{\partial(\lambda_1, \lambda_2 \ldots \lambda_n)}{\partial(x_1, x_2 \ldots x_n)}$ is positive at, and therefore near, P. Hence we can express the x's as functions of the λ's. The equations (3) then become

$$\lambda_r = R\psi_r(\lambda_1, \ldots \lambda_n) \qquad r = 1, 2, \ldots n.$$

For the denominator $\Sigma\Sigma \frac{\partial \lambda_s}{\partial x_r} x_r x_s$ is a negative definite form with d^2u and so cannot vanish near P (and therefore also $\theta > 0$). The Jacobian of these last equations with regard to the λ's will tend to 1 as R tends to 0, and they will therefore have a unique solution $\lambda_1, \ldots \lambda_n$ which tends to $0, 0 \ldots 0$ as R tends to 0. Hence the equations (3) have a unique solution tending to P as $R \to 0$.

We have now to consider the conditions for a maximum which are obtained most simply by Lagrange's multipliers.

If we consider $u + KR$

we should have $$\frac{\partial u}{\partial x_r} + K\frac{\partial R}{\partial x_r} = 0$$

or $1 + K - \frac{K}{\theta} = 0$ if θ has the meaning it has in equations (3).

or $$K = \frac{+\theta}{1-\theta}.$$

Then $$d^2u = d^2\left(u + \frac{\theta}{1-\theta}R\right)$$
$$= d^2u + \frac{\theta}{1-\theta}d^2R$$

(calculated as if the variables x were independent [1]), and in a sufficiently small neighbourhood of P we shall have $\theta <$ any assigned positive constant and so $d^2u + \frac{\theta}{1-\theta}d^2R$ negative definite with d^2u. This establishes the desired result.[2]

(6) Suppose now R and the λ's can be regarded as infinitesimals; then putting

$$\lambda_r = \sum_s \frac{\partial \lambda_r}{\partial x_s} dx_s$$

equations (3) give us, using (2),

[1] See, *e.g.*, de la Vallée Poussin, *Cours d'Analyse*, 4th ed., t. 1, p. 149.

[2] Clearly also we shall get a maximum at any point for which d^2R is negative and $\theta < 1$; *i.e.*, if d^2R is everywhere negative (3) will give a maximum for all values of θ up to $\theta = 1$, which gives a maximum of R. This covers the case treated in Part II and so also any case approximating to that.

$$\frac{\sum_s \frac{\partial \lambda_r}{\partial x_s} dx_s}{\sum_s \frac{\partial \lambda_r}{\partial x_s} x_s} = \qquad = \qquad = -\theta = \frac{R}{\Sigma\Sigma x_r x_s \frac{\partial \lambda_r}{\partial x_s}} < 0,$$

and their solution is evidently given by

$$\frac{dx_1}{x_1} = \frac{dx_2}{x_2} = \qquad = \frac{dx_n}{x_n} = -\theta < 0 \quad . \quad . \quad . \quad (4)$$

i.e., the production of each commodity should be diminished in the same proportion.

(7) It is interesting to extend these results to the case of a given revenue to be raised by taxing certain commodities only. If the utility were the sum of two functions, one of the taxed and the other of the untaxed commodities, it is obvious that our conclusions would be the same as before. But in the general case the question is by no means so simple.

Let us denote the quantities of the commodities to be taxed by $x_1 \ . \ . \ . \ x_n$, and those not to be taxed by $y_1 \ . \ . \ . \ y_n$.

If $\quad \lambda_r = \frac{\partial u}{\partial x_r}$ then λ_r is the tax per unit on x_r,

and if $\quad \mu_r = \frac{\partial u}{\partial y_r}, \ \mu_r = 0$ (λ's and μ's functions of x's and y's),

also as before

$$\frac{\partial \lambda_r}{\partial x_s} = \frac{\partial \lambda_s}{\partial x_r}, \ \frac{\partial \mu_r}{\partial y_s} = \frac{\partial \mu_s}{\partial y_r}, \text{ and } \frac{\partial \lambda_r}{\partial y_s} = \frac{\partial \mu_s}{\partial x_r} \quad . \quad . \quad . \quad (5)$$

and we have to maximise u subject to

$$\sum_{r=1}^{n} \lambda_r x_r = R, \ \mu_t = 0, \ t = 1, \ . \ . \ . \ m.$$

We have

$$0 = du = \sum_r \lambda_r dx_r$$

$$0 = dR = \sum_r \lambda_r dx_r + \sum_s \sum_r x_s \frac{\partial \lambda_s}{\partial x_r} dx_r + \sum_s \sum_t x_s \frac{\partial \lambda_s}{\partial y_t} dy_t$$

$$0 = d\mu_t = \sum_r \frac{\partial \mu_t}{\partial x_r} dx_r + \sum_u \frac{\partial \mu_t}{\partial y_u} dy_u, \qquad t = 1, \ . \ . \ . \ m.$$

Solving these last equations ($d\mu_t = 0$) for the dy's we obtain

$$dy_t = \sum_r \chi_{tr} dx_r \quad . \quad . \quad . \quad . \quad . \quad . \quad . \quad (6)$$

where $\quad \frac{\partial \mu_t}{\partial x_r} + \sum_{u=1}^{m} \frac{\partial \mu_t}{\partial y_u} \chi_{ur} = 0 \begin{Bmatrix} r = 1, \ . \ . \ . \ n \\ t = 1, \ . \ . \ . \ m \end{Bmatrix} \quad . \quad . \quad . \quad (7)$

(The possibility of solution is guaranteed by the discriminants of d^2u not vanishing.)

Whence $\quad 0 = dR = \sum_r dx_r \left(\lambda_r + \sum_s x_s \frac{\partial \lambda_s}{\partial x_r} + \sum_s \sum_t x_s \frac{\partial \lambda_s}{\partial y_t} \chi_{tr} \right).$

E 2

∴ instead of equations (3) we have

$$\frac{\lambda_r}{\sum_{s=1}^{n} x_s\left(\frac{\partial\lambda_s}{\partial x_r} + \sum_{t=1}^{m} \chi_{tr}\frac{\partial\lambda_s}{\partial y_t}\right)} = \quad = \quad . \quad . \quad (3')$$

It can be shown that these give a maximum of u with the same sort of limitations as equations (3) do.

(8) And if the λ's are infinitesimal

$$\lambda_r = \sum_s \frac{\partial\lambda_r}{\partial x_s} dx_s + \sum_t \frac{\partial\lambda_r}{\partial y_t} dy_t$$

$$= \sum_{s=1}^{n} dx_s\left(\frac{\partial\lambda_s}{\partial x_r} + \sum_{t=1}^{m} \chi_{ts}\frac{\partial\mu_t}{\partial x_r}\right) \text{ by (5), (6).}$$

But $$\sum_t \chi_{ts}\frac{\partial\mu_t}{\partial x_r} = -\sum_t\sum_u \frac{\partial\mu_t}{\partial y_u}\chi_{ts}\chi_{ur} \text{ by (7)}$$

$$= \sum_t \chi_{tr}\frac{\partial\mu_t}{\partial x_s}\left(\text{by symmetry since } \frac{\partial\mu_t}{\partial y_u} = \frac{\partial\mu_u}{\partial y_t}\right).$$

So $$\lambda_r = \sum_s dx_s\left(\frac{\partial\lambda_s}{\partial x_r} + \sum_t \chi_{tr}\frac{\partial\lambda_s}{\partial y_t}\right), \text{ since } \frac{\partial\lambda_s}{\partial y_t} = \frac{\partial\mu_t}{\partial x_s},$$

and so equations (3′) are satisfied by

$$\frac{dx_1}{x_1} = \quad = \frac{dx_n}{x_n},$$

i.e., as before the taxes should be such as to reduce in the same proportion the production of each *taxed* commodity.

(9) Further than this it is difficult to go without making some new assumption. The assumption I propose is perhaps unnecessarily restrictive, but it still allows scope for all possible first-order relations between commodities in respect of joint supply or joint demand, and it has the great merit of rendering the problem completely soluble.

I shall assume that the utility is a non-homogeneous quadratic function of the x's, or that the λ's are linear. This assumption simplifies the problem in precisely the same way as we have previously simplified it by supposing the taxes to be infinitesimal. We shall, however, make this new assumption the occasion for exhibiting a method of interpreting our formulae geometrically in a manner which makes their meaning and mutual relations considerably clearer.

It is not, of course, necessary, nor would it be sensible to suppose the utility function quadratic for all values of the variables; we need only suppose it so for a certain range of values round the point P, such that there is no question of imposing taxes large enough to move the production point (values of the

x's) outside this range. If we were concerned with independent commodities, this assumption would mean that the taxes were small enough for us to treat the supply and demand curves as straight lines.

Part II

(10) Let $u = \text{constant} + \Sigma a_r x_r + \Sigma\Sigma \beta_{rs} x_r x_s$, $(\beta_{rs} = \beta_{sr})$, and let us regard the x's as rectangular Cartesian co-ordinates of points in n-dimensional space.

The point $P(\bar{x}_1, \ldots \bar{x}_n)$ is given by $\dfrac{\partial u}{\partial x_r} = 0$,

and at that point

$$d^2u = 2\Sigma\Sigma\beta_{rs}dx_r dx_s \text{ is a negative definite form.}$$

$$\therefore \Sigma\Sigma\beta_{rs}x_r x_s \text{ is a negative definite form,}$$

and the loci $u = \text{constant}$ are hyper-ellipsoids with the point P for centre.

Since
$$\lambda_r = \frac{\partial u}{\partial x_r} = a_r + 2\sum_s \beta_{rs} x_s \quad \ldots \ldots \quad (8)$$

$$R = \Sigma\lambda_r x_r = \Sigma a_r x_r + 2\Sigma\Sigma\beta_{rs}x_r x_s \quad \ldots \quad (9)$$

and the loci $R = \text{constant}$ are hyper-ellipsoids with the point Q, whose co-ordinates are $\frac{1}{2}\bar{x}_1, \frac{1}{2}\bar{x}_2 \ldots \frac{1}{2}\bar{x}_n$, for centre.

(The equations for Q are those for P with their first degree terms doubled and their constant terms unaltered.)

Moreover, the hyper-ellipsoids $u = \text{constant}$, $R = \text{constant}$ are all similar and similarly situated. The figure shows these relations for the case of two commodities only.

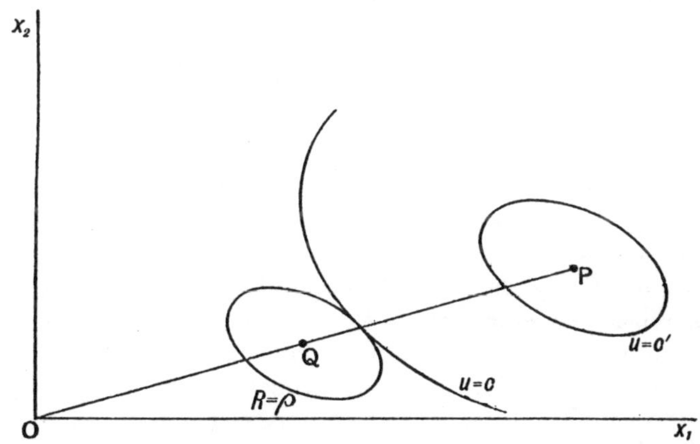

(11) If we are to raise a revenue ρ we must depress production to some point on the hyper-ellipsoid $R = \rho$.[1]

[1] We can depress production to any point we please because the connection between the x's and λ's is one-one.

To do this so as to make u a maximum we must choose a point on this hyper-ellipsoid at which it touches an ellipsoid of the family $u =$ constant. There will be two such points which will lie on the line PQ: one between Q and P making u a maximum, the other between O and Q making u a minimum. For the point of contact of two similar and similarly situated hyper-ellipsoids must lie on the line joining their centres. Since the maximum of u is given by a point on OP we have as before that

The taxes should be such as to diminish the production of all commodities in the same proportion.

And this result is now valid not merely for an infinitesimal revenue but for any revenue which it is possible to raise at all.

The maximum revenue will be obtained by diminishing the production of each commodity to one-half of its previous amount, *i.e.*, to the point Q.

(12) If in accordance with this rule we impose taxes reducing production from $\bar{x}_1, \bar{x}_2 \ldots \bar{x}_n$ to $(1 - k)\bar{x}_1, (1 - k)\bar{x}_2 \ldots (1 - k)\bar{x}_n$.

We get from (8) $\lambda_r = a_r + 2(1 - k)\sum_s \beta_{rs}\bar{x}_r$,

but at P $\qquad \lambda_r = 0$, so that $0 = a_r + 2\sum_r \beta_{rs}\bar{x}_r$;

therefore $\qquad \lambda_r = ka_r \quad . \quad . \quad . \quad . \quad . \quad . \quad . \quad . \quad (10)$

i.e., the taxes should be in the fixed proportions $\lambda_1 : \lambda_2 : : \lambda_n : : a_1 : a_2 : a_n$ independent of the revenue to be raised.

$$\text{Also } R = \Sigma\lambda_r x_r = k(1 - k)\Sigma a_r \bar{x}_r,$$
$$= 4k(1 - k) \times \text{the maximum revenue (got by putting } k = \tfrac{1}{2}).$$

(13) Since k is positive it follows from (10) that the sign of λ_r is the same as that of a_r, and unless the a_r are all positive some of the λ_r will be negative, and the most expedient way of raising a revenue will be by placing bounties on some commodities and taxes on others.

The sort of case in which this might occur is that of sugar and particularly sour fruits, *e.g.* damsons. A tax on sugar might reduce the consumption of damsons more than in proportion to the reduction in the total consumption of sugar and so require to be offset by a bounty on damsons.

(14) We can now consider the more general problem: a given revenue is to be raised by means of fixed taxes $\mu_1 \ldots \mu_m$ on m commodities and by taxes to be chosen at discretion on the remainder. How should they be chosen in order that utility may be a maximum?

We have $\lambda_1 = \mu_1, \ldots \lambda_m = \mu_m$, m hyperplanes ($n - 1$ folds) whose intersection is a plane $n - m$ fold which we will call S. S will cut the hyper-ellipsoids $u =$ constant, $R =$ constant in hyper-ellipsoids which are similar and similarly situated and whose centres are the points P', and Q' in which S is met by the m-folds through P and Q conjugate to S in $u = c$ or $R = c$. As before the required maximum is given by the point of contact of two of these hyper-ellipsoids in S, which must lie upon the line $P'Q'$.

Now the hyperplane $\lambda_1 = \mu_1$ or $\frac{\partial u}{\partial x_1} = \mu_1$ is conjugate in $u = c$ to the diameter

$$x_2 = \bar{x}_2,\ x_3 = \bar{x}_3,\ \ldots\ x_n = \bar{x}_n.$$

Hence S is conjugate to the m-fold

$$x_{m+1} = \bar{x}_{m+},\ \ldots,\ x_n = \bar{x}_n,$$

and the co-ordinates of P' satisfy these equations, since they lie on this m-fold.

Similarly the co-ordinates of Q' satisfy

$$x_{m+1} = \tfrac{1}{2}\bar{x}_{m+1},\ \ldots\ x_n = \tfrac{1}{2}\bar{x}_n.$$

And so the desired production point lying on the line $P'Q'$ satisfies

$$\frac{x_{m+1}}{\bar{x}_{m+1}} = \frac{x_{m+2}}{\bar{x}_{m+2}} = \qquad = \frac{x_n}{\bar{x}_n},$$

i.e., the whole system of taxes must be such as to reduce in the same proportion the production of the commodities taxed at discretion.

PART III

(15) I propose now to explain what our results reduce to in certain special cases. First suppose that all the commodities are independent and have their own supply and demand equations, *i.e.*, we have for the rth commodity the demand price

$$p_r = \phi_r(x_r)$$

and the supply price $\qquad q_r = f_r(x_r).$

$\therefore \qquad \lambda_r = p_r - q_r = \phi_r(x_r) - f_r(x_r),$

and equations (3) become, since $\frac{\partial \lambda_r}{\partial x_s} = 0,\ r \neq s,$

$$\frac{\lambda_1}{x_1\{\phi_1'(x_1) - f_1'(x_1)\}} = \frac{\lambda_2}{x_2\{\phi_2'(x_2) - f_2'(x_2)\}} = \ldots = -\theta.$$

These equations we can express in terms of elasticities in the following way.

Suppose the tax *ad valorem* (reckoned on the price got by the producer) on the rth commodity is μ_r, then

$$\lambda_r = \mu_r q_r = \mu_r f_r(x_r),$$

and $$\phi_r(x_r) = f_r(x_r) + \lambda_r = (1 + \mu_r) f_r(x_r).$$

$$\therefore \qquad \theta = \frac{-\lambda_r}{x_r\{\phi_r'(x_r) - f_r'(x_r)\}} = \frac{+\mu_r}{x_r \dfrac{f_r'(x_r)}{f_r(x_r)} - (1 + \mu_r) x_r \dfrac{\phi_r'(x_r)}{\phi_r(x_r)}},$$

now $x_r \dfrac{f_r'(x_r)}{f_r(x_r)}$ is the reciprocal of the elasticity of supply of the commodity reckoned positive for diminishing returns, and $-x_r \dfrac{\phi_r'(x_r)}{\phi_r(x_r)}$ is the reciprocal of the elasticity of demand, reckoned positive in the normal case.

Hence if we denote by ρ_r and ϵ_r the elasticities of demand and supply,

$$\mu_r = \theta\left(\frac{1}{\epsilon_r} + \frac{1 + \mu_r}{\rho_r}\right),$$

or $$\mu_r = \frac{\left(\dfrac{1}{\epsilon_r} + \dfrac{1}{\rho_r}\right)\theta}{1 - \dfrac{\theta}{\rho_r}} \quad . \quad . \quad . \quad . \quad . \quad . \quad . \quad (11)$$

(valid provided the revenue is small enough, see § 5).

For infinitesimal taxes θ is infinitesimal and

$$\frac{\mu_1}{\dfrac{1}{\epsilon_1} + \dfrac{1}{\rho_1}} = \qquad = \qquad = \frac{\mu_n}{\dfrac{1}{\epsilon_n} + \dfrac{1}{\rho_n}} \quad . \quad . \quad (12)$$

i.e., the tax *ad valorem* on each commodity should be proportional to the sum of the reciprocals of its supply and demand elasticities.

(16) It is easy to see

(1) that the same rule (12) applies if the revenue is to be collected off certain commodities only, which have supply and demand schedules independent of each other and all other commodities, even when the other commodities are not independent of one another.

(2) The rule does not justify any bounties; for in stable equilibrium, although $\dfrac{1}{\epsilon_r}$ may be negative, $\dfrac{1}{\rho_r} + \dfrac{1}{\epsilon_r}$ must be positive.

(3) If any one commodity is absolutely inelastic, either for supply or for demand, the whole of the revenue should be

collected off it. This is independently obvious, for taxing such a commodity does not diminish utility at all. If there are several such commodities the whole revenue should be collected off them, it does not matter in what proportions.

(17) Let us next take the case in which all the commodities have independent demand schedules but are complete substitutes for supply; *i.e.*, with appropriate units the demand price

$$p_r = \phi_r(x_r),$$

the supply price $$q_r = f(x_1 + \quad + x_n).$$

Let us put $$z = x_1 + \quad + x_n.$$

We can imagine this case as that of a country in which all commodities are produced at constant returns by the application of one kind of labour only, the increase in the supply price arising solely from the increasing marginal disutility of labour, and the commodities satisfying independent needs. Then z will represent the amount of labour.

Equations (3) give us

$$-\theta = \frac{\lambda_r}{x_r\phi_r'(x_r) - zf'(z)}.$$

Or if μ_r represents the tax *ad valorem* and ρ_r the elasticity of demand for the rth commodity and ϵ the elasticity of supply of things in general, we get, by a similar process to that of § 15,

$$\mu_r = \frac{\left(\frac{1}{\rho_r} + \frac{1}{\epsilon}\right)\theta}{1 - \frac{\theta}{\rho_r}} \quad . \quad . \quad . \quad . \quad . \quad . \quad (13)$$

If the taxes are infinitesimal we have

$$\frac{\mu_r}{\frac{1}{\rho_r} + \frac{1}{\epsilon}} = \quad = \quad = \theta \quad . \quad . \quad . \quad . \quad (14)$$

In this case we see that if the supply of labour is fixed (absolutely inelastic, $\epsilon \to 0$) the taxes should be at the same *ad valorem* rate on all commodities.

(19) If some commodities only are to be taxed it is easier to work from the result proved in § 8 for an infinitesimal revenue, that the production of the commodities taxed should be diminished in the same ratio.

Suppose, then, $x_1, \ldots x_m$ are to be taxed, $x_{m+1} \ldots x_n$ untaxed.

Let $$dx_1 = -kx_1, \ldots, dx_m = -kx_m.$$

Let
$$z' = x_1 + x_2 + \ldots + x_m$$
$$z'' = x_{m+1} + \ldots + x_n.$$
$$\lambda_1 = \phi_1(x + dx_1) - zf(z + dz)$$
$$= \phi_1'(x_1)dx_1 - f'(z)dz.$$

$$\therefore \qquad \mu_1 = \frac{k}{\rho_1} - \frac{dz}{z\epsilon} \ldots, \mu_m = \frac{k}{\rho_m} - \frac{dz}{\epsilon z},$$

now
$$dz = dz' + dz'' = -kz' + dz'',$$

also
$$0 = -\frac{dx_{m+1}}{\rho_{m+1}x_{m+1}} - \frac{dz}{\epsilon z}.$$

$$\therefore \qquad \frac{dx_{m+1}}{\rho_{m+1}x_{m+1}} = \frac{dx_{m+2}}{\rho_{m+2}x_{m+2}} = \frac{dx_n}{\rho_n x_n} = -\frac{dz}{\epsilon z} = \frac{dz''}{\sum_{m+1}^{n}\rho_r x_r} = \frac{kz'}{\epsilon z + \sum_{m+1}^{n}\rho_r x_r}.$$

$$\therefore \qquad \mu_1 = k\left(\frac{1}{\rho_1} + \frac{\sum_{1}^{m}x_r}{\epsilon\sum_{1}^{n}x_r + \sum_{m+1}^{n}\rho_r x_r}\right), \text{ etc.}$$

As before we see that of two commodities that should be taxed most which has the least elasticity of demand, but that if the supply of labour is absolutely inelastic all the commodities should be taxed equally.

Part IV

(20) We come now to applications of our theory; these cannot be made at all exactly without data which I, at any rate, do not possess. The simplest result is the one which we have proved in the general case for an infinitesimal revenue (§ 8); this means that it is approximately true for small revenues, and that the approximation approaches perfection as the revenue approaches zero. It is thus logically similar to the theorem that the period of oscillation of a pendulum is independent of the amplitude. We have also extended the result to any revenue which does not take the production point outside a region in which the utility may be taken to be quadratic, *i.e.*, the supply and demand schedules linear.

The sort of cases in which our theory may be useful are the following:

(21) (*a*) If a commodity is produced by several different methods or in several different places between which there is no mobility of resources, it is shown that it will be advantageous to discriminate between them and tax most the source of supply which is least elastic. For this will be necessary if we are to maintain unchanged the proportion of production between the two sources (result analogous to § 19 with supply and demand interchanged).

(*b*) If several commodities which are independent for demand require precisely the same resources for their production, that should be taxed most for which the elasticity of demand is least (§ 19).

(*c*) In taxing commodities which are rivals for demand, like wine, beer and spirits, or complementary like tea and sugar, the rule to be observed is that the taxes should be such as to leave unaltered the proportions in which they are consumed (§ 14). Whether the present taxes satisfy this criterion I do not know.

(*d*) In the case of the motor taxes we must separate off so much of the taxation as is offset by damage to the roads. This part should be so far as possible equal to the damage done. The remainder is a genuine tax and should be distributed according to our theory; that is to say, it should be placed partly on petrol and partly on motor-cars, so as to preserve unchanged the proportion between their consumption, and should be distributed between Fords and Morrises, so as to reduce their output in the same ratio. The present system fails in both these respects.

(22) (*e*) Another possible application of our theory is to the question of exempting savings from income-tax.[1] We may consider two uses of income only, saving and spending, and supposing them independent we may use the result (13) in § 17. We must suppose the taxes imposed only for a very short time [2] and that they raise no expectation of similar taxation in the future; since otherwise we require a mathematical theory considerably more difficult than anything in this paper.

On these assumptions, since the amount of saving in the very short time cannot be sufficient to alter appreciably the marginal utility of capital, the elasticity of demand for saving will be infinite, and we have

$$\mu_1 \text{ (tax on spending)} = \frac{\left(\frac{1}{\rho_1} + \frac{1}{\epsilon}\right)\theta}{1 - \frac{\theta}{\rho_1}},$$

$$\mu_2 \text{ (tax on saving)} = \frac{1}{\epsilon}\theta,$$

and we see that income-tax should be partially but not wholly remitted on savings. The case for remission would, however,

[1] No account is taken of graduation in this.

[2] Strictly, we consider the limit as this time tends to zero.

be strengthened enormously by taking into account the expectation of taxation in the future.

(23) It should be emphasized in conclusion that the results about "infinitesimal" taxes can only claim to be approximately true for small taxes, how small depending on data which are not obtainable. It is perfectly possible that a tax of 500% on whisky could for the present purpose be regarded as small. The unknown factors are the curvatures of the supply and demand curves; if these are zero our results will be true for any revenue whatever, but the greater the curvatures the narrower the range of "small" taxes.

On the other hand, the more complicated results contained in equations (3), (3′), (11), (13) may well be valid under still wider conditions. But these are, in the general case, too complicated to be worth setting down in the absence of practical data to compare with them.

APPENDIX

We can also say something about the more general problem in which the State wishes to raise a revenue for two purposes; first, as before, a fixed money revenue, R_1, which is transferred to rentiers or otherwise without effect on the demand schedules; and secondly, an additional revenue, R_2, sufficient to purchase fixed quantities, $a_1, a_2, \ldots a_n$ of each commodity.

Let us denote by p_r, q_r, as before, the demand and supply prices of the rth commodity, and the tax on it by λ_r. Then if x_r is the amount of the rth commodity consumed by the public (or by the State out of R_1), $x_r + a_r$ is the amount produced, and we have

$$\frac{\partial u}{\partial x_r} = \lambda_r = p_r(x_1, x_2, \ldots, x_n) - q_r(x_1 + a_1, x_2 + a_2, \ldots, x_n + a_n),$$

$$R_1 + R_2 = \Sigma \lambda_r x_r, \quad R_2 = \Sigma a_r q_r;$$

so that u is to be a maximum subject to

$$\Sigma \lambda_r x_r - \Sigma a_r q_r = R_1 = \text{constant},$$

whence

$$\frac{\lambda_r}{\sum_s x_s \frac{\partial \lambda_s}{\partial x_r} - \sum_s a_s \frac{\partial q_s}{\partial x_r}} = \quad = \quad = -\theta$$

or

$$\frac{\lambda_r}{\sum_s (a_s + x_s)\frac{\partial q_s}{\partial x_r} - \sum_s x_s \frac{\partial p_s}{\partial x_r}} = \theta, \text{ which replace equations (3).}$$

Although these equations do not give such simple results as we previously obtained for an infinitesimal revenue or a quadratic utility function, in the cases considered in § 15 and § 17 they lead us again to the equations (11) and (13).

For, taking the case of § 15, in which the commodities are independent both for demand and supply, and, as before, denoting by μ_r the rate of tax *ad valorem* on the rth commodity and by ρ_r, ϵ_r its elasticities of demand and supply for the amounts x_r, $x_r + a_r$ respectively consumed and produced by the public, we have

$$\frac{\mu_r}{\dfrac{x_r + a_r}{q_r}\dfrac{dq_r}{d(x_r + a_r)} - \dfrac{x_r}{q_r}\dfrac{dp_r}{dx_r}} = \theta$$

or

$$\frac{\mu_r}{\dfrac{1}{\epsilon_r} + \dfrac{1 + \mu_r}{\rho_r}} = \theta$$

whence $\mu_r = \dfrac{\left(\dfrac{1}{\epsilon_r} + \dfrac{1}{\rho_r}\right)\theta}{1 - \dfrac{\theta}{\rho_r}}$, which is equation (11) again. And we can similarly derive equation (13) from the assumption of independence for demand and equivalence for supply.

F. P. RAMSEY

[10]

On the Management of Public Monopolies Subject to Budgetary Constraints*

M. Boiteux

Le Directeur Général, Electricité de France, 2, Rue Louis Murat, Paris, 8e France

Received September 18, 1969

1. Problem and Method

1.1. The writings on social welfare or "collective benefit" call for the firm to operate as though it were maximizing its profits at constant prices. In the case of monopolies, this requires the entrepreneur to substitute for his natural behavior the marginal cost pricing rule. However, this rule often turns out to be inapplicable, at least to public enterprises, for it can lead either to systematic deficits which the public authorities refuse to underwrite, or to profits, which these same public authorities, whether for misguided reasons or on good grounds, insist be returned to consumers in the form of lower selling prices.

One is therefore left with the problem of determining how to amend the marginal cost pricing rule when the firm is subjected to a budgetary condition incompatible with this decision rule.

1.2. Problems of this variety can be analyzed with the aid of an expression that gives the social (opportunity) loss associated (with any pricing arrangement) [11; 1, p. 637; 5; 8]. One then seeks, in the neighborhood of the optimum, the economic state compatible with the constraint that minimizes the loss thus defined.[1] But aside from the difficulties encountered in defining that loss, the method suffers from the defect that it limits investigations to infinitesimal variations in the

* The translation from French to English is by William J. Baumol and David F. Bradford, Department of Economics, Princeton University, Princeton, New Jersey 08540. Minor changes have been made to correct typographical errors and inconsistencies in the original. The article first appeared as "Sur la gestion des Monopoles Publics astreints à l'équilibre budgétaire," *Econometrica*, Volume 24, No. 1, January 1956, pp 22–40.

[1] We utilized this approach to deal with the same problem in Section 4 of an earlier article [5] and obtained for the neighborhood of the optimum the same formulae as those given below. But our expression for the loss was rendered obsolete by that given by Debreu several months later. This raised a number of questions about the rigor of the derivations in Section 4.

642/3/3-1

neighborhood of the optimal solution, a serious shortcoming since it implies that the constraints are infinitesimally close to the "natural" conditions in the optimal situation under consideration.

The method proposed here avoids these difficulties; it consists in the addition of the imposed constraints to the natural relationships that limit the freedom of the variables of the economic system, and the writing of the Pareto optimality conditions in the framework of these various relationships.

The procedure appears quite natural when the constraints imposed are physical conditions among the quantities exchanged (import quotas, arrangements circumscribing international trades). But it is equally applicable when the supplementary constraints deal with values. It suffices to consider that the variables of the system include, beside the quantities of goods and services usually considered, the individual prices and incomes. The structure of the economic system is then defined by the classical quantitative relations and by the constraints relating quantities and prices which determine the nature of the behavior imputed to those economic entities whose activity is not taken into account. The supplementary constraints which will be studied (the regulated and unregulated sectors, taxes, etc.) must be added to the preceding structural constraints. The problem consists of the determination of the behavior of those economic entities whose rules of action constitute our unknowns, in order to yield results for the economic system that are optimal within the constraints.

It is this method, with its more general range, that we propose to apply to the study of the problem described in 1.1.

2. Notation and Model

2.1. Each individual $k = 1,\ldots, m$ consumes (furnishes) per unit of time the vector Q^k whose elements are the quantities q_i^k of the goods or services $i, j = 1,\ldots, n$ (the services supplied are represented by negative quantities).

The satisfaction yielded to the individual by this consumption is

$$S^k = S^k(Q^k) \qquad (k = 1,\ldots, m). \tag{1}$$

The individual k maximizes his satisfaction, taking into account the vector of prices P (whose elements are $p_1, p_2, \ldots, p_n$) and the income

r^k which he receives over and above the wages of his labor, so that

$$P' \cdot Q^k = r^k \qquad (k = 1, \ldots, m), \tag{2}$$

$$\frac{\partial S^k / \partial q_i^k}{p_i} = \frac{\partial S^k / \partial q_j^k}{p_j} \qquad (k = 1, \ldots, m; \quad i, j = 1, \ldots, n). \tag{3}$$

2.2. The productive system contains two sectors. In the first, each enterprise $h = 1, \ldots, v$ produces (consumes) the vector[2] X^h whose elements are the quantities x_i^h, which are positive if i is produced by enterprise h, and negative if it is consumed there. The production function of firm h is

$$f^h(X^h) = 0 \qquad (h = 1, \ldots, v). \tag{4}$$

The firms in the first sector maximize their incomes taking into account the set of prices P. Letting f_i^h designate the derivative of f^h with respect to x_i^h

$$f_i^h / p_i = f_j^h / p_j \qquad (h = 1, \ldots, v; \quad i, j = 1, \ldots, n). \tag{5}$$

From this manner of operation, each firm h derives some profit (or loss) not subject to any particular requirement.

2.3. In the second production sector, each firm $h = 1, \ldots, w$ produces (consumes) the vector Y^h. Its production function is

$$g^h(Y^h) = 0 \qquad (h = 1, \ldots, w). \tag{6}$$

We seek to determine *what the rules of operation of the firms of this second sector ought to be*, in order for it to serve most effectively the general interest within the framework of a budgetary constraint given for each enterprise:

$$P' \cdot Y^h = b^h \qquad (h = 1, \ldots, w). \tag{7}$$

(Put in another way, behavior, in the first sector, is given—maximization of profits subject to constant prices—and profits are subject to no restriction. In the second, behavior constitutes the unknown of the problem, but profits are fixed.)

2.4. The equations of equilibrium of the flows produced and consumed are

$$\sum_k q_i^k = \sum_h x_i^h + \sum_h y_i^h \qquad (i = 1, \ldots, n). \tag{8}$$

[2] All of the vectors $Q^k (k = 1, \ldots, m)$, $X^h (h = 1, \ldots, v)$, $Y^h (h = 1, \ldots, w)$ belong to the same space, one of n dimensions, as that of goods $i, j = 1, \ldots, n$.

2.5. Let us take as our criterion of general welfare the Pareto criterion according to which a situation is optimal if it is impossible to modify the quantities exchanged in a way that increase the satisfaction of one individual without necessarily reducing that of some other. The behavior of the firms of the second sector will be determined in requiring one of the levels of satisfaction S^k to be maximal, given the interrelationships of the system, if all other levels of satisfaction are fixed.

The given elements of the system are therefore $m - 1$ values of satisfactions (utilities) S^k, and the w values of the profits b^h of the firms in the second section.

The variables are one of the S^k, the mn quantities q_i^k, the n prices p_i, the m incomes r^k, the nv quantities x_i^h, and the nw quantities y_i^h. But since the prices enter in a homogeneous manner throughout the system the n prices constitute no more than $n - 1$ independent variables[3] so that there are, in total,

$$1 + mn + n - 1 + m + nv + nw \text{ independent variables.}$$

The relationships among the variables consist of

- m utility functions (1),
- mn relationships (2) and (3) which define consumers' behavior,
- nv relationships (4) and (5) which describe the behavior of the v firms in the first sector,
- $2w$ relationships (6) and (7) which define the constraints to which the undetermined behavior of the w firms of the second sector are subject,
- n relationships of flow equilibrium (8),

making, in total, $m + mn + nv + 2w + n$ relationships among the variables.

The degrees of freedom are therefore $(n - 2)w$, *corresponding to* $(n - 2)$ *conditions to be obtained in determining the rules of optimal management of the firms in the second group*, with $n - 2$ conditions per firm.

3. Interpretation of the Model

3.1. Individuals are assumed to satisfy precisely their marginal relationships (3).

The firms of the first group maximize their profits at constant prices

[3] To eliminate the arbitrariness of the price level, in what follows we will take the price p_n to be fixed. Good n therefore plays the role of a standard commodity.

(relations 5); their behavior is that which would be adopted on their own volition by perfectly competitive firms, both in the sale of their products and in the purchases of their inputs.

One recognizes, on the contrary, that the firms of the second group can be subjected to the administrative rules which this study will show to be optimal.

The model just described thus schematizes the situation in which both private and publicly operated enterprises find themselves. The former tend to maximize their profits in freedom, while the latter are assigned the mission of serving *consciously* the general welfare without violating the budgetary constraints imposed on them by the public authorities.

In fact, the behavior of private firms differs for a variety of reasons from that of enterprises operating under perfect competition. This is particularly apparent in the case of firms enjoying a natural monopoly in their sales or their purchases.

But all of these problems cannot be resolved simultaneously. We assume here that the nonnationalized enterprises exhibit "perfect behavior," but we leave ourselves free to study later the problem of "an imperfect environment" [7, pp. 158–185].

We can, alternatively, interpret our model in another way. The first group here is composed of those firms which can be assumed to operate under conditions approximating those of perfect competition. The object of the study is then to determine the administrative rules which are appropriately imposed on the remaining firms, whether nationalized or not, which best serve the general welfare, if each is required to satisfy a budgetary equilibrium condition.

Under the first interpretation, one determines, for the nationalized firms, administrative rules which the public authorities have the power to impose. But these rules are subject to the warning that they rest on an assumption of perfect competition among private firms. The second interpretation leads to rules resting on a firmer foundation, but which remain academic to the extent that the number of firms to which they must be applied exceeds that which can effectively be dealt with by the public authorities.

When we want to offer a specific interpretation of the results, we will generally utilize the former interpretation.

3.2. As will be shown subsequently, in the absence of budgetary constraints the optimal administrative rules for firms in the second group become the same as the maximization of profit with fixed prices, and thus they require both the equality of product prices to their marginal costs, and the equality of input prices to their marginal products.

The optimal behavior of firms of the second group, then, may be described by relationships of the following type:

$$g_i^h/p_i = g_j^h/p_j \qquad (h = 1,..., w; \quad i, j = 1,..., n).$$

The supplementary constraints imposed by the budgetary requirements cause modifications in the optimal output and input quantities for the firms h of the second group, and the preceding conditions will, as a consequence, no longer hold. Instead of being proportionate to the elements of the price vector P the partial derivatives of the production function g^h will be proportioned to the components of a certain vector Π^h, and it is our task to determine its elements.

In effect, knowledge of vector Π^h suffices to define the behavior of firm h since the quantities of its outputs (inputs) are the solution of the system

$$g^h(Y^h) = 0 \qquad (h = 1,..., w),$$
$$g_i^h/\pi_i^h = g_j^h/\pi_j^h \qquad (i, j = 1,..., n).$$

In this system, the elements of vector Π^h take the form of a set of prices.

Determination of the optimal behavior of firms of the second sector is thus equivalent to determination of the vectors of "fictitious prices" Π^h on whose basis each firm h ought to maximize its profits.

3.3. The vector Π^h is defined only up to a factor of proportionality. To remove this arbitrary element, we adopt the convention of taking its n-th component to be equal to the reference price p_n. Thus

$$\pi_n^h = p_n ,$$

whereby $\pi_i^h = p_n g_i^h/g_n^h$.

In fact, the calculations that follow do not determine the vector Π^h itself, but its difference T^h from the price vector P:

$$T^h = P - \Pi^h,$$

a vector whose components consequently take the form

$$t_i^h = p_i - \pi_i^h = p_i - p_n g_i^h/g_n^h \qquad (i = 1,..., n - 1; \quad h = 1,..., w). \quad (9)$$

4. Transformation of the Model's Relationships

4.1. Equations (2) and (3) determine the individual demand (supply) functions

$$Q^k = Q^k(P, r^k), \qquad (10)$$

among whose properties the following are noteworthy:

(i) The (utility) function $S^k(P, r^k) \equiv S^k[Q^k(P, r^k)]$ satisfies identically [12] the relationship

$$S_i^k + q_i^k S_r^k \equiv 0, \tag{11}$$

where S_i^k represents the partial derivative of $S^k(P, r^k)$ with respect to p_i and S_r^k its partial derivative with respect to r^k;

(ii) The [Hicksian] substitution term of goods i and j for individual k,[4]

$$(ij)^k = (ji)^k = \frac{\partial q_i^k}{\partial p_j} + q_j^k \frac{\partial q_i^k}{\partial r^k},$$

satisfy identically [13, p. 107] the relationship

$$\sum_i p_i(ij)^k \equiv 0. \tag{12}$$

One can, therefore, substitute for relationships (2) and (3) the relationship (10), taking note of the identities (11) and (12).

4.2. Equations (4) and (5) determine the supply (demand) functions for firm h, i.e.,

$$X^h = X^h(P), \tag{13}$$

which, in particular, satisfy [13, p. 68][5] the property

$$\sum_i p_i(ij)^h \equiv 0, \tag{14}$$

where $(ij)^h = (ji)^h = \partial x_i^h/\partial p_j$ represents the coefficient of substitution between goods i and j in firm h.

One can, therefore, substitute for Eqs. (4) and (5) the Eqs. (13), taking note of identity (14).

4.3. Designating relationships by use of the Greek letters that will

[4] I.e., $\partial x_i/\partial p_j = \partial x_j/\partial p_i$ when income effects have been removed. Boiteux calls it the "coefficient of substitution," a usage to which we will adhere [trans.].

[5] While this property can be derived from Samuelson's discussion near the page cited it does not appear there explicitly [trans.].

serve as the corresponding Lagrange multipliers, the constraints of the model finally take the following form:

$$(\lambda^k) \qquad S^k - S^k(P, r^k) = 0 \qquad (k = 1,..., m),$$

$$(\mu_i) \qquad \sum_k q_i^k(P, r^k) - \sum_h x_i^h(P) - \sum_h y_i^h = 0 \qquad (i = 1,..., n),$$

$$(\phi^h) \qquad g^h(Y^h) = 0 \qquad (h = 1,..., w),$$

$$(\beta^h) \qquad P' \cdot Y^h - b^h = 0 \qquad (h = 1,..., w),$$

where the functions $S^k(P, r^k)$, $Q^k(P, r^k)$ and $X^h(P)$ satisfy identically the relationships (11), (12) and (14).

5. Maximization

The $(n - 2)w$ conditions that we seek are obtained by maximizing the sum of the first members of the relationships of the model multiplied, respectively, by the Lagrange multipliers by which they are designated, and then eliminating these coefficients.[6]

5.1. The condition obtained by setting equal to zero the coefficient of dp_j in the total differential of this sum will be labelled $\underline{(dp_j)}$. The same notation will be used for the other variables.

$$\underline{(dp_j)} \qquad -\sum_k \lambda^k S_j^k + \sum_i \mu_i \left[\left(\sum_k \frac{\partial q_i^k}{\partial p_j} - \sum_h \frac{\partial x_i^h}{\partial p_j}\right)\right] + \sum_h \beta^h y_j^h = 0$$

$$(j = 1,..., n - 1)^7,$$

$$\underline{(dr^k)} \qquad -\lambda^k S_r^k + \sum_i \mu_i \frac{\partial q_i^k}{\partial r^k} = 0 \qquad (k = 1,..., m).$$

The combination $\underline{(dp_j)} + \sum_k q_j^k \underline{(dr^k)}$ leads to the relationship

$$-\sum_k \lambda^k (S_j^k + q_j^k S_r^k) + \sum_i \mu_i (ij) + \sum_h \beta^h y_j^h = 0,$$

where one has set

$$(ij) = \sum_k \left[\left(\frac{\partial q_i^k}{\partial p_j} + q_j^k \frac{\partial q_i^k}{\partial r^k}\right)\right] - \sum_h \frac{\partial x_i^h}{\partial p_j} = \sum_k (ij)^k - \sum_h (ij)^h.$$

[6] We will not concern ourselves here with the second-order maximum conditions.

[7] p_n being fixed to eliminate the arbitrariness in the price level, there is no relationship (dp_n).

Here $(ij)^k$ designates the coefficient of substitution of goods i and j for individual k so that $\sum_k (ij)^k$ is the coefficient of substitution of goods i and j for the entire set of household consumers (suppliers). Similarly, $\sum_h (ij)^h$ is the global coefficient of substitution between i and j for firms of the first category. (ij) is, therefore, the overall coefficient of substitution between i and j for the set of consumers and suppliers (domestic and industrial) other than those of the second category, i.e., *the coefficient of substitution between goods i and j for the clientele (suppliers) of firms in the second group.*

By properties (12) and (14), the coefficient of substitution (ij) also satisfies the identity

$$\sum_i p_i(ij) \equiv 0. \tag{15}$$

Returning to the condition obtained by the formation of the combination $(\underline{dp_j}) + \sum_k q_j^k(\underline{dr^k})$ we note that the λ^k are eliminated when we take into account the identity (11). Then, there remains only

$$\sum_i \mu_i(ij) = -\sum_h \beta^h y_j^h \qquad (j = 1,..., n-1). \tag{16}$$

These equations take the form of a system of $n - 1$ equations in n unknowns, the μ_i. But identity (15) can be written[8]

$$\sum_i^n p_i(ij) + p_n(nj) \equiv 0.$$

On substituting this value of (nj) into Eqs. (16) and writing

$$z_i = \mu_i - \mu_n(p_i/p_n) \qquad (i = 1,..., n - 1), \tag{17}$$

these relationships finally constitute a system of $n - 1$ equations in $n - 1$ unknowns, the z_i:

$$\sum_i^n z_i(ij) = -\sum_h \beta^h y_j^h \qquad (j = 1,..., n-1). \tag{18}$$

5.2. Setting equal to zero the coefficient of dy_i^l one obtains the relationship

$$(\underline{dy_j^l}) \qquad \mu_i = \phi^l g_i^l + \beta^l p_i,$$

so that, by (17),

$$z_i = (\beta^l - \mu_n/p_n)(p_i - g_i^l p_n/g_n^l).$$

[8] The symbol Σ_i^j represents a sum extending over $i = 1,..., n$ except for j.

Since the Lagrange multipliers enter all these relationships homogeneously, it is possible to assign an arbitrary value to one of them. One can, e.g., set $\mu_n = -p_n$.

Taking account of (9), one can, therefore, write

$$z_i = (1 + \beta^l)\, t_i^l \qquad (i = 1,..., n-1; \quad l = 1,..., w), \tag{19}$$

where t_i^l represents, as was said earlier, the deviation between the actual price p_i and the fictitious price π_i^l which defines the behavior of firm l (see 3.3).

5.3. One verifies that in the absence of budgetary constraints, i.e. (see 4.3), for

$$\beta^h = 0 \qquad (h = 1,..., w),$$

the system (18) permits only the trivial solution

$$z_i = 0 \qquad (i = 1,..., n-1),$$

and the relations (19) yield

$$t_i^l = 0 \qquad (l = 1,..., w; \quad i = 1,..., n-1).$$

The vector Π^l characterizing the behavior of firm l is thus identical with the price vector P. Firms of the second category should then maximize their profits at constant prices equal to the market prices, from which there follow the classical equalities between prices, marginal costs and marginal products.

6. Case of a Single Budgetary Condition for the Entire Nationalized Sector

6.1. Before embarking on the study of formulas (18) and (19) in their most general form, it is interesting to examine what becomes of them in the case where there is substituted for the w conditions of budgetary equilibrium,

$$(\beta^h) \qquad P' \cdot Y^h - b^h = 0,$$

a condition of overall equilibrium for the nationalized sector

$$(\beta) \qquad P' \cdot Y - b = 0,$$

where $Y = \sum_h Y^h$ designates the net output (consumption) of the nationalized sector.

One verifies readily that this simply requires us to substitute β for β^h in the preceding formulas. Relation (18) becomes

$$\sum_i^n z_i(ij) = -\beta y_j \qquad (j = 1,\dots, n-1), \tag{20}$$

and relationship (19) becomes

$$t_i^l = z_i/(1+\beta) \qquad (l = 1,\dots, w;\quad i = 1,\dots, n-1). \tag{21}$$

6.2. One deduces from (21) that all of the vectors T^l are equal, and, therefore, so are all the vectors Π^l. Thus, *the nationalized firms should maximize their profits on the basis of a set of fictitious prices that are the same for every firm.*

6.3. The components of the deviation T between the real prices and the fictitious prices Π are the solution to the system

$$\sum_i^n t_i(ij) = \frac{-\beta}{1+\beta} y_j \qquad (j = 1,\dots, n-1). \tag{22}$$

Let us interpret this system of equations.

Consider a variation[9] dP in the prices P *accompanied by a compensating variation in income to offset the "income effect."* The dr^k are then defined by the relationship

$$dr^k = \sum_i q_i^k \, dp_i \, .$$

The "compensated" variations in the quantities of goods $j = 1,\dots, n-1$ consumed by individuals $k = 1,\dots, m$, variations which we represent by δ, are

$$\delta q_j^k = \sum_i^n \frac{\partial q_j^k}{\partial p_i} dp_i + \frac{\partial q_j^k}{\partial r^k} dr^k = \sum_i^n (ij)^k \, dp_i \, .$$

The variations in the quantities x_j^h produced by the firms in the first group are

$$\delta x_j^h = \sum_i^n \frac{\partial x_j^h}{\partial p_i} dp_i = \sum_i^n (ij)^h \, dp_i \, .$$

The compensated variation in net demand for good i by the clientele

[9] The element p_n remaining unchanged.

of the nationalized firms is, therefore, by virtue of the definition (see 5.1) of the coefficient (ij),

$$\delta y_j = \sum_k \delta q_j{}^k - \sum_h \delta x_j{}^h = \sum_i^n (ij)\, dp_i \qquad (j = 1,..., n - 1).$$

If one desires that these net variations in demand be proportioned to the outputs of the goods demanded, i.e.,

$$\delta y_j = \lambda y_j \qquad (j = 1,..., n - 1), \tag{23}$$

the variations in price dp_i must be a solution to the system

$$\sum_i^n (ij)\, dp_i = \lambda y_j \qquad (j = 1,..., n - 1),$$

whose form is identical with that of the system (22).

The elements of the deviation T, between the true prices P and the fictitious prices Π in relation to which the nationalized industries should maximize their profits, *are proportionate to the infinitesimal variations in price that, when accompanied by compensating variations in incomes, entail the same proportionate change in the demands (supplies) of the goods produced (consumed) by the nationalized sector*—with the exception of the standard item whose price is fixed and whose variation in demand (supply) remains free.

6.4. The uniqueness of the vector Π for all the nationalized firms represents $(n - 2)(w - 1)$ conditions. The results which we have just obtained define T uniquely up to a factor of proportionality, giving $n - 2$ conditions. Finally, one arrives at the required $(n - 2)w$ conditions.

One determines the vector T in practice by choosing the coefficient of proportionality, that it requires, in such a way that the budgetary constraint imposed on the nationalized sector (condition β) is satisfied.

6.5. We must still examine whether, and under what conditions, the solutions are acceptable, and, in particular, whether the prices corresponding to the equilibrium, thus determined, are positive. We will not deal with this issue; see [3] and [9].

7. Case of a Separate Budgetary Requirement for Each Firm

The elements t_i^l of the vectors T^l are determined by the conditions (18) and (19) reproduced below,

$$\sum_i^n z_i(ij) = -\sum_h \beta^h y_j^h \qquad (j = 1,..., n-1), \tag{18}$$

$$t_i^l = z_i/(1+\beta^l) \qquad (i = 1,..., n-1; \quad l = 1,..., w), \tag{19}$$

between which one eliminates the z_i.

7.1. The elimination of the β^l and the z_i among the relationships (19) leads to the equations

$$t_i^h/t_j^h = t_i^l/t_j^l \qquad (i, j = 1,..., n-1; \quad h, l = 1,..., w),$$

which indicate that *the deviations t for any two goods must have the same ratio for all firms in the sector.*

7.2. Let z_i^h $(i = 1,..., n-1)$ be the solution of the system

$$\sum_i^n z_i^h(ij) = -y_j^h. \tag{24}$$

One has, with this notation, $z_i = \sum_h \beta^h z_i^h$, whereby

$$t_i^l = \frac{\sum_h \beta^h z_i^h}{1+\beta^l} \qquad (l = 1,..., w; \quad i = 1,..., n-1), \tag{25}$$

which constitute $(n-1)w$ relationships containing w unknown coefficients β^h, thus yielding the desired $(n-2)w$ conditions.

One determines the values of the β^h in such a way that the budgetary conditions imposed on each of the firms of the sector are satisfied.[10]

7.3. The practical interpretation of the z_i^h is analogous to that given of the z_i in 6.3. *The z_i^h pertaining to firm h are proportional to the infinitesimal variations in price which yield a "compensated" variation in the demand (supply) of the nationalized sector that is proportional to the production (consumption) of the firm under consideration*—an exception being the standard commodity whose price is fixed and any change in whose demand (supply) is unrestricted.

[10] Same remark as in 6.5.

8. Results

The results obtained are thus the following:

Firms of the second category (nationalized firms) should maximize their profits on the basis of a set of fictitious prices.

8.1. *If the firms in question are subject to an overall budgetary constraint with no other restriction on each enterprise's profits, this set of fictitious prices will be the same for the entire sector.* This implies, for example, that if the fictitious price for the sale of coal which is to be used by the "Charbonnages de France" is 1000 francs per ton below the effective market price, then "Électricité de France" should utilize its heating equipment and its central facilities on the basis of the same fictitious price equal to the market price minus 1000 francs.

If each nationalized enterprise is subjected to a budgetary constraint pertaining to itself alone, say, e.g., the requirement of strict budgetary equilibrium, a set of fictitious prices is associated with each firm. These sets of fictitious prices are interrelated by the condition that the differences between the real and the fictitious prices for the same two goods must have the same ratio for all firms in the sector. Stated otherwise, once we know the set of fictitious prices associated with one of the nationalized firms, and hence the deviations between its fictitious and its market prices, the deviations associated with every other nationalized firm are equal to those of the first firm aside from a factor of proportionality whose magnitude is determined by the condition of budgetary equilibrium imposed on the firm.

Suppose, for example, that for Charbonnages de France the deviation between the market price and the fictitious price for coal is 1000 francs per ton, and the deviation between market purchase price and fictitious purchase price of electricity furnished by "Électricité de France" is 1 franc per kW hr, then, if the budgetary condition applicable to "Électricité de France" leads it to consider for coal a fictitious price 750 francs below the price which is charged to it by "charbonnages," the deviation between the real price and the fictitious price which should be used by "Électricité de France" should be 0.75 francs per kW hr.

8.2. *In the case of a single overall budgetary constraint* for the entire nationalized sector, the set of fictitious prices to be utilized by all the firms of the sector is defined by the following condition: *the deviations between the real and the fictitious prices are proportional to the variations in price that, when accompanied by a compensating variation in incomes, entail the same relative change in net demand (net supply) of the goods produced (supplied) by the nationalized sector*—with the exception of the standard good, whose price is fixed and whose demand (supply) is free to vary.

The coefficient of proportionality is chosen to assure satisfaction of the budgetary constraint.

In the case of a separate budgetary constraint for each nationalized firm, the deviations t_i^l *between the market prices and the fictitious prices associated with a firm l of this sector are equal to a linear combination of the basic relative deviations* z_i^h *for each firm h in the sector.*

The basic relative deviations z_i^h $(i = 1,..., n)$ *for firm h are proportionate to the variations in price that, when accompanied by a compensating variation in incomes, lead to the same [proportionate] change in total demand (total supply) of the goods produced (consumed) by firm h*—with the exception of a standard good whose price is fixed and whose demand (supply) remains free to vary.

The coefficients of the linear combinations of the basic deviations are the same for all goods and, except for a factor of proportionality, the same for all firms. They should be chosen in a manner that assures satisfaction of the budgetary requirement for each firm.

8.3. Thus one can offer a concrete interpretation of the calculations of the preceding sections—and that is doubtless a considerable step toward practical application of the results. But that application still faces serious difficulties; the general lines of an approximative solution can be the following:

(i) It is evident, and can be demonstrated, that the deviations t_i^l pertaining to two perfect substitutes i and j should be proportionate to the prices of these substitutes.

(ii) If one groups the various goods produced (consumed) by each firm into "complexes" composed of close substitutes, one can show that the equations relating to these complexes are the same as those obtained for separate goods in the preceding sections, provided one assumes that the goods in any such complex are perfect substitutes for one another.

(iii) On that hypothesis, each complex being treated as a separate good, and taking account of the fact that in reality the activity of a firm relates to a relatively small number of such complexes, one can attempt to evaluate the elasticities of substitution between complexes and to solve the resulting equations numerically.

(iv) Returning to the goods making up the complexes, one associates with each of these a deviation t_i^l whose ratio to price p_i is the same as the relative deviation t_I^l/p_I applicable to complex I to which this good i belongs.

(v) Thus one obtains an approximative solution which can be improved upon by trying out a combination of complexes slightly different from the preceding.

8.4. The results thus obtained would be approximative in character. Furthermore the hypotheses upon which their validity rests should not be forgotten: perfect competition or equivalent behavior in the non-nationalized sector. The realism of these hypotheses themselves gives us little encouragement.

Approximation in the implementation of conclusions themselves based on hypotheses of questionable realism... One may ask whether the practical application of the results obtained is of any real interest. Without wishing to open anew a debate which would take us too far [7, pp. 217–229], we should emphasize that, given the normative character of the hypotheses of perfect competition, this type of hypothesis is of particular interest relative to all the unrealistic hypotheses one might have taken, and, furthermore, that the solutions which have heretofore been proposed to the problem under study are based more or less explicitly on the same hypotheses.

M. Allais has advocated [2, p. 10] the solution pure and simple of the proportionality of price to marginal cost. In opposition, those holding to the Marshalian analysis and the [consumers' and producers'] surplus theory defend the proportionality of the divergence between price and marginal cost to the elasticity of demand. It is, incidentally, much more to contend against the abuses to which this solution leads than for theoretical reasons that Allais has proposed the simple rule of proportionality. It would therefore seem unnecessary to present a criticism of the latter rule. We note simply that it is only rigorous in the case of close substitutes or under the heroic assumption of a region of uniform substitutability.

We shall examine in greater detail the rules derived from surplus theory.

9. The Surplus Method

9.1 In its simplest form the surplus method appears as follows: Let Q, with components $q_1, q_2, \ldots, q_N$, be the *production* of the enterprise under consideration, and let $D(Q)$ be the corresponding expenditure. $c_i = \partial D/\partial q_i$ is the marginal cost of production of good i. If we limit ourselves in this sketch of the surplus method to the case in which the demands for the goods produced are independent, we can define, for each demand, a "demand curve" $p_i = p_i(q_i)$.

The "surplus" arising for the collectivity from the production of the vector Q is

$$S(Q) = \int_0^q \sum_i p_i(q_i)\, dq_i - D(Q).$$

The budget constraint imposed on the enterprise may be written

$$\sum_i q_i p_i(q_i) - D(Q) = b.$$

Maximization of surplus subject to this budget constraint leads to the relationships

$$p_i - C_i + \lambda(p_i - c_i + q_i dp_i/dq_i) = 0 \; (i = 1,..., N)$$

thus further, setting $k = -\lambda/(1 + \lambda)$:

$$(p_i - c_i)/p_i = k\eta_i \tag{26}$$

where $\eta_i = (q_i/p_i)(dp_i/dq_i)$ is the elasticity of the price of good i with respect to changes in its quantity. In words: *the relative divergence between price and marginal cost should be proportional to the elasticity of the good considered. The constant of proportionality is chosen as required to realize the desired budgetary equilibrium.*

On this principle is based the traditional policy of public monopolies and, notably, of railroads, of charging *ad valorem* tariffs. Leaving aside certain confusions about the notion of marginal cost attached to a guaranteed supply [6], this policy consists in taxing a market the more heavily the less elastic is its demand, and of applying the profit thus acquired to cover the deficit from sale at marginal cost of goods whose demand is very elastic. In the case of railroad transport this leads to charging each sort of traffic "what the traffic will bear" according to the most classic commercial principles.

9.2. Under the same summary hypotheses, the variation of price which induces a variation δq_i in the demand for good i is

$$\delta p_i = p_i \eta_i \, \delta q_i / q_i$$

The variations δp_i which lead to an equal relative increase in the demand for all goods

$$\delta q_i / q_i = k' \; (i = 1,..., N)$$

are thus determined by the relationships

$$\delta p_i = k' p_i \eta_i \; (i = 1,..., N)$$

which are analogous to equations (26) put into the form

$$p_i - c_i = kp_i\eta_i .$$

We deduce therefrom an alternative version of the rule established in 9.1: *the divergences between price and marginal cost should be proportional to the variations in price which would lead to an equal relative increase in demand for all goods produced by the enterprise.*

This result bears a certain family resemblance to those derived in the preceding sections. One is perhaps tempted by this coincidence to feel some justification, at least approximatively, for the traditional policies of public monopolies. It is nevertheless important to note some important differences.

9.3. First of all, the (consumers' surplus) calculations deal in terms of *deviations between product prices and marginal costs of inputs*. The cost function is a given function of the output. The pricing of factors is thus not considered. If the markets for these inputs are "perfect," the firm equates the prices of these inputs to their marginal products, while it accepts a distortion between output prices and their marginal costs. But if the firm does not pursue maximum profits, there is no justification for failing to question the pricing of inputs right along with the investigation of the production program. There can be no doubt that *the loss of welfare caused by the imposition of a budgetary constraint will be smaller, the larger the number of variables (including both input and output quantities) that this constraint is permitted to affect.*

9.4. The method of surpluses leads to a rule determining the deviations between output prices and marginal costs. But because in our calculations in the preceding sections, input policy is reconsidered simultaneously with the planning of production, *the vector Π (see 3.2) is no longer a vector of costs or marginal products.* To demonstrate this we will deal with the case of a single firm using the same notation as in Sections 2 to 7.

Letting Π represent the vector of fictitious prices relative to which the firm maximizes its profits, one knows that the relations $f(Q) = 0$ and $f_i = \lambda\pi_i$ define the vector Q as a function of Π, i.e.,

$$q_i = q_i(\Pi) \qquad (i = 1,..., n)$$

functions that satisfy identically the relationship

$$\sum_i \pi_i(ij) = 0,$$

where $(ij) = \partial q_i/\partial p_j = (ji)$ is the substitution coefficient for goods i and j in the firm.

Suppose π_j varies by $\delta\pi_j$, the other fictitious prices remaining unchanged. The q_i vary by

$$\delta q_i = \frac{\partial q_i}{\partial p_j}\,\delta\pi_j = (ij)\,\delta\pi_j\,.$$

The variation in net expenditure resulting from the increase δq_j in production of q_j is

$$\delta d_j = \sum_i^j p_i\,\delta q_i = -\sum_i^j p_i(ij)\,\delta\pi_j\,,$$

and the marginal cost of q_j is

$$c_j = \frac{\delta d_j}{\delta q_j} = \frac{-\sum_i^j p_i(ij)\,\delta\pi_j}{(jj)\,\delta\bar{\pi}_j} = p_j - \frac{1}{(jj)}\sum_i p_i(\underline{ij}).$$

By virtue of the identity $\sum_i \pi_i(ij) \equiv 0$, this can be written

$$p_j - c_j = \frac{1}{(jj)}\sum_i t_i(ij),$$

whence

$$\pi_j - c_j = \frac{1}{(jj)}\sum_i^j t_i(ij).$$

The vector of fictitious prices Π (whose elements are π_j) and the vector of marginal costs (products) with elements c_j coincide only if all of the t_i are zero so that P and Π coincide—which precludes the case of an (effective) budgetary constraint.

On the other hand, if marginal costs (or products) are calculated on the basis of the fictitious prices Π this vector constitutes precisely the vector of marginal costs (products). Thus

$$c_j' = \frac{\delta d_j'}{\delta q_j} = \frac{-\sum_i^j \pi_i(ij)\,\delta\pi_j}{(jj)\,\delta\pi_j} = \frac{\pi_j(jj)\,\delta\pi_j}{(jj)\,\delta\pi_j} = \pi_j\,.$$

To summarize, our results relate to the deviations between the "fictitious" marginal costs (or products) and not the deviations between price and real marginal costs as in the (consumers') surplus theory.

9.5. Surplus theory tells us that the deviations between prices and marginal costs should be proportionate to the variations in price that yield the same relative increases in the demands for the firm's outputs.

But the results derived in 6.2 carry an important specification which one does not find here, namely, the variations in price considered must be accompanied by a compensating variation in income equal to the change in outlay caused by the variation in price when quantities purchased are unchanged. With each variation dP in P there must be associated a variation dr^k in the r^k equal to

$$dr^k = dP' \cdot Q^k.$$

If the good considered is used only for industrial purposes (originates only from industry) the income effect is zero and this stipulation has no consequences. But if, on the contrary, it involves a consumer demand (supply) the income effect may become predominant and, consequently, one cannot neglect it "as a first approximation."

9.6. It is true that surplus analysis can be improved [10] to take account of the income effects. But one last difficulty remains if one decides, as one should, to consider simultaneously inputs and outputs. For then the prices P can no longer be taken to be functions of the quantities demanded.

In effect, (i) consumer demands are functions of prices and incomes:

$$Q^k = Q^k(P, r^k),$$

a homogeneous function of degree zero in P and r^k.

(ii) Each variation in price is accompanied by changes in incomes

$$r^k = r^k(P),$$

which are homogeneous functions of degree one.

(iii) The individual-compensated demands are thus homogeneous functions of degree zero in prices P alone:

$$Q^k = Q^k[P, r^k(P)] = Q^k(P),$$

and the same is true of collective demands $Q = \sum_k Q^k$.

The demand (supply) functions $X^h(P)$ for the firm are themselves homogeneous. The net demand for the nationalized sector $Y = Q - X$ is then also a homogeneous function of degree zero in the prices

$$Y = Y(P).$$

It follows that this function cannot be inverted into the form $P = P(Y)$ which permits the definition of a generalized surplus that excludes income effects.

Recollect that things are quite different when incomes are taken as given. The individuals' demand functions $Q^k = Q^k(P)$ appear as nonhomogeneous functions and, as a consequence, so do the collective demands. Hence, it is possible to invert the demand functions, writing them as functions of quantities.

There is one consequence that arises explicitly when we deal with demands corrected for the income effects, a phenomenon that entered our calculation every time we found ourselves with a system of equations whose coefficient matrix was that of the (ij), whose determinant is zero. It was as a result of this situation that we had to assign to one of the goods (item n) the role of "standard commodity" [see, particularly, relations (9) and (17)].

Thus, for example, if we had wished to do the calculation given in 6.3 utilizing n equations $j = 1,\ldots, n$, and n variations in price dp_i $(i = 1,\ldots, n)$, conditions (23) would have taken the form

$$\sum_i (ij)\, dp_i = \lambda y_j \qquad (j = 1,\ldots, n).$$

This system of equations, in general, has no solution (adding term by term the n equations multiplied, respectively, by p_j, one obtains $\sum_i dp_i[\sum_j p_j(ij)] = \lambda \sum_j p_j y_j$, in which the left side is identically zero, while the right side is generally different from zero). That is why the n-th equation had to be suppressed, and the variation dp_n in price p_n was assumed to be zero. *There does not exist, in general, a variation in* [all] *prices—accompanied by a compensating variation in incomes—that can yield the same relative increase in the demand* (*supply*) *of every good.*

The asymmetry in the role of the various goods that is thereby introduced is not very satisfactory aesthetically. It results, in sum, from the fact that the vectors Π and P are defined up to a factor of proportionality, that is, in direction but not in magnitude. This remark suggests that we may wish to seek to substitute for the given price p_n a symmetric condition determining the absolute magnitudes of the vectors under consideration. Our attempts in this direction have so far yielded results whose interpretation is much less simple than those which we obtained in Sections 6, 7 and 8.

References

1. M. Allais, "Traité d'Économie Pure," Imprimerie Nationale, Paris 1943.
2. M. Allais, Le problème de la coordination des transports et la théorie économique, *Rev. Econ. Politique* **58** (1948), 212–271.
3. K. J. Arrow, An extension of the basic theorems of welfare economics, Proc. Second Berkeley Symp. Math. Statist. Probability, pp. 507, Univ. Calif. Press., Berkeley, 1951.

4. M. Boiteux, Communication au congrès de la société européenne d'économétrie, La Haye, août, 1948.
5. M. Boiteux, Le revenue distribuable et les pertes économiques, *Econometrica* **19** (1951), 112–133.
6. M. Boiteux, La tarification au coût marginal et les demandes aléatoires, *Cahiers Sem. Econ.* **1** (1951), 56–69.
7. De Bernis, "Essai sur la Tarification dans les Exploitations Industrielles de l'État du Secteur Monopolistique," These soutenue le 21 décembre 1953 devant la Faculté de Droit de l'Université de Paris.
8. G. Debreu, The classical tax-subsidy problem, *Econometrica* **20** (1952), 100.
9. G. Debreu, Existence of an equilibrium for a competitive economy, *Econometrica* **22** (1954), 265.
10. J. R. Hicks, The generalized theory of consumer's surplus, *Rev. Econ. Stud.* **13** (1945–1946), 68–74.
11. H. Hotelling, The general welfare in relation to problems of taxation and railway and utility rates, *Econometrica* **6** (1938), 242–269.
12. R. Roy, La distribution des revenus entre les divers biens, *Econometrica* **15** (1947), 205–225.
13. P. A. Samuelson, "Foundations of Economic Analysis," pp. 447 Harvard University Press, Cambridge, Mass., 1947.

[11]

Optimal Departures From Marginal Cost Pricing

By WILLIAM J. BAUMOL AND DAVID F. BRADFORD*

The need for this paper is a paradox in itself and indeed it might be subtitled: *The Purloined Proposition or The Mystery of the Mislaid Maxim.* For the results which it describes have appeared many times in the literature and have been reported by most eminent economists in very prominent journals. Yet these results may well come as a surprise to many readers who will consider them to be at variance with ideas which they have long accepted.

The proposition in question asserts that, *generally, prices which deviate in a systematic manner from marginal costs will be required for an optimal allocation of resources, even in the absence of externalities.* The reason for the difficulty into which marginal cost pricing is likely to fall is rather well known. What is not widely recognized is that there exists a highly sophisticated and well-developed body of literature indicating what should be done in such circumstances.

To see how the problem arises, consider an economy in which all industry has been nationalized and in which the central planning agency is dedicated to the maximization of social welfare. Suppose, accordingly, that it is decided to set all prices *equal* to marginal costs and to make up any deficits by subsidy out of the governmental treasury. If these funds are derived by excise taxes this is obviously a decision to make some prices depart from marginal costs after all. Or if it is obtained by an income tax, it is the price of labor which is forced away from its marginal cost. Any tax, except a Pigouvian poll tax—which might perhaps more felicitously be called an "inescapable tax"—will unavoidably affect some price. There is no way out of it. Any level of tax revenue which the government is determined to collect, whether as a means to make up a deficit resulting from a marginal cost pricing arrangement or for any other purpose, must in practice produce some price distortion.

Once this difficulty is recognized it becomes clear that one is dealing with a problem in the area of the second best. We are now faced with a problem involving maximization *in the presence of an added constraint.* Resource allocation is to be optimal under the constraint that governmental revenues suffice to make up for the deficits (surpluses)[1] of the individual firms that constitute the economy.

* The authors are members of the department of economics, Princeton University. We are grateful to the National Science Foundation whose grant greatly facilitated completion of this paper. We must also express deep appreciation to our colleagues, Charles Berry, Stanley Black, William Branson, and W. Arthur Lewis, and to Ralph Turvey, whose comments and suggestions helped enormously in the development of its ideas.

[1] Presumably, as a practical matter, there is an asymmetry between the problems posed by surpluses and those resulting from deficits. The real difficulty arises when we try to collect resources to cover the deficits without distorting consumers' and producers' choices. Since it is not possible in practice to levy lump sum taxes whose magnitude is independent of the decisions of those who pay them, we are forced to consider second-best solutions to the tax problem. A surplus can presumably be distributed more easily in a "lump sum" manner. One can, for example, distribute shares in future surpluses to all members of the economy on the basis of their incomes at some point in the past, or one can simply divide them equally among all individuals.

It should be emphasized also that the deficit problem need not arise only in the case of decreasing costs where

The theorems which have been developed to deal with this issue derive added interest from the fact that they are (virtually) the only concrete prescriptions for any second-best problem which have so far appeared in the literature. The discussion of this paper differs from the earlier writings in several ways. First, it deals with an important case not explicitly covered in most of the other papers in the area: quasi-optimal pricing when commodity prices throughout the economy are all adjusted as far as is possible. Second, it attempts a simplified exposition which is, of course, possible only at a cost in terms of loss of generality. Third, it brings together, explicitly, all three strands of the discussion: the welfare theoretic, the regulatory, and the public finance contributions. Finally, as far as we know, it offers the first overview of the extensive literature that has grown up in the area.

I. *Sources of the Analysis*

The preceding formulation of the problem suggests why the results described in this paper are not widely recognized. For they arise not out of the literature of welfare economics but from two more specialized fields—the theory of taxation and the analysis of public utility regulation.

The connection of the analysis with the theory of taxation is easy to understand. For the investigation, as it has just been described, is tantamount to a study of a system of optimal excise and income taxes. Only a small modification in our statement is needed for this purpose: instead of requiring the governmental revenue to equal the (algebraic) sum of the deficits of the firms constituting the economy, the revenue constraint can be generalized to require the tax system to bring in whatever revenues the government has decided it needs. The taxes which are optimal subject to this more general revenue requirement constraint then can be shown to follow the same necessary condition as that which replaces the marginal cost pricing rule in our previous discussion.

Similarly, there is a direct line between the more general welfare analysis and the theory of public utility regulation. For one reason or another, various public or regulated private monopolistic or partially monopolistic enterprises are operated under what amounts to a fixed profit constraint. Examples are turnpike authorities (required to cover costs and pay back invested capital), and regulated electricity, water, and telephone systems. The enterprises cited as examples are all firms that market a number of commodities. The turnpike sells easy driving between many different pairs of points, and, perhaps more important, at various times of day. Similarly, the telephone system sells ordinary telephone services for various uses over various distances and at various times, and, in addition, sells private wire, teletype, television signal transmission, and other services related to, but not identical with, telephone services as usually conceived. In each example the demands for the different services are very obviously strongly interrelated, and they are obviously produced under conditions involving common costs.

If we assume that the net revenue allowed these enterprises is less than the amount profit maximization would yield, some degree of freedom is introduced into the pricing of the commodities produced.[2] A wide variety of output combinations and

---

the revenue yielded by marginal cost pricing will fall short of the total costs of the firm. For example, in practice revenue requirements of the firm are often based on historical accounting cost figures which management feels it must recover. Similarly, governmental tax requirements may exceed any profits obtained from nationalized firms subject to diminishing returns when they price at marginal costs.

[2] Of course, some amount of freedom is also introduced into the choice of method of production. We assume throughout that good will, pride of service, patriotism or the shrewdness of regulators assure that whatever output combination is chosen is produced at minimum cost.

sets of prices can then be chosen, each of which would just meet the net revenue constraint. The problem, then, is to determine which of these is optimal (second best) from the point of view of the use of resources to serve consumer desires. A similar problem obviously arises in a nationalized industry which is required to earn enough to cover its costs.

II. *The Nature of the Theorem*

In this section we shall describe the rules indicating whether a particular price-output combination that satisfies the profit constraint is socially optimal, i.e., whether from the point of view of the economy it yields the most effective allocation of resources permitted by the constraint.[3] A solution to this constrained maximum problem will be called "quasi-optimal," because it is a second-best solution forced upon us by the revenue requirement.

A problem such as ours is usually framed in terms of the determination of appropriate output levels, but it can also be treated in terms of the choice of a price set for the outputs. Given the relevant demand functions, the choice of prices is tantamount to the choice of (salable) output levels. The two problems are, of course, formally identical, but, as we shall show, the pricing decision approach avoids a number of difficulties and yields a surprisingly simple optimality rule. In most conventional and familiar terms this rule asserts that Pareto optimal utilization of resources in the presence of an absolute profit constraint requires (considering substitution effects alone) that all outputs be reduced by the same proportion from the quantities that would be demanded at prices equal to the corresponding marginal costs. The rule takes an even simpler form in the event cross elasticities of demand are zero. It then requires that each price be set so that its percentage deviation from marginal cost is inversely proportionate to the item's price elasticity of demand. According to this result, the social welfare will be served most effectively not by setting prices equal or even proportionate to marginal costs, but by causing unequal deviations in which items with elastic demands are priced at levels close to their marginal costs. The prices of items whose demands are inelastic diverge from their marginal costs by relatively wider margins.

This result is surely not immediately acceptable through intuition. It strikes us as curious, if for no other reason, because it seems to say that ordinary price discrimination might well set relative prices at least roughly in the manner required for maximal social welfare in the presence of a profit constraint. Since the objective of the analysis can be described as the determination of the optimally discriminatory set of prices needed to obtain the required profit, some degree of resemblance is perhaps to be expected. The case studied here is, thus, in a sense the obverse of the problem of profit maximizing price discrimination, and while the two solutions bear some qualitative resemblance, it can be shown that they may in fact differ substantially in quantity.

The theorem can be reformulated and generalized in a number of ways. Instead of utilizing the producers' and consumers' surplus concepts with all their theoretical limitations, the analysis can be framed in terms of the Hicksian compensating variation. Or a Pareto optimality approach can be utilized, both of these procedures obviating any need for interpersonal utility

[3] It is not suggested that profit-constrained firms will by themselves tend to institute such optimal policies. When profits are eliminated or reduced in importance, other objectives presumably guide decision makers. For one thing, they may be able to afford stupidity in production decisions as pointed out by Harvey Leibenstein. A well-known alternative goal is sales maximization, the implications of which have been discussed *ad nauseam* by one of the present authors. Other possibilities have been examined by Herbert Simon, Robin Marris, Oliver Williamson, Armen Alchian, and Reuben Kessel and by others. For a bibliography and an excellent discussion see Williamson.

comparisons. Similarly, the theorem has been extended to cover cases involving nonzero cross-elasticities of demand, to deal with input prices and the prices of intermediate goods, etc. Of course, once this is done the result loses some of its simplicity and the preceding statement requires considerable modification. But even then, surprisingly simple versions remain possible, as we shall see.

III. *The Formal Theorem*

In previous discussions, the basic theorem has been stated in a number of different ways. The objective itself has been described alternatively as: a) maximization of the sum of consumers' and producers' surpluses; b) determination of a set of prices from which it is *not* possible to change in a way that permits the gainers to compensate the losers; and c) maximization of the level of satisfaction of any one individual, given the utility level of each other individual (Pareto quasi-optimality). Each of these maximizations is, of course, constrained by the revenue requirement.

We will discuss the following four variants of the theorem, each of which gives a set of necessary conditions for quasi-optimal pricing:

1) If prices are quasi-optimal the ratio between the marginal profit yields of unit changes in the *prices* of any two goods will be equal to the ratio between their output levels.

2) For each product, the deviation of the quasi-optimal price from marginal cost must be proportionate to the difference between the product's marginal cost and marginal revenue (i.e., its marginal social welfare cost must be proportionate to its marginal contribution to the profit requirement). This result holds only in the case where cross-elasticities are all zero.

3) For each product, the percentage deviation of quasi-optimal price from marginal cost must be inversely proportionate to its price elasticity of demand. This result also holds only where cross-elasticities of demand are zero.

4) Quasi-optimal prices must yield outputs that deviate by (approximately) the same proportion from those which would result from pricing at the marginal costs corresponding to the quasi-optimal output levels. This last form of the proposition, which is the variant most frequently encountered in the literature, is more general than the second and third versions of the theorem.

In demonstrating these propositions we shall utilize a comparatively straightforward manner of proof which has not previously appeared in the literature.[4] To facilitate the exposition we start with a partial equilibrium approach. That is, we demonstrate that socially optimal pricing by a multi-product monopolist operating under a profit constraint is described by the preceding propositions. The monopolist is assumed able to set the prices of his final good outputs, but to purchase inputs at prices which remain fixed throughout the analysis. It will be clear that his optimal policy is the same as that which would be induced by the imposition of excise taxes equal to the derived divergence between output price and the marginal costs which would obtain if the outputs were to be produced by perfect competitors. This establishes the correspondence between the monopoly regulation and the excise taxation interpretations of the theorems.

If the monopolist is taken to be very large (e.g., if substantially all of the economy is operated by the government), or correspondingly, if the commodities taxed account for a large share of total output, the assumption of fixed input

[4] To simplify the exposition we have dispensed with some theoretical niceties in the proof presented here, especially in the definition of the objective function. These are discussed and the objective function is examined in greater detail in our forthcoming paper.

prices must clearly be relaxed. This has been recognized and dealt with in the literature (for a simple statement see A. C. Pigou (1947, pp. 105–09); a sophisticated treatment is found in M. Boiteux 1956). We do not go into detail on this problem, but we do show in a subsequent section that the same line of reasoning used in our proof can readily be extended to a general equlibrium model.

The demonstration proceeds as follows: Let $p_1, \ldots, p_n$ and $x_1, \ldots, x_n$ be the prices and outputs of the n commodities produced by the monopolist and, as indicated above, take as fixed the prices of his inputs. Let $Z(p_1, \ldots, p_n)$ be our (unspecified) measure of consumer benefit which is to be maximized subject to the profit constraint[5] $\Pi(p_1, \ldots, p_n) = M$ where the profit function has now been expressed in terms of prices rather than outputs. As usual in such constrained maximization problems, Z will be maximal subject to this constraint only if

$$(1)\quad \frac{\partial Z}{\partial p_i} = \lambda \frac{\partial \Pi}{\partial p_i}, \quad (i = 1, 2, \ldots, n)$$

That is the intuitively obvious first-order requirement that the marginal welfare gain from a given price change (price reduction) must be proportionate to its marginal profit cost.

[5] If the revenues permitted by regulation are based on total investment rather than being fixed in absolute amount, this constraint may require some modification. If (as is at least ostensibly the goal of regulation) gross profits are required to be no greater than the cost of capital, then net profits (over the cost of capital) will be zero and the constraint will hold as stated with $M=0$. If, however, the profit rate is permitted to exceed the cost of capital and the firm's total capital varies with output levels we may end up with M, the total profit permitted by regulation, itself varying with output levels. Our formal results remain unchanged if in the profit constraint $\Pi = R - C = M$ (where R = total revenue and C = total cost) we use C^* to represent $M + C$ and rewrite the constraint as $\Pi = R - C^* = 0$. We can then express all of our results in terms of C^* instead of C. Economic interpretations are, however, clouded by this modification.

We can make the preceding equation much more explicit by examining more specifically the nature of the consumer benefit function $Z(p_1, \ldots, p_n)$. While we will not be able to say much about that function itself, we can be rather specific about its partial derivatives, which is all we need for our present purposes.

We need a basis on which to estimate the gain to consumers from price-quantity data. A one dollar reduction in the price of a commodity will enable a consumer who is presently consuming x units of that commodity to continue buying exactly his original bundle of goods with a budget that is smaller by x dollars than his original budget. Thus x dollars is a lower limit to the relevant compensating variation since this is the least he would be willing to pay for that price change, and he would probably pay more since the x dollar reduction in his budget accompanied by the one dollar reduction in the specified price would certainly permit him to buy his original bundle and might perhaps enable him to buy one which he prefers but which he could not previously afford. Similarly, if an individual is currently purchasing the respective amounts $x_1, \ldots, x_n$ of our n commodities at prices $p_1, \ldots, p_n$, the amount he would pay to confront instead prices $p_1 + \Delta p_1, p_2, \ldots, p_n$ will be at least $-x_1 \Delta p_1$. John Hicks (p. 330 ff.) shows rigorously in this same general manner that the *rate* of consumer gain per dollar *increase* in the price of any commodity is precisely the negative of the amount of the commodity initially consumed, times one dollar. We may then take as our expression for the derivative of the benefit function the compensating variation corresponding to the price change

$$\partial Z / \partial p_i = -x_i$$

Hence, substitution into the previous equation (1) yields

$$(2)\quad -x_i = \lambda \partial \Pi / \partial p_i$$

or, dividing by the corresponding condition for any other item j, we obtain

$$\frac{1}{x_i}\frac{\partial\Pi}{\partial p_i} = \frac{1}{x_j}\frac{\partial\Pi}{\partial p_j} \tag{2a}$$

as the required condition for quasi-optimality.

Equation (2a), then, is the first of the four variants of the theorem described at the beginning of this section. This necessary condition for quasi-optimality requires marginal profit yields of price changes to be proportionate to output levels. It may perhaps claim the virtue that it is relatively operational. If the firm has some notion of the likely marginal profit yield of a change in any one of its product prices, management can readily check whether (2a) is approximately satisfied.

We can now proceed directly from (2) to a derivation of the other variants of the basic theorem. We use MR_i, MC_i, and E_i to represent, respectively, the marginal revenue, marginal cost, and price elasticity of demand of output i, and for simplicity assume that all cross-elasticities of demand are zero, though this is not necessary for the more general analysis, and is certainly not required for the preceding variant of the theorem.

Since[6]

$$MR_i = p_i + x_i \partial p_i/\partial x_i \tag{3}$$

then

$$\partial\Pi/\partial p_i = (MR_i - MC_i)dx_i/dp_i$$
$$= (p_i + x_i\partial p_i/\partial x_i - MC_i)dx_i/dp_i$$

Substituting this into our basic condition (2) we have

$$-x_i dp_i/dx_i = \lambda(p_i + x_i dp_i/dx_i - MC_i)$$

or adding $(p_i + x_i dp_i/dx_i - MC_i)$ to both sides we obtain

$$p_i - MC_i = (1+\lambda)(p_i + x_i dp_i/dx_i - MC_i)$$
$$= (1+\lambda)(MR_i - MC_i)$$

This is the second form of the quasi-optimality theorem: the difference between price and marginal cost[7] should be proportionate to the difference between marginal revenue and marginal cost.

Next we may rewrite the preceding equation as

$$-\lambda(p_i - MC_i) = (1+\lambda)x_i dp_i/dx_i \tag{4}$$

or

$$\frac{p_i - MC_i}{p_i} = \frac{1+\lambda}{\lambda}\frac{1}{E_i}$$

since by the usual formula, $E_i = -(p_i/x_i)(dx_i/dp_i)$ which is the third form of the result.[8] Note that it implies that if all elasticities in question are equal, prices

[6] It is here that the zero cross-elasticities enter our exposition. In the more general case, of course, $MR_i = p_i + \sum_j x_j \partial p_j/\partial x_i$. In our forthcoming paper we have dealt in some detail with this more general case which clearly complicates the analysis but does not change its nature in any fundamental way.

[7] Some care must be exercised in interpreting the various forms of the theorem described here because marginal costs are not generally constant. Let $MC_i(q)$ represent marginal costs corresponding to the quasi-optimal output levels while $MC_i(M)$ represent the marginal costs corresponding to the equilibrium outputs when all prices are set equal to marginal costs. Then in our proposition we have $\Delta p_i = p_i - MC_i(q)$ and they are thus *not* necessarily equal to the $p_i - MC_i(M)$. That is, the propositions do not contrast quasi-optimal prices with the prices corresponding to a marginal cost pricing equilibrium as ordinarily conceived. They refer instead to the differences between the quasi-optimal prices and the marginal costs corresponding to the quasi-optimal output levels.

[8] It should be reemphasized that this form of the derivation deliberately ignores the supply side for the sake of expository simplicity. However, the analysis is easily extended to take supply into account, and this was done from the very beginning of the discussion, by Frank Ramsey and by A. C. Pigou in 1947. For example, Pigou states "Writing η (defined as negative) for the elasticity of demand in respect of pre-tax output, e_r for the corresponding elasticity of supply of the rth commodity and t_r for the ad valorem rate of tax on it, it can be proved that, in the conditions supposed (the optimum system of such taxes yielding a given revenue require) rates of tax . . . such that $t_r/(1/e_r - 1/\eta)$ has the same value for all values of r" (pp. 107–08).

should be set proportional to marginal costs.

For the final form of the proposition, write the deviation of price from marginal cost as Δp_i, i.e., set $p_i - MC_i = \Delta p_i$. Then equation (4) can be written after a minor rearrangement of terms as

$$\frac{dx_i}{dp_i}\Delta p_i = -\frac{1+\lambda}{\lambda}x_i$$

But the left-hand side of the preceding equation may be interpreted as an approximation to the change, Δx_i, in the ith commodity demanded which would result from a shift from the actual prices to current marginal cost levels. We thus obtain the last version of our theorem:

$$\Delta x_i = kx_i, \quad \text{where } k = (1+\lambda)/\lambda.$$

The more sophisticated discussions have generally emphasized this last form of the theorem, the assertion that quasi-optimal pricing requires (after compensation for income effects) a proportionate change in all purchases from the levels that would be observed if prices were set at marginal costs.[9] This interpretation has usually been preferred to the two variants that precede it because, as has been shown by M. Boiteux (1956), Paul Samuelson (1951), and others, this form of the theorem holds quite generally and does not depend on the simplifying assumptions needed to arrive at the two special forms of the theorem described before this last variant. Only our first relationship (2a), which requires the marginal profit yields of commodity price changes to be proportionate to their output levels, is of the same order of generality.[10]

IV. *Intuitive Rationale*

Though at first blush the rationale underlying the preceding propositions may not be entirely transparent, it is not too difficult to account for them intuitively. The last form of the theorem is perhaps the most helpful in offering us a grasp of the entire matter. We need merely think of the consequence of a deviation of price from marginal cost as a distortion of relative demand patterns. This immediately suggests the last form of the theorem for it implies that the damage to welfare resulting from departures from marginal cost pricing will be minimized if the *relative* quantities of the various goods sold are kept unchanged from their marginal cost pricing proportions. If we accept this plausibility argument, then the elasticity form of the theorem clearly follows. If we propose to (say) contract the demands for A and B each by precisely k percent, then if A's demand is much more elastic than B's, clearly A's price must be raised by a substantially smaller percentage than that of B.

A bit more light is shed on the matter by a simple graphic discussion that follows rather loosely an analysis first presented by Ursula Hicks (p. 167 ff) and developed

[9] In accord with the comments of fn. 6, this third form of the theorem should be read as follows: a change in prices from their quasi-optimal levels to *the corresponding marginal cost levels* should reduce all outputs in (approximately) the same proportions.

If we estimate demand changes on the assumption that the slope of each demand curve is constant over the relevant range, our proposition is valid for large as well as for small price changes. It now asserts that the divergence between price and marginal cost must be such that the estimated percentage changes in demand resulting from a drop in all prices to the given marginal cost levels are the same for all commodities.

[10] Note that application of the theorem in any of its forms does not rule out a two-part or a multi-part tariff. On the contrary, it tells us how to determine the quasi-optimal value for each of the multiplicity of prices that composes such a tariff. For example, when the consumer pays one charge for the rental of a telephone and another for each of his calls, this can be interpreted either as a two-part tariff or as a pair of prices for two distinct but related services each of which has a quasi-optimal price. This discussion is, of course, based on the observation that one cannot in reality impose a Pigouvian poll tax as one part of the multi-part tariff. Indeed, if such a lump sum tax were possible there clearly would be no need for the theorems under discussion. Marginal cost prices plus lump sum taxes could then satisfy the revenue requirement and yield an optimal allocation.

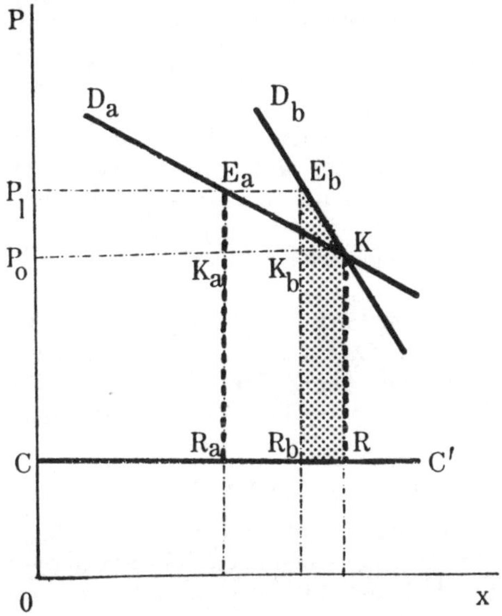

FIGURE 1

fully by William Vickrey in 1968. In Figure 1 consider the segments of two demand curves D_aK and D_bK through point K. Let us use the Marshallian measure of consumers' surplus to compare the psychic loss to consumers from a given price (tax) rise with the resulting increase in (tax) revenues. Then, if demand is in fact given by the less elastic curve D_bK and price rises from P_o to P_1, the loss of consumers' surplus will be $P_oKE_bP_1$. On the other hand, assuming for simplicity that marginal costs are constant at level OC, net revenue will be increased as a result of the price change by the quantity $P_oK_bE_bP_1$ minus R_bRKK_b. Thus the positive portion of the net revenue change, $P_oK_bE_bP_1$, may be considered to be offset by an approximately equivalent loss to consumers. This means that with the less elastic demand curve the rise in price will have caused a net reduction in net revenue plus consumers' surplus that is measured by the shaded area, R_bRKE_b.

Similarly, with the more elastic demand curve, D_aK, the rise in price from P_o to P_1 will decrease the sum of the revenue net of consumers' surplus by the greater area R_aRKE_a. In general, then (with marginal costs constant), a given price rise will exact a larger social cost in consumers' surplus not offset by increased revenues the more elastic the demand curve. That is essentially the reason for the theorem that calls for a relatively small deviation between the price and marginal cost of any commodity whose demand is comparatively elastic.

V. *A Simple General Equilibrium Model*

Our interest in conveying the central results of the literature discussed in our paper to a wide readership in an intuitively convincing fashion leads us to couch our argument of Section IV in terms of partial equilibrium analysis. It is desirable, however, to sketch out the way it all works in general equilibrium terms. A simple reinterpretation of the terms used in the derivation of the theorems will show that our proof is sufficient to establish the propositions in the special general equilibrium case in which there is only one input factor, labor, and all the productive activities are in the hands of the government. Accordingly, let $p_1, \ldots, p_n$, be the prices in terms of labor hours at which the n final outputs other than leisure, $x_1, \ldots, x_n$, all produced by the government, are sold to the consumer-laborers. The government is assumed to operate with a profit constraint in the form of a fixed number, M (which may be zero), of units of labor. In addition, of course, there is a production constraint, which we may write as[11]

[11] Notice that in putting this constraint in the form of an equality, we have ruled out production inefficiency. Although this is a plausible requirement and makes things easier, it is not always innocuous when more is meant by "consumer benefit" than attainment of Pareto optimality—the concept utilized here. See

(5) $$C = F(x_1, \ldots, x_n),$$

where C is the minimum labor input sufficient to produce the output vector, $x_1, \ldots, x_n$. The problem is to maximize "consumer benefit" subject to this production relation and the profit constraint,

(6) $$\pi = p_1x_1 + \ldots + p_nx_n - C = M$$

Now let us treat the government as an ordinary firm that imagines it can buy all the labor it wants at a price of one per unit. The additional labor it would have to buy to produce an additional unit of good is then the marginal cost of that good, both in the accounting sense and in the sense of its leisure opportunity cost, all other outputs held constant.

There will be, in general, a large set of price vectors compatible with both (a) clearing of the markets for goods and factors and (b) satisfaction of the government's profit constraint. It is useful to spell this statement out in somewhat more detail. If the aggregate labor sold is L, we can write the set of demand equations as

$$L = L(p_1, \ldots, p_n)$$
$$x_1 = x_1(p_1, \ldots, p_n)$$
$$\cdots\cdots\cdots$$
$$x_n = x_n(p_1, \ldots, p_n),$$

where, necessarily (Walras' Law),

$$p_1x_1 + \cdots + p_nx_n = L$$

For a set of prices to be market-clearing, the government must buy exactly the specified amount of labor and produce exactly the specified quantities of goods. By (5) and (6) "feasible price vectors" are those which satisfy the profit constraint conditions

$$L - F(x_1, \ldots, x_n) = M,$$

or, equivalently,

$$p_1x_1 + \cdots + p_nx_n - F(x_1, \ldots, x_n) = M$$

The task is to find among these an optimal price vector, where we have taken this to mean a vector which consumers in the aggregate would be unwilling (after costless negotiation among themselves) to bribe the government to change. The solution to this problem is found in the propositions set forth in Section III above. The entire analysis in that section continues to hold when the profit constraint as just described is used in place of the usual partial equilibrium construct.

VI. *The Taxed and the Untaxed Sectors*

Now we are equipped with a genuine, if very simple, general equilibrium apparatus, but one which in most respects can be manipulated in partial equilibrium terms. The key to this is the form in which we have expressed the production relation (as a cost function), the fixing of the government's profit constraint in terms of labor, and the corresponding choice of labor as price numeraire (so that the price of the single input factor, the "all other prices" of partial equilibrium analysis, is fixed at unity). In this model the government can be taken to tax the output of producers of the n non-leisure goods (where the tax is the difference between price and marginal cost), and hence these goods make up the "taxed sector." The untaxed sector here may reasonably be described as the production of negative labor input to the taxed goods-production sector, i.e., the production of leisure. In a rather trivial sense, in the latter sector marginal cost and price are always equal at unity.

It is illuminating at this point to reconsider "our" results in light of the following comment by Abba Lerner, who derives two special rules for quasi-optimality, each applicable to a special case:

[One] rule [equalize tax elasticities] is

Peter Diamond and James Mirrlees for a proof that production efficiency will be called for under almost all "reasonable" assumptions about production, individual utility, and social welfare relations.

> appropriate where the shifting is only from a taxed to an untaxed sector, while the [other] rule [maintain proportionality of price to marginal cost] is appropriate where the shifting is only to another part of the taxed sector (as would be the case if all uses of resources could be, and were, taxed).
>
> What we need is a rule that is applicable whether the resources shifted by a tax remain in the taxed sector or go to the untaxed sector or are divided between the two sectors. [p. 285]

Documentation of the fact that a general rule for optimal excise taxation has long been available in the literature, and presentation of a simplified derivation of several forms of such a rule are precisely our objectives. It is easy to show that in those situations where Lerner recommends prices in proportion to marginal cost, our theorems do likewise; where Lerner recommends equalization of tax elasticities, so do our theorems; and where Lerner calls for something in between the two, our theorems provide an exact prescription.

In the case of the model which has just been described,[12] the statement that a tax change has as its only effect a shifting of resources from taxed to untaxed sectors is clearly equivalent to the assertion that the only output affected in the taxed sector is the one whose tax rate has changed. If the effect of varying any one tax is only to shift resources into the non-taxed sector then only own elasticities of the taxed goods, and not their cross-elasticities with one another, can be non-zero. In this case, Lerner and we (most directly in variant 3 of the theorem) conclude that the percentage deviation of price of any taxed commodity from marginal cost should be inversely proportional to its own price elasticity of demand.

We turn now to the next case where the alternative use of resources induced by tax changes can be said to be entirely in the taxed sector. This is obviously equivalent to the assertion that labor is perfectly inelastically supplied over a wide range of price vectors.[13] In this situation, Lerner and our theorems agree that prices proportional to marginal costs, i.e., relative prices equal to marginal rates of transformation between (non-leisure) commodities, is clearly optimal. This result follows easily for the case when cross-elasticities between (non-leisure) goods are all zero. Then, since a change in the price of a given good results in no change in either the purchases of other goods or of labor sold, it must lead to no change at all in labor expenditure on the good in question. That is, all goods must be demanded with equal, in fact, with unit elasticity. Our third form of the theorem states that in this case the relative deviation of price from marginal cost should be the same for all commodities.

More generally, admitting non-zero cross elasticities, the zero elasticity of labor supply means that any change in profit resulting from a price change comes purely from the change in labor cost of goods sold, since there can be no change in the

[12] Two things should be noted. First, when Lerner speaks of "tax elasticity" he is referring to what might better be called "own tax elasticity," that is, the relative change in the tax revenue (here, profit) collected on commodity x_i when the tax on x_i (divergence between price and marginal cost of x_i) is raised by one unit. The change in tax revenue collected on other commodities, which arises via cross-elasticity of demand, is not included.

Second, it should be observed that although the term "resources" is often not definable in general equilibrium models of the type described above (since choice is made from among alternative vectors of social aggregates of final goods, without reference to the underlying mechanics of production), in this simple case we may presumably equate them with "labor."

[13] Note that unless this inelasticity of supply results from some kind of artificial constraint, such as a legal maximum working day, or from a kink in the individuals' utility functions, commodity taxes will in this case *not* yield the same result as lump sum taxes. For if the inelasticity results from the offsetting of income and substitution effects, a doubling of prices will generally have a different effect from the subtraction of half (or any other portion) of the individuals' original labor income, leaving prices unchanged. This is obviously so because the (alternative) new price lines will not have the same slope and so they cannot be tangent to the same indifference curve at the same point.

total revenue received by the firm or government: the fixed quantity of labor offered in exchange for their products. We have, for all price vectors in question, by the inelasticity of labor supply at quantity L_0:

$$\sum_j p_j x_j(p) = L_0;$$
$$(7) \qquad \text{i.e.,} \quad \sum_j p_j \frac{\partial x_j}{\partial p_i} + x_i = 0$$

for all i. Furthermore, as just noted, price changes can affect profits only through their effect on costs:

$$(8) \qquad \frac{\partial \pi}{\partial p_i} = \frac{\partial}{\partial p_i}\left(\sum_j p_j x_j - C\right) = 0 - \sum_j \frac{\partial C}{\partial x_j}\frac{\partial x_j}{\partial p_i}$$

Recall now the first form of "our" theorem which asserts that optimality requires, for all i,

$$-x_i = \lambda \frac{\partial \pi}{\partial p_i}$$

In the case now under consideration, this becomes by (8)

$$-x_i = -\lambda \sum_j \frac{\partial C}{\partial x_j}\frac{\partial x_j}{\partial p_i}$$

But by (7)

$$-x_i = \sum_j p_j \frac{\partial x_j}{\partial p_i}$$

Together these results imply that the first-order conditions can be written for all i,

$$\sum_j \left(p_j + \lambda \frac{\partial C}{\partial x_j}\right)\frac{\partial x_j}{\partial p_i} = 0$$

Since $\partial C/\partial x_j$ is the marginal cost of x_j, this asserts that prices bearing the proportion $-\lambda$ to marginal cost satisfy the first-order conditions.

In the more general case where shifting takes place both between sectors ($\partial C/\partial p_i \neq 0$) and within the taxed sector ($\partial x_i/\partial p_j \neq 0$, at least sometimes), an analogous algebraic chain of steps leads to the following first-order conditions, for all i:

$$(9) \qquad \sum_j \left(p_j + \lambda \frac{\partial C}{\partial x_j}\right)\frac{\partial x_j}{\partial p_i} = (1 + \lambda)\frac{\partial L}{\partial p_i}$$

Only by chance will these conditions be satisfied by prices proportional to marginal cost, or by prices deviating from proportionality by a simple function of own elasticity. In this we agree with Lerner. However, the theorems prescribe definite prices which do optimize, given the constraints, and there is no necessity to resort to a rough compromise between two polar rules. One rule prescribes for the polar situations as well as for intermediate ones. This does not mean that a more precise spelling out of Lerner's compromise would not yield the same (correct) conclusions: it means only that the task which remains is not to find the general rule. That is already accomplished by (9). Rather, it is only necessary to translate this rule into a form compatible with Professor Lerner's very illuminating intuitions.

VII. *The Case Where All Items are Taxable*

Finally, we must yet deal with the case, excluded from our discussion thus far, in which "*all* uses of resources" can be taxed. In view of our preceding agreement with Lerner that when tax changes result in resource shifts only within the taxed sector, prices proportional to marginal costs are optimal, our assertion that this is generally not the case when all goods are taxable may come as a surprise. The explanation is, however, relatively simple: overall marginal cost pricing will not, as a rule, yield the necessary revenue.[14] This

[14] We shall say that "overall marginal cost pricing" prevails when the price vector confronting consumers is a scalar multiple of the vector of first partial derivatives of the transformation function evaluated at the associated social total net output vector.

follows from a basic assumption of the entire analysis: that lump sum taxes are impossible. In terms of our general equilibrium this requires (by Walras law) that the net value of consumers' sales and purchases of all commodities, *including labor*, add up to zero. In that case, a proportionate tax, leading to a proportionate change in prices, will still leave the net consumer expenditures at zero and hence will yield no revenue to the government.

In formal terms, let P_i be the price of commodity i $(i=1, \ldots, n)$ facing the consumer, no longer expressed in labor terms, and let P_L be the price of labor. Following the sign convention that positive numbers represent net purchases of desired goods, negative numbers, net sales, let $a_1, \ldots, a_n, a_L$, be the vector of net transactions carried out by a consumer. Our no-lump sum tax assumption can be expressed as the requirement that $P_1a_1 + P_2a_2 + \ldots + P_na_n + P_La_L = 0$. (This implies, of course, that the aggregate net transactions vector, summed over all consumers, satisfies the same condition, expressed above as the condition on the demand functions $p_1x_1 + \ldots + p_nx_n = L$, where prices were expressed in labor terms.) Obviously, here it makes absolutely no difference to the consumer whether he faces prices $P_1, \ldots, P_n, P_L$ or prices ten times as high; only relative prices count. If the government were to collect the difference between these two price vectors (P and $10P$) as a tax, it would collect precisely $9(\sum_i P_ia_i + P_La_L)$, which is zero. A tax vector which is a scalar multiple of the price vector facing consumers will, under our zero-transfer assumption, *always* yield zero revenue.

With consumer budgets equated to zero, the vector of taxes thus cannot be proportional to consumer prices if there is to be any tax yield, and hence consumer prices cannot be proportional to marginal costs. Now we are back where we started. If the government wishes to obtain, say, a quantity M of labor for its own uses, and can only work with commodity taxes, it must get consumers to settle at an equilibrium with an aggregate net transaction vector $x_1, \ldots, x_n, -L$, satisfying $L - F(x_1, \ldots, x_n) = M$, i.e., such that the leisure given up for production exceeds that necessary to produce the other desired goods by M.

VIII. *An Analysis in Terms of Quantity Changes*

Some readers may find it instructive to see a derivation of the propositions carried out explicitly in a general equilibrium context and in terms of quantity changes rather than price changes. This is easily done within our present model if it is assumed that lump sum redistributions maintain a socially optimal distribution of alternative social totals of goods and leisure. Then we can employ a Samuelsonian social utility function relating social welfare to these totals, with the property that the tangent plane to any social indifference surface is also a "budget plane" associated with prices at which that point will be sustained as a competitive equilibrium. Thus prices can be written as a function of quantities. The analysis is made more transparent if we assume that there is a certain fixed total, $\bar{L}$, of labor time which must be allocated among production, leisure, R (for recreation), and government surplus, yielding the constraint:

$$F(x_1, \ldots, x_n) + R + M = \bar{L}$$

where $F(x_1, \cdots, x_n)$ is obviously the (labor) cost function for the output bundle $(x_1, \cdots, x_n)$.

The problem is to maximize over output-leisure bundles the social utility function, $U(x_1, \cdots, x_n, R)$, subject to this constraint, and subject to the constraint that exactly the required government surplus is obtained as profit:

$$\sum_{i=1}^{n} p_i x_i - F(x_1, \ldots, x_n) = M,$$

where the p's are equilibrium labor-prices associated with the chosen output-leisure bundle. Associating the Lagrange multiplier λ with the first constraint, and the multiplier, μ, with the second, we can write out the Lagrangian expression:

$$\begin{aligned} V(x_1, \ldots, x_n, R, \lambda, \mu) \\ = U(x_1, \ldots, x_n, R) \\ + \lambda[\bar{L} - F(x_1, \ldots, x_n) - R - M] \\ + \mu\left[M - \sum_{i=1}^{n} p_i x_i + F(x_1, \ldots, x_n)\right] \end{aligned}$$

Taking partial derivatives we obtain the first-order conditions:

$$\frac{\partial U}{\partial x_i} - \lambda \frac{\partial F}{\partial x_i} - \mu\left[\frac{\partial}{\partial x_i}\left(\sum_{j=1}^{n} p_j x_j\right) - \frac{\partial F}{\partial x_i}\right] = 0, \quad i = 1, \ldots, n$$

$$\frac{\partial U}{\partial R} - \lambda = 0$$

Dividing each of the first n conditions by the $(n+1)$st and noting that equilibrium of the consumer requires $\partial U/\partial x_i/\partial U/\partial R = p_i/p_r = p_i$ (since labor is the numeraire, its price unity) we have

$$p_i - \frac{\partial F}{\partial x_i} = \frac{\mu}{\lambda}\left[\frac{\partial}{\partial x_i}\left(\sum_{j=1}^{n} p_j x_j\right) - \frac{\partial F}{\partial x_i}\right].$$

Employing, with their usual meanings, the symbols MC and MR (the latter including the effect on revenue of variations in *all* prices), the preceding condition implies

$$p_i - MC_i = \frac{\mu}{\lambda}(MR_i - MC_i), \quad i = 1, \ldots, n$$

which is the second form of our theorem from which the other forms can be obtained exactly as before. Thus we have derived the results explicitly from a general equilibrium model. Note that the term "marginal revenue" is definable here because we have normalized prices to labor dimensions and have assumed behind-the-scenes income distribution, making determinate the effect on equilibrium prices of changes in any of the desired outputs. Note also that under these conditions, the second version of the theorem, proved in Section III for the case of independent demands, is shown to hold generally.

IX. *Notes on the History of the Discussion*

There is some point in going briefly into the antecedents of the discussion because this history makes it all the more difficult to understand why the propositions in question have achieved so little recognition by the profession. The general line of argument has appeared widely for the better part of a century. The formal theorems themselves date back more than forty years. As we will see, this work has appeared in some of our leading journals under the authorship of some of the luminaries of our profession and was clearly not limited to a backwater of the literature.

There is an informal proposition very closely related to the results under examination that has a long history going back at least to the 1870's. With the establishment of the Railway and Canal Commission in England in 1873, and of the discussion preceding the establishment of the Interstate Commerce Commission in the subsequent decade there arose a rich literature examining utility pricing in relation to the public interest. A number of authors advocated prices that vary directly with demand *in*elasticity ("value of service").[15]

[15] For some examples see A. T. Hadley (ch. 6); E. Porter Alexander (esp. pp. 2–5, 10–11) and W. M. Acworth (ch. 3, esp. pp. 57–60). Hadley, the American

The mainstay of the early discussion was an argument only loosely related to the formal propositions in which we are interested. In brief, it was maintained that a relatively low price in elastic markets, provided it covers more than incremental cost, may well permit lower prices in other markets and hence be beneficial to everyone. For (particularly if the firm is subject to a constraint on its overall profit) the opening of a market which makes any net contribution may permit or may even require a reduction in prices elsewhere.[16]

Discussion along these lines has since appeared throughout the literature of public utility economics. (See, e.g., James Bonbright, esp. chs. 5, 17–20.) The various forms of the proposition have also appeared at least implicitly in a number of the standard writings of economic theory, notably in Joan Robinson's work and that of W. Arthur Lewis.[17]

However, the formal mathematical propositions which are derived from optimality considerations and which are the subject of this paper, themselves have a substantial history. As propositions on optimal taxation they first appear in 1927 in Frank Ramsey's pathbreaking article on taxation.[18] Thus, more than a decade before the publication of Hotelling's historic discussion of marginal cost pricing, Ramsey had in another context provided at least implicitly a solution to the optimal pricing problem for an industry in which marginal cost prices do not cover total costs.

A. C. Pigou took up the Ramsey discussion in the following year in his book on public finance, providing a very lucid and rather extensive summary of the argument. It was independently approached by Ursula Hicks in her 1947 book on the same subject. Her analysis is largely diagrammatic and is based entirely on the Marshallian consumers' surplus, just as Ramsey's and Pigou's had been. However, as far as we have been able to tell, the formal anal-

economist who went on to become a president of Yale, is the author of what is apparently the classic discussion of the period, in which he coined the phrase "not charging what the traffic can *not* bear." There is in fact a hint of the argument much earlier than this in the work of Dupuit who advocates the separation of consumers into different classes each paying a different price, remarking "suppose that (railroads) offered nothing but first class tickets, what a loss for the public and for the companies" (pp. 124–27).

[16] "If the (New York to San Francisco) price is more than the *additional outlay* involved in doing it, as against leaving it alone, it is profitable to the railroad, and the business is moreover advantageous to the whole inland community served by the railroad. For it adds to the number of men employed along the line and . . . the more prosperous the road, the lower the local rates may be made" E. P. Alexander (p. 4) (author's italics). The author adds (p. 5) that between the limits of "unreasonable" profits and net loss, actual profit rates "should be adjusted in proportion to value of service rendered" (*in*-elasticity of demand).

[17] See Joan Robinson (p. 207). Since she is dealing with a single product and does not utilize any explicit revenue constraint, the result she gives is not quite what is needed for our purposes but it is closely related to the theorem under discussion.

Lewis' statement (pp. 20–21), on the other hand, is precisely on target:

> The principle . . . is that those who cannot escape must make the largest contribution to indivisible cost, and those to whom the commodity does not matter much . . . get off lightly. . . . When there are escapable indivisible expenses to be covered the case for discrimination is clear. It secures an output nearer the optimum and levies the indivisible cost on those who get the greatest benefit (measured by their consumers' surplus). . . . Moreover, it is possible in some cases that the net result may be that everyone pays a lower price. . . . *If the undertaking is out merely to cover its costs* . . . reducing the price to some persons with elastic demands may increase the surplus over marginal cost which they contribute. . . . (emphasis added).

[18] The theorem seems to have made its greatest impact on the literature of public finance. A. C. Pigou (1928, pp. 126–28); (1947, pp. 105–09) reports Ramsey's results, offers an intuitive explanation and translates the theorem into elasticity terms. He also argues that except in the case of linear supply and demand functions the argument holds only if the taxes are small.

Ursula Hicks (pp. 167 ff) provides a very similar result on the basis of an elementary graphic argument. Yet even Richard Musgrave in his classic volume (p. 148) devotes only a footnote to the theorem and dismisses it as being "arrived at within the framework of the old welfare economics of interpersonal utility comparison " His characterization of the argument as part of the ability-to-pay approach is surely rather misleading. Cf. R. Bishop's comment on Musgrave, p. 212n.

ysis did not reappear until 1951 in an article by M. Boiteux which was the first to dispense with the notion of consumers' surplus. Apparently in the same year, Paul Samuelson submitted to the U.S. Treasury a closely related paper containing a generalization of Ramsey's results.[19] Samuelson's approach differs from that which we are discussing in that he employs no explicit revenue requirement. Instead he requires some preselected quantity of each output to be left unused by the private sector and made available to the government. His result, however, is essentially the same as those of the other contributors under discussion.

In 1952 there appeared a particularly simple derivation of the theorem in its most elementary form in a note by Alan Manne. His discussion assumes that cross-elasticities of demand are all zero and it measures and aggregates consumers' and producers' surplus in an unabashed Marshallian manner, but his derivation compensates for these simplifications by its great lucidity. Boiteux and Manne were also the first to present the analysis in the form of a discussion of public utility pricing. One year later Marcus Fleming provided an independent and illuminating derivation.

Meanwhile, Gerard Debreu had contributed analytic materials which led Boiteux to employ a Pareto optimality approach to the matter. On this basis Boiteux was then able to complete his definitive analysis of the subject. In Boiteux' classic 1956 article the analysis is, as a result, independent of any interpersonal comparison. The notions of consumers' and producers' surplus are dispensed with altogether. He is able to deal with goods whose demands are interdependent, with the pricing of inputs and intermediate goods as well as with outputs. It has also been emphasized by a subsequent writer (Jacques Drèze) that by his general equilibrium approach to the matter, Boiteux was contributing an explicit second-best solution, one of the few to be found to date in any area of welfare economics. Of course, no piece of analysis can answer every relevant question, and Boiteux left unsettled some matters of detail. There is a moderately mysterious role played in his analysis by the numéraire commodity; he has not dealt with problems of nonnegativity of outputs, etc. All this has left room for subsequent work by R. Rees, William Vickrey (*Testimony* and other unpublished work), the present authors, and by a number of others.[20]

[19] Samuelson's own brief description of the history of the analysis (1964) is worth reproducing:

> . . . Consider an optimal *laissez faire* situation that maximizes a social welfare function with zero government expenditure and taxes. Now introduce government services as a (vector) function of a small or large parameter y, $G(y)$. Suppose excise taxes (on goods or services) to be alone feasible, and introduce a (vector) pattern of excises $T(y)$ sufficient to provide resources for the G. What is the optimal $T(y)$ pattern to maximize the welfare function $W(y)=W(T, G)$? This is the problem set by Pigou to Frank Ramsey in the 1920's. Approximate answers were given by Ramsey, Boiteux (and in unpublished form by Hotelling and Hicks). In a pearl cast before the U.S. Treasury in 1950, I gave an exact solution for large and small programs; namely, that the optimal pattern is the one at which the response of all goods and factors to a further compensated-Slutsky price distortion would result in equal percentage (virtual) reductions.
>
> My literary wording is loose, but there is no need for approximative consumer's surplus at all. . . .

Though the reported date of the Samuelson memorandum may seem to imply some ambiguity about the order of appearance of this and the first Boiteux article, this issue is cleared up by Samuelson's explicit reference to the Boiteux article on page 5 of his memorandum in which he expresses his debt to the "brilliant analysis by M. Boiteux."

[20] Among those who have also written on the subject are Diamond and Mirrlees and Bishop. Recall in this connection Samuelson's reference to unpublished work by Hicks and Hotelling, on which more light is shed by the following excerpt from a letter which the authors received from Professor Hicks:

> It was just as well that you sent me the cutting from Samuelson [the preceding footnote], or I should have found it hard to recollect the matter. But with this refreshment it comes back. I think the story is as follows.

However, there is no need to go beyond Boiteux' work for a basis for the welfare discussion contained in this paper. The generalization to optimal pricing for an entire economy requires only one small modification in Boiteux' two-sector analysis. In his model there are two sets of firms, the first composed exclusively of perfect competitors, while the second are subject to the author's rules for quasi-optimal pricing. For our purpose we need merely take all firms to fall into the second category and our interpretation follows at once. In sum, it follows for the economy as a whole that unless marginal cost pricing happens to provide returns sufficient to meet the social (governmentally determined?) revenue requirement, a quasi-optimal allocation calls for systematic deviations of prices from marginal costs *throughout the economy* in the manner specified by the theorems that this paper has described.

X. *Concluding Comment*

We conclude our survey of the relevant literature as we began—at a loss to explain how a set of results flowing from the pens of so distinguished a set of authors and appearing and reappearing in the profession's leading journals, should so long have escaped general notice. This is all the more curious in light of the importance of the subject and the elegance of the theory.

As a theoretical matter, the theorem we have discussed seems fundamental not only for the analysis of public finance and the regulation of utilities, but also for some of the basic precepts of welfare economics. Earlier we spoke of the result as a proposition in the theory of the second best. But it is more than this. In a world in which marginal cost pricing without excise or income taxes is normally not feasible, the solution we have usually considered to characterize the "best" is none too good, because it is simply unattainable. In that case, the systematic deviations between prices and marginal costs that the theorem calls for may truly be optimal because they constitute the best we can do within the limitations imposed by normal economic circumstances.

Appendix

Comments On Lerner's Appendix

In the Appendix to his paper, Lerner asserts that our analysis over-emphasized demand elasticities. In addition, the Appendix contains a wider range of lesser criticisms. To deal in depth with all of these would require us to impose on the reader's time and patience. We propose to touch briefly on what appear to us to be the more important issues raised by Lerner, and trust that our failure to respond to other points will not be taken as a sign of general agreement.

Two criticisms appear recurringly in Lerner's Appendix and they are best disposed of at the outset. The first is that we have somehow used as a standard of welfare a measure of *consumers' loss*, and have left out any measure of *social damage*. Since our economy was taken to consist entirely of consumers, i.e., we use the terms "consumer" and "person with utility function" here

---

In December 1946 (in the last week of my first visit to the United States) I stayed for a couple of days with Hotelling at Chapel Hill. I then told him that I had worked out (using a quite crude consumers' surplus method) that if a given sum had to be raised in excise taxes, the least-sacrifice way of doing it was the proportional all-round reduction in consumption, as compared with an optimum position. For if the burden of the tax is

$$\frac{1}{2}\sum q_{ij}dp_i dp_j$$

this is minimised subject to $G=\Sigma q_i dp_i$ if

$$dq_i = \sum q_{ij}dp_j = \lambda q_i$$

where λ is the Lagrange multiplier. Not much more than this, except that I had allowed (in the spirit of the old Hotelling article) that the q_{ij} could incorporate supply as well as demand reactions.

I remember he told me I ought to publish this, but I didn't—mainly, I suppose, because I was conscious of the qualifications to which Samuelson alludes in his paper, and which, if I had set them out in my style, would have whittled away the result so near to nothing.

interchangeably, we would use the two terms "consumers' loss" and "social damage" interchangeably as well. We would use neither without a grain of salt. The touchstone of quasi-optimality is plain and simple Pareto optimality, given the profit or tax revenue constraint. As is by now generally recognized, Pareto optimality cannot be comfortably equated with a "higher ethical good," and we apologize if we give the impression that a quasi-optimal price structure (for the monopolist) or tax structure was "good" in any sense other than Pareto optimality.

The second assertion that occurs in several places is that our analysis assumes constant marginal costs. This is simply incorrect. The only point at which marginal costs are taken to be constant is in our Section IV, the graphical presentation, which is intended solely as an aid to intuition. Elsewhere there is no assumption of any sort about marginal costs and none of the results depend on such an assumption. Lerner seems to suggest that our assumption that the prices of inputs are fixed can be equated to the premise that marginal cost is constant. We fail to see any connection between the two. Our assumption that input prices are constant is another, perhaps mistaken, compromise in the direction of intuitive appeal.[21]

Incidentally, the point of our footnote 7 is not, as Lerner suggests, to acknowledge in passing that marginal costs might in fact be variable. Rather, it is intended to point out that the marginal costs in question in the various forms of the theorem are *not* those which prevail in some initial situation before any taxes are imposed, but those which in fact rule at the solution values. Rather than apologizing for assuming marginal costs constant, we are, on the contrary, saying that marginal costs will very likely change as taxes are varied, so one must watch out and be sure to use the correct values in testing for optimality.

The basic task undertaken by Lerner in his Appendix relevant to the discussion here is derivation of our four forms of the "mislaid maxim" from his second rule. Since all four are derivable from either the first ($\partial\pi/\partial p_i=\lambda x_i$, all i) or the fourth ($\Sigma_j(\partial x_i/\partial p_j)(p_j-MC_j)=\gamma x_i$, all i) it is reasonable that he should be able to do this. It is nevertheless somewhat surprising that he did not in the process notice that his second rule takes into account only "own tax elasticity" and hence implicitly assumes the zero cross elasticities which he finds so objectionable in our second and third forms. It is probably because of this that he comes to the conclusion that our first form holds only when cross-elasticities are zero, which is simply incorrect.

Lerner's handling of our first form of the theorem (which, incidentally, is the one form we did *not* distill from the literature although since deriving it, we have seen essentially the same variant in Diamond and Mirrlees) is altogether curious. Almost paradigmatic of the economist's approach to a welfare problem, say, how large a park to build, is the following: "Clearly our rule should be, enlarge the park until the incremental social gain from enlargement by an additional unit is just balanced by the social loss from the space and other resources thereby foregone. But that is, of course, purely tautological. What we now need to do is clothe the concepts of social gain and social loss with operational measures. . . ." In this case Lerner goes backwards: "The equalization of the ratio between marginal yield and output level turns out to be an obscure way of expressing the equalization of marginal tax yield and marginal social damage—an equalization that minimizes the total social damage for a given total tax yield" (p. 289). We were, as it happens, especially pleased with the first form of the theorem which we think is new, precisely

[21] Analytically, it does serve to a set a price level so that the government profit constraint in pecuniary form is pinned down. In the case of more than one input factor it does, however, hide rather strong assumptions about the transformation function in a full general equilibrium treatment. In any event, the pecuniary variant of the government's budget constraint is perhaps not the most felicitous for use in such a treatment. The theorems in question are, however, in no way sensitive to these assumptions. Again we recommend perusal of the literature on this point.

because it seemed to promise more than the others a degree of operational applicability. Our feeling was that experienced tax officials (or monopoly managers) would have a much better chance of estimating at least roughly the magnitudes that enter that expression—the effect on the total tax take (profit) (including cross effects) of a change in a given tax (price) than econometricians would have of estimating the full matrix of cross elasticities, just as it seems plausible that a businessman may come close to maximizing profits even though he is pretty vague about quantities such as marginal cost and marginal revenue. If this is misplaced faith it doesn't matter, because the first form of the theorem, being equivalent to the others (and for more forms see our forthcoming paper), is at least no harder than they to put into practice. One thing is clear, the operational meaning of the first form is easier than the others (except, perhaps, for the fourth) to explain to a non-economist.

The derivations of the second and third forms of our theorem, like those of the first and fourth, make no use of and in no way depend upon constancy of marginal cost. The second and third variants do, however, involve an assumption of zero cross elasticities of demand among the goods whose prices are in question. Lerner is quite properly disturbed by the implication of extending this assumption to *all* goods. The demand relationship being traced out by variations in the price vector is simply the aggregate offer curve of the economy with the initial commodity vector of each citizen specified (generally at zero) and no net transfers. Independent demands for the individual goods are impossible here except in the trivial case in which the demanded vector is completely independent of the price vector, a vector which would in turn have to be the zero net transactions vector. The implication is not that the results are incorrect but that the second and third forms are not relevant when all goods are taxable and there are no net transfers.

Again, contrary to Lerner, the fourth form of the theorem is as general as the first, and more general than the second and third (*not* because it doesn't depend upon constant costs—they don't either—but because it does not assume zero cross-elasticities). Given the parenthetical word "approximately" its generality would seem assured. But we were willing to go farther than that, and took great pains to make precise in Section III, in the algebraic development of the fourth variant, what operationally was meant by "approximately" here. In footnote 9 we spell this out still further.

REFERENCES

W. M. Acworth, *The Railways and the Traders*. London 1891.

E. P. Alexander, *Railway Practice*. New York 1887.

R. Bishop, "The Effects of Specific and ad valorem Taxes," *Quart. J. Econ.*, May 1968, *82*, 198-218.

D. F. Bradford and W. J. Baumol, "Quasi-optimal Pricing with Regulated Profit and Interdependent Demands," forthcoming.

M. Boiteux, "Le 'revenue distribuable' et les pertes économiques," *Econometrica*, Apr. 1951, *19*, 112-33.

———, "Sur la gestion des Monopoles Publics astreints à l'équilibre budgétaire," *Econometrica*, Jan. 1956, *24*, 22-40.

J. Bonbright, *Principles of Public Utility Rates*. New York 1961.

G. Debreu, "The Classical Tax-Subsidy Problem," *Econometrica*, Jan. 1952, *20*, 100.

P. A. Diamond and J. A. Mirrlees, "Optimal Taxation and Public Production," mimeo. working paper 22, M.I.T. 1968.

J. H. Drèze, "Some Postwar Contributions of French Economists to Theory and Public Policy, with Special Emphasis on Problems of Resource Allocation," *Amer. Econ. Rev.*, June 1964, *54*, 1-64.

J. Dupuit, *Traité théorique et pratique de la conduite et de la distribution des eaux*. Paris 1854.

J. M. Fleming, "Optimal Production with Fixed Profits," *Economica*, Aug. 1953, N.S. *20*, 215-36.

A. T. Hadley, *Railroad Transportation*. New York and London 1886.

J. R. Hicks, *Value and Capital*, 2d ed, New York 1956.

Ursala Hicks, *Public Finance*. New York 1947.

H. Hotelling, "The General Welfare in Relation to Problems of Taxation and of Railway and Utility Rates," *Econometrica*, July 1938, *6*, 242-69.

H. Leibenstein, "Allocative Efficiency vs. 'X-Efficiency,'" *Amer. Econ. Rev.*, June 1966, *56*, 392-415.

A. P. Lerner, "On Optimal Taxes With an Untaxable Sector," *Amer. Econ. Rev.*, June 1970, *60*, 284-94.

W. A. Lewis, *Overhead Costs*. London 1949.

A. Manne, "Multiple-Purpose Public Enterprises—Criteria for Pricing," *Economica*, Aug. 1952, N.S. *19*, 322-26.

R. Musgrave, *The Theory of Public Finance*. New York 1957.

A. C. Pigou, *A Study of Public Finance*, (a) 1st ed., London 1928; (b) 3d ed., London 1947.

F. Ramsey, "A Contribution to the Theory of Taxation," *Econ. J.*, Mar. 1927, *37*, 47-61.

R. Rees, "Second-Best Rules for Public Enterprise Pricing," *Economica*, Aug. 1968, N.S. *35*, 260-73.

Joan Robinson, *The Economics of Imperfect Competition*. London 1933.

P. A. Samuelson, "Theory of Optimal Taxation," unpublished, approx. 1951.

———, "Principles of Efficiency—Discussion," *Amer. Econ. Rev. Proc.*, May 1964, *54*, 94-95.

W. Vickrey, *Testimony*, F. C. C. Docket No. 16258, Networks Exhibit No. 5, Appendix I. Washington 1968.

O. Williamson, *The Economics of Discretionary Behavior*. Englewood Cliffs 1964.

[12]

Optimal Taxation and Public Production I: Production Efficiency

By PETER A. DIAMOND AND JAMES A. MIRRLEES*

Theories of optimal production in a planned economy have usually assumed that the tax system can allow the government to achieve any desired redistribution of property.[1] On the other hand, some recent discussions of public investment criteria have tended to ignore taxation as a complementary method of controlling the economy.[2] Although lump sum transfers of the kind required for full optimality[3] are not feasible today, commodity and income taxes can certainly be used to increase welfare.[4] We shall therefore examine the maximization of social welfare using both taxes and public production as control variables. In doing so, we intend to bring together the theories of taxation, public investment, and welfare economics.

There are two main results of the study: the demonstration of the desirability of aggregate production efficiency in a wide variety of circumstances provided that taxes are set at the optimal level; and an examination of that optimal tax structure. It is widely known that aggregate production efficiency is desired as one part of achieving a Pareto optimum. It is also widely known that when the desired Pareto optimum cannot be achieved, aggregate production efficiency may not be desirable. Our conclusion differs from these results in that production efficiency is desirable although a full Pareto optimum is not achieved. In the optimum position, the presence of commodity taxes implies that marginal rates of substitution are not equal to marginal rates of transformation. Furthermore, the absence of lump sum taxes implies that the income distribution is not the best that can be conceived. Yet, the presence of optimal commodity taxes will be shown to imply the desirability of aggregate production efficiency.

This result is similar to that derived by Marcel Boiteux, although he considered an economy where lump sum redistributions of income were possible. Boiteux also examined the optimal tax structure that was necessary for this result. The optimal tax structure for the case of a single consumer (or equivalently with lump sum redistribution) has also been examined by Frank

* The authors are at Massachusetts Institute of Technology and Nuffield College, Oxford, respectively. During some of the work, Diamond was at Churchill College, Cambridge and Nuffield College, Oxford and Mirrlees was at M.I.T. Earlier versions of this paper were given at Econometric Society winter meetings at Washington and Blaricum, 1967, at the University Social Science Council Conference, Kampala, Uganda, December 1968, and to the Game Theory and Mathematical Economics Seminar, Hebrew University, Jerusalem. The authors wish to thank M.A.H. Dempster, D. K. Foley, P. A. Samuelson, K. Shell, and participants in these seminars for helpful discussions on this subject, and referees for valuable comments. Diamond was supported in part by the National Science Foundation under grant GS 1585. The authors bear sole responsibility for opinions and errors.

[1] For a discussion of this literature, see Abram Bergson.

[2] For a survey of this literature, see Alan Prest and Ralph Turvey.

[3] We wish to distinguish here between lump sum taxes, which may vary from individual to individual while being unaffected by the individual's behavior, and poll taxes which are the same for all individuals, or perhaps for all individuals within several large groups, distinguished perhaps by age, sex, or region.

[4] For another study of the general equilibrium impact of taxation, which does not explore the optimality question, see Gerard Debreu (1954).

Ramsey and Paul Samuelson.[5] Our results move beyond theirs in considering the problem of income redistribution together with that of raising revenue. Even in the absence of government revenue requirements, if lump sum redistribution is impossible, the government will want to use its excise tax powers to improve income distribution. It will subsidize and tax different goods so as to alter individual real incomes. The optimal redistribution by this method occurs when there is a balance between the equity improvements and the efficiency losses from further taxation.

The general situation we want to discuss is an economy in which there are many consumers, public and private production, public consumption, and many different kinds of feasible tax instruments. We think that it is easier to understand the problem if we present the analysis first for a single consumer, no public consumption, and only commodity taxation, although this case has little intrinsic interest. The main point of the paper is that the analysis of this special case carries over in the main to the general case.

The first two sections are devoted to this special case. In the first, the situation is portrayed geometrically (for a two-commodity world with no private production); in the second, production efficiency and conditions for the optimal taxes are derived by application of the calculus. The use of the calculus here and elsewhere is not perfectly rigorous for the usual reasons. These issues are taken up in Section IV. In the third section, we extend the analysis of production to an economy with many consumers, elucidating precise conditions under which production efficiency is desirable (and presenting certain exceptions). Section IV provides a rigorous statement of the theorems. In the fifth section, we discuss briefly certain applications and extensions of the basic efficiency result.

A following paper, referred to here as Diamond-Mirrlees II, will appear in the June 1971 *Review*. In it we will examine the optimality rules for commodity taxes, for other taxes including income taxes, and for public consumption. We will also give a rigorous statement of conditions under which the first-order conditions obtained (heuristically) below are indeed necessary conditions.

I. One-Consumer Economy—Geometric Analysis

We begin by considering an economy with a single, price-taking consumer and two commodities. We assume, for the moment, that all production possibilities are controlled by the government. While there is no scope for redistribution of income in this economy, the government might need to raise revenue to cover losses if there are increasing returns to scale or if there are fixed expenditures (such as defense) and constant returns to scale. Alternatively, the technology might exhibit decreasing returns to scale, facing the government with the problem of disposing of a surplus if all transactions are carried out at market prices. The optimal solution to either raising or disposing of revenue is well known. A poll tax or subsidy, as the case may be, will permit the hiring of the needed resources and permit the economy to achieve a Pareto optimum, which, in a one-consumer economy, is equivalent to the maximization of the consumer's utility. While this is a reasonable possibility in a one-consumer economy, lump sum taxes varying from individual to individual do not seem feasible in a much larger economy. An identical problem of distributing a surplus among many people arises if it is desired to improve income distribution.

[5] For a detailed history of analysis of this problem, see William Baumol and David Bradford. A summary and discussion of the work of Boiteux has been given by Jacques Drèze.

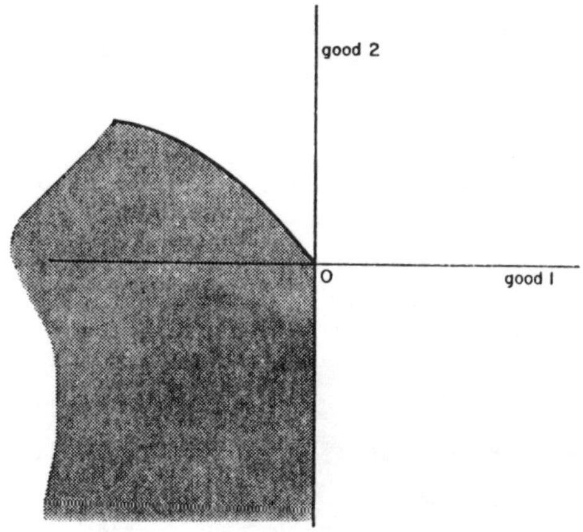

FIGURE 1

Thus we shall consider the use of commodity taxes when lump sum taxes are not permitted to the government, not for the intrinsic interest of this question in a one-consumer economy, but as an introduction to the many-consumer case. Furthermore we shall hold constant the government expenditure pattern which directly affects consumer utility. Thus we can ignore it, since the utility function already reflects its impact. The addition of choice for public consumption will be considered in Diamond-Mirrlees II.

Assuming free disposal, the technological constraint on the planner is that the government supply be on or under the production frontier. Such a constraint is shown by the shaded area in Figure 1. Let us measure on the axes the quantities supplied to the consumer. Thus, the output being produced (good 2) is measured positively, while the input (good 1) is measured negatively. The case drawn is the familiar one of decreasing returns to scale. If the government needed a fixed bundle of resources, for national defense say, then the production possibility frontier (describing the potential transactions with the consumer) would not pass through the origin. With constant returns to scale this might appear as in Figure 2, where a units of good 1 are needed for defense. (It is perhaps convenient to think of good 1 as labor and good 2 as a consumption good.)

In a totally planned economy, where the planner selects a fixed consumption bundle (including labor to be supplied) for each consumer, the planner would have no further constraint and could choose any point that was technologically feasible. Again, this is not implausible for the planner in a one-consumer economy, but becomes so as the number of households grows. A more realistic assumption, then, is to assume that the planner can only deal with consumers through the market place, hiring labor and selling the consumer good. Assume further that the planner is constrained to charge uniform prices. The planner must now set the price of the consumer good relative to the wage (or inversely the real wage), and is constrained to transactions which the consumer is willing to undertake at some relative price. The locus of consumption bundles which the consumer is willing to achieve by trade from the origin is the offer curve or price-consumption locus. It represents the

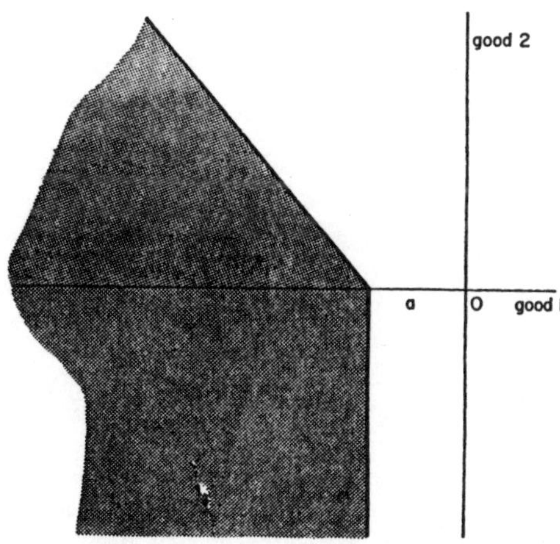

FIGURE 2

bundles of goods that the consumer would purchase at different possible price ratios. Figure 3 contains an example of an offer curve with several hypothetical budget lines and the corresponding indifference curves drawn in. The planner thus has two constraints: he must choose a point which is both technologically feasible and an equilibrium bundle from the point of view of the consumer. Combining these two constraints, the range of consumption bundles which are both feasible and potential consumer equilibria is shown as the heavy line in Figure 4.

We can state these two constraints algebraically. Let us denote by $z = (z_1, \ldots, z_n)$ the vector of government supply. The production constraint is then written

(1) $G(z) \leqq 0$, or, equivalently,

$$z_1 \leqq g(z_2, z_3, \ldots, z_n)$$

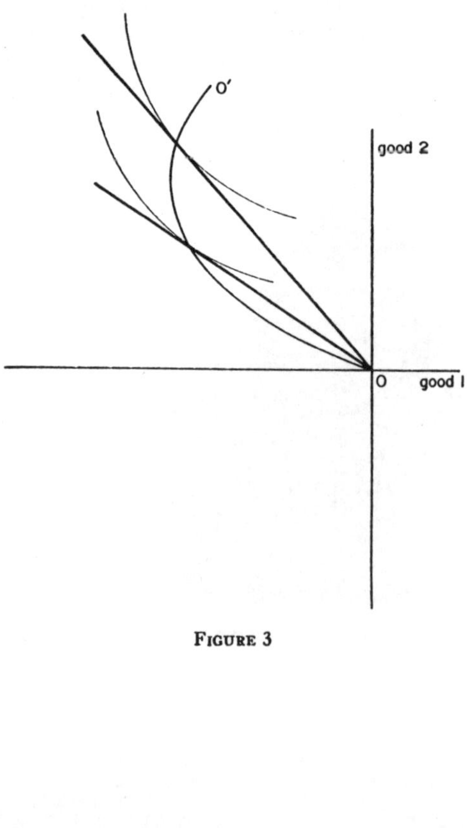

FIGURE 3

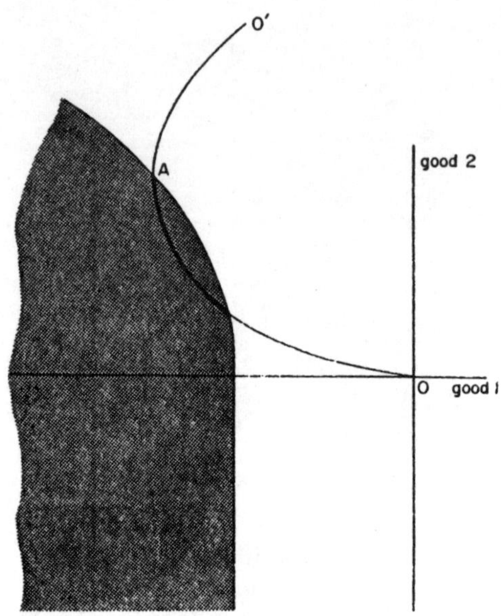

FIGURE 4

The constraint that the government supply equal the consumer demand for some price can be written in vector notation

(2) $$x(q) = z,$$

where $x = (x_1, \ldots, x_n)$ is the vector of consumer demands and $q = (q_1, \ldots, q_n)$ is the vector of prices faced by the consumer.

Now consider the government's objectives. Since the consumer's equilibrium position is determined by the prices he faces, we can, in the usual circumstances, describe the objective function as a function of prices, say $v(q)$. The problem is to choose q so as to

(3) Maximize $v(q)$

subject to $G(x(q)) \leqq 0$

This simply formulated problem is the focus of attention of the paper and can take on a variety of interpretations. The reader may note that the consideration of many consumers does not alter the form of this problem. This is a major advantage

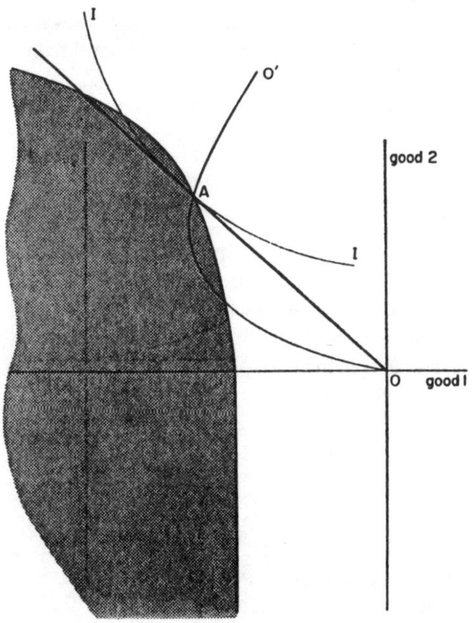

FIGURE 5

of using prices rather than quantities as the focus of the analysis.

Let us consider the case where the planner seeks to maximize the same function of consumption as the consumer's utility function. The welfare function is said to be ***individualistic***, or to respect individual preferences, since welfare can be written as a function of individual utility. Returning to Figure 3 we see that the consumer moves to higher indifference curves as he proceeds along the offer curve away from the origin. Thus, in Figure 4 we wish to move as far along *OO′* as possible, subject to the constraint of the shaded production possibility set. The optimal point is therefore *A*, where the offer curve and the production frontier intersect.

The prices which will induce the consumer to purchase the optimal consumption bundle are defined by the budget line *OA*. In Figure 5 we show the optimal point and the implied budget line, and indifference curve *II*. All the points above *II* and in the shaded production set are Pareto-superior to *A* and technologically feasible, but not attainable by market transactions without lump sum transfers. For contrast, in Figure 6, we show the Pareto optimal point, *B*, and the implied budget line, and indifference curve *I′I′*, which will permit decentralization. In the case drawn, the consumer's budget line does not pass through the origin; this represents his payment of a lump sum tax to cover government expenditures in excess of profits from production.

We see that the optimal point is on the production possibility frontier of the economy, not inside it. This important property of the optimum can easily be seen to carry over to the case of many commodities, but still one consumer. With many commodities, the offer curve is a union of loci, each of which is obtained by holding the prices of all but one commodity constant and varying the price of that one commodity. Doing this for each com-

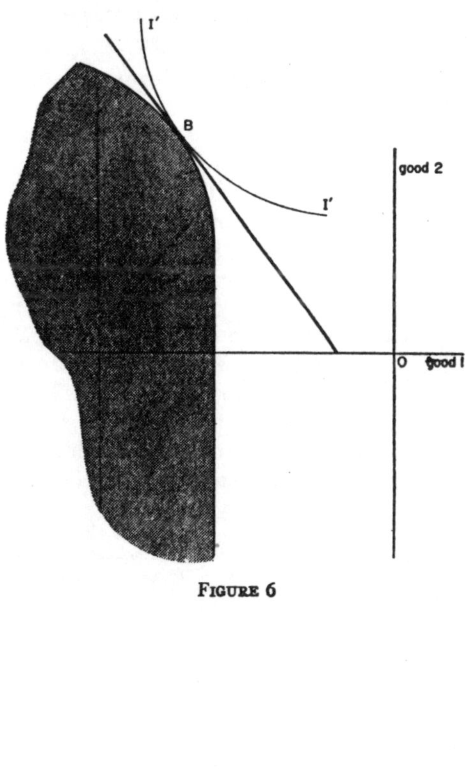

FIGURE 6

modity, and for all possible configurations of prices for the other commodities, generates all the loci. The offer curve is the union of such loci. On each locus, the point which is also on the production frontier is better than the other points on the locus. Thus, any point which is not on the production frontier is dominated by some point which is on the frontier. Therefore, the optimal point is one of the points on the frontier. The implications of this result will be seen more clearly below, when we consider both public and private production. For this result to carry over to the case of many consumers requires one further, mild assumption which will be discussed in the third section. First, we treat the one consumer economy algebraically, with both public and private production, showing by calculus the desirability of aggregate production efficiency, and obtaining the optimal relationship between consumer prices and the slope of the production possibilities. This relationship defines the optimal tax structure.

II. One-Consumer Economy—Algebraic Analysis

We assume constant returns to scale in the private production sector and the presence of competitive conditions there. In equilibrium there are, therefore, no profits. (This is a critical assumption for the efficiency analysis.) We also assume, for the present, that the only taxes used by the government are commodity taxes.[6] Consumer prices, q, therefore determine the choices available to the consumer, and we may write the welfare function as a function of consumer prices, $v(q)$. Notice that this covers the case where the government's assessment of welfare does not coincide with the consumer's utility, although depending on what he consumes. In the special case where social preferences coincide with those of the single consumer, his utility may be taken to measure welfare. Then we have

$$v(q) = u(x(q)) \tag{4}$$

We shall not use this special form for $v(q)$ in the analysis below until we come to evaluate the tax structure explicitly. Until that point, the analysis applies also to welfare functions that are not individualistic. For later use let us express the derivatives of v in this special case. Writing $v_k = \partial v/\partial q_k$, $u_i = \partial u/\partial x_i$, and using (4), we have

$$v_k = \sum u_i \frac{\partial x_i}{\partial q_k} = -\alpha x_k, \tag{5}$$

where α is a positive constant (i.e., independent of k), the marginal utility of income. Equation (5) follows from the budget constraint,

$$\sum q_i x_i = 0, \tag{6}$$

which on differentiation with respect to q_k yields

$$x_k + \sum q_i \frac{\partial x_i}{\partial q_k} = 0 \tag{7}$$

Since utility-maximization implies that $u_i = \alpha q_i$, (5) now follows from (7).

Production

Let us denote the vector of prices faced by private producers by $p = (p_1, \ldots, p_n)$. Because of taxes, t, these may differ from the prices faced by consumers: $q_i = p_i + t_i$ $(i = 1, \ldots, n)$. $y = (y_1, \ldots, y_n)$ is the vector of commodities privately supplied (inputs will thus appear as negative supplies), and we write the private production constraint,

$$y_1 = f(y_2, \ldots, y_n) \tag{8}$$

Notice that we assume *equality* in the

[6] This assumption is made solely for simplicity. In Diamond-Mirrlees II, the general principles will be seen to carry over with additional taxes, including a progressive income tax.

production constraint, that is, that production is efficient in the private sector. This follows from profit maximization if there are no zero prices. We assume that f is a differentiable function, and that $y_i \neq 0$ $(i=1, \ldots, n)$. Then, profit maximization means that

$$p_i = -p_1 f_i(y_2, \ldots, y_n), \quad (i = 2, \ldots, n) \tag{9}$$

where f_i denotes the derivative of f with respect to y_i. Also, by the assumption of constant returns to scale, maximized profits are zero in equilibrium:

$$\sum p_i y_i = 0 \tag{10}$$

So that we may conveniently employ calculus, we shall assume that the government production constraint, (1), is satisfied with an equality rather than an inequality:

$$z_1 = g(z_2, \ldots, z_n) \tag{11}$$

Thus we do not give the government the option of inefficient government production. Rather, we shift our attention to *aggregate* production efficiency. Efficiency will be present if marginal rates of transformation are the same in publicly and privately controlled production. It will then be seen quite easily that the assumption of efficiency in the public sector is justified.

Walras' Law

We have chosen an objective function and expressed the government's production constraint above. To complete the formulation of the maximization problem, it remains to add the requirement that the economy be in equilibrium. The conditions that all markets clear can be stated in terms of the vectors x, y, and z.

$$x(q) = y + z \tag{12}$$

The reader may be puzzled that at no place in this formulation has a budget constraint been introduced for the government. (Other readers may be puzzled by our failure to include only $n-1$ markets in our market clearance equations. These are aspects of the same phenomenon.) Walras' Law implies that if all economic agents satisfy their budget constraints and all markets but one are in equilibrium, then the last market is also in equilibrium. It also implies that when all markets clear and all economic agents but one are on their budget constraints, then the last economic agent is on his budget constraint. In setting up our problem, we have assumed that the household and the private firms are on their budget constraints. Thus, if we assume that all markets clear, this will imply that the government is satisfying its budget constraint,[7] which we can express as

$$\sum (q_i - p_i)x_i + \sum p_i z_i = 0 = \sum t_i x_i + \sum p_i z_i \tag{13}$$

Alternatively, if we consider the government budget balance as one of the constraints, then it is only necessary to impose market clearance in $n-1$ of the markets.

In this model we can make two price normalizations, one for each price structure. Since both consumer demand and firm supply are homogeneous of degree zero in their respective prices, changing either price level without altering relative prices leaves the equilibrium unchanged. As normalizations let us assume,

$$p_1 = 1, \qquad q_1 = 1, \qquad t_1 = 0 \tag{14}$$

It may seem surprising that it does not matter whether the government can tax good one. But the reader should remember the budget balance of the consumer. Since there are no lump sum transfers to the

[7] In an intertemporal interpretation of this model, the government budget is in balance over the horizon of the model, not year by year.

consumer, net expenditures are zero. Thus, levying a tax at a fixed proportional rate on all consumer transactions results in no revenue. (It should be noticed that a positive tax rate applied to a good supplied by the consumer is in effect a subsidy and results in a loss of revenue to the government.)

Welfare Maximization

We can now state the maximization problem. In the statement we shall use the two sets of prices as control variables. It would be a more natural approach to use the taxes which the government actually controls as decision variables. However, once we have determined the optimal p and q vectors we have determined the optimal taxes. Using taxes as decision variables complicates the mathematical formulation and leads to a control problem since the tax vector may not uniquely determine equilibrium.

Rather than calculate the first-order conditions from the formulation spelled out above, we shall alter the problem to simplify the derivation. We have to choose

$$(15) \quad q_2, \ldots, q_n, \quad p_2, \ldots, p_n, \quad z_1, \ldots, z_n$$

to maximize $v(q)$ subject to

$$x_i(q) - y_i - z_i = 0 \qquad (i = 1, 2, \ldots, n),$$

where y maximizes $\sum p_i y_i$ subject to

$$y_1 = f(y_2, \ldots, y_n),$$

and

$$z_1 = g(z_2, \ldots, z_n)$$

Since the choice of producer prices can be used to obtain any desired behavior on the part of private producers, we can use any vector y consistent with the production constraint (8). Producer prices are then determined by equation (9). Using the equations

$$y_2 = x_2 - z_2, \ldots, y_n = x_n - z_n,$$

we reduce the constraints in (15) to the single constraint

$$x_1(q) = y_1 + z_1$$
$$= f(x_2 - z_2, \ldots, x_n - z_n) + g(z_2, \ldots, z_n)$$

We have therefore simplified the problem (15) to:

$$(16) \quad \text{Choose } q_2, \ldots, q_n, \qquad z_2, \ldots, z_n$$

to maximize $v(q)$ subject to

$$x_1(q) - f(x_2(q) - z_2, \ldots, x_n(q) - z_n) - g(z_2, \ldots, z_n) = 0$$

Forming a Lagrangian expression from (16), with multiplier λ,

$$(17) \quad L = v(q) - \lambda[x_1(q) - f(x_2 - z_2, \ldots, x_n - z_n) - g(z_2, \ldots, z_n)],$$

we can differentiate with respect to q_k:

$$(18) \quad v_k - \lambda\left(\frac{\partial x_1}{\partial q_k} - \sum_{i=2}^{n} f_i \frac{\partial x_i}{\partial q_k}\right) = 0 \qquad k = 2, 3, \ldots, n$$

Making use of the equations (9) for producer prices, this can be written

$$(19) \quad v_k - \lambda \sum_{i=1}^{n} p_i \frac{\partial x_i}{\partial q_k} = 0 \qquad k = 2, 3, \ldots, n$$

Differentiating L with respect to z_k we have

$$(20) \quad \lambda(f_k - g_k) = 0 \qquad k = 2, 3, \ldots, n$$

Provided that λ is unequal to zero (i.e., that there is a social cost to a marginal need for additional resources), equation (20) implies equal marginal rates of transformation in public and private production and thus aggregate production efficiency as was argued above. The assumption that $\lambda \neq 0$ needs justification. This is provided by the rigorous arguments of Sections III and IV.

If we had introduced *several* public

production sectors, each described by a constraint like (11), we should have obtained an equation of the form (20) for *each* sector. Thus marginal rates of transformation in all public sectors should be equal, since they are all to be equal to the private marginal rates of transformation. This argument—which we only sketch here, since the conclusion will be proved more directly in the next section—justifies our assumption that there should be production efficiency in the public sector.

Optimal Tax Structure

The relations (19) determine the optimal tax structure, since they show how producer and consumer prices should be related. These equations show that consumer prices should be at a level such that further increases in any price result in an increase in social welfare, v_k, which is the same ratio, λ, to the cost of satisfying the change in demand arising from the price increase. Reintroducing taxes explicitly into the problem we can obtain an alternative interpretation for the first-order conditions.

Since x_i is a function of $p+t$,

$$\frac{\partial x_i}{\partial q_k} = \frac{\partial x_i}{\partial t_k}$$

(p is held constant in this latter derivative.) Consequently, the optimal tax structure, (19), can be rewritten:

$$(21) \qquad v_k = \lambda \sum p_i \frac{\partial x_i}{\partial t_k} = \lambda \frac{\partial}{\partial t_k} \sum p_i x_i$$

Since $\sum p_i x_i = \sum q_i x_i - \sum t_i x_i = -\sum t_i x_i$ (by the consumer's budget constraint (6)), we have

$$(22) \qquad v_k = -\lambda \frac{\partial}{\partial t_k} (\sum t_i x_i)$$

This last set of equations asserts the proportionality of the marginal utility of a change in the price of a commodity to the change in tax revenue resulting from a change in the corresponding tax rate, calculated at constant producer prices. Like the first-order conditions for the optimum in standard welfare economics, our first-order conditions are expressions in constant prices. The tax administrator, like the production planner, need not be concerned with the response of prices to government action when looking at the first-order conditions.

If we now make the further assumption that the welfare function is individualistic, we can use equation (5) to replace v_k. The first-order conditions then become

$$(23) \qquad x_k = \frac{\lambda}{\alpha} \frac{\partial(\sum t_i x_i)}{\partial t_k}$$

Thus for all commodities the ratio of marginal tax revenue from an increase in the tax on that commodity to the quantity of the commodity is a constant. This form of the first-order conditions has the advantage of showing the information needed to test whether a tax structure is optimal. The amount of information does not seem excessive relative to the data and knowledge which a planner in an advanced country should have.

The statements of the first-order conditions thus far do not directly indicate the size of the tax rates required, nor the impact upon demand that the optimal tax rates would have. In his pioneering study of optimal tax structure, Frank Ramsey manipulated the first-order conditions so as to shed light on the latter question. He employed the concept of demand curves calculated at a constant marginal utility of income. Paul Samuelson reformulated this using the more familiar demand curves calculated at a constant level of utility. We shall return to this question in Diamond-Mirrlees II.

III. Production Efficiency in the Many-Consumer Economy

We have remarked already that many of the results carry over directly to an economy of many consumers, even when lump sum taxation is excluded. We notice at once that the device of expressing welfare as a function of the prices, q, faced by consumers can be used perfectly well. Explicitly, we assume that there are H households, with utility and demand functions u^h and x^h ($h=1, 2, \ldots, H$). If, as we may generally suppose, in the absence of externalities from producers to consumers, social welfare can be expressed as a function of the consumption of the various consumers in the economy, $U(x^1, x^2, \ldots, x^H)$, it may also be written

$$(24)\quad V(q) = U(x^1(q), x^2(q), \ldots, x^H(q)),$$

where we assume that there are no lump sum incomes or transfers that would be influenced by producer prices or government policy. In the case where social welfare depends only on individual utility and there are no externalities, we can write

$$(25)\quad V(q) = W[u^1(x^1(q)), u^2(x^2(q)), \ldots, u^H(x^H(q))],$$

where W is presumed to be strictly increasing in each of its arguments.

Using this indirect welfare function, we can carry out the analysis already presented for the one-consumer economy, and conclude in the same way that aggregate production efficiency is desirable. For that argument to be correct, we must confirm that the Lagrange multiplier λ is not zero. Rather than attempt to do this directly, we shall present a different argument for the desirability of production efficiency. A further condition will be required to secure our conclusion. In considering this problem, we shall concentrate on the case where all production is under government control. The desirability of production efficiency in this case will be seen to imply the same conclusion when there is also a private sector (provided that private producers are price takers, and profits, if any, are transferred to the government). Assume then (as we did in Section I) that all production takes place in the public sector: our problem is to find q that will

$$(26)\quad \text{Maximize } V(q), \qquad \text{subject to } G(X(q)) \leqq 0,$$

where we define $X(q) = \sum_h x^h(q)$ as aggregate demand at prices q. We shall also express the production constraint a little more generally by saying that $X(q)$ is to belong to the production set G, the set of technologically feasible production plans. (Thus the letter G denotes both the production set, and also the function that can be used to describe it; but we shall hardly ever use the *function* G explicitly).

Suppose we establish that, at the optimum for problem (26), production is efficient. Consider an economy with the same technolgical possibilities, partly under the control of private, competitive producers. The government can induce private firms to produce any efficient net output bundle by suitable choice of producer prices p. In particular, it can obtain the production plan that would be optimal if the government controlled all production. The choice of p does not affect consumer demands or welfare, since pure profit arising from decreasing returns to scale go to the government, and since, any commodity taxes being possible, q can be chosen independently of p. Thus, if the solution to (26) is efficient, the same equilibrium can be achieved when some production is under private control, and is optimal in that case too. Proof that production efficiency is desirable in the "special" case (26) therefore implies that production efficiency is desirable in the more general case.

Examples of Inefficiency

Before considering the argument for efficiency, it is useful to consider some limitations on that argument as demonstrated by the following examples of desired inefficiency. It will be recollected that a production plan is efficient if any other feasible production plan provides a smaller net supply of at least one commodity. We shall use a different concept: we say that a production plan is *weakly efficient* if it is on the production frontier. It is possible for a production plan to be weakly efficient without being efficient if the production frontier has vertical or horizontal portions. For matters of economic importance, such as the existence of shadow prices, weak efficiency is all that is required. It is easy to see that if all the prices corresponding to a weakly efficient production plan are positive, the plan is in fact efficient in the usual sense.

Even with this slightly weakened concept of efficiency, it is not necessarily true that, when an optimum exists, optimal production has to be weakly efficient. We present two examples.

Example a is portrayed in Figure 7. It is a one-consumer economy where social preferences, as depicted in the social indifference curve II, do not coincide with individual preferences. It is evident that, in the case shown, the optimal production plan is actually in the interior of the production set.

In the second example, social preferences do respect household preferences, but again optimal production lies in the interior of the production set, and is therefore not weakly efficient: suitable producer prices cannot be found, and the social optimum cannot be obtained when there is private control of production.

Example b. There are two commodities and two households. One has utility function x^2y, the other has utility function xy^2; each has the nonnegative quadrant $\{(x, y) \mid x \geqq 0,\ y \geqq 0\}$ as consumption set. The first consumer has three units of the first commodity initially; the second, one unit of the second commodity. The welfare function is

$$-\frac{1}{x_1y_1}-\frac{1}{x_2y_2}$$

The second commodity can be transformed into the first according to the production relation $x+10y \leqq 0$, $(x \geqq 0)$. Let the prices of the commodities be q_1, q_2. Then the first household's net demands are

$$-\ 1 \text{ of the first commodity,}$$

$$q_1/q_2 \text{ of the second commodity.}$$

The second household has net demands

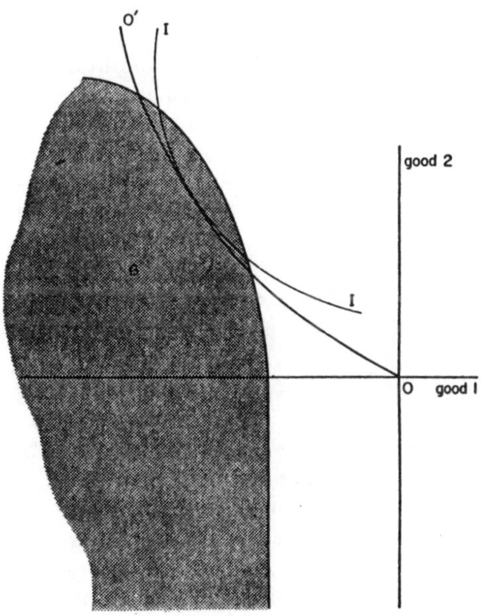

FIGURE 7

$\frac{1}{3}(q_2/q_1)$ and $-\frac{1}{3}$

Thus, the net market demand for the commodities is

$$x = \tfrac{1}{3}(q_2/q_1) - 1 \quad \text{and} \quad y = (q_1/q_2) - \tfrac{1}{3}$$

These must satisfy

$$x + 10y \leqq 0, \qquad x \geqq 0$$

Welfare is $-q_2/4q_1 - 27q_1/4q_2$ which is maximized when $q_2/q_1 = 3\sqrt{3}$: the corresponding production vector $\sqrt{3}-1, \frac{1}{3}(\sqrt{\frac{1}{3}} -1)$ is actually interior to the production set, not on the frontier. This example has the unimportant peculiarity that initial endowments of the consumers are on the frontiers of their consumption sets. More complicated examples avoiding the peculiarity have been constructed.

The Efficiency Argument

Despite these examples, the following argument shows that optimal production will generally be on the production frontier. Suppose that the aggregate demand functions, $X(q)$, are continuous. Then any small change in the prices, q, will not change aggregate production requirements by much. Therefore, if optimal production were in the interior of the production set, small changes in consumer prices would still result in technologically feasible aggregate demands. Thus, if we are at the optimum, small changes in consumer prices cannot increase welfare. If we can argue that, at the optimum, there exists a small price change which would increase $V(q)$, we can conclude that production for the optimum must occur on the production frontier. For any unsatiated single consumer, utility can be increased either by lowering the price of a supplied good or raising the price of a demanded good (as we can see, algebraically, in equation (5)). With a single consumer, we need not argue further, provided the equilibrium involves some trade. When there are many consumers, we can be certain of increasing welfare if we raise some consumer's utility without lowering that of anyone else. If there is a commodity that no consumer purchases, but some consumer supplies (such as certain labour skills); or a good (with positive price) which no consumer supplies, but some consumer purchases (such as electricity), we could alter the price of that commodity in such a way as to bring about an unambiguous increase in welfare. In that case, we conclude that efficient production is required for the maximization of individualistic social welfare. In example *b*, it will be seen that neither of the commodities is supplied, or demanded, by both consumers. The very simplicity of the case appears to be misleading.

A formal presentation of this argument is given in the next section: these technical details can be omitted without loss of continuity. We conclude this section by introducing further taxes into the discussion.

First, consider the case of a poll tax (or subsidy)—that is, a tax is paid by a household on the basis of some unalterable property, such as its sex or age distribution. Such a tax is, of course, a lump sum tax, although its availability is not, in general, sufficient to enable the full optimum to be achieved. To fix ideas, suppose there is a single transfer, τ, to be made to all households. Then welfare can be written $V(q, \tau)$, and we are to

(27) Maximize $V(q, \tau)$

subject to $X(q, \tau)$ being in G

The standard efficiency argument can be used. Let (q^*, τ^*) be the optimum: if any small change in q or τ would increase V, optimal production, $X(q^*, \tau^*)$ must be on the production frontier (assuming that X is a continuous function). Now a poll subsidy must make everyone better off, unless some are already satiated, and so must a small increase in subsidy. Thus so long as a poll subsidy is possible (and it surely is) and not every household is satiated, optimal production must be on the frontier.

Adding further tax instruments to the government's armoury in no way weakens the efficiency conclusion. We simply note that if there are other tax variables which are independent of producer prices and quantities, denoted collectively by ζ, we can hold them constant at their optimum values ζ^*, and then apply the efficiency argument to the problem (27) or (26), where V and X are evaluated for $\zeta=\zeta^*$.

Our final conclusion is that whatever the class of possible tax systems, if all possible commodity taxes are available to the government, then in general, and certainly if a poll subsidy is possible, optimal production is weakly efficient. We would not expect this conclusion to be valid if there were constraints on the possibilities of commodity taxation, or more generally, on the possible relationship between producer prices and consumer demand. The presence of pure profits is one example of such a relationship. To show what goes wrong, suppose, by way of another example, that *no* commodity taxes are possible, but a poll tax is possible, and that part of production is privately controlled, in such a way that it is uniquely determined by producer prices. Then we have to choose a public production vector z and a poll tax τ to

(28) Maximize $V(p, \tau)$

subject to $X(p, \tau) - y(p) = z$ being in G,

where $y(p)$ is the private production vector when prices are p. Following the argument used above, we consider τ smaller than τ^*, the optimum level, and note that $V(p^*, \tau)>V(p^*, \tau^*)$. This implies that $X(p^*, \tau)-y(p^*)$ is not in G, and therefore z^*, the optimal z, is efficient in G. But the argument does not imply that the aggregate optimal production plan, $y(p^*)+z^*$ is efficient. Of course, in an economy where all production is under public control, these problems do not arise. Even when some of the q_k are fixed, the efficiency argument holds, for there can be no necessary relation between q and p.

IV. Theorems on Optimal Production

In this section, we explore the existence of the optimum, and the efficiency of optimal production, rigorously. We rely on Debreu (1959) for the results of general equilibrium theory that are required.

Assumptions

There are H households in the economy, each household choosing a preferred net consumption vector x from his consumption set C subject to the budget constraint $q\cdot x\leqq 0$ where q is the vector of prices charged to consumers. (Consumption is measured net of initial endowment for convenience, since the latter is unaltered in the analysis.) As usual the net demand vector x has, in general, both positive and negative components corresponding to purchases and sales by the household.

The assumptions used below will be selected from the following list (the superscript h refers to the index of households; all assumptions, when made, hold for all h):

(a.1) C^h is closed, convex, bounded below by a vector a^h, and contains a vector with every component negative.

(a.2) The preference ordering is continuous.

(a.3) The preference ordering is strongly convex. Formally, if x^2 is preferred or indifferent to x^1 and $0<t<1$, then $tx^2+(1-t)x^1$ is strictly preferred to x^1.

(a.4) There is no satiation consumption in C^h.

Assumptions (a.1) and (a.2) guarantee the existence of continuous utility functions, which we shall write u^h (see Debreu Section 4.6). Furthermore, under (a.1)–(a.3), when the demand vector $x^h(q)$ is defined, it is uniquely defined. When C^h is bounded, assumptions (a.1)–(a.3) imply that $x^h(q)$ is defined and continuous at all non-zero nonnegative q. (See Debreu, Section 4.10.)

Let us denote aggregate demand by $X(q)=\sum_h x^h(q)$.

It is assumed that all production is controlled by the government. The assumptions on the production possibility set, G, will be taken from the following set:

(b.1) Every production plan in which nothing is produced in a positive quantity is possible: i.e., if $z\leqq 0$, z is in G.

(b.2) Complete inactivity is possible: i.e., 0 is in G.

(b.3) G is closed.

(b.4) There exists a vector $\bar{a}$ such that $z\leqq\bar{a}$ for all nonnegative z in the convex closure of G. (i.e., the closure of the convex hull of G).[8]

(b.5) G is convex.

The welfare function will be denoted by $U(x^1, \ldots, x^H)$. When demands are functions of prices only we can define the indirect welfare function as

$$V(q) = U(x^1(q), \ldots, x^H(q))$$

Similarly we can define an individual's indirect utility function by

$$v^h(q) = u^h(x^h(q))$$

We shall say that the welfare function *respects household preferences* when U can be written

$$U(x^1, \ldots, x^H) = W(u^1(x^1), \ldots, u^H(x^H))$$

[8] When G is convex, this assumption is similar to the assumption that inputs are required to obtain outputs, but permits the government to own a vector of inputs.

with W increasing in each argument. We shall assume

(c.1) U is a continuous function of $(x^1, \ldots, x^H)$

We can now state our problem as trying to find q^* to maximize $V(q)$ subject to $X(q)$ being in G. A commodity vector will be called *attainable* if it is feasible and if there exists prices such that aggregate demand equals the vector. The set of all such vectors, the *attainable set*, is the intersection of G with the set of vectors $X(q)$ for all nonnegative q.

Existence of an Optimum

If we assume that the attainable set is nonempty and bounded, we obtain

THEOREM 1. *If assumptions* (a.1)–(a.3), (b.3), *and* (c.1) *hold, and if the attainable set is nonempty and bounded, an optimum exists.*

PROOF:

Consider an economy in which the consumption sets are truncated by removing from them all points x with $\|x\|>M$, where all vectors in the attainable set satisfy $\|x\|<M$. For this truncated economy, the demand functions are continuous at all price vectors not equal to zero. Since the attainable set, and demands for any q corresponding to an attainable vector, are the same in the original and truncated economies, an optimum for the truncated economy is an optimum for the original economy. In other words, we may, without loss of generality, assume that demands are continuous at $q\neq 0$. Since the demand functions are homogeneous of degree zero in the prices, we can restrict our attention to q satisfying $q\geqq 0$ and $\sum_i q_i=1$.

We next demonstrate that the set $\{q|X(q)$ in $G\}$ is closed. Let q_n be a sequence of price vectors converging to q', with $X(q_n)$ in G for all n. Let x' be a limit point of $\{X(q_n)\}$. Since G is closed, x' is

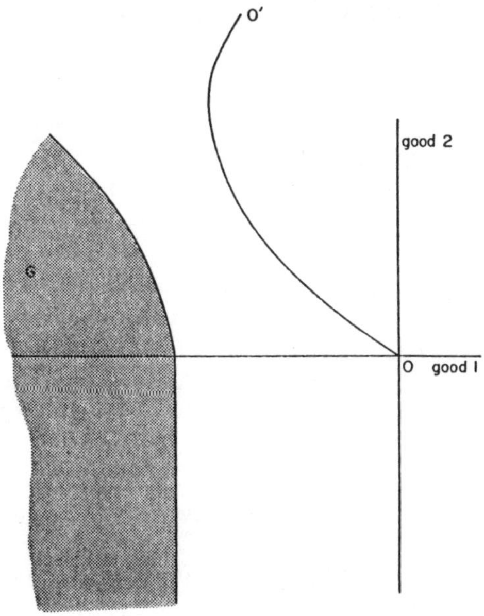

FIGURE 8

in G. At the same time, $x'=X(q')$, by the continuity of X. Thus q' is in $\{q|X(q) \text{ in } G\}$, which is therefore closed.

Since the attainable set is nonempty, and prices are in any case bounded, $\{q|X(q) \text{ in } G\}$ is closed, bounded, and nonempty. By the continuity of the demand functions, and assumption (c.1), V is a continuous function of q, which therefore attains its maximum on the set $\{q|X(q) \text{ in } G\}$.

One criterion for the attainable set to be nonempty follows immediately from the existence of competitive equilibrium in an exchange economy:

THEOREM 2. *If assumptions* (a.1)–(a.4) *and* (b.1) *hold, the attainable set is nonempty.*

PROOF:

See Debreu (Section 5.7) for a proof that there exists an equilibrium for the exchange economy with these consumers. The equilibrium prices result in a feasible demand.

If the production set is taken to be the set of possible production vectors net of government consumption, the assumption that zero production is possible is excessively strong, especially for governments with large military establishments. But it is easy to construct examples of economies not satisfying (b.1) in which there is no attainable point. Consider the one-consumer economy depicted in example *c* shown in Figure 8.

The boundedness of the attainable set would be implied by the boundedness of the consumption sets, or the boundedness of production, but the following case is more appealing:

THEOREM 3. *If assumptions* (a.1) *and* (b.2)–(b.4) *hold, then the attainable set is bounded.*[9]

PROOF:

Suppose the attainable set is not bounded. Then there exists a sequence of attainable vectors x_n such that $\|x_n\|$ is an unbounded increasing sequence of real numbers. There exists an n' such that $\|x_{n'}\| > \|\bar{a}\|$, where $\bar{a}$ is the vector employed in (b.4). Consider the sequence of vectors $(\|x_{n'}\|/\|x_n\|)x_n$ for $n \geq n'$. Each vector is in the convex hull of G (being a convex combination of the origin and x_n). Further the sequence is bounded. Thus there is a limit point, ξ, which is in the convex closure of G and satisfies $\|\xi\| > \|\bar{a}\|$. Let $b=\sum_h a_h$, where a_h are the vectors employed in (a.1). Then $x_n=\sum_h x_n^h \geqq \sum_h a_h = b$. Further $(\|x_{n'}\|/\|x_n\|)x_n \geqq (\|x_{n'}\|/\|x_n\|)b$. But the latter sequence of vectors converges to zero. Thus $\xi \geqq 0$. This is a contradiction.

[9] The attainable set will also be bounded if (b.2)–(b.4) hold for the true production set, *gross* of government consumption, rather than the net production set, G. Thus the assumption that zero production is possible is not of great consequence.

Finally, we should remark that the strong convexity assumption, (a.3), which was made in Theorem 1 can be changed to convexity without affecting the conclusion. All that is required is to replace the continuous functions of the proof by upper semi-continuous correspondences. On the other hand, one can easily construct examples in which an optimum fails to exist because of the absence of continuity.

Efficiency

The following lemma provides two criteria for optimal production to be on the frontier of the production set. It will be used to deduce a theorem about the case where household preferences are respected.

LEMMA 1: *Assume an optimum, q^*, exists. If aggregate demand functions and the indirect welfare function are continuous in the neighborhood of the optimal prices; and if either*

(1) *for some i, V is a strictly increasing function of q_i in the neighborhood of q^*; or*

(2) *for some i with $q^*>0$, V is a strictly decreasing function of q_i in the neighborhood of q^*,*

then $X(q^*)$ is on the frontier of G.

PROOF:

Let l_i be the vector with all zero components except the ith, which is one. In case 1, for ϵ sufficiently small $V(q^*+\epsilon l_i) > V(q^*)$. Hence $X(q^*+\epsilon l_i)$ is not in G. Letting ϵ decrease to zero, the continuity of X shows that $X(q^*)$ is a limit of points not in G, and therefore belongs to the boundary of G. In case 2, a similar argument can be made using $V(q^*-\epsilon l_i)$.

These conditions are weak. They are, naturally, independent of production possibilities. It may also be noticed that, when V is a differentiable function of prices, the stated conditions are equivalent to assuming that

(29) It is not the case that $V'(q^*) \leqq 0$

Here $V'(q)$ is the vector of first derivatives of V with respect to prices. The equivalence of the conditions of the theorem and (29) is clear if we remember that

$$V'(q)\cdot q = \sum \frac{\partial V}{\partial q_k} q_k = 0, \tag{30}$$

since V is homogeneous of degree zero in q. Therefore $V' \leqq 0$ if, and only if, $\partial V/\partial q_k = 0$ when $q_k > 0$ and $\partial V/\partial q_k \leqq 0$ in any case.

In the following theorem, we strengthen the assumptions in a different way: they remain notably weak.

THEOREM 4. *If* (a.1)–(a.4) *and* (c.1) *hold; if social welfare respects individual preferences; and if either*

(1) *for some i, $x_i^h \leqq 0$ for all h, and $x_i^{h'} < 0$ for some h'; or*

(2) *for some i, with $q_i > 0$, $x_i^h \geqq 0$ for all h and $x_i^{h'} > 0$ for some h';*

Then if an optimum exists, production for the optimum is on the frontier of the feasible set.

PROOF:

Individual demand functions are continuous in the neighborhood of the optimum and thus aggregate demands and the indirect welfare function are continuous. Since social welfare respects preferences, indirect social welfare can be written as an increasing function of indirect utilities. In case 1, indirect utilities are a nondecreasing function of q_i in the neighborhood of q^* for all h while the indirect utility function of h' is strictly increasing in q_i. Thus V increases with q_i. Case 2 follows similarly.

The assumption of strictly convex preferences made in Theorem 4 is required in the theorem as stated.

Example d: Consider an economy with one consumer whose indifference curves have

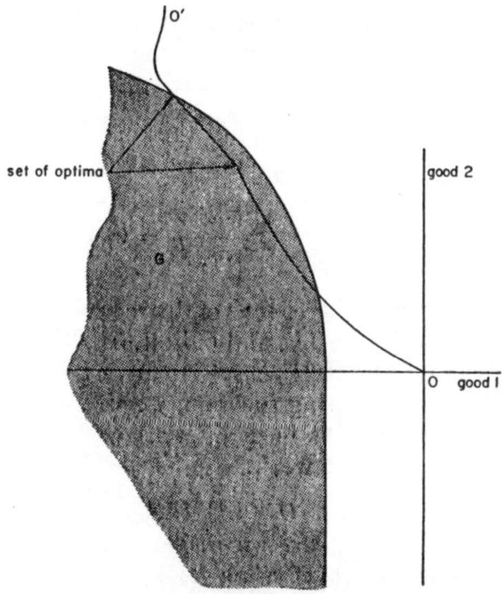

FIGURE 9

a linear section. Then the offer curve may coincide with the linear part of an indifference curve, giving a set of optima, only one of which is on the production frontier. As an illustration, see Figure 9.

The example suggests that we weaken the conclusion of Theorem 4 to say that there exists an optimum on the frontier of G: this generalization is indeed correct if we merely assume convexity of preferences. The proof follows that of Theorem 4, with upper semi-continuity of the demand correspondence replacing continuity of demand functions.

V. Extensions

We can summarize the efficiency result by considering an economy with three sectors—consumers, private producers, public producers. We assumed that only the equilibrium position of the consumer sector enters the welfare function, and that only market transactions take place between sectors, while the government has power to tax any intersector transaction at any desired rate. One conclusion was that all sectors not containing consumers should be viewed as a single sector, and treated so that aggregate production efficiency is achieved. By regrouping the parts of the economy according to this schematic division, we can extend the efficiency result to several other problems. In each case, we indicate briefly how application of this schematic view shows the relationship of the extension to the basic model.

Intermediate Good Taxation

The model, as presented above, left no scope for intermediate good taxation. If we separate private production possibilities into two (or many) sectors, we introduce the possibility of taxing transactions between firms. In the schematic view presented above, we could consider a consumer sector and two, constant returns to scale, private production sectors. We conclude that we want efficiency for these private production possibilities taken together. Therefore the optimal tax structure includes no intermediate good taxes, since these would prevent efficiency. (Similarly we conclude that government sales to firms should be untaxed while those to consumers are taxed.)

There is a straightforward interpretation of this result, which helps to explain the desirability of production efficiency. In the absence of profits, taxation of intermediate goods must be reflected in changes in final good prices. Therefore, the revenue could have been collected by final good taxation, causing no greater change in final good prices and avoiding production inefficiency. This interpretation highlights the necessity of our assumption of constant returns to scale in privately controlled production.

However, it may well be desirable to tax transactions between consumers or to charge different taxes on producer sales to different consumers. There are two ways in which we can consider doing this. The country might be geographically partitioned with different consumer prices in different regions. Ignoring migration, and consumers making purchases in neighboring regions, our analysis can be applied to determine taxes region by region. In general the tax structure will vary over the country.

Alternatively, we might consider taxation on all consumer-consumer transactions. Here, too, we would expect to be able to increase social welfare by having these additional tax controls. Neither addition to the available tax structure alters the desirability of production efficiency.

Untaxable Sectors

One problem that arises with a model considering taxation of all transactions is that some transactions may not be taxable, practically or legally. An example of the former might be subsistence agriculture where transactions with consumers are hard to tax while those with firms are not. If the introduction of other taxes (e.g., on land or output) is ruled out, we can accommodate this problem in the model by including subsistence agriculture in the consumer rather than producer sector (or treating it as a second consumer sector). Efficiency would then be desired for the modern and government production sectors taken together; while the tax structure rules would be stated in terms of demand derivatives of the augmented consumer sector rather than of just the true consumers.

Similarly, in an economy without taxes, a public producer subject to a budget constraint is unable to charge different prices to consumers and producers. Lumping together the entire private sector as a single consumer sector, we obtain the conditions for optimal public production of an industry regulated in this manner. This is the problem considered by Boiteux in the context of costless income redistribution. He also analyzed such an economy with several firms, each limited by a budget constraint.

Foreigners

It is not easy to provide a satisfactory welfare economics for a world of many countries. The study of world welfare maximization is interesting, and, one may hope, "relevant." But it has the serious limitation that its results can seldom be applied to the actions of governments. However altruistic the principles on which a government seeks to act, it has to allow for the actions other governments may take, based on different principles, or for different reasons. (A somewhat analogous problem arises in intertemporal welfare economics.) In the following two subsections, we shall, in order to keep the discussion brief, refer only to the case where the reactions of all other countries are well-defined functions of the actions of the country directly considered. Thus we neglect, reluctantly, those situations that have come to be called "game-theoretic." Also, we shall not consider the problem of formulating a social welfare function in an international setting.

International Trade

So long as we are completely indifferent to the welfare of the rest of the world, and so long as the reactions of other countries are well-defined, international trade simply provides us with additional possibilities for transforming some goods and services into others. The efficiency result then implies that we would want to equate marginal rates of transformation between producing and importing. If there is a monopoly position to be exploited, it should be. If international prices are unaffected by this country's demand, intermediate goods should not be subject to a tariff, but final good sales direct to consumers should be subject to a tariff equal to the tax on the same sale by a domestic producer.

Sometimes it is not possible to sell goods to foreigners at prices different from those at which they are sold to domestic consumers, although the theory just outlined suggests that foreigners should be treated like producers. As examples, we may cite tourists and commodities covered by special kinds of international agreement. If tourism, say, is an important trading opportunity for the country, and tourists have to be charged the same prices as domestic consumers, this will affect the optimal level of taxes on certain commodities. The general efficiency result is not upset, however. The analysis can be performed by treating tourists as consumers whose income does not affect social welfare.

The authors do not, of course, recommend indifference to the welfare of the rest of the world; although it happens to make the results somewhat neater. International trade provides the country with another set of consumers who can trade with it at prices different from its own consumers: the case (when foreign reactions are well-defined) is similar to the possibility of using different consumer prices in different regions of the same economy. In that case, there is no reason why optimal international trade prices should be the same as producer prices, p, or domestic consumer prices, q.

Migration

In all that has gone before, we have been holding constant the set of consumers in the economy. We can introduce migration in a straightforward manner. Social welfare may be a function of the consumption of every household in the world. Changes in the consumer prices charged in the home country cause migration in one direction or another, and therefore affect welfare in ways we have not previously discussed (such as the effect on the inhabitants of another country of having additional taxpayers join them). But we can still define an indirect welfare function $V(q)$, so long as the reactions of the rest of the world are well-defined. Similarly we can define aggregate demand functions $X(q)$, but these are no longer continuous. For, when a man decides to emigrate, his contribution to aggregate demand changes from x^h to 0.[10] But the number of migrants arising from a small price change may, quite reasonably, be assumed small relative to the population as a whole. We can therefore adequately approximate this situation by considering a continuum of consumers. In this way we can restore continuity to aggregate demand, and to the indirect welfare function. It is to be expected, then, that production efficiency is still desired. Since the derivatives of the demand functions, and possibly also the derivatives of V, will be different when the possibility of migration is allowed for, the optimal tax structure will be changed to reflect the loss of tax revenue when net taxpayers, for example, leave the country. While we do not wish to examine this problem in detail here, we believe that these ideas provide an interesting approach to the analysis.

Consumption Externalities

The schematic view of this problem given above suggests that the basic structure of the results, although not the specific optimal taxes, are unchanged by complications which occur wholly within the consumer sector. Thus, if we introduce consumption externalities that leave aggregate demand continuous we will still obtain production efficiency at the optimum, if we can argue that $V(q)$ has no unconstrained local maximum for finite q.

[10] A similar discontinuity problem arises in the case of tourists' decisions not to visit the country.

The conditions used above are no longer sufficient for this argument since the direct effects of a price change might be offset by the change in the pattern of externalities induced by the price change. Although we have not examined this case in detail, there are a number of cases where arguments similar to those in the no-externality case will be valid.[11] Furthermore it seems quite likely to us that efficiency will be desired in realistic settings.

Capital Market Imperfections

While some capital market imperfections affecting firms are complicated to deal with, some imperfections relevant only for consumers can be described as elements solely within the consumer sector. For example, consider the constraint that consumers can lend but not borrow. We must then rewrite consumer utility maximization as subject to a set of budget constraints for the different time periods. In the case of two periods, for example, it would appear as

$$\text{(31)}\qquad \begin{aligned} &\text{Maximize } u(x^1, x^2) \\ &\text{subject to } q^1x^1 + s \leqq 0 \\ &\qquad\qquad q^2x^2 - s \leqq 0 \\ &\qquad\qquad s \geqq 0 \end{aligned}$$

where s represents first period savings. From this consumer problem, we still have utility and demand expressible in terms of prices. We expect that the efficiency result continues to hold. In calculating the optimal formula, though, it becomes necessary to distinguish the time period of the good in question for there are now two Lagrange multipliers giving the marginal utility of income in each of the two periods. For this consumer we have

$$\text{(32)}\qquad \frac{\partial v}{\partial q_k^1} = -\alpha^1 x_k^1, \quad \frac{\partial v}{\partial q_k^2} = -\alpha^2 x_k^2$$

Since savings are allowed $\alpha^1 \geqq \alpha^2$. If the consumer would borrow if he could, $\alpha^1 > \alpha^2$ and the optimal tax structure is altered by this market limitation.

[11] We have benefited from discussions with Elisha Pazner on this subject.

REFERENCES

W. Baumol and D. Bradford, "Optimal Departures From Marginal Cost Pricing," *Amer. Econ. Rev.*, June 1970, *69*, 265–83.

A. Bergson, "Market Socialism Revisited," *J. Polit. Econ.*, Oct. 1967, *75*, 431–49.

M. Boiteux, "Sur la gestion des monopoles public astreints à l'équilibre budgétaire," *Econometrica*, Jan. 1956, *24*, 22–40.

G. Debreu, "A Classical Tax-Subsidy Problem," *Econometrica*, Jan. 1954, *22*, 14–22.

———, *Theory of Value*, New York 1959.

J. Drèze, "Postwar Contributions of French Economists," *Amer. Econ. Rev. Supp.*, June 1964, *54*, 1–64.

A. Prest and R. Turvey, "Cost-Benefit Analysis: A Survey," *Econ. J.*, Dec. 1965, *75*, 683–735.

F. Ramsey, "A Contribution to the Theory of Taxation," *Econ. J.*, Mar. 1927, *37*, 47–61.

P. Samuelson, "Memorandum for U.S. Treasury, 1951," unpublished.

[13]

Optimal Taxation and Public Production II: Tax Rules

By PETER A. DIAMOND AND JAMES A. MIRRLEES*

In Part I of this paper which appeared in the March 1971 issue of this *Review*, we set out the problem of using taxation and government production to maximize a social welfare function. We derived the first-order conditions, and considered the argument for efficiency in aggregate production. Here in Part II we consider the structure of optimal taxes in more detail. Part I contained five sections, and Part II begins at Section VI. In the sixth and seventh sections we consider commodity taxation in one- and many-consumer economies. In the eighth section we consider other kinds of taxes; and in the ninth, public consumption. In the tenth section we consider a rigorous treatment of the problem, giving a sufficient condition for the validity of the first-order conditions. To begin, we shall restate the notation and basic problem.

Notation

p	producer prices
q	consumer prices
t	taxes $(t=q-p)$
$x^h(q)$	net demand by consumer h (incomes are assumed to equal zero) $h=1, 2, \ldots, H$
$u^h(x^h)$	utility function of consumer h
$v^h(q)$	indirect utility function of consumer h $v^h(q)=u^h(x^h(q))$
$X(q)$	aggregate net demand $X(q)=\sum_h x^h(q)$
$U(x^1, \ldots, x^H)$	social welfare function
$V(q)$	indirect social welfare function $V(q)=U(x^1(q), \ldots, x^H(q))$
$W(u^1, \ldots, u^H)$	special case of an individualistic social welfare function, assumed for some of the analysis below.

With this notation before us again, we can restate the welfare maximization problem as that of selecting q to

$$\text{Maximize } V(q) \quad \text{subject to } G(X(q)) \leqq 0 \tag{33}$$

where G represents the aggregate production constraint. This problem gave rise to the first-order conditions ((19) and (22)) which were equivalently stated as

$$\frac{\partial V}{\partial q_k} = \lambda \sum p_i \frac{\partial X_i}{\partial q_k} = -\lambda \frac{\partial}{\partial t_k}\left(\sum t_i X_i\right) \qquad (k = 1, 2, \ldots, n) \tag{34}$$

Equations (34) were derived only for $k=2, \ldots, n$. But we can see that they hold also for $k=1$; for, on multiplying by q_k and adding, we have

$$\sum_{k=1}^{n}\left[\frac{\partial V}{\partial q_k} - \lambda \sum_i p_i \frac{\partial X_i}{\partial q_k}\right] q_k = 0$$

by the homogeneity of degree 0 of V and the X_i. Equation (34) states that the impact of a price rise on social welfare is proportional to the cost of meeting the change

* Massachusetts Institute of Technology and Nuffield College, respectively. The remainder of the matching footnote in Part I is appropriate here too.

in demand induced by the price rise. Alternatively the impact of a tax increase on social welfare is proportional to the induced change in tax revenue (all calculated at fixed producer prices).

VI. Optimal Tax Structure—One-Consumer Economy

For one consumer and an individualistic welfare function (so that V coincides with v, the indirect utility function of the only consumer in the economy), we can express directly the derivative of social welfare with respect to q_k ($v_k = -\alpha x_k$ where α is the marginal utility of income—see equation (5) of Part I). For this case we can then explore the structure of taxation in more detail. The formulation of the first-order conditions using compensated demand derivatives is due to Paul Samuelson (1951). We begin by stating the familiar Slutsky equation:

$$\frac{\partial x_i}{\partial q_k} = s_{ik} - x_k \frac{\partial x_i}{\partial I} \tag{35}$$

where s_{ik} is the derivative of the compensated demand curve for i with respect to q_k, and $\partial x_i/\partial I$ is the derivative of the uncompensated demand with respect to income (evaluated at $I=0$ in our case). We shall make use of the well-known result that $s_{ik}=s_{ki}$.

Substituting into the first-order conditions (34) we have:

$$\begin{aligned} -\alpha x_k &= -\lambda \frac{\partial}{\partial t_k}\left(\sum t_i x_i\right) \\ &= -\lambda\left(x_k + \sum t_i \frac{\partial x_i}{\partial t_k}\right) \\ &= -\lambda x_k - \lambda \sum t_i s_{ik} \\ &\quad + \lambda x_k \sum t_i \frac{\partial x_i}{\partial I} \\ & \qquad k = 1, 2, \ldots, n \end{aligned} \tag{36}$$

Rearranging terms, we can write this in the form:

$$\frac{\sum_i t_i s_{ik}}{x_k} = \frac{\alpha + \lambda - \lambda \sum t_i \frac{\partial x_i}{\partial I}}{\lambda} \tag{37}$$

The point to be noticed is that the right-hand side of this equation is independent of k. Call it $-\theta$. Finally, using the symmetry of the Slutsky matrix, we write the first-order conditions as:

$$\frac{\sum_i s_{ki} t_i}{x_k} = -\theta \tag{38}$$

Multiplying by $t_k x_k$ and summing, we obtain

$$\theta \sum_k t_k x_k = -\sum_{k,i} t_k s_{ki} t_i \geq 0, \tag{39}$$

by the negative semi-definiteness of the Slutsky matrix. Thus θ has the same sign as net government revenue.

The left-hand side of (38) is the percentage change in the demand for good k that would result from the tax change if producer prices were constant, the consumer were compensated so as to stay on the same indifference curve, and the derivatives of the compensated demand curves were constant at the same level as at the optimum point:

$$\begin{aligned} \Delta x_k &= \sum_i \int_0^{t_i} \frac{\partial x_k}{\partial t_i} dt_i = \sum_i \int_0^{t_i} s_{ki} dt_i \\ &= \sum_i s_{ki} \int_0^{t_i} dt_i = \sum_i s_{ki} t_i \end{aligned} \tag{40}$$

In fact, it is not possible for all these derivatives to be constant. But if the optimal taxes are small, it is approximately true that the optimal tax structure implies an equal percentage change in compensated demand at constant producer prices.

We can also calculate the actual changes in demand arising from the tax structure (assuming price derivatives of demand and production prices are constant) by resubstituting from the Slutsky equation (35). Then, upon substitution, we have:

$$\sum_i \frac{\partial x_k}{\partial q_i} t_i + \frac{\partial x_k}{\partial I} \sum t_i x_i = -\theta x_k;$$

or

$$\frac{\sum_i \frac{\partial x_k}{\partial q_i} t_i}{x_k} = -\theta - x_k^{-1} \frac{\partial x_k}{\partial I} \sum t_i x_i \tag{41}$$

The actual changes in demand (again assuming constant derivatives) induced by the tax structure differ from proportionality with a larger than average percentage fall in demand for goods with a large income derivative.

Three-Good Economy

In the case of a three-good economy, we can obtain an expression for the relative ad valorem tax rates of the two taxed goods. This argument is similar to that of W. J. Corlett and D. C. Hague, who discussed the direction of movement away from proportional taxation that would increase utility. In the three-good case, with good one untaxed, the first-order conditions (38) become

$$\begin{aligned} s_{22}t_2 + s_{23}t_3 &= -\theta x_2 \\ s_{32}t_2 + s_{33}t_3 &= -\theta x_3 \end{aligned} \tag{42}$$

Solving these equations we have

$$t_2 = \theta \frac{s_{23}x_3 - s_{33}x_2}{s_{22}s_{33} - s_{23}^2}, \quad t_3 = \theta \frac{s_{32}x_2 - s_{22}x_3}{s_{22}s_{33} - s_{23}^2} \tag{43}$$

Notice that the denominator here is positive, by the properties of the Slutsky matrix. We convert these into elasticity expressions, defining the elasticity of compensated demand by

$$\sigma_{ij} = \frac{q_j s_{ij}}{x_i} \tag{44}$$

Equation (43) can then be written

$$\frac{t_2}{q_2} = \theta'(\sigma_{23} - \sigma_{33}), \quad \frac{t_3}{q_3} = \theta'(\sigma_{32} - \sigma_{22}), \tag{45}$$

where

$$\theta' = \frac{\theta x_2 x_3}{q_2 q_3 (s_{22}s_{33} - s_{23}^2)}$$

We now substitute for σ_{23} and σ_{33}, using the adding-up properties of compensated elasticities,

$$\begin{aligned} \sigma_{23} &= -\sigma_{22} - \sigma_{21}, \\ \sigma_{32} &= -\sigma_{33} - \sigma_{31} \end{aligned} \tag{46}$$

This gives us

$$\begin{aligned} \frac{t_2}{q_2} &= \theta'(\sigma_{21} + \sigma_{22} + \sigma_{33}), \\ \frac{t_3}{q_3} &= \theta'(\sigma_{31} + \sigma_{22} + \sigma_{33}) \end{aligned} \tag{47}$$

The interesting case to consider is where labor ($x_1 < 0$) is the untaxed good, while goods 2 and 3 are consumer goods ($x_2 > 0$, $x_3 > 0$). Then θ' has the same sign as net government revenue. For definiteness, suppose that government revenue is positive so that $\theta' > 0$. Equation (47) shows that

$$\frac{t_2}{q_2} \gtreqless \frac{t_3}{q_3} \text{ according as } \sigma_{21} \lesseqgtr \sigma_{31} \tag{48}$$

The tax rate is proportionally greater for the good with the smaller cross-elasticity of compensated demand with the price of labor. (It is possible that one commodity is subsidized, but it has to be the one with the greater cross-elasticity.)

Examples

The implications of the above model are very diverse, depending upon the nature of the demand functions. A simple example will show how the theory can be used. If we define ordinary demand elasticities by the usual formula

$$\epsilon_{ik} = q_k x_i^{-1} \frac{\partial x_i}{\partial q_k}, \tag{49}$$

we can rewrite the optimal taxation formula in the form

$$v_k = q_k^{-1} \lambda \sum p_i x_i \epsilon_{ik} \tag{50}$$

When the welfare function is individualistic, equation (5) applies, so that equation (50) may be written as

$$(51) \qquad -\alpha q_k x_k = \lambda \sum p_i x_i \epsilon_{ik}$$

or

$$q_k p_k^{-1} = -\frac{\lambda}{\alpha} \sum_i \frac{p_i x_i}{p_k x_k} \epsilon_{ik}$$

If we have a good whose price does not affect other demands (implying a unitary own price elasticity), equation (51) simplifies to yield the optimal tax of that good:

$$(52) \qquad \text{If } \epsilon_{ik} = 0 \ (i \neq k) \quad \text{and} \quad \epsilon_{kk} = -1, \quad \text{then } q_k p_k^{-1} = \lambda \alpha^{-1}$$

where $q_k p_k^{-1}$ equals one plus the percentage tax rate. Recalling that α is the marginal utility of income while λ reflects the change in welfare from allowing a government deficit financed from some outside source, their ratio gives a marginal cost (in terms of the numeraire good) of raising revenue. Thus the optimal tax rate on such a good gives the cost to society of raising the marginal dollar of tax.

An example of a utility function exhibiting such demand curves is the Cobb-Douglas, where only labor is supplied. As an example consider:

$$(53) \qquad u(x) = b_1 \log (x_1 + \omega_1) + \sum_{i=2}^{n} b_i \log x_i$$

If we choose labor as the untaxed numeraire, all other goods satisfy (52) and we see that the optimal tax structure is a proportional tax structure.

It is easy to exhibit examples where the optimal tax structure is not proportional. Consider the example:

$$(54) \qquad u(x) = \sum b_i \log (x_i + \omega_i), \qquad \sum b_i = 1, \ \omega_i \neq 0$$

The demands arising from these preferences are:

$$(55) \qquad x_i = q_i^{-1} b_i \sum q_j \omega_j - \omega_i$$

Therefore the demand elasticities are:

$$(56) \qquad \epsilon_{ik} = b_i \omega_k x_i^{-1} \frac{q_k}{q_i} \quad (k \neq i)$$
$$\epsilon_{kk} = -b_k x_k^{-1} \sum_{j \neq k} \omega_j \frac{q_j}{q_k}$$

Substituting in the formula for the optimal taxes,

$$(57) \qquad -\alpha q_k x_k = \lambda \left[\sum_{j \neq k} b_j \frac{p_j}{q_j} \omega_k q_k - b_k \frac{p_k}{q_k} \sum_{j \neq k} \omega_j q_j \right] = \lambda \sum_j \left[b_j \omega_k \frac{p_j q_k}{q_j} - b_k \omega_j \frac{p_k q_j}{q_k} \right]$$

Since the assumption $\sum b_j = 1$ allows us to write the demand functions (55) in the form:

$$(58) \qquad q_k x_k = \sum_j [b_k \omega_j q_j - b_j \omega_k q_k],$$

we can deduce from (57) and (58) that

$$(59) \qquad \sum_j \left[b_j \omega_k q_k \left(\frac{p_j}{q_j} - \frac{\alpha}{\lambda} \right) - b_k \omega_j q_j \left(\frac{p_k}{q_k} - \frac{\alpha}{\lambda} \right) \right] = 0$$

These equations allow us to calculate p for any given q, and in that way give the optimal taxation rules. In general, taxes will not be proportional. As one example of this, consider the following three-good case.

Sample Calculation

Let us combine the above two examples by considering a three-good economy (one-consumer good and two types of labor) with preferences as in (54). This example will be used to show that limited tax possibilities (represented by the same proportional tax on goods 2 and 3) introduces the desirability of aggregate production inefficiency.

Example e. Assume that preferences satisfy

$$(60a)\quad u = \log x_1 + \log (x_2 + 1) + \log (x_3 + 2)$$

$$x_1 > 0, \quad x_2 > 1, \quad x_3 > -2;$$

while private production possibilities are

$$(60b)\quad y_1 + y_2 + y_3 \leqq 0,$$

$$y_1 \geqq 0, \quad y_2 \leqq 0, \quad y_3 \leqq 0;$$

and the government constraint is

$$(60c)\quad 1.02z_1 + z_2 \leqq 0$$

$$z_1 \geqq 0, \quad z_2 \leqq 0, \quad z_3 \leqq -0.1$$

Thus the government needs good 3 for public use and can produce good 1 from good 2, but only less efficiently than the private sector can.

Since we know that production efficiency is desired, we have

$$q_1 = p_1 = p_2 = 1, \qquad z_1 = z_2 = 0$$

From the first-order conditions (59) and market clearance given the demands (58), we obtain two equations to determine q_2 and q_3:

$$q_2(q_3^{-1} - 1) = 2q_3(q_2^{-1} - 1)$$

$$(q_2 + 2q_3)(q_2^{-1} + q_3^{-1} + 1) = 8.7$$

These have a unique positive solution

$$q_2 = 0.94494, \quad q_3 = 0.90008$$

which give

$$x_1 = 0.9150, \quad x_2 = -0.0316, \quad x_3 = -0.9834$$

$$u = -0.1045$$

If we now require the same tax rate on goods 2 and 3 and at the same time impose production efficiency, then $q_2 = q_3 = q$, and the tax rate is determined by the market clearance equation. We obtain

$$3q + 6 = 8.7; \qquad \text{i.e., } q = 0.9$$

Then demands are

$$x_1 = 0.9, \quad x_2 = 0, \quad x_3 = -1$$

and

$$u = -0.1054$$

Notice that the economy is still on the production frontier even though both input prices are lower in this case. If we introduce inefficiency with $p_2 > 1$, so that $y_2 = 0$ and $x_2 = z_2$, we can increase utility. Market clearance now requires

$$(q_2 + 2q_3)((1.02)^{-1}q_2^{-1} + q_3^{-1} + 1) = 8.7$$

At prices $q_2 = .92$, $q_3 = .90008$ for example, we have, $x_1 = 0.9067$, $x_2 = -0.0144$, $x_3 = -0.9926$, and $u = -0.1051$.

VII. Optimal Tax Structure—Many-Consumer Economy

As we noted in Section III of Part I, the equations for optimal taxation with a single consumer which do not reflect the particular form of V are also valid for many consumers. To pursue the analysis further, we must find an expression for V_k, the derivative of social welfare with respect to the kth consumer price.

With an individualistic welfare function, we have

$$(61)\quad V(q) = W(v^1(q), v^2(q), \ldots, v^H(q))$$

Differentiating with respect to q_k, we obtain

$$(62)\quad V_k = \sum_h \frac{\partial W}{\partial u^h} v_k^h = -\sum_h \frac{\partial W}{\partial u^h} \alpha^h x_k^h$$

The term α^h is the marginal utility of income of consumer h. Therefore

$$(63)\quad \beta^h = \frac{\partial W}{\partial u^h} \alpha^h$$

is the increase in social welfare from a unit increase in the income of consumer h. We have

$$(64)\quad -V_k = \sum_h \beta^h x_k^h,$$

or the derivative of welfare with respect to a price equals the "welfare-weighted" net consumer demand for commodity k. The necessary condition for optimal taxation makes V_k proportional to the marginal contribution to tax revenue from raising the tax on good k.

$$\sum_h \beta^h x_k^h = \lambda \frac{\partial T}{\partial t_k}, \tag{65}$$

where $T=\sum t_i X_i$ is total tax revenue, and the derivative is evaluated at constant producer prices (i.e., on the basis of consumer excess demand functions alone). We also have the alternative formula

$$\sum_h \beta^h x_k^h = -\lambda \sum_i p_i \frac{\partial X_i}{\partial q_k} \tag{66}$$

Example f. Before turning to interpretations of the optimal tax formulae like those above, let us consider an example.

We will assume that each consumer has a Cobb-Douglas utility function,

$$u^h = b_1^h \log (x_1^h + \omega^h) + \sum_2^n b_i^h \log x_i^h, \qquad \sum_1^n b_i^h = 1 \tag{67}$$

Choosing good 1 as numeraire, we saw in Section VI that with a one-consumer economy, taxation would be proportional. This will not, in general, be true in a many-consumer economy where each consumer has this utility function. The individual demand curves arising from this utility function are:

$$\begin{aligned} x_i^h &= q_i^{-1} b_i^h q_1 \omega^h, \qquad i = 2, 3, \ldots, n \\ x_1^h &= -(1 - b_1^h)\omega^h \end{aligned} \tag{68}$$

Notice that $\partial x_i^h/\partial q_k = 0 \,(k \neq i \neq 1)$ and $\partial x_i^h/\partial q_i = -x_i^h/q_i \;(i \neq 1)$.

Assuming an individualistic welfare function, the first-order conditions (66) are in this case

$$\sum_h \beta^h x_k^h = \lambda p_k q_k^{-1} \sum_h x_k^h \qquad (k = 2, \ldots, n) \tag{69}$$

This implies the following formula:

$$\frac{q_k}{p_k} = \lambda \frac{\sum_h x_k^h}{\sum_h \beta^h x_k^h} = \lambda \frac{\sum_h b_k^h \omega^h}{\sum_h \beta^h b_k^h \omega^h} \qquad (k = 2, \ldots, n) \tag{70}$$

To complete the determination of the optimal taxes, we must find the relationship between λ, p_1, and q_1. This is obtained from the Walras identity. The value of net consumer demand in producer prices is equal to minus the profit in production. (Alternatively, we could determine λ so that the government budget is balanced.) That is

$$-p_1 \sum_h (1 - b_1^h)\omega^h + \sum_{i=2}^n \sum_h p_i q_i^{-1} b_i^h q_1 \omega^h = \gamma, \tag{71}$$

where γ is the maximized profit of production net of government needs $(=\sum_{i=1}^n p_i z_i)$. Substituting from (70) and rearranging, we obtain

$$\begin{aligned} \frac{q_1}{p_1} &= \lambda \frac{\sum_h (1 - b_1^h)\omega^h + \gamma p_1^{-1}}{\sum_{i=2}^n \sum_h \beta^h b_i^h \omega^h} \\ &= \lambda \frac{\sum (1 - b_1^h)\omega^h + \gamma p_1^{-1}}{\sum \beta^h (1 - b_1^h)\omega^h} \end{aligned} \tag{72}$$

The number γp^{-1} is determined by the technology and the government expenditure decision, and therefore depends on p (unless $\gamma = 0$).

Equations (70) and (72) determine the optimal tax rates. If the social marginal utilities, β^h, are independent of taxation, the optimal tax rates can be read off at once. This is true if W has the special form $\sum_h v^h$; for in that case $\beta^h = 1/\omega^h$. It should be noticed that, although each household's social marginal utility of income is unaffected by taxation, it is desirable to have taxation in general. If households with relatively low social marginal utility of income predominate among the purchasers of a commodity, that commodity should be relatively highly taxed. Although such taxation does nothing to bring social marginal utilities of income closer together, it does increase total welfare.

In general, taxation does affect social marginal utilities of income. The β^h depend on the tax rates, and equations (70) do not, therefore, give explicit formulae for the optimum taxes. In the case $W = -\mu^{-1}\sum_h e^{-\mu v^h}$, $\mu > 0$, so that there is a stronger bias toward equality than in the additive case, it can be verified quite easily that the optimum taxes have to satisfy

$$(73)\qquad \frac{q_k}{p_k}\sum_h b_k^h(\omega^h)^{-\mu}\prod_{i=2}^{n}(b_i^h)^{-\mu b_i^h} q_i^{\mu b_i^h} = \lambda \sum_h b_k^h \omega^h \qquad (k = 2, 3, \ldots, n)$$

In this case, marginal utilities of income are brought closer together.[1] It is not immediately obvious from the equations (10) that the q are determined given the p. However, it can be shown that, in the present example, the first-order conditions must have a unique solution.[2] In fact, the relations (70) (along with (72)) would, if followed by government, certainly lead to maximum welfare if production were perfectly competitive, since any state of the economy satisfying these conditions maximizes welfare, and the maximum is unique for the welfare function considered. Unfortunately this convenient property is not general.

From equation (70) we can identify two cases where optimal taxation is proportional. If the social marginal utility of income is the same for everyone ($\beta^h = \beta$, for all h), then equation (70) reduces to $q_k p_k^{-1} = \lambda/\beta$. In this case there is no welfare gain to be achieved by redistributing income, and so no need to tax differently (on average) the expenditures of different individuals. Thus the optimal tax formula has the same form as in the one-consumer case. When the β^h do differ, taxes are greater on commodities purchased more heavily by individuals with a low social marginal utility of income. If, for example, the welfare function treats all individuals symmetrically and if there is diminishing social marginal utility with income, then there is greater taxation on goods purchased more heavily by the rich.

The second case leading to proportional taxation occurs when demand vectors are proportional for all individuals, $x^h = \rho^h x$, and thus $b_k^h = b_k$ for all h. With all individuals demanding goods in the same proportions, it is impossible to redistribute income by commodity taxation implying that the tax structure again assumes the form it has in a one-consumer economy.

Optimal Tax Formulae

The description in Section VI of some possible interpretations of the optimal tax formula carries over to the many-consumer case. Thus, as was true there con-

[1] If $\mu < 0$, utilities and marginal utilities are moved further apart.

[2] It is easily verified that $v^h = \delta_h + \sum_i b_i \log(q_1/q_i)$, where the δ_h are constants. Consequently

$$V(q) = -\mu^{-1}\sum_h e^{-\mu\delta_h}\prod_i (q_1/q_i)^{-\mu b_i^h}$$

which is a concave function of $(q_1/q_2, q_1/q_2, \ldots, q_1/q_n)$. Also, aggregate demand is

$$X_i(q) = \sum_h b_i^h \omega^h \cdot (q_1/q_i),\quad X_1(q) = -\sum_h (1 - \alpha_i^h)\omega^h$$

If the production set is convex, the set of $(q_1/q_2, \ldots, q_1/q_n)$ for which $(X_1, X_2, \ldots, X_n)$ is feasible is also convex. Thus the optimum q is obtained by maximizing a concave function of $(q_1/q_2, \ldots, q_1/q_n)$ over a convex set, and is therefore uniquely defined by the first-order conditions.

sumer price elasticities but not producer price elasticities enter the equations, and at the optimum the social marginal utility of a price change is proportional to the marginal change in tax revenue from raising that tax, calculated at constant producer prices. Analysis of the change in demand can also be carried out, but is naturally more complicated. Assuming an individualistic welfare function, the first-order conditions can be written[3]

$$(74)\qquad \sum \beta^h x_k^h = \lambda \sum_h \sum_i t_i \frac{\partial x_i^h}{\partial q_k} + \lambda \sum_h x_k^h$$

From the Slutsky equation, we know that

$$(75)\qquad \begin{aligned} \frac{\partial x_i}{\partial q_k} &= s_{ik} - x_k \frac{\partial x_i}{\partial I} = s_{ki} - x_k \frac{\partial x_i}{\partial I} \\ &= \frac{\partial x_k}{\partial q_i} - x_k \frac{\partial x_i}{\partial I} + x_i \frac{\partial x_k}{\partial I} \end{aligned}$$

Substituting from (75) in (74) we can write the optimal tax formula as equation (76). Rearranging terms we can write equation (76) as (77). With constant producer prices, equation (77) gives the change in demand as a result of taxation for a good with constant price-derivatives of the demand function (or for small taxes). Considering two such goods, we see that the percentage decrease in demand is greater for the good the demand for which is concentrated among:

(1) individuals with low social marginal utility of income,
(2) individuals with small decreases in taxes paid with a decrease in income,
(3) individuals for whom the product of the income derivative of demand for good k and taxes paid are large.

VIII. Other Taxes

Thus far we have examined the combined use of public production and commodity taxation as control variables. It is natural to reexamine the analysis when additional tax variables are included in those controlled by the government. In particular, in the next subsection we will briefly consider income taxation; but first, let us examine a general class of taxes such that the consumer budget constraint depends on consumer prices and on tax variables. We shall replace the budget constraint $\sum q_i x_i = 0$ by the more general constraint $\phi(x, q, \zeta) = 0$, where ζ represents a shift parameter to reflect the choice among different systems of additional taxation (for example, the degree of progression in the income tax). Let us note that this formulation continues to assume that all taxes are levied on consumers and that there are no profits in the economy.

The key assumption to permit an extension of the analysis above is an independence of the two constraints on the planner. We need to assume that the choice of tax variables does not affect the production

[3] We neglect the possibility of a free good when the first-order condition would be an inequality.

$$(76)\qquad \sum_h \beta^h x_k^h = \lambda \sum_h \sum_i t_i \frac{\partial x_k^h}{\partial q_i} + \lambda \sum_h \sum_i t_i \left(x_i^h \frac{\partial x_k^h}{\partial I} - x_k^h \frac{\partial x_i^h}{\partial I} \right) + \lambda \sum_h x_k^h$$

$$(77)\qquad \frac{\sum_h \sum_i t_i \frac{\partial x_i^h}{\partial q_i}}{\sum_h x_k^h} = \frac{1}{\lambda} \frac{\sum_h \beta^h x_k^h}{\sum_h x_k^h} - 1 + \frac{\sum_h \left(\sum_i t_i \frac{\partial x_i^h}{\partial I} \right) x_k^h}{\sum_h x_k^h} - \frac{\sum_h \left(\sum_i t_i x_i^h \right) \frac{\partial x_k^h}{\partial I}}{\sum_h x_k^h}$$

possibilities, and further that the choice of a production point does not affect the set of possible demand configurations. In particular, this formulation implies that producer prices do not affect consumer budget constraints. Thus the income tax, to fit this formulation, needs to be levied on the wages that consumers receive, not on the cost of wages to the firm. Similarly it is assumed that there are no sales tax deductions from the income tax base.

We know already that in such a case, optimal production is efficient. We may therefore concentrate upon the case in which all production is controlled by the government, and the production constraint is that $x_1 = g(x_2, x_3, \ldots, x_n)$. We have to choose $q_2, q_3, \ldots, q_n, \zeta$ to

(78) maximize $V(q, \zeta)$ subject to $X_1(q, \zeta) = g(X_2(q, \zeta), \ldots, X_n(q, \zeta))$

As before we introduce a Lagrange multiplier λ. Differentiation with respect to q_k yields the familiar

$$V_k = \lambda \sum_i p_i \frac{\partial X_i}{\partial q_k}, \tag{79}$$

where the producer price p_i is $\partial g / \partial x_i$ $(i = 2, 3, \ldots, n)$, and $p_1 = 1$. Differentiation with respect to the new tax variable provides the similar equation

$$\frac{\partial V}{\partial \zeta} = \lambda \sum_i p_i \frac{\partial X_i}{\partial \zeta} \tag{80}$$

We have an alternative form for (79), namely,

$$V_k = -\lambda \frac{\partial T}{\partial t_k} \tag{81}$$

In exactly the same way, we obtain from (80) a formula involving the effect of the new tax on total tax revenue,

$$V_\zeta = -\lambda \frac{\partial T}{\partial \zeta} \tag{82}$$

Income Taxation

Nothing that we have said suggests that commodity taxation is superior to income taxation. The analysis has only considered the best use of commodity taxation. It is natural to go on to ask how one employs both commodity taxation and income taxation. The formulation of income taxation raises a problem. If the planners are free to select any income tax structure and if there are a finite number of tax payers, the tax structure can be selected so that the marginal tax rate is zero for each taxpayer at his equilibrium income (although this does not necessarily bring the economy to the full welfare maximum). This eliminates much of our problem, but like lump sum taxation, seems to be beyond the policy tools available in a large economy. The natural formulation of this problem is for a continuum of tax payers, since then no man can have a tax schedule tailor-made for him. (This approach is taken by Mirrlees.) However, we shall here take the alternative route by assuming a limited set of alternatives for the income tax structure.

If only commodity taxation is possible, the tax paid by a household that purchases a vector x^h is

$$T^h = \sum_i t_i x_i^h \tag{83}$$

To add income taxation to the tax structure, we can select a subset of commodities, L, e.g., labor services, and tax the value of transactions on this subset, so that

$$I^h = \sum_{i \text{ in } L} q_i x_i^h$$

where I is "taxable income." Then

$$T^h = \sum_i t_i x_i^h + \tau(I^h, \zeta), \tag{84}$$

where τ is a fixed continuously differentiable function depending on a parameter ζ, and is the same for all consumers. With a tax on services (x_i negative) we would expect τ to be decreasing in its tax base, with a derivative between zero and minus one. In terms of the notation employed above, we can define the budget constraint $\phi(x^h, q, \zeta)$ by

$$\phi(x^h, q, \zeta) \tag{85}$$
$$= \sum p_i x_i^h + T^h$$
$$= \sum q_i x_i^h + \tau\left(\sum_{i \text{ in } L} q_i x_i^h, \zeta \right)$$

Here we can regard q and ζ as the policy variables. Thus the consumer's budget constraint can be expressed in a form depending on consumer prices and independent of producer prices.

The first-order conditions for optimal income taxation are just the conditions (79) and (80), interpreted for this special case. The social marginal utility of a tax variable change is proportional to the marginal change in tax revenue calculated at constant producer prices. In the case of an individualistic welfare function, we can give more explicit formulae for the welfare derivatives, V_k and V_ζ:

$$V_k = \sum_h \beta^h x_k^h \left(1 + \delta_k \frac{\partial \tau^h}{\partial I}\right) \tag{86}$$

$$V_\zeta = \sum_h \beta^h \frac{\partial \tau^h}{\partial \zeta}, \tag{87}$$

where $\delta_k = 1$ if k is in L, 0 if k is not in L; and $\tau^h = \tau(I^h, \zeta)$.

These equations are derived from the first-order conditions for maximizing u^h subject to $\phi = 0$, noticing that, for example, the budget constraint implies that

$$\sum_k \frac{\partial \phi}{\partial x_k} \frac{\partial x_k}{\partial \zeta} + \frac{\partial \phi}{\partial \zeta} = 0$$

Combining (82) and (87), we obtain

$$\sum \beta^h \frac{\partial \tau^h}{\partial \zeta} = \lambda \frac{\partial T}{\partial \zeta} \tag{88}$$

Thus, at the optimum, for any two different kinds of change in the income tax structure, the social-marginal-utility weighted changes in taxation (consumer behavior held constant) are proportional to the changes in total tax revenue (both income and commodity tax revenue, calculated at fixed producer prices, with consumer behavior responding to the price change).

IX. Public Consumption

From the start, we have considered the government production decision as constrained by $G(z) \leqq 0$. The presence of a fixed bundle of public consumption was therefore included in the model (and would show itself by $G(0)$ being positive). This is unsatisfactory and was assumed to keep as uncluttered as possible a naturally complicated problem. We can now consider a choice among vectors of public consumption which affect social welfare directly. (We shall assume that the government controls all production, thus ignoring public expenditures which affect private production rather than consumer utility.) Let us denote by e the vector of public consumption expenditures. (Items of public consumption which are difficult to measure can be described by the inputs into their production.) The presence of public consumption alters our problem in three ways. First, public consumption represents public production (or purchases) which are not supplied to the market. Thus market clearance becomes $X = z - e$.

Second, the presence of public consumption affects private net demand, which must now be written $X(q, e)$. Third, the level of public consumption directly affects the social welfare function (by affecting individual utility in the case of an individualistic welfare function).

We can restate the basic maximization problem as

(89) $\underset{q,e}{\text{Maximize}}\ V(q, e)$

subject to $G(X(q, e) + e) \leqq 0$

The presence of e in the problem will not affect the equations obtained by differentiating a Lagrangian expression with respect to q. Thus the presence of alternative bundles of public consumption does not alter the rules for the optimal tax structure. Nor would we expect it to affect the conditions which imply production efficiency at the optimum. We can therefore replace the inequality in (89) with an equality and differentiate the Lagrangian expression with respect to e_k:

$$(90)\quad \frac{\partial V}{\partial e_k} - \lambda\left[\sum G_i \frac{\partial X_i}{\partial e_k} + G_k\right] = 0$$

Since

$$(91)\quad \sum G_i \frac{\partial X_i}{\partial e_k}$$

$$= \sum p_i \frac{\partial X_i}{\partial e_k} = \sum (q_i - t_i)\frac{\partial X_i}{\partial e_k}$$

$$= \frac{\partial}{\partial e_k}\left(\sum q_i X_i - \sum t_i X_i\right)$$

$$= -\frac{\partial}{\partial e_k}\left(\sum t_i X_i\right),$$

we can write (90) as

$$(92)\quad \frac{\partial V}{\partial e_k} = -\lambda \frac{\partial}{\partial e_k}\left(\sum t_i X_i\right) + \lambda G_k$$

Equations (92) show how the optimal level of public consumption depends on:

(i) the direct contribution of public consumption to welfare (measured by $\partial V/\partial e_k$);

(ii) the effect of public consumption on tax revenue (measured by $\partial \sum t_i X_i/\partial e_k$); and

(iii) the direct cost of public consumption (G_k).

There are three differences between this theory and that of public goods in the presence of lump sum taxation (as developed, for example, by Samuelson (1954)). Because social marginal utilities of income are not equated, the expression $\partial V/\partial e_k$ cannot be reduced to a sum of marginal rates of substitution, but depends on the weights given to the different beneficiaries of public consumption:

$$(93)\quad \frac{\partial V}{\partial e_k} = \sum_h \frac{\partial W}{\partial u^h}\frac{\partial u^h}{\partial e_k}$$

Second, the cost associated with the raising of government revenue implies that the impact of public consumption on revenue is a relevant part of the first-order conditions. Third, for the same reason, the cost of public consumption is measured in terms of the cost to the government of raising revenue to finance the expenditures (in terms of the one-consumer equation, λ may not be equal to α, the marginal utility of income).

The first-order conditions for the provision of public goods can be expressed in another way, showing the relationships between the marginal cost and "willingness to pay." Write r_k^h for the marginal rate of substitution between public good k and income for the hth household. Then $\partial u^h/\partial e_k = \alpha^h r_k^h$, where α^h is the hth household's marginal utility of income. The social marginal utility of the hth household's income, β^h, is $(\partial W/\partial u^h)\alpha^h$. Consequently, from (93)

$$(94)\quad \frac{\partial V}{\partial e_k} = \sum_h \beta^h r_k^h$$

Then, from (92)

$$(95)\quad G_k = \sum_h \left[\frac{\beta^h}{\lambda} r_k^h + \frac{\partial}{\partial e_k}\sum_i t_i x_i^h\right]$$

Thus the marginal cost of producing the public good should be equated to a sum, over all households, of the price which the household is just willing to pay for a marginal increment in the level of provision, weighted by the marginal "social worth" of the household's income, and adjusted for the effect of the level of provision on net tax payments by the household.[4]

In the discussion of public consumption thus far it has been assumed that there were no possible fees associated with the provision of public goods. This would be appropriate for national defense or preventive medicine, but not for goods where licenses can be required from users. The optimal level of license fees will not, in general, be zero. Indeed we may be able to associate with any good more complicated pricing mechanisms than the single fixed price considered above. In particular, there are the familiar examples of two-part tariffs (a license fee for use of a facility plus a per unit charge on the amount of use), and prices depending on quantity of sales. Formally these can be treated in a fashion similar to the income taxes considered above; the set of goods over which the tax is defined is now a consumption good rather than labor. With a two-part tariff, this would imply a tax function which was not continuous at the origin.

Presumably the introduction of more general pricing and taxing schemes gives an opportunity for increasing social welfare, just as the progressive income tax gives such an opportunity. In practice, the ignored costs of tax administration may severely limit the number of complicated pricing schemes which can increase welfare. We would expect the analysis done above to be basically unchanged by the addition of these possibilities, although a two-part tariff will cause aggregate demand to have discontinuities. In practice we would expect these discontinuities to be small relative to aggregate demand, and formally, they could be eliminated by the device of a continuum of consumers.

[4] Another case can be treated in a similar manner: that of limited government production of a good, which is also being produced privately, when government production is given away rather than being sold. Since the government production rule given above does not reduce to the first-order condition in producer prices, we would not find aggregate production efficiency for the sum of these two sources of production.

X. The Optimal Taxation Theorem

In the earlier discussion, we employed calculus techniques to obtain the first-order conditions for the optimal tax structure. However, the valid use of Lagrange multipliers is subject to certain restrictions, which in the present case have no very obvious economic significance. This section provides a rigorous analysis of conditions under which the tax formulae (34) are indeed necessary conditions for optimality, and in particular provides economically meaningful assumptions that ensure their validity. The reader should be warned that the discussion is highly technical.

One might hope to provide a rigorous analysis by using the well-known Kuhn-Tucker theorem for differentiable (not necessarily concave) functions. This theorem requires a certain "constraint qualification" to be satisfied. Let us apply it and see how far we get. We wish to

$$\text{Maximize } V(q)$$
$$\text{subject to } g(X(q)) \leqq 0 \quad \text{and} \quad q \geqq 0,$$

where g is a (vector) production constraint such that $g(X) \leqq 0$ if, and only if, X is in G. Given that V, X, and g are differentiable, and that the Kuhn-Tucker constraint qualification is satisfied, we have the first-order conditions

$$(96) \quad V'(q^*) = \frac{\partial V}{\partial q} \leqq p \cdot \frac{\partial X}{\partial q} = p \cdot X'(q^*),$$

where $p = \lambda \cdot g'(X(q^*))$ for a vector of Lagrange multipliers λ, and is therefore a support or tangent hyperplane to G at $X(q^*)$. Since V and X are homogeneous of degree zero, $[V'(q^*)-p\cdot X'(q^*)]\cdot q^*=0$: consequently $\partial V/\partial q_i=p\cdot(\partial X/\partial q_i)$ for i such that $q_i^*>0$.

To express the first-order conditions in this form, we naturally expect to assume that V and X are continuously differentiable: to that extent, the differentiability assumptions are innocuous. The assumption that the production set can be described by a finite number of continuously differentiable inequality constraints that satisfy the constraint qualification is less satisfactory. The constraint qualification is an assumption about the functions g: one can violate it by changing the functions g without changing the actual constraint set, G. Some such assumption is required to avoid not unreasonable counter-examples, as we shall see below. But it is not at all obvious how one would check whether a particular example that failed to satisfy the constraint qualification could be put right by describing G by a better behaved set of inequalities. We should like to use a constraint qualification that depends on the properties of the set G (and X) rather than the particular functions g; and we should like the assumption to be more amenable to economic interpretation. The theorem we prove below contains such an assumption, for the case where G is convex and has an interior.

Before stating the theorem let us consider an example in which the first-order conditions are not satisfied at the optimum.

Example g. Consider the one-consumer economy. In the case shown in Figure 10, the offer curve is tangent to the production frontier at the optimum production point. As q varies, the vector $X(q)$ traces out the offer curve. Thus, holding q_2 constant, the vector $\partial X(q)/\partial q_1$ is tangent to the offer curve at $X(q^*)$. Therefore if p is the vector of producer prices, which is tangent to the production frontier at $X(q^*)$, $p\cdot\partial X(q^*)/\partial q_1=0$. The same is true for the derivatives with respect to q_2. But there is no reason why $V'(q^*)$ should be zero: therefore the above first-order conditions may not be satisfied at the optimum.

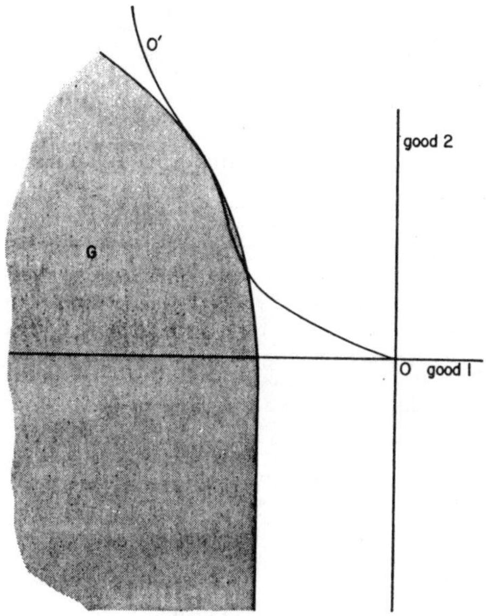

FIGURE 10

We shall make an assumption ruling out tangency between the frontier of the production set and the offer curve:

> For any p, q ($q\geqq 0$, $p\neq 0$) such that $X(q)$ is in G and $p\cdot X(q)\geqq p\cdot x$ for all x in G, $p\cdot X'(q)\geqq 0$.

The qualification takes this particular form because we also have the constraint $q\geqq 0$. Let us note that for $q>0$ the condition $p\cdot X(q)\geqq 0$ is equivalent to $p\cdot X'(q)\neq 0$, because X is homogeneous of degree zero. The qualification asserts that *for any possible competitive equilibrium (under commodity taxation) there is a consumer price change which will decrease the value of equilibrium demand, measured in producer prices*. By the aggregate consumer budget constraint, $q \cdot X = (p+t) \cdot X = 0$. Therefore the assumption says that at any possible equilibrium point on the production frontier, it is possible to increase tax revenue. Thus the first-order conditions may not be applicable if the optimal point represents a local tax revenue maximum. Returning to example *g*, we see that $p \cdot X' = 0$ at the optimum, or equivalently $\partial(t \cdot X)/\partial t = 0$, although the derivatives of V are not necessarily zero there.

We now state and prove the theorem.[5]

THEOREM 5: *Assume an optimum, (X^*, q^*) exists; that $V(q)$ and $X(q)$ are continuously differentiable; and that G is convex and has a nonempty interior. Assume furthermore that there is no pair of price vectors (p, q) for which*

$$(97) \qquad \begin{aligned} &X(q) \textit{ maximizes } p \cdot x \textit{ for } x \textit{ in } G, \\ &p \neq 0, \quad \textit{and} \\ &p \cdot X'(q) \geqq 0 \end{aligned}$$

Then there exists p^* such that

$$\begin{aligned} &X^* \textit{ maximizes } p^* \cdot x \textit{ for } x \textit{ in } G, \quad \textit{and} \\ &V'(q^*) \leqq p^* \cdot X'(q^*) \end{aligned}$$

PROOF:

Let $P = \{p \mid p \cdot X^* \geqq p \cdot x, \text{ all } x \text{ in } G\}$. P is the cone of normals to G at X^*, including the zero vector. It is a nonempty, closed, convex cone.

[5] It should be noticed that when the constrained optimum is (locally) an unconstrained maximum, the producer prices satisfying the theorem are zero. This happens if optimal production is in the interior of the production set and may happen if it is on the frontier. The theorem can be weakened in a complicated manner by replacing the nontangency qualification by two conditions. One is an analog of the Kuhn-Tucker Constraint Qualification providing for the existence of an arc in the attainable set. The other use of nontangency occurs when V' is in $\bar{B}$ but not in B. If it is assumed that when there is tangency, the cone of normals is polyhedral, B will be closed. The Kuhn-Tucker theorem is then a special case of the weakened version of theorem 5 when G is the nonnegative orthant. The Kuhn-Tucker theorem is very much easier to prove, however.

We write V' for $V'(q^*)$ and X' for $X'(q^*)$. Consider the set

$$B = \{v \mid v \leqq p \cdot X', \text{ some } p \text{ in } P\}$$

We have to show that V' is in B. We do this by showing first, that if V' is in $\bar{B}$, the closure of B, in fact V' is in B; and then that V' must be in $\bar{B}$.

If V' is in $\bar{B}$, there exist sequences $\{v_n\}$ and $\{p_n\}$, p_n in P, such that

$$(98) \qquad \begin{aligned} &v_n \leqq p_n \cdot X', \\ &v_n \to V' \qquad (n \to \infty) \end{aligned}$$

Either $\{p_n\}$ is bounded or it is not. If not, we can find a subsequence on which

$$\|p_n\| \to \infty, \qquad \frac{p_n}{\|p_n\|} \to \bar{p} \neq 0$$

Then, dividing (98) by $\|p_n\|$ and letting $n \to \infty$ on the subsequence, we obtain $\bar{p} \cdot X' \geqq 0$ while $\bar{p}$, $\neq 0$, is in P. This possibility is excluded by assumption (97). Therefore $\{p_n\}$ is bounded, and has a limit point p, in P. Equation (98) implies that $V' \leqq p \cdot X'$. The conclusion of the theorem is thus established on the assumption that V' is in $\bar{B}$.

Suppose, on the contrary, that V' is not in $\bar{B}$. We shall derive a contradiction by a sequence of lemmas.

LEMMA 5.1:

$\bar{B}$ is pointed. That is, v and $-v$ both belong to $\bar{B}$ only if $v = 0$.

PROOF:

If v, $-v$ is in $\bar{B}$, we have sequences such that

$$(99) \qquad \overset{1}{v}_n \leqq \overset{1}{p}_n \cdot X', \qquad \overset{2}{v}_n \leqq \overset{2}{p}_n \cdot X',$$

$$(100) \qquad \overset{1}{v}_n \to v, \qquad \overset{2}{v}_n \to -v$$

If $v \neq 0$, it cannot be the case that p_n^1 and p_n^2 both tend to zero. Suppose, for example, p_n^1 does not, and take a subsequence on which

$$\|p_n^1\| \to \pi_1 \leqq \infty,$$

$$p_n^1/\|p_n^1\| \to p^1, \neq 0$$

If $p_n^1+p_n^2 \to 0$, $p_n^2/\|p_n^1\| \to -p^1$, and therefore $-p^1$ is in P. This is impossible, since, G having a nonempty interior, P is pointed. (If p, $-p$ are in P, $p \cdot x$ is constant for x in G, but a hyperplane has no interior.) We can therefore take a subsequence on which

$$\|p_n^1 + p_n^2\| \to \pi, \qquad 0 < \pi \leqq \infty,$$

$$\frac{p_n^1 + p_n^2}{\|p_n^1 + p_n^2\|} \to p, \neq 0, \in P$$

From (99) (adding and dividing by $\|p_n^1+p_n^2\|$) and (100), we now have

$$p \cdot X' \geqq \operatorname{Lim} \frac{v_n^1 + v_n^2}{\|p_n^1 + p_n^2\|} \tag{101}$$
$$= 0$$

This contradicts (97), since p is in P and $p \neq 0$, and thereby establishes the lemma.

LEMMA 5.2: *If C is a pointed, closed, convex cone, there exists a vector p such that for all non-zero z in C, $p \cdot z < 0$.*

PROOF:

By the duality theorem for convex cones $C^{++}=C$, where C^+ is the dual cone, $\{p \mid p \cdot z \leqq 0,\ z \text{ is in } C\}$. Clearly, if C^+ is pointed, C has a nonempty interior: for if interior C is empty, $p \cdot z = 0$ for some non-zero p and all z in C, and then p and $-p$ both belong to C^+. Under the assumptions of the theorem, C is closed and pointed. Therefore C^{++} is pointed, and C^+ has an interior point p.

$$p \cdot z < 0 \quad (\text{all nonzero } z \text{ in } C)$$

Otherwise, if $p \cdot z = 0$, we can easily find a sequence $\{p_n\}$ on which $p_n \to p$ and $p_n \cdot z > 0$, so that p_n is not in C^+.

LEMMA 5.3: *If V' is not in $\overline{B}$, there exists r such that*

(102) $\quad V' \cdot r > 0$

(103) $\quad v \cdot r < 0 \qquad (v \in B)$

PROOF:

The closed convex cone $\overline{B} + \{\lambda V' \mid \lambda \leqq 0\}$ is pointed. Thus there exists an r such that

$$v \cdot r + \lambda V' \cdot r < 0$$
$$(v \in \overline{B},\ \lambda \leqq 0,\ v, \lambda \text{ not both zero})$$

Putting $v=0$ and $\lambda=-1$ we obtain (102); putting $\lambda=0$ we obtain (103).

LEMMA 5.4: *Let r be a vector satisfying (102) and (103). For some $\delta>0$,*

(104) $\quad X(q^* + \theta r) \in G \quad (0 \leqq \theta \leqq \delta)$

PROOF:

Assume not. Then for some sequence $\{\theta_n\}$, $\theta_n > 0$, $\theta_n \to 0$,

$$X(q^* + \theta_n r) \notin G$$

Since G is convex, this implies that

$$X(q^*) + \frac{\lambda}{\theta_n}\left[X(q^* + \theta_n r) - X(q^*)\right] \notin G$$

for $\lambda \geqq \theta_n$. Letting $n \to \infty$, we deduce, for any $\lambda > 0$, that

$$X(q^*) + \lambda X' \cdot r$$
$$= \operatorname*{Lim}_{n \to \infty}\left[X(q^*) + \lambda \frac{X(q^* + \theta_n r) - X(q^*)}{\theta_n}\right]$$

is not in the interior of G. It follows that the half-line $\{X(q^*) + \lambda X' \cdot r \mid \lambda > 0\}$ can be separated from the interior of G by a hyperplane with normal $p \neq 0$:

$$p \cdot X(q^*) + \lambda p \cdot X' \cdot r \geqq p \cdot x$$
$$(\lambda > 0,\ x \in \operatorname{Int} G)$$

Letting $\lambda \to 0$ we have $p \in P$. Letting $x \to X^*$ we have

$$p \cdot X' \cdot r \geqq 0,$$

which contradicts (103) since $p \cdot X'$ is in B. The lemma is proved.

Since q^* is optimal, (104) implies that

$$V(q^* + \theta r) \leqq V(q^*) \qquad (0 \leqq \theta \leqq \delta)$$

Therefore,

$$V' \cdot r = \lim_{\theta \to 0} \frac{1}{\theta} [V(q^* + \theta r) - V(q^*)] \leqq 0$$

This, however, contradicts (102). The hypothesis of Lemma 5.3, that $V' \in \overline{B}$, is therefore false. The proof of the theorem is thus complete.

In reaching our results that the first-order conditions for optimum taxes (96) hold in general, we have assumed that the production set, G, is convex. But one common argument for government control of production is nonconvexity of the production set. This is not a question we are primarily concerned with in this paper. However, some extensions of the theorem do hold. As an example, assume the frontier of G is differentiable at X^*, so that p can be uniquely defined as the normal at X^* and that G is not thin in the neighborhood of X^*—i.e., there exists a ball with center on the normal through X^*, contained in G and containing X^*. Applying the theorem to this ball we get the validity of the first-order conditions (96) using the producer prices defined by the normal.

As in general welfare economics, two uniqueness problems may arise when considering the application of the first-order conditions to achieve an optimum. In the first place, there may be more than one pair of price vectors, (p, q), that satisfy the first-order conditions and allow markets to be cleared. This is similar to the problem that arises when we attempt to define optimum production and distribution by first-order conditions in the presence of a non-convex production set. It is noteworthy that, if lump sum transfers are excluded as a feasible policy, this problem may arise even when the production set is convex. There is no reason why the demand functions should have any of the nice convexity properties which ensure that first-order conditions imply global maximization. Only in particular cases, such as that discussed in footnote 2 above (where rigorous argument is possible without appeal to theorem 5), will the first-order conditions lead to a unique solution.

The second problem is that the tax policies one might like to employ may not uniquely determine the behavior of the system. The lump sum redistribution of wealth required in standard welfare economics does not carry with it any guarantee that the desired competitive equilibrium is the unique one consistent with the optimal wealth distribution (although if the wrong equilibrium is achieved, this should be easily noticed). Similarly, in the present case, if we employ taxes rather than consumer prices as the government control variables, the equilibrium of the economy may not be unique.[6] But if consumer prices are used as the control variables—and why not?—the demand functions give us a unique equilibrium position, so long as preferences are strictly convex.

XI. Concluding Remarks

Welfare economics has usually been concerned with characterizing the best of attainable worlds, accepting only the basic technological constraints. As economists have been aware, the omitted constraints on communication, calculation, and administration of an economy (not to mention political constraints) limit the direct applicability of the implications of this theory to policy problems, although great insight into these problems has certainly been acquired. We have not at-

[6] For a discussion of multiple equilibria in a related problem, see E. Foster and H. Sonnenschein.

tempted to come directly to grips with the problem of incorporating these complications into economic theory. Instead, we have explored the implications of viewing these constraints as limits on the set of policy tools that can be applied. There are many sets of policy tools which might be examined in this way. Specifically, we have assumed that the policy tools available to the government include commodity taxation (and subsidization) to any extent. For these tools we have derived the rules for optimal tax policy and have shown the desirability of aggregate production efficiency, in the presence of optimal taxation. We have also considered expansion of the set of policy tools in such a way that we continue to have the condition that production decisions do not change the class of possible budget constraints. For example, this condition is still preserved when one includes poll taxes, progressive income taxation, regional differences in taxation, taxation on transactions between consumers, and most kinds of rationing. This type of expansion of the set of policy tools does not alter the desirability of production efficiency, nor does it alter the conditions for the optimal commodity tax structure, although in general the tax rates themselves will change. We have, unfortunately, ignored the cost of administering taxes. Presumably optimization by means of sets of policy tools that do not, because the cost of administration, include the full scope of commodity taxation, will not lead to the same conclusions.

Let us briefly consider the type of policy implications that are raised by our analysis. In the context of a planned economy our analysis implies the desirability of using a single price vector in all production decisions, although these prices will, in general, differ from the prices at which commodities are sold to consumers.

As an application of this analysis to a mixed economy, let us briefly examine the discussion of a proper criterion for public investment decisions. As has been widely noted, there are considerable differences in western economies between the intertemporal marginal rates of transformation and substitution. This has been the basis of analyses leading to investment criteria which would imply aggregate production inefficiency because they employ an interest rate for determining the margins of public production which differs from the private marginal rate of transformation. One argument used against these criteria is that the government, recognizing the divergence between rates of transformation and substitution, should use its power to achieve the full Pareto optimum, bringing these rates into equality. When this is done, the single interest rate then existing will be the appropriate rate to use in public investment decisions. We begin by presuming that the government does not have the power to achieve any Pareto optimum that it chooses. Then from the maximization of a social welfare function, we argued that the government will, in general, prefer one of the non-Pareto optima to the Pareto optima, if any, that can be achieved. At the constrained optimum, which is the social welfare function maximizing position of the economy for the available policy tools, we saw that the economy will still be characterized by a divergence between marginal rates of substitution and transformation, not just intertemporally, but also elsewhere, e.g., in the choice between leisure and goods. However, we concluded that in this situation we desired aggregate production efficiency. This implies the use of interest rates for public investment decisions which equate public and private marginal rates of transformation.

We have obtained the first-order conditions for public production, but we have not considered the correct method of evaluating indivisible investments. This is one problem that deserves examination. In examining the optimal tax structure, we have briefly considered the tax rates implied by particular utility functions. This analysis should be extended to more general and more interesting sets of consumers. Further, we have not examined in any detail the uniqueness and stability of equilibrium, that is, the question whether there are means of achieving in practice an equilibrium which is close to the optimum.

Finally, we would like to emphasize the assumptions which seem to us most seriously to limit the applications of this theory.[7] We have assumed no costs of tax administration and no tax evasion. And we have assumed constant-returns-to-scale and price-taking, profit-maximizing behavior in private production. Pure profits (or losses) associated with the violation of these assumptions imply that private production decisions directly influence social welfare by affecting household incomes. In such a case, it would presumably be desirable to add a profits tax to the set of policy instruments. Nevertheless, aggregate production efficiency would no longer be desirable in general; although it may be possible to get close to the optimum with efficient production if pure profits are small. We hope, nevertheless, that the methods and results of this paper have shown that economic analysis need not depend on the simplifying, but unrealistic, assumption that the perfect capital levy has taken place.[8]

[7] These assumptions are viewed in the context of equilibrium theory. There is no need here to go into the limitations inherent in current equilibrium theory.

[8] A recent paper by Clarence Morrison also deals with marginal cost pricing as a special case of optimal pricing.

REFERENCES

W. J. Corlett and D. C. Hague, "Complementarity and the Excess Burden of Taxation," *Rev. Econ. Stud.*, 1953, *21*, No. 1, 21–30.

E. Foster and H. Sonnenschein, "Price Distortion and Economic Welfare," *Econometrica*, Mar. 1970, *38*, 281–97.

H. Kuhn and A. Tucker, "Nonlinear Programming," in J. Neyman, ed., *Proceedings of the Second Berkeley Symposium on Mathematical Statistics and Probability*, Berkeley 1951.

J. A. Mirrlees, "An Exploration in the Theory of Optimum Income Taxation," *Rev. Econ. Stud.*, Apr. 1971, *38*, forthcoming.

C. C. Morrison, "Marginal Cost Pricing and the Theory of Second Best," *Western Econ. J.*, June 1969, *7*, 145–52.

P. A. Samuelson, "Memorandum for U.S. Treasury, 1951," unpublished.

———, "The Pure Theory of Public Expenditure," *Rev. Econ. Statist.*, Nov. 1954, *36*, 387–89.

Part III
Predatory Pricing

[14]

PREDATORY PRICING AND RELATED PRACTICES UNDER SECTION 2 OF THE SHERMAN ACT †

Phillip Areeda * *and Donald F. Turner* **

A firm may reduce its prices in an attempt to destroy its rivals or to deter new entry. Although the Sherman Act has long been construed to prohibit this practice, the case law on predatory pricing has been characterized by vagueness and a paucity of economic analysis. In this Article, Professors Areeda and Turner analyze the predatory pricing offense in terms of its economic underpinnings. After briefly reviewing the fundamental economic concepts of cost-measurement and profit-maximization, the authors examine the relationship between a firm's prices and its costs in order to define a rational dividing line between legitimately competitive prices and prices that are properly regarded as predatory. They then apply their analytical framework to possible techniques of predation other than general price reductions.

ALTHOUGH antitrust law is not usually concerned with setting a limit on price competition, under certain conditions low prices may have anticompetitive effects. A firm which drives out or excludes rivals by selling at unremunerative prices is not competing on the merits, but engaging in behavior that may properly be called predatory. There is, therefore, good reason for including a "predatory pricing" antitrust offense within the proscription of monopolization or attempts to monopolize in section 2 of the Sherman Act.[1]

Treatment of predatory pricing in the cases and the literature,

---

 This Article is an adaptation of part of a treatise on antitrust law that is being prepared for publication by the authors.

* Professor of Law, Harvard University (on leave). A.B., Harvard, 1951; LL.B. 1954. Professor Areeda is currently Counsel to the President of the United States. This Article was drafted before he became associated with the federal government and does not reflect the views of any government agency.

** Professor of Law, Harvard University. B.A., Northwestern University, 1941; Ph.D., Harvard University, 1947; LL.B., Yale University, 1950.

[1] 15 U.S.C. § 2 (1970); *see, e.g.*, United States v. American Tobacco Co., 221 U.S. 106, 182 (1911); Standard Oil Co. v. United States, 221 U.S. 1, 43 (1910). The Clayton Act, as amended by the Robinson-Patman Act, also provides a safeguard against predation in its prohibition of price discrimination. 15 U.S.C. § 13 (1970); *see, e.g.*, Moore v. Mead's Fine Bread Co., 348 U.S. 115 (1954); Porto Rican American Tobacco Co. v. American Tobacco Co., 30 F.2d 234 (2d Cir.), *cert. denied*, 279 U.S. 858 (1929). *See also* 15 U.S.C. § 13a (1970) (unlawful to "sell . . . at unreasonably low prices for the purpose of destroying competition or eliminating a competitor"). Although most of our discussion will be based on the reach of the Sherman Act, § 2, the issues are substantially the same under the Clayton Act insofar as that statute is concerned with predatory pricing. *See* pp. 724–28 *infra*.

however, has commonly suffered from two interrelated defects: failure to delineate clearly and correctly what practices should constitute the offense,[2] and exaggerated fears that large firms will be inclined to engage in it.[3] Unhappy rivals may automatically assume predation when a competitor's price is below their costs, disregarding the possibility that the alleged predator's cost is well below theirs and more than covered by his price. Moreover, "selling at a loss" might be viewed as improper even though the seller would incur greater losses if it attempted to charge a higher price or if it ceased production altogether.[4]

These vague formulations of the offense overlook the fact that predation in any meaningful sense cannot exist unless there is a temporary sacrifice of net revenues in the expectation of greater future gains. Indeed, the classically-feared case of predation has been the deliberate sacrifice of present revenues for the purpose of driving rivals out of the market and then recouping the losses through higher profits earned in the absence of competition.[5] Thus, predatory pricing would make little economic sense to a potential predator unless he had (1) greater financial staying power than his rivals, and (2) a very substantial prospect that the losses he incurs in the predatory campaign will be exceeded by the profits to be earned after his rivals have been destroyed.

As for the first prerequisite, it should, of course, be recognized that predation cannot be successful, and therefore is unlikely to occur, when the predators' rivals possess resources comparable to his own. Even when an alleged predator has greater staying power, however, attention must also be given to the second prerequisite, which is less likely to occur. Although a predator may drive competitors into bankruptcy, their durable assets may remain in the market in the hands of others. Moreover, a firm can anticipate monopoly profits for only so long as its monopoly prices

---

[2] *See, e.g.*, Atlas Bldg. Prod. Co. v. Diamond Block & Gravel Co., 269 F.2d 950 (10th Cir. 1959), *cert. denied*, 363 U.S. 843 (1960); Maryland Baking Co. v. FTC, 243 F.2d 716 (4th Cir. 1957).

[3] *See, e.g.*, Reynolds Metal Co. v. FTC, 309 F.2d 223, 229–30 (D.C. Cir. 1962); Foremost Dairies, Inc., 60 F.T.C. 944, 1083–84 (1962); MacIntyre & Volhard, *Predatory Pricing Legislation — Is It Necessary?*, 14 B.C. IND. & COM. L. REV. 1 (1972). One commentator has suggested that predatory pricing is likely to be used in combination with attempts to merge or with cartelization, but includes all pricing that is not profit-maximizing in his definition of "predatory." *See* Yamey, *Predatory Price Cutting: Notes & Comments*, 15 J. L. & ECON. 129 (1972).

[4] *See* note 20 *infra*.

[5] A large firm may also "sell at a loss" for the purpose of disciplining smaller rivals for undercutting its monopoly price. Although this practice may not drive rivals out of the market, it does enable the disciplining firm, if successful, to regain losses it incurred during the period of discipline. *See* pp. 706–09 *infra*; note 35 *infra*.

do not attract new entry. Losses incurred through predation could be regained in markets with very high barriers to entry. In many markets, however, and especially in those having a number of small rivals, entry barriers may be nonexistent or at least too low to preclude entry. Admittedly, a demonstrated willingness to indulge in predatory pricing might itself deter some smaller potential entrants, but it is unlikely to inhibit firms with resources comparable to those of the predator. Repeated predation in the same market, moreover, is not only costly but is likely to be easily detectable and thus the occasion for severe antitrust sanctions. The prospects of an adequate future payoff, therefore, will seldom be sufficient to motivate predation.[6] Indeed, proven cases of predatory pricing have been extremely rare.[7]

That predatory pricing seems highly unlikely does not necessarily mean that there should be no antitrust rules against it. But it does suggest that extreme care be taken in formulating such rules, lest the threat of litigation, particularly by private parties, materially deter legitimate, competitive pricing. Courts in predatory pricing cases have generally turned to such empty formulae as "below cost" pricing,[8] ruinous competition,[9] or predatory intent [10] in adjudicating liability. These standards provide little, if any, basis for analyzing the predatory pricing offense. In this Article we will attempt to formulate meaningful and workable tests for distinguishing between predatory and competitive pricing by examining the relationship between a firm's costs and its

---

[6] It has also been argued that predatory pricing to drive out rivals is unlikely because the alternatives of acquiring rivals by merger or forming a price cartel are less costly. *See* McGee, *Predatory Price Cutting: The Standard Oil (N.J.) Case*, 1 J. L. & ECON. 137, 138–43 (1958); Telser, *Cutthroat Competition and the Long Purse*, 9 J. L. & ECON. 259 (1966). In the early years of the Sherman Act predatory pricing was used to coerce rivals into merger with the predator or into joining a price cartel. *See, e.g.*, Standard Oil Co. v. United States, 221 U.S. 1 (1910); United States v. E.I. du Pont de Nemours & Co., 188 F. 127, 140 (Cir. Ct. Del. 1911). When these alternatives are also illegal and either more visible or more difficult to effect, however, the argument that they will supplant predatory pricing is unpersuasive.

[7] *See* Koller, *The Myth of Predatory Pricing — An Empirical Study*, 4 ANTITRUST L. & ECON. REV. 105 (Summer 1971).

[8] *See, e.g.*, National Dairy Prod. Corp. v. United States, 350 F.2d 321, 327 (8th Cir. 1965), *vacated and remanded on other grounds*, 384 U.S. 883 (1966); Forster Mfg. Co. v. FTC, 335 F.2d 47, 53 (1st Cir. 1964), *cert. denied*, 380 U.S. 906 (1965); E. B. Muller Co. v. FTC, 142 F.2d 511, 517 (6th Cir. 1944).

[9] Porto Rican American Tobacco Co. v. American Tobacco Co., 30 F.2d 234, 236 (2d Cir.), *cert. denied*, 279 U.S. 858 (1929).

[10] *See, e.g.*, Moore v. Mead's Fine Bread Co., 348 U.S. 115, 118 (1954); Forster Mfg. Co. v. FTC, 335 F.2d 47, 52 (1st Cir. 1964), *cert. denied*, 380 U.S. 906 (1965); Maryland Baking Co. v. FTC, 243 F.2d 716, 718 (4th Cir. 1957); E. B. Muller & Co. v. FTC, 142 F.2d 511, 517 (6th Cir. 1944).

prices. We will first review some rudimentary economic distinctions among various measures of cost and their relevance to profit-maximization. We will then discuss which measurements of cost should be used to determine when a firm is engaging in predatory pricing. Finally we will examine predatory devices other than general price reductions.[11]

I. Alternative Measures of Cost [12]

The economic costs facing a firm differ in an important respect: some are "fixed," and others are "variable." Fixed costs are costs that do not vary with changes in output. They typically include most management expenses, interest on bonded debt, depreciation (to the extent that equipment is not consumed by using it), property taxes, and other irreducible overhead. And though not an accounting cost, fixed costs should be deemed to include the return on investment that would currently be necessary to attract capital to the firm — what the economist refers to as the opportunity cost to the owners of the firm. In short, it is reasonably accurate to say that fixed costs are costs that would continue even if the firm produced no output at all.

Variable costs, as the name implies, are costs that vary with changes in output. They typically include such items as materials, fuel, labor directly used to produce the product, indirect labor such as foremen, clerks, and custodial help, utilities, repair and maintenance, and per unit royalties and license fees. The average variable cost is the sum of all variable costs divided by output.

Marginal cost is the increment to total cost that results from producing an additional increment of output. It is a function solely of variable costs, since fixed costs, by definition, are costs unaffected by changes in output. Marginal cost usually decreases over low levels of output and increases as production approaches plant capacity.[13]

Average cost is the sum of fixed cost and total variable cost, divided by output. It is, by definition, higher than average variable

---

[11] The bulk of our analysis focuses on what should be deemed to be a predatory practice by a monopolist, since that is the "worst case." Practices acceptable for the monopolist are a fortiori acceptable for firms with less market power. However, we shall also indicate the respects in which nonmonopoly firms should have wider latitude.

[12] *See generally* R. Dorfman, Prices and Markets (2d ed. 1972).

[13] If variable costs are strictly proportional to output, marginal cost will equal average variable cost at all outputs. If not, marginal cost will be lower than average variable cost at some (usually low) outputs and higher at other (usually high) outputs.

cost at all outputs, but will typically be below marginal cost at very high levels of output, when the plant is strained beyond efficient operating capacity.[14]

Which costs are fixed and which are variable (and hence marginal) is a function of both (1) the magnitude of the contemplated change in output, and (2) time. Virtually all costs are variable when a firm, operating at capacity, plans to double its output by constructing new plants and purchasing new equipment. Moreover, more costs become variable as the time period increases. The variable costs described above are those incurred in what is usually termed the "short run," namely, the period in which the firm cannot replace or increase plant or equipment. Conversely, in the "long run" the firm can vary quantities of *all* inputs (plant and equipment as well as shortrun variable inputs); thus, all costs are variable over the long run.[15]

In order to determine which of these various costs is relevant to predatory, "below cost," selling, we must first ask what costs are relevant to the firm which is seeking to maximize profits or minimize losses, since a firm which seeks to do so is normally responding to acceptable economic incentives and thus is not engaging in predatory behavior. The profit-maximizing or loss-minimizing output for any firm, whether competitive or monopolistic, is that where any increase in output would add more to costs than to revenues and any decrease in output would reduce revenues more than costs. In short, in deciding whether it would increase or decrease output, the firm looks to the *incremental*

[14] The different categories of cost and their relationship can be portrayed by the following classic diagram:

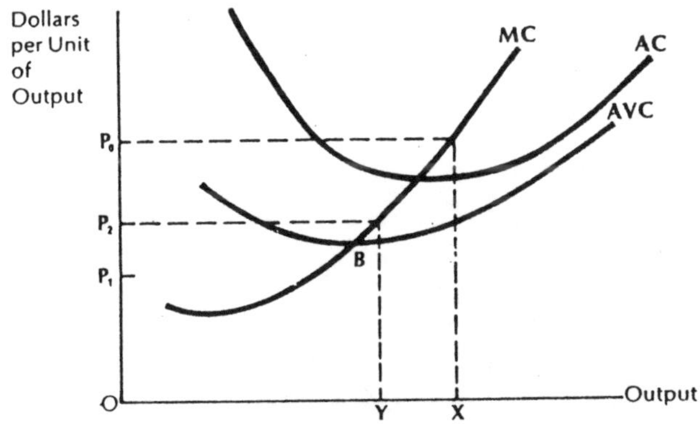

Marginal cost (MC) is equal to average variable cost (AVC) when AVC is at a minimum and is equal to average cost (AC) when AC is at a minimum.

[15] There is, of course, no single time period that determines the short or long run. As the time period lengthens, more fixed costs become variable.

effects on revenues and costs. Thus, the relevant cost is marginal cost.[16]

Under conditions of perfect competition, a firm always maximizes profits (or minimizes losses) by producing that output at which its marginal cost equals the market price.[17] This occurs because the perfectly competitive firm accepts the market price as given since it is, by definition, too small to affect market price by any variations in output. Accordingly, its incremental or marginal revenue from selling any additional unit of output is equal to the market price itself. Thus, when price is equal to marginal cost, changes in output will reduce profits. This solution in the perfectly competitive world also produces an efficient allocation of resources: market price reflects what consumers are willing to pay for the last unit of output; marginal cost reflects the full current cost of resources needed to produce it; a higher price would result in a reduction in output and thus deprive some buyers of a commodity for which they were willing to pay the cost of production.[18]

The firm with monopoly power, however, has, by definition, captured a sufficiently large part of a market to determine market

[16] Since fixed costs do not vary with changes in output, they are irrelevant to a determination of the profit-maximizing or loss-minimizing output. The size of the fixed costs determines only whether, at the best output, the firm will earn excess, normal, or below-normal returns. Of course, if the firm can at best make below-normal returns, and the prospects remain the same when the time comes for plant or equipment to be replaced, the rational firm would not make the reinvestment and its output would decline or cease. But at the time that such a decision is made, the fixed costs would no longer be fixed but would have become a part of variable cost, since they would then be affected by variations in output.

[17] If, however, price is below average variable cost at all levels of output, the firm can minimize losses only by ceasing operations. Since the average cost of production of each unit is greater than the revenue realized from its sale, any output greater than zero increases the firm's losses. At price P_1 on the diagram in note 14 *supra*, the loss-minimizing firm will shut down.

[18] The following diagram shows the profit-maximizing price for the perfectly competitive firm:

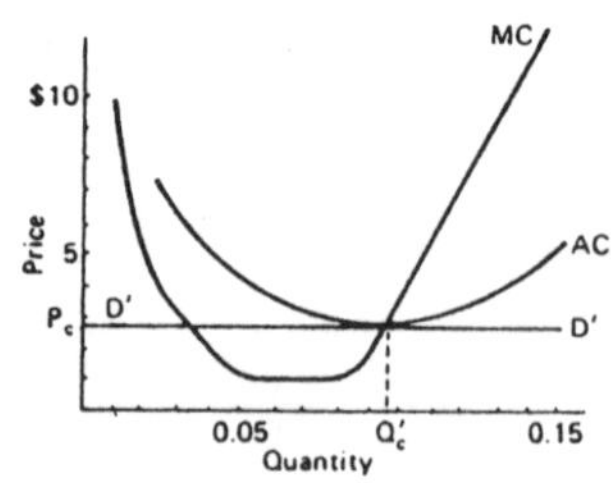

Since the firm is unable to affect price by changes in its output, it faces a horizontal demand curve. The firm maximizes profit when price (P_c) is equal to marginal cost (MC).

price by varying its output. For the monopolist facing the usual "downward sloping" demand curve (and unable to engage in significant price discrimination), an increase in output will reduce the market price. Thus, the incremental revenue to the monopolist from selling an additional unit is the lower price received for that unit, minus the revenue lost from selling all other units at the lower price. For him, therefore, marginal revenue is always below price, with the result that the output at which marginal cost equals marginal revenue will generate a price that exceeds marginal cost.[19] The monopolist's price is thus higher, and its output lower, than the social optimum; any higher output and lower price would be an improvement in resource use up to the point where, as in a competitive market, price equals marginal cost.

II. Predatory Pricing in General

A. The Problem

We are now able to characterize more precisely the predatory pricing problem. We would normally expect a profit-maximizing firm, within the limits of data and convenience, to attempt to maximize profits or minimize losses in the short run — the competitive firm by producing where marginal cost equals price, and the monopolist by producing where marginal cost equals marginal revenue. The firm that is selling at a shortrun profit-maximizing (or loss-minimizing) price is clearly not a predator. A necessary, but, as we will subsequently argue, not sufficient condition of predation is the sacrifice of shortrun profits.

---

[19] Because the monopolist can affect market price by varying its output, it faces a downward sloping demand curve (D):

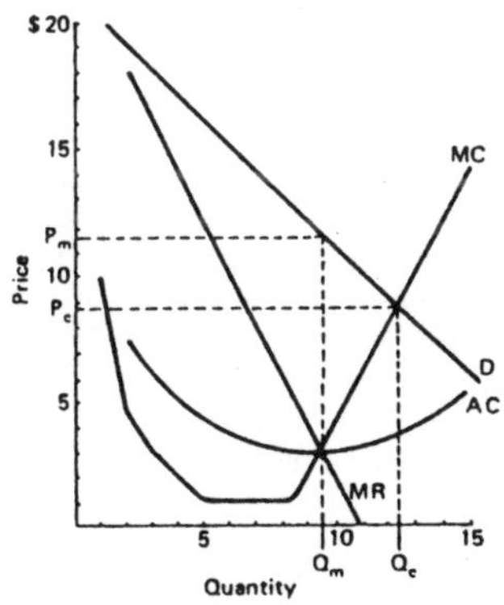

The monopolist maximizes profit when marginal revenue (MR) is equal to marginal cost (MC). Thus, in the illustration, the profit-maximizing monopolist will produce quantity Q_m and sell at price P_m, which is higher than marginal cost.

Shortrun profit-maximizing may adversely affect profitability in the longer run. A firm may correctly calculate that shortrun losses will be more than repaid by the higher monopoly prices that can be charged after competitors have been driven out. Accordingly, longrun profit-maximizing should not be an absolute or automatic defense to allegedly predatory, shortrun profit-sacrificing. However, not all deliberate sacrificing of shortrun profits is illegitimate. A firm may voluntarily assume shortrun losses in situations where monopoly is neither sought nor possible, and where, as in the case of a new entrant seeking to become established in a market, such action promotes rather than retards competition. Thus, a standard based upon shortrun profit-maximizing is not an adequate means of defining the legitimate price floor for firms in general. Indeed, even for a monopolist, a profit-maximization standard is inappropriate. Definition of a proper price floor requires an understanding of the relationship between a firm's prices and various measures of cost.

B. *Prices At or Above Average Cost*

When price is equal to average cost, the firm is at the "break even" point — that is, total revenues just cover total costs, including normal returns on investment. The relationship between price and average cost does not, however, determine whether a firm is profit-maximizing; it shows only whether the firm is making excess, normal, or below-normal returns.

When a monopolist sells at a price at or above average cost, but could earn higher shortrun profits at a higher price, the necessary element of predation is presumably present.[20] Unless acting irrationally or out of ignorance, the firm is likely to be charging the lower price in order to preserve or enhance its market share by deterring rivals.[21] Such pricing may take two forms: (1) the

[20] When a firm sells at a price *below* average cost it is incurring a loss. The mere fact that the firm is not recovering full costs, however, is not grounds for concluding that its price is predatory. Losses are sometimes inevitable; demand conditions may dictate that a firm earn its maximum net revenue over variable costs at a price below average cost. For example, in the diagram in note 14 *supra*, a firm may be loss-minimizing at price P_2. While not recovering full fixed costs, such a firm is not sacrificing available present returns for any anti-competitive objective. The shortrun, loss-minimizing price cannot, therefore, be considered predatory or otherwise objectionable by antitrust law.

This proposition will not resolve many real cases. It will be exceedingly difficult to know what is or is not a loss-minimizing price. Nevertheless, the proposition is an important one in principle, for it serves to remind us that the defendant's failure to earn profits or even to recover his full cost is not necessarily objectionable.

[21] The firm may also be keeping price down to reasonable levels during periods of high demand in order to preserve customer goodwill.

firm may permanently charge less than a profit-maximizing price in order to deter entry or to destroy rivals; or (2) it may first charge a profit-maximizing price, lower the price when rivals appear, and then raise the price when the rivals are extinguished. However, in both instances, we conclude that such pricing behavior should be deemed non-predatory so long as the prices equal or exceed average total cost. Our analysis of each variation follows. In each instance we assume that the price is equal to or greater than both average cost and marginal cost.[22]

1. Limit Pricing. — A monopolist protected by an insurmountable barrier to the entry of others can charge whatever price will maximize his profit. The ability of other firms to overcome entry barriers may, however, affect the monopolist's price. To oversimplify a bit, suppose that the monopolist's profit-maximizing price is $100 per unit, but a $100 price would attract entry while a $90 price would not. Average total costs (including a normal return on investment) at an efficient scale of output might be $80 to the monopolist but $91 for newcomers. In that event, the monopolist will have to choose between inducing entry at the profit-maximizing price of $100 and retaining the entire market at the $90 price. If the discounted income stream at the lower price exceeds that from sharing the market at the higher price, the monopolist will charge the lower price. Although the lower price would thus be the longrun, profit-maximizing price, it is usually called a "limit price" and contrasted with the higher, shortrun, profit-maximizing price determined without reference to possible entry.[23]

The limit price is intended by the monopolist to impair the opportunities of rivals, and, if successful, it does prevent competition from arising. In the absence of limit pricing, competition might arise and force the price down to the former limit price or even lower, if the presence of additional firms induces cost paring, reduction of "slack," and, in the long run, more efficient production. Without limit pricing other benefits of competition may also arise. More firms in the market might, for example, lead to more invention and innovation and a quicker dispersion of existing innovations throughout the economy.

We do not, however, believe that these arguments justify a prohibition against limit pricing. Superior products or service, successful innovation, or other effective competition on the merits always tends to exclude rivals. Without them, more competitors might arise and eventually achieve comparable or better results,

---

[22] The unusual case where price equals or exceeds average cost but is less than marginal cost is discussed at pages 712–13 *infra*.

[23] *See generally* J. BAIN, INDUSTRIAL ORGANIZATION 269–76 (2d ed. 1968).

but we do not accept such speculative possibilities in exchange for the present benefits of superior competitive performance. Exclusion by charging prices equal to average cost is also competition on the merits — only those potential entrants who cannot survive at the efficiency-related price are kept out.[24] And the lower prices, higher output, and fuller use of the monopolist's productive capacity are, of course, socially beneficial.

In sum, without even considering the formidable administrative problems which supervising a monopolist's pricing policies would impose,[25] we conclude that more-or-less permanently "low" prices are competition on the merits and not an abuse of power or exclusionary behavior for the purposes of section two of the Sherman Act.[26]

2. *Temporary Price Reduction to Average Cost.* — Where entry is easy and relatively costless, the monopolist would have to maintain the lower price to forestall renewed entry. But where a new entrant must make a large investment in facilities, personnel training, distribution development, or product promotion, he will not enter without the prospect of survival for a period sufficiently long to recover at least those initial costs. The potential entrant who cannot survive at a price covering the monopolist's costs will not, therefore, enter when he thinks it probable that the monopolist will adopt that lower price in response to entry. If the monopolist reduces his price once or twice, he will discourage future entry. In such circumstances, monopoly may be maintained without a permanent price reduction, and thus consumers will not receive the long-term benefit of the higher output at lower price by which rivalry was destroyed or prevented. This result is certainly not a happy one.

Nevertheless, despite the loss of long-term benefits to consumers, this case is analytically indistinguishable from the preceding case. Temporary price reductions are no more exclusionary than permanent low prices, and may be even less so since some entrants may have the staying power to meet the monopolist's temporary, low price. In either case, the low price at or above

[24] Similarly, only less efficient, existing rivals will be eliminated by the monopolist's limit price.

[25] *See* pp. 707–09, 711 *infra*.

[26] Our conclusion that it makes no legal sense to compel a monopolist to invite entry by exploiting consumers, or to force a firm to forego price competition on the merits with existing rivals is no less applicable when a firm permanently reduces an earlier and higher price to a price at or above average cost even though he would earn larger, shortrun profits at the higher price. The fact that a firm once restricted output or exploited buyers, generates no social interest in continued exploitation. Moreover, the fact that the lower price is relatively permanent provides some assurance that the firm is making a normal return, since otherwise it would be unlikely to maintain the lower price.

average cost is competition on the merits and excludes only less efficient rivals. Even if this were not fully convincing we would still conclude that temporary price reductions in response to rivalry or threatened rivalry should not be judged unlawfully exclusionary under the Sherman Act because of the formidable administrative problems in attempting to control such temporary price reductions adequately, efficiently, and without interfering unduly with desirable pricing behavior.

We see no satisfactory method of control. One might try to forbid the high monopoly price and thereby assure that consumers always have the benefit of competitive prices. There are, however, serious theoretical and practical difficulties in determining what is a "reasonable" (nonmonopoly) price, as the history of public ratemaking makes painfully manifest. Determination of a reasonable price would require continuing supervision as cost, demand, and technological functions change. Antitrust courts have rightly resisted undertaking the heavy, continuous, and unguided burden of supervising the economic performance of business firms.[27] Moreover, a monopolist whose power was legitimately acquired by patents cannot be denied monopoly profits without subverting the purpose of the patent laws. Similarly, denying monopoly profits to those whose power was obtained by superior skill, foresight, and industry could eliminate the primary incentive to develop such competitive skill. Finally, price restrictions would have perverse effects on the efficiency and innovation aspects of a monopolist's on-going performance by eliminating the reward.[28]

Alternatively, one might try to forbid a monopolist from lowering his price below the price charged by a rival or announced by

---

[27] The conclusions of the Supreme Court in rejecting a "reasonable price" defense to a price-fixing agreement are equally apposite here:

> The reasonable price fixed today may through economic and business changes become the unreasonable price of tomorrow. Once established, it may be maintained unchanged because of the absence of competition secured by the agreement for a price reasonable when fixed. Agreements which create such potential power may well be held to be in themselves unreasonable or unlawful restraints, without the necessity of minute inquiry whether a particular price is reasonable or unreasonable as fixed and without placing on the government in enforcing the Sherman Law the burden of ascertaining from day to day whether it has become unreasonable through the mere variation of economic conditions. Moreover, in the absence of express legislation requiring it, we should hesitate to adopt a construction making the difference between legal and illegal conduct in the field of business relations depend upon so uncertain a test as whether prices are reasonable — a determination which can be satisfactorily made only after a complete survey of our economic organization and a choice between rival philosophies.

United States v. Trenton Potteries Co., 273 U.S. 392, 397–98 (1927).

[28] For a discussion of the relationship between monopoly and innovation see F. Scherer, Industrial Market Structure and Economic Performance 363–77 (1970).

an entrant. This would guarantee the entrant or the rival protection from any competitive price initiatives on the part of the monopolist. The administrative problems with this method, however, are also substantial. Relative qualities and consumer preferences have to be assessed in order to determine when a particular price in fact merely meets rather than effectively undercuts the rival's price.[29] Moreover, a time limit would have to be placed on the constraint, since otherwise new entrants would be motivated to maintain monopoly prices and the constraint itself would have an anticompetitive effect. The constraint might last only until new entrants recover start-up costs, thereby assuring the survival of entrants able to produce as efficiently as the firm with monopoly power. It would, however, be difficult to determine the time needed for recovery of start-up costs, and the longer the constraint lasts the more likely that it will encourage waste by the new entrants. Moreover, even a temporary imposition of a price floor could encourage entry of inefficient firms.[30]

Finally, one might forbid the reversal of a price decrease and thereby either discourage temporary price reductions from the outset or at least give consumers the permanent benefit of the lower prices by which a monopolist destroyed his rivals or prevented their entry. Although this method is perhaps the most feasible, we feel that it should be rejected for a number of reasons. First, forbidding reversal of a price decrease would greatly increase the likelihood that a monopolist would elect to forego the price reduction and maximize his monopoly profits until such time as entry or expansion of rivals eliminates them. Foregoing the reduction would encourage the entry of less efficient rivals.

Second, enforcement of such a rule would require adjustments to cope with subsequent changes in costs or demand. Most obviously, the price ceiling would have to be raised with an increase in such factor costs as wage rates or materials, or with an increase in demand that could only be met at marginal costs above the price ceiling. In such events, failure to raise the ceiling would result either in (1) uneconomically high output (where price is less than marginal cost) or (2) insufficient output to meet the demand at the ceiling price, which would in turn lead to private rationing or a "gray" market in which resales took place at higher prices.

[29] *See* p. 716 & note 41 *infra*.

[30] Alternatively, the pricing constraint on the monopolist might be maintained until new entrants or rivals had acquired a specified market share. Such a limit, however, would not only encourage entry of less efficient firms seeking to take advantage of a guaranteed market share, but would also provide an incentive for rivals to restrict output just short of the specified share in order to maintain high prices.

Moreover, enforcing a price ceiling would raise the problem of reduced profits or even losses for the monopolist in the event of a decrease in demand. Theory might suggest no relief or even a price reduction, on the ground that if competition had not been excluded the same result would have obtained. But it is at least doubtful that so ruthless an approach would be acceptable even under legislatively authorized "public utility" regulation. And such a policy would further discourage a monopolist from making any price reductions.

In sum, a rule forbidding reversal of a price reduction would impose on enforcement agencies and the courts administrative burdens that are not justified by the speculative benefits such a rule might bring. Accordingly, we conclude that a price at or above average cost should be demed non-predatory, and not in law exclusionary, whether permanent or not.

We are under no illusions that a rule permitting prices at or above average cost is easily applied. Average cost includes a "normal" return on investment, a figure usually not determinable with any precision. But the principle that average-cost pricing is legitimately competitive is an important one and may serve to dispose quickly of cases in which the alleged predator's rate of return is normal by any reasonable test.[31]

C. *Marginal-Cost Pricing*

In the previous Section we considered the threat to rivals and new entrants posed by a price that is profitable to the monopolist but not to the rival. In some instances, however, the monopolist's price may both generate below-normal returns — that is, it may be below average cost — and be below the loss-minimizing price. Because such a price yields less than the normal return on capital, it can threaten the survival of equally efficient rivals with less staying power than the monopolist enjoys. We will consider these loss-producing prices in two categories: (1) those equal to or greater than marginal cost and (2) those less than marginal cost.

1. Prices At or Above Marginal Cost. — At the outset we can eliminate from our consideration situations in which the monopolist is producing beyond the output at which his plant functions most efficiently, since at such high levels of production, marginal cost will exceed average cost. In such cases, pricing at or above marginal cost will not eliminate equally efficient rivals or potential

[31] The district court in Telex Corp. v. IBM, 367 F. Supp. 258 (N.D. Okla. 1973), apparently failed to recognize this principle. Despite a lack of evidence that IBM reduced prices below cost and a reasonable profit, and despite IBM's anticipation of returns "in excess of 20%," the court found that IBM had engaged in predatory pricing. *Id.* at 306.

entrants, who may freely restrict their ouput to efficient levels, and thus make substantial profits at the monopolist's price.

We need consider, then, only instances when marginal cost is below average cost, a situation which will not occur unless the monopolist possesses "excess capacity." [32] Only then will the monopolist's marginal cost price deprive equally efficient rivals, actual or potential, of "normal" returns on their capital.[33]

Although narrowed, the problem remains: the equally efficient rival might be destroyed or dissuaded from entering not because he is less efficient but because he has less capital. Consider two illustrations. First, suppose that the monopolist occupies an entire market by himself and that his plant has excess capacity. Suppose further that the monopolist could maximize profits at a price exceeding average cost but chooses to dissuade entry by pricing at marginal cost, which is now below average cost. Although it may preserve a monopoly, this price seems socially appropriate, because the construction of additional capacity where excess capacity already exists would waste social resources. Indeed, a price higher than marginal cost would yield a smaller output and would waste present resources. Existing capacity, that could be used to produce at a cost less than the added value to consumers, would be idled.

Second, suppose that (1) a monopolist and his smaller rival have identical cost curves, (2) both have been producing at full capacity and earning significant profits, (3) demand falls during a temporary, two-year recession, (4) the monopolist would maximize profits at a price above average cost, (5) the monopolist chooses to price at marginal cost, which is now below average cost, (6) the rival has insufficient liquid resources or access to new capital to cover his losses and service his capital debt, (7) the rival thereby expires, (8) his assets and business are withdrawn from the market, and (9) subsequent new entry is difficult. In this set of circumstances, marginal-cost pricing by the monopolist does not merely discourage the addition of immediately redundant capacity, but has the effect of destroying an equally efficient rival.[34]

---

[32] A firm has excess capacity (and marginal cost is below average cost) when the demand curve intersects the average cost curve to the left of minimum average cost, *i.e.*, prior to the point where marginal cost equals average cost.

[33] We also do not consider here loss-minimizing prices below average cost. As we have noted, *see* note 20 *supra*, such prices lack the predatory element of sacrificing current revenues.

[34] This illustration is not meant to suggest that facts number four and number five will actually occur with any frequency; nor is it inevitable that the rival will fail to ride out the recession, that his assets will in fact be withdrawn from the

Nevertheless, we conclude that prices at or above marginal cost, even though they are not profit-maximizing, should not be considered predatory. If a monopolist produces to a point where price equals marginal cost, only less efficient firms will suffer larger losses per unit of output; more efficient firms will be losing less or even operating profitably. Admittedly, the destruction of an equally efficient rival, and the deterrence of entry of firms which are equally efficient, poses some threat to competition in the long run; if demand increases to its former level, only the monopolist will occupy the market which he formerly shared with the rival. However, we see no satisfactory method of eliminating this risk. Establishing a price floor above marginal cost would permit survival not only of equally efficient firms, but less efficient ones as well. And in the short run, at least, entry even by equally efficient firms will be undesirable since excess capacity already exists.

Furthermore, to force the firm to charge a higher price would reduce industry output and waste economic resources in the short run. Output that could be produced at a cost lower than its value to consumers would be eliminated. Thus, pricing at marginal cost is the competitive and socially optimal result.

Finally, enforcement of a prohibition against marginal-cost pricing would create serious administrative problems. If the monopolist were prohibited from dropping his price down to marginal cost, then some price floor above marginal cost would be required. Such a floor should be set no higher than a monopolist's loss-minimizing price since a higher price is not predatory and would require the monopolist to incur greater losses. Yet, a floor so defined would be more difficult to administer or comply with than a marginal-cost floor. Difficult as it may be for a firm to calculate marginal cost, it is vastly more difficult to calculate in advance what the loss-minimizing price would be. In addition to marginal costs, the firm would have to estimate what the shape and position of its demand curve will be, which would in turn require an estimate, among other things, of the price and output responses of rivals to various prices it might charge. To hold the monopolist responsible, after-the-fact, for reasonable miscalculations would be an intolerable burden, and encourage a high-price policy in order to be safe. And it is likely to be nearly as difficult to make after-the-fact determinations of what would have been the loss-minimizing price as it was to make them a priori.

Thus, we conclude that a prohibition of marginal-cost pricing

industry, or that reentry will be difficult. Nevertheless, we are posing a testing case in order to examine the principle that marginal-cost pricing should be considered lawful.

cannot be justified either by economic theory or administrative convenience.[35]

2. *Prices Below Marginal Cost.* — By definition, a firm producing at an output where marginal cost exceeds price is selling at least part of that output at an out-of-pocket loss. It could eliminate that loss by reducing its output or, where the highest obtainable price is below average variable cost at all levels of output, by ceasing operations altogether.[36]

We have concluded above that marginal-cost pricing by a monopolist should be tolerated even though losses could be minimized or profits increased at a lower output and higher price, for the reasons, among others, that marginal-cost pricing leads to a proper resource allocation and is consistent with competition on the merits. Neither reason obtains when the monopolist prices below marginal cost. The monopolist is not only incurring private losses but wasting social resources when marginal costs exceed the value of what is produced. And pricing below marginal cost greatly increases the possibility that rivalry will be extinguished or prevented for reasons unrelated to the efficiency of the monopolist. Accordingly, a monopolist pricing below marginal cost should be presumed to have engaged in a predatory or exclusionary practice.[37]

We would make one exception to this rule, namely, when the price, though below marginal cost, is at or above average cost.

[35] It is possible that a firm may temporarily reduce its price to marginal cost in order to punish competitors for shading its higher price. If the firm's marginal-cost price merely meets that of its competitors, we see no justification for finding a predatory offense. Meeting a rival's price with a price above marginal cost is competition on the merits and prohibition of that practice would coerce a firm into giving up a portion of its market share whenever rivals choose to cut their prices.

Price reductions below that of a rival are more objectionable, but even here identification of the violation will be difficult in many instances. In an oligopoly situation it would be difficult if not impossible to distinguish "disciplinary" price-cutting from an outbreak of competitive pricing under the pressures of excess capacity. It would be plainly perverse to impose a constraint on competitive pricing, and thus reinforce the innate tendencies of oligopolists to maintain non-competitive prices by cooperation or collusion.

When a monopolist engages in temporary marginal-cost pricing to discipline small rivals, predation is more easily inferred. Nevertheless, because of the difficulties of drawing the lines between monopoly and oligopoly and between "meeting" and "beating" a rival's price, *see* note 41 *infra*, and because of the administrative problems inherent in setting any price floor above marginal cost, we conclude that disciplinary price cuts to levels above marginal cost should be disregarded.

[36] *See* note 17 *supra*.

[37] Because of the substantial problems involved in determining a firm's marginal cost, we suggest below that average variable cost be used as a surrogate for marginal cost in distinguishing between predatory and non-predatory prices. *See* pp. 716–18 *infra*.

This is not justifiable "on principle," since production to the point where marginal cost exceeds price is wasteful whether or not price exceeds average cost. Nevertheless, practical reasons suggest that the case can be disregarded, for it seems unlikely to have any significant anticompetitive consequences. The case could occur, by definition, only when demand exceeds what the firm can produce at minimum average cost. If the excess demand is temporary, there is little need for new entry. If permanent, pricing below marginal cost, with its consequent high output, may have some deterrent effect on new entry and some adverse effect on existing rivals. The harmful effect, however, will be minimal, since the price is higher than the monopolist's average cost at most efficient levels of output, and equally efficient rivals or entrants would be making above-normal profits at that price.[38] Thus, it is unlikely that the monopolist would continue that pricing policy for any substantial length of time, because the prospects of recovering profits lost through attempted predation would be dim.

Pricing above average cost is, however, the only exception we would make to a prohibition of below-marginal-cost prices. A monopolist may attempt to justify prices below marginal cost by claiming either that the price is being used for promotional purposes or that he is simply meeting an equally low price of a rival. We conclude, however, that these justifications are either so rarely applicable or of such dubious merit for a monopolist that the presumption of illegality for prices below both marginal and average cost should be conclusive.

(*a*) *Promotional Pricing.* — A promotional price is a temporary, low price designed to induce patronage with the expectation that the customer will continue purchasing the product in the future at a higher price. The promotional price may be below cost and is most easily illustrated by the seller who gives his product away without charge to some or all would-be customers.

Unless continued over a long period of time, in which case it is no longer promotional, promotional pricing by new entrants or small firms without monopoly power threatens little or no harm. Promotional pricing can facilitate new entry or the expansion of small rivals in an industry dominated by one or a few large firms. Entrenched consumer loyalties to established brands constitute barriers to entry and to a small firm's growth. For new or even established firms, promotional pricing serves the purely informational function of advertising by alerting consumers to the existence of new products. The low promotional price is preferable to advertising, for it gives the consumer a better buy during

[38] *See* pp. 709–10 *supra*.

the period of promotion and allows him to judge the product on its merits. Of course, the promotion may on occasion temporarily divert demand from better products or more efficient producers, but the diversion will last only long enough for consumers to judge and reject the inferior, promoted product.[39]

The monopolist can make no such case for promotional pricing. His promotion would not usually intensify competition but would only decrease it — existing rivals will be damaged or driven out, and new entry deterred. In contrast to new entrants or small rivals, he has little need to resort to extreme price reductions to acquaint existing consumers with the merits of his brand.[40]

The only other apparent arguments a monopolist could make are (1) that pricing below marginal cost is necessary to raise the overall market demand by attracting new customers who have not heretofore known or been interested in the product or (2) that it is necessary to enable a firm with declining costs to move to a more efficient level of output. The arguments might be held to justify selective reductions to new customers or in new geographical markets, but as a defense to a general price reduction to present as well as new customers, we find these arguments unpersuasive.

As to the first argument, it is possible but seems highly improbable that an established monopolist would find a general price reduction below marginal cost worthwhile solely because it attracts new customers to the market and thus generates a permanent increase in market demand. The monopolist has a number of alternatives for achieving this goal besides pricing below marginal cost. First, a marginal-cost price itself would ordinarily be a substantial reduction below the shortrun profit-maximizing price for any firm with significant monopoly power, and would thus have a substantial promotional effect. Second, the monopolist may be able to make selective price reductions to marginal cost to new customers or in new geographical areas and thus minimize his shortrun losses from the promotion. Finally, there are the alternatives of selective advertising or other sales efforts. The general price-cut will inevitably draw customers away from rivals as well as attract new buyers, and the effect on those rivals and on new entry will be more severe than any of the alternatives.

[39] After short-term promotion, a firm might eventually become so dominant as to obtain monopoly power, but it would have obtained its power because of competitive superiority, and the mere fact that the initial promotion got the firm going is no reason for condemning the promotion.

[40] It is conceivable that some consumers may have acquired strong loyalties to the brands of small rivals without ever having purchased the monopolist's product. In such event, promotional pricing by a monopolist might be thought defensible. But we consider the case too unlikely to warrant recognition given the risks of abuse that allowing the defense would entail.

We find the declining costs justification for promotional pricing equally unconvincing. Pricing below marginal cost might be rational for a brief period of time for a new producer of an existing product with a very large and much more efficient plant that could supply the entire market at an average cost well below those of existing producers. Similarly, a new producer with a monopoly on an entirely new product might also find it rational to set an initial price below the high marginal costs incurred at early low outputs. But no defense is needed for these declining cost cases. They can be taken care of by a sensible interpretation of the rule that a monopolist is entitled to price at or above *reasonably anticipated* marginal costs. In other words, to establish predatory pricing, it should be necessary to show that a monopolist has priced both below immediate marginal cost and below the marginal cost at the output which he reasonably anticipated he would attain within a reasonable period of time.

(*b*) *Meeting Competition as a Defense.* — We would not permit a monopolist to price below marginal cost in order to meet the lawful price of a rival. Although there are grounds for permitting him to price below marginal cost in order to meet a rival's unlawful price, the administrative difficulties presented by the necessity of distinguishing the two cases are so great as to lead us to reject the defense altogether.

The first proposition, although questionable, seems correct, particularly where the rival is a new entrant. The fact that the rival's low price may be legitimately promotional, and hence a proper competitive tactic, does not make legitimate the response of a monopolist whose product is already well known. The monopolist who goes below marginal cost to meet a rival's promotion is not competing on the merits; the response will destroy or greatly reduce the effects of the rival's promotional effort, a result likely to be particularly serious for the new entrant, whose usual problem is precisely that of obtaining a profitable volume quickly enough to make start-up losses bearable.

The monopolist might attempt to justify a below-marginal-cost price to meet a rival by claiming that he believed he could rapidly reduce his costs to or below those of his rival, and that it would cost him less to hold his organization and patronage intact than to recover them in the future. This contention, however, would be made in every case, and it would be difficult for the monopolist to know or the court to determine that the monopolist could achieve cost parity, that it would be less expensive to suffer such interim out-of-pocket losses than to bear the future costs of rebuilding his organization and recovering lost patronage, or indeed, that there would be any such future costs at all. Furthermore, the complex problems of defining meeting-rather-than-beating the rival's price would have to be faced.[41] Courts would have to undertake the difficult task of assessing differences in product quality and thus become involved in speculation about consumer preferences.

There is some basis for allowing a monopolist to meet a rival's unlawful price. The rival's unlawful price is not competition on the merits, and there is no strong reason for denying even a monopolist the opportunity to defend himself from predatory attack. Retaliation may possibly increase the waste of productive resources in the short run, but it is likely to serve the useful purpose of bringing the predator's unlawful pricing to a quicker end. Nevertheless, we would reject even this limited defense for the monopolist when his price is below marginal cost. The administrative problems of defining a price that meets the rival would be further compounded by the need to determine whether the rival's price were indeed unlawful. There is, after all, consolation for the monopolist in his relative security from serious injury at the hands of a smaller rival unlawfully pricing below marginal cost, in the relative infrequency of that challenge to him, and in his ability to bring a private antitrust suit for injunction or damages.

D. Average Variable Cost as a Surrogate for Marginal Cost

In our analysis of predatory pricing we have concluded that marginal-cost pricing is the economically sound division between acceptable, competitive behavior and "below-cost" predation. Thus, we have suggested a prohibition of prices below marginal cost. The primary administrative impediment to enforcing that prohibition is the difficulty of ascertaining a firm's marginal cost. The incremental cost of making and selling the last unit cannot readily be inferred from conventional business accounts, which typically go no further than showing observed average variable cost. Consequently, it may well be necessary to use the latter as an indicator of marginal cost.

An average variable cost rule, like a marginal cost rule, should be flexible enough to allow a defendant to demonstrate that its price was equal to or above a reasonably anticipated average variable cost. A firm may legitimately determine its price and output levels according to expected future costs rather than historical accounting costs. Of course, historical costs may be the

[41] For a discussion of the difficulties encountered by the courts in applying the "meeting competition" defense of the Robinson-Patman Act, 15 U.S.C. § 13(b) (1970), see F. Rowe, Price Discrimination Under the Robinson-Patman Act 207–64 (1962).

best approximation of costs for the near future, but a defendant should be permitted to show why it anticipated lower costs in the future.

The consequences of substituting average variable cost for marginal cost depend on the relationship between the two cost measurements. Marginal cost may be equal to, below, or above average variable cost: marginal cost will be equal to average variable cost when the latter is constant, less when it is declining, and greater when it is rising. By reference to the marginal-cost standard, accordingly, reliance on average variable cost may be identical, more prohibitive, or more permissive.

There is no a priori reason to expect any particular firm to be operating at the point where marginal cost equals average variable cost,[42] but when the two costs measures are identical over the relevant range of output, employing one as a proxy for the other plainly raises no difficulties.

Whenever unit variable cost declines as output expands, the marginal or incremental variable cost of the next unit is necessarily less than the average of the preceding units. Thus, whenever a firm can reduce unit variable cost by expanding output, a price at average variable cost must exceed marginal cost.[43] Although an average variable cost standard is more prohibitive in these circumstances, it is the correct test on principle, since a firm that sells below its average variable cost is clearly not loss-minimizing. At a price less than average variable cost the firm is earning no return and could incur fewer losses by ceasing operations.[44] The primary nonpredatory justification for prices below

[42] For the usual firm, average variable cost falls and then ultimately rises as output expands. At its low point, the average variable cost curve will be intersected by marginal cost. At that output or range of outputs, the two will be identical. A firm might experience constant variable costs over the full output range, or over the range beyond some minimum efficient scale, or only over the wide or narrow range lying between the realization of scale economies and diseconomies. There is some evidence of relatively constant variable costs over wide ranges of intermediate outputs for many industries. *See* J. JOHNSTON, STATISTICAL COST ANALYSIS 13, 73, 96, 168 (1960); Scitovsky, *Economic Theory and the Measurement of Concentration*, in BUSINESS CONCENTRATION AND PRICE POLICY, 105 (1955).

[43] This might occur (a) over the entire range of outputs in declining cost industries or (b) over that portion of a firm's output preceding the full realization of those economies of scale implicit in its plant in the short run or in industry technology over the long run. The first case is the "natural monopoly" and is relatively rare. The second situation may describe a firm opening a new plant that has not yet won its way in the market. It may also describe a firm with declining demand that has forced production to be cut back well below the efficient scale at which it previously operated. In sum, average variable cost will typically exceed marginal cost only when a plant is operating below efficient use of capacity.

[44] *See* note 17 *supra*.

average variable cost is that the firm is just starting up and has not yet reached expected production levels. Firms in this situation, however, will not be in violation of a rule that prohibits prices below reasonably anticipated average variable cost.

When marginal cost exceeds average variable cost, adopting the latter as the standard runs the risk of allowing a firm to sell at a price below marginal cost while meeting the average variable cost standard. Thus, the surrogate is even more permissive than our exception from marginal cost pricing when the price is at or above average cost.[45] Nevertheless, a permissive exception is justified for similar reasons. Marginal cost is likely to be higher than average variable cost only when output nears the firm's optimum.[46] When capacity is thus strained, predation is especially unlikely, since the loss of profits would be most severe and new demand could not be easily absorbed by the predator. Moreover, given the relatively rare occurrence of predatory pricing, we believe that a slightly permissive rule is acceptable since the threat of litigation under any rule on predatory pricing is more likely to discourage proper pricing than predation, and the benefit of any doubts should go toward protecting the seller, instead of increasing his vulnerability.

In sum, despite the possibility that average variable cost will differ from marginal cost, it is a useful surrogate for predatory pricing analysis.

E. *Predatory Investment in the Monopoly Market*

In theory, the principles applied to define shortrun predatory pricing are applicable to the longer run when funds are invested or reinvested in plant and equipment and hence become part of marginal cost. If it is appropriate to permit a monopolist to expand output in the short run to the point where marginal cost equals price, it should be equally appropriate to permit him to expand capacity to the point where longrun marginal cost equals price, even though that expansion reduces his overall rate of return and even though it limits or forecloses the opportunities of rivals or new entrants. Similarly, if it is appropriate to condemn a monopolist for pricing below marginal cost in the short run, it would seem equally appropriate to condemn him for adding new facilities when he anticipates that the revenue to be obtained from

[45] *See* pp. 712–13 *supra*.

[46] Whenever unit variable cost increases as output expands, the marginal or incremental variable cost of the next unit is necessarily more than the average of the preceding units. This occurs when output nears the optimum for which the plant was designed, thus requiring the use of less efficient manpower or other resources, or exerting upward pressure on factor prices (*e.g.*, the payment of overtime wage rates).

them over their useful life will not cover all costs, including a normal rate of return.

Nevertheless, while we adhere to the first proposition, we reject the second and believe that antitrust law should ignore the possibility of predatory investment in a monopolized product. Our reasons are two. First, construction and perpetuation of excess capacity would be extremely costly, particularly if it fails to deter new entry or expansion of rivals. Investment for predatory purposes is thus an extremely unlikely possibility. Second, the practical difficulties of attempting to distinguish between innocent and predatory expansion are much more severe than those of evaluating shortrun pricing.

Our suggested test for shortrun predation is pricing below reasonably anticipated average variable cost. The firm knows the price it is currently charging; and though "reasonable anticipation" is not precise, it should not pose serious difficulties in application. The firm knows its recent variable costs and should become quickly aware of any substantial changes in such cost elements as wages or materials. However, when a firm is attempting to determine its probable return on new facilities over their useful life, it faces uncertainties of a much higher order. It cannot be sure as to the long-term future course of wage, material, and other variable costs. Nor can it be certain of the prices it will be able to charge over the life of the new facility; accurate estimates of future market-wide demand for its product are difficult, if not impossible, to make with precision, and the firm has no control over, or perhaps even knowledge of, construction or expansion of capacity by others or the development of new substitutes for its product. Thus, there is little basis for inferring predation from the fact that a monopolist has invested in new facilities which later turn out to be unprofitable.

When a monopolist does have excess capacity, it is almost certain to have innocent explanations: (1) new capacity becoming operational sooner than expected; (2) failure of demand to grow as much as anticipated; (3) unanticipated declines in demand attributable to general economic fluctuations or to unexpectedly serious competition from producers of the same or substitute products; (4) increased variable costs; or (5) modernization that substitutes new, lower-cost capacity for old facilities that are worth maintaining for peak demands or as break-down reserve. We can see no workable rule that will satisfactorily distinguish between these legitimate cases of excess capacity and cases of predatory investment. Even a narrow prohibition, requiring clear proof of a deliberate choice to invest despite the anticipation of losses, would subject innocent firms to the threat of baseless but costly litigation. We do not believe that the slight possibility of predation justifies the potential abuse of a rule against predatory investment.

To conclude that there should be a rule against predatory pricing but not against predatory investment requires that a workable line be drawn between the short run and the long run. In theory this is difficult since fixed costs become variable over a continuum,[47] but we think that the issue is practically resolvable. Since the offense is limited to predatory pricing, the relevant question is which costs were variable during the period of alleged predation. Normal accounting procedures will usually supply the answer: costs charged as a direct expense should be treated as variable; costs charged as an investment for depreciation and tax purposes should be treated as fixed. A firm is not likely to alter its accounting procedures in order to validate shortrun predatory pricing. And if it does, or if it has unusual accounting procedures well before the period of alleged predation, it would have a heavy burden of explanation.[48]

III. Predation in Other Contexts

Our discussion in Part II has focused on the problem of predation in a firm's general pricing policy. Devices other than a general price-cut may, however, be the subject of suits for predation. A firm may cut its prices on only selected products or in a few geographical markets. Or a firm may engage in practices that force rivals to raise costs above price in order to maintain their market shares. In this Part we will examine four possibly predatory practices: earning differential returns (including "predatory investment" in new products), price discrimination, excessive promotional spending, and excessive product variation. Despite the different forms of these practices, in most instances the analytical framework developed in Parts I and II will serve to distinguish between predatory and nonpredatory behavior.

A. *Differential Returns on Different Products*

When a firm earns a different return on its investment in different product lines there may be some concern that the lower rate of return reflects predatory pricing in that product line. Two separate situations are relevant here: (1) different rates of return

[47] *See* p. 701 & note 15 *supra*.

[48] There are, of course, situations in which proper accounting procedures are in reasonable dispute; treatment of advertising, as we later note, *see* pp. 728–729 *infra*, is one example. Nevertheless, it seems highly unlikely that a firm will significantly distort its accounting practices over time in anticipation of defending against a charge of predatory pricing.

in the short run, that is, where investment in plant and facilities has already been made, and (2) so-called "predatory investment," namely, new investment that produces or is expected to produce a rate of return lower than the firm is earning from its existing plants and facilities.

1. Different Rates of Return in the Short Run. — The easiest shortrun case is that of differential returns on unrelated products. This might occur in the conglomerate firm situation, in which the subsidiaries or divisions of a single firm produce a number of unrelated products. One would not expect all divisions of a firm to be earning the same return at any particular time; temporary variations in demand and costs in different industries will most likely result in some differences in returns. Moreover, when the firm has a monopoly in one of the products, it is not unusual for it to earn substantially more on that product than on those it sells in competitive markets. Thus, the mere fact of differential returns proves nothing of any antitrust significance regarding the firm's pricing policy.

Of course, to use the common but usually misapplied description, a firm may be "subsidizing" low returns in a competitive market with higher returns on a monopolized product. But as long as a firm is turning a profit on each additional sale, a subsidy is not necessary. Thus, just as in the case of the single-product monopolist, illicit pricing can be established only by showing that in the competitive market the firm is pricing below marginal cost or the "surrogate" average variable cost.

Even when it appears that the monopolist has priced below average variable cost in the competitive market for an unrelated product, he should be entitled to any defenses — such as "promotional" pricing — to which a nonmonopolist would be entitled. The monopolist, using revenues from the monopolized product, might be thought more likely to indulge in "excessive" promotional pricing than a single-product producer. But revenues from monopoly are no different from superior resources derived from any other source and their existence should not affect the determination of whether the below-marginal-cost price is indeed promotional.

The more difficult case of shortrun differential returns arises when the product earning a lower return is related to a product on which the firm has a monopoly. The products may be related in that they are produced with some common facilities, are sold to and used together by the same consumers, or both. In this situation marginal-cost pricing on the competitive product may adversely affect firms that are the most likely potential rivals in the monopolized-product market. By applying pressure through marginal-cost pricing on the firms in the competitive market, entry into the monopoly market may be deferred or completely discouraged.

Yet this raises no issues that we have not already covered. If the related-product market is competitive, marginal-cost pricing is the norm and should not be discouraged. If the firm has monopoly power in the related-product market, the question is the same as that raised by marginal-cost pricing by any monopolist — whether possible gains from an umbrella price are worth the shortrun economic costs of under-utilization of resources and the severe administrative difficulties of applying a test other than marginal (or average variable) cost.[49]

2. *"Predatory Investment" in New Product Lines.* — To this point, we have been discussing differential returns on different products in the short run, that is, where the monopolist has already invested in plant and equipment. Suppose the monopolist invests or reinvests in facilities in the "competitive" line in expectation of earning an aftertax return of, say, ten percent as compared to the twenty percent he has been earning in the monopoly line. In so doing, he may have an exclusionary purpose, namely to impair the capacity of potential rivals to enter the monopoly field by keeping them under competitive pressure in their particular line. But what may appropriately be deemed illegally "exclusionary" is neither easy to specify nor easy to prove. The difficulties with a predatory investment rule that we discussed earlier in connection with investment in the monopoly line[50] are applicable here and are, we believe, dispositive. But there are other problems as well.

The monopolist may have nonexclusionary reasons for making the new investment. Notwithstanding the past profit rate in the monopolized product, investment in the competitive line might be an equally or more profitable choice quite apart from any exclusionary effects. Additional investment and output in the monopoly may so reduce prices and profits that the marginal return on the new investment would be ten percent or less. Moreover, investment in the competitive line might contribute more to profits than is shown by the estimated revenue-cost relationship on that line only. The ability to offer a fuller line of complementary products may increase the sales of each, either because consumers prefer to deal with a single seller or because the fuller line enhances the seller's image. Finally, even though the new investment might appear to be less profitable than additional investment in the monopoly line, it is possible that it is rational when the two antici-

---

[49] *See* pp. 709–16 *supra*.

[50] *See* pp. 718–20 *supra*.

pated rates of return are discounted for risks. The monopolist may stand to lose more from possible invasion of his monopoly line than he would from adverse developments in the competitive line, or adverse developments may be more likely in the former.

Even if the new investment would appear to be less profitable after taking risks into account, it should not be deemed predatory so long as the expected return equals or exceeds the "normal" return for the product line concerned. To be sure, the "opportunity" cost of the monopolist's capital is measured by the rate of return, say fifteen percent, that could be earned on an alternative investment in the monopoly line. And, unlike the case of the monopolist engaged in shortrun marginal-cost (or below profit-maximizing) pricing, which leads to a better use of resources, it would appear to be a misuse of *capital* resources to devote them to a less profitable pursuit. But it simply makes no sense to adopt a rule forcing a monopolist to invest further in production of the monopolized product merely because the rate of return exceeds the expected return on alternative product-line investments. Such a rule would have the effect of forcing profits on the monopolized product down toward a competitive rate of return, like the maximum price constraint we have earlier rejected;[51] or it would eliminate monopolists as potential entrants in other product lines, which would in turn protect high profits and restricted output in those lines. Moreover, prohibiting the monopolist from investing in alternative product lines would be inefficient when there are economies in product integration.

If the monopolist can earn a normal or higher return on the new investment: (1) the rivals are earning supranormal profits (or would be if he did not invest); (2) he is more efficient than they; or (3) his continued presence or new entry is on too small a scale to have any effect on them. If the monopolist's entry would have no effect, there is no reason to stop him. If he is more efficient, his entry is to be encouraged. If rivals in the competitive line are earning high returns and capital markets are imperfect, they might more easily enter the monopoly product line, but it is not at all clear that the possibility of competition in the monopoly line outweighs the disadvantages of protectionism in the competitive line.

The case against a monopolist's investment which is expected to generate below-normal returns is stronger. Logically it is as predatory for a monopolist to invest in a competitive line in the expectation of receiving below-normal returns as it is for him to engage in shortrun pricing below marginal cost. Prohibition of such a practice, however, would be hindered by all the difficulties

[51] *See* p. 707 *supra*.

we noted in our discussion of investment in the monopoly product line.[52] In light of these difficulties, we are inclined to reject a "predatory investment" rule. The possibility that anyone, even a monopolist, would make such an investment seems far too remote to warrant the ill-founded litigation that a protective rule would promote.

B. Price Discrimination

Price discrimination involves charging different prices on different sales of the same product despite identical costs.[53] The monopolist may discriminate in price between different markets or between different customers in the same market. In either case price discrimination might be thought to increase the likelihood of predation by risking only a portion of the defendant's business while threatening the entire business of smaller rivals who are confined to the geographic area in which the selective price cut was made or who serve primarily those customers who will benefit from the price reduction. Thus, in cases of price discrimination the predation requirement of greater staying power may more frequently be met.

1. Price Discrimination Between Different Geographic Markets. — Oversimplifying somewhat, there are two situations: (1) where the monopolist supplies each geographic market from a separate plant; and (2) where he supplies all markets from the same plant.

Where the monopolist supplies different markets from different plants, we would ordinarily expect different prices in markets with different demands, costs, and degrees of competitiveness. This case is virtually indistinguishable from that of the monopolist who earns higher returns in the monopoly-product market than in one or more competitive-product markets. Indeed, but for the accident of common ownership of plants in several markets, the term "price discrimination" would not even be used. Thus, here too, the low price in one market should be considered predatory only if below marginal cost, and in the competitive markets the monopolist should be entitled to any defenses available to any other seller.

Where a firm that monopolizes one geographic market supplies other geographic markets from the same plant, the analysis is

[52] *See* pp. 718–20 *supra*.

[53] In economic terms, intraproduct discrimination also includes charging the same price on all sales despite variations in cost (usually distribution costs), or, more generally, any variation in price-cost relationships. The analysis is the same regardless of the form. To simplify the discussion we deal only with price differentials where costs are identical.

more complex and the outcome perhaps more debatable. Suppose *M* has a plant in market *A* and a monopoly there. At his profit-maximizing price and output in that market (where marginal revenue is equal to marginal cost), he has excess capacity. Any further sales in that market would, by definition, reduce his net returns, but sales in another, more competitive market would increase his net returns up to the point where the price in that market equals marginal cost. *M* therefore may sell in market *B* at some price substantially below his monopoly price in market *A*.

This is clearly price discrimination; if anything, costs on sales in market *B* are likely to be higher because of transportation costs, so that the price difference understates the amount of discrimination. As with general price-cuts, however, the low price lacks the necessary element of predation except where *M*'s price is lower than his short-run, profit-maximizing price in market *B*. And even when the monopolist is not profit-maximizing, we see no good reason to depart from a marginal (or average variable) cost test. Price discrimination will not always have adverse effects in market *B*. The discrimination will have beneficial effects if, because of a shortage in capacity, the firms in *B* are earning abnormally high profits and *M*'s sales merely bring the *B* price down toward a competitive level. Even when profits are at a competitive level in market *B*, discrimination will have no adverse effects if *M*'s sales in market *B* are of insufficient volume to significantly affect the price, or if discrimination leads to the displacement of only one or two of an ample number of competitors. If *M*'s sales do affect the price in market *B* and drive out enough rivals to give *M* a monopoly in that market, there still must be barriers to entry in order for *M* to reap the benefits of any alleged predation.

We would, therefore, adhere to the general rule permitting pricing at or above reasonably anticipated average variable cost, and permitting any defenses (such as promotional) available to any seller. The deterrent effect of a more severe constraint would, we conclude, be likely to cause more economic harm than good.

2. *Price Discrimination in the Same Geographic Market.*— If, as we have contended, a monopolist should be permitted to make a general price reduction so long as his price equals or exceeds marginal cost, we are unable to see a persuasive case for prohibiting selective price-cutting to retain or obtain particular customers. Selective price-cutting cannot possibly be more harmful to small competitors than a general price reduction to the same level.[54] And since any additional sale at a price at or above

---

[54] Selective price-cutting might, however, be more likely to occur than general price-cuts, since the monopolist's losses on selective reductions would be smaller.

marginal cost does not decrease shortrun net returns, the necessary element of predation is missing.

The only possible argument for an antidiscrimination rule is a pragmatic one. Such a rule would confront the monopolist facing price-cuts by small competitors with two choices: (1) a general price-cut, which would preserve his market share but at a heavy cost in profits; (2) maintaining his price, which would preserve high profits on his sales but lead to a smaller market share. Faced with that choice, the monopolist, at least up to a point, would often elect to maintain his price, thus facilitating the growth of competitors and the erosion of his monopoly. But this is simply an argument for inducing umbrella pricing by the monopolist, an approach we have rejected for reasons earlier explained.[55]

3. The Relevance of the Robinson-Patman Act. — Subject to affirmative defenses of cost justification and meeting competition, the Robinson-Patman Act prohibits price discrimination in sales of the same product [56]

> where the effect . . . may be substantially to lessen competition or tend to create a monopoly in any line of commerce, or to injure, destroy, or prevent competition with any person who either grants or knowingly receives the benefit of such discrimination, or with customers of either of them . . . .

The only Robinson-Patman Act issue relevant to our discussion is that of primary-line injury, that is, injury to competition between the discriminating seller and his competitors. While there have been relatively few Robinson-Patman Act cases dealing with primary-line injury, they suggest a far broader prohibition of discriminatorily low prices than the marginal-cost test we have defended here. In some cases, it has been held that the requisite "injury to competition" is established merely by proof that the lower price diverted a substantial number of sales from competitors.[57] And in *Utah Pie Co. v. Continental Baking Co.*,[58] the Supreme Court found rather brief local price-cutting by three

[55] *See* p. 711 *supra*. The administrative difficulties with a prohibition of selective price-cuts are not as severe as those involved in prohibiting nondiscriminatory price-cuts, since the proscription would focus on discrimination in pricing rather than absolute price levels. However, a cost defense, essential to any rational antidiscrimination rule, raises complex problems of proof, as litigation under the Robinson-Patman Act has shown. *See generally* F. ROWE, *supra* note 41, at 273–312.

[56] 15 U.S.C. § 13(a) (1970).

[57] *See, e.g.*, Samuel H. Moss, Inc. v. FTC, 148 F.2d 378 (2d Cir.), *cert. denied*, 326 U.S. 734 (1945). *But see* Anheuser-Busch, Inc. v. FTC, 289 F.2d 835 (7th Cir. 1961).

[58] 386 U.S. 685 (1967).

"large" national firms to be a violation despite the fact that the plaintiff, a "small" local firm, held the bulk of the market, enjoyed substantially increasing sales, and earned substantial profits throughout the period covered by the complaint. Two of the firms were found to have sold "below cost," but apparently only below average cost.[59] They were also vaguely condemned for having contributed to a "deteriorating price structure." [60]

We respectfully suggest that in these cases the courts have failed to focus on the important issues. The basic substantive issues raised by the Robinson-Patman Act's concern with primary-line injury to competition and by the Sherman Act's concern with predatory pricing are identical. If the Sherman Act is properly interpreted to permit a monopolist to discriminate in price so long as his lower price equals or exceeds marginal cost, such discrimination is a fortiori permissible for firms with lesser degrees of market power, and the Robinson-Patman Act should be interpreted no differently in primary-line cases unless the statutory language or compelling legislative history dictates otherwise.

Without fully elucidating the point, we see nothing that compels a more restrictive substantive interpretation of the Robinson-Patman Act. The phrase "where the effect may be substantially to lessen competition" does not; if marginal-cost pricing cannot reasonably be construed as a "lessening of competition," the "may be" issue is never reached. The original Clayton Act was indeed primarily a response to fears of predatory pricing and primary-line effects;[61] but the original language referred to effects on "competition" only, not individual competitors.[62] The concern expressed in the legislative history of the Robinson-Patman Act for the fate of individual competitors was primarily, if not exclusively, directed to secondary-line competition.[63] Nor does the intent of Congress in passing the original Clayton Act to go beyond the Sherman Act have any great significance, given that no one knew what the Sherman Act rule on predatory pricing was or would come to be and that Congress may well have been operating on pessimistic assumptions.

---

[59] The Court was unclear on which cost measurement it used to find "below-cost" pricing. In one instance it referred to direct cost plus allocated overhead, apparently a measure of average cost. *Id.* at 698.

[60] *Id.* at 690.

[61] *See* FTC v. Anheuser-Busch, Inc., 363 U.S. 536, 543 & n.6 (1960); H.R. REP. No. 627, 63d Cong., 2d Sess. 89 (1914).

[62] Clayton Act, ch. 323, § 2, 38 Stat. 730 (1914).

[63] F.T.C., CHAIN STORES, FINAL REPORT ON THE CHAIN-STORE INVESTIGATION, S. Doc. No. 4, 74th Cong., 1st Sess. 85–86 (1935). *See generally* F. ROWE, *supra* note 41, at 11–23.

There is superficial merit in the argument that effective enforcement of the Robinson-Patman Act requires a more readily determinable test than "marginal cost." We have suggested the use of average variable cost as a surrogate for marginal cost to mitigate the administrative difficulties of enforcement.[64] But even though determinations of cost may remain a substantial problem, it seems clear to us that in this instance it is unavoidable. In the vast majority of situations, discriminatory price-cutting — insofar as primary-line competition is concerned — will be profitable to the firm concerned and pro-competitive. Thus any such simple test as "diversion" or "deteriorating price structure" would be wrong most of the time. We should not pay that price for administrative simplicity.

C. *"Excessive" Promotional Spending*

1. Predatory Spending. — Rather than cutting its price, a firm may undertake advertising campaigns or provide special services and conveniences to consumers with no price increase. These expenditures, of course, increase the firm's costs. The expenditures may impose a burden too great for smaller rivals to maintain and thus result in diminishing their market share or completely driving them out of the market. In theory, the principles we have proposed for defining and dealing with predatory pricing and predatory investment should also apply to "excessive" advertising and other promotional expenditures. If the additional promotional costs raise the firm's average variable cost above its price, then the promotional spending is predatory. There are, however, additional conceptual and practical difficulties in policing excessive promotional spending.

Conceptually, it is extremely difficult to determine whether any given advertising expenditure should be classified as a current expense attributable to current sales, or as a capital investment in goodwill designed to maintain or increase the level of sales over some longer period. Usually, it will or was designed to do both. The problem of allocating advertising and promotional expenditures between fixed and variable costs is not peculiar to instances of "excessive" promotional spending. Application of our average variable cost test requires that some allocation be made for all of the firm's advertising expenditures. For the usual and continuing expenditures, however, the firm's past accounting practices should provide an adequate basis for allocation. It is unlikely that over a long period of time a firm will bias its treatment of normal advertising costs in anticipation of defending itself against allegations of predation.

[64] *See* pp. 716–18 *supra*.

The relatively rare, large promotional expenditure is, however, more problematic. A firm may have no established accounting practice for such expenditures and may choose to capitalize the costs of one-time promotional campaigns, either because it views the promotion as a legitimate investment in goodwill or because it seeks to avoid a suit for predatory spending. Moreover, as a practical matter, it may be difficult to determine whether the monopolist could have "reasonably anticipated" that the increased advertising or other promotional expenditure would lower his net revenues in whatever shortrun period is thought to be appropriate. The probable consequence of pricing below anticipated marginal cost (or average variable cost) is clear — it will lower net returns. The probable consequence of a stepped-up promotional campaign will usually be much more speculative, and in all but clear cases, a judicial determination would involve speculation about speculation.

The ambiguous character of short-term promotional expenditures and the uncertainty of their effect prevents relying solely on our variable cost analysis. Accordingly, decisions in cases involving substantial shortrun increases in promotional spending would have to incorporate at least one additional consideration, namely timing. The timing of the promotion suggests the possibility of predation if the campaign begins with the appearance of an entrant (or coincides with a rival's promotion) and terminates when the entrant leaves the market (or the rival's efforts cease). In such cases, it seems reasonable to us to consider all the increased expenses as part of variable costs, and to conclude presumptively that predation has occurred if average variable costs, during the period of the promotion, exceed price.[65] Needless to say, predation is negated when the promotion yields a substantial increase in net revenues, or even leaves them unaffected.

We are not wholly satisfied with this solution, but are reluctant to reach the only other plausible conclusion, which is to impose no legal check on predatory spending.

2. *Nonpredatory Spending.* — It could be argued that "excessive" promotional expenditures should be deemed unlawfully exclusionary though they yield an increase in net revenues. We reject the argument because of severe theoretical and practical difficulties.

We assume that heavy promotional expenditures by a monopolist may impair the ability of small rivals to compete. We

---

[65] As in the case of alleged predatory pricing, the presumption would be rebuttable on a showing that average variable costs exceeded what was reasonably anticipated. *See* pp. 716–17 *supra*.

also assume that they may in some cases discourage entry by building up durable consumer preferences that can only be broken down by a very large initial investment in counterpromotion.[66] But if the expenditures are nonpredatory — if they increase net revenues over the appropriate timespan for making that determination — we find no basis for making them an antitrust offense.

While one might believe that "persuasive" as distinct from "informative" advertising is a waste of economic resources, such a judgment in all but exceptional cases must rest on a noneconomic value judgment. To the extent that promotional expenditures cause consumers to pay a higher price for a product or buy more of it at the same price, the product is worth that much more to them and the increase in worth is economically indistinguishable from an increase attributable to product improvement. One might judge that consumers should not be so "deluded," but no such legislative judgment has been made for products generally, apart from the prohibition of false and misleading representations[67] — a category that covers but a fraction of "persuasive" advertising. It seems wholly inappropriate to make such a disputable judgment in an antitrust case.

Moreover, there would be insurmountable problems in implementing it: "informational" and "persuasive" elements in advertising are usually inextricably mixed. Nor is there any evident satisfactory standard for determining when nonpredatory promotional expenditures are "excessive." The number of variables seems far too large and nonquantifiable to enable one to find a "similar" market to use as a benchmark. And without such a benchmark, the issue becomes almost wholly subjective.

The deficiencies of advertising — that it supplies inadequate information and may contribute to monopoly problems — may call for some solution: neutral sources of accurate and complete information is a possible one. But apart from predatory spending, antitrust law should ignore the problem.

D. *"Excessive" Product Variation*

Like excessive promotional expenditures, excessive product variation may increase the difficulties of smaller rivals or newcomers and thereby reduce competition. Such variations might exceed what consumers would truly desire if they were fully

[66] *See* J. Bain, Barriers to New Competition 114–17 (1956).

[67] False and misleading representations are prohibited as "unfair methods of competition" under the Federal Trade Commission Act, § 5(a)(1), 15 U.S.C. § 45(a)(1) (1970). *See, e.g.*, Continental Wax Corp. v. FTC, 330 F.2d 475 (2d Cir. 1964); Giant Food, Inc. v. FTC, 322 F.2d 977 (D.C. Cir. 1963), *cert. dismissed*, 376 U.S. 967 (1964); Bakers Franchise Corp. v. FTC, 302 F.2d 258 (3d Cir. 1962).

aware of the consequences of their purchasing decisions. Although legislation can explicitly substitute a social judgment for that of the marketplace, antitrust law is not the appropriate vehicle for such a substitution and should accept marketplace decisions as the expression of consumer preference. Accordingly, product variations should be ignored in the search for "exclusionary" behavior. Our reasons follow.

1. Multiple Product Variations. — A large firm might attempt to destroy its rivals by offering variations on a basic product. To operate at equivalent costs, smaller rivals may have to concentrate their entire output on one subtype. For example, stamping machines may be too specialized to permit production of more than one product type, and a firm with a small output may be unable to operate two or more machines at full capacity. Thus, if the smaller firm were to produce more product types its operation would be more costly than that of the large firm.

It is also true, however, that product diversity could create more opportunities for the success of smaller rivals or newcomers who could satisfy some corner of the market without provoking competitive retaliation from the dominant firm. Such rivals may succeed under the dominant firm's "price umbrella" and ultimately grow strong, branch out, and vitalize competition in widening portions of the market.

On the other hand, small rivals suffer if a full line confers important advantages. Consumers who are uncertain of which product subtype best serves their needs may prefer to consult with the broad-line supplier. While independent dealers might serve that function, they might choose to deal exclusively in one manufacturer's product, and such dealers would prefer the full-line supplier. But even if product diversity reduces the intensity of competition and perhaps discourages entry by those unable to offer similar diversity, that result may merely reveal the importance consumers attach to product variety. It is possible that buyers never "voted" between diversity and greater competition; that is, buyers might prefer diversity to uniformity when other things are equal, but not at the expense of market dominance with little price competition. Buyers may not necessarily realize that indulging a preference for diversity may discourage an outsider from entering at all. And concern about lack of genuine consumer choice may be strongest where the variations seem to be of little intrinsic importance, as in mere style variations.

Yet, we know that many consumers with a true choice between cheaper uniformity and more costly style variations do in fact choose the latter, and this may well be the usual case. Thus, although we may question whether the market reflects informed consumer choice, we cannot assume that consumers would surrender diversity in order to enjoy the benefits of a larger number of competing suppliers. Accordingly, we cannot condemn a monopolist who succeeds in varying his product in ways that buyers, whether well-advised or not, find desirable.

2. *Frequent Product Changes.* — The vitality of rivals can also be impaired by frequent product changes, whether functional or merely style changes. The design, engineering, and retooling costs of any particular variation will obviously be less costly per unit when spread over a larger volume of production. The larger the output, moreover, the sooner certain machines or dies will wear out. If those replaced in a style or other variation are nearly worn out anyway, the incremental cost of the alteration will be less than for a smaller volume producer whose machines and dies are nowhere near retirement.

Yet the disadvantages from which small rivals may suffer do not warrant antitrust attack on the monopolist who exploits them. The small-volume producer has the option of maintaining an unchanged product while offering buyers the benefit of the costs saved by avoiding changeovers. If the cost savings are negligible as compared to costs of the large producer who does changeover, the small rival is simply the victim of economies of scale. And if buyers prefer the variation to the cost saving, consumer welfare is presumably being served by the frequent changes. Although, as in the case of multiple product variations, the market judgment may reflect inadequate knowledge of the consequences of reduced competition, and although we may doubt the wisdom of preferring "insubstantial" variations to incremental competition, we cannot determine or even assert the impropriety of the practice with sufficient clarity to hold it exclusionary for section two purposes.[68]

IV. Conclusions

We reach the following conclusions regarding a monopolist's general (nondiscriminatory) pricing in the market in which he has monopoly power:

1. On principle, we conclude that:
   (a) A shortrun profit-maximizing (or loss-minimizing) price is nonpredatory even though below average cost.
   (b) A price at or above average cost should be deemed non-

[68] For the reasons given, we are quite unpersuaded by the arguments in Note, *Annual Style Change in the Automobile Industry as an Unfair Method of Competition*, 80 Yale L.J. 567 (1971). *See also* Selander, *Is Annual Style Change in the Automobile Industry an Unfair Method of Competition? A Rebuttal*, 82 Yale L.J. 691 (1973).

predatory even though not profit-maximizing in the short run.

(c) A price at or above reasonably anticipated shortrun marginal and average variable costs should be deemed nonpredatory even though not loss-minimizing in the short run.

(d) Unless at or above average cost, a price below reasonably anticipated (1) shortrun marginal costs or (2) average variable costs should be deemed predatory, and the monopolist may not defend on the grounds that his price was "promotional" or merely met an equally low price of a competitor.

2. Recognizing that marginal cost data are typically unavailable, we conclude that:

(a) A price at or above reasonably anticipated average variable cost should be conclusively presumed lawful.

(b) A price below reasonably anticipated average variable cost should be conclusively presumed unlawful.

As to "predatory" devices other than general price reductions we conclude that:

3. The above conclusions apply to differential returns on different products and to price discrimination, whether between different geographic markets or in the same market, except that a monopolist should have the benefit of any defenses — such as "promotional" pricing or "meeting competition" — available to other sellers in any market in which he lacks monopoly power.
4. There should be no prohibition of investment whether in a new product line or in the monopoly product line.
5. Promotional spending should be deemed predatory when timed to coincide with entry or promotion by a rival, and when average variable cost, including the promotional expenditure, exceeds price.
6. There should be no prohibition of nonpredatory spending or of product variation.

[15]

An Economic Definition of Predation: Pricing and Product Innovation*

Janusz A. Ordover† and Robert D. Willig††

Many forms of business conduct have been attacked as predatory since the passage of the Sherman Act[1] in 1890. Neither the courts[2] nor legal and economic scholars,[3] however, agree on a general definition of predatory behavior.

Section I of this paper presents a definition of predation[4] that is economically sound, judicially workable, and broadly applicable to a wide variety of business practices. Section II shows how the well-known cost-based tests for predatory pricing can be derived from this general standard. It also clarifies these cost-based tests, and expands their applicability to encompass multi-product firms.

Sections III-V contain the most novel aspect of this paper—the derivation from our general standard of specific tests that distinguish between predatory and procompetitive product innovations. These sections argue that even genuine innovations—new products that in some ways are superior to existing products in the eyes of both engineers and consumers—are in some circumstances anticompetitive. Such innovations do not provide benefits to consumers that are worth the cost, and are motivated solely by

* This article is a substantially revised and expanded version of our paper, *An Economic Definition of Predatory Product Innovation,* in STRATEGY, PREDATION, AND ANTITRUST ANALYSIS (S. Salop ed. 1981). We are grateful to the National Science Foundation and to the Federal Trade Commission for their financial support of the research reported here. We are also grateful for helpful and stimulating comments from F. Easterbrook and S. Salop, and from E. Bailey, C. Berry, G. Faulhaber, E. Fox, J. Gelman, A. Klevorick, D. Kreps, and F. M. Scherer. Motty Perry provided able research assistance.

† Associate Professor of Economics, New York University.

†† Professor of Economics and Public Affairs, Princeton University.

1. 15 U.S.C. §§ 1-7 (1976). Predatory behavior also comes within the purview of the Clayton Act, 15 U.S.C. §§ 12-17 (1976), the Robinson-Patman Act, 15 U.S.C. §§ 13-13b, 21a (1976), and the Federal Trade Commission Act, 15 U.S.C. §§ 41-58 (1976).

2. *See* L. SULLIVAN, HANDBOOK OF THE LAW OF ANTITRUST 108-13 (1977) (reviewing early predation cases). *See also* ABA ANTITRUST SECTION MONOGRAPH NO. 4, THE ROBINSON-PATMAN ACT: POLICY AND LAW VOLUME I (1980); Hurwitz, Kovacic, Sheehan & Lande, *Current Legal Standards of Predation,* in STRATEGY, PREDATION, AND ANTITRUST ANALYSIS (S. Salop ed. 1981) (reviewing post-Areeda-Turner cases) [hereinafter cited as Hurwitz].

3. The recent outpouring of writing on predation has been stimulated by Areeda & Turner, *Predatory Pricing and Related Practices under Section 2 of the Sherman Act,* 88 HARV. L. REV. 697 (1975). *See* Joskow & Klevorick, *A Framework for Analyzing Predatory Pricing Policy,* 89 YALE L.J. 213 (1979) (critically analyzing responses to Areeda & Turner); McGee, *Predatory Pricing Revisited,* 23 J. L. & ECON. 289 (1980) (same).

4. *See* Ordover & Willig, An Economic Definition of Predation (1981) (unpublished paper on file with *Yale Law Journal*).

Predatory Product Innovation

the monopoly profit attendant on the exit that they induce.

Two types of product innovations are identified as potentially anticompetitive. The first involves the introduction of a new product that is a substitute for the products of a rival firm, and that endangers the rival's viability by diverting its sales. Although this tactic has not been extensively scrutinized in antitrust litigation, it is related to a second type of product innovation that has been the subject of an important and rapidly growing line of cases. Firms adopting this second method of product innovation, a form of "systems rivalry," introduce new systems of components that are incompatible with components manufactured by rivals, and constrict the supply of components that are compatible with those made by rivals. Sections III-V develop workable tests for determining whether or not such tactics are predatory,[5] and show that these tests can deter anticompetitive product innovation without distorting incentives for procompetitive innovation and without unduly taxing scarce judicial resources. Finally, the Appendix employs the general standard of predatory behavior to analyze the possible anticompetitive effects of product "preannouncements."

I. A General Standard of Predatory Behavior

Assuming that businessmen know how their actions affect their profitability and the profitability of their rivals,[6] predatory objectives are present if a practice would be unprofitable without the exit it causes, but profitable with the exit. Thus, although a practice may cause a rival's exit, it is predatory only if the practice would not be profitable without the additional monopoly power resulting from the exit.

When a firm reduces price below cost, that firm exhibits a predatory objective if it can recover the consequent losses of net revenue only by exercising the additional monopoly power generated by a rival's induced exit. Similarly, the introduction of a new product exhibits a predatory objective if the firm can only recoup its investment by the exercise of such additional monopoly power. It follows that predatory behavior is a response to a rival that sacrifices part of the profit[7] that could be earned

5. Our tests for predatory product innovation suggest the importance of two factors that have not been analyzed in prior works on predatory behavior. First, the tests require scrutiny of the research and development (R&D) investment in product innovations. Second, they imply that, in the context of systems rivalry, the predatory act may be the *upward repricing or withdrawal* of preexisting components that are complementary to the rivals' products.

6. *See* note 19 *infra* (relating to plausibility of this assumption); note 20 *infra* (discussing modification of analysis to accommodate uncertainty).

7. Some commentators prefer not to focus on profit-sacrifice in testing for predation, but instead focus on behavior that is detrimental to social welfare. *See* Scherer, *Predatory Pricing and the Sherman Act: A Comment*, 89 HARV. L. REV. 869, 883-84 (1976). Easterbrook characterizes the Scherer approach as "nebulous," although he agrees that for a practice to be predatory it must reduce con-

under competitive circumstances, were the rival to remain viable, in order to induce exit[8] and gain consequent additional monopoly profit.[9]

An important aspect of the proposed standard is the stipulation that the sacrifice of profit must be assessed with reference to "competitive circumstances." Sacrifice should not be inferred if the incumbent avoids a cartel-like response that yields greater profits both for him and for his rival.[10] Instead, the profitability of the incumbent's actual and alternative responses should be assessed on the assumption that the rival reacts to them in a competitive fashion. A cartel-like response would not benefit the incumbent under this assumption because the rival's competitive reaction would undermine its profitability. Therefore, the proposed standard does not penalize the incumbent for legitimate competitive responses, even if they damage the rival, and the standard does not protect a rival that cannot prosper under competitive circumstances.

For a practice that induces a rival's exit to generate additional monop-

sumer welfare. *See* Easterbrook, *Predatory Strategies and Counterstrategies*, 48 U. CHI. L. REV. 263, 264 n.6, 266 (1981). Scherer and Easterbrook disagree sharply, however, as to whether the fact-finder in an antitrust case can perform the requisite welfare calculations. *Cf.* Joskow & Klevorick, *supra* note 3, at 222, 282-87 (discussing problem of errors in enforcement of welfare-based tests for predation).

8. The definition applies only to behavior that may cause existing rivals to exit the industry; behavior that merely deters entry is beyond its scope.

9. The proposed definition of predation is similar in some respects to that proposed by other authors. For example, Areeda and Turner state that

> predation in any meaningful sense cannot exist unless there is a temporary sacrifice of net revenues in the expectation of greater future gains. Indeed, the classically-feared case of predation has been the deliberate sacrifice of current profits for the purpose of driving rivals out of the market and then recouping the losses through higher profits earned in the absence of competition.

Areeda & Turner, *supra* note 3, at 698 (footnote omitted). This view of predation was embraced explicitly by the court in Janich Bros., Inc. v. American Distilling Co., 570 F.2d 848, 856 (9th Cir. 1977), *cert. denied*, 439 U.S. 829 (1978). *See* R. BORK, THE ANTITRUST PARADOX 144-45 (1978) (predation "provisionally" defined as behavior not profit-maximizing unless rivals are driven from market or chastened not to behave competitively); Baumol, *Quasi-Permanence of Price Reductions: A Policy for Prevention of Predatory Pricing*, 89 YALE L.J. 1, 5 (1979) (arguing that if quasi-permanence of price cuts is required, established firm will adjust its price in face of entry only if value of resulting competitive gain exceeds long-run permanent reduction in price); Williamson, *Predatory Pricing: A Strategic and Welfare Analysis*, 87 YALE L.J. 284 (1977) (arguing that predation is intertemporal phenomenon entailing strategic response to actual or potential entry—response is only profitable if it can be rescinded once entry threat subsides or entrant actually exits).

Our definition of predation is superior to the formulation offered by Areeda and Turner for several reasons. First, it explicitly proposes a profit benchmark against which to measure the profit sacrifice. *See* p. 13 *infra*. Second, if long-run profits are calculated on the premise of the continued viability of a rival, the proposed definition suggests that predation may entail a sacrifice of long-run profits rather than short-run profits. *See* note 21 *infra*. Third, it suggests that analysis of exit inducement should be distinguished from analysis of behavior that deters entry without causing the exit of actual rivals; the profit benchmark that is appropriate to test for predation against actual entrants may not be the benchmark to test for entry deterrence.

10. Such a response might involve a curtailment of output by the incumbent firm to a level low enough for the market to accommodate the entrant's output at a price that allows the entrant to make a profit. An entrant cannot complain of predation, however, if his entry destroys the collusive discipline of an industry and his profits are lower than he anticipated on the basis of industry history.

oly power, and perhaps thereby to violate the proposed standard of predatory behavior, a market must have several structural characteristics. First, the market must be horizontally concentrated. In an unconcentrated market, there is sufficient competitive discipline from the remaining rivals to preclude monopoly power, irrespective of the exit of one firm.

Second, the market must be protected by a form of entry barriers that we term *entry hurdles*. These hurdles exist whenever the prospective entrant is cost-disadvantaged relative to the incumbent solely because the incumbent is already functioning as a going concern, and the entrant has not yet committed the requisite resources.[11] In general, entry hurdles arise when investments are not fully reversible.[12] The need to incur the irreversible portion of the investment, and thereby to put that amount at risk, confronts the prospective entrant with a cost disadvantage relative to the incumbent whose resources are already committed.[13] Thus, an incumbent may have an incentive to induce the exit of an entrant, who would then

11. Entry barriers that are not entry hurdles present a firm with a cost disadvantage vis-a-vis an incumbent regardless of whether the firm is a prospective or an actual entrant. For example, a firm with an inferior technology faces a cost disadvantage that would persist after its entry. Thus, it does not matter to the incumbent whether rivalry from such a firm is active or prospective.

12. *See* Baumol & Willig, *Fixed Costs, Sunk Costs, Entry Barriers, and the Sustainability of Monopoly*, 96 Q. J. ECON. 405 (1981) (discussing importance to market organization and performance of distinction between sunk costs and other fixed costs). Baumol and Willig show that the need for an entrant to sink costs can be a barrier to entry that permits incumbents to hold prices above costs. In contrast, fixed costs that are not sunk costs do not impede the power of potential entry to induce efficient operation and pricing on the part of incumbents. *See* W. BAUMOL, J. PANZAR & R. WILLIG, CONTESTABLE MARKETS AND THE THEORY OF INDUSTRY STRUCTURE (forthcoming); Bailey, *Contestability and the Design of Regulatory and Antitrust Policy*, 71 AM. ECON. REV. 178, 178-79 (1981).

13. There are many types of entry hurdles due to the fact that many capital investments are highly specialized, and their value in alternative uses is much lower than their value in the use for which they were originally designed. For such investments, the liquidation value is well below the original cost (adjusted for depreciation), and the difference is a source of risk for the potential entrant.

Before entry, the entrant must foresee an expected return that is sufficiently large to compensate him for the risk of losing the irreversible portion of his investment. For the incumbent, in contrast, the irreversible portion of his investment is already sunk, and the riskiness of his position is concomitantly lower. In addition, the market may have been less risky to the incumbent when he entered because there was less competition at that time. Consequently, the cost of capital to the prospective entrant may be higher than it is for the incumbent. *See, e.g.*, C. VON WEIZSACKER, BARRIERS TO ENTRY 123-44 (1980); Williamson, *supra* note 9, at 295 n.36.

This type of entry hurdle is especially common if there are few prospective buyers in the resale market for the entrant's capital stock, or if the entrant's capital is totally firm-specific and would have no value to other firms. For example, advertising expenditures that are incurred in promoting an entrant's product cannot be recouped if the product fails and the entrant exits the market. Similarly, costs required to assemble a firm's labor force, to establish its reputation, and to acquire its technological and market "know-how" are irreversible firm-specific investments. Costs required to construct a firm's plant also may be irreversible if the plant cannot be resold intact.

Another type of irreversible investment may arise when an entrant has to acquire rights or licenses in order to commence operation. Such acquisition costs will be sunk investments if their unexpired portion is non-refundable. *See* United States v. Columbia Pictures Indus., Inc., 507 F. Supp. 412 (S.D.N.Y. 1980) (defendants argued that need to acquire costly, non-transferrable pay-television movie rights created entry hurdles into pay-television network programming).

face an entry hurdle afresh. If there are no entry hurdles, however, there can be no incentives for predation because prospective entrants constrain the market power of the incumbent just as effectively as actual competitors.

A third structural characteristic that is necessary for successful predation is the presence of *reentry barriers.*[14] A reentry barrier may be defined as the cost that a firm that has exited a market must incur to resume production. If the firm can costlessly reassemble the physical and human capital that was retooled or dispersed upon the firm's exit, then no reentry barrier exists. Under such conditions, a firm confronted with predatory behavior by a rival can shut down its operations, and costlessly reenter the market when the predator attempts to recoup the profits that he sacrificed during the predatory campaign. If reentry barriers are truly inconsequential, therefore, a predator cannot recoup lost profits because its rivals remain viable even after they cease production. Hence, there can be no motive for predation.[15]

Other structural factors may also be relevant to the threshold assessment of whether successful predation is feasible in a particular market. For example, it is implausible that a relatively small firm could engage in predation against a rival with a strong market position that could not be rapidly eroded. Similarly, it is implausible that a firm with limited financial resources could successfully engage in predation through price cutting against a better-financed rival.[16]

In a market characterized by the structural factors noted above, actual and potential competitors are equally effective at constraining the market power of incumbent firms—whatever the fate of the particular rivals whose exit is at issue—and allegations of predatory behavior in that market should be dismissed. The process of determining whether the market has these characteristics is a structural test[17] that should be performed

14. If reentry is equivalent to de novo entry, then reentry barriers are the same as entry barriers, including entry hurdles. In some instances, however, reentry may be less costly than new entry because some elements of tangible and intangible capital do not lose all value in the interval between exit and reentry.

15. Bork's argument that successful predation is impossible, or unlikely, *see* R. BORK, THE ANTITRUST PARADOX 149-154 (1978), depends to some extent on the unstated assumption that rivals of the alleged predator do not face significant reentry barriers. Reentry barriers are fairly common and significant, however, and exist to the extent that the capital formerly amassed by a firm has been irreversibly dispersed or depreciated before reentry occurs. For example, salvaged and retooled equipment, dispersed labor force and management, discontinued advertising, and unmaintained reputation can only be replaced or readapted to their former uses at substantial cost. Such costs constitute reentry barriers. *See, e.g.*, G. BECKER, HUMAN CAPITAL (1964) (discussing depreciation of investments in human capital and specific on-the-job training); M. PORTER, INTERBRAND CHOICE, STRATEGY AND MARKET POWER (1976) (discussing advertising).

16. Predatory innovation, however, can entail a precommitment to sunk R&D costs that renders financial staying power irrelevant.

17. In advocating a structural test, we agree with the two-tier approach suggested by Joskow &

prior to the application of tests for predatory behavior. Concededly, one rarely observes markets with no concentration, no entry hurdles, and no reentry barriers, but structural tests nevertheless are useful. In general, the benefit of predation to a firm is smaller the less concentrated its market is (after the exit at issue occurs), the lower the entry hurdles are, and the lower the reentry barriers are. Thus, the relevant structural test is whether the conceivable gains from predation can outweigh the costs to the incumbent of the allegedly predatory conduct. If not, there can be no motive for predation and it is unnecessary to scrutinize allegedly predatory conduct for anticompetitive effect or intent.

In markets in which structural factors permit successful predation, a firm may rationally attempt to induce the exit of a rival in order to gain additional monopoly profits. The mere fact of a rival's exit from such markets, however, does not constitute sufficient proof of predation. To the contrary, exit-inducing actions are not predatory if they are part of legitimate competitive interactions. Differences between firms in efficiency virtually guarantee that some firms will fail in a sufficiently competitive marketplace. These inefficient firms can be induced to exit by actions that efficient firms find profitable regardless of their effects on rivals' viability. Such actions are not predatory.

This distinction between predatory and non-predatory exit-inducing behavior is captured by our proposed standard of predatory conduct. Under that standard, predatory sacrifice of profit is assessed on the premise of the continued viability of the rival. This potentially counterfactual premise assumes that the rival remains able to produce without incurring new start-up costs, whether or not the rival has actually ceased production. Thus, the continued-viability premise is equivalent to assuming the absence of reentry barriers,[18] and a firm's action entails predatory sacrifice of profit if there is some alternative action that would yield greater profit if there were no reentry barriers. The existence of such an alternative action indicates that the firm's actual action was motivated by the desire for the monopoly profits attendant on the exit of the rival.[19]

Table 1 illustrates these concepts. It lists the present discounted values of the incumbent's profits for three scenarios: the actual action of the incumbent that induces the exit of the rival; the actual action of the incum-

Klevorick, *supra* note 3, at 242.

18. *But see* pp. 41-42 *infra* (allowing for certain analytic complications that arise in the context of systems rivalry).

19. It is unlikely that the alternative action is not known or immediately apparent to the alleged predator. Indeed, in many contexts it is obvious what constitutes such an action. In the case of predatory pricing, for example, an alternative action is a reduction of current output by the incumbent firm, and a commensurate increase in price. In the case of sytems rivalry, the alternative action might be to *lower* the price on the system components that are compatible with the products of the rival.

bent under the counterfactual premise that the rival remains viable; and the alternative action of the incumbent that allows the rival to remain viable.

Firm A has an incentive to choose the exit-inducing "actual action," because it yields him a profit of 110, while the alternative yields only 105. In this example, the incumbent's choice is predatory because under the counter-factual premise that the rival remains viable, the actual action yields a profit of only 100, or a profit sacrifice of 5 relative to the alternative action.[20]

Table 1

Incumbent's Profits

	Firm A		Firm B	
	Actual Action	Alternative Action	Actual Action	Alternative Action
Rival Viable	100	105	100	95
Rival Exits	110		110	

Firm B's choice of the actual action is not predatory, however, even though it induces exit. Again, the incumbent has an incentive to make this choice, because it yields him a profit of 110, while the alternative action yields only 95. Because the actual action yields a higher profit (100) than the alternative action under the premise of the continued viability of the rival, however, it entails no predatory sacrifice of profit.[21]

Of course, the proposed standard would be difficult to administer if its application required data like those presented in Table 1. Fortunately, one can identify circumstances that are readily observable and that logically imply a predatory sacrifice of profit. Therefore, although the proposed definition of predation is not itself a workable test, it provides a unifying, general, and open-ended standard from which specific and

20. Uncertainty in the rival's response can be readily incorporated into the test for predation by regarding the profit figures as expected values. *See* Ordover & Willig, *supra* note 4 (treatment of predation under uncertainty).

21. Contrary to the analysis of other writers, *see* Areeda & Turner, *supra* note 3, at 698, 703, this definition of predatory profit sacrifice does not necessarily imply that short-run profit is sacrificed for future monopoly gain. For example, the actual action in Table 1 might earn current period profits of 10, while the alternative action earns only 5. Despite the fact that the actual action maximizes short-run profit, however, it is predatory because it would not maximize overall profit if the rival remained viable. Concededly, an effect of this kind is implausible in the context of predatory price-cutting, in which the incumbent sets a low price designed to induce exit and thereby suffers an immediate loss of net revenues. If the predatory action involves investments, however— for example, in plant capacity or in R&D—the profit sacrifice may occur after the action is taken. In the context of systems rivalry, for example, a predator may respond to entry by shifting from a relatively expensive R&D program aimed at significant quality improvement of his products to a cheaper R&D program aimed at exclusionary redesign of his products. Such an investment decision may raise short-run profit and raise expected long-run profit (because of the additional monopoly power), but lower long-run profit under the premise that the new rival remains viable.

workable tests can be derived. In the case of single product firms, the standard suggests a number of tests akin to those proposed by Areeda and Turner.[22] Similar tests can be derived for multiproduct firms.

II. Application of the General Standard to Predatory Price-Cutting

The well-known cost-based tests for predatory price-cutting, and useful new variants of these tests, can be derived from the proposed standard.

A. *Price Floors for Single Product Firms*

Consider, as a stereotype, a dominant incumbent firm that drops its price in response to entry, and thereby endangers the viability of the entrant. Our proposed standard of predatory behavior requires first that the structure of the relevant market be examined for concentration, entry hurdles, and reentry barriers. If the market exhibits all of these structural features, and if the price cut raises the probability of the entrant's exit to a dangerous level, then the standard directs attention to the question of whether the incumbent's response to entry, which includes his decisions about price, output, capital investment, and marketing activities, entails a predatory sacrifice of profit. If an alternative response would earn greater profit for the incumbent under the premise of the continued viability of the rival, a finding of predation would be appropriate.

In the simplest possible case, the issue of whether the incumbent's response to entry entails predatory sacrifice of profit reduces to the issue of whether an alternative response, less threatening to the entrant's viability, would yield a higher level of current profit under competitive circumstances. This simple case arises when the response at issue has no impact on the incumbent's future profits apart from effects on the degree of competition offered by the rival. For this condition to hold, there must be no intertemporal demand effects, such as those that motivate promotional pricing, and current output and investment must have no effect on future profitability. Such effects on future profits may sometimes exist, however, and although the proposed standard can readily account for them,[23] we

22. Areeda & Turner, *supra* note 3.

23. For example, when an incumbent's response includes a change in his investment policy, an effect on future profits will typically result. Workable tests that apply when the incumbent's response includes investment or disinvestment in capital facilities can be derived from the general standard. *See* Ordover & Willig, *supra* note 4, at 80. *See also* pp. 26-28 *inra* (discussing responses that include R&D investment).

Areeda & Turner doubt whether such effects on future profitability can be incorporated into the analysis in a practical manner. *See* Areeda & Turner, *supra* note 3, at 718-19. Concededly, neither the legal and economic commentators nor the courts have heretofore developed a theoretical framework with which to analyze such practices. Our framework can be adapted to this purpose, however, and once it is so adapted, fact-finders will be able to determine whether it can be applied in a practical manner.

assume for simplicity that under the continued-viability premise, the response to the rival affects only the current profits of the incumbent. Then, the actual response of the incumbent exhibits predatory sacrifice of profit if an alternative price and output response would increase the incumbent's current profits under competitive circumstances and would lower the probability of the rival's exit.

When the response to entry involves price-cutting, the relevant alternative responses entail smaller levels of output than that actually chosen by the incumbent, say by δ, and commensurately higher prices. Of course, the price that would result under competitive circumstances from an output reduction of δ depends upon the precise nature of market demand and rivals' production costs. Under the plausible assumption that an output reduction does not result in a lower price, however, a cost-based test for predatory profit sacrifice does not require a determination of the new price level. Instead, observe that the incumbent's cutback of δ from his actual level of production would reduce his revenues by no more than his original price, p, multiplied by the cutback, δ.[24] If the incumbent's output cutback would not affect price at all, the revenue reduction is exactly equal to $p\delta$. If the cutback would cause the price to rise, the revenue reduction would be less than $p\delta$ because of the additional revenue earned on the remaining units of output.

The output cutback of δ from the incumbent's actual production, which is less damaging to the rival, will increase the incumbent's profits under the continued viability premise if it yields him a savings of production costs that exceeds the reduction of the incumbent's revenues. Thus, predatory sacrifice of profit is present if the cost saving from the hypothetical output cutback is larger than $p\delta$—an underestimate of the revenue reduction if price increases, and an exact estimate if price remains constant. Concomitantly, predatory sacrifice is present if the incumbent's actual price, p, is less than the average savings in costs due to the output cutback, where the average is taken over the size of the hypothetical cutback, δ, for any possible value of δ.[25]

Several specific values of δ narrow this general test to especially useful cost-based price floors. For the value of δ that corresponds to elimination of the incumbent's entire output, the test for predatory sacrifice is whether the incumbent's price is below the average avoidable cost of the product

24. Let p′ and p be the alternative and actual prices, respectively, and let $q^0 - \delta$ and q^0 be the alternative and actual levels of output. Then, the reduction in revenues is $pq^0 - p'(q^0 - \delta)$. But, with $p' \geq p$, this expression is less than or equal to $pq^0 - p(q^0 - \delta) = p\delta$, as stated in the text.

25. If $C(q^0)$ and $C(q^0 - \delta)$ denote total production cost for output levels q^0 and $q^0 - \delta$, respectively, predatory sacrifice is present if $p < \frac{C(q^0) - C(q^0 - \delta)}{\delta}$.

line in question. For the value of δ that corresponds to the smallest possible output cutback, the test is whether the price is below the marginal (avoidable) cost.[26]

Thus, the cost-based tests for predatory pricing advanced by other writers may be derived from our proposed standard.[27] But contrary to the suggestion of Areeda and Turner that the average cost price floor is merely an approximation to the theoretically superior marginal cost price floor,[28] our standard implies that both average cost and marginal cost define correct price floors.[29] In particular, if the incumbent's price is below marginal cost, a slight reduction of the incumbent's output flow would raise profits under the premise of the continued viability of the rival. If the price is below average cost, an elimination of the incumbent's output flow would raise his profits under the same premise. Because either of these alternatives is less threatening to the rival's viability than the incumbent's actual response, both define correct tests of predatory sacrifice under the proposed standard.[30]

Our approach to the derivation of these cost-based tests also clarifies the appropriate cost concepts. Whatever the cost-based test at issue, it is the cost saving from an output contraction that must be compared with the associated revenue reduction. Hence, advertising and other marketing costs, for example, should be included in the average cost test to the extent that they can be avoided if the incumbent ceases production.

Similarly, there are circumstances in which capital costs should be in-

26. Other hypothetical cutbacks yield additional cost-based price floors that are germane to various circumstances. For example, if the incumbent increases his output following the rival's entry, an interesting and important hypothetical cutback is equal to the post-entry output expansion. The resultant cost-based test for predatory sacrifice is whether the actual price is below the average cost of the post-entry output expansion. *See* Ordover & Willig, *supra* note 4.

27. Cost-based tests for predatory pricing were first derived by Areeda & Turner, *supra* note 3, and amplified by Baumol, *supra* note 5, and Joskow & Klevorick, *supra* note 3. Leading court cases that have applied these tests include Berkey Photo, Inc. v. Eastman Kodak Co., 603 F.2d 263 (2d Cir. 1979), *cert. denied,* 444 U.S. 1093 (1980); Janich Bros., Inc. v. American Distilling Co., 570 F.2d 848 (9th Cir. 1977), *cert. denied,* 439 U.S. 829 (1978); International Air Indus., Inc. v. American Excelsior Co., 517 F.2d 714 (5th Cir. 1975), *cert. denied,* 424 U.S. 943 (1976); California Computer Prods., Inc. v. IBM, 613 F.2d 727 (9th Cir. 1979); Transamerica Computer Co. v. IBM, 459 F. Supp. 626 (N.D. Cal. 1978), 481 F. Supp. 965 (N.D. Cal. 1979), *appeal docketed,* No. 80-4048 (9th Cir. Jan. 31, 1980); ILC Peripherals Leasing Corp. v. IBM Corp., 458 F. Supp. 423 (N.D. Cal. 1978), *aff'd. sub nom.* Memorex Corp. v. IBM, 636 F.2d 1188 (9th Cir. 1980). *See also* Pacific Eng'r & Prod. Co. v. Kerr-McGee Corp., 551 F.2d 790 (10th Cir.), *cert. denied,* 434 U.S. 879 (1977). A useful and up-to-date compendium of predatory pricing cases is Hurwitz, *supra* note 2.

28. Areeda & Turner, *supra* note 3, at 716-18.

29. This result, of course, depends upon our stated assumption that relevant alternative responses by the alleged predator have no effects on his future profitability, other than those that stem from the exit of rivals. *See* pp. 15-16 *supra.*

30. The relative stringency of these two tests will depend upon the circumstances in which they are applied. For example, if there are economies of scale in avoidable costs, then the average cost test is the more stringent one—that is, it defines a higher price floor than the marginal cost test.

cluded in the calculation of the cost-based price floors.[31] If capital has alternative uses, either internal or external to the firm, output contractions can save capital costs by freeing equipment for use elsewhere. These avoidable capital costs should always be included in the calculation of price floors. Moreover, even if capital costs are not avoidable after they are first incurred, they should still be included in the price floor that applies when the firm has expanded output as part of its allegedly predatory conduct—the firm could have avoided such costs by maintaining the original level of output. Capital costs should be included to some extent under these circumstances regardless of whether the firm expanded its capital stock concurrently with its output expansion.[32] Thus, although output expansion in response to entry is not necessarily predatory under the proposed standard, output expansion can lead to a higher cost-based price floor, and to a more stringent test for predatory price cutting.[33]

Given the appropriate cost concepts, these tests for predatory pricing protect and enhance competition without simultaneously interfering with its workings. The tests condemn behavior that induces exit and that is not a part of the normal competitive process, but they do not mistake a normal competitive response for a predatory response—competitive responses entail no sacrifice of profit under the premise of the continued viability of the rival.

Furthermore, one can demonstrate in a variety of theoretical settings that the proposed standard protects rivals that would profitably produce in the socially optimal allocation of production among extant firms, but does not protect inefficient firms that would not profitably produce at the social optimum.[34] Suppose, for example, that both the incumbent and the rival have constant marginal and average costs. If the costs of the incumbent are lower than those of the rival, then the latter would not profitably produce in the socially optimal allocation of productive resources. Without violating the standard of predation, therefore, the incumbent can induce the rival's exit by lowering price to a level just below the rival's cost.

31. *See* Ordover & Willig, *supra* note 4, at 81.

32. If the firm expanded its capital stock concurrently with the output expansion, then an alternative and less damaging response to its rival would be to lower output and to lower or at least postpone investment. Under these circumstances, the added capital costs are directly attributable to the actual output expansion. If the output expansion is not accompanied by additional investment, then the price floor calculation should still include any increase in the costs of producing the preexpansion level of output caused by the congestion of capital facilities. A conservative estimate of this amount is the cost of the capital that eventually would be purchased to alleviate such congestion.

33. *See* Williamson, *supra* note 5, at 114-16 (arguing that output expansion by incumbent firm following entry of rival may be predatory).

34. Application of the proposed standard does not necessarily raise the level of social welfare if the incumbent and his rivals do not actively compete. In fact, one can construct examples in which all extant firms exhibit non-competitive behavior, and although the standard may protect an existing firm from induced exit, such exit would raise social welfare.

Predatory Product Innovation

Because a higher price would be undercut by the rival, no alternative price, less damaging to the rival, earns the incumbent greater current profit under competitive circumstances. A price just below the rival's cost entails no profit sacrifice, therefore, and it does not violate our standard of predation even though it induces exit.

Now suppose that the costs of the incumbent exceed those of the rival. Then only the rival would profitably produce at the social optimum. The incumbent nonetheless may have an incentive to induce the exit of the rival to gain market power and to permit prices in excess of the rival's costs. If his staying power is greater than the rival's,[35] it is possible that the incumbent will successfully induce exit, and thus reduce social welfare because, by hypothesis, the rival should produce at the social optimum. An exit-inducing action by the incumbent under these conditions, however, entails predatory sacrifice, because a price below the rival's cost will cause the incumbent to earn a negative profit that is less than his profit under any one of the following alternative responses that are less damaging to the rival: a small cutback in output; a total elimination of production; or an increase in price to a level that covers production costs. Of course, if the incumbent's actual action succeeds in driving the rival out of the market, it may be the incumbent's most profitable action. Under the premise of the continued viability of the rival, however, the actual price is not the most profitable price, and it is predatory under the proposed standard.[36]

35. The incumbent may have greater staying power than the more efficient rival if he has better internal financing or has more tangible assets available to secure debt. Concomitantly, external financing is not always available to the rival simply because he is more efficient. This fact does not necessarily reflect imperfections in the operation of capital markets, but rather it may reflect the intrinsic inability of outsiders to appraise the market situation with certainty, and their resulting unwillingness to provide funds without charging a substantial risk premium.

36. To elaborate on the welfare analysis of the proposed standard, consider an industry in which the socially optimal allocation of productive resources requires production by an arbitrary number of firms, n, indexed by i = 1,2, . . ., n. At the social optimum, each firm charges the market price, p^*, produces q_i^* where $C_i'(q_i^*)$, the firm's marginal production cost, is equal to p^*, and earns a nonnegative profit given by $\pi_i^* = p^*q_i^* - C_i(q_i^*) \geq 0$. To induce the exit of a rival who would produce at this social optimum, it is necessary that a firm (say firm l) set price at a level below p^*, or set price at p^* while producing more output than q_1^*, thereby leaving the rival with smaller demand than it needs to cover its costs. Otherwise, the rival, i, would earn at least $\pi_i^* \geq 0$, and would continue to produce.

Either of these exit-inducing tactics, however, entails a predatory sacrifice of profit on the part of firm 1. An alternative action for firm 1, less damaging to the rival, is to charge p^* and produce q_1^*. The competitive response to this action by each other firm, j, is to produce q_j^* and charge p^*, so that p^* indeed will be the market price under competitive circumstances.

The price p^* and the output q_1^* earns a higher profit for firm 1, under competitive circumstances and with the continued viability of the rival, than a price below p^* or an output above q_1^* at price p^*: Define $\pi_1^*(p)$ to be the maximium profit that firm 1 can earn if the market price is p. This maximum corresponds to a choice of output $q_1^*(p)$ at which marginal cost, $C'_1[q_1^*(p)]$, is equal to p. Therefore, $\pi_1^* = p^*q_1^* - C_1(q_1^*) = \pi_1^*(p^*)$. Moreover, because $\pi_1^*(p)$ decreases as p decreases, if firm 1 sets a price that is lower than p^*, or produces an output that is greater than q_1^* at the price p^*, it will earn a profit smaller than $\pi_1^*(p^*)$, the profit it would earn at the social optimum. The exit-inducing tactics

B. *Price Floors for Multiproduct Firms*

This section develops a test for predatory price-cutting that is applicable to multiproduct firms.[37] It shows how cost-based price floors should be adjusted for demand interrelationships between products.

The analysis again focuses on the response by a dominant incumbent firm to the entry of a new rival. The incumbent is assumed to be a multiproduct firm, however, and the product whose price or output level is allegedly predatory is assumed to be cross-elastic with another of the incumbent's products. The multiproduct nature of the firm does not alter the basic test for predatory sacrifice—whether an output contraction of size δ, along with a commensurate increase in price, would increase the current profit of the incumbent under competitive circumstances.

As above, assume that the output contraction does not cause price to fall, so that $p\delta$ is a conservative estimate of the loss of revenue from the sales of the product, and the associated cost savings less $p\delta$ is an overestimate of the increase in the incumbent's current profit on the product. In the multiproduct case, however, the effects of the output contraction on the incumbent's profit also depend upon its effects on revenue and production costs for the cross-elastic product. Let w be the initial price of the cross-elastic good before the output contraction, and let Δy be the change in sales of the cross-elastic good due to the output contraction, δ. An estimate of the effect of the output contraction on profit from sales of the cross-elastic good that leads to a conservative test for profit sacrifice is the approximate change in revenue, $w\Delta y$, less the change in production cost for the cross-elastic good attributable to the change in its output.[38]

Predation exists under our standard if the conservative estimate of the loss of direct revenues from the hypothetical output contraction, $p\delta$, is less than the sum of the direct cost saving from the contraction and the estimate of the net effect on profit from the sales of the cross-elastic product.

of setting price below p^* or producing output greater than q_i^* at price p^*, therefore, earn less profit under competitive circumstances and with the continued viability of the rival than the alternative of producing q_i^* at price p^*. Hence, the use of exit-inducing tactics against a firm that would produce at the social optimum entails predatory sacrifice of profit under the proposed standard of predation.

On the other hand, a firm can induce the exit of another firm that would not produce at the social optimum without predatory sacrifice of profit. In this model, such a result can be derived by analyzing a series of price reductions and output increases culminating in the attainment of the optimum. Under competitive circumstances, these actions by firms that would survive at the optimum *increase* their profits, and hence do not entail predatory sacrifice.

37. The courts have had difficulty with this problem. *See* Transamerica Computer Co. v. IBM, 459 F. Supp. 626, 631-32 (N.D. Cal. 1978) (suggesting that adjustments to cost-based tests to reflect cross-elasticity are impermissible as a matter of law).

38. Considering w to be unchanged leads to a conservative test for sacrifice because if the output contraction of δ increases profit (under the viability premise) with w unchanged, then it would also increase profit with w readjusted to maximize profit concurrently with the output contraction. *Cf.* P. SAMUELSON, FOUNDATIONS OF ECONOMIC ANALYSIS (1947) (discussion of Le Chatelier principle).

Equivalently, the test for predatory sacrifice is whether the price at issue is below the cost saving from the hypothetical cutback, averaged over the size of the cutback, plus an adjustment for the cross-elastic effects. This adjustment is the ratio of the induced output change, Δy, to the cutback, δ, multiplied by the margin between the price, w, and the average cost change associated with the cross-elastic good.[39]

To analyze the effects of this adjustment on the cost-based price floors for multiproduct firms, relative to the floors that would be used for single product firms, assume that the price of the cross-elastic good is not less than its average incremental cost.[40] If the cross-elastic product is a substitute[41] for the good in question, the adjustment for cross-elasticity raises the cost-based price floor because price cuts have an additional negative effect on the incumbent's current profits due to the diversion of profitable sales from the substitute product. If the cross-elastic product is a complement to the good in question, however, the adjustment lowers the price floor because price cuts have an additional positive effect on the incumbent's current profits by stimulating profitable sales of the complementary product. In both cases, the size of the adjustment to the price floor is greater, the larger is the mark-up of price over cost on the cross-elastic good, and the more sensitive are the sales of the cross-elastic good to the price and output of the good in question. If there is no significant cross-elastic effect, or if there is no significant mark-up over average incremental costs on the cross-elastic good, the adjustment for cross-elastic effects may be ignored.[42]

39. To be precise, let q^0 and y^0 be the actual output levels of the two goods. An output contraction of δ would increase the incumbent's current profit if $p'(q^0 - \delta) + w(y^0+\Delta y) - C(q^0 - \delta, y^0 + \Delta y) > pq^0 + wy^0 - C(q^0, y^0)$, where C now denotes the multiproduct cost function. With $p' \geq p$, a sufficient condition for this inequality to hold is:

$$p < \frac{C(q^0,y^0)-C(q^0-\delta,y^0)}{\delta} + \frac{\Delta y}{\delta}\left[w - \frac{C(q^0-\delta,y^0+\Delta y)-C(q^0-\delta,y^0)}{\Delta y} \right]$$

40. This assumption is likely to be correct because the price of the cross-elastic good is not being tested for predation —absent predatory intent, it would not pay the incumbent to maintain that price below average incremental cost.

41. Two goods are "substitutes" if an increase in the price of one good increases the demand for the other. For example, mid-size Chevrolets and mid-size Buicks are likely to be substitutes. Two goods are "complements" if an increase in the price of one good decreases the demand for the other. Computer peripherals and central processing units are likely to be complements, as are cameras and film.

The degree of substitutability or complementarity between two goods is measured by their cross-elasticity of demand, which equals the percentage change in the quantity demanded of one commodity that results from a one-percent change in the price of the other commodity. If the cross-elasticity is positive, then the two goods are substitutes; if it is negative, then the two good are complements.

42. It is not correct, however, to base the tests of price predation for a multiproduct firm on a product-specific average cost. For a multiproduct firm, average cost is not a meaningful concept, because its calculation implicitly requires that fixed costs, including some R&D costs, be allocated among product lines. There are no economically sound methods for allocating such common costs, however, and as shown above, *see* note 29 *supra*, average incremental cost is the appropriate measure of a product's cost for purposes of predation analysis. *See In Re Coal Rate Guidelines*—Nationwide Proceedings before the ICC, Ex Parte No. 347 (Sub-No. 1) (May 11, 1981)(statement of W. Baumol

III. Predatory Product Innovations

Predatory pricing is only one of the strategies that a firm may use to induce the exit of a competitor. The introduction of a new product can also be anticompetitive and predatory. Indeed, such a tactic may be more effective than predatory price-cutting as a way of inducing exit.[43] Of course, the introduction of a new product can also be procompetitive, as well as directly beneficial to consumers who prefer the new product to the existing ones.

Unlike a price cut, however, the introduction of a new product is a composite strategy. It involves at a minimum the following fundamental decisions: (a) the choice of the product design; (b) the choice of the time to announce the new product; (c) the choice of the price for the new product; (d) the choice of the size and content of research and development (R & D) and promotional budgets; and (e) in a multiproduct firm, the choice of the associated adjustments in the prices of existing products. Each of these choices can affect the viability of competitors. To test the introduction of a new product for predation, therefore, it is necessary to scrutinize these choices both singly and jointly as components of the overall strategy.[44]

Our analysis considers two tactics that may or may not be predatory. One tactic is the introduction of a new product that is a substitute for the products of the rival firm, and that endangers the rival's viability by diverting its sales. The second tactic, employed in the context of *systems rivalry*, involves the constriction of the supply of components that consumers must purchase in order to use the product of the rival, and a concur-

& R. Willig, economists); Braeutigam, *An Analysis of Fully Distributed Cost Pricing in Regulated Industries*, 11 BELL J. ECON. 182 (1980); Cole, *A Note on Fully Distributed Cost Prices*, 12 BELL J. ECON. 329 (1981). *But see* Transamerica Computer Co. v. IBM, 459 F. Supp. 626, 631 (arguing that appropriate method of cost allocation is factual question).

43. Product innovation may be more effective than price-cutting in inducing the exit of a rival because the associated costs to the firm are largely fixed and irreversible. After a firm commits the requisite R&D and other fixed costs, the remaining reversible costs of the product introduction may be so small that the firm would not abandon its tactic whatever the rival's response. Aware of this fact, rivals may quickly exit. In contrast, a rival's dogged refusal to exit can always motivate a firm to rescind a price cut. Thus, rivals may persevere in order to test the resolve of the price-cutter.

Areeda and Turner argue against extensive antitrust scrutiny of investments in new products or product lines. *See* Areeda & Turner, *supra* note 3, at 719, 722, 730. Even in the absence of antitrust sanctions, however, manipulation of the product set can be more effective than price-cutting as an anticompetitive tactic. There is a strong policy reason not to exclude the introduction of new products from antitrust scrutiny, therefore, unless reasonable tests for predation are infeasible.

44. Under the Areeda-Turner test, a new product is not predatory if its price satisfies the de minimis requirement that it equal or exceed the short-run marginal cost (or, if marginal costs cannot be computed, the short-run average variable cost). Short-run marginal cost and short-run variable cost, however, are not correct cost-based price floors for new products. To illustrate, consider a new product whose demand in the presence of competition permits a price above these floors, but does not permit a price high enough to recoup the requisite R&D outlays. The social benefits from such an R&D investment are questionable. *See* pp. 26-28 *infra*. In addition, a firm may undertake such an R&D investment in order to induce the exit of rivals, increase its monopoly power, and thereby recoup R&D outlays through price increases made possible by the weakening of competition.

rent introduction of new systems components that provide consumers with an alternative to the rival's products.

Each of these tactics can have three effects. First, each may increase the variety or the quality of the products available to consumers. Second, each may facilitate the procompetitive entry of new firms, or the procompetitive expansion of the number of competing products. Third, however, each may undermine competition by eliminating rivals whose viability is essential to competition.

A. *The Introduction of Substitute Products as a Form of Predation*

This section discusses in detail the phenomenon of competition through the introduction of substitute products. Although the introduction of substitutes has not been a subject of extensive antitrust scrutiny, the tests for predatory innovation developed in this section are necessary to the development of tests for predatory systems rivalry, which has been the subject of extensive litigation.

1. *Introduction to Theoretical and Practical Issues*

The prototypical instance of predation through the introduction of a substitute product may be described as follows. The dominant manufacturer of widgets in a concentrated industry introduces a new and superior model. The price of the new model is set low enough to induce a large percentage of buyers to switch from previous models, among which there is significant competition. Because of declining sales and declining net revenues, rival manufacturers abandon the production of widgets, and disperse their productive assets. After exit occurs, the innovating firm readjusts its prices and earns additional monopoly profits that are protected by entry hurdles and reentry barriers.

It is not surprising that predatory product innovation may occur in a scenario of this kind. If a dominant firm can engage in predatory price-cutting, with the quality of its product left unchanged, an obvious alternative tactic is to improve the product's quality without changing its price. Because consumers may divert their purchases of the rival's goods to the new product in response to the quality improvement, the qualitative effect on a rival of predatory product innovation is much the same as the qualitative effect of predatory price-cutting.

An important conceptual distinction between the two tactics, however, is that although predatory price-cutting may reduce price below cost, predatory product innovation may increase cost above price. Such a cost increase may consist of an increase in variable cost, an increase in expenditure for R&D and other fixed costs necessary to bring the new product to market, or both. It is the second group of costs that raise practical and theoretical issues beyond the issues already discussed in connection with predatory pricing. The proposed general standard of predation, however, does suggest a proper test for predatory product introduction that incorporates such costs. Essentially, the test inquires whether R&D and other fixed outlays that are incurred for the new product can be recouped through profits on the new product, under the premise of the continued viability of the rival. Of course, an important problem in the application of this test is to distinguish between predatory R & D expenditures, and R & D expenditures for unsuccessful projects that are undertaken for legitimate purposes. These practical aspects of implementing the test are discussed in Section III. C below, after a demonstration of the welfare optimality of the test in the context of a simple model.

2. *A Model of Predation through Substitute Product Innovation and its Welfare Implications*

Consider the following scenario: Immediately after the entry of a rival, the dominant firm (firm A) sells N_A units of output, and the rival firm (firm B) sells N_B units of a product that substitutes perfectly in the perceptions of consumers for the output of firm A. Each firm receives a price of *p* per unit, and each consumer values[45] a unit of either firm's product at *b*. The unit production cost for firm A is c_A, which is less than or equal to the unit production cost for firm B, c_B. The rival, firm B, equates price and unit cost so that $c_B = p$.

Suppose that in response to the entry of firm B, firm A expends the sum of R on an annual basis[46] to introduce a new substitute product. The new product yields to each consumer a value of b' per unit, and has a variable unit production cost of c'_A. Firm A markets the new product at the highest possible price that induces all consumers to purchase the new product instead of the old product. This price, p', is just below b'-b+p because, at this level, the net benefit to a consumer from purchasing the new good, b'-p', just exceeds the net benefit from purchasing the old good, b-p.[47] As a result, firm B loses all of its sales and exits from the market. Afterwards, in the presence of reentry barriers, firm A can raise its price without concern for the competition of firm B, and can thereby earn

45. The "value" of one unit of a product to a consumer is equal to the maximum amount the consumer will pay for it.

46. That is, the actual R&D expenses of firm A are equivalent in present value to annual expenses of R over the anticipated life of the new product. Thus, R can be viewed as the present value of R&D expenditures multiplied by the sum of the rate of return and the appropriate depreciation rate.

47. That is, if $p' < (b'-b+p)$, then $b'-p' > b'-(b'-b+p) = b-p$.

greater profit.

Under the proposed general standard of predation, the introduction of the new product is not predatory if the investment required to introduce the product is recoverable under the premise of the continued viability of firm B. Under that premise, B continues to make its product available at the competitive price of *p*, and firm A can obtain a price no higher than $p' = b'-b+p$ for the new good. Then, under the continued viability premise, one can show that the annualized investment cost of R is exceeded by the increase in firm A's net revenues from the new product if and only if the investment is socially desirable. That is, the social benefits from the new product exceed its costs if and only if the introduction of the product is profitable under the premise of the continued viability of the rival.[48] Thus the proposed test for predation is indeed conducive to social welfare.

Of course, our demonstration of the welfare optimality of the proposed predation standard rests on the assumptions of this simple model. Nevertheless, the analysis has a number of general implications. First, even if a new product is successful in the market, it may either increase or decrease social welfare, depending upon the magnitude of R&D costs and other investments. Second, a dominant firm may profit from the introduction of a new product, whether or not it is socially beneficial, if it induces the exit of a rival and thereby increases the firm's monopoly power. Third, application of the proposed standard of predation may reduce the incentives for anticompetitive product innovation, without diminishing the incentives for procompetitive innovations.

3. *General Application of the Proposed Standard*

General application of the proposed standard to the introduction of substitute products raises a number of issues that require further discussion. Under the continued viability premise, the assessment of the profitability of a new product must take account of the loss in net revenues from the innovator's old product. In other words, the introduction of a new substitute product may be predatory if the revenues from its sales fail to exceed the incremental costs of its production plus the reduction in net revenues

48. The algebraic proof is as follows: Prior to the introduction of the new product and the investment in its development, firm A earns a profit of $\pi_0 = N_A(p-c_A)$. After the new product is introduced, and under the continued viability premise, the new price is $p' = b'-b+p$. Firm A displaces the sales of firm B, and hence firm A's new profit level under the continued viability premise is $\pi_1 = (N_A + N_B)(b'-b+p-c'_A)-R$. If the innovation is to be profitable under the continued viability premise, then $\pi_1 - \pi_0 > 0$. This inequality implies that $N_A(b'-b+c_A-c'_A)+N_B(b'-b+p-c'_A)-R>0$. Recall that $p=c_B$. Then, this inequality can be written as $N_A[(b'-c'_A)-(b-c_A)] + N_B[(b'-c'_A)-(b-c_B)]-R>0$. The expression on the left-hand side, however, is precisely the change in net social welfare due to the investment and new product introduction, as measured by the sum of consumers' and producers' surplus. Thus, $\pi_1 - {}_0 > 0$ holds if and only if the investment and innovation increase social welfare.

caused by the diversion of sales from the preexisting products of the innovator. If revenues fall short of this level, there is prima facie evidence that the product introduction entails a predatory sacrifice of profit under the continued viability premise.[49]

The existence of a profit sacrifice, however, is not itself sufficient for a finding of predation. The likelihood of the rival's exit must be substantially raised by the product introduction, and the additional monopoly profit that would accrue to the innovator after the exit of the rival must be sufficient to make the introduction of the new product profitable for the innovator. This element of the test for predatory product innovation requires the existence of a motive for predation. Clearly, there can be no motive for predation absent the structural conditions of horizontal concentration, entry hurdles, and reentry barriers. In addition, a finding that R&D costs exceed the increment in net revenues earned under the viability premise does not establish a motive for predation if these costs also exceed the increment in net revenues *with* the rival's exit. Such a finding establishes only that the innovating firm overestimated the benefits it would obtain from its R&D investment.

As this last observation suggests, both the character and the details of the proposed test depend to a large extent on the significance of post-entry R&D costs. If these costs are small relative to the other incremental costs of the new product, then the test for predatory price reduction by a multiproduct firm is directly applicable.[50] If post-entry R&D expenditures are

49. This issue arose in Transamerica Computer Co. v. IBM, 459 F. Supp. 626 (1978). The plaintiff (TCC) asked the court to consider the effects of a new product introduction on the profitability of preexisting product lines in calculating the cost-based price floor for ascertaining profit sacrifice. TCC urged that "impact cost," measured as "the reduction in anticipated future profits on an existing product line caused by the introduction of a new product line," should be subtracted from the new product's profit in "determining whether the price set was predatory and below cost." *Id.* at 630. The inclusion of impact costs was ruled to be impermissible as a matter of law on the ground that such inclusion would constitute a drawback to research and innovation and that impact costs are difficult to calculate. *Id.* at 631.

This ruling is at variance with the economic analysis of tests for predatory profit sacrifice presented in this article. We argue that the introduction of a new product (or a price reduction on an existing product) can divert sales from preexisting products. The forgone profits from diverted sales should be netted out from the expected gross revenues that accrue to the firm from the introduction of a new product, or, equivalently, should be added to the incremental costs incurred for the product introduction. Absent an anticompetitive objective, a firm would not engage in the development and marketing of a new product if the new product were not expected to generate revenues sufficient to recoup its operating and fixed costs, including R&D and marketing costs, and also to compensate the innovator for profits lost through sales diversion. As Judge Schnacke observed at trial, IBM had engaged in a very thorough financial analysis of the expected profitability of each of its new products. Transamerica Computer Co. v. IBM, 481 F. Supp. 965, 997-1002 (1979). Consequently, assessments of the impact costs were feasible. More importantly, however, impact costs would have been an important component of an economically sound test for predatory product innovations in the Transamerica litigation. The ruling to exclude such costs was inconsistent with our view that exit-inducing profit sacrifice for the sake of future monopoly gain is predatory.

50. *See* pp. 20-21 *supra*.

significant, however, then the decision to undertake the R&D investment must be tested for predation along with the innovator's pricing strategy.

When R&D costs are at issue, the purpose of the test is to determine the objective underlying the R&D investment decision. This determination requires scrutiny of the level of profits with and without the viability of the entrant and net of the post-entry R&D costs that are allocable to the innovation and were foreseeable at the time the investment was made.

As a defense to a charge of predation, the defendant may show that his inability to recover the full incremental cost of the newly introduced product, including the post-entry R&D costs, stems from an exaggerated expectation of consumers' demand for the new product.[51] A possible element of proof in this argument is a showing that the defendant *attempted* to recoup the initial outlay on R&D. A high initial price, followed by price reductions to bolster sales, is indicative of such an attempt if supported by the appropriate marketing evidence.

The defendant's investment planning process may be the most useful source of data concerning the firm's expectations. Decisions to commit substantial funds to R&D projects are likely to be supported by internal analyses of prospective costs and financial benefits.[52] These analyses often identify the objectives of an R&D project, such as bringing a preconceived product to market, or generating basic research whose market applicability is as yet unknown. Because the costs of basic research cannot be attributed to specific products, such costs should be excluded from the tests for predatory sacrifice of profit. On the other hand, R&D expeditures for preconceived products are relevant to the proposed tests of predatory sacrifice.

Of course, R&D projects are endemically subject to uncertainty both with regard to the cost necessary to achieve a given outcome, and the usable output achieved from a given outlay. This uncertainty exists for the firm at the time of its investment decision, as well as for factfinders seeking to determine the objective of that decision. The firm's objective is properly assessed in terms of the costs and benefits expected by the firm—which inform the firm's investment decision and which are reflected in the firm's internal analyses.

Once the relevant R&D expenditures are isolated, the proposed stan-

51. Of course, if the new product is truly unwanted by consumers, it is unlikely to cause the exit of a rival who produces a substitute product, and it is unlikely, therefore, that a charge of predatory innovation would ever be brought. Even an unsuccessful product, however, should be required to pass cost-based price tests that exclude considerations of post-entry R&D costs; the mere fact that the product sells poorly should not preclude a charge of predatory conduct.

52. For example, the record in *Berkey* is replete with information about Kodak's R&D investment decisions. *See* Berkey Photo, Inc. v. Eastman Kodak Co., 603 F.2d 263, 276-79 (2d Cir. 1979), *cert. denied*, 444 U.S. 1093 (1980).

dard requires identification of the market conditions under which the innovator expects to recoup those expenditures. Market conditions play a central role in a firm's assessment of the expected benefits to be derived from R&D. This assessment reflects the price that consumers are expected to be willing to pay for a new product, and the quantity that they are expected to purchase at a given price. These expectations must be based on knowledge of the array of substitute products available in the market and their prices. If an innovator's R&D decision is actually based on an assessment of expected benefits that posits the continuing availability of rivals' products, then that decision is free of predatory sacrifice.

4. *The Dangers of "Off-the-Shelf" Product Innovations*

As shown above, whether a new product passes the proposed test for predation can depend significantly on the extent to which R&D costs are included in the cost-based price floor. The proper allocation of these costs, however, depends upon when the allegedly predatory innovation was undertaken. If a new product is developed before entry occurs, and is introduced "off-the-shelf" after entry occurs, then the R&D costs for the product were sunk prior to entry and should not be included in the cost-based floor. Otherwise, innovators would be accused of predation against rivals who did not exist at the time of the allegedly predatory conduct.

Concededly, this treatment of R&D costs may give an innovator incentives to accumulate new product designs in anticipation of entry,[53] and then to wait and introduce the designs after entry occurs. The magnitude of such incentives is generally small, however, because it is costly to withold product innovations from the market in anticipation of uncertain entry. First, the innovator must forego revenue from the sale of the new products until the time of entry. Second, the innovator must forego the return that would have been earned by investing the R&D funds elsewhere. Third, there is a risk that actual or potential rivals may bring new products to market before the innovator, and thereby render the innovator's new product less profitable than it would have been if introduced earlier.

Moreover, innovating firms may have countervailing incentives to introduce products early to create artificial entry barriers.[54] If incumbents fill the spectrum of products that match the diverse tastes of consumers, prospective entrants may find it difficult to create a new product that would

53. *See* Gilbert, *Patents and Entry Deterrence*, in STRATEGY, PREDATION, AND ANTITRUST ANALYSIS (S. Salop ed. 1981) (discussing entry deterrence through accumulation of unused product designs).

54. *See* Schmalensee, *Entry Deterrence in the Ready-To-Eat Breakfast Cereal Industry*, 9 BELL J. ECON. 305 (1978) (arguing that brand proliferation, product differentiation, and intensive advertising create barriers to entry).

make entry profitable. Thus, according to the entry-deterrence theory of product competition, incumbent firms may offer an excessive, socially inefficient variety of products to prevent the entry of new rivals.[55] In view of this countervailing incentive, and in view of the other costs of witholding innovations from the market, the incentives for over-accumulation of product designs are probably small.

To further reduce these incentives, plaintiffs might be permitted to introduce evidence of off-the-shelf innovation as proof of predation. The plaintiff might argue that the exit-inducing aspect of the product introduction made the introduction profitable, even though it was unprofitable prior to the plaintiff's entry. If so, the product introduction entailed a sacrifice of profit under the continued viability premise.

Despite the strength of this argument, however, off-the-shelf product introductions in response to entry are not necessarily predatory. The change in market structure due to entry can have a number of effects on the profitability of a product introduction. For instance, the introduction may be more profitable post-entry than pre-entry because with more products in the market, the new product diverts fewer sales from the innovator's own substitute products. In some instances, therefore, off-the-shelf product introductions may be part of socially desirable product competition. Consequently, it would be socially counterproductive to place undue weight on the fact that a product introduction is taken off-the-shelf. Rather, off-the-shelf innovation should be treated like other innovation. The R&D costs to be tested for predation should be limited to those incurred after the innovator became aware of the rival's actual or impending entry. The plaintiff may utilize the fact that the innovator found the product introduction unprofitable prior to entry, however, to bolster the showing of predatory profit sacrifice.

5. *Summary*

Because technological progress is desirable and should not be stifled by the antitrust laws, it may be tempting to follow the view that if engineering data suggest that a new product is superior to the product it replaces, antitrust inquiry should end.[56] Such products, however, do not always generate higher social welfare.[57] Under the proposed standard, the rele-

55. Entry-deterrence theory and its relevance to antitrust policy is criticized in Easterbrook, *supra* note 7, at 282-97. *But see* Williamson, Antitrust Enforcement: Where It's Been; Where It's Going (University of Pennsylvania Working Paper, May 1981) (on file with *Yale Law Journal*) (concluding that entry deterrence theory is useful to antitrust analysis).

56. *See* ILC Peripherals Leasing Corp. v. IBM, 458 F. Supp. 423, 439 (N.D. Cal. 1978), *aff'd sub nom.* Memorex Corp. v. IBM, 636 F.2d 1188 (9th Cir. 1980).

57. We have argued that a profitable new product may not be socially beneficial if its R&D costs can be defrayed only by the additional monopoly profit attendant on the exit of rivals. Other authors

vant question is whether the innovator anticipated positive incremental profit for the new product, given the continued viability of the rival. The incremental profit measure should be calculated net of the losses resulting from diversions of sales from the innovator's preexisting products, and net of all post-entry R&D costs. If the post-entry R&D costs are small because the new product was introduced "off-the-shelf," the plaintiff may attempt to show anticompetitive conduct from the fact that the off-the-shelf design was introduced only in response to entry.

B. *Predatory Systems Rivalry*

Most of the recent cases pertaining to predatory product innovations deal with the phenomenon of systems rivalry.[58] Typically, the defendant was a firm that had been offering systems components that were *compatible* with the components produced by a rival, as well as systems components that were *competitive* with the components produced by the rival. The defendant then introduced a new system of components that were incompatible with those of the rival, thereby threatening the rival's viability.

To illustrate, consider a market for widget systems in which consumers derive utility from appropriate combinations of widgets and widget accessories. The dominant manufacturer of widgets, firm A, also manufactures widget accessories, as does a rival firm, firm B. At some point in time, however, firm A introduces a new line of widgets and compatible accessories that threatens the viability of firm B because the new widgets are incompatible with firm B's accessories. If firm A's new widget system is sufficiently superior to the old widget system in the perceptions of consumers, firm B may be driven out of the widget systems market even if the price of the old systems remains the same. Firm A can increase the likelihood of firm B's exit, however, by increasing the price of the old-style widgets or by discontinuing their production.

This section provides workable tests to determine whether the introduc-

have shown that a profitable new product may lower social welfare if it diverts demand from substitute products that are produced with significant economies of scale. *See, e.g.*, E. CHAMBERLIN, THE THEORY OF MONOPOLISTIC COMPETITION (6th ed. 1948); R. WILLIG, WELFARE ANALYSIS OF POLICIES AFFECTING PRICES AND PRODUCTS (1979); Dixit & Stiglitz, *Monopolistic Competition and Optimum Product Diversity*, 67 AM. ECON. REV. 297 (1977); Spence, *Product Selection, Fixed Costs, and Monopolistic Competition*, 43 REV. ECON. STUD. 217 (1976).

58. California Computer Prods., Inc. v. IBM, 613 F.2d 727 (9th Cir. 1979); Telex Corp. v. IBM, 510 F.2d 894 (10th Cir. 1975), *cert. dismissed*, 423 U.S. 802 (1975); Transamerica Computer Co. v. IBM, 459 F. Supp. 626 (N.D. Cal. 1978), 481 F. Supp. 965 (N.D. Cal. 1979), *appeal docketed*, No. 80-4048 (9th Cir. Jan. 31, 1980). *See also* Berkey Photo, Inc. v. Eastman Kodak, Co., 603 F.2d 263 (2d Cir. 1979), *cert. denied* 444 U.S. 1093 (1980); MCI Communications Corp. v. AT&T, 969 ANTITRUST & TRADE REG. REP. (BNA) A-3 (N.D. Ill. June 19, 1980), *appeal docketed*, No. 80-2171 (7th Cir. Aug. 27, 1980); ILC Peripherals Leasing Corp. v. IBM, 458 F. Supp. 423 (N.D. Cal. 1978), *aff'd sub nom.* Memorex Corp. v. IBM, 636 F.2d 1188 (9th Cir. 1980).

Predatory Product Innovation

tion of a new system into an existing systems market, coupled with price adjustments on components of the old system, is anticompetitive. Under the proposed general standard of predation, a finding of predatory conduct requires both a showing of motive and a showing of profit sacrifice. There is no clear motive for predatory systems rivalry if the dominant firm can earn all of the monopoly profits obtainable in the market by charging an elevated price for the component of the system over which the dominant firm already possesses monopoly power. Monopoly power over one component of a system, however, is not always sufficient for a dominant firm to extract all the monopoly profits obtainable in the systems market. In such instances, the dominant firm can increase its profit by inducing the exit of a rival and thereby extending its monopoly power to other systems components.[59] We argue that the conditions necessary for this incentive for predation are the rule rather than the exception, and hence that courts should presume their existence. Of course, a motive for predation also requires that the systems market is concentrated and protected by entry hurdles and reentry barriers.

Once the existence of a motive is established, the test for profit sacrifice proceeds in two stages. The first stage requires an examination of the post-innovation prices of the components that are compatible with the products of the rival. The innovator's behavior is free of profit sacrifice only if he offers to provide his rivals with the necessary compatible components at compensatory prices, in preference to making far fewer sales at higher prices or to making the components unavailable. The prices of old components are compensatory if they cover the cost of supplying the old component and yield the same incremental profit as the displaced cross-elastic sales of new and other components, assuming the rival remains viable in the systems market. Compensatory prices of old components should not reflect the additional monopoly profits that the innovator would earn if a rival were irreversibly driven out of the market.

The second stage of the test for profit sacrifice examines the rationality of the R&D investment in the new system, under the assumption that the

59. Other writers contend that a firm has no incentive to "lever" its market power from one market to another. Under this theory, the nature of vertical relations between firms is entirely determined by efficiency considerations. *See* R. POSNER, ANTITRUST LAW: AN ECONOMIC PERSPECTIVE 173-74 (1976) (weakness of leverage theory is inability to explain why firm with monopoly over one product would want to monopolize complementary products); Easterbrook, *supra* note 5, at 308 (concluding that dominant firm cannot lever its market power through innovations since attempts at leverage impose costs on purchasers of goods). *But see* Ordover & Willig, Notes on Non-price Anticompetitive Practices by Dominant Firms (unpublished paper prepared for the 9th Annual Telecommunications Policy Research Conference, April 27-30, 1981) (on file with *Yale Law Journal*). The *Berkey* case holds, however, that a new system can be predatory if it would enable a firm with monopoly power to lever this power into competitive advantage in another market. Berkey Photo, Inc. v. Eastman Kodak Co., 603 F. 2d 263, 275-76, 285-88 (2d Cir. 1979), *cert. denied*, 444 U.S. 1093 (1980).

innovator offers the old components at compensatory prices. This stage of the test, therefore, is conceptually equivalent to the tests developed in section III A that dealt with the introduction of substitute products.

1. *Basic Concepts in Systems Rivalry*

A "system" is a collection or package of complementary products that are combined by a manufacturer, or a consumer, to yield a final product. Because the components of the system are complementary products, an increase in the price of one component reduces the demand for the other components.[60]

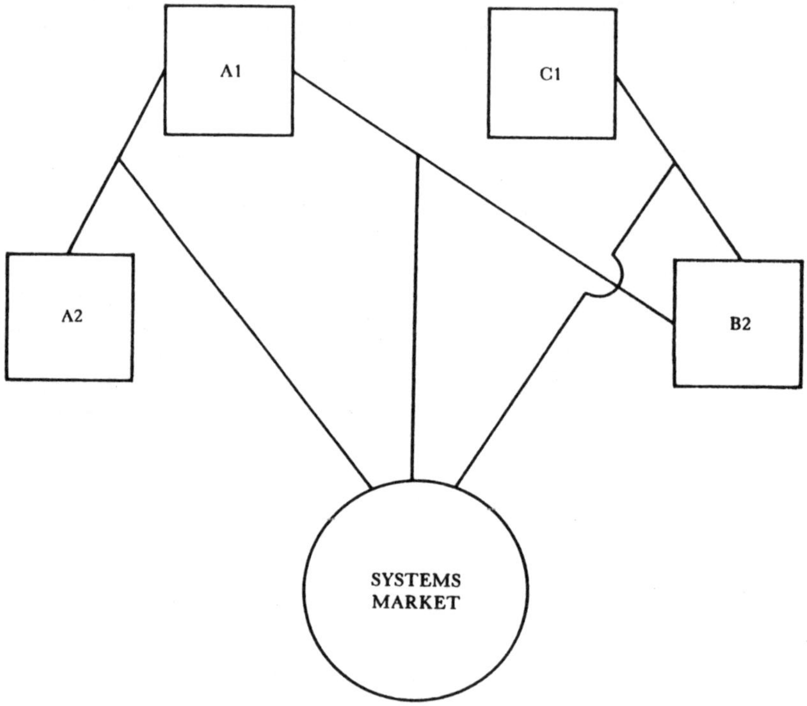

Figure 1

Frequently, a system can be assembled from complementary compo-

60. For example, an increase in camera prices tends to reduce the demand for film, and an increase in prices of computer central processing units tends to reduce the demand for the associated peripheral equipment.

nents that are produced by different manufacturers, as long as the various components are "compatible" with each other—that is, as long as the components of various manufacturers are interchangeable without much loss in their efficiency. If the components of various manufacturers are compatible, then competition in the systems market is enhanced. Concomitantly, incompatibilities reduce competition, and the creation of incompatibilities may increase the monopoly profits of a firm that has monopoly power over one or more of the components.

Figure 1 diagrammatically summarizes the basic elements of systems rivalry. Each system consists of two complementary components, denoted by the numbers 1 and 2. The three manufacturers are denoted by the letters A, B, and C. Thus, A1 stands for the first component manufactured by firm A, and B2 stands for the second component manufacturered by firm B. A line joining two components indicates that the two components are compatible. The absence of a line indicates incompatibility. Thus, in Figure 1, A1 and B2 are compatible, but C1 and A2 are not compatible. There is substantial intersystem rivalry in the final systems market, because consumers can select from three distinct systems, all of which may be perfect substitutes for each other.

In Figure 2, however, firm A has a monopoly over the first component, A1, and also produces a compatible second component, A2. Firm B specializes in the production of the second component, which is compatible with A1. In this market scenario, two business decisions by firm A may disadvantage the rival firm B, whatever firm A's underlying motive, and irrespective of the effects of its decisions on competition. First, firm A can refuse to deal[61] with firm B by withholding the complementary component from the open market and selling it exclusively as a part of a system.[62] Second, firm A may engage in the related tactic of price discrimination. A price discriminating firm sets two prices—a high price on components that are sold to a rival or its customers, and a low price on components that are sold to customers who do not purchase components from a rival. The extreme form of this strategem is a price that chokes off all effective demand for separate sales of the relevant component; such a price has the same effect on the rival as a pure refusal to deal.

61. *See generally* Note, *Refusals to Deal by Vertically Integrated Monopolists*, 87 HARV. L. REV. 1720 (1974).

62. In Figure 1, the refusal to deal by firm A may have little impact on the ability of firm B to compete with firm A, because firm C is an alternative source for the complementary component. Specifically, the impact of firm A's decision is minimized if component C1 is a good substitute for Al in the opinion of consumers; component B2 can easily be made compatible with component C1; and manufacturer C does not increase the price of C1 after the refusal to deal by firm A. In Figure 2, however, firm A is the only source of component 1, and a refusal to deal may drive firm B out of the market unless a new entrant into the market commences production of component 1.

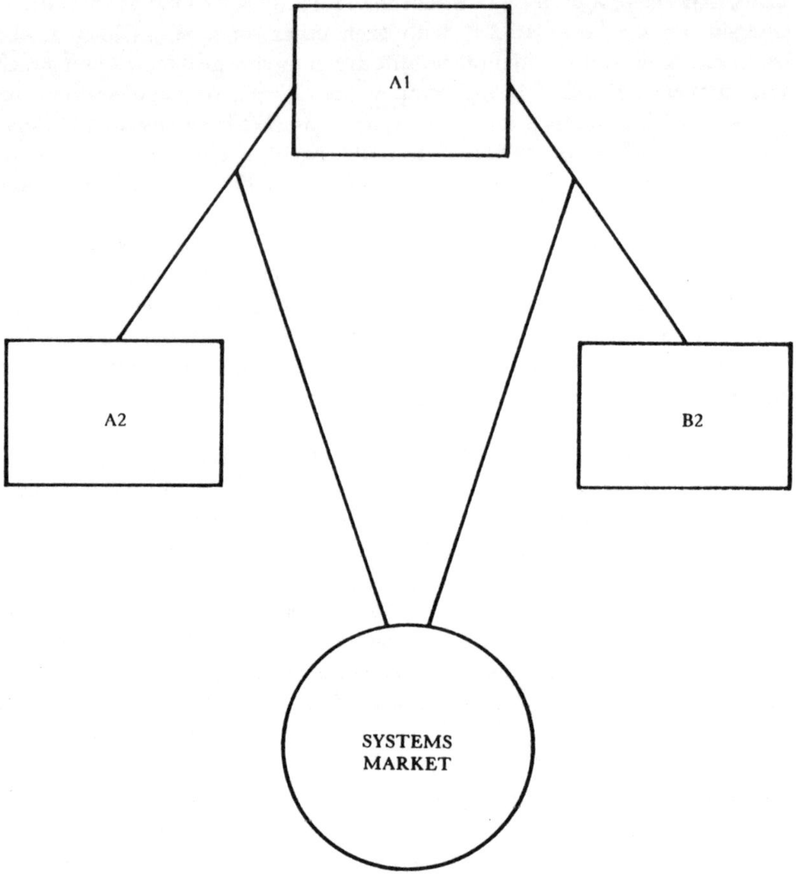

Figure 2

Refusal to deal and price discrimination may be procompetitive regardless of their effects on rivals. Both practices would be procompetitive, for example, if they were necessary to maintain the system's reputation for quality, the product differentiation of the system,[63] or the supply of requi-

63. In the presence of product differentiation, consumers have the opportunity to choose among the various aspects of product design for which tastes and needs may differ. Other things being equal, therefore, product differentiation benefits consumers. Moreover, product differentiation may promote competition. For example, product differentiation may be essential to new entrants who cannot compete with existing firms merely by mimicking their products. By assembling a system that is distinct from those of their rivals, entrants may avoid head-on price competition, at least until after they can establish themselves in the market. If firms are compelled to sell the unique components of their

site system components.

In other instances, however, the two strategies may be anticompetitive, and transparently without a business justification other than the pursuit of monopoly power. To avoid the appearance of anticompetitive intent, a firm may employ a less obviously anticompetitive strategy that still permits the extension of its monopoly power over one component into monopoly power over the entire systems market. The introduction of new systems can be a camouflaged anticompetitive strategy, precisely because the introduction of new products or systems is typically regarded as procompetitive and beneficial to consumer welfare.[64]

The introduction of a new system can disadvantage rivals in at least two ways. First, if the new system is superior to existing systems, demand for the existing systems will decline. Second, the innovator may constrict the supply[65] of the components that are compatible with those of the rival by increasing the prices of preexisting components, or discontinuing their production. Discontinuance of the old components is particularly damaging to the rival's profits; the more incompatible the rival's components are with the new components, the more costly it is for the rival to introduce components that are compatible with the innovator's new components, and the more costly or inferior are the substitute components available from other producers in the market. Although these injuries to rivals may be incidental to socially beneficial product innovation, they are the primary motivation for predatory product innovations.

If the innovating dominant firm continues to supply the old components at compensatory prices, the introduction of the new system can be tested for predation using the tests developed in Section III A. Distinct issues arise, however, if the defendant increases the prices of existing components above their compensatory level; because the potentially predatory conduct does not involve a price cut, but rather a price increase, the standard comparison between prices and costs is inappropriate.

systems to rivals, however, product differentiation may not be feasible. *See* U.S. v. Columbia Pictures Indus., Inc., 507 F. Supp. 412 (S.D.N.Y. 1980).

64. *See* Berkey Photo Inc. v. Eastman Kodak Co., 603 F.2d 263, 287 (2d Cir. 1979)(concluding that market acceptance of innovation is best indicator of product quality and of benefit to public as long as market permits free choice of consumers); ILC Peripherals Leasing Corp. v. IBM, 458 F. Supp. 423, 439 (N.D. Cal. 1978), *aff'd sub nom.* Memorex Corp. v. IBM, 636 F.2d 1188 (9th Cir. 1980) (same, with proviso that consumer's choices have not been manipulated by the monopolist); Comment, *Antitrust Scrutiny of Monopolists' Innovations: Berkey Photo Inc. v. Eastman Kodak Co.*, 93 HARV. L. REV. 408, 414-15 n.60 (1979) (concurring with view expressed in Berkey).

65. In general, an innovator can constrict the supply of compatible components in several ways: refusing to deal with the rival; selling the components only as a complete system; pricing the components in a way that discriminates against rivals; selling the components as a complete system in combination with high individual prices for the compatible components if sold separately; underpricing components that compete with the components of rivals; overpricing components that are compatible with the components of rivals; or, as suggested in the text, introducing a new system that is incompatible with rivals' products while overpricing or withdrawing the necessary preexisting components.

Nonetheless, the proposed general standard of predatory behavior yields workable tests for predatory systems rivalry. For conduct involving the introduction of a new system and an attendant price revision to be predatory, the dominant firm must have a motive for inducing the exit of a rival, the challenged conduct must substantially increase the probability that the rival will exit, and the conduct must entail a profit sacrifice in comparison to the profits that could be earned, with the continued viability of the rival, if the innovator pursued an alternative strategy.

2. *Motives for Predation: The Economics of Vertical Price Squeezes*

When a firm has monopoly power over one component in a system, conventional economic wisdom suggests that the firm can extract all the monopoly profit available in the systems market by charging a sufficiently high price for the monopolized component—that is, by executing a *vertical price squeeze*. If that is true, why should the firm bother to engage in predation against a rival manufacturer of a complementary component? The answer to this question is critical to the understanding of the profit motive for tactical exit inducement in the systems' context, and also to the construction of tests for predatory profit sacrifice.

Consider a market scenario in which a firm with market power has no motive to induce the exit of its rival. In Figure 3, the dominant firm can extract all the monopoly profit that is available in the systems market by subjecting the rival to a carefully designed vertical price squeeze. The unit incremental cost of the first component is equal to *c*, and the unit incremental cost of the second component is equal to *a*, regardless of who produces it. Assume that all consumers are identical and have a maximum willingness to pay of *b* for either system. If the system price is *b* or less, each consumer will buy one system. If the price exceeds *b*, consumers will not buy any systems.

In this scenario, the viability of firm B need not diminish the monopoly profits of firm A.[66] To see this, consider the profits that firm A can earn in the absence of firm B, and then consider the profits that firm A can earn with a perfect price squeeze against a viable firm B.

In the absence of firm B, firm A will maximize its profit by selling systems to consumers at the highest possible price—their willingness to pay of *b*. Since each system costs c+a to produce, each sale yields a profit margin of b-(c+a). Firm A's total profit is equal to b-(c+a) multiplied by the number of sales in the entire systems market.

66. In fact, if the rival is a more efficient producer of component two, then the profits of firm A are larger if firm B remains viable. *See* note 67 *infra*.

Predatory Product Innovation

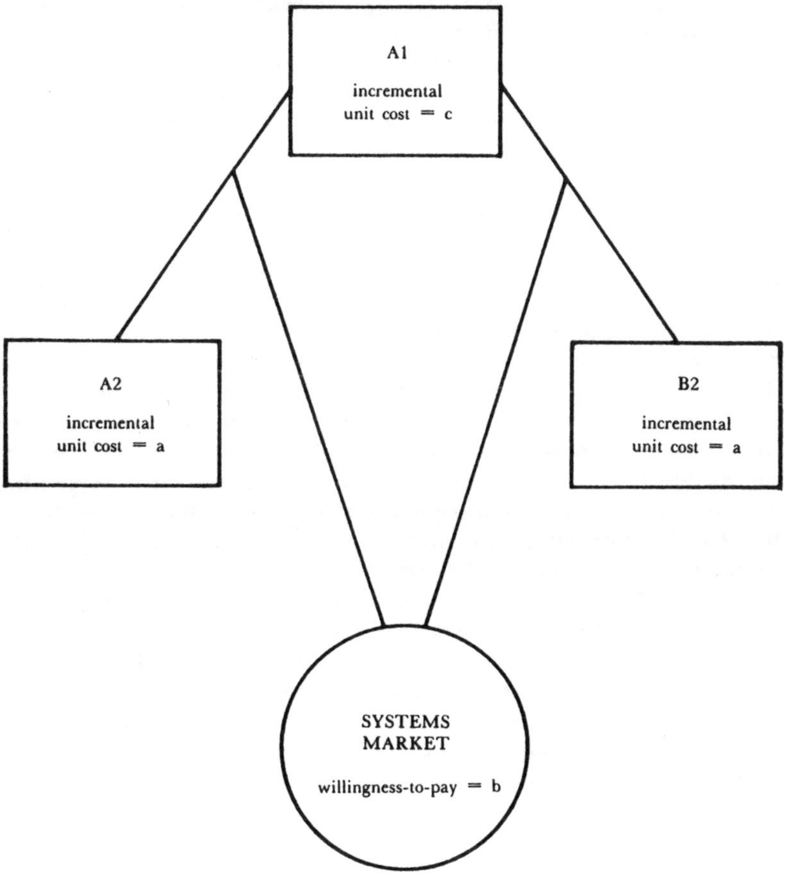

Figure 3

Now suppose that firm B is a viable competitor of firm A. The presence of firm B constrains the equilibrium price of type-two components to *a*, their unit cost. Nonetheless, firm A can extend its monopoly power over type-one components to the entire systems market by charging a price of *b* for entire systems, a price of b-a in the open market for type-one components, and a price of *a* in the open market for type-two components. Then, a direct sale of a whole system by firm A has b-(c+a) as its profit margin. A system that is comprised of components A1 and B2 yields to firm A a profit of (b-a)-c, through its sale of component A1 at the price of (b-a) and with the cost of *c*. Finally, a system assembled by consumers that is comprised of components A1 and A2 yields to firm A a profit of (b-a)-c on its sale of A1 and no profit on its sale of A2 at cost. Thus, with a perfect price squeeze, firm A does not lose profits if consumers choose systems that include the rival's component rather than systems that are wholly comprised of firm A's own components,[67] and firm A has no incentive to extend its monopoly power to the second component.

Such a perfect price squeeze, however, requires that all of the profits available in the systems market be captured through the markup on the monopolized component. One impediment to the execution of such a price squeeze may arise when system components can be utilized in different mixes by different consumers. For example, consumers who demand relatively more of the non-monopolized components for their systems may have a more than proportionately greater willingness-to-pay for systems. Then, only prices that embody a relatively high markup on the non-monopolized component and a relatively low markup on the monopolized component can transfer to suppliers the willingness-to-pay of these consumers along with the smaller willingness-to-pay of other consumers. Such prices constitute a form of price discrimination in the systems market between the different groups of consumers. They are infeasible in the presence of competition in the sale of the non-monopolized component, however, and are inconsistent with the use of a price squeeze. Thus, if this type of price discrimination is necessary for a monopolist to derive maximum profits from the systems market, a firm with monopoly power over one component has incentives to extend its power to other components.

The desire to price discriminate, however, is not the only obstacle to the implementation of a price squeeze. Regulated firms, for example, may be unable to charge the unbalanced markups needed to implement a perfect price squeeze. Alternatively, consumers may underestimate their demand for the components subject to competition and this circumstance may enlarge the profit-maximizing markup on those components. In addition, consumer uncertainty about the value of a given system may call for promotional pricing of the very component that must carry a high markup in a price squeeze.

The most important type of impediment to the use of a price squeeze, however, is the existence of an alternative source of supply of the monopo-

67. If firm B can produce type two components at a lower cost than firm A, say a', firm A can extract the maximum profits available in the systems market only if firm B remains viable. The profit maximizing tactic for firm A is to set a price for A1 of b-a', and a price for the entire system just above *b*. Then, firm B cannot price B2 above a', because a higher price would raise the total cost of a system above consumers' willingness to pay. Hence, firm A would not sell any units of A2, and would earn a profit of b-a'-c on each sale of A1. This is the maximum profit available in the systems market, and it exceeds b-a-c, which is the maximum profit in the absence of firm B.

lized component, which is of inferior quality or which incurs a higher cost of production, but which limits the markup that the market will bear on the monopolized component. Figure 4 depicts a market scenario in which the monopoly power of the dominant firm is limited by an inferior source of supply.[68] There are now three firms in the market: the dominant firm A, which manufactures both system components, and the specialized firms, B and C, which manufacture only one component. Assume that the dominant firm has a relatively small cost advantage over the other manufacturer of the first component, equal to *d*.

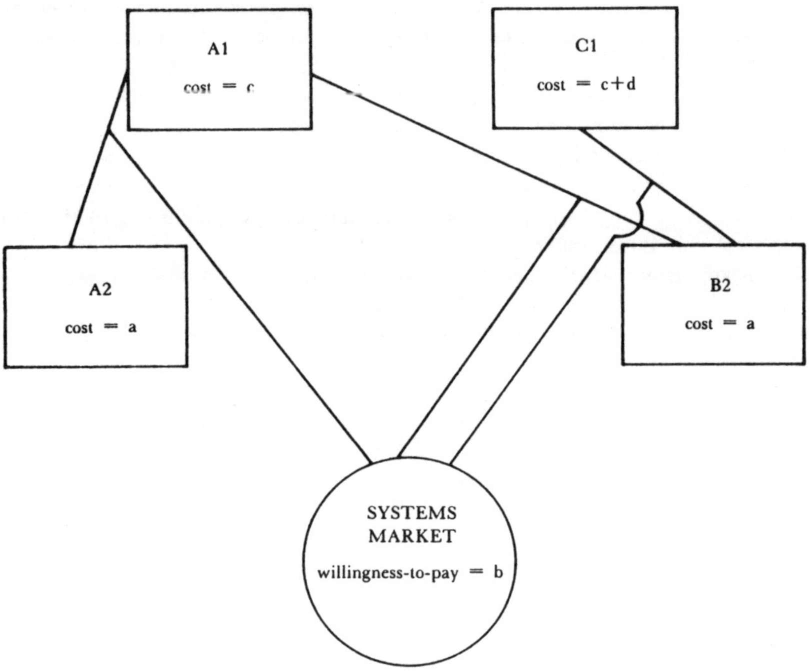

Figure 4

Absent the rival manufacturer of the second component, firm B, firm A's small cost advantage over firm C could be levered into substantial monopoly profits. Firm A could set the system price at *b* and earn the maximum profit of b-(a+c) on each system sold.[69] With firm B in the market, however, the competing perfect substitute system of C1 and B2

68. The model in the text applies whether the inferior source of supply is an actual or a potential rival of the dominant firm A.
69. *See* pp. 36-37 *supra*.

can be sold for a total price of a+c+d, and this amount is then the maximum that firm A can charge for a system. At that price, the profit margin for firm A is only *d*. Of course, in the absence of both of the competing firms B and C, firm A could earn b-(a+c) on each system—the full monopoly profit available in the systems market.

In some instances, the most effective way for firm A to earn the full monopoly profit is to drive firm C out of the market. In particular, a nonpredatory price of *c* for component A1 would divert all sales of component one from firm C to firm A, and might thereby induce firm C's exit. The viability of firm C, however, may not rest on events in the market in question. Instead, component C1 may have alternative uses for which A1 does not suffice. Thus, firm C might survive despite the postulated cost advantage of component A1 over component C1 in this market.[70] Alternatively, firm C may face very low reentry barriers. Under such circumstances, only the exit of firm B will enable firm A to capture the full monopoly profit available in the systems market,[71] and the existence of an inferior source of supply provides the dominant firm with a motive for tactical exit inducement.

In applying the proposed test for predation, courts should not require a detailed, dispositive showing of alternative though inferior sources of supply, because such sources of supply are common in actual systems markets.[72] To satisfy the motive element of the test for predation, however, a

70. Firm C can survive in the long-run either because its product has purposes for which component A1 is ill-suited or because its productive capacity has other uses. Of course, if the viability of firm C depends upon sales of C1 in the market with A1, it cannot withstand competition from firm A, and it will exit the market. Because of the other uses for firm C's products or capacity, however, it remains a potential competitor, and constrains the market power of firm A as long as firm B remains viable.

71. In this scenario, the most direct way for firm A to induce the exit of firm B involves a refusal to deal and a low systems price: firm A refuses to sell the first component in the open market, and prices its complete system just below a+c+d. At this price, consumers will not demand systems assembled from components C1 and B2 unless firms B or C are willing to sell their components below cost.

If the dominant firm cannot refuse to deal with firm B, however, it may still induce the exit of firm B by selling the second component below cost. For example, firm A can sell the first component for c+d, and price the second component below *a*, its incremental unit cost. This tactic obviously violates the Areeda-Turner test, as well as the cost-based price floors proposed in this article. *See* pp. 15-19 *supra*.

Alternatively, firm A may induce the exit of firm B by charging in the open market a discriminatory price for A1 that is slightly below c+d, while setting a lower internal transfer price for A1 and an internal price for A2 equal to *a*. In so doing, firm A can sell a complete system in the market for less than consumers must pay for a system comprised of A1 and B2. The unit production cost of A2 provides a "conservative" estimate for the imputed internal price of A2 because it results in a larger estimate of the imputed price for A1 than would any other figure not below the cost of A2. Then, if this estimate of the imputed price for A1 is smaller than the actual price charged for A1 in the open market, the latter price is discriminatory and has the effect of excluding firm B from the market to the advantage of firm A.

72. There is an alternative source of supply if the rival's components can be utilized in the systems market with components other than those supplied by the defendant firm. These alternatives may be newly developed products, or newly modified versions of products with other uses. All that is

demonstration of other structural conditions in the system market remains necessary. First, the defendant must possess monopoly power over some of the components of the system. Second, entry hurdles into the overall systems market must exist. Third, if there are alternative, inferior sources of supply of the components over which the defendant exercises monopoly power, there must be entry hurdles and reentry barriers into the production of the other components needed to complete a system. Finally, if implicit price discrimination would be profitable, entry hurdles and reentry barriers into the supply of components that would undermine implicit price discrimination must exist. The existence of all of these structural conditions may create a motive for predatory exit inducement.

3. *Predatory Systems Rivalry, Compensatory Pricing of Complementary Components, and the Analysis of Research and Development Investments*

The introduction of a new system is predatory only if it entails a sacrifice of profit given the continued viability of the rival.[73] Because competition in the systems market as a whole protects the interests of consumers, the relevant market for the definition of a rival's viability is the final systems market.[74] Consequently, the continued viability premise implies more than an absence of reentry barriers; even if the productive assets of the rival remain available for production, the rival is not viable in the systems market if compatible components are unavailable.[75] The absence of com-

necessary is that some alternative system would become economical if the dominant firm attempted to raise the prices on its preexisting component to the point where they would extract the total monopoly profit from the systems market. Hence, the alternative will not always be identifiable by the uses to which it is presently put, because the dominant firm will have incentives to maintain its prices below the point at which it becomes economical. For example, in *Telex*, the court noted that Telex's peripherals *could* be made compatible with Burroughs' CPU's, even though this was not the economic choice in view of the pricing policy of IBM. Telex Corp. v. IBM, 510 F.2d 894, 916 (10th Cir. 1975), *cert. dismissed*, 423 U.S. 802 (1975).

73. *See* note 75 *infra* (meaning of viability in context of systems rivalry).

74. Concededly, the systems market is not always the relevant market. For example, after a durable product is purchased by consumers, there may be a distinct market for replacement parts or for accessories compatible with the product. For consumers who are not locked-in to a particular system, however, the systems market is the appropriate market for antitrust scrutiny.

Similarly, if consumers underestimate their need for a system component, they will place too little weight on its price in choosing which system to purchase. Hence, in addition to competition in the systems market, competition in the supply of that component is necessary. With correctly informed consumers, however, the relevant market again is the systems market.

75. One could define viability narrowly in terms of the rival's ability to offer components that are compatible with the new system, rather than in terms of the rival's ability to compete in the systems market. This pro-rival conception of viability, however, suffers from irresolvable difficulties. In many instances, the rival's preexisting components may be technologically incompatible with the new system, and the narrower definition of viability would imply that the rival has access to the innovative designs embodied in the new system. Such access could unduly constrict the temporary quasi-monopoly profits available to the innovator, however and thereby chill socially beneficial innovation. That is, for an innovating firm to recoup its initial outlay on R&D, it must be assured some respite from

patible components implies that: the defendant refuses to sell the components at compensatory prices; there are no existing alternative suppliers of compatible components; there are barriers that prevent the entry of an alternative supplier; and the rival is unable to produce, quickly and at sufficiently low cost, components that are compatible with the new system.

Profit sacrifice is present if there exists an alternative action, less damaging to the rival, that yields to the incumbent a higher level of profit under the continued viability premise. If the rival is a manufacturer of complementary products, the less damaging alternative action involves prices that are *lower* than the actual prices of the necessary complementary components. The repricing or withdrawal policy of the innovator exhibits profit sacrifice if a lower price is feasible[76] and yields no less profit on the premise of the continued viability of the rival.

A lower price on the preexisting component has four distinct effects on the profits of the innovator. First, it increases profit by the markups on the additional sales of the preexisting component, and by the markups on the innovator's additional sales of complementary products. Second, it reduces profit from sales of the preexisting component that would have been made at the higher price. Third, it reduces profit by the markups on the diverted sales of the new components. Fourth, because a lower price on the preexisting component is less likely to induce the rival's exit, it reduces the future profits of the innovator by diminishing his future monopoly power (if any) in the systems market.

This fourth effect may provide a motive to induce exit by the introduction of new components and the repricing of old components. This effect on profit, however, is eliminated under the premise of the continued viability of the rival in the systems market.[77] Thus, the test for predatory profit sacrifice should disregard profits that are only possible as a result of the actual exclusion of the rival.[78]

imitation—an "imitation lag." If the imitation lag shrinks to zero, rivals can generally undersell the innovator and still make a positive incremental profit because their expenditures on imitative R&D are generally lower than the R&D expenditures of the innovator. To cope with this problem, a court would have to determine the socially optimal duration of the imitation lag for each new system, and would have to decide whether the innovating firm has unduly lengthened the imitation lag. Such findings would inevitably contain substantial errors; prospective innovators might reduce their investments in R&D in fear of such errors, thereby stifling the innovative process.

76. If the costs of providing the preexisting components are prohibitive, the compensatory price will be prohibitive. This may occur if the production of the old components renders the production of the new components physically impossible, or vice-versa.

77. In making the profit assessment, data that pertain to the period following the introduction of the innovation but preceding the actual exclusion of the rival are the most useful. When the attribution of incremental profits to various components is ambiguous due to data limitations, conservative methods should be chosen so as to bias the scrutiny of profit sacrifice in favor of the innovator. A useful rule of thumb may be to exclude from consideration any loss of profits on the part of the innovator from new line components that substitute for the rival's components.

78. Similar analysis applies in the context of predatory pricing. For example, a price below cost

Predatory Product Innovation

a. *Compensatory Prices*

The *compensatory* price for a preexisting component is the lowest price that would compensate the innovator for making the component available, under the continued viability premise. Thus, an innovator who substantially damages rivals by refusing to sell preexisting components, rather than selling them at compensatory prices, is sacrificing profit under the proposed standard. Although the innovator may set a price above the compensatory level if such a price yields an even higher profit contingent on the rival's viability, prices higher than the compensatory level may entail predatory profit sacrifice.

For example, if sales of the old component divert sales of the new component on a one-to-one basis, and if sales of the old component have no other effects on the innovator's profits, then the compensatory price contains a markup over cost exactly equal to the markup over cost on the new-line component. In this simple case, the one-to-one diversion of sales occurs if the price differential between a system comprised of new components and a system comprised of old components exceeds consumers' evaluation of the quality differential between the two systems. Predatory profit sacrifice is present if the rival must exit because the incumbent sets a price above the compensatory level, and if the rival or its customers would purchase the preexisting component at a lower but supra-compensatory price. By the definition of a compensatory price, a lower price above the compensatory level would increase the profits of the innovator under the continued viability premise, because the markup on the additional sales of the preexisting component would exceed the markup on the diverted sales of the new-line component.[79]

The following model of a market with an inferior source of supply[80] illustrates the calculation of the compensatory price under these assumptions. Figure 5 provides the structure of this hypothetical market. The symbols A1′ and A2′ denote the components of the new system introduced by the dominant firm A. The associated unit costs are c′ and a′, and con-

may be defended as a promotional device. *Cf.* M. PORTER, INTERBRAND CHOICE, STRATEGY AND BILATERAL MARKET POWER (1976) (extensive up-to-date discussion of promotional strategies). If future sales are complementary to current sales, a low or even negative markup on current sales may be justified by higher future revenues. When complementarity exists, however, the future markups used to assess profit sacrifice should reflect the assumed viability of the rival; otherwise, predation would be logically impossible.

79. If the diversion of sales is not one-to-one, or the sales of the old component have other effects on the innovator's profits, then the equal markup rule for compensatory pricing must be modified. For example, if the sale of one preexisting component diverts the sale of more than one new-line component, the compensatory markup must equal the sum of the markups on those diverted sales. In general, the compensatory price must reflect all three of the effects that the post-innovation price of old-line components has on the innovator's profits under the continued viability premise. *See* p. 42 *supra*.

80. *See* pp. 38-41 *supra*.

sumers' willingness-to-pay for the new system is b′. As indicated, the new components are incompatible with the old components of all three manufacturers. Nothing is assumed at this point about the technological or economic superiority of the new system.

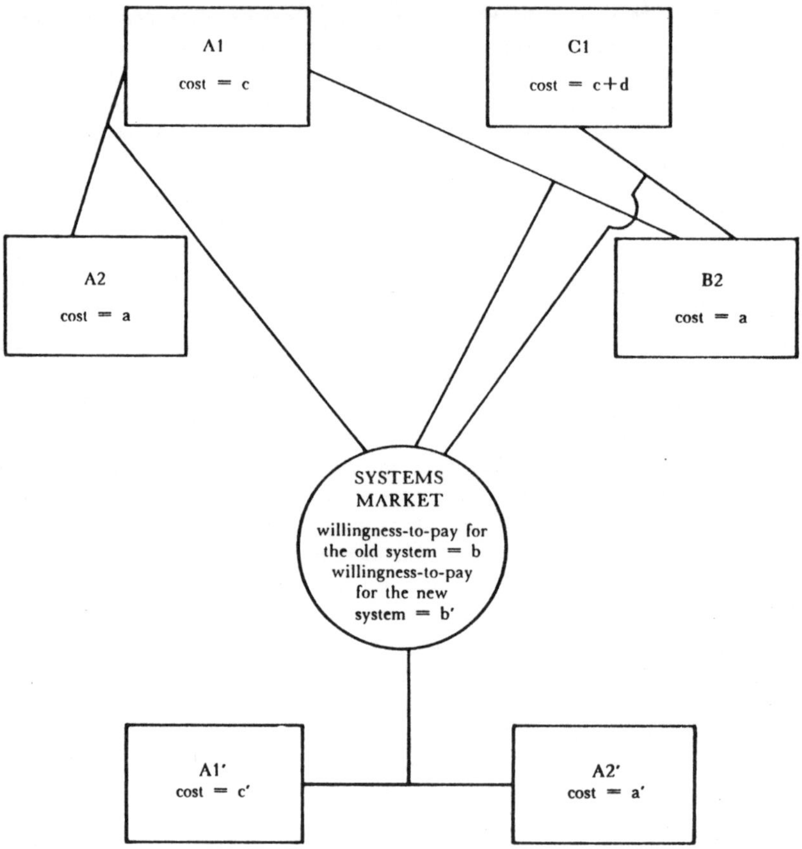

Figure 5

In this scenario, firm A can induce the exit of firm B with the following two-part tactic: First, firm A sets the price of A1 at a level denoted by *p*. Second, firm A offers the new system, composed of A1′ and A2′, at a price p'_s that is low enough to induce all consumers to choose the new system over the preexisting system comprised of A1 and B2, sold at a price of p+a, and over the preexisting system comprised of C1 and B2, even if that system is sold at its cost of c+d+a. Thus, p'_s is set such that b'-p'_s, the consumer surplus[81] from the new system, is greater than both b - (p+a) and b - (c+d+a), which represent the consumer surplus from the systems comprised of A1 and B2, and C1 and B2, respectively. As a consequence, the sales of component B2 fall to zero, and the viability of firm B is threatened. As noted above, firm A's motive for exit inducement in this scenario may be the additional monopoly profit attendant on the irreversible exit of firm B.

To determine whether predatory profit sacrifice has occurred, one must inquire whether a price for A1 lower than *p*, the price actually charged, would be less damaging to firm B and would increase the profit of firm A given the continued viability of firm B. Due to the presence in the market of the component C1, firm B is viable[82] until the dispersal of its productive assets. Thus, the test for profit sacrifice can utilize data from the time period between the introduction of the new system and the exit of firm B.

During this period, a price for component A1 that induces the exit of firm B eliminates sales of both B2 and A1. Hence, if a lower price for A1 would stimulate sales of A1 at a markup greater than the markup on the diverted sales of the new system, the actual price of A1 entails predatory profit sacrifice.

The price of A1 that compensates firm A for lost sales of the new system, the *compensatory price*, can be calculated as follows:[83] The profit on the sale of each new system is p'_s-a'-c'. If each sale of A1 displaces the sale of one new system, then the compensatory price must provide firm A with a profit per unit just equal to the lost profit on a new system. Thus, because the cost of A1 is *c*, the compensatory price is c+p'_s-a'-c'. Firm A is guilty of predatory profit sacrifice if it refuses to reduce the price of A1 to this compensatory level, and maintains instead a higher actual price, thereby choking off all sales of A1.

Of course, the compensatory price for A1 may be above its actual price of *p*. A price for A1 that induces the exit of firm B, however, can be less than or equal to the compensatory price if and only if the new system is economically superior to the old system, without consideration (yet) of the R&D costs for the new system.[84] Thus, in this model of systems rivalry,

81. Consumer surplus is equal to the difference between the maximum amount that a consumer will pay for a given quantity of a good and the amount actually paid for that quantity of the good. *See* Willig, *Consumer's Surplus Without Apology,* 66 AM. ECON. REV. 589 (1976).

82. *See* pp. 41-42 *supra*.

83. Alternatively, the compensatory price can be calculated as the price that yields the same markup on A1 as the markup on the parallel new component, A1', when the latter markup is calculated conservatively. *See* note 77 *supra*. Both calculations yield the same result.

84. Specifically, one can find values of p and p'_s such that (i) b-(p+a) $<$ b'-p'_s; (ii) b-(c+d+a) $<$ b'-p'_s; and (iii) p$<$c+p'_s-a'-c', if and only if b'-(c'+a') $>$ b-(c+a). Condition (i) is that consumers prefer the new system to A1 and B2, when B2 is priced at cost; (ii) is that consumers prefer the new system to C1 and B2, when they are both priced at cost; and (iii) is that the price of A1 does

the compensatory price test protects social welfare.

To establish this proposition, assume first that b'-(c'+a'), the net social benefit from the production and consumption of a new system (exclusive of initial R&D outlays), exceeds b-(c+a), the corresponding net social benefit from the old system. Then, firm A can induce the exit of firm B by setting p'_s just below (b'-b)+(c+d+a), while setting p at the corresponding compensatory level just below (b'-(c'+a'))-(b-(c+a))+(c+d).[85] These exit-inducing prices have the following interpretation: the new system price, p'_s, is just below the cost of producing a system comprised of components manufactured by A's rivals, (c+d+a), plus consumers' evaluation of the quality advantage of the new system over the old system, (b'-b). Thus (b'-b)+(c+d+a) is the maximum amount that consumers are willing to pay for the new system *if* the rivals of firm A, firms B and C, are viable competitors in the systems market. The corresponding compensatory price for A1 is equal to the difference between the maximum profit that can be earned on the sale of a new system, (b'-(c'+a')), and the maximum profit on the sale of an old system, (b-(c+a)), plus the cost of the inferior supplier, (c+d). Note that (b'-(c'+a')) and (b-(c+a)) also represent the net social benefits, exclusive of R&D costs, from a new and an old system, respectively, and that c+d is the maximum price that firm A can charge for A1 in the face of competition from C1. Thus, the compensatory price yields to firm A the maximum possible price for A1 given the viability of firm C, (c+d), plus a profit increment equal to the difference in potential profitability between a sale of the new system and a sale of the old system. If that profit increment is positive, as postulated above, the compensatory price is above (c+d).

At these prices for A1 and for the new system, firm B cannot sell B2 at any price at or above production cost, because the consumer's surplus from the C1, B2 system offered at cost, b-(c+d+a), is just below the consumer's surplus from the new system, b'-p'_s. Moreover, because the actual price for A1, *p*, (through compensatory) is above (c+d), consumers prefer C1 offered at (c+d) to A1 offered at *p*. Thus, firm A can induce the exit of firm B without violating the compensatory price test.

not exceed its compensatory level. The relationship b'-(c'+a') > b-(c+a) implies that the net social benefit from the production and consumption of a new system exceeds that from the old system. The truth of this proposition can be established by straightforward algebra.

85. Firm A earns a profit of p'_s - (a'+c') on each sale of the new system. Given the hypothesized value of p'_s, the profit on such a sale is (b'-b+c+d+a) - (a'+c'). Firm A loses one sale of a new system for every consumer purchase of an old system comprised of one unit of B2 or A2 and one unit of A1. Consequently, in the absence of anticompetitive objectives, firm A willingly would sell A1 at a markup at least equal to the profit lost on a diverted sale of the new system. If *p* is the price of A1, then firm A earns a profit of p-c on each sale of A1. Hence, if *p* is set compensatorily, p-c will equal (b'-b+c+d+a) -(a'+c'). From this equality, the compensatory level of *p* can be calculated as (b'-(a'+c')) - (b-(a+c)) + (c+d), as stated in the text.

Predatory Product Innovation

Now assume that the old system is economically superior to the new system, even without accounting for the R&D costs of the new system, so that b-(c+a) exceeds b'-(c'+a'). Then, firm A cannot induce firm B's exit without violating the compensatory price test. Suppose first that firm A sets the price of A1, *p* above c+d, so that C1, sold at cost, is preferred to A1. To induce all consumers to purchase the new system rather than the system comprised of C1 and B2, firm A must then set p'_s such that b'-p'_s exceeds b-(c+d+a)—that is, such that the consumer surplus from a new system exceeds the consumer surplus from an old system comprised of C1 and B2. Therefore, p'_s must be less than b'-b+c+d+a, which is the maximum amount that consumers are willing to pay for the new system if the old system is sold at cost. Consequently, the corresponding compensatory price of A1, p'_s-a'-c'+c, must be less than (b'-b+c+d+a) -a'-c'+c. The latter expression is equivalent to (c+d) + (b'-a'-c') - (b-a-c), which is less than (c+d) under the hypothesis that (b-a-c) exceeds (b'-a'-c'). Hence, the compensatory price of A1 is less than c+d, and because (by hypothesis) the actual price, *p*, is above c+d, the actual price of A1 exceeds the compensatory price. Thus, if firm A sets *p* above (c+d), and sets p'_s to divert all sales from the economically superior old system, the price of A1, *p*, fails the compensatory price test.

Suppose instead that firm A sets *p* below c+d, so that the systems comprised of A1 and B2 or A1 and A2 are the consumers' best alternatives to the new system. Then, for firm A to drive the demand for B2 to zero, p'_s must be set such that b'-p'_s exceeds b-(p+a)—that is, such that the consumer surplus from a new system exceeds the consumer surplus from an old system comprised of A1 and either A2 or B2. If b'-p'_s exceeds b-(p+a), *p* exceeds p'_s+b-a-b'. But the latter quantity exceeds the compensatory price for A1, p'_s-a'-c'+c, by (b-c-a)-(b'-c'-a'), which (by hypothesis) is positive. Hence, if firm A sets *p* below (c+d) and sets p'_s in order to divert all sales from the economically superior old system, the price of A1 again fails the compensatory price test.

In summary, firm A can set prices such that: all consumers prefer the new system to the old; firm B is driven from the market; and the price of A1 satisfies the compensatory price test, if and only if the displacement of the old system by the new system is socially beneficial, treating R&D costs for the new system as sunk costs that cannot be recovered.

b. *Research and Development Costs*

The second part of the test for predatory profit sacrifice examines the motive for the R&D investment in the new system. The proposed general standard implies that R&D expenses are not predatory if they are less than the anticipated additional net revenues made possible by the innovation, given a compensatory price for A1. Assume, in the context of the model above, that b′-(c′+a′) exceeds b-(c+a), so that the induced exit of firm B is consistent with compensatory pricing of A1.

Firm A's net revenues are maximized by the highest level of p'_s that is feasible with the continued viability of firms B and C, i.e., b′-b+c+d+a. The corresponding net revenue per system is (b′-b+c+d+a)-(a′+c′), or (b′-a′-c′)-(b-a-c)+d. Absent the development of the new system, the maximum net revenue available to firm A is *d* per system. Therefore, the incremental net revenue per system attributable to the innovation, under the continued viability premise, is the difference between these two figures—(b′-c′-a′)-(b-c-a).

The test for predatory sacrifice is whether this difference in net revenue per system, as anticipated at the time of the R&D investment decision, is large enough to justify the R&D outlay. If so, then the R&D investment is justified by an innocent profit motive, even though it results in the exit of firm B. If not, however, only predatory objectives can rationalize the R&D expenditures. This test coincides exactly with the test of whether the R&D investment is socially warranted; the social benefits from the displacement of the old system by the new system exceed the costs of the innovation if and only if (b′-c′-a′) - (b-c-a) times the number of systems customers exceeds the R&D expense.[86]

Thus, the proposed tests for compensatory pricing and for the R&D motive conduce to social welfare. They permit socially desirable innova-

86. The results in the text implicitly assume that the production costs of A1 are not changed by the introduction of the new system. If the production costs of A1 change due to the introduction of the new line, however, say from *c* to *e*, the tests remain socially optimal if modified slightly. Specifically, one can show that there exist values of p'_s and p_1 (the new price of A1) such that (i) $p'_s \geqq a'+c'$; (ii) $b'-p'_s \geqq b-(a+c+d)$; (iii) $b'-p'_s \geqq b-(a+p_1)$; and (iv) $p_1-e \geqq p'_s-(a'+c')$ if and only if (v) $b'-(a'+c') \geqq b-(a+e)$ and (vi) $b'-(a'+c') \geqq b-(a+c+d)$. The interpretations of these relationships are as follows: (i) the new system is priced at or above production costs; (ii) the consumer surplus from the new system equals or exceeds that from C1 and B2 sold at cost; (iii) the consumer surplus from the new system equals or exceeds that from A1 and B2; (iv) the markup on A1 relative to its new cost does not exceed that on the new system, so that p_1 is not supra-compensatory; and (v) and (vi) the net social benefits from the consumption and production of the new system equal or exceed those from an old system comprised of either A1 and B2 or C1 and B2, where the relevant cost of A1 is its new level, *e*. Thus, firm A can induce the exit of firm B by diverting all sales to the new system with prices that are compensatory and cover costs, if and only if the new system is socially preferable to the old system, without consideration of R&D costs, and with reference to the new level of production costs for the old system.

One can also show that firm A's profit-maximizing prices, among those that cover production costs, are compensatory, and divert all sales to the new system (that is, which satisfy (i)-(iv) above), yield profits equal to N[(b′-a′-c′) - (b-a-c-d)]-R, where N is the number of system customers. Because the maximum profits from the old system are Nd, the change in the innovator's profits is N[(b′-a′-c′)-(b-a-c)]-R, given compensatory prices not below costs, and the continued viability premise. This quantity is exactly equal to the change in net social benefits attributable to the innovation. Hence, when production costs for the old components are altered by the innovation, the proposed tests for predation promote social welfare if they are augmented by the stipulation that the price of the new system must cover its production costs.

Predatory Product Innovation

tions, whatever their effects on market structure, and they simultaneously restrain socially wasteful innovations whose only motivation is the additional monopoly profits attendant on their anticompetitive effects. For example, if the new system is technologically inferior to the old one, and if its incremental production cost is not substantially lower, then the compensatory price for the old component enables an equally efficient rival to sell the old system at a price that yields consumers greater net benefits than the purchase of a new system. Thus, the predatory and socially wasteful R&D investment in the new system is deterred.

Moreover, the technological superiority of a new system does not preclude a finding of predatory product innovation. Instead, the requisite R&D investment must be scrutinized for the underlying motive by comparing the anticipated costs of the innovation with its anticipated incremental net revenues, calculated on the premise that the rival has continued access to necessary preexisting components. Under this standard, a new system is immune from a finding of predation if and only if the value to consumers of the new system relative to the preexisting system is greater than the required development costs.[87]

C. *An Alternative Test*

Another test for predatory product introduction is applicable in some special circumstances. This test inquires whether an alternative, less exclusionary design of the new product would yield a higher incremental profit to the innovator than the design actually chosen, under the premise of the continued viability of the rival. More often than not, this test is too speculative to be of legal value, but in some instances an alternative design that is less exclusionary, less costly, and no less desirable to consumers may be evident.[88] The decision by a defendant to reject such a design en-

87. Concededly, the optimality properties of the proposed tests have not been formally analyzed in models more general and complex than those developed in the text.

88. In a recent case, the plaintiff urged the court as part of the predation test to incorporate the profits that the innovator sacrificed by selecting the actual product design over an available less exclusionary design. Transamerica Computer Co. v. IBM, 459 F. Supp. 626 (1978). In that case the plaintiff, Transamerica, argued that to test for predatory profit sacrifice it is necessary "to subtract from the profits IBM predicted it would realize on a particular product the estimated profits that might have been realized on a product that could have been produced in its stead." *Id.* at 631. These forgone profits are referred to as *opportunity costs. Id.* Judge Schnacke ruled that the use of the concept of opportunity costs is improper as a matter of law. *Id.*

The analysis in this article suggests that the positions taken by TCC and by Judge Schnacke are both incorrect. In contrast to the rule proposed by Transamerica, our standard implies that the relevant comparison is between the profits the discarded design would have earned under the premise of the continued viability of the innovator's rivals and the profits that the adopted design would have earned under the same premise. And, contrary to Judge Schnacke's ruling, our analysis shows that if the *correctly* calculated opportunity costs are sufficiently large, then the chosen product design may entail predatory profit sacrifice, which is the hallmark of predatory behavior. At the same time, Judge Schnacke correctly recognized that calculation of the profits that would be generated by an alternative

tails a predatory sacrifice of profit.

When applicable, this test also promotes social welfare. Specifically, an exclusionary new design is socially preferable to an alternative design that is compatible with a rival's component, if and only if the former would be more profitable than the latter under the continued viability premise, with preexisting components offered at compensatory prices, and net of R&D costs.[89] Thus, an exclusionary design may be socially optimal even if a less-exclusionary alternative design exists. On the other hand, an exclusionary design may be motivated by the prospect of additional monopoly power attendant on the exit of a rival. Such designs waste social resources and entail a predatory profit sacrifice.

D. *The Burden of Proof*

Although antitrust scrutiny of product innovation *in principle* can promote social welfare,[90] the possibility exists that judicial adoption of the proffered standard might spur excessive, costly litigation over product innovations. In our opinion, however, the danger of excessive litigation is small due to the burden of proof that the standard places on prospective

product design may be highly speculative. For this reason, if a chosen design earns at least a normal rate of profit under the premise of continued viability, it perhaps should be viewed as free of predatory profit sacrifice, unless there is an evident alternative that is less exclusionary and *clearly* more profitable under the viability premise. *See* Berkey Photo, Inc. v. Eastman Kodak Co., 603 F. 2d 263, 288-89 (2d Cir. 1979), *cert. denied*, 100 S. Ct. 1061 (1980); Note, *An Economic and Legal Analysis of Physical Tie-Ins*, 89 YALE L.J. 769, 793-94 n.115 (1980).

89. As shown above, *see* note 85 *supra*, if the preexisting component, A1, is available to the rival at a compensatory price, the maximum profits per system customer that the innovator can earn (gross of R&D costs) from the exclusionary new system are (b'-a'-c') - (b-a-c)+d. This quantity must be compared with the maximum profit that the innovator can earn from an alternative new design that is compatible with the rival's component, B2. Let the consumers' willingness-to-pay for this alternative system equal b'', let the production cost of the alternative monopolized component, A1'', equal c'', and let the R&D costs of this component equal R''. Because A1'' is compatible both with B2 and A2, the introduction of the alternative system would not endanger the viability of firm B, would not require firm A to maintain a compensatory price for A1, and would not affect the competitive price of a for both B2 and A2. The maximum price at which the new system can be sold is p''_s, where $b''-p''_s = b-(c+d+a)$; at a higher price, consumers would derive greater consumer surplus from purchasing the old system, C1 and B2, sold at cost. Thus, $p''_s = b''-b+(c+d+a)$. The corresponding profit on the alternative system is $p''_s-c''-a=(b''-a-c'') - (b-a-c)+d$ per systems customer, less the total R&D costs R''. The innovator can earn all of this profit by selling A1'' for p''_s-a, or by selling bundled systems for p''_s. Consequently, the difference between the innovator's profits from the exclusionary design under the continued viability premise and the innovator's profits from the alternative design is (b'-a'-c') -(b''-a-c'') per systems customer, less the difference in R&D costs, (R-R''). This is precisely equal to the difference between the net social benefits from the consumption, production, and development of the two system designs.

90. In the model that we have analyzed in this article, the *only* possible cause of social inefficiency is predatory behavior. We conjecture that this implicit assumption enables our proposed tests to achieve social optimality. In fact, however, there are other causes of social inefficiency aside from predation. *See* note 57 *supra* (discussing other reasons why profitable product introductions may be socially inefficient). We would not be surprised or disillusioned to discover that our proposed tests may sometimes ameliorate and may sometimes exacerbate the social inefficiency caused by other imperfections in market performance.

plaintiffs.

First, the standard narrowly limits the circumstances in which the *behavior* of an innovating firm is to be examined. Moreover, because innovation is generally beneficial, the plaintiff should carry the burden of establishing the preconditions for the scrutiny of behavior. Thus, under our standard the plaintiff must establish that the defendant possesses monopoly power over certain system components; that there are entry hurdles and reentry barriers into the final systems market and into the production of relevant individual components; and that the rival's exit would substantially weaken competition in the systems market.[91] In addition, the plaintiff must convincingly show that the rival's exit[92] from the systems market is likely,[93] and that the defendant's actions substantially increase the likelihood of exit.

If the plaintiff alleges that the defendant's repricing or withdrawal of complementary components is predatory, the plaintiff must show that the components are in fact vital to the viability of the defendant's rivals. Thus, the components must be shown to be strongly complementary to those of the rivals, and to be the most preferred complements of the rival's offerings (even in relation to alternatives that the rival could produce himself).

If the plaintiff establishes all of the aforementioned facts, he then may argue that the defendant's post-innovation behavior entails predatory profit sacrifice. One way for the plaintiff to succeed in this argument is to demonstrate that the defendant's rival (or his customers) was willing to purchase compatible components at prices that were at least compensatory, but that the defendant was unwilling to sell the components at such prices.[94] Alternatively, if the plaintiff cannot show that the defendant vio-

91. The proposed standard avoids the repression of socially valuable innovations by defining the relevant market as the market for systems, not the market for components that are compatible with those of the alleged predator. The narrower market definition would erroneously suggest that the introduction of a new system may be anticompetitive merely because it creates incompatibilities between the products of the rival and those of the alleged predator. Innovators require temporary, quasi-monopoly profits from new designs to recover R&D investments, *see* app. *infra*, and hence a focus on the creation of incompatibilities is inappropriate.

92. Exit may entail either the dispersal of the rival's productive assets or the unavailability of components that are compatible with the rival's components. *See* pp. 41-42 *supra*.

93. The social costs of litigation under our standard will be smaller, the more demanding are the burden of proof requirements imposed on the plaintiff. The procompetitive benefits from the application of our standard, however, derive from the forestalled exit of socially desirable competitors. We feel that an appropriate balance is struck by requiring a truly dangerous probability of exit; such a requirement would prevent excessive litigation without destroying the standard's efficacy.

94. The requirement that the innovator offer to sell the old components at compensatory prices may appear quite harsh, but in fact the opposite is true. First, even if the monopolist refuses to provide the needed components at compensatory prices, he can nevertheless defend against a charge of predation by showing that his refusal was part of a bargaining strategy designed to secure supra-compensatory prices for the components. For this defense to be credible, the monopolist must demonstrate that he and his rivals engaged in good-faith bargaining over the relevant prices.

Second, the offer to sell at a compensatory price need only be of limited duration. If rivals do not

lated the compensatory price test, he may prove that the R&D investment was anticompetitive, in that it entailed a predatory profit sacrifice. Whichever argument the plaintiff makes, however, he should carry the burden of proof, to discourage socially wasteful litigation, to conserve judicial resources, and to avoid chilling the innovative process.

Conclusion

This article has proposed an economic definition of predation, and has derived from that definition workable tests for predatory price-cutting and product innovation. These tests go beyond existing tests for predation to encompass conduct that has proven troublesome to analyze in the past. The new tests enhance social welfare by deterring exit-inducing anti-competitive conduct, without deterring procompetitive conduct, and without stimulating excessive litigation.

Appendix: Product Preannouncements

Often, to inform consumers about a new product, an innovator preannounces the product before it becomes commercially available. In several recent cases, the innovator's timing of the announcement has been challenged as an anticompetitive tactic.[95]

In at least one instance, a product announcement was alleged to be anticompetitive because it was made substantially ahead of the actual introduction of the new product.[96] In other instances, however, announcements were attacked for precisely the opposite reason—because they were not issued suffficiently ahead of

avail themselves of the option during twelve months, say, the offer can be discontinued without further culpability. Concededly, this rule raises the possiblity that the innovator will set the price of the new system low during the period the offer is in force, only to raise it when the offer expires. For two reasons, however, this danger is not terribly worrisome. First, compensatory prices are linked to the prices of new components—if the latter prices decline, so do the former prices—and hence a temporary reduction in the price of the new system confers a benefit on the rival in terms of a lower compensatory price. Second, if the price of the new system is set low, the price structure may fail the predation test that requires that the R&D investment yield sufficiently large incremental profit.

Finally, the compensatory pricing rule is not unduly burdensome on the innovator because compensatory prices are determined on the basis of current unit costs. These costs include any capital costs that are attributable to the provision of capital equipment; if the capital equipment used to produce the old components is also used to produce the new system, it may be more scarce and congested than prior to the innovation. If so, the compensatory price increases. Also, to assure that capital costs for the production of the old component will be covered, the innovator may require a long-term purchase agreement.

95. Berkey Photo, Inc. v. Eastman Kodak Corp., 603 F.2d 263 (2d Cir. 1979), *cert. denied*, 444 U.S. 1093 (1980); United States v. IBM, No. 69-200 (S.D.N.Y., filed Jan. 12, 1969) (Complaint at 20-21); ILC Periperals Leasing Corp. v. IBM, 458 F. Supp. 423, 436 (N.D. Cal. 1978), *aff'd sub nom.* Memorex Corp. v. IBM, 636 F.2d 1188 (9th Cir. 1980). *See generally* Note, *Berkey Photo, Inc., v. Eastman Kodak Co.: The Predisclosure Requirement—A New Remedy for Predatory Marketing of Product Innovations*, 10 RUT.-CAM. L.J. 395 (1979).

96. *See* U.S. v. IBM, No. 69-200 (S.D.N.Y., filed Jan. 12, 1969)(Complaint at 20-21).

the actual introduction of the new product.[97]

This disparity of views as to the proper timing of announcements portends the difficulty of developing workable tests for the legality of product announcements. Under the standard proposed in this article, the trier of fact would have to determine whether the timing of the announcement would have been different had the innovator assumed the continued viability of the rival.

Although several considerations determine the timing of a product announcement, one possibly anticompetitive consideration is the negative effect that a preannouncement can have on the revenues of a rival. If, as a result of an early announcement, prospective buyers postpone their purchases until the new model becomes commercially available, rivals may experience substantial reductions in their cash flows, and their viability may be endangered. Moreover, if the innovator anticipates that a rival may exit, a product announcement may be advanced for several reasons. If the rival exits before the new product is introduced, some sales are diverted to the preexisting products of the innovator that compete with the rival. To some extent, this gain offsets the loss of sales to consumers who react to the preannouncement of the new product by postponing their purchases. Second, the incremental profit on the new product is increased by the early exit of rivals because some of their sales are diverted to the new offering. Hence, the anticipated exit of rivals may increase the benefits and reduce the costs of early preannouncement, and to this extent, exit inducement may be a motive for early preannouncement.

On the other hand, early preannouncement of an innovation may be procompetitive. If the new product is part of a system, the innovator may wish to provide other firms with the lead time necessary to the production of complementary components. Moreover, even under the continued viability premise, it may be profitable to inform consumers of a forthcoming innovation to encourage them to postpone their purchases. Accurate information of this kind can benefit consumers by promoting better planning and decisionmaking.

Other legitimate considerations, however, justify delay in the timing of a product announcement. Because an innovator requires a temporary "quasi-monopoly" on new products to recoup the costs of R&D, preannouncement may deprive him of the necessary lead time over his competitors. Thus, to require preannouncements may repress socially beneficial innovation.

We conclude, therefore, that any timing of a product preannouncement should be presumed legal. The diversity of considerations that underlie the decision to predisclose the new product make it impossible to fashion an implementable test for anticompetitive product preannouncements. Furthermore, the need for such a test is substantially reduced by a requirement that innovating firms provide their rivals with complementary components at compensatory prices.

97. Berkey Photo, Inc. v. Eastman Kodak Corp., 603 F.2d 263 (2d Cir. 1979), *cert. denied*, 444 U.S. 1093 (1980); ILC Peripherals Leasing Corp. v. IBM, 458 F. Supp. 423, 436 (N.D. Cal. 1978), *aff'd sub nom.* Memorex Corp. v. IBM, 636 F.2d 1188 (9th Cir. 1980).

[16]

PREDATION AND THE LOGIC OF THE AVERAGE VARIABLE COST TEST*

WILLIAM J. BAUMOL
New York University

ABSTRACT

This article explores principles for execution of the widely accepted Areeda-Turner test of predatory pricing. Defining an Areeda-Turner price as one that does not threaten to exclude any more-efficient supplier, I conclude that (1) any individual price that is not below average avoidable cost cannot be predatory; (2) thus, *average avoidable cost,* not *marginal cost,* is crucial in testing predation; (3) sets of prices of different products of the firm can violate the test if the revenues of any *combinations* of the firm's products fall short of the combined avoidable costs of those products; and (4) a firm's failure to maximize its profits during some relatively brief period is not by itself legitimate evidence of predation.

EVER since the appearance in 1975 of the classic Areeda-Turner article, average variable cost (AVC) has played a key role in adjudication of charges of predatory pricing. This is so despite the conclusion by Phillip Areeda and Donald Turner that it is *marginal* cost (MC) rather than any form of average cost that constitutes the defensible borderline between a price that is predatory and one that is not.[1] As in their article, the courts have accepted the view that marginal cost is exceedingly difficult to determine in practice, so that, faute de mieux, one must apologetically accept average variable cost as an imperfect proxy, even though one knows full well that the magnitudes of the two costs can differ substantially.

I have previously suggested that, in taking this position, those authors and their followers had undervalued average variable cost itself as an independent and perfectly legitimate test for the purpose.[2] This article presents what I believe to be even stronger grounds for that position and for the more unorthodox view that some variant of the AVC test is more to the point than one based on marginal cost.

* I am extremely grateful to Holly J. Gregory of Weil, Gotshal and Manges for her very valuable comments. I must also thank the C. V. Starr Center for Applied Economics, New York University, for its support of the preparation of this article.

[1] Phillip Areeda & Donald Turner, Predatory Pricing and Related Practices under Section 2 of the Sherman Act, 88 Harv. L. Rev. 637 (1975).

[2] William J. Baumol, Superfairness: Applications and Theory 126–27 (1986).

[*Journal of Law & Economics*, vol. XXXIX (April 1996)]
 0022-2186/96/3901-0002$01.50

Perhaps the more important objective of this article is to explore the principles that should guide proper execution of the Areeda-Turner test, thereby dealing with a number of issues that have been matters of contention in the courts.[3] Starting from the premise that a proper Areeda-Turner price is one that does not threaten the existence (or at least the presence) of any equally efficient or more efficient supplier, this analysis leads to the following rules: (1) no price that equals or exceeds average avoidable cost can be predatory; (2) "average total cost" is a figure that is undefinable and unmeasurable in a multiproduct firm and must therefore be rejected as part of any legitimate test of predatory pricing; (3) the firm can violate the Areeda-Turner test not only if the price of an individual product is below average variable (avoidable) cost, but also if, at the prices in question, the revenues of any *combinations* of the firm's products fall short of the combined avoidable costs of those products; (4) the time period appropriate for use in an Areeda-Turner test is either the period during which the price at issue actually prevailed or the period during which it could, ex ante, reasonably have been expected to prevail; (5) where the firm practices differential pricing—for example, by negotiating different contract terms with different customers—sales of a product at different prices should be treated as sales of different products and subjected to combinatorial rule 3; (6) a firm's failure to maximize its profits during some relatively brief period is normal and beneficial business practice and is not legitimate evidence of predation; and (7) the average avoidable cost used in the Areeda-Turner test should include any opportunity costs incurred when proprietors of the firm supply inputs to the firm but should not include revenue forgone if the price at issue entails a reduction from some previous price because the previous price is irrelevant for determining whether the price at issue is a threat to the viability of an efficient competitor.

In all this it should be recognized that the problem of determining an

[3] Thus, it is not the purpose of this article to reexamine the issue of predation in general and to review the large body of literature of the subject, encompassing such noteworthy contributions as John S. McGee, Predatory Price Cutting: The Standard Oil (New Jersey) Case, 1 J. Law & Econ. 137 (1958); Lester G. Telser, Economic Theory and the Core (1978); Oliver E. Williamson, Predatory Pricing: A Strategic and Welfare Analysis, 87 Yale L. J. 284 (1977); and Paul L. Joskow & Alvin K. Klevorick, A Framework for Analyzing Predatory Pricing Policy, 89 Yale L. J. 213 (1979). Moreover, this article makes no attempt to follow up on the view I have suggested elsewhere in William J. Baumol, Quasi-Permanence of Price Reductions: A Policy for Prevention of Predatory Pricing, 89 Yale L. J. 1 (1979), that there is much to be said for an intertemporal analysis of the process of predation, considering the sequence of deliberate losses by the predator, the exit of rivals, and the subsequent attempt at recoupment of the earlier losses as a useful basis for rules for the prevention of predatory acts. Here, however, my focus is on the widely adopted Areeda-Turner rule, its logic, and its proper execution.

appropriate lower bound for price, as the Areeda-Turner test of predatory pricing undertakes to do, is very much like the problem of selecting such a price floor as a criterion of cross subsidy. That is why much of the content of this article is apt to remind the reader of the literature on price regulation that clearly has suggested a number of the conclusions offered here.

I. In Praise of Areeda-Turner

Before getting to the substance of my discussion it is important for me to emphasize that nothing said here is intended in any way to undermine or even to criticize the Areeda-Turner test. It is easy, with years of afterthought, to quibble with details of their original argument, and that will occur here. But none of what is said is intended to belittle the authors' accomplishment or to advocate restriction of the use of their standard. In a world in which vigorous competition is all too easily mistaken for predation, and in which firms can unintentionally overstep the line, it is important to provide managers with guidelines as unambiguous as the issue permits, to enable them to tailor their decisions in a way that ensures compliance with the law and minimizes vulnerability to anticompetitive lawsuits intended to handicap vigorous competition. Of course, in the complex world of reality, one cannot hope to formulate a test that does so with perfection, but Areeda-Turner comes as close to success in doing so as could reasonably have been hoped, and more. There seems to be general consensus among informed observers that genuine cases of predation are very rare birds. As Areeda and Turner note, that does not relieve us of the necessity of guarding against those rare occurrences, of taking steps to prevent them and to rectify any damage they produce. But there is a painful trade-off here. Rules that make it excessively easy to secure conviction on charges of predation invite anticompetitive and rent-seeking litigation. Such rules tempt firms that cannot make it in the marketplace by virtue of superior products or greater efficiency and lower costs, to seek success over their more efficient rivals in the courts instead. There they can hope to constrain the vigor of rivalrous acts by competitors and to transmogrify the character of their rivals from energetic enterprise to timidity and hesitance. This can sometimes be accomplished by mere threat of a lawsuit, but if the lawsuit is indeed undertaken and won there is a rich additional bonus awaiting the plaintiff—trebled damages, which, in a total victory, can amount to many years of net earnings by either the plaintiff or the defendant. Long study of the subject has led me to the conclusion that litigation of this sort is a major handicap to the growth and competitiveness of the nation's economy. Thus, I conclude that Areeda and Turner have made a substantial contribution to our economic well-being by helping to reduce ambiguity in the concept of predatory pricing and decreasing the vulnerability of vigorous competitors to lawsuits that threaten to undermine the effectiveness of their competition and their entrepreneurship.

Still, there are a number of instances in which the odor of predation is strong, as when an entrant airline with its six-plane fleet, operating on almost as many routes, proposes to fly a route coveted by a large incumbent airline, whereon the latter announces that it will open for business (for the first time) along each of the most promising of the entrant's routes. Analogous examples in which predatory *pricing* is the issue are also easily imagined. There is reason to provide the entrant in such a scenario effective recourse against overaggressive acts by the large incumbent. Accordingly, the rules for proper execution of an average variable cost test that are described in this article are designed not to offer undue protection to the firm suspected of predatory pricing. Indeed, we will see that some of those rules facilitate the task of the plaintiff, by making clearer what that entity must prove, just as an Areeda-Turner type of rule makes clearer to the firm making a pricing decision what it must do to ensure that its choice of price is free of any taint of predation.

II. Two Possible Roles of Cost Tests of Predatory Pricing

Discussions of the subject can generally be interpreted to imply that there are three necessary conditions that must be satisfied before a price can legitimately be deemed to be predatory. Indeed, one can, perhaps, *define* a price to be predatory if and only if it meets all three of the following conditions. First, the choice of that price must have no legitimate business purpose.[4] Second, that price must threaten the existence or the entry of rivals that are at least as efficient as the firm (call it "firm F") that has adopted the price at issue ("price *P*"). Third, there must be a reasonable prospect of recoupment of at least whatever initial costs to firm F were entailed in the company's adoption of the price in question, that recoupment taking the form of monopoly profits made possible by reduction (as a result of price *P*) in the number of competitors facing F.

[4] In an article in the American Lawyer, Roger Parloff takes issue with my views on legitimate business purpose, saying, "There is, of course, no 'legitimate business purpose' exemption in the antitrust laws" (Roger Parloff, Fare's Fair, 65 Am. Law. (October 1993)). But, then, the laws, so far as I know, also provide no exemption for prices that exceed AVC, yet many courts clearly accept that criterion. Moreover, the courts have, I believe, repeatedly emphasized that normal business acts undertaken in pursuit of profit constitute no violation of the law, even if they *happen* to harm rivals incidentally. But that is just what I mean by legitimate business purpose.

Here, I will not be concerned with the third of these necessary conditions for pricing to be deemed predatory—the prospect of recoupment. Rather, I will focus on the other two necessary conditions, to which I will refer, respectively, as *legitimate business purpose* and *threat to efficient rivals*. I will suggest that the *cost* tests of predatory pricing have generally been interpreted to direct themselves to the first of these two requirements, while, in my view, they throw light far more dependably on the second. If this is granted, I will show that it is to AVC, or one of its close relatives, rather than to MC, that we must turn for guidance.

III. Areeda-Turner and Legitimate Business Purpose

The original Areeda-Turner article never seems to come down squarely on one of the two roles as primary justification for the test. However, one comes away with the distinct impression that legitimate business purpose is a foundation on which the authors propose to rest their argument. This seems implicit in their criterion of predation that rests on the relationship between price and marginal cost where, I note for later discussion, marginal cost (as well as marginal revenue) must, of course, include the present values of the effects of today's decisions on future costs (or revenues). It is implied that a price as low as marginal cost is legitimate business practice because, in equilibrium in a regime of perfect competition (the economist's theoretically ideal—if practically unattainable—state of affairs), the firm will always adopt a price that is equal to marginal cost, and "a higher price would result in a reduction in output and thus deprive some buyers of a commodity for which they were willing to pay the cost of production."[5] At the other extreme, the monopolist will maximize profit by selecting an output at which marginal cost is equal to marginal revenue. Since, as is well known, when the demand curve is downward sloping, as is normally assumed, price will necessarily exceed marginal revenue, that price will always exceed marginal cost as well.[6] And, it may be added, if the demand curve, though downward sloping, is nearly horizontal (a small rise in price reduces quantity demanded substantially) price, marginal revenue and, hence, marginal cost will all very nearly be equal. Thus, even for the monopolist, a normal pricing act will entail $P >$ MC, though possibly by a very small amount. In contrast, "[b]y definition, a firm producing at an output where marginal cost exceeds price is selling at least part of that output at an out-of-pocket loss. It could eliminate that loss by reducing its output."[7] The authors

[5] Areeda & Turner, *supra* note 1, at 702.

[6] *Id.* at 703.

[7] *Id.* at 712.

go on to note, "A monopolist may attempt to justify prices below marginal cost by claiming either that the price is being used for promotional purposes or that he is simply meeting an equally low price of a rival. We conclude, however, that these justifications are either so rarely applicable or of such dubious merit for a monopolist that the presumption of illegality for prices below both marginal and average cost[8] should be conclusive."[9]

To sum up, the argument seems to be that in normal and legitimate business transactions price will at least sometimes exceed marginal cost by only a very small amount but that it will only very rarely fall short of marginal cost in transactions that are clearly legitimate. The inference that seems to be drawn from this is that marginal cost is the knife-edge border between pricing that constitutes legitimate business practice and pricing that can be presumed to constitute acts of predation.

Yet the choice of marginal cost as the borderline between price as legitimate and illegitimate business act is not altogether convincing. It is at once too permissive and excessively demanding. At the one extreme, suppose demand for the product at issue happens to be brisk and that it is clearly profitable for the firm to price 50 percent above MC. Is it then normal and legitimate business practice for the firm to eschew this profit opportunity and select a price that exceeds MC by, say, only 2 percent? Such a decision does not imply that the choice is predatory, but it also does not constitute proof that it constitutes legitimate business practice. In contrast, it is hard to imagine a firm that has never found it expedient or even necessary to sell products for at least a brief period at a price below marginal cost, for reasons ranging from product introduction to distress sales of products that are perishable or subject to obsolescence. Thus, on the one side, we cannot casually accept the unsupported assertion that sales at prices below marginal costs constitute a presumption that the act is without legitimate business purpose. On the other side, we cannot confidently conclude that any sale at a price above marginal cost has a legitimate business purpose.

The problem with use of marginal cost as the criterion for testing legiti-

[8] As I presently show, the concept "average cost" in a multiproduct firm is treacherous nonsense. Because costs that are fixed and common are characteristically substantial, and because they can only be allocated among the firm's different products on a totally arbitrary basis, they have always been subject to manipulation by "creative accounting procedures" and have commonly been used to inhibit competition.

[9] *Id.* at 713. A curious feature of the Areeda-Turner article is its exclusive focus on the two polar cases of monopoly and perfect competition, with little said about anything in between. This is particularly surprising since (hardly by accident) litigation on predatory pricing usually arises in industries composed of a multiplicity of firms whose number can be fairly small.

macy of business purpose is that it simply does not get at the issue. We can define an act by a firm to have a legitimate business purpose if it promises to yield a net addition to the firm's profits over the long run, a profit that does not depend on the exit of any at least equally efficient rivals or on prevention of entry of efficient firms. But there is simply no way in which one can infer from the fact that the firm adopts a price that exceeds MC that this will constitute a net addition to long-run profits relative to what the firm might otherwise have earned, nor can one legitimately conclude that a price that falls short of MC must reduce those profits in the absence of destruction of competitors or entrants. Promotional prices for new products are examples that are real and exceedingly common, and the temporary losses they entail are a feature they share with heavy outlays on innovation, or radical plant modernization and retooling, and a host of other patently legitimate business acts that are prime examples of productive entrepreneurship. Mere comparison of price and marginal cost is simply not very effective in discriminating between legitimate and illegitimate business acts.

IV. Areeda-Turner as Test of Threat to Efficient Rivals

I will argue now that the Areeda-Turner test is entirely defensible as a criterion to determine whether the price at issue constitutes a threat to efficient rivals of firm F. But I will show that for this purpose it is average variable cost or a near relative, rather than marginal cost, that provides the requisite information.

Areeda and Turner do discuss the role of their criterion in helping to distinguish whether efficient rivals are threatened by price *P*. They conclude, quite correctly, that the marginal cost test performs this task imperfectly. They consider "instances where marginal cost is below average cost, a situation that will not occur unless the monopolist possesses 'excess capacity.' Only then will the monopolist's marginal cost price deprive equally efficient rivals, actual or potential, of 'normal' returns on their capital. Although narrowed, the problem remains: the equally efficient rival might be destroyed or dissuaded from entering. . . . Admittedly [this] poses some threat to competition in the long run. . . . However, we see no satisfactory method of eliminating this risk."[10]

There is, however, a method that is satisfactory, and, as a matter of fact, it is the method by which the courts have chosen to carry out the Areeda-Turner test. For there is a well-known principle in elementary economics telling us that a firm will minimize its losses (maximize its

[10] *Id.* at 710–11.

profits) by exiting from a market (using the term in an economic rather than a legal sense) when and only when the total revenue it can obtain by remaining in that market falls short of its total *variable* cost. If that revenue exceeds the firm's variable cost it should nevertheless remain in the market even though by doing so it does not cover its *total* cost. Here, the term "variable cost" is defined to include all *fixed* costs that are not *sunk,* so that they can be escaped if the firm exits from the market.

To see this,[11] we must first examine the relation between cost and the incentive for exit that faces a firm. It will be recalled that costs are defined to be sunk if the firm cannot escape them in the short run, either because of a contract (say, with the landlord or the union) or because it has already signed a contract to buy the item whose cost is sunk (for example, a machine). If the firm stops producing, its revenue will fall to zero. Its short-run variable costs will also fall to zero. But its sunk costs—such as rent—will remain to plague it. If the firm is losing money, it will be better off continuing to operate if the resulting revenues produce *any* surplus above variable costs, thereby making *some* contribution to sunk cost. However, it should be obvious that, if the revenues the firm can earn by remaining in operation fall short of variable costs the shortfall will simply add to the losses resulting from its sunk-cost obligations.

The pertinence of all this for the Areeda-Turner test as a criterion of threat to efficient rivals follows from one more observation. Consider two firms, A and B, that are vying to serve as suppliers of a given quantity, Q, of some good or service. Which of them will be the more efficient supplier of Q? The answer is that it will be the firm for which the supply of Q causes the smallest addition to cost. That addition to cost is what economists call the *incremental cost* of Q. For the moment, let us simply equate AIC (average incremental cost) with average variable cost (a subject to which we will return presently). Then, if $\mathrm{AVC}(Q)_{\mathrm{A}}$ is the average variable cost of Q when produced by firm A, and so on, firm B will be the more efficient supplier of Q if and only if

$$\mathrm{AVC}(Q)_{\mathrm{B}} < \mathrm{AVC}(Q)_{\mathrm{A}}.$$

But, then, if A charges a price P_{A} for Q that at least equals its average variable cost of Q production, then that price cannot possibly drive its efficient competitor B out of business because then

$$P_{\mathrm{A}} > \mathrm{AVC}(Q)_{\mathrm{A}} > \mathrm{AVC}(Q)_{\mathrm{B}}.$$

[11] The next few paragraphs contain material that is obvious to an economist. However, since the point is central to my argument, and because a number of wise and erudite lawyers with whom I have worked have nevertheless wanted the matter explained, I have not excised the material altogether.

For, then, B can charge a price equal to A's or even a little lower, and still cover its own variable cost, which, as we have seen, ensures that exit is not the more profitable alternative for firm B. We obtain the generalized Areeda-Turner result:

RULE 1. Any price above the pertinent average variable cost for the output quantity in question cannot be predatory because it can never cause the exit (prevent the entry) of an efficient, profit-seeking rival.[12]

This rule is still vague in two respects. It has not yet indicated what output quantity is pertinent, and it has not shown what average variable cost is relevant. The latter, for example, entails the proper choice of time period (the pertinent short run) in which to calculate the cost. The output quantity issue is this: is the relevant quantity that of firm F, whose price is under investigation, or is it the output of its complaining rival? Perhaps surprisingly, I argue later that, at least for part of the role of the test, it is the output quantity of the rival that matters.

V. WHICH COST? AVERAGE VARIABLE COST? AVERAGE INCREMENTAL COST? AVERAGE AVOIDABLE COST?

Though average variable cost is the concept that seems to be used universally in carrying out the Areeda-Turner test, that cost is not well defined. It seems to refer to the variable portion of the total cost of production of the entire quantity of a commodity supplied by a firm divided by that output quantity. But this statement is not as clear-cut as it appears. First, it does not make clear what is to be done about outlays that have been called "product-specific fixed costs,"[13] that is, costs that

[12] One can still object that a price that just equals or slightly exceeds the firm's average variable cost can be used to drive out a rival that is marginally less efficient than the incumbent. If the latter then is able to raise its price well above the competitive level, one may have good reason to conclude that the original price was predatory in its consequences. Elsewhere I have recognized the pertinence of such intertemporal pricing patterns and have proposed a criterion of predatory behavior to deal with them (Baumol, *supra* note 3). Such a possibility, however, affects *every* cost test that is designed to determine the borderline between a level of price that is predatory and one that is not. For any price that is above the selected borderline can nevertheless serve to drive out a firm so inefficient that it cannot meet the price set at that level. It seems to me that despite the valid concern raised here, the average variable cost criterion remains a legitimate borderline.

[13] There is considerable confusion in the literature about two pertinent concepts, fixed costs and sunk costs, which are really very different. There are, in fact four types of cost that are relevant here, and they can be defined thus: *fixed costs* are costs that must be incurred in a lump in order for any output at all to be provided, and they do not vary when the magnitude of output changes. These costs are not variable either in the short or the long run. Any cost that is not fixed is defined to be *variable*. A *sunk cost*, however, is a cost that cannot be avoided for some limited period of time, but after that period it becomes *avoidable* or *escapable*. A cost that is fixed may or may not be sunk, and a cost that is sunk may not be fixed. For example, one cannot operate an airline between, say, New York and Milwaukee without investing in at least one airplane, an outlay whose amount

are incurred *exclusively* on behalf of one particular product but whose magnitude is not increased when the output of that product rises.

The economist's concept, average incremental cost, is unambiguous on this subject. The average incremental cost of any given increment in output always includes *any* product-specific outlay (that is, any outlay that does not serve several products in common) that is caused by the output increment in question. It seems clear that, if one is testing whether price P is in some sense compensatory, such incremental costs must be included in the calculation, even if they are fixed in character. But that is not quite the answer we seek. The issue, in terms of the notation of the preceding section, is whether P_A, the price charged by firm A, can drive an efficient firm, B, out of the field of endeavor. The pertinent cost here is what may be thought of as the decremental rather than the incremental cost to firm B if it decides to exit. That is, the issue is the cost that B can *escape* or *avoid* by leaving. Thus P_A will not be able to drive firm B from the production of X (or some portion of the production of X) if it exceeds AAC_B, firm B's average avoidable cost (AAC) incurred in producing the pertinent increment of X (in the discussion that follows, the terms "avoidable cost" and "escapable cost" will be used interchangeably).

Now, it will generally be true that AAC $\leq$ AIC for any given quantity of output. That is, when expanding output X by a given increment, it is necessary to incur some sunk outlays (that are typically quite substantial and) that cannot entirely be escaped or avoided except in the very long run. So AIC includes those sunk outlays, but AAC does not. Thus, a price that exceeds the average incremental cost of some output can confidently be expected to exceed its average avoidable cost. Thus we arrive at:

RULE 2. The proper AVC figure to be used in the Areeda-Turner test to determine whether some price constitutes a threat to an efficient rival is the average avoidable cost of the pertinent output increment (decrement). If the average incremental cost is used instead, and the price nevertheless passes the test, one can be confident that the price is not predatory, because in general AIC $\geq$ AAC. The AAC figure must, how-

does not vary with number of passengers until capacity is reached. Thus, this cost is fixed, and does not become variable even in the long run, because one cannot run an airline on the route with zero airplanes. In contrast, this cost is not sunk because, if traffic between New York and Milwaukee declines drastically, the plane can be shifted to serve another route. A large factory with a 10-year useful life, however, constitutes a cost that is sunk for that period, but it need not be fixed because at the end of 10 years it may be desirable to produce less than before, using a smaller factory whose investment cost is lower. The distinction is not mere semantics—the two types of cost have very different implications for market performance and economic efficiency.

ever, include all pertinent portions of the product-specific fixed but avoidable costs, that is, all portions of such costs that can be escaped in the pertinent period of time.

VI. Digression: Nonexistence of Average Total Cost in Multiproduct Firms

Since the concept of "average total cost" (ATC) intrudes so often in discussions of predation, it is worth noting briefly that in the case of a multiproduct firm it violates all economic logic. Outside a textbook, there probably exists no such thing as a single-product firm, and all multiproduct firms have fixed costs incurred in common on behalf of two or more of their products. There is, however, no economically defensible way of dividing such costs up among the firm's various products. As is well known, all methods for the allocation of common fixed costs are arbitrary.

Before the courts or regulatory agencies, ATC (fully allocated costs) are always manipulated to produce whatever answers are desired by the party that puts them forward. Moreover, as I show elsewhere,[14] the amounts by which these contrived cost figures can easily be manipulated is enormous. Thus, though to economists it may seem obvious, for practitioners in the antitrust arena it is hardly redundant to suggest:

Rule 3. Any conclusion about the predatory character of a price that is based on a calculation of average total cost must be disregarded. The ATC numbers can offer absolutely no substantive economic information, and they are apt to constitute an invitation to anticompetitive action.

VII. Product Combinations and the AVC Test

How, then, should fixed and common costs be dealt with? Are the fuel bill and the pilot's salary simply to be ignored in a test to determine whether air fares are predatory? Surely, those costs are avoidable. By canceling a flight the fuel expenditure can be avoided and perhaps also the salary of the pilot. Economists have, indeed, worked out a rigorously defensible way to take them into account. To make the procedure clear one must begin the explanation, as it were, one step earlier. We must start off with the incremental cost (or the avoidable cost) of the individual services supplied by the airline—in this case, the two services: first-class transportation and economy transportation. The point is that for *neither*

[14] See William J. Baumol, Michael F. Koehn, & Robert D. Willig, How Arbitrary Is Arbitrary?—or, Toward the Deserved Demise of Full Cost Allocation, 120 Pub. Util. Fortnightly 16 (September 3, 1987).

of these services does the incremental cost or the avoidable cost include any of the pilot's income or any (substantial) part of the fuel bill. If the airplane is to fly in order to transport the economy passengers, it adds little or nothing to either of those costs to fly the first-class passengers as well. The same argument holds for the incremental (avoidable) cost of flying the economy passengers. Thus, none of the common fixed cost enters the incremental cost of any *one* individual service.

However, matters are quite different if we consider the cost of the two services together, which, it will be remembered, are assumed to constitute the full set of services offered by our hypothetical airline. The incremental cost of transporting both first-class and economy passengers combined clearly includes both pilot compensation and fuel outlay on the flight, and much of that combined cost could be avoided if the airline chose not to serve first-class and economy passengers alike, and simply canceled the flight. Thus, these common fixed costs must be included in their entirety in the incremental cost of the *combination* of the two airline services, and whatever portion of those costs is escapable in the pertinent period must be included in the avoidable cost of the service combination.

It is easy to see now that the price of first-class service can exceed its average avoidable cost, and the same can be true for the economy fare, yet the two together may fail to cover their combined avoidable cost. A numerical example will make that clear. Suppose that the incremental food, ticketing, and other avoidable costs for the trip in question is $50 for each of the 200 economy passengers and $80 for each of the 40 first-class passengers, and that the escapable portion of the fuel and pilot costs amount to $15,000. Then an economy fare of $60 and a first-class fare of $100 will clearly cover their average incremental (avoidable) costs, which are $50 and $80, respectively. But at those prices the total incremental revenue yielded by the flight is 200 × $60 + 40 × $100 = $16,000, and hardly covers the total escapable cost whose amount is 200 × $50 + 40 × $80 + $15,000 = $28,200. For the individual fares together do not contribute enough to cover the common escapable costs.

The implication of all this is the following. The price of an individual product may fail what we may call the *generalized Areeda-Turner test* if it does not cover the average avoidable cost of that product alone. But it can also fail the test if the incremental revenues provided by that service together with that of any subset of the company's other services are insufficient in total to cover the avoidable costs of that combination of services. Thus, a firm that supplies, say, five different services can fail the test on the basis of the price of some individual service, or because it fails the corresponding test for any pair of the firm's services, or because it does so for any triad of the firm's services, and so on.

Of course, it is totally impractical, and an unreasonable burden, for a defendant to be required to supply an estimate of the avoidable cost for each and every combination of such services. Indeed, such a requirement would invite anticompetitive "fishing expeditions" by prospective plaintiffs. However, this combinatorial feature of the generalized Areeda-Turner test does offer that plaintiff a very legitimate advantage. As is done in regulatory arenas that use such combinatorial criteria to determine whether prices are compensatory, the plaintiff is required to specify, *in advance,* what service or what one combination of services he believes to have predatory prices, and the plaintiff and defendant alike are expected to provide avoidable cost information about the one service or the one combination of services that has been deemed predatory in the complaint. Sometimes this test can, in practice, be extended to encompass several services or service combinations, but that set is always required to be small, and the procedure is, consequently, entirely manageable, as experience in regulation has demonstrated. This leads to:

RULE 4. The proper Areeda-Turner test to determine whether a firm's prices constitute a threat to an efficient rival must extend to combinations of the firm's products. The price of each product by itself must equal or exceed that item's average avoidable cost. Moreover, any combination of the firm's products must be priced so as to yield an incremental revenue that exceeds the avoidable cost incurred by that combination of products. In practice, a plaintiff should be required to specify in advance what products or product combinations it has reason to believe will fail this criterion, and litigation should take into consideration only the avoidable costs of the preselected products or product combinations.

VIII. SEQUENCES OF TIME PERIODS AND THE AREEDA-TURNER TEST

Just as the generalized Areeda-Turner test must logically be extendible to combinations of products, it must also be extendible to sequences of time periods. The issue arises because the magnitude of avoidable cost for a product or combination of products varies with the time period under consideration. Generally, the longer the pertinent time period, the greater the total avoidable cost and average avoidable cost figures will be. The reason is that as time passes, the larger the set of costs that were formerly sunk now become escapable. A firm may have signed a 2-year lease for a building, for example. At the end of the 2-year period, if the firm wants to remain in production, it will have to continue the rent payments. But only then, if it decides to cease production, can it escape those outlays altogether. Similarly, as time passes the firm has more of an opportunity to sell or lease redundant equipment, thus avoiding part of the cost which it cannot escape in a shorter period.

Since the longer the period considered, the higher we can expect avoidable cost to be, in a predation case we can expect the plaintiffs to press for a long period as the time interval suitable for the cost calculation, while the defendant can be relied on to argue for a brief period. The choice, however, is not arbitrary, and the principle for its selection follows unambiguously from the use of the Areeda-Turner criterion to determine whether a price or a combination of prices is a threat to an efficient rival. The answer, simply, is that, if the price at issue is in force for, say, 3 months, the period pertinent to the cost calculation is 3 months. For if that price alone is to drive a competitor from the arena, it then has just 3 months in which to do so. And on the principle explained in an earlier section, it will be capable of driving a rival from the field only if that price is less than the per-unit cost that a rival can escape in that period—it is the average avoidable cost calculated for a 3-month horizon. Logic permits no other answer.

However, that is not the end of the story. Suppose that the defendant adopted a $50 price for 3 months, a $52 price for the following 2 months, and a $47 price for the 5 months following that. Suppose, moreover, that the three prices in combination are claimed to be predatory, on the hypothesis that no one of them or no pair of them could have driven out an efficient rival but that, by persistently proffering such a sequence of low prices, the rival allegedly could be forced from the arena. This is clearly a tenable hypothesis that can justify examination on its merits. And this can be done in a manner analogous with the procedure for combinations of outputs. That is, one must compare the incremental revenue provided by the sales that occurred at those prices to the firm that charged them, with the costs escapable over the entire period during which the prices prevailed. That is, one should compare the discounted present value of the incremental revenues with the discounted present value of the costs that could have been escaped, taking each such cost avoided to occur at the date at which the escape could reasonably be expected to occur. We then have:

RULE 5. The time horizon pertinent for the calculation of the AAC for an Areeda-Turner test is the time period over which the price in question prevailed or could reasonably have been expected to prevail. Where a sequence of prices is alleged to be predatory in combination the pertinent horizon is the end of all the time periods during which those prices prevailed, and the test should require that the present value of the incremental revenues for this extended period equal or exceed the present value of the avoidable costs. Once again, it should be the obligation of the plaintiff to specify in advance what pertinent time period or sequence of time periods it is challenging.

IX. The Size of the Pertinent Increment (Decrement) under Differential Pricing

Up to this point I have spoken of a comparison of *the* (unique) price of the product in question with the average avoidable cost entailed in continued production of that good or service. In practice, however, firms often do not charge the same price for a given product to all customers. For example, if the product serves primarily as an input to the production processes of a number of large business customers, each of the buyers may negotiate its own contract, with its purchase price dependent on the outcome of the negotiations and possibly quite different from the prices paid by other purchaser firms. This is said to entail *differential pricing*. It is also referred to as "price discrimination." Because differential pricing is so widespread in industries with scale economies, and arises so often in regulatory arenas, in the next section I will digress once more to see why such differential pricing may be necessary for the achievement of economic efficiency. That is, the discussion in the next section will show why one cannot solve simply by prohibition of differential pricing any special problems related to predatory pricing that may arise because differential prices are present. Here, however, we will simply recognize the existence of such prices and see what they imply for the choice of output increment to be used in the calculation of AAC for use in the Areeda-Turner test.

To illustrate the point, suppose that the firm sells 7,000 units of commodity X at a price of \$500 and that, in addition, it sells 3,000 units of the same good at a price of \$375. What price, or what incremental revenue, is appropriately to be compared with what avoidable cost? The answer, in brief, is that the two sales should be treated as the sales of two different commodities sold by the same firm. That is, the appropriate rule for the generalized Areeda-Turner test for this case is rule 4 above. Thus, the \$500 sale of 7,000 units of X must cover its own avoidable cost, and the same must be true of the sales at the \$375 price. In addition, the combined sales must provide enough incremental revenue to cover their combined incremental costs. The reason is straightforward. Consider an efficient rival that is competing for one or both of our firm's customer groups. Since, by definition of efficiency, that rival firm must have avoidable cost no higher than our firm's, it follows that, if the prices at issue pass the generalized Areeda-Turner test procedure just described, that rival cannot be driven out of the competition for either customer group or from competition for their combined purchases.

Here a confusion can easily arise. If there are scale economies in the production of X, a rival that seeks to compete only, say, for the business of the \$500 customers will find itself at a cost disadvantage because it seeks to produce only the 3,000 units demanded by those customers at that price, while our firm produces the 10,000 units demanded by the two customer groups together. But this simply means that the rival is *not* an efficient supplier of the 3,000 units of product by themselves. The issue for customers is which of the two sellers can provide them with good *X* more cheaply, regardless of the reason that explains why one firm happens to produce at a lower cost than the other. Superior efficiency may be attributable to harder work or greater ability, but it may also result from luck (for example, one of the firms happened to pick what later turned out to be a better location, say, one closer to a superhighway entrance that had not been constructed or even planned when the site was chosen). Similarly, large scale (or, sometimes, small scale) can give one of the firms a cost advantage. But all of that is immaterial to customers—they simply want the lower-priced supplier regardless of whether its efficiency was achieved by merit or happenstance, and the market mechanism parcels out its rewards accordingly. We obtain:

RULE 6. Where differential pricing is practiced, the generalized Areeda-Turner test should be carried out in accord with rule 4, treating sales of a given product at different prices as sales of different commodities supplied by the same firm.

Before leaving the subject of the pertinent increment (decrement) to be considered in the Areeda-Turner test, I note that one additional observation is appropriate, this time for the case where differential pricing is not practiced. The point to be made now is offered for analytical completeness, though in practice it will probably prove wise to disregard it. Consider a case in which the defendant, firm D, is producing 8,000 units of good *X*, while the plaintiff, firm P, is producing only 2,500 units. The efficiency issue entailed in the possibility that the plaintiff will be forced to exit is whether the public is better off if the 2,500-unit output continues to be produced by firm P or if that production is taken over by D. Obviously, the public will be better off when P stays in the business if P has the lower incremental cost of producing 2,500 units. Moreover, if the same is true of avoidable costs, a price by D that covers its own incremental or avoidable costs of producing the 2,500 units cannot threaten the existence of firm P. The point to be noted here is that the avoidable cost to be considered in the test is that of the defendant and that is the cost that has usually been examined in practice in carrying out the Areeda-Turner test. But the output quantity in question is not the 8,000-unit output of the defendant, *but the 2,500 unit output quantity of the plaintiff.*[15] The reason for this rather surprising observation is that the pertinent

[15] That is, the pertinent cost is the defendant's avoidable cost entailed in producing the 2,500 units after they are, hypothetically, added to its initial 8,000-unit output.

issue for the public interest here is who is the more efficient producer of the plaintiff's output because the choice of producer of the defendant's output is simply not at issue. Yet, as has been noted, this observation is probably only of theoretical interest. In practice, it will probably not be easy to determine the incremental or avoidable cost that would be incurred by the defendant if it were, hypothetically, to take over the production of the plaintiff, in addition to its own. Moreover, unless there are very sharp scale economies or sharp diseconomies in the production of the good at issue, the cost figure will not be affected much by the choice between the output quantities of the two firms as the increment in output to be used in the calculation. In any event, if average variable cost is being used to determine, not whether a particular price by firm Y is a threat to its competitor, but to investigate whether it is compensatory to Y and, hence, a legitimate business decision, then it is clear that it is the output of Y, and not that of a rival, that is pertinent.

X. Digression: Differential Pricing and Economic Efficiency

Let us pause to see now why it is not in the public interest to rule out differential pricing altogether. For simplicity, the discussion of this section will deal with the imaginary case of single-product firms. I will show that a role arises for differential (that is, discriminatory) prices if, as is widely considered to be the normal case, the firm's average cost[16] curve is U-shaped. Figure 1 represents a case of two-firm production (by firms 1 and 2) with a U-shaped AC curve for each of the firms. The graph is a bit unusual in that the horizontal axis does not measure physical output but instead measures the share of total industry output that accrues to each firm. For example, the 60 percent point on the x-axis means that at that point firm 1 produces 60 percent of total industry output, so that firm 2 produces the remainder, 40 percent, of that output. At the left end of the axis, there is the 0 percent point at which firm 1 produces nothing, and so firm 2 produces 100 percent of industry output, while at the right end of the axis, at the 100 percent point, the opposite is true. The purpose of this somewhat unusual construction is that it enables us to compare the costs and sales of the two firms directly. For firm 1, rising output share means moving from left to right on the graph, in the usual manner. For firm 2, however, rising output share means moving from right to left.

Clearly, the allocation of the task of production will be efficient at point b on the horizontal axis, where the marginal costs of the two firms are

[16] Note that here we are entitled to talk about average costs (or average total costs) because we are dealing with single-product firms for which there can be no unattributable common costs (see Section VI *supra*).

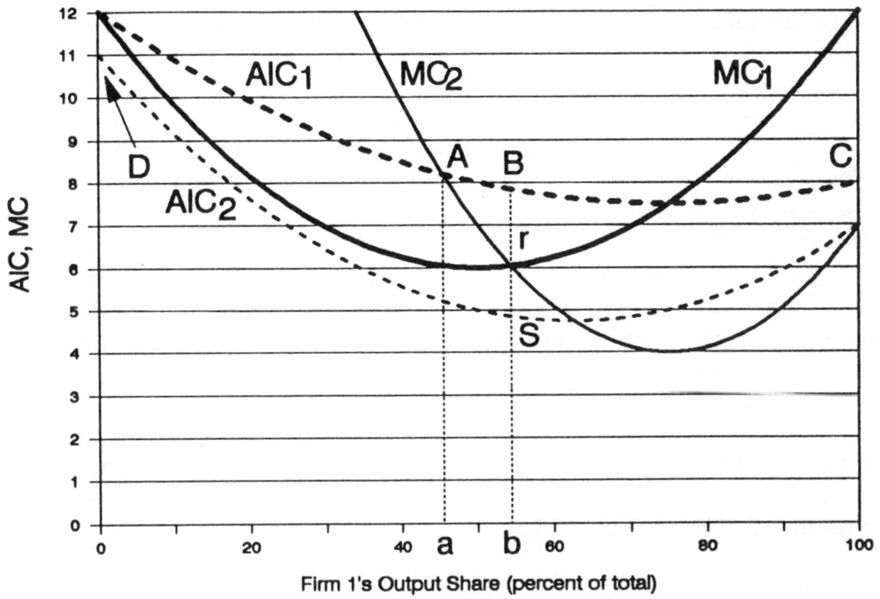

FIGURE 1.—Differential pricing required for efficiency

equal (point *r*). For in this case sharing of the output task clearly results in lower total output cost than production of the entire product by either firm alone. This is clear because at efficient output share *b* the average cost of firm 1 (point *B*) is lower than when firm 1 serves 100 percent of the market (point *C*), and the same is true for firm 2 (point *S* is substantially lower than *D*).

Yet there is no undifferentiated price that will lead to efficiency. It is true that a fixed price equal to the common marginal cost at point *r* will lead both firms to select the outputs that place them at the efficient output-share point, *b*. But since *r* lies below *B*, it is clear that this price will be below the average cost of firm 1. This means, most obviously, that firm 1 will be unable to survive at the marginal-cost price, so that, even though it is inefficient, the industry will be driven to monopoly, or a price will have to be set at some level above *r*—a level that is incompatible with an efficient allocation of output between the two firms. Moreover, even if firm 1 is able to survive a price equal to *r* by virtue of some form of subsidy, that price can exclude a third firm more efficient than firm 1; that is, it will exclude a third firm whose average cost of producing firm 1's output at point *b* is less than 1's average cost, *B*, but higher than the marginal-cost price, *r*.

Differential pricing can, however, solve all these problems. For example, firm 1 could charge different prices for its product to 10 different customer groups, with each group's price set to pass the Areeda-Turner test for the increment in firm 1's production constituted by that group's purchases. In this way, one group could be charged a price very close to the common marginal cost level, *r*, while the incremental revenues from all customer groups together cover the total costs of firm 1. Because the prices are set so as to pass the generalized Areeda-Turner test, no more-efficient firm can be excluded by them. Moreover, if there is no third firm available that is more efficient than firm 1, at those prices the latter enterprise will be able to survive indefinitely, and without the aid of any subsidy.

It should be recognized that this need not be a rare and pathological example. It can easily be true of any product that is produced most efficiently by several firms, in which the number of enterprises is small. That is why economic efficiency would not be served by a rule that simply prohibited differential pricing.[17]

XI. On Short-Run Profit Maximization Criteria of Predatory Pricing

Two ancillary topics remain to be dealt with here. One is the role of short-run profit maximization in a test of predatory pricing, an issue that has arisen in several discussions. The second is the proper role of opportunity cost in the generalized Areeda-Turner test.

The notion that failure to maximize short-run profits is somehow associated with predation has arisen in the Areeda-Turner discussion from the very beginning. Thus, Areeda and Turner themselves remark, "A necessary but . . . not sufficient condition of predation is the sacrifice of short-run profits."[18] However, the U.S. Court of Appeals, Fifth Circuit, has gone well beyond Areeda-Turner on this matter. It has asserted that, to prevail in a complaint of predation, "a plaintiff must at least show that either (1) a competitor is charging a price below his average variable cost in the competitive market or (2) the competitor is charging a price below its short-run, profit-maximizing price and barriers to entry are great

[17] It should be noted that the famous Ramsey pricing rule, which is the recognized rule for efficient pricing in circumstances where prices equal to marginal costs are incompatible with survival of the firm, uses differential pricing to obtain its optimality results. That is, Ramsey analysis shows that, where marginal-cost prices are not feasible financially, then differential pricing is required for optimality. On all this see, for example, William J. Baumol & J. Gregory Sidak, Toward Competition in Local Telephony ch. 3 (1994).

[18] Areeda & Turner, *supra* note 1, at 703.

enough to enable the discriminator to reap the benefits of predation before new entry is possible."[19] This would seem to imply that in the circumstances noted, failure to maximize profit is also *sufficient* to prove predation.

Now, there is a sensible interpretation of this short-run profit-maximization test, and there is also one that makes no sense. If one means by it that normal business behavior requires the firm always to seek the price that maximizes the profits that the firm will earn before some nearby horizon date, then the proposition is, indeed, nonsense. Every rational and successful firm has at some time forgone near-term profits in the expectation that the temporary sacrifice constitutes what amounts to an investment that will later pay off in spades. Rare is the firm that did not lose money during the weeks or months after it was first established. Every firm that decides to shut down a factory in order to retool and modernize deliberately elects to sacrifice short-term profits in the sense we are now using the term. Every firm that undertakes to invest heavily on an innovation whose payoff is expected only several years in the future is making a similar choice. It is not only silly but destructive of effective exercise of entrepreneurship to determine that such an act is suspect. As said, if this view were accepted, there would be few if any firms that would not qualify as suspects.

There is, however, a second interpretation of the term, "failure to maximize short-run profits." This sensible connotation is the adoption for some limited period of a price that reduces the present value of the firm's future profits. Here, the term "short-run" pertains to the limited period of time the price is in force. It places no time constraint on the period during which any resulting effects on the profits that are earned can be taken into consideration. In this sense, a new product price that will last for 2 weeks, and that entails $10,000 in net costs during those 2 weeks, but which is expected eventually to stimulate demand sufficiently to make up for this outlay many-fold, need not be a departure from short-run profit maximization. Only if that 2-week outlay cannot reasonably be expected to be made up in the future, or if it can be made up only through later monopoly profits after rivals are driven from the field by the price cut, is that requirement violated. There is, indeed, some reason to suspect predatory behavior if short-run profits are deliberately satisfied in the second of these senses, but not in the first. These observations can be summarized as:

RULE 7. There is absolutely nothing predatory about a price decision

[19] International Air Ind. Inc. v. American Excelsior Co. 517 F.2d 714, 724 (5th Cir. 1975); Adjustors Replace-A-Car v. Agency Rent-A-Car, Inc. 739 F.2d 884, 889–90 (5th Cir. 1984).

by a firm that fails to maximize the profits it can expect to earn during some brief proximate time period, provided that this price passes the (average variable cost) Areeda-Turner test and that this act can be expected to yield returns in the future that make up for whatever has been sacrificed in this way.

However, one can perhaps agree that a "necessary . . . condition of predation" is the adoption for some limited period of a price that will reduce the present value of the firm's stream of expected future profits, constituting a short-run action by the firm that is inconsistent with maximization of the present value of present and future profits.

Some courts have taken the position that the preceding argument is troublesome. For it seems to allow a defense holding that short-run losses are acceptable if only they raise the present discounted value of the firm. However, this is precisely what rational predation does. How, then, does one distinguish between predation and its absence if short-run losses are considered unobjectionable? Surely, the average variable cost test is the appropriate way to deal with the dilemma. That is, a price that exceeds average variable cost as defined here cannot be predatory, even if it does not maximize short-run profit. For, as has been shown in Section IV above, no price by an incumbent that at least equals its average variable cost can force the exit or prevent the entry of any rival that is at least equally efficient in terms of the incremental cost of the output in question.

XII. On the Role of Opportunity Costs in the Areeda-Turner Test

Economists agree that the type of sacrifice that they call "opportunity cost" is a legitimate part of any cost calculation. Indeed, they (including myself) assert that any cost calculation that totally ignores the opportunity cost component is likely to be illegitimate. The courts have not generally committed themselves on this issue in their dealings with the Areeda-Turner test. I show here that the matter is somewhat complex and that if the test is used to determine whether the price at issue constitutes a threat to the existence of an efficient rival, the opportunity cost component of avoidable cost must be treated in a particular way that will be spelled out presently.

The *opportunity cost* of an act such as the adoption of some price is defined to consist of any earnings implicitly or explicitly forgone as a result of that decision. For example, the opportunity cost of a student's decision to attend college includes any earnings forgone because that decision prevents the student from accepting full-time employment. It is a real cost that must be weighed in the decision to attend college because, if that decision is not taken, the prospective student will be better off financially by the amount of those wages. This, then, must be weighed in along with the other costs and the benefits of college attendance.

In business decisions, opportunity cost takes two primary forms that play an important and very different role in our discussion. The first is the opportunity cost of *owner-supplied inputs,* and the second is the cost of *revenues forgone* as a result of the decision in question. For example, suppose a single-proprietor firm decides to reduce the price of its product and this results in an increase in sales whose production requires some additional investment. If the owner supplies the funds out of her own savings, those funds cannot be considered to be free. The decision to tie them up in the company means that they cannot be invested in bonds where they would have earned, say, $9,000 per year in interest. On this account, then, the proprietor is $9,000 per annum poorer than she otherwise might have been, and failure to take this into consideration can clearly lead to an irrational decision.

The same price cut means that the goods that would otherwise have been sold at the previous higher price—say, 1,000 units of product at a price of $30 per unit—will now be sold at the reduced price of $25, for example, resulting in a forgone revenue of $5 × 1,000 units = $5,000. This loss of revenue, that is, this opportunity cost, too, must be weighed against the other gains and losses that can be expected to stem from the price cut before deciding whether or not the price reduction should be adopted.

Turning now to our central issue, suppose it is alleged that the price cut is predatory and that the new price should consequently be subjected to an Areeda-Turner test comparing the price with avoidable cost. Obviously, the inclusion of opportunity cost can only increase the avoidable cost figure and make the Areeda-Turner test more difficult to pass. Should all the opportunity costs be included in the calculation?

The answer, that may be unexpected to economists, is that if the Areeda-Turner test is used (as it is argued here it should be) to determine whether the price constitutes a threat to efficient competitors, then the opportunity cost of owner-supplied inputs *should* be included, but the revenues forgone as a result of the price cut *should not.*

The reason the cost of the owner-supplied income should be included is that any funds that our firm uses to produce its pertinent input must have their counterpart if that same output is instead produced by an efficient rival. If additional investment is required to provide that output, the rival, too, will have to provide such funds, either by borrowing or some other such means or by obtaining them from the rival's proprietors. If our firm's price does not cover the cost of its own invested funds, it is also likely to be unable to cover the rival's required investment cost, even if the rival is the more efficient supplier and can carry out its production cost with a (slightly) lower investment. In other words, a price of firm F that does not cover the opportunity cost of that firm's avoidable investment can constitute a threat to a more efficient rival and should be considered to fail the generalized Areeda-Turner test.

In contrast, the revenue firm F forgoes by reducing its price has no relevance to determination of whether the new price constitutes a threat to the presence of an efficient rival. If, in our example, the new price of $25 covers all of firm F's pertinent and avoidable input costs, both its opportunity costs and its other costs, then that price should by definition cover the corresponding costs of the lower input quantities needed by an efficient rival to produce the output in question. True, the higher revenue that the higher $30 price would have offered might also have constituted a benefit to the rival, but it is irrelevant to whether the lower price, in itself, is or is not a threat to an efficient rival. That gives us, finally:

RULE 8. In carrying out the generalized Areeda-Turner test of a price or set of prices, it is essential to include all opportunity costs of owner-supplied inputs in the calculation of associated avoidable cost, but it is necessary to omit the opportunity cost of any revenue forgone if the price in question constitutes a reduction from an earlier price.[20]

XIII. FINAL COMMENT: THE HETERODOX POSITIONS ON AREEDA-TURNER

This article has departed from standard views of the Areeda-Turner test in a number of ways. For example, the possibility that combinations of services can fail the modified Areeda-Turner test, even if all the individual services pass, seems not to have arisen in the literature. Still, it should be recognized that in practice courts do seem to have been willing to consider the prices of a set of outputs in combination or an intertemporal sequence of prices in predation lawsuits, just as my proposed rule on this subject requires. Similar comments apply to other rules in this article, such as that on the proper role of opportunity cost in the Areeda-Turner calculation. Perhaps the most novel element in the discussion is the proposed treatment of the Areeda-Turner test as a means to determine whether the price at issue constitutes (or constituted) a threat to efficient rivals, and my deduction from this point of departure that average vari-

[20] There are at least two cases in which the courts have explicitly rejected forgone revenues of profits as a type of opportunity cost that must be considered in a predatory pricing case. These are Continental Airlines, Inc. v. American Airlines, Inc., 824 F. Supp. 689 (S.D. Tex. 1993) (in a predatory pricing case, rejecting forgone revenues as an opportunity cost that must be included in determining defendant's relevant costs); In re IBM Peripheral EDP Devices Antitrust Litigation, 459 F. Supp. 626 (N.D. Cal. 1978) (same).

able cost, interpreted as average avoidable cost, is really the pertinent criterion, and not merely an inferior proxy for marginal cost.

Bibliography

Areeda, Phillip, and Turner, Donald. "Predatory Pricing and Related Practices under Section 2 of the Sherman Act." *Harvard Law Review* 88 (1975): 637–733.

Baumol, William J. "Quasi-Permanence of Price Reductions: A Policy for Prevention of Predatory Pricing." *Yale Law Journal* 89 (1979): 1–26.

Baumol, William J. *Superfairness: Applications and Theory*. Cambridge, Mass.: MIT Press, 1986.

Baumol, William J.; Koehn, Michael F.; and Willig, Robert D. "How Arbitrary Is Arbitrary?—or, Toward the Deserved Demise of Full Cost Allocation." *Public Utilities Fortnightly* 120 (September 3, 1987): 16–21.

Baumol, William J., and Sidak, J. Gregory. *Toward Competition in Local Telephony*. Cambridge, Mass.: MIT Press, 1994.

Joskow, Paul L., and Klevorick, Alvin K. "A Framework for Analyzing Predatory Pricing Policy." *Yale Law Journal* 89 (1979): 213–70.

McGee, John S. "Predatory Price Cutting: The Standard Oil (New Jersey) Case." *Journal of Law and Economics* 1 (1958): 137–69.

Parloff, Roger. "Fare's Fair." *American Lawyer* 65 (October 1993): 60–66.

Telser, Lester G. *Economic Theory and the Core*. Chicago and London: University of Chicago Press, 1978.

Williamson, Oliver E. "Predatory Pricing: A Strategic and Welfare Analysis." *Yale Law Journal* 87 (1977): 284–340.

Part IV
Regulation of Prices

A
Traditional Regulation

[17]

BEHAVIOR OF THE FIRM UNDER REGULATORY CONSTRAINT

By HARVEY AVERCH AND LELAND L. JOHNSON*

In judging the level of prices charged by firms for services subject to public control, government regulatory agencies commonly employ a "fair rate of return" criterion: After the firm substracts its operating expenses from gross revenues, the remaining net revenue should be just sufficient to compensate the firm for its investment in plant and equipment. If the rate of return, computed as the ratio of net revenue to the value of plant and equipment (the rate base), is judged to be excessive, pressure is brought to bear on the firm to reduce prices. If the rate is considered to be too low, the firm is permitted to increase prices.

The purpose here is (a) to develop a theory of the monopoly firm seeking to maximize profit but subject to such a constraint on its rate of return, and (b) to apply the model to one particular regulated industry—the domestic telephone and telegraph industry. We conclude in the theoretical analysis that a "regulatory bias" operates in the following manner: (1) The firm does not equate marginal rates of factor substitution to the ratio of factor costs; therefore the firm operates inefficiently in the sense that (social) cost is not minimized at the output it selects. (2) The firm has an incentive to expand into other regulated markets, even if it operates at a (long-run) loss in these markets; therefore, it may drive out other firms, or discourage their entry into these other markets, even though the competing firms may be lower-cost producers. Applying the theoretical analysis to the telephone and telegraph industry, we find that the model does raise issues relevant to evaluating market behavior.

I. *The Single-Market Model*

First we shall consider a geometrical and a mathematical framework showing the effect of the regulatory constraint on the cost curves of the

* The authors, research economists at The RAND Corporation, are indebted to Kenneth Arrow who suggested a mathematical framework when the ideas in this paper were in an early state of development. Any views expressed in this paper are those of the authors. They should not be interpreted as reflecting the views of The RAND Corporation or the official opinion or policy of any of its governmental or private research sponsors. An earlier version of this paper was presented at the Econometric Society meetings on December 28, 1961 in New York.

firm employing two factors. The essential characteristic to be demonstrated is: if the rate of return allowed by the regulatory agency is greater than the cost of capital but is less than the rate of return that would be enjoyed by the firm were it free to maximize profit without regulatory constraint, then the firm will substitute capital for the other factor of production and operate at an output where cost is not minimized.

Figure 1 denotes the firm's production where capital x_1 is plotted on the horizontal axis and labor x_2 on the vertical axis. The market or

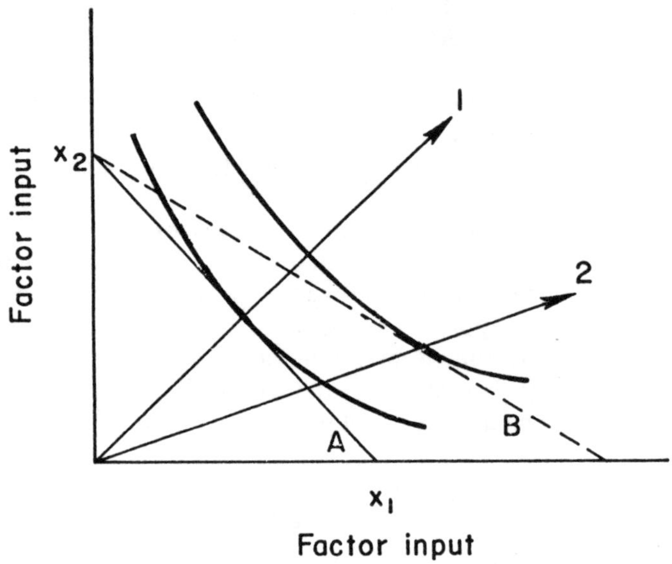

FIGURE 1

"social" cost of capital and labor generates the isocost curve *A* and the *unregulated* firm would move along expansion path 1 where market cost is minimized for any given output. With regulation, however, the cost of capital to the firm—the "private" cost—is no longer equal to market cost. For each additional unit of capital input, the firm is permitted to earn a profit (equal to the difference between the market cost of capital and rate of return allowed by the regulatory agency) that it otherwise would have to forego. Therefore, private cost is less than market cost by an amount equal to this difference. The effect of regulation is analogous to that of changing the relative prices of capital x_1 and labor x_2: isocost curve *B* becomes relevant and the firm moves along expansion path 2—a path along which market cost is not minimized for any given output. The firm finds path 2 advantageous simply because it is along

that path that the firm is able to maximize total profit given the constraint on its rate of return.

Treating the problem mathematically, we now consider a monopoly producing a single homogeneous product using two inputs. Define

$$z = z(x_1, x_2), \qquad x_1 \geq 0, \qquad x_2 \geq 0$$

$$(1) \qquad \frac{\partial z}{\partial x_1} > 0, \qquad \frac{\partial z}{\partial x_2} > 0,$$

$$z(0, x_2) = z(x_1, 0) = 0$$

as the firm's production function. That is, marginal products are positive, and production requires both inputs.

We write the inverse demand function as

$$(2) \qquad p = p(z).$$

Profit is defined by

$$(3) \qquad \pi = pz - r_1x_1 - r_2x_2$$

where the r_i $(i=1, 2)$ are factor costs presumed constant for all levels of factor input.

Let x_1 denote the physical quantity of plant and equipment in the rate base, c_1 the acquisition cost per unit of plant and equipment in the rate base, u_1 the value of depreciation of plant and equipment during a time period in question, and U_1 the cumulative value of depreciation. Let x_2 denote the quantity of labor input and r_2 the labor wage rate. The regulatory constraint is:

$$(4) \qquad \frac{pz - r_2x_2 - u_1}{c_1x_1 - U_1} \leq s_1$$

where the profit net of labor cost and capital depreciation constitutes a percentage of the rate base (net of depreciation) no greater than a specified maximum s_1.

For simplicity, we assume that depreciation (u_1 and U_1) is zero and we define capital so that its acquisition cost or value c_1 is equal to 1, i.e., the value of the rate base is equal to the physical quantity of capital.[1] The "cost of capital" r_1 (to be distinguished from the acquisition cost of plant and equipment measured by c_1) is the interest cost involved in holding plant and equipment. The allowable rate of return s_1 is the rate of return allowed by the regulatory agency on plant and equipment in order to compensate the firm for the cost of capital—the interest

[1] Alternatively, one could construct a dynamic rather than a static model and consider positive values for depreciation; but to do so would complicate the results without contributing much additional insight into the behavior of the firm.

cost—involved in holding plant and equipment. Therefore, the constraint may be rewritten as

$$\frac{pz - r_2x_2}{x_1} \leq s_1 \tag{5}$$

or

$$pz - s_1x_1 - r_2x_2 \leq 0. \tag{6}$$

For $s_1 < r_1$, the allowable rate of return is less than the actual cost of capital, and the firm withdraws from the market. For, from (6), if $x_1 > 0$,

$$pz - r_1x_1 - r_2x_2 = pz - s_1x_1 + (s_1 - r_1)x_1 - r_2x_2 \leq (s_1 - r_1)x_1 < 0.$$

If $x_1 = 0$, $\pi = -r_2x_2$ from (3), and the firm can further reduce its loss by setting $x_2 = 0$. Then $\pi = 0$. Therefore, $s_1 \geq r_1$; the allowable rate of return must at least cover the actual cost of capital.

The problem then is to maximize (3) subject to (6).[2] Define the Lagrangian expression:

$$L(x_1, x_2, \lambda) = pz - r_1x_1 - r_2x_2 - \lambda[pz - s_1x_1 - r_2x_2]. \tag{7}$$

The Kuhn-Tucker necessary conditions[3] for a maximum at $\bar{x}_1$, $\bar{x}_2$, $\bar{\lambda}$ are

$$r_1 \geq (1 - \lambda)\left[p + z\frac{dp}{dz}\right]\frac{\partial z}{\partial x_1} + \lambda s_1, \qquad x_1 \geq 0 \tag{8.1}$$

$$r_1 > (1 - \lambda)\left[p + z\frac{dp}{dp}\right]\frac{\partial z}{\partial x_1} + \lambda s_1 \quad \text{implies} \quad \bar{x}_1 = 0 \tag{8.2}$$

$$(1 - \lambda)r_2 \geq (1 - \lambda)\left[p + z\frac{dp}{dz}\right]\frac{\partial z}{\partial x_2}, \qquad \bar{x}_2 \geq 0 \tag{8.3}$$

$$(1 - \lambda)r_2 > (1 - \lambda)\left[p + z\frac{dp}{dz}\right]\frac{\partial z}{\partial x_2} \quad \text{implies} \quad \bar{x}_2 = 0 \tag{8.4}$$

$$pz - s_1x_1 - r_2x_2 \leq 0, \qquad \bar{\lambda} \geq 0 \tag{8.5}$$

$$pz - r_2x_2 < s_1x_1 \quad \text{implies} \quad \bar{\lambda} = 0. \tag{8.6}$$

Assuming $\bar{\lambda} > 0$, it is clear from (8.1) that $\lambda = 1$ if and only if $r_1 = s_1$. If $\lambda = 1$, $r_1 = s_1$. This does not involve any variables, and it follows that any x_1, x_2 which satisfies (8.5) is a solution.

[2] Since (6) is an inequality, we are faced with a nonlinear programming problem. However, the similarity of the results to ordinary marginal conditions is obvious.

[3] If the total revenue function, pz, is concave in the relevant range of operation, it is clear that the Kuhn-Tucker conditions in this case are also sufficient. Given a concave pz, it is possible to define the dynamic gradient process corresponding to the static Kuhn-Tucker conditions showing the firm's input variation over time. But we do not do this here since we are primarily interested in equilibrium and the optimal inputs under regulation.

For $s_1 > r_1$, which is the interesting case, it follows that $0 \leq \lambda < 1$: From (8.6), s_1 may be chosen large enough so that $\lambda = 0$ (i.e., at some high level of allowable rate of return s_1, the value $x_1 (s_1 - r_1)$ exceeds the level of unconditionally maximized profit, and the constraint is ineffective). If we now let $s_1 \to r_1$, λ varies continuously, and since $\lambda \neq 1$, we have $0 < \lambda < 1$. For the unregulated monopoly, the marginal conditions are:

$$(9) \qquad r_i = \left[p + z \frac{dp}{dz} \right] \frac{\partial z}{\partial x_i}, \qquad (i = 1, 2).$$

Under conditions of effective regulatory constraint ($\lambda > 0$) equations (8.3) and (9) disclose that, as in the case of unregulated monopoly, the input of x_2 is such that its marginal cost r_2 is equal to its marginal value product. In contrast, equations (8.1) and (9) disclose that the input of x_1 is such that its marginal cost r_1 is greater than its marginal value product,[4] i.e., its use is expanded beyond the point at which its marginal cost would be equal to its marginal value product.

From equations (8.1) and (8.3) when the equalities hold, the marginal rate of substitution of factor 1 for factor 2 is:

$$(10) \qquad \frac{-dx_2}{dx_1} = \frac{r_1}{r_2} - \frac{\lambda}{(1 - \lambda)} \frac{(s_1 - r_1)}{r_2}.$$

Since

$$\frac{\lambda}{(1 - \lambda)} \frac{(s_1 - r_1)}{r_2} > 0, \qquad \lambda > 0, \qquad s_1 > r_1,$$

then

$$(11) \qquad \frac{-dx_2}{dx_1} < \frac{r_1}{r_2}.$$

The firm adjusts to the constraint, then, by substituting capital for the cooperating factor and by expanding total output. Comparative equilibrum outputs are shown in Figure 2. If the regulated firm were constrained to move along the socially efficient expansion path 1 in Figure 1, it would operate at *OC* in Figure 2. Here price is slightly above

[4] Clearly

$$\frac{r_1 - \lambda s_1}{1 - \lambda} = r_1 - \frac{\lambda}{1 - \lambda} (s_1 - r_1) \geq \left[p + z \frac{dp}{dz} \right] \frac{\partial z}{\partial x_1}.$$

Since $0 < \lambda < 1$, $s_1 > r_1$, it follows immediately that:

$$r_1 > \left[p + z \frac{dp}{dz} \right] \frac{\partial z}{\partial x_1}.$$

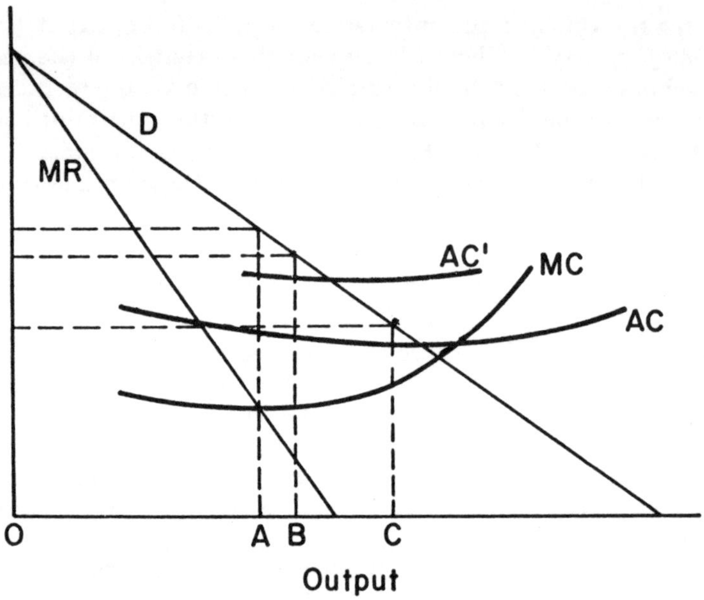

FIGURE 2

average cost AC to reflect the fact that $s_1 > r_1$ (profit is not entirely eliminated). Since the regulated firm moves along path 2, the social cost curve rises from AC to AC', and the regulatory constraint is satisfied at the lower output OB. The effect of regulation is to force the firm to expand output from the unregulated position OA, but output does not expand to C because a portion of what would otherwise be profit is absorbed by cost. The extent to which regulation affects output depends upon the nature of the production function. If it involves fixed proportions, i.e., min $\left(\frac{x_1}{a}, \frac{x_2}{b}\right)$, the regulated firm is constrained to the efficient expansion path and it moves all the way to OC. If the production function is linear and if the iso-output curves have a slope equal to $-\frac{r_1}{r_2}$, the firm could substitute x_1 for x_2 and, with no change in marginal rate of substitution, hold output constant. In this case it could remain at OA, the unregulated monopoly output, under the condition that at output OA

$$pz - s_1x_1 - r_2x_2 \leq 0, \qquad x_2 = 0.$$

II. *The Multimarket Case*

Suppose that in addition to operating in a single market, the firm can also enter other regulated markets, and that the regulatory agency bases its "fair rate of return" criterion on the firm's over-all value of plant and equipment for all markets taken together rather than computing a separate rate of return for each market. In this case the firm may have an incentive (that it would not have in the absence of regulation) to enter these other markets, even if the cost of so doing exceeds the additional revenues. Expanding into other markets may enable the firm to inflate its rate base to satisfy the constraint and permit it to earn a greater total constrained profit than would have been possible in the absence of second markets.

A noteworthy implication is that the firm operating in oligopolistic second markets may have an advantage over competing firms. The regulated firm can "afford" to take (long-run) losses in these second markets while competing firms cannot. Under these circumstances, it is conceivable that the firm could drive out lower-cost producers—the loss it willingly takes in second markets could exceed the difference between its costs and the lower costs of other firms. It may succeed, therefore, in either driving lower cost firms out of these markets or of discouraging their entry into them. This is unlike the textbook case of "predatory price-cutting" where the regulated monopolist may temporarily cut prices in outside competitive markets to drive out rivals and subsequently raise prices to monopoly levels. The monopolist would ordinarily engage in such a practice only if he had the expectation that in the long run he would make a positive profit in these additional markets; but here even in the case of a long-run loss the regulated firm may find operations in such markets to be advantageous as long as the firm is permitted to include its capital input in these markets in its rate base.

Moving to a mathematical treatment, let us consider an extreme example where operating in a second market permits the firm to act as an unconstrained monopoly in the first market, i.e., operating in the second market permits satisfaction of the regulatory constraint such that the firm can operate in the first market at output *OA* in Figure 2. We shall assume that for any combination of factors along the socially optimal expansion path in market 2 the firm is just able to break even in that market. That is, for any equilibrium x_{12}, x_{22}

$$p_2z_2 - r_1x_{12} - r_2x_{22} = 0. \tag{12}$$

The constraint for n markets is written:

$$\sum_{i=1}^{n} p_iz_i - s_1 \sum_{i=1}^{n} x_{1i} - r_2 \sum_{i=1}^{n} x_{2i} \leq 0. \tag{13}$$

Denoting output and factor inputs in market 1 as $\bar{z}_{11}$ and $\bar{x}_{11}$, $\bar{x}_{21}$ respectively at the output at which profit is unconditionally maximized in market 1, we have

$$p_1\bar{z}_1 - s_1\bar{x}_{11} - r_2\bar{x}_{21} = m, \qquad m > 0 \tag{14}$$

where m is the value of "excess" profit in market 1 that would violate the constraint (13) if the firm operated only in market 1. However, by moving along its expansion path in market 2 the firm can choose a level of capital input such that

$$p_2\bar{z}_2 - s_1\bar{x}_{12} - r_2\bar{x}_{22} = - m. \tag{15}$$

Adding (14) and (15) we see that the firm can now satisfy constraint (13) without foregoing any profit in market 1. While the unregulated firm would be indifferent about operating in market 2, the regulated firm in this example finds market 2 attractive because it can add capital to the rate base at "no loss"; i.e., for any capital input in market 2 the output generates revenues just equal to factor cost. Since in market 2 the actual cost of capital is below the allowed rate of return, the firm can apply the difference in satisfying the constraint in market 1 and thereby enjoy additional profit equal to $s_1 - r_1$ for each unit of capital in market 2.

This analysis suggests that even if the firm suffers a loss in market 2 (measured in terms of social costs r_1 and r_2) it may still operate there provided the value of x_{12} $(s_1 - r_1)$ exceeds this level of loss. If it suffers a loss it would no longer operate in market 1 at the profit-maximizing output *OA* in Figure 1; seeking to equate the marginal value product of capital in both markets, it would move toward *OB*.

In the literature on public utility economics, concern is frequently expressed that the firm will attempt to inflate its rate base to increase its profit. However, the problem is generally viewed as one of proper valuation of rate base, i.e., the firm would always have an incentive to have its property stated at a value higher than its cost. The problem has given rise to a great deal of controversy about proper valuation, especially concerning original versus reproduction cost, and depreciation policy.[5] In the present study the problem of rate-base inflation is not viewed as one of valuation but rather as one of *acquisition*—quite apart from the problem of placing a valuation upon the rate base, the firm has an incentive to acquire additional capital if the allowable rate of return exceeds the cost of capital.

III. *The Telephone and Telegraph Industry*

Turning to the domestic telephone and telegraph industry, we find that the market structure and the regulatory setting are consistent with

[5] For examples of the manner in which the problems has previously been treated see [5, Ch. 19, 20] [10, Ch. 12, 17] [14, pp. 515–16].

those described in the model. And the implications drawn from the model, concerning relative factor inputs and incentives to operate in some markets even at a loss, raise issues relevant to assessing market behavior of firms in the industry.

For our purposes, the notable feature of the industry's market structure is that the degree of competition does vary from one subsector to another. Common carriers have monopoly positions with regard to public message telephone and telegraph services, while they compete with each other in supplying private line services to customers who, in addition, are free to construct private wire facilities for their own use as an alternative to purchasing from the common carriers.

The principal supplier of public message telephone service is the Bell Telephone System. Besides the parent corporation, American Telephone and Telegraph Company, the Bell system includes 22 subsidiary "associated" companies of which 20 are primarily or wholly owned by AT&T. Each of the associated carriers provides local exchange and toll service within the state or group of (contiguous) states that comprises its "operating territory."[6] The Bell system holds about 98 per cent of all facilities employed in long-distance message toll telephone service in the United States, and about 85 per cent of all facilities employed in local telephone service. The remaining 15 per cent of local exchange facilities are in the hands of about 3,200 "independent" telephone firms, most of which are very small. These carriers connect with the Bell system, under service- and revenue-sharing agreements, and provide an integrated nationwide network. Competition does not exist among firms in the public message telephone business. Although many firms are in the industry, each has its own exclusive local marketing area.[7]

In the telegraph field, in contrast to telephone, public message telegraph service is offered only by the Western Union Telegraph Company. This is a much smaller subsector in terms of revenues than public message telephone service. In 1959 Western Union revenues for the former were about $170 million, while Bell and independent connecting carrier revenues for the latter were $7 billion.

Bell and Western Union compete in common markets in providing other services. Until recently Bell (together with independent connecting carriers) was sole supplier of private-line telephone service. How-

[6] AT&T, through its Long Lines Department, provides interstate line and radio facilities to connect the separate operating territories of the associated companies; in addition, in some cases Long Lines participates in providing interstate service internally within the territories of the multistate associated companies.

[7] A good description of the industry and its present-day market structure is contained in [8, pp. 4-34].

ever, in 1961 Bell and Western Union negotiated facilities contracts[8] that enable Western Union to offer private-line telephone service in competition with Bell. Western Union and Bell both provide telegraph exchange service and private-line telegraph service—Bell's teletypewriter or TWX service is similar to Western Union's Telex, and Bell's teletype private-wire service is similar to Western Union's leased circuit teleprinter offering. In addition, a new competitive element has recently been introduced: as an alternative to purchasing private-line telephone and telegraph services from the common carriers, firms outside the communications industry may now operate their own microwave facilities to provide communication among their geographically separated plants.[9]

Intrastate services of the common carriers are regulated by individual state regulatory commissions; interstate operations are regulated by the Federal Communications Commission. These agencies use a "fair rate of return" criterion in regulating prices within their respective jurisdictions. The services of each common carrier are generally lumped together in computing the rate of return to be regulated. For example, in regulating Bell's service the FCC routinely considers together all revenues, plant investment, and operating costs of Bell's interstate services in computing a rate of return to serve as the basis for decisions about price adjustments.[10] Likewise, most state agencies compute an over-all rate of return for each carrier for all of its intrastate operations within the state in question.

Since the interesting implications of the model rest on the assumption that the allowable rate of return exceeds the actual cost of capital, the question arises as to whether revenues of the industry do exceed factor costs. While it is impossible to treat this question exhaustively here, there is some reason to believe that revenues are generally in excess of costs. We have been told by representatives in both the industry and in regulatory agencies that justification exists for allowing a return in excess of cost to give firms an incentive to develop and adopt cost-saving techniques. If the firm is left only indifferent as among a wide range of activities it has no positive incentive to mini-

[8] These contracts permit Western Union to lease Bell communications facilities in order to enter markets that it could not feasibly serve if confined to its own facilities.

[9] While railroads and public utilities, the so called "right-of-way" companies, have historically been permitted by law to employ privately owned radio communications facilities for their internal needs, it was not until 1960 that the way was cleared (by a final decision of the Federal Communications Commission in Docket 11866) for other firms to provide their own communications facilities.

[10] It is true that special studies of the separate services are occasionally made by the FCC in order to determine individual rates of return. Evidence from one such study will be presented below.

mize costs for any given activity. Consequently, regulatory agencies do not typically view with disfavor rates of return which are (within broad limits) somewhat in excess of rates they would judge to reflect cost. Positive profit is sometimes generated by the "regulatory lag" phenomenon: As the firm adopts new cost-saving technology or as its business volume rises for output subject to decreasing costs, its rate of return rises. However, the regulatory agency does not react immediately to force prices down. Rather, a lag of years may be involved. An example of this can be drawn from the interstate telephone operations of the Bell System. In its over-all interstate operations Bell experienced a decline in its rate of return from 7.5 per cent to 5.2 per cent from 1950 to 1953. Reasoning that a rate in the neighborhood of 5 per cent was too low, it filed revised tariff schedules increasing interstate message toll rates by about 8 per cent—an increase expected to bring the rate of return up to about 6.5 per cent. The FCC, agreeing that earnings under the old tariff were inadequate, allowed the new tariff to go into effect. There is a strong implication in the FCC staff memoranda written at the time that a fair rate of return was considered to be in the neighborhood of 6 per cent.[11] After the increase went into effect in 1953, the rate of return rose to 6.6 per cent in 1954, 7.7 per cent in 1955, reached a peak of 8.5 per cent in early 1956, and continued in excess of 7 per cent during 1957 and 1958. Despite an interstate toll rate reduction in 1959, the rate of return amounted to almost 8 per cent in 1959 and 1960. The fact that the rate of return remained above a 6 per cent level during most of the decade meant that for a number of years revenues in interstate operations exceeded the FCC Staff estimate of cost.[12]

One implication drawn from the model is that the firm increases its ratio of capital input to cooperating factor input in a manner that increases social costs at the equilibrium output. Do the common carriers in this industry overinvest in this fashion? Unfortunately, empirical evidence is not available to us on the issue of bias in favor of investment

[11] A clear, concise account of the manner in which the FCC regulates interstate telephone and telegraph services is contained in [12, pp. 3427–45].

[12] The rise in Bell's rate of return is partly attributable to Bell's striking success in developing and adopting new cost-saving technology. The average book cost per circuit mile of Long Lines plant declined from roughly $230 in 1925 to $30 in 1960. The strong long-run incentives apparent in Bell's activities to cut costs may be construed as prima-facie evidence that it enjoys positive profits. Of course, one could argue that another factor is present—entrepreneurship—whose cost would more or less offset the postive profit; i.e., in the economic sense (in contrast to the accounting sense) revenue may just cover cost and the firm still has incentive to minimize cost. But here we are concerned with the *marginal* cost of capital to the firm compared to the *marginal* return to capital allowed by the regulatory agency. If the latter exceeds the former, the "regulatory bias" emerges regardless of whether total cost includes a fixed charge attributable to an additional factor.

in plant and equipment. However, one point should be made: the regulatory agencies exert little direct control over investment decisions that would force the firm to follow the socially optimal expansion path. The FCC, for example, follows a "used and useful" criterion in judging whether a given item is to be included in the rate base of plant and equipment. If the item is being employed in operations, and if it is useful (judged partially on subjective grounds), it is included. While common carriers are required routinely to provide a formidable list of reports concerning current operations, the relatively small staffs of the regulatory agencies available for research and investigative tasks, the lack of satisfactory criteria upon which to make judgments, and the heterogeneity of both factor inputs and service outputs would make extremely difficult if not impossible the task of detecting such bias.

The second implication drawn from the model is that due to the nature of regulation the firm has an incentive to operate in some markets even at a loss. Again, there is no clear-cut evidence which shows whether common carriers in this industry do, in fact, operate at a loss in some markets. However, evidence is available disclosing that (1) fears of "unfair" competition based on operations at "noncompensating" prices play a prominent role as a source of conflict between the carriers themselves and between the carriers and the FCC; and (2) in attempting to establish a commercial communications satellite system, the federal government has enacted a law containing provisions that (to serve "public ends") appear to exploit the willingness of common carriers to operate in markets at a loss. We shall now discuss some of this evidence.

The FCC undertook a study in 1956 of interstate private-line services offered by the common carriers in order to determine the relationship between price and cost for these services on a more precise basis than is possible by considering only the over-all rate of return for each carrier on all its interstate services. In the course of the study Bell submitted data (based on 1955 operations) showing that its telephone grade services were earning at a rate of 11.7 per cent, and its teletypewriter (telegraph) grade services at 2.6 per cent.[13] On the basis of this evidence, the FCC ordered interim price reductions in telephone grade services (in which Bell at the time was sole supplier) and permitted an increase for both Bell and Western Union for telegraph services (in which the two carriers do compete). The FCC expected the price adjustments to reduce substantially the spread between Bell's rates of return on telephone and telegraph grade services and to increase Western Union's rate of return on telegraph services.

[13] The initial decision of the FCC staff in this study (not adopted by the Commission at this writing) is contained in [6].

During the study Western Union criticized Bell's behavior that allegedly resulted in Bell's relatively low rate of return on the telegraph services competitive with Western Union's own offerings. In the words of the FCC staff [6, p. 54]:

> Western Union refers to evidence of record indicating that during the twenty-year period preceding this investigation, all principal private line telegraph rate adjustments were initiated by AT&T and, with one exception, all were rate reductions. Western Union alleges that AT&T has received a noncompensatory return on its private line telegraph service while enjoying a substantial return from services not competitive with Western Union. . . . According to Western Union, it follows that AT&T has engaged in unfair competition by maintaining unreasonably low rates for a competitive service and shifting the resulting financial burden to other services.[14]

Western Union's allegations, if true, would indicate that in conformity with the model, Bell is operating in private-line telegraph at a loss. However, it is impossible, for two reasons, to determine from the evidence in the FCC study whether this is in fact the case. First, the evidence in the record is simply not sufficient to determine what earnings level is "proper", i.e., what earnings level would just cover the cost of capital.[15] Second, the rates of return quoted above are based on "fully allocated cost" as opposed to marginal cost. In our model, the firm operates at a loss in a market only if the additional revenues it receives by operating in that market are below the additional costs it incurs. And whether operations in that market impose a "financial burden" (to use Western Union's words) on the other services depends on whether additional revenues do cover the additional costs.[16] But fully allocated costs are something else again. These include the costs of facilities used solely for the service in question and, in addition, they include an allocation of the "common" costs incurred by the carrier. For example, the telephone instrument itself is necessary in providing both intrastate and interstate message toll service as well as local exchange service; a transcontinental microwave system carries both public message toll and private-line traffic. In computing a rate of return for each of these services, it is necessary to allocate the costs of facilities having multiple uses. In general, the FCC allocates these costs in accordance with relative time of use. If a given facility is employed by service A 50 per

[14] For AT&T's reply see [4, pp. 14-18].

[15] The FCC staff concluded that AT&T's proper earnings levels is 7¼ per cent and for Western Union 9 per cent. This conclusion was contested by Bell in its reply brief: "These [FCC staff] findings are made despite the fact that there is not a word of testimony in the record concerning the over-all costs of capital to either carrier, much less the costs of capital for their private line services" [4, p. 3]. See also [2, p. 27].

[16] A good statement of this point is contained in [1, pp. 7-10].

cent of the time and by service B 50 per cent of the time, the cost of the facility is split equally between A and B. For our purposes, however, the crucial question is whether the cost of the facility could have been cut in half if either service A or service B had not been offered.[17] Is allocation on the basis of relative time in use an accurate reflection of marginal costs generated by each service? We may presume an affirmative answer only if the industry is subject to constant costs. However, the available evidence is not sufficient to determine whether the industry is, in general, subject to constant costs in the relevant range of output. If, on the contrary, it is subject either to decreasing or to increasing costs, use of the conventional cost allocation procedures would tend either to overstate or to understate marginal costs for particular services. Because of these possibilities, the rates of return commonly quoted for a particular communications service cannot be used as a reliable guide in determining whether a loss, in the relevant sense, is being incurred in providing that service and whether a financial burden is thereby being imposed upon the other services.

Competition between Bell and Western Union will probably continue to be a lively issue in future FCC investigations. In February 1962, the FCC was reported to have had "under consideration for some time an over-all study of telephone vs. telegraph competition"; in the same month the American Communications Association (a union representing Western Union employees) "formally petitioned for an investigation into the extent and effect of participation by the American Telephone and Telegraph Co. in domestic and international telegraph communications."[18]

Our model suggests that apprehension about the nature of competition in the industry is justified since a common carrier, regulated as described above, would (under certain conditions) have an incentive to operate at a loss in competitive markets and to shift the financial burden to its other services. In this sense, it would have an "unfair" advantage over other firms which do not have other markets sufficiently profitable to bear the loss of competing with it.[19] Unfortunately, however, the FCC and other regulatory bodies are so wedded to the fully allocated cost criteria rather than to marginal cost criteria in judging the "fairness" of competition, that evidence drawn from future hearings and investigations will probably not throw much light on the question

[17] For purposes of this simple illustration, we are assuming a zero elasticity of demand substitution between A and B.

[18] [9, February 26, 1962, p. 1].

[19] That is, the unconditionally maximized profits of the other regulated firms may be sufficiently low so that imposition of the regulatory constraint does not induce them to operate at a loss in competitive markets.

whether common carriers in some markets do, in fact, operate at a loss measured in the relevant economic sense.

Finally, the model appears useful in treating economic implications of the Communications Satellite Act passed by Congress in August 1962, after long and bitter debate[13]. The Act specifies establishment of a new, private corporation regulated as a separate entity by the FCC to develop and operate the satellite system. The corporation is to be financed in two ways: (1) It may issue capital stock, carrying voting rights and eligible for dividends, to be sold "in a manner to encourage the widest distribution to the American public [13, Sec. 304 (a)]. Purchase of this stock is also permitted by "authorized" communications common carriers[20] subject to the constraint that the aggregate of shares held by these carriers together not exceed 50 per cent of the total shares issued and outstanding. This stock is *not* eligible for inclusion in the carrier's rate base. For convenience in subsequent analysis we shall refer to these securities as "type I securities." (2) The Corporation may issue "nonvoting securities, bonds, debentures and other certificates of indebtedness as it may determine." Communications common carriers are permitted to hold these securities without specified limit, and these securities *are* eligible for inclusion in the rate base of the carrier "to the extent allowed by the Commission [FCC]" [13, Sec. 304 (b)]. For convenience we shall refer to these as "type II securities."

The model suggests that, given the provisions of the Act, communications common carriers would have a special incentive to invest in type II securities, and that their financial support might consititue a partial subsidy for the satellite corporation. By holding type II securities the common carrier incurs an interest cost (r_1) and collects whatever interest or dividends are forthcoming on type II securities (r_1'). Were the carrier unregulated or were the securities not eligible for inclusion in its rate base it would purchase securities only under the condition that $r_1' \geq r_1$. Since, however, the investment in type II securities can be included in the over-all rate base of the carrier, the carrier has an incentive (again under certain conditions) to invest more than would otherwise be the case.

Consider the example where the carrier receives a zero return on its investment in type II securities, i.e., $r_1' = 0$ at all levels of investment; therefore, the carrier suffers a loss of r_1 for each dollar of investment. If, however, the allowable rate of return (s_1) is greater than the interest cost (r_1) the regulatory constraint on the carrier's other services is relaxed, permitting prices and profits to be raised in the other

[20] Authorized common carriers presumably would include AT&T, Western Union and eight U.S. overseas radio and cable telegraph companies.

sectors. For each dollar in type II securities, the carrier's over-all profit would *rise* by the value $(s_1 - r_1)$: The loss involved in the investment in type II securities would be more than offset by the increased profits elsewhere resulting from inflation of the rate base and relaxation of the regulatory constraint. The carrier, then, may have an incentive to hold type II securities even if a direct loss is involved.

Two closely related implications arise from this analysis: First, the costs to the satellite corporation of obtaining money capital will fall if it can sell type II securities to common carriers at a return that is below their own interest cost (and if their own rate of interest is no higher than that which the satellite corporation would otherwise have to pay). To the extent that these funds provided at reduced cost to the satellite corporation permit a shift downward in its cost curves, the communications toll rates it charges to users of satellite services would also fall below the level that would have been established had the satellite corporation been forced to resort to conventional financing.[21]

Interestingly, a reduction in satellite communications toll rates by reducing financing costs to the satellite corporation, shifting the burden to other services, was intended by the sponsors of the bill that led to the Satellite Act. Senator Kerr, when introducing the bill to the Senate in February 1962, stated [11, p. 1670]:

> [This bill strives for] . . . a privately owned corporation in which the existing American companies engaged in the international communications business would be able to invest, with their investments treated the same as the acquisition of new equipment and thus includable in their rate bases. This important feature permitting the rate of return for all communication services to be spread over a broad base would insure lower charges for communication satellite services.

Second, inclusion of type II securities in the carrier's rate base may permit the satellite corporation to operate even if its total revenues do not cover total market costs. In this case type I securities issues may be small, since little if any dividends would be earned, and the bulk of financial support might come from common carriers holding type II securities at a return below the market rate of interest.[22] Again, the losses in satellite operations would be covered by revenues from telephone and telegraph services provided by the carriers.

[21] These users include both U.S. and foreign international common carriers who would employ the satellite relays primarily for transoceanic communications links in combination with or as a substitute for submarine cable and radio. To the extent that users of the satellite system are the same carriers which invest in type II securities, their subsidy to the satellite corporation would be more or less offset by the reduction in toll rates they pay to the satellite corporation. However the Act specifies no particular relationship between the amount of type II securities they respectively hold and their relative use of the satellite system.

[22] In this case type I securities would be attractive primarily because of the voting rights they confer.

IV. *Conclusions*

The preceding analysis discloses that a misallocation of economic resources may result from the use by regulatory agencies of the rate-of-return constraint for price control. The firm has an incentive to substitute between factors in an uneconomic fashion that is difficult for the regulatory agency to detect. Moreover, if a large element of common costs exists for the firm's outputs in the various markets, the widely used "fully allocated" cost basis for rate-of-return computation is likely to prove unsatisfactory in determining whether the firm is operating at a loss in any given market, or whether its activities in some markets tend to restrict competition in an undesirable manner. At the same time, regulatory practices that provide an incentive for the firm to operate in some markets even at a loss may constitute a convenient mechanism through which certain activities of the firm judged to be in the "public interest" can be subsidized.

Our analysis suggests lines of further inquiry: We have considered only the telephone and telegraph industry, but the issues raised by the model may be relevant to evaluating market behavior in other industries as well. It is notable that Gardner Means in a recent study [7] has advocated that certain large nonregulated firms judged to be "collective enterprises" be encouraged, by tax incentive, to engage in "target pricing" where they aim for a profit equal to a fair rate of return on investment. By following this approach to pricing, which is similar to that employed in public utilities, the danger exisits (which he does not recognize) that these firms would be exposed to the same pressures discussed above of inflating their rate bases by substituting capital for labor and by expanding into unprofitable new lines in order to satisfy the authorities that they were using "proper" target pricing. It might prove worthwhile to examine the effect of target pricing in steel and other industries discussed by Means in the light of the preceding analysis. Furthermore, it might be interesting to explore alternative forms of government control that, by avoiding the return-on-investment criterion for price regulation, do not generate the bias disclosed here.

References

1. American Telephone and Telegraph Co., *Brief of Bell System Respondents in Support of Lawfulness of Revised Telpak Tariff under Section 202(a) of the Communications Act*, regarding FCC Docket No. 14251. 1961.
2. ———, *Exceptions of Bell System Companies to the Initial Decision Released July 14, 1961*, regarding FCC Docket Nos. 11645, 11646, 12194. 1961.
3. ———, *Proposed Findings and Conclusions of the Bell System Companies*, regarding FCC Docket Nos. 11645, 11646. 1960.

4. ———, *Reply Brief of the Bell System Companies,* regarding FCC Docket Nos. 11645, 11646, 12194. 1961.
5. J. M. Clark, *Social Control of Business,* 2nd ed. New York 1939.
6. Federal Communications Commission, *Initial Decision* (adopted July 6, 1961), regarding Docket Nos. 11645, 11646, 12194. 1961.
7. G. C. Means, *Pricing Power and the Public Interest.* New York 1962.
8. National Association of Railroad and Utilities Commissioners, *Message Toll Telephone Rates and Disparities.* Washington 1951.
9. *Telecommunications Reports* (Washington), weekly news service covering telephone, telegraph and radio communications.
10. Emery Troxel, *Economics of Public Utilities,* New York 1947.
11. U.S. Congress, *Congressional Record* (Senate), Feb. 7, 1962, 87th Cong., 2nd sess. Washington 1962.
12. ———, *Consent Decree Program of the Department of Justice.* Hearings before the Anti-Trust Subcommittee of the House Committee on the Judiciary, 85th Cong., 2nd sess. Washington 1958. Pt. 2, American Telephone and Telegraph Co. (3 vols.).
13. U. S. Public Law 87-624, Communications Satellite Act of 1962, 87th Cong. Aug. 31, 1962.
14. Clair Wilcox, *Public Policies toward Business.* Chicago 1955.

[18]

The Traditional Issues in the Pricing of Public Utility Services

The essence of regulation is the explicit replacement of competition with governmental orders as the principal institutional device for assuring good performance. The regulatory agency determines specifically who shall be permitted to serve; and when it licenses more than one supplier, it typically imposes rigid limitations on their freedom to compete. So the two prime requirements of competition as the governing market institution—freedom of entry and independence of action—are deliberately replaced. Instead the government determines price, quality and conditions of service, and imposes an obligation to serve.

The licensure of entry in most public utility industries tends to be an infrequent, once-and-for-all or almost-all determination. Franchises legally may have to be renewed, and new firms may seek to be licensed; in radio and television, and trucking this is a frequent occurrence. But even in those cases, and even more so in others, the tendency is to rely on the same chosen instruments, year after year and decade after decade; the structure of the market and identity of the firms selected to serve remain essentially unchanging. And what public utility commissions mainly *do* (though not in broadcasting) is to fix the prices the chosen instruments may charge—not just a ceiling, as in the case of permissible interest rates paid on time deposits or as prescribed in usury laws, or a floor, such as a minimum wage—but a set of specific prices. It is through the regulation of price that the limitation of profits is purportedly achieved; it is incident to the regulation of price that the levels and permissible kinds of cost are controlled, by allowing or disallowing payments for various inputs, by supervising methods of financing and controlling financial structures. Price regulation is the heart of public utility regulation.

This assertion might strike a constitutional lawyer or anyone who has read Chapter 1 as strangely old-fashioned. It sounds like something the United States Supreme Court would have said 40 to 50 years ago, when it was systematically striking down legislative attempts to regulate prices or wages outside the traditional "industries affected with a public interest" on the ground that the right to set prices free of public control was at the heart of the freedom of contract protected by the Fourteenth Amendment.[1] In 1934, in *Nebbia v. New York*, the Supreme Court finally rejected the notion that there was anything constitutionally sacrosanct about private price-determination, and declared that if any industry could, for good and sufficient reasons, be subjected to public regulation, there was no constitutional bar to its being subjected to price regulation in particular.[2]

Our assertion may seem irrational also to the economist. And to some extent it is. One purpose of regulation is to protect buyers from monopolistic exploitation—but buyers can be exploited just as effectively by giving them poor or unsafe service as by charging them excessive prices. Another purpose is to prevent destructive competition—but it would seem that sellers can compete just as destructively by offering better or more service for the same price as by offering the same service at lower prices. Price really has no meaning except in terms of an assumed quality of service; price is a ratio, with money in the numerator and some physical unit of given or assumed quantity and quality in the denominator. Price regulation alone is economically meaningless. Moreover, the nature of our dependence on public utility services is typically such that customers may correctly be *more* interested in the denominator than in the numerator—in the reliability, continuity, and safety of the service than in the price they have to pay.[3]

This relatively greater concentration on price than on quality of service is one reflection of the severe limitations of regulation as an institution of social control of industry. In this chapter we examine the major traditional components of that effort. In addition to laying the necessary factual foundation for our subsequent analysis, the purpose of this preliminary survey is to suggest (1) the limited resemblance between what regulation, as traditionally practiced, tries to do and the principles of normative microeconomic theory, thus providing the justification for our alternative approach, in Part II, and (2) the severe limitations of this institutional device for achieving optimal economic results, which provides the background for Volume 2.

THE LIMITED ATTENTION TO QUALITY OF SERVICE

The regulatory process devotes considerable attention to the denominator of the money-quantum-of-service ratio.[4] The governing statutes generally empower commissions to investigate and issue findings on whether the service offered under their jurisdiction is "unjust, unsafe, improper, inadequate or insufficient," and to promulgate rules for its improvement. The rules adopted

[1] See notes 11–20, Chapter 1. In *Adkins v. Children's Hospital*, the Court struck down a law fixing minimum wages for women in the District of Columbia in these terms:

"The essential characteristics of the statute now under consideration, which differentiate it from the laws fixing hours of labor. . . . [are] that the latter . . . deal with incidents of the employment having no necessary effect upon the heart of the contract; that is, the amount of wages. . . .

"If now, in the light furnished by the foregoing exceptions to the general rule forbidding legislative interference with freedom of contract, we examine and analyze the statute in question, we shall see that it differs from them in every material respect. It is not a law dealing with any business charged with a public interest. . . . It has nothing to do with the character, methods, or periods of wage payments. It does not prescribe hours of labor or conditions under which labor is to be done. . . . It is simply and exclusively a price-fixing law. . . ." 261 U.S. 525, 553–554 (1923).

[2] 291 U.S. 502, 531–532, 536–537 (1934).

[3] See Irston R. Barnes, *The Economics of Public Utility Regulation* (New York: Appleton-Century-Crofts, 1942), 742–743.

[4] For a useful survey, see Charles F. Phillips, Jr., *op. cit.*, 400–438.

cover matters such as safety standards, minimum physical specifications (accuracy of meters, voltage of electricity, heating value of gas), the requirements of prompt meeting of customer demands, extension of service to new customers, controls on abandonment of service, provision of special facilities and arrangements, and certification of new entrants.[5]

But it is far more true of quality of service than of price that the primary responsibility remains with the supplying company instead of with the regulatory agency, and that the agencies, in turn, have devoted much more attention to the latter than to the former. The reasons for this are fairly clear. Service standards are often much more difficult to specify by the promulgation of rules. Where they can be specified, they are often essentially uncontroversial. Where they cannot—and this is particularly the case when it comes to innovations, to the dynamic improvement of service—in a system in which the private companies do the managing and the government the supervision, there is no choice but to leave the initiative with the company itself. The only role the regulatory commission can typically play is a negative one—formulating minimum standards and using periodic inspections to see that they are met; investigating customer complaints and issuing orders when service has been obviously poor, when management or subordinates have been blatantly inefficient or unfair, or when it wishes to insist that the companies take on or retain unremunerative business.[6]

This authority is by no means negligible. The aggressive commission has available to it the ability to penalize offending companies by holding permissible rates at less remunerative levels than it would otherwise be prepared to allow—subject to the constraint, however, that it would be self-defeating to punish them so severely as to impair their financial capacity to institute the desired improvements. And commissions frequently do use this weapon.[7]

Still, their role is essentially a negative one and this raises fundamental questions about the efficacy of the entire process. If, as far as quality of service is concerned, the principal responsibility rests with the private monopolist,

[5] "Public utility commissions are constantly passing upon questions of service. The determination of a rate without a determination of the quality of the service rendered would be similar to an individual's agreeing to pay a stipulated sum of money for a commodity without specifying the kind or grade of commodity he expects to receive in return for his outlay. A very large portion of the commissions' time is, then, necessarily devoted to the determination of the quality of service rendered by the utilities under their jurisdiction. Most states which have active commissions now have state-wide service standards. . . . Where there are departures from these standards the utility is obviously derelict in the performance of its duties, and unless excused by the commission because of unusual circumstances is subject to its disapproval." Charles Stillman Morgan, ***Regulation and the Management of Public Utilities*** (Boston: Houghton Mifflin, 1923), 270–271.

[6] The question of whether and in what circumstances a utility company may be required to extend service to new customers and areas, or be forbidden to discontinue services may of course be regarded as an aspect of the regulation of service and is usually so treated. But the issue here is usually quite explicitly one of price or of the relation of revenues to costs, present or prospective: to what extent may utilities be required to take on new, or continue to serve old markets that they think are or will be unremunerative; to what extent should profitable business subsidize unprofitable extensions or continuations? These issues are thus embraced (sometimes explicitly, sometimes implicitly) in our later discussions of cost-price relationships. Of course, as we have already suggested, all regulations of service quality are in economic effect also regulations of price.

[7] For example,

"The testimony given in the gas service case hearing at Neenah was conclusive that the quality of service rendered is totally inadequate. . . . The Commission finds therefore that no increase in rates for gas should be given consideration until the service rendered in the gas department shall conform in a reasonable manner to the standard laid down by the Commission. . . . That no increase in rates for the electric and street railway departments of this utility should be granted until the service in each of them shall be shown to be reasonably satisfactory, and the burden of proof of so doing shall be put on the company. . . ." Morgan, *op. cit.*, 272.

Or, to turn to more recent examples:

"We are receiving numerous complaints from portions of the territory served by Southern Bell. In some areas . . . installation intervals, or the time required to install service, fall well below a reasonable standard. Operator answering time consistently meets Bell's requirements but does not meet the standards recently adopted by this commission. By far the biggest complaint . . . is the length of time required to obtain service. . . . These are problems that can and must be resolved. We have recently adopted uniform standards for telephone service, and have prescribed administrative rules requiring periodic reports which, together with field inspections, will keep the commission fully advised concerning the quality and sufficiency of telephone service being provided. . . . Any rate adjustments, including the one in this docket, will be on a temporary basis for a reasonable period of time pending any necessary improvements in the quality and sufficiency of service. . . .

"Southern Bell will be required to furnish a good and sufficient surety bond conditioned on the prompt and full refund of the difference, if any, between the rates collected by it on a temporary basis pursuant to this order, and the rates ultimately prescribed or approved . . . . as a result of any further order that may be entered in this docket reducing such temporary rates because of service deficiencies."

Re Southern Bell Telephone and Telegraph Company, Florida Public Service Commission, Order No. 4462, November 26, 1968, 76 *Public Utility Reports* 3rd, 412–413.

"We make the following findings:

1. The present earnings of United Telephone Company of Florida are far below a reasonable level and said utility is entitled to some relief on a temporary and emergency basis.
2. United Telephone's present earnings of 3.15 per cent will not support the additional financing that is necessary to enable it to complete its improvement program.
3. The telephone service presently being rendered . . . by United Telephone has improved substantially during the past several months, but is not sufficiently adequate and efficient to justify the full increases requested. . . .
4. The company has virtually completed 64 per cent of its current 3-year (1967–1969) improvement program and, thus, has been able to bring about substantial improvement in service. On that basis, it is fair and reasonable to allow the utility 64 per cent of the requested increases in local exchange rates. . . .
5. The emergency increases authorized by this order will not result at this time in a fair and reasonable return for United Telephone Company, but will improve its financial position so that it should be able to finance the remainder of its improvement program. . . ."

Re United Telephone Company of Florida, Florida Public Service Commission, Order No. 4451, November 12, 1968, 76 PUR 3rd, 471.
For other examples, see *ibid.*, 441–451 and 461.

"After years of deliberation, the Federal Communications Commission has decided to tackle the controversial question of how fast Western Union Telegraph Co. should be required to deliver telegrams. . . .

"Communications experts say the commission's involvement could lead to the first Government-mandated standards regulating the speed of domestic telegram deliveries. . . .

"Western Union Telegraph has come under increasing fire in recent years from critics who complain that the cost of telegrams keeps going up while the quality of service declines. . . .

"The FCC's decision to consider the speed-of-service issue cropped up as a little-noticed part of the FCC's current investigation of telegram rate increases proposed by Western Union Telegraph. In announcing the inquiry, the FCC said it would consider not only the rate boosts, but also the 'speed, quality and adequacy' of the company's telegram service.

"FCC officials say this phrase means the commission probably will deal with a number of service-related telegram issues in its investigation, such as how many telegraph offices Western Union Telegraph should maintain, and whether it should be investing more money in its telegram service. But a key question, these sources maintain, is whether the FCC should force Western Union to meet certain speed requirements in its telegram deliveries. . . ." *Wall Street Journal*, October 18, 1968.

Again, in 1969 the New York State Public Service Commission ordered the Penn Central Company to take more than a dozen specific steps to provide "safe, adequate, just and reasonable service" on its Harlem and Hudson commuter lines, including the purchase or lease of at least 80 new cars and 24 new engines, assuring that each of its 340 weekday trains runs on time at lest 80% of the time each month, and providing enough telephone lines and employees

and the government supervisor can intervene only where objective standards can be set or, after the event, when the monopolist's performance has been *obviously bad*,[8] do we have an adequate assurance—comparable to the assurance provided by competition in other sectors of the economy—that his performance will be *positively good* and continuously as good as possible? If poor service is economically the equivalent of high price, why is there not just as great a danger that monopoly power will involve the one as the other? If monopoly carries the danger of sluggishness with respect both to efficiency and to dynamic cost-reduction, is there not the danger of sluggishness as well in improving the quality and extending the scope of service?

These problems are real. Although, as we shall see later, they can never be wholly solved within the regulatory framework, they deserve more creative and active attention from commissions than they now receive.[9] But there is another reason why public utility commissions have been willing, and to some extent justified, to leave the quality of service, far more than price, to the companies themselves—the latter will typically have a strong interest in providing good, ample, and expanding service, as long as they can recoup its costs in the prices they charge. In this respect, far more than in the matter of price, the interest of the monopolist on the one hand and the consumer on the other are more nearly coincident than in conflict.[10] Why so?

1. Maintaining and improving the quality and quantity of service typically is costly. Any regulated monopolist who is prevented by regulation from fully exploiting the inelasticity of his demand but assured (albeit with a regulatory lag) of his ability to incorporate these additional costs in his cost-of-service and hence of recouping them in his price, will presumably be less hesitant than a nonregulated monopolist to incur them.[11]
2. Improvement and extension of service will often involve an expansion of the company's invested capital—that is, its "rate base"—on which it is entitled to a return. The regulated monopolist therefore will have some

---

so that passengers phoning to check on train schedules "receive a prompt response." *The New York Times*, June 6, 1969, 1. In response, the company petitioned for a rehearing. *Ibid.*, July 4, 1969, 1.

For a more general discussion of the way in which service standards and orders may be enforced and particularly of the authority of commissions to condition rate increases on specified improvements or extensions of service, see "The Duty of a Public Utility to Render Adequate Service: Its Scope and Enforcement," *Columbia Law Rev.* (Feb. 1962), LXII: 312, 327–331.

[8] See the astonishing intention of Senator Pastore, chairman of the U.S. Senate Subcommittee on Communications, explicitly to confine the powers of the Federal Communications Commission in precisely this manner in deciding whether or not to renew broadcasting station licenses. He would prohibit challenges to renewals unless the FCC first determines that the station has violated the "public interest." Daniel Zwerdling, "FCC Impropriety," *The New Republic*, June 21, 1969, 10–11. See also note 134, Chapter 2, Volume 2.

[9] For the case of radio and television, and for a novel case involving the quality of passenger rail service, see Chapter 2 of Volume 2.

[10] Indeed, the greater danger might be that the companies place excessive instead of inadequate emphasis on providing high-quality service, at the expense of economy, for reasons that follow. See also the discussion in Chapter 5, Volume 2, of whether the public utilities reflect a general tendency for limitations on price competition to be associated with an intensification of quality competition.

[11] The unregulated monopolist also will have an incentive to improve his product or diversify his product offerings, to the extent that his demand is sufficiently responsive to offset the additional costs of his so doing. But if he is a profit maximizer presumably he will have set his price-quality combination at the profit-maximizing point, beyond which superior service will add more to costs than to revenues. A public utility, in contrast, if prevented from fixing its price at the profit-maximizing level, has a reserve of incompletely exploited monopoly power; in the

temptation to err in the direction of expanding and improving his services, and thus increasing his rate base beyond the point of economic optimality instead of the reverse.[12]

3. A public utility company is peculiarly exposed to public criticism if its service is inadequate. This exposure is increased by the possibility of customers complaining to regulatory commissions. Possibly associated with this consideration may be a tendency for managers of such companies to assume a quasi-professional responsibility for giving the best possible service, even at the expense of profit maximization.[13] Although customers may have very definite opinions about whether the prices they pay are too high, the determination of whether in fact they are doing so is a complicated matter, as we shall see. But they need no complex investigative and adjudicatory processes to tell them when they are suffering from a power failure, or a refusal of a railroad to make freight cars available to them, or when they keep getting busy signals or wrong numbers on the telephone.[14] Adequate levels of service can be guaranteed more satisfactorily than price by customer complaints, on the one hand, and the "conscience of the corporation," on the other.[15]

It is doubtful that these pressures are as reliable as those exerted by competition; and an unregulated monopolist will surely be subject to similar influences. Still, motivations such as these do to some extent take the place of competition in inducing the franchised monopolist to have a favorable attitude toward providing good and ever-improving service to his captive customers.

The customer may have a fair notion of whether the service he gets is satisfactory. He is likely to find it much more difficult to judge whether its quality and variety are *improving* at a satisfactory rate, because in making such a judgment it would not be pertinent to compare the quality of what he is receiving with what he has been accustomed to expect. But it is precisely these questions about dynamic performance, with respect not only to the quality of service but also to costs and price, that the regulatory commission also is least competent to answer decisively. Although it is in this respect that there may be the greatest danger of inadequate monopoly performance—or *excessive* performance, for the reason suggested under (2), above—this danger is not one to which the commissions have typically been able to devote effective attention.

REGULATING THE RATE LEVEL

Public utility commissions spend the major part of their time, by far, directly or indirectly regulating price. This task has two major aspects and the commissions have tended typically to treat them quite distinctly. The first has to do with the level of rates, taken as a group. The second has to do with the structure of rates—the specific charges on different categories of

same circumstances it will therefore have less disincentive to improve service, since any additional costs involved can serve as the justification for raising price correspondingly.

[12] On this particular distortion, see the section on the "A-J-W Effect," in Chapter 2, Volume 2.

[13] See, for example, Troxel, *Economics of Public Utilities*, 464–465, 557–560.

[14] See the flurry of complaints in New York City in July of 1969 over the annoying frequency of busy signals in the New York Telephone Company's Plaza 8 exchange. See, for instance, *New York Times*, July 14, 1969, 22.

[15] But see Glaeser, *op cit.*, 115, emphasizing the need for regulation, to overcome consumer ignorance and managerial inertia.

service and the relationship between them. Outside of the transportation field, the former task has claimed much the greater share of commission attention.

"The rate level," like "the general price level," is a statistical abstraction. It could be expressed only as some sort of index number, summarizing the numerous individual rates for the various classifications of service provided by each company: there are some 43 trillion railroad rates on file with the Interstate Commerce Commission![16] Its real economic meaning is disclosed when these separate prices are translated into total company revenues or into total profits expressed as a percent of owners' investments. Actually the regulatory process works the other way around. The commissions decide what total revenues the companies are entitled to take in, then adjust permitted "rate levels," either selectively or across the board, to yield these totals.

They typically do this by undertaking a thorough examination and appraisal of total company costs in a recent, "test" year.[17] In this way, item by item, they build up an estimate of total permissible "revenue requirements." On the basis of this total, adjusted as much as possible for known or readily predictable changes between the test year and the period for which rates are to be ascertained, the company is ordered or permitted to propose the required adjustments in its rate schedules. Therefore, discussions of rate levels are really discussions of total revenues.

The process of determining permissible revenues falls traditionally into the following three parts or steps, each of them involving an enormous variety of problems and boasting a correspondingly rich history of legal and economic controversy.

Supervision and Control of Operating Costs and Capital Outlays

Just as competition is supposed to hold prices down to the cost of production (ignore for a moment the question of precisely what that means) so regulation takes cost as its standard of the "revenue requirements" of public utility companies, hence the "just and reasonable" rates that the typical controlling statute enjoins them to maintain. It became clear that if the commissions were to be something more than rubber stamps they had to exercise their own judgment about the propriety of the items presented to them as the major components of the cost of service. To do so, first, they had to require the companies to keep uniform systems of accounts, according to procedures and rules stipulated by the commissions, and subject to their audit.[18] Then they needed to make determinations about which costs they were prepared

---

[16] C. F. Phillips, *op. cit.*, 314.

[17] They may do so regularly or only once in a long while, in a major general rate investigation, or never. If only occasionally, they may employ more limited checks in the intervening years, possibly permitting rate changes on the basis of estimates of cost changes since the "test year." For an illuminating case study of "The General Passenger Fare Investigation," the first undertaken by the Civil Aeronautics Board, about 15 years after passage of its enabling act (a delay for which it was criticized), see the case study of that title by Emmette S. Redford, in Edwin A. Bock, ed., *Government Regulation of Business: A Casebook* (Englewood Cliffs: Prentice-Hall, 1962), 336–411. On the Federal Communications Commission's "continuous surveillance" over the telephone industry, see Chapter 2, Volume 2, at note 37.

[18] Commissions cannot review costs unless the regulated companies keep their records in some uniform and prescribed fashion. Accounting regulations become necessary also to prescribe those elements of outlay that are to be charged

to authorize for inclusion in the computed company cost-of-service; and, of these, which could be charged directly as operating expenses and thus included in annual revenue requirements dollar for dollar, and which capitalized, thus entering the cost of service in the form of annual allowances for depreciation and return on the undepreciated portion of the investment. Since mere disallowance of certain outlays after the fact could have the effect of reducing excessively the companies' rates of return, and hence of threatening their ability to attract additional capital, commissions came to insist also on the authority to control company expenditure in advance, supervising and passing on their budgets.

Why should it be necessary for commissions to involve themselves in passing on the operating costs of public utility companies? Presumably even an unregulated profit-maximizing monopolist would wish to hold his costs to a minimum, entirely on his own initiative. Could not the commissions then leave such matters to the self-interest of the company managers themselves? Answers can be framed at several levels.

First, there is the simple danger of concealment of profits by exaggeration of costs. Whatever his *actual* level of costs, it obviously pays a regulated monopolist to exaggerate his estimated cost of service. As long as regulation is effective in holding his profits lower than they otherwise could be, he can more completely exploit his monopoly power by fooling the commission into permitting him higher rates than his actual costs justify. Such exaggerations might be expected to show up, after the event, in excessive rates of earnings. But profits can be computed only from accounting records; if there are no understandings about how costs are to be computed and recorded, expenditures to be audited, and the capital value of the stockholders' investment to be measured, there is no way of appraising those records, and supernormal rates of profit can be concealed in padded expense figures and inflated capital accounts.

Second, the charge for depreciation represents not an objective datum but an imputation, an attribution to the production in any given accounting period of responsibility for the using up or obsolescence of capital assets. Similar to the cost of capital itself—that is, the requisite return on invested capital that must likewise be included in the cost of production—there is room for differences of judgment about its proper level. It is obviously in the interest of the regulated company to exaggerate its gross cost of capital—depreciation plus return on investment—and for the commission to hold it to the minimum, as we shall see more fully presently.

Third, it might be in the interest of the company—always assuming that regulation is effective in holding its profits below the levels that the market would otherwise permit—to incur actually greater costs than is in the best interest of the consumer, provided it is then permitted to incorporate those costs in the regulated price. One example would be heavy expenditures for advertising and public relations, since the companies might receive numerous

---

directly to income and those that are to be capitalized. The appropriate charges for depreciation cannot be determined and reviewed unless the depreciable property accounts are kept in some comprehensible fashion. Accounting rules are also necessary with respect to the valuation of property, which plays an extremely important role in determining the final cost of service, as we shall see. They are similarly necessary if the utility company itself or the commission is to use cost intelligently in the devising of rate structures.

benefits therefrom while passing the costs on to the consuming public. Public utility companies advertise in the hope of influencing regulatory commissions to treat them generously, and electric companies have financed expensive propaganda campaigns in opposition to competing public power projects.[19] Similar purposes might be served by large charitable contributions; with these, as with advertising outlays, commissions have had to decide how much, if any, is properly charged to the consumer and how much should be borne by the stockholders. A similar need for regulatory supervision could be created by the possible temptation of utility companies—to which we have already alluded, and which we will analyze more fully below—to use capital wastefully in order to inflate their rate bases and hence their total permissible profits.

Fourth, the regulated companies—even more, their promoters and managers—have extracted some of these potential monopoly profits by paying excessive prices to affiliated, unregulated companies for equipment, supplies, financial advice and underwriting, engineering, and managerial services—charges included in the cost of service and recovered from customers.[20]

Fifth, since the public utilities are typically not subject to intensive price competition, they are probably not under the same pressures as firms in more competitive industries to hold their costs down. It is understandable, therefore, that regulatory commissions, charged with taking the place of competition, should make some efforts in the same direction. The necessity for their doing so is accentuated, finally, by the unusually high degree of

[19] See Ernest Gruening, *The Public Pays: A Study of Power Propaganda*, rev. ed. (New York: Vanguard, 1964), *passim*. Gruening includes (xxix-xliii) the *Memorandum Opinion* of the Federal Power Commission, *In the Matter of Northwestern Electric Company et al.*, Docket No. IT–5647, Opinion No. 59, 1941, reporting on its investigation of the accounting disposition of expenditures for political purposes by five electric companies. Merle Fainsod and Lincoln Gordon report an estimate that the costs of the "educational" campaign by utility companies after World War I "to 'sell' their industry to the public and to convince the American people of the adequacy of existing regulatory techniques and of the dangers of further penetration of government into the utility business" ran $25–30 millions a year, "all charged off as proper advertising expenses . . . and computed in the rates which the public was required to pay." *Government and The American Economy* (New York: Norton, 1941), 308. And those were Coolidge and Hoover, not Nixon, dollars. The problem, although ancient, has not disappeared: "Five Manhattan State Senators protested yesterday what they called the Consolidated Edison Company's 'gigantic' advertising and promotion campaigns in connection with its request for higher electricity charges." According to the Company's own estimate, its expenditures for institutional advertising would have come to some $2.1 millions in 1965. *New York Times*, August 23, 1966, 27.

Utility companies engage in commercial as well as political and "institutional" advertising, and the former expenditures may well be economically legitimate (see, for example, note 16, Chapter 4). American Telephone and Telegraph (AT&T) and its affiliated companies ranked fourteenth among the nation's advertisers in 1965 with total expenditures of $70 million. But this was a relatively modest 0.6% of the system's total revenues, of $11.3 billion. *Advertising Age*, August 29, 1966, 44, 61.

For a summary of the regulatory treatment of such expenditures, see A. J. G. Priest, *Principles of Public Utility Regulation*, 59–65; also "Trends and Topics, Promotional Programs," *Public Utilities Fortnightly* (June 23, 1966), LXXVII: 65.

[20] See, for example, Louis D. Brandeis, *Other People's Money and How the Bankers Use It* (Washington: The McClure Publications, 1913); James C. Bonbright and Gardner C. Means, *The Holding Company: Its Public Significance and its Regulation* (New York: McGraw-Hill, 1932), esp. Chapter 6. The holding company in some ways has contributed to greater efficiency; but it was also used as a device for milking the (controlled) operating companies, and through them the rate-payers. The relation of the various Bell System companies to their parent, AT&T, and to its wholly-owned subsidiary and equipment

separation of ownership and managerial control in these companies.[21] This fact, taken in conjunction with the lesser pressures of price competition and the possibility of recouping higher costs in higher prices along an inelastic demand curve, creates a particular danger that, in the absence of regulatory scrutiny, managements may vote themselves unusually large salaries, expense accounts and other perquisites, as well as engage in other methods of exploiting their position for their own personal profit or nonpecuniary advantage, as in fact they have from time to time in the past.[22]

Manifestly, the operating expenses and capital outlays of public utility companies are by far the most important component of their rate levels, on the one hand, and the efficiency with which they make use of society's resources on the other. Therefore, in terms of their quantitative importance, it would be reasonable to expect regulatory commissions to give these costs the major part of their attention. But in fact they have not done so; they have given their principal attention instead to the limitation of profits.

The reasons for this perverse distribution of effort illustrate once again the inherent limitations of regulation as an institution of effective social control of industry. Effective regulation of operating expenses and capital outlays

supplier, Western Electric Company, has thus been a subject of continuing regulatory concern. In one of the landmark United States Supreme Court decisions in the 1920s the Court refused to permit the Public Service Commission of Missouri to disallow certain payments by the local Bell company to AT&T for rentals and services. *Southwestern Bell Telephone Company v. Public Service Commission of Missouri*, 262 U.S. 276, 288–289 (1923). The Court reversed itself on this matter in *Smith v. Illinois Bell Telephone Co.*, 282 U.S. 133, 152–153 (1930), and the general rule is that these charges must be justified in terms of the costs to AT&T of performing the services. Similarly, numerous state commissions check on the payments by their various Bell companies for Western Electric equipment and supplies, and the *Smith v. Illinois Bell* decision required that this scrutiny take into account Western's profits from these sales. The Michigan Commission has in the past scaled down the payments when it found that the rate of return on Western Electric's capital exceeded the rate of return that it permitted the Michigan Bell Company to earn. C. Emery Troxel, "Telephone Regulation in Michigan," in William G. Shepherd and Thomas G. Gies, ed., *Utility Regulation: New Directions in Theory and Policy* (New York: Random House, 1966), 168–169. But the overwhelming majority of commissions have found Western's charges reasonable and have permitted them to enter the operating companies' cost of service without adjustment. For a fuller discussion, see Chapter 6, Volume 2.

[21] Distribution of 176 large corporations, according to the proportion of voting stock owned by managements, September 30, 1939, by industrial classes:

Percent of Stock Outstanding	Industrial	Public Utility	Railroad
0–1	66	33	21
1–5	29	3	1
5–10	7	2	1
10–20	6	—	—
20–30	2	—	—
30–40	—	—	—
40–50	1	—	—
50 plus	4	—	—
Total	115	38	23

Source. Robert Aaron Gordon, *Business Leadership in the Large Corporation* (Washington: The Brookings Institution, 1945), 27.

A later study of the 200 largest nonfinancial corporations found that in 1963 18% of the industrial corporations were controlled by owners of more than 10% of their stock; the corresponding figures for public utility and railroad corporations were 2% and 4% respectively. At the other extreme, management-controlled companies were 78% of the industrial and 98% of the public utility group. In the case of railroads the percentage was 83, but if one adds in the corporations found to be controlled by a legal device such as pyramiding or the use of voting trusts, that figure rises to 97%, while the ratio for industrials rises only to 82%. Robert J. Larner, "Ownership and Control in the 200 Largest Nonfinancial Corporations, 1929 and 1963," *Amer. Econ. Rev.* (September 1966), LVI: 781.

[22] See Barnes, *Economics of Public Utility Regulation*, 618–619 and the cases cited there. Following up a finding by Gary S. Becker that monopolistic

would require a detailed, day-by-day, transaction-by-transaction, and decision-by-decision review of every aspect of the company's operation. Commissions could do so only if they were prepared completely to duplicate the role of management itself. This society has never been willing to have commissions fill the role of management and doubtless with good reason: it is difficult to see how any company could function under two separate, coequal managements, each with an equally pervasive role in its operations. Therefore, when the controlling decisions are made, they are made in the first instance by private management itself. Regulation can do little more than review the major decisions after the fact, permitting here and disallowing there. In these circumstances they have been unable as a general practice to substitute their judgments for those of management; and often when they have tried, the courts have denied them the authority to do so, except in cases of obvious and gross mismanagement.[23] Profits, in contrast, are merely a markup, something added to the sum total of expenses. This does not mean that profit control is noncontroversial—quite the contrary. But their regulation does not involve the same type of detailed and pervasive supervision as would a comparable control of the decisions that determine a company's efficiency.

---

enterprises discriminate against blacks more frequently than competitive ones, Armen A. Alchian and Reuben A. Kessel developed the more general hypothesis that the managements of companies whose pecuniary profits are limited by regulation (or similar pressures) will be under strong temptation to take out any possibilities of monopoly profit that remain unexploited in the form of "nonpecuniary gains," one category of which is "the indulgence of one's tastes in the kind of people with whom one prefers to associate. Specifically, this may take the form of pretty secretaries, pleasant, well-dressed congenial people who never say anything annoying, of lavish offices, of large expense accounts, of shorter working hours, of costly administrative procedures that reduce the wear and tear on executives . . . having secretaries available on a moment's notice . . . and of many others." "Competition, Monopoly, and the Pursuit of Pecuniary Gain," in Universities-National Bureau Committee for Economic Research, *Aspects of Labor Economics* (Princeton University Press: Princeton, 1962), 163. The likelihood of this managerial behavior may not be significantly greater for regulated public utility companies than in the case of unregulated companies with market power. See Oliver E. Williamson, "Managerial Discretion and Business Behavior," *Amer. Econ. Rev.* (December 1963), LIII: 1032–1057, and William G. Shepherd, "Market Power and Racial Discrimination in White-Collar Employment," *Antitrust Bulletin* (Spring 1969), XIV: 141–161 and, with particular reference to regulated companies, 155–157.

[23] See, for example, William K. Jones, *Cases and Materials on Regulated Industries* (Brooklyn: The Foundation Press, 1967), 175–186.

"Good faith is to be presumed on the part of the managers of a business. . . . In the absence of a showing of inefficiency or improvidence, a court will not substitute its judgment for theirs as to the measure of a prudent outlay." *West Ohio Gas Co. v. Public Utilities Commission* 294 U.S. 63, 72 (1935). See the exhaustive summary of the case law in Priest, *Principles of Public Utility Regulation*, I, Chapter 3.

On the other hand:

"The Alaska commission upheld disallowance of $50,000 of expenses to compensate for inefficiencies in an electric company's operation. Comparison of the company's expense with that of automated companies . . . showed the cost to be one and one-half to seven times that of the other companies designated as comparable. . . .

"[According to the hearing officer:] It was not out of place for the commission to disallow expenses claimed to be excessive because available advances in technology had been ignored and the capacity and efficiency of the plant had been eroded through years of inadequate maintenance. . . .

"It was not so much a matter of how the company stacked up in relation to the efficiency of other companies, but a measurement of how it operated at present compared to how it would have operated if suggested recommendations had been put into effect. . . .

"The company had adequate notice and opportunity to institute procedures recommended by engineers it had hired as consultants, which it had neglected to do."

"Expense Reduction to Compensate for Inefficiencies Upheld," *Public Utilities Fortnightly*, March 27, 1969, 60–61.

The process has focused primarily on profits, also, because these are politically the most visible—excessive profits the most obvious danger and sign of consumer exploitation, in the absence of effective competition, regulated profits the most obvious and comforting evidence that regulation can be "effective."[24]

And in those numerous, though comparatively unimportant instances in which commissions do in fact decide whether or not to disallow some item of expenditure, the governing consideration turns out to be what policy would be most "fair" to stockholders on the one hand and consumers on the other—a constantly recurring theme in the regulatory process.[25] It is certainly not suggested here that considerations such as these are irrelevant in what is, inescapably, a political determination—that is, a determination of who gets what and how much (and the "who" may include not just stockholders, managers, and customers but, for example, the colleges, churches, or minority groups that might benefit from contributions or other such expenditures that the corporation may be unable to justify on a purely economic basis).[26] But it is important to recognize that criteria such as these may or may not coincide with the type of results competition would produce, or with what would be economically optimal.[27]

---

[24] The analogous situation prevails with respect to weapons acquisition by the Department of Defense:

"a workable definition of efficiency requires considering all of the costs generated in a weapons program, profit . . . being just one special form of cost. Herein lies the second reason for the emphasis on minimum profits as an indicator of weapons acquisition efficiency. It is usually much easier for government negotiators or auditors to say that profits are too high than to claim that the cost of developing some technically complex item of equipment is excessive. Government personnel recognize that if any item in the weapons bill can be attacked and perhaps reduced, it is the profit item. However, this Machiavellian realism ignores the 90% or more of the bill in which a much greater potential for efficiency improvements typically exists." Merton J. Peck and Frederic M. Scherer, *The Weapons Acquisition Process: An Economic Analysis*, Division of Research, Graduate School of Business Administration (Boston: Harvard University, 1962), 509.

[25] It frequently recurs outside the regulatory area as well. A striking example is to be found in the field of antitrust policy, where precisely the same issues arise about the compatibility of "fair competition" and economic efficiency. See, for example, Joel B. Dirlam and Alfred E. Kahn, *Fair Competition, The Law and Economics of Antitrust Policy* (Ithaca: Cornell University Press, 1954), which is addressed to this issue.

[26] This means that the process, being essentially political, is capable of generating violent emotions or at least rhetoric, on the part both of the industry, in its efforts to reduce the load of regulation, to justify its managements' compensation and its own performance against the threat of government competition, and of its critics, who see regulation as ineffective and the consumer subjected to merciless gouging. For a fine example of the latter, see Lee Metcalf and Vic Reinemer, *Overcharge* (New York: David McKay Company, 1967), *passim*, and, specifically on cost items such as charitable contributions, managerial compensation, and political advertising, Chapters 6, 8, and 9. It is no condescension to point out that the book's economic analysis and appraisals are neither objective nor thorough; but its argument cannot be ignored.

[27] See, for example, the survey of the policies of regulatory commissions with respect to the allowance or disallowance of promotional, public relations, or charitable expenditures in C. F. Phillips, *op. cit.*, 186–188. Or see the very interesting conflicting majority, concurring, and dissenting opinions on the subject of contributions in *Pacific Telephone and Telegraph Co. v. Public Utilities Commission of the State of California et al.*, 401 P. 2d 353, 374–375, 379–382 (1965). It is very difficult to detect any consistent consideration, let alone application, of economic criteria, of the kind to be developed in Part II. Instead there is a mushy mixture of questions such as: Do these outlays benefit the company? Or the community at large? Or the stockholders, mainly? Are they properly part of the utility business? What would be fair? These observations are by no means intended to suggest that application of "strictly economic" criteria would provide any simple answers to these problems either.

Therefore, although efficient operation and continuous improvement therein are, quantitatively, the most important aspects of industrial performance, the principal reliance for securing these results cannot, in the nature of the case, be placed on the regulatory process itself. The major contribution that regulation can make, and it is a modest one, can only be the providing of incentives—or taking care not to remove incentives—for private managements to exert themselves continuously in this direction. Whether such incentives can ever be sufficient, once the spur of competition has been drastically attenuated, is the fundamental question with which we deal in Volume 2.

The allowance for depreciation expenses is of quite a different character. Operating expenses involve actual money outlays, which can be automatically recorded in company accounts and transferred into the computed cost of service. Depreciation, too, goes into cost of service and price; but it is not a money outlay in the year it is charged. It is an imputed cost, introduced to take account of the fact that the economic life of capital assets is limited; to distribute the decline in their value—which is a genuine cost of production—over their economic life, in order to assure its recoupment from customers. So the portion of total revenues it permits the company to earn does not, as is the case with normal operating expenses, go out in payments to outside parties—suppliers of raw materials, workers and so on. It belongs to the owners; it is part of the gross return they are permitted to earn on their investment.

The return to capital, in other words, has two parts: the return *of* the money capital invested over the estimated economic life of the investment and the return (interest and net profit) *on* the portion of investment that remains outstanding. The two are arithmetically linked, since according to the usual (but not universal) regulatory practice the size of the net investment, on which a return is permitted, depends at any given time on the aggregate amount of depreciation expense allowed in the previous years—that is, the amount of investment that remains depends on how much of it has been recouped by annual depreciation charges previously. And the two are linked economically, since the rate at which owners are permitted to get their capital out helps determine the true rate of return that they earn on their original investment. To the extent—as happens in some jurisdictions—that accrued depreciation is not fully deducted from the rate base, the regulated companies in effect are being permitted a higher rate of profit; and the same result could be achieved by allowing a higher nominal rate on original investment cost less full depreciation.

Any economic discussion of depreciation should really consider it along with the return on investment. In many contexts it must take into account also the changing provisions of the corporation income tax law concerning allowable rates of depreciation for tax purposes. Consider, for instance, the three-fold effect on the cost of service, hence on allowable rates of return, of provisions for accelerated depreciation in the income tax laws, such as were enacted in 1964, via (1) what it may do to the appropriate level of annual depreciation expense allowed by the regulatory commission, (2) the effect of different rates of annual depreciation on the net remaining investment, on which the net return is permitted, and (3) the amount of income taxes that ought to be included in the cost of service. That requires some explanation.

The effect of accelerated tax depreciation is not to reduce total taxes paid over the life of any particular piece of capital equipment, but only to change its timing. Only the original cost of the equipment can be charged off, in total, over its life. When a company charges a disproportionately large part of the total in the earlier years for tax purposes—which has the effect of reducing taxable income, hence taxes—this means it will be able to charge off correspondingly less, hence will be forced to pay equivalently higher taxes, in later years. Assuming no change in tax rates in the interim, the taxes saved in the early years have to be paid back in full in the later years. But the postponement is beneficial to the taxpayer; in effect, accelerated depreciation means the Treasury Department is giving him an interest-free loan, during the period of the postponement. It increases the real rate (after tax) of return on investment, if one is permitted to keep more of his profits for a while, before having to hand them over to the government.

So regulatory commissions have had to decide whether the taxes to be incorporated in price should be only those actually paid—in which event the benefits of accelerated depreciation are passed on entirely to customers in the years of tax saving—or "normalized" over the life of the investment (higher than actual taxes in the early years, lower in the later)—in which event the interest-free loan is retained by the company. If the latter is chosen, commissions have had to decide also what treatment should be given to the revenues recouped from consumers in excess of the taxes actually paid in the earlier years. These "phantom taxes" are typically segregated in a special reserve for deferred taxes, in recognition of the fact that taxes will in later years exceed these "normalized" recoupments from customers. But the controversial question is whether the amount of that reserve should be deducted from the company's net investment or rate base, on the ground that, as with depreciation, these monies have been retrieved from customers and that it would be double recoupment to permit the company also to earn a return on that portion of its undepreciated investment; or whether it should be left in the rate base, because Congress intended the tax savings to benefit investors and by so doing to encourage additional investment. The more frequent practice is to permit the company no return on the assets represented by the tax reserve; but many commissions permit a small return (for example, 1.5%, in contrast with 6.5% on the normal rate base), and some allow the full return—that is, they do not reduce the rate base by the accumulations of deferred taxes at all.[28]

Advocates of including in the cost of service only the taxes actually paid, which involves "flowing through" the benefits of accelerated depreciation to the customers, argue that the benefits are likely to be permanent—that is, that the amount of taxes saved is not really postponed but is, in effect, forgiven. And they are more right than wrong, *provided* the company's total investments grow over time at a sufficiently rapid rate. In that event, the tax postponements on its newer (and ever larger) investments will always exceed the higher taxes continually coming due on the older (and smaller) investments. Indeed, as long as total company assets grow at all, taxes will always be lower under accelerated amortization than they would be otherwise. Opponents of flow-through, assuming instead that the tax is merely postponed, maintain that this method confers a windfall of rate reductions on

[28] See Eugene F. Brigham, "Public Utility Depreciation Practices and Policies," *National Tax J.* (June 1966), XIX: 149.

current customers at the expense of future customers. And, indeed, under almost any assumption about future growth of the company, rates under flow-through *will* have to be increased at some time in the future—although, as long as growth is positive, not to the levels that would have to be charged all the way along by a company that failed to take advantage of this tax privilege.

Rate-payers benefit from normalization also, as long as the accumulated tax reserve is deducted in whole or in part from the rate base, since they no longer have to pay a return on that part of the company's total assets represented by those accumulated tax-savings. Flow-through gives them the greatest immediate benefit. Whether in the long run rates end up lower under flow-through than normalization depends, for the reasons already indicated, on how rapidly the company's total assets grow.[29]

Not surprisingly, there has been continuous controversy and litigation over which of these methods, if either, utility commissions ought to adopt; and, if they adopt flow-through, whether regulated companies can be required to avail themselves of the tax privileges, although they retain none of the benefits and run the risk of having to ask for rate increases in the future.[30] These are really questions of the appropriate return to be permitted on capital investment. When company spokesmen argue against flowing-through or deducting the deferred-tax reserves from their allowable rate base, they are in effect arguing for a larger return on investment. When consumer representatives argue on the other side, their contention, at least implicitly, is that regulation must in any case provide a sufficient rate of return—in which event these additional incentives are unnecessary and ought to be passed on in lower rates.

Another issue associated with the determination of depreciation expense is whether the number of dollars that investors are permitted in this fashion to recoup from customers should be the amounts originally invested, or whether that total should be adjusted over time to reflect the changing purchasing power of those dollars. Here, again, the question is really one of what type of return investors ought to be permitted; in economic essence, it is the same issue in another form as whether the rate base, on which the

[29] For a general survey of the issues, see Garfield and Lovejoy, *Public Utility Economics*, 109–114. For a very lucid account and analysis of the pattern of rates over time under the various possible systems and under different growth rate assumptions, see Eugene F. Brigham, "The Effects of Alternative Tax Depreciation Policies on Public Utility Rate Structures," *National Tax J.* (June 1967), XX: 204–218.

[30] A survey at the outset of 1970 showed that commissions in 20 states required normalization, in 17 flowing-through, and in 12 had taken no action at all. Both the Federal Power Commission and the Interstate Commerce Commission have ordered flow-through; the Civil Aeronautics Board, normalization; and the Federal Communications Commission has taken no stand, except to declare that the failure of a regulated company to take advantage of accelerated depreciation for tax purposes would be taken into account in fixing the rate of return. "States Split on Accelerated Depreciation," *Electrical World*, January 20, 1969, 73, and *ibid.*, January 12, 1970, 12. FPC decisions requiring flow-through and computing company costs of service *as though* the companies had availed themselves of the tax privileges even though they had ceased to do so, have been sustained in the courts. See *Alabama-Tennessee Natural Gas Co. v. Federal Power Commission*, 359 F. 2d 318 (1966), cert. denied, 385 U.S. 847 (1967); *Natural Gas Pipeline Co. of America v. Federal Power Commission*, 385 F. 2d 629 (1967); and *Midwestern Gas Transmission et al. v. Federal Power Commission*, 388 F. 2d 444 (1968), cert. denied 392 U.S. 928 (1968). But the ability of commissions to require flowing-through was severely curtailed by the 1969 income tax law revision. Public Law 91–172, 91st Congress, December 30, 1969, 83 Stat. 487, 625–628.

allowable return is to be computed, should be similarly adjusted—to which we turn shortly.

The treatment of depreciation expense under public utility regulation provides an early illustration of the respects in which pricing here departs from the norms of microeconomic theory. It is an elementary proposition of that model and one aspect of its central rule, as we shall see more fully in Chapter 3, that price ideally should be set at marginal cost—that is, at short-run marginal cost. But that marginal cost is a measure of changes in *variable* costs alone; it does not include (most of) depreciation, or any part of the net return on investment, as such. Nor do monopolists, who are supposed to equate marginal cost to marginal revenue, take depreciation into account either in their pricing decisions—again according to the traditional theory of the firm, which assumes continuous, short-run profit maximization. In both cases this means, roughly, that the businessman must cover his variable costs, if he is to continue to operate at all; and so far as gross return on investment is concerned, he takes as much as he can get, over and above the variable costs—sometimes much, sometimes little—whatever the market will bear. It is only in the long run, over the life of investments, that prices, thus set, are expected to be high enough on the average to cover fixed costs. Therefore, when regulatory commissions include fixed costs such as depreciation and return on investment in their cost of service computations, and hence in the permissible rates, they are in effect requiring not marginal-cost but average-cost or full-cost pricing—a practice widely followed in unregulated industries as well. How serious this departure from optimum pricing is in practice is a major topic of Part II.

Determination of the "Rate Base"

Since the production of public utility services typically is unusually capital-intensive,[31] the element of cost represented by the return on invested capital necessarily bulks larger in their final selling price than in unregulated

[31] Garfield and Lovejoy offer as typical the following capital turnover ratios (gross revenues divided by capital investment).

Electric utilities	0.30
Natural gas utilities	0.60
Natural gas pipelines	0.40
Bell Telephone System	0.40
Water utilities	0.20
Total manufacturing	2.00

Source. *Op. cit.*, 23.

A clearer impression of the unusually heavy utilization of capital in the public utility industries is provided by the following skeletal financial data taken from the Annual Reports of a public utility, a steel, and a grocery retailing company. Note the wide range in the ratios of their capital to sales, whether the former is measured by total assets, fixed assets —land, plant, and equipment—or, on the liability side, by total invested capital—that is, long-term debt and owners' equity. Or, to describe the same relationship by its reciprocal, note the differences in the number of times their capital "turns over" each year in the form of sales.

	Pacific Gas and Electric Co.	United States Steel Corp.	The Great Atlantic & Pacific Tea Co. (A&P)
Current assets	236	2,091	558
Land, plant, and equipment, net	3,551	3,446	326
Other assets	28	854	—
Total assets	3,815	6,391	884

industries generally.[32] And since it is this element in the cost of service that determines the size of the company's profit, it is not surprising that its determination has been by far the most hotly contested aspect of regulation,[33] consuming by far the greatest amount of time of both commissions and courts.

The number of dollars of investment return are, of course, a product of the aggregate investment, on which some return is to be allowed, and the percentage rate permitted. Arithmetically, the two factors are of equal importance; the result can be changed by increasing or decreasing one just as well as the other. But, largely for constitutional reasons, the traditional emphasis and focus of most of the litigation in the American regulatory experience has been on the former, the "rate base."

It was not always so. In its historic *Munn v. Illinois* decision, the Supreme Court addressed itself to the contention of the appellants that it was up to the courts to determine whether the rates prescribed—in this case by the legislature itself—were reasonable or unreasonable. It specifically declined to do so:

"It is insisted, however, that the owner of property is entitled to a reason-

	Pacific Gas and Electric Co.	United States Steel Corp.	The Great Atlantic & Pacific Tea Co. (A&P)
Long term debt	1,830	—	—
Owners equity	1,625	3,344	627
Total invested capital	3,456	3,344	627
Sales	1,005	4,609	5,459
Ratios to sales:			
Total assets	3.8	1.4	0.16
Fixed assets	3.5	0.7	0.06
Invested capital	3.4	0.7	0.11

Source. The P.G.&E. and U.S. Steel figures are for 1968, the A&P for the fiscal year 1967–68; balance sheet items are for the end of those years. From their *Annual Reports*.

[32] Capital costs as a percentage of sales, 1965.

	Net Income After Taxes Plus Interest Paid %[a]	Depreciation Plus Income Taxes %[b]
Transportation	5.9	9.7
Communications	13.4	18.6
Electric, gas, and sanitary services	15.4	19.3
Total manufacturing	5.1	6.3

Source. Computed from U.S. Treasury Department, Internal Revenue Service, *Statistics of Income, 1965, Corporation Income Tax Returns*, Washington, 1969, 17, 20.

[a] This column presents net return on investment (equity plus borrowed capital) as a percentage of total business receipts. Interest alone represented the following portions of the total return in the four industry groups: 41, 21, 38 and 14%, respectively.

[b] These are shown additionally in consideration of the fact, already noted, that they are also part of the gross costs of capital. The percentages in the two columns should therefore be added to obtain a fuller indication of the relative importance of all capital costs in these various industries.

[33] This generalization, along with the generalization that commissions have devoted their major attention to the general level of rates, does not apply to transportation, where, for more than four decades, profits (at least of railroads) have typically been below levels that regulatory commissions would have regarded as reasonable, and primary attention has gone instead to rate structures and the conditions of inter-carrier competition. See p. 170, below.

able compensation for its use, even though it be clothed with a public interest, and that what is reasonable is a judicial and not a legislative question.

". . . the practice has been otherwise. In countries where the common law prevails, it has been customary from time immemorial for the legislature to declare what shall be a reasonable compensation under such circumstances, or, perhaps more properly speaking, to fix a maximum beyond which any charge made would be unreasonable. . . .

"We know that this is a power which may be abused; but that is no argument against its existence. For protection against abuses by legislatures the people must resort to the polls, not to the courts."[34]

Thirteen years later, however, the Court took the opposite position:

"The question of the reasonableness of a rate of charge for transportation by a railroad company, involving as it does the element of reasonableness both as regards the company and as regards the public, is eminently a question for judicial investigation, requiring due process of law for its determination."[35]

Finally, in *Smyth v. Ames*, in 1898, the Court not only strongly reaffirmed its responsibility under the Fourteenth Amendment's due process clause to review the reasonableness of rates set by state commissions, but it proceeded to specify its criteria of reasonableness:

"We hold . . . that the basis of all calculations as to the reasonableness of rates to be charged by a corporation maintaining a highway under legislative sanction [the case in question involved a railroad] must be the *fair value* of the property being used by it for the convenience of the public. And in order to ascertain that value, the original cost of construction, the amount expended in permanent improvements, the amount and market value of its bonds and stock, *the present as compared with the original cost of construction*, the probable earning capacity of the property under particular rates prescribed by statute, and the sum required to meet operating expenses, are all matters for consideration, and are to be given such weight as may be just and right in each case. We do not say that there may not be other matters to be regarded in estimating the value of the property. What the company is entitled to ask is a fair return upon the value of that which it employs for the public convenience."[36]

The "specification" was hardly precise; several of the listed "matters for consideration" were distressingly vague, and the Court was also vague about how it wanted all of them, along with the "other matters," combined into a composite "fair value" figure. Nor were regulatory commissions thereafter much clearer about how they were following those instructions, as Ben W. Lewis has caustically observed:

"A word should be said at this point with reference to the hybrid 'fair value' ('trance') method. . . . The 'fair value' method consists of an examination by the commission of evidence relating to reproduction cost and prudent investment, together with evidence of intangible values and observed condition of the property, the application of judgment whose processes defy

[34] 94 U.S. 113, 133–134 (1877).

[35] *Chicago, Milwaukee & St. Paul Railway Company v. Minnesota*, 134 U.S. 418, 458 (1890). For a compendium of the leading cases concerning the judicial review of utility regulation, see Barnes, *Cases on Public Utility Regulation*, Chapter 3.

[36] Stress supplied. 169 U.S. 466, 546–547 (1898).

analysis or description, and the selection of a final value figure which bears no derivative relation to any figures in evidence and no ascertainable relation to any functional purpose of rate making. The determination is typically accompanied by explicit denials that a formula was employed or that the result is a compromise, together with a statement that the commission is quite incapable of retracing and setting forth the processes by which the value figure was reached."[37]

It was not only its lack of precision that made *Smyth v. Ames* the bane of public utility regulation for the next 50 years, embroiling commissions and courts in endless controversies about the definition and measurement of fair value. It was also its specific insistence that stockholders were entitled to a return not on the dollars they had actually invested—a quantity easily recorded in the company accounts, hence readily ascertainable—or "prudently invested," but on the current value of their investment. The first thing wrong with such a standard is its possible circularity. As the Supreme Court pointed out 46 years later, in overturning *Smyth v. Ames*, "fair value" cannot serve as the basis for rate regulation if it is taken to mean market value, since the market value of any enterprise or of its common stock depends on its earnings or anticipated earnings, which in turn depend on the rates that are allowed it: "'fair value' is the end product of the process of rate-making not the starting point. . . . "[38]This objection is sound, however, only if "fair value" is to be measured in terms of the market value of the enterprise. It is incorrect if applied to the customary interpretation that measured fair value (at least in part) with reference to the cost of reproducing the company's assets, as *Smyth v. Ames* likewise instructed commissions to do. Whatever the problems of applying the reproduction cost standard, and they were great, circularity was not one of them. The current cost of duplicating the existing facilities or others capable of giving the same service does not move up or down so as to validate whatever levels of rates and earnings are permitted.[39]

---

[37] In Leverett S. Lyon and Victor Abramson, *Government and Economic Life: Development and Current Issues of American Public Policy* (Washington: The Brookings Institution, 1940), 2: 692.

[38] "The heart of the matter is that rates cannot be made to depend upon 'fair value' when the value of the going enterprise depends on earnings under whatever rates may be anticipated." *Federal Power Commission v. Hope Natural Gas Co.*, 320 U.S. 591, 601 (1944).

The "market value of its bonds and stock" was one of the considerations that the Supreme Court said had to go into the determination of "fair value" in *Smyth v. Ames*.

[39] There *is* some causal connection between rates and reproduction costs. Higher or lower rates will mean a greater or lesser volume of sales, hence a need for greater or lesser production capacity. To the extent that capacity is supplied under conditions of increasing or decreasing cost, its reproduction cost will vary depending on whether a greater or lesser volume is demanded, hence on the level of rates. In principle, this relationship does not preclude a single determinate solution, with a level of rates set in order to permit the desired return on the current cost of producing the capacity required to satisfy the demand elicited by that rate level (and structure). In contrast, there are any number of possible rate levels compatible with earning that return on the *market value* of investment, since—if demand is sufficiently inelastic—higher rates will mean a correspondingly higher market value, low rates a lower market value. Indeed, in perfectly functioning capital markets the market value of the company will move up and down, whatever the level of rates set, sufficiently to keep the rate of return earned on that market value at a constant level. (If investors are satisfied with a 10% return on investment, the market value of any company or of its securities will be ten times its permitted earnings, no matter what the rates it is permitted to charge; so its earnings will always be equal to 10% on its "fair value," thus defined, no matter what their absolute level.)

As we shall see, a strong economic case can be made for basing rate levels on "the present as compared with the original cost of construction," as *Smyth v. Ames* suggested. But as it developed in practice it had a fatal flaw: it invited endless controversy over the proper valuation of sunk capital, in direct contradiction of the economic principle that sunk investment costs are prominent among the "bygones" that ought to be ignored in price making.[40]

"It is not too much to say that in terms of cost, delay, uncertainty, and the arousing of animosity and contention, the performance of the reproduction cost method falls little short of a public scandal; by far the greater part of the grotesque and costly ponderosity which characterizes modern rate regulation is to be attributed directly and solely to the reproduction cost approach. There is no occasion here to recite details of the maneuvering in a typical rate proceeding. The months and years spent by contending parties, commissions, and courts over such hypothetical factors as pricing, conditions of construction, labor performance, overheads, intangibles; the huge sums paid to engineers and accountants and other professional experts, directed in their claims and counter-claims by high-priced attorneys skilled in the art of rate case strategy; the highly charged, politico-legal-mystic character of the whole performance—this is all accepted practice under the reproduction cost method, yet it seems far removed from the essential business of setting the price of a single service in a single community under conditions of simple monopoly."[41]

It is ironic that when the Supreme Court insisted on the relevance of current or reproduction cost, in *Smyth v. Ames*, it did so in the interest of effective regulation, and specifically in order to preserve "the right of the public to be exempt from unreasonable exactions."[42] For obvious reasons, the respective enthusiasms for original and reproduction cost on the part of regulatory commissions and regulated companies has varied depending on the trend of prices and construction costs. *Smyth v. Ames* came at a time when the general price level had fallen to its secular low point as a result of the deflations following the Civil War and the extended Depressions of the 1870s and the 1890s. It was the state of Nebraska that argued for the use of present value, as measured by (the lower) reproduction cost, and the railroads that argued for book or historical cost. In supporting the position of the former, the Court had in mind not only the long-term decline of construction costs, hence of fair value relative to original investment, but also the common complaint that railroad capital structures, on the liability side, and property valuations, on the asset side, were vastly inflated because of excessive payments to contractors and promoters and inadequate accounting for depreciation.[43]

[40] This does not mean that the returns permitted on past investments are irrelevant to the optimal pricing of public utility services. It means that endless controversies over the proper valuation and continual revaluation of capital investments made in the past are a deplorably inefficient and indirect way of approaching the task of devising economically efficient rates. (See the discussion on pp. 109–117, Chapter 4).

[41] Lyon and Abramson, *op. cit.*, 2: 691. For a more recent appraisal, see Lewis' "Emphasis and Misemphasis in Regulatory Policy," in Shepherd and Gies, *op. cit.*, 229–236. A place of high honor in these evaluations must be accorded also to Justice Louis D. Brandeis, who made many of the same observations as long ago as 1923; see his famous dissenting opinion in the *Southwestern Bell Telephone* case, 262 U.S. 276, 289–312 (1923).

[42] 169 U.S. 466, 544 (1898).

[43] See *ibid.*, 544–545, and Justice Brandeis, in *Southwestern Bell Telephone*, *op. cit.*, 298.

During and after World Wars I and II, the positions of the contending agencies were reversed: inflation and the introduction of more effective controls over book (historical) property valuations and company capitalizations converted regulated companies into enthusiasts for reproduction cost, and most commissions and advocates of effective regulation the other way—into proponents of a rate or earnings base measured by "prudent investment"—the number of dollars originally, prudently invested in the property used and usable in public service, less accumulated depreciation.[44]

It was not until 1944, in the *Hope Natural Gas* case,[45] that the Supreme Court at last decided, in the immortal words of Lord Mountararat, to "withhold its legislative hand," when it explicitly declined to tie the Federal Power Commission to any particular prescribed formula for the fixing of reasonable public utility rates. Rejecting fair value on grounds of circularity, the Court asserted that it would no longer insist on commissions taking reproduction cost into account in fixing permissible rates, either.

> "Under the statutory standard of 'just and reasonable' it is the result reached not the method employed which is controlling."[46]

What "end results" were relevant? The tests would henceforth be economic and pragmatic:

> "Rates which enable the company to operate successfully, to maintain its financial integrity, to attract capital, and to compensate its investors for the risks assumed certainly cannot be condemned as invalid, even though they might produce only a meager return on the so-called 'fair value' rate base."[47]

As long as regulation treats investors sufficiently well, by the acid test of the competitive capital-market place, to enable the regulated companies to raise whatever funds they need to provide acceptable service, the Court seemed to say, it would pose no additional tests or obstacles.[48]

The Court has been true to its promise. Outside of the novel area of natural gas production, it has entertained no public-utility rate-level case of the traditional kind since *Hope*.[49] State regulatory commissions have responded,

---

[44] See, among others, John Bauer and Nathaniel Gold, *Public Utility Valuation for Purposes of Rate Control* (New York: The Macmillan Co., 1934), Chapter 3; Barnes, *The Economics of Public Utility Regulation*, Chapters 11–17, an especially thorough analysis; Troxel, *Economics of Public Utilities*, Chapter 13; Eli Winston Clemens, *Economics and Public Utilities* (New York: Appleton Century-Crofts, 1950), 157–158; Wilcox, *Public Policies Toward Business*, 311–314; James C. Bonbright, *Principles of Public Utility Rates* (New York: Columbia University Press, 1961), Chapters 11–12; C. F. Phillips, *op. cit.*, 231–240.

[45] *Federal Power Commission v. Hope Natural Gas Co.*, 320 U.S. 591 (1944).

[46] *Ibid.*, 602.

[47] *Ibid.*, 605.

[48] Even in applying that primary test, it indicated it would give heavy weight to the "expert judgment" of the regulatory commission:

> "Moreover, the Commission's order. . . . is the product of expert judgment which carries a presumption of validity." *Ibid.*, 602.

[49] Information by courtesy of Edward M. Barrett. In the natural gas cases, the Federal Power Commission was attempting to evolve some system for fixing the field prices of a commodity produced at widely varying costs by a large number of producers. The Supreme Court had to decide a number of issues, the most important of which was whether the Commission had to make the traditional type of cost of service determinations, company by company, or might instead shift, as it wished to do, to setting area-wide rates applicable to all companies regardless of their individual costs. In general, following the philosophy of *Hope*, the Court sustained the Commission's exercise of its own "expertise." See *Wisconsin v. Federal Power Commission*, 373 U.S. 294 (1962) and *Permian Basin Area Rate Cases*, 390 U.S. 747 (1968). For a similar decision in a case involving the ICC's use of multi-company costs in determining the proper division

in varying degree, by shifting their attention from a preoccupation with the rate base to the more manageable question of the appropriate rate of return.[50] In a sense, the change is completely insubstantial: the substantive question of how much return on investment should be incorporated in the total cost of service is the same whether it focuses on one or the other of the two factors by which it is determined. And, as for administrative practicability, since it is the aggregate of dollar profits that concerns the parties to regulatory proceedings, it would seem there would be just as much opportunity for controversy over the percentage rate as there was in the past over the principal sum to which that rate was to be applied. The battle has not abated but merely shifted ground. As regulatory attention has turned from the rate base to the rate of return, and the latter has become less and less an essentially conventional 6% or so, the litigants have become increasingly skilled and assiduous in developing prolonged, complex, and inconclusive testimony about its proper measurement.[51]

Nevertheless the transformation of the rate base by most state commissions from a hypothetical or imaginary to an actual book figure,[52] representing actual money outlays, introduced a strong element of stability and predictability into the regulatory process. While the question of what constitutes a "fair" rate of return, as an ethical or political matter, would seem to be just as potentially productive of controversy as the question of what constitutes "fair value," the economic question, though in a sense unchanged and no easier to solve than before, is at least subject to the pragmatic test suggested by the Supreme Court itself—are the regulated companies succeeding in attracting the capital they require?[53]

of revenues for multi-line freight service, see *Chicago & North Western Railway Co. et al. v. Atchison, Topeka & Santa Fe Railway Co. et al.*, 387 U.S. 326 (1966).

[50] This does not mean that they have been permitted to ignore the rate base. On the contrary, as long as the courts continue to review commission rate orders at all, it is difficult to see how they can avoid insisting on some evaluation of the property on which a reasonable return must be permitted. This has been the continuing practice of such courts as have spoken since *Hope*. See Francis X. Welch, "The Rate Base is Here to Stay!" *Public Utilities Fortnightly* (October 22, 1953), LII: 635–641.

[51] See, for example, the possibly jaundiced view of Ben Lewis:

"as we begin in sheer disgust to move away from the debacle of valuation, we will probably substitute a new form of Roman holiday—long-drawn-out, costly, confusing, expert-contrived presentations, in which the simple directions of the *Hope* and *Bluefield* cases are turned into veritable witches' brews of statistical elaboration and manipulation. . . . We do not need to do this sort of thing to regulation; we do not need to do it to ourselves. The behavior of investors will tell us, day by day, all we need to know about 'comparability.'" In Shepherd and Gies, *op. cit.*, 242–243. Copyright, 1966, by Random House, Inc.

[52] On the imaginary character of the reproduction cost calculation, see Wilcox, *op. cit.*, 317.

[53] Controversy over the rate base has by no means disappeared. With price levels increasing secularly since the *Hope* decision, it has paid regulated companies to argue for some incorporation of reproduction cost in their rate bases. The state commissions have to some extent acceded: as of 1967, 31 of them (including the District of Columbia) used original cost (or "prudent investment") in regulating electric and gas utilities, 12 used fair value—a compromise between original and reproduction cost—one called its method "average net investment," and one used reproduction cost specifically. Of the remaining six states, four had no state commissions to regulate gas and electric utilities (see note 36, chapter 1) and two commissions had no established procedures. U.S. Senate, Committee on Government Operations, Subcommittee on Inter-governmental Relations, *State Utility Commissions*, *op. cit.*, 37–40. See also Federal Power Commission, *Federal and State Commission Jurisdiction and Regulation: Electric, Gas, and Telephone Utilities*, *op. cit.*, 11–12, which gives a slightly different tabulation; and Joseph R. Rose on "Confusion in Valuation for Public Utility Rate Making," *Minnesota Law Review* (1962),

Selection of the Permitted Rate of Return

In essence, every part of the regulatory price making exercise involves determining the proper level of earnings to be permitted the regulated companies. This is obviously true of the explicit determination of return, whether concentrating, as it traditionally has, on the valuation of the property on which a more or less conventional rate of return is to be allowed, or, as has become the practice in the majority of jurisdictions, on the rate of return to be permitted on the dollars actually invested in the enterprise. It is also the consequence of a commission's deciding whether or not to include items such as public relations expenditures in the cost of service, or how to measure depreciation, or how to treat income tax costs when accelerated depreciation is available. The process has inevitably reflected a complex mixture of political and economic considerations. Governmental price-fixing is an act of political economy. And, it bears repeating, this means that it necessarily and quite properly involves the striking of a balance between conflicting economic interests, influenced by political considerations in both the crassest and the broadest possible senses, and informed by community standards of fairness. Therefore, from time to time, the courts and commissions have characterized the entire task of setting "just and reasonable rates," and particularly that portion representing return to shareholders, in terms of reaching an acceptable compromise between the interests of investors on the one hand and consumers on the other.[54] The conception is that there is no single, scientifically correct rate of return, but a "zone of reasonableness," within which judgment must be exercised.

What are the limits of this zone? The bottom limit is an economic one, set by the necessity of continuing to attract capital; but, as we shall see, even that limit is an elastic one, depending on how much capital is required and how well one wishes to treat the company's existing stockholders.[55] The upper

XLVII: 1, whose analysis demonstrates that the foregoing simple designations conceal considerable differences in application. In a few instances, for example, "original cost" states have applied the permissible rate of return to an *undepreciated* rate base. For a thorough survey of actual valuation practices and rates of return allowed, see *Return Allowed in Public Utility Rate Cases, 1915–54* and *1955–61*, 2 vols., Arthur Andersen & Co. (place and date of publication not indicated); also A. J. G. Priest, "The Public Utility Rate Base," *Iowa Law Review* (Winter 1966), LI: 283–303, yielding a count of 31 original cost, and 19 fair value jurisdictions.

This continued emphasis on the rate base might seem irrational: inflation can be taken into account just as effectively by varying the permissible rate of return as by continuing to fight the old valuation controversies. To some extent this is what has happened. State commissions continuing to employ original cost have tended to compensate by allowing higher rates of return than the states that have either continued to use or have turned to fair value. But the compensation has been only partial. There continues to be a strong element of convention and tradition in the allowable rates of return; confined to something like a 5.5 to 8% interval, their variation has not been a complete substitute for alterations in the rate base as well. See C. F. Phillips, Jr., *op. cit.*, 268–271, Garfield and Lovejoy, *op. cit.*, 133–134, and the sources cited by both.

[54] See, for example, the words of Justice Douglas, speaking for the Supreme Court majority in the *Hope* case, 320 U.S. 591, 603 (1944).

[55] A firm can continue to attract outside capital, within limits, even though its overall rate of return is held well below the rate that new investors will require if they are to make funds available to it. If it does so, it will be at the expense of its present stockholders. See note 64, p. 46. Its managers will therefore be reluctant to do so in those circumstances, to the extent that they are interested in the welfare of their stockholders. The bottom limit can be lower if it is defined as how much the firm must be permitted to earn on its total investment in order for it to be *able* to pay new investors enough to have them willingly supply the firm with additional funds than if it is defined as the rate that will make a company *willing*, without

limit has been either what it was estimated capital was obtaining in investments of similar risk elsewhere or, even higher, at whatever it was deemed the traffic would bear. As Justice Holmes once commented, rate regulation

". . . has to steer between Scylla and Charybdis. On the one side, if the franchise is taken to mean that the most profitable return that could be got, free from competition, is protected by the Fourteenth Amendment, then the power to regulate is null. On the other hand, if the power to regulate withdraws the protection of the Amendment altogether, then the property is nought. *This is not a matter of economic theory, but of fair interpretation of a bargain.* Neither extreme can have been meant. A midway between them must be hit."[56]

Such a view of regulation, as a sort of collective bargaining process, with the commission mediating between investors and consumers, may be justified on two quite distinct bases. The first is that there really *is* such a thing as the correct rate of return, but that it is impossible to *measure* it precisely. The economist, taking as his model the equating of price and marginal cost, would ordinarily begin[57] by identifying as the "correct" return the one that covers the costs of (incremental) capital.[58] But as we shall see there is no objective, unequivocal method of ascertaining the cost of capital, even for a particular regulated company at a particular time and place; the process requires the exercise of a good deal of judgment, and judgments will inevitably differ as to the result.

---

coercion by the regulatory authorities, to seek outside capital. And it can be lower, still, if the company does not need *outside* capital. The point in either case is that, by virtue of their power to control the distribution of dividends and both to prohibit the discontinuance and to require extensions of service, commissions can compel public utility companies to reinvest internally generated funds or to seek outside funds despite the fact that allowed returns are less than sufficient to induce such investment on a voluntary basis. If the supply of capital thus obtained sufficed to provide the desired quantity and quality of service, it would not be necessary to give shareholders a return as high as would be demanded by suppliers of new capital. This is merely a recognition of the fact that capital irretrievably sunk in an enterprise has a lower opportunity cost than incremental capital. See pp. 70–73, 118.

This was one consideration underlying the decision of the Federal Power Commission in 1965 to introduce a two-price system for natural gas, with a lower price for gas discovered in the past and already committed under existing contracts, and a higher price for new, additional supplies of gas committed in new interstate contracts. The differentiation in this case took the form not of allowing different nominal rates of return but of using different cost computations for old and new gas, with the price for the latter being set at the estimated full current cost of new, additional supplies. The justification, proffered by this writer and accepted by the Commission, was that it was both undesirable and unnecessary to extend that higher price to the old gas—undesirable because to do so would confer windfalls on the owners of reserves discovered and developed at lower costs in the past (a noneconomic argument), and unnecessary because the investments in the old gas had already been made (an economic consideration). *Area Rate Proceeding, Claude E. Aikman, et al.*, 34 FPC 159, 185–192 and *passim* (1965), sustained in *Permian Basin Area Rate Cases*, 390 U.S. 747 (1968).

[56] Stress supplied. *Cedar Rapids Gas Light Co. v. Cedar Rapids*, 223 U.S. 655, 669 (1912).

[57] On the reasons why he will not necessarily stop there, see pp. 44 and 69–70.

[58] This was one of the criteria listed by the Supreme Court in its leading decision in the *Bluefield* case, back in 1923:

"The return should be reasonably sufficient to assure confidence in the financial soundness of the utility and should be adequate, under efficient and economical management, to maintain and support its credit and enable it to raise the money necessary for the proper discharge of its public duties." *Bluefield Water Works & Improv. Co. v. Public Service Commission of West Virginia*, 262 U.S. 679, 693 (1923).

It was also one of the standards set forth by the Supreme Court majority in the *Hope* decision. See p. 40.

The other view would be that the proper return that the regulatory process seeks and should seek to ascertain is not itself an objective phenomenon: what is a "just" or "fair and reasonable" return is a political, not a scientific question. This view is certainly not incorrect, either as a description of the rate making process or as prescription. A model of the price system in the modern, impurely competitive economy constructed in terms of the interplay of various organized groups, each with some degree of market power, with the results determined by the equilibrium of power relations, on the one hand, and influenced by considerations of "just price," on the other, is in some ways more relevant than one in which the transacting parties are conceived of as individuals, each a pecuniary profit-maximizer whose actions are entirely dictated by the objective constraints of the impersonal market. In any event, the economist cannot claim that such a vision of regulation as an essentially political process is "wrong;" all he can do is point out the costs to society of departing from purely economic standards.

Economists could make such an argument with better grace and greater forcefulness if they could themselves declare unequivocally what rate of return those purely economic standards dictate. The problem is that even if we confine ourselves to economic criteria we find that the very *idea* of the "correct" rate is elusive. The cost of capital is only the beginning point, for two reasons, both of which we will be explaining and exploring at a later point. (1) If perfect competition does not prevail in the real world, non-regulated industries generally may earn more (or less) than that minimum return. If so, it would produce misallocation to hold the prices of regulated services down (or up) to that level: this is the problem of the so-called "second best."[59] (2) The microeconomic model that calls for equating all prices to (marginal) cost and profits to the (marginal) cost of capital, which we describe in Chapter 3, is a static one. It tells us how to make the most satisfactory use of our limited resources with given tastes and a given technology. But it does not necessarily tell us how best to promote economic progress. The provision of incentives and the wherewithal for dynamic improvements in efficiency and innovations in service may require allowing returns to exceed that level: this was the essence of Joseph A. Schumpeter's classic defense of monopoly.[60] Thus, the rate of return must fulfill what we may term an *institutional* function: it somehow must provide the incentives to private management that competition and profit-maximization are supposed to provide in the nonregulated private economy generally. We have already identified this as a central problem of regulation.[61] There is as yet no scientific way even of defining the rate of return arrangements that would achieve this more complex definition of economic optimality, not to mention measuring them.

In keeping with the purpose of this entire chapter, the following survey of

[59] See pp. 69–70, Chapter 3 and p. 195, Chapter 7.

[60] See his *Capitalism, Socialism and Democracy* (New York: Harper & Brothers, 1942), Chapters 7–9.

[61] This is not to suggest that it is only through the rate of return that the necessary incentives are best provided. Given the divorce between ownership and management, the rewards might better be offered to, and penalties assessed against, the managers themselves, for example, in the form of variable bonuses proportioned to some measure of performance. See the section on "Incentive Plans," Chapter 2, Volume 2.

the major problems and issues in determining the proper rate of return (we assume, for simplicity, that the investment to which it is to be applied is valued at original cost less depreciation) is intended principally to illustrate the foregoing observations. While summarizing the major traditional issues in price regulation, as background for our own, alternative approach in Part II, it should demonstrate also (1) the problems in measuring the minimum cost to which prices would be held by effective competition, which regulation is supposed to emulate; (2) the important influence of noneconomic considerations, and especially of conceptions of what is "fair;" and (3) the elusiveness of the proper economic standards, for the reasons just identified—the problem of "second best" and the institutional function of the rate of return.

Problems in Measuring the Cost of Capital. The public utility company competes with all other companies in the economy for the various inputs of its production process—for labor, materials, and capital. To the extent that these are supplied in open markets (instead of, for example, under negotiated bids), in principle there ought to be readily available objective measures of the prices of these inputs that have to be incorporated in the cost of service. This is clearly true of the capital input: since the regulated company must go to the open capital market and sell its securities in competition with every other would-be issuer, there clearly is a market price (a rate of interest on borrowed funds, an expected return on equity) that it must be permitted and enabled to pay for the capital it requires. Of course, the costs that go into its price (or rate levels) are a function not only of the unit prices of its inputs (for example, the price of a ton of coal, delivered to the generating plant, or the interest rate on its bonds) but also of the efficiency with which they are employed (for example, the number of tons of coal or the number of dollars of capital investment required to generate a kilowatt hour of electricity); and we have already alluded to the problem of assuring maximum efficiency under regulation and to the important role that the allowable rate of return may play in providing an incentive for managers to run their companies as efficiently as possible. But the proper starting point is clearly the competitive price—in this case, the so called "cost of capital."

1. But whose cost of capital? Should it be the cost to the individual company under consideration? Or of a representative group of companies? If the latter, what constitutes a representative group? The concept of regulation as seeking to keep prices at the lowest possible level consistent with the company's supplying the amount and quality of service demanded at that price—which is surely the competitive ideal, also—would argue for measuring the actual cost of capital to that company alone. But suppose one company is so well run (or promises to become so much more so) that investors, having particularly great confidence in it (or in the stability or growth of its future earnings) are willing to make capital available to it at a price (for example, at current or promised rates of return) less than the average for other regulated companies? If the unusually efficient company's resultant lower cost of capital is automatically translated into lower permitted profits per dollar of invested capital—something that would *not* automatically happen under pure competition—will it not have been deprived of the incentive to be efficient, or to become more so? Its owners, and therefore conceivably its managers, would have been deprived

of the supernormal rewards (quasi-rents) that constitute in nonregulated markets a prime spur to efficiency.[62]

2. Should it be the cost of capital at a particular moment in time, or an average over some period in the past? If the former, what moment? If the latter, how long a period? Is what is sought the *historical* cost of capital, as of the time when it was raised? Or the current cost? The reader will recognize the relatedness of these questions to the question of whether the rate base and depreciation should likewise be measured at original or at current cost.[63] The usual practice is to combine the actual or historical interest cost, as far as debt capital and preferred stock are concerned, with the (estimated) current cost of raising money by sale of common stock. Does this make economic sense? Is it fair? How do these various possible approaches compare with the results that would be produced by competition? And, in such a comparison, *what* "competition" is relevant—"ideal" pure or perfect competition? Or the highly imperfect mixtures of competition and monopoly that actually prevail in unregulated markets?
3. The usual starting point for measuring the cost of equity capital is the ratio of earnings to market prices of the common stocks of the company or companies selected. The logic of this procedure—and it is persuasive—is that the price investors are willing to pay in the open securities markets for shares of stock with known levels of earnings provides an objective measure of the terms on which they are willing to make their money available to the companies in question. If, for example, the common stock sells at 10 times annual earnings, the earnings/price ratio is 10% and that may (subject to the very serious qualifications to be noted) be taken as the cost of capital—the rate of return that the companies must be able to earn on any additional dollars invested in them if they are going to be willing and able to raise those dollars in the capital markets.[64]

   However, the principal difficulty is that what investors are capitalizing in the purchase price of the securities they buy is not current but antici-

[62] Of course, some diminution of the incentive to efficiency is inherent in any system of regulation that holds rates of return to some prescribed level, regardless of how or where that level is set. Still, if the more efficient and progressive company is permitted some sort of higher, industry-average rate of return, instead of its own, low cost of capital, it is on this account rewarded for its own, deserved, above-average attractiveness to investors, and retains an incentive to improve its efficiency in hope of increasing that reward.

[63] He is reminded, too, that we consider the economics of these interrelated choices in the following chapters—in particular, Chapter 4.

[64] As we have already suggested, a company *can* raise capital even if it is allowed a rate of return below the cost of capital, but only at the expense of its existing stockholders. The common sense of this should be apparent: if a company sells its new stock on terms that give the new stockholders, for instance, a 10% return on their investment—the cost of capital being 10%, they will pay only ten times the prospective earnings for each share—and invests the funds in assets on which it is permitted to earn only 7 1/2%, clearly the other 2 1/2% must be coming out of earnings previously available to its existing stockholders. This is what is known as dilution—dilution of the share in equity (that is, in the claim on net assets of the firm) of existing stockholders.

Suppose, for example, the firm had the following skeleton balance sheet before the new stock issue:

Assets		**Liabilities**	
Net plant	$100	Net worth	
		Common stock (10 shares)	$50
		Surplus	50

And suppose its permitted rate of return (r) and cost of equity capital (k) were, as above, 7½% and 10%, respectively. In this event, its permitted earnings would be $0.75 per share, and investors

pated earnings;[65] and there is no objective measure of what their anticipations were or are. Thus, computed contemporaneous earnings/price ratios will either underestimate or overestimate the actual cost of capital, depending on the extent to which investors were expecting earnings to rise or fall from current levels when they paid those prices. From the late 1940s on, for example, security prices in the United States soared relative to earnings; this sharp drop in earnings/price ratios continued all through the 1950s, leveling off during 1960–1965 at the 5 to 6% level, which was well below the average of the preceding half-century.[66] There can be little doubt that these trends partly reflected the anticipation of increasing earnings and future appreciation of security values; those anticipations were an important consideration in the high and rising prices investors were willing to pay for each dollar of current earnings.[67] If so, the contemporaneous earnings/price ratios must have understated the true cost of equity capital: investors *thought* they were getting a better return

---

would pay only $7.50 for a share. (The market value would thus be below the book value of $10 per share, precisely because r is less than k; see note 69.) Now suppose the company sought to raise another $100 to invest in plant. It would be permitted to earn an additional $7.50 on this investment, or a total of $15. How many shares would it have to sell and at what price would they sell? Let x be the required additional number of shares. Then earnings per share will end at $15/(10+x)$. These earnings would be capitalized at 10%—that is, investors would pay 10 times those earnings for each new share of stock, assuming they expected per share earnings to remain thenceforth at that level. So the price of each share would be (10) ($15)/(10+x) and x shares would have to be sold at that price to raise the required $100:

$$\frac{(10)\ (\$15)}{10+x}\,x = \$100$$

$$x = 20$$

Therefore 20 additional shares would have to be sold to raise the added $100, at a price of $5. The price per share would thus have dropped from $7.50 to $5; the total permitted earnings of $15 would now be distributed among 30 shares, yielding $0.50 per share, capitalized at 10%. Assuming they predicted accurately the trend in earnings per share, the new investors would be in a position to demand the 10% k—they would pay only $5 for a share promising earnings of $0.50. But sale of the stock in these circumstances would *dilute* the share in ownership of the holders of the 10 original shares of stock: their share in book equity would decline from the original $10 per share to $6.67, the new total equity of $200 being distributed now among 30 shares. The 33⅓% decline in the market value of their stock would reflect this corresponding dilution of their equity.

A company *can*, thus, raise more capital when r is below k (within limits—try to work out the above example if r is only 5%) but only at the expense of its existing stockholders. This is something its management would ordinarily be unwilling to do.

[65] It is uncertain to what extent and in what direction investors' appraisal of earnings is altered by variations of the proportions respectively distributed in dividends and reinvested in the business. The weight of informed opinion since the early 1950s seems to be that it is total earnings instead of dividends alone that investors value in purchasing securities; that pay-out ratios have little if any effect—that is, that investors are essentially indifferent to what percentage of earnings is distributed in dividends. See Fred P. Morrisey, "Current Aspects of the Cost of Capital to Utilities," *Public Utilities Fortnightly* (August 14, 1958), LXII: 217–227; Merton H. Miller and Franco Modigliani, "Some Estimates of the Cost of Capital to the Electric Utility Industry," *Amer. Econ. Rev.* (June 1966), LVI: 368–370; Irwin Friend and Marshall Puckett, "Dividends and Stock Prices," *ibid.* (September 1964), LIV: 656–682; cf. E. W. Clemens, "Some Aspects of the Rate-of-Return Problem," *Land Econ.* (February 1954), XXX: 32–43.

[66] Dividend/price ratios showed a similar trend, and between 1955 and 1965 were lower relative to levels of the preceding half-century than were earnings/price ratios. Board of Governors of the Federal Reserve System, *Historical Chart Book, 1967*, Washington, 37.

[67] It can be demonstrated that, under not unreasonable assumptions, the market price of a share of stock (P) will be equal to current dividends (D) divided by (the cost of capital, k, minus the anticipated annual percentage growth in dividends, g): $P = D/(k-g)$. Or, in other words, that the cost of capital is equal to the

than would be indicated by that ratio.[68] Any successful effort by utility commissions to hold earnings on the companies' rate bases thereafter to the low rates suggested by those ratios would surely have resulted in a deflation of security prices, and, by thus increasing earnings/price ratios, have demonstrated that the true cost of capital was higher than they had originally inferred.[69] But how much higher, it is impossible to say with any precision.[70]

4. Is there need for consistency between the basis on which the cost of equity capital is determined and the rate base to which it is then applied? If the

---

current dividend/price ratio plus that anticipated percentage growth: $k = D/P + g$. For a fuller explanation, see the Appendix to this chapter, which reproduces a very lucid account by Herman G. Roseman.

To some extent, g results merely from the reinvestment of earnings. If a company earns 9% on book equity, distributes 2/3 and reinvests 1/3 (that is, 6% and 3% of book equity, respectively), the book value of each share of stock will grow 3% a year and dividends may therefore be expected to do the same on this account, *ceteris paribus*. If 9% is also the cost of capital, the market value of the stock will be equal to book (see footnote 69, below) and $(D/P) + g$ (in this case 6% + 3%) will, as far as this source of growth is concerned, be the same as the earnings/price ratio, E/P (9%). The problem arises when g is expected to be greater or less than what would result merely from the reinvestment of earnings. See for example the estimates referred to in note 70.

[68] That certainly had been their experience during the preceding years. An investment of equal amounts in every stock traded on the New York Stock Exchange in December 1950 would have yielded an investor 15.0% compounded annually, in dividends and capital appreciation, by December 1960; a similar investment in December 1955 would have yielded 11.1% by the later date. See L. Fisher and J. H. Lorie, "Rates of Return on Investments in Common Stocks," *Jour. of Bus.* (January 1964), XXXVII: 5. During the first period E/P ratios dropped continuously from over 15 to less than 5%, during the second its range was from about 8 to 5%. Board of Governors, *op. cit.*, note 66. Obviously what dropped E/P ratios was investor expectations that they would continue to see this kind of growth in earnings and market value of their investments.

[69] On the other hand, the sharp appreciation in the prices of public utility stocks, to one and a half and then two times their book value during this period, reflected also a growing recognition that the companies in question were in fact being permitted to earn considerably more than their cost of capital. Perhaps, indeed, the discrepancy was growing over time: as the data in note 76 demonstrate, the return on equity among the public utilities increased markedly relative to manufacturing in the two decades after World War II. See Miller and Modigliani, *op. cit.*, *Amer. Econ. Rev.* (June 1966), LVI: 386; David A. Kosh, "Recent Trends in the Cost of Capital," *Public Utilities Fortnightly* (September 26, 1963), LXXII: 19–26. Suppose, for example, the following skeletal balance sheet of a regulated company:

Net plant	100	Equity	
		Common stock (10 shares)	50
		Surplus	50

And suppose the true cost of capital is 10%. If the regulatory commission permits the company to earn 10% on its net plant, valued at original cost, the profits will be \$1 a share, and, *ceteris paribus*, investors will buy those shares for \$10: market value and book value will coincide. But the market value will exceed book value if the commission permits a return in excess of the cost of capital: if, for example, it allows 15%, this will yield \$1.50 a share, for which investors will bid \$15.

But suppose, to illustrate the point in the text, the commission had been allowing only the true cost of capital, 10% or \$1 a share, but investors had bid share prices up to \$15, yielding currently only $6\frac{2}{3}$%, because they expected to get the other $3\frac{1}{3}$% from future increases in earnings and appreciation of the securities' prices. If in this event the commission took the $6\frac{2}{3}$% earnings/price ratio to represent the cost of capital, it would permit earnings of ony \$0.67 per share, and the market price of the securities would collapse either to the book value of \$10, if investor confidence in future trends continued unshaken, or down to \$6.67, if those favorable anticipations were now destroyed.

[70] Since the true cost of capital (k) may be taken as equal to $(D/P) + g$ (see note 67), some company witnesses in regulatory proceedings have attempted in various ways to make plausible

cost of equity capital is determined on the basis of the ratio of earnings to the *market price* of the company's common stock, is there not some inconsistency in applying that rate of return to a rate base as valued in the company's *books*—that is, at original or historic cost—when, as has been true for well over a decade, the market value of most public utility shares has far exceeded their book value? If, for example, earnings per share were $5, the market price $100, and the book value $50, the E/P ratio would suggest a 5% cost of capital; if that 5% were applied to the book value of (the equity portion of) the rate base, this would produce a return of only $2.50—thus eliminating the justification for the $100 market price.

The answer is that there would be an inconsistency in this case, but only because it involves inconsistent assumptions about regulatory policy.

---

estimates of the g investors had in mind in purchasing the company stock, in order to come up with an estimate of k (since D and P are of course known). See, for instance, the testimony of Irwin Friend, May 26, 1966, in Federal Communications Commission, *In the Matter of American Telephone and Telegraph Company*, Docket 16258, and of Roseman before the Pennsylvania Public Utility Commission, Re: *The Peoples Natural Gas Company*, Docket No. 18527, Exhibit No. 16, 1968. Roseman's basic approach, for example, is to determine statistically which measure of growth (average annual growth in earnings, in dividends, in book equity, in revenue, or in net plant, all over various time periods up to the present) correlates most closely with the current evaluation placed by the market on dividends—that is, with the D/P ratios—of 21 gas distribution companies. The correlation is negative: the higher the anticipated g, the higher the price investors will pay for a dollar of current dividends, so the lower is the D/P ratio. Then, having in this way identified the measure of actual past growth with the highest negative correlation with D/P, he proposes that for his measure of the (anticipated) g component of k. Applying this method for each of the 20 companies (in addition to the one for which he was testifying), he obtained an average estimate for k of 9.8%, compared with an *earnings*/price ratio of 7.6%. Roseman describes this method also in "Measuring the Cost of Equity Capital for Public Utilities," ABA, *Annual Report, Section of Public Utility Law*, 1969, 54–67.

Two other writers have suggested an alternative solution that would permit the use of E/P ratios alone as the measure of k. Their reasoning is that whenever regulated companies purchase their inputs in competitive markets, regulatory commissions correctly accept the prices thus determined for incorporation in the cost of service. Capital markets are highly competitive; they, too, therefore, should be able to provide commissions with a very accurate measure of the competitive, minimum necessary cost of capital. The problem at present is that commissions have no way of telling what are the terms of the equity share contract. That is, when investors pay x dollars for a share of stock, they are buying not just current earnings but some unmeasurable amount of growth over and above the growth that occurs because of the mere reinvestment of earnings. (As we have already seen, if dividends are expected to grow only because of reinvestment of earnings, $(D/P)+g$ is the same as E/P, and the latter is a correct measure of k. See note 67, above. It is the expectation of greater—or lesser—growth than this that renders E/P an inaccurate measure of k.) The first key to a solution to this problem is to be found in the fact that when earnings are expected to grow over time merely because of reinvestment of earnings, the market and book values of a share of company stock will grow together; there is no reason for such growth to produce any discrepancy between them. It is the expectation of a capital gain resulting from a *discrepancy* between market and book values, thus, that makes E/P an inaccurate measure of k, and so makes the latter so difficult to measure. The second key to the solution is that if the allowed rate of return (r) is held at the cost of capital (k), market value will tend to equal book value (see note 69), and the possibility of a discrepancy between them is greatly diminished.

Therefore, the authors suggest, if regulatory commissions were to put investors on notice that henceforth they would allow a return equal only to whatever earnings/price ratio the securities markets set when the market value of the common stock equaled its book value (at which point presumably r equals k), they could greatly diminish, if not eradicate, the expectation of capital gains or losses arising from divergencies of market and book value and thereby cause the current earnings/price ratios to give them a much more accurate reflection of the true cost of

That is, it assumes at one and the same time that the commission allows returns on equity (r) in *excess* of and equal to the cost of capital (k). The source of the discrepancy between market and book value has been that commissions have been allowing r's in excess of k; if instead they had set r equal to k, or proceeded at some point to do so, both the discrepancy between market and book value and the inconsistency would have disappeared, or would never have arisen.[71] The fact that market value has remained above book value indicates that in most jurisdictions r has been high enough, relative to k, so that its application to the lower book value, in determining allowable earnings, has not destroyed the willingness of investors to continue to pay above book value for public utility company shares.[72]

5. To what extent does the cost of capital, which is a weighted average of the separate costs of obtaining funds by sale of bonds, preferred stock, and common stock, depend on the particular mixture of sources of financing selected? There is general agreement that up to a point the composite cost will be reduced by resorting to borrowing, because the interest costs of borrowed capital may be deducted from taxable income, whereas the return on equity capital—which is no less a genuine economic cost of production—is subject to the corporation income tax.[73] But some commentators have maintained that, apart from this tax aspect, the capital structure has no effect on the composite cost of capital; that the more a company resorts to borrowing, typically at lower contractual interest rates than the rates of return it has to promise to common stockholders, the correspondingly higher is its true cost of equity capital, in reflection of the greater risks to stockholders of having a larger and larger share of aggregate earnings subject to the prior, contractual claim of the bond holders.[74] The more traditional view is that up to some point

capital. Thereafter, when investors purchased the stock they would be buying only current earnings plus such anticipated growth as would result from reinvestment of profits, which would raise book and market value per share simultaneously. They would no longer be paying also for the expectation that the market value per share might rise relative to the number of stockholder dollars actually invested in the enterprise. Regulatory commissions could presumably obtain successive approximations to the true cost of capital by reducing permitted rates of return (r) sufficiently to bring market prices down to book value per share, and then adjusting r to the earnings/price ratios that emerged on announcement of the policy that destroyed anticipations of market price diverging from book.

In brief, what the commissions would be doing in this way would be specifying the terms of the equity share contract. If they succeeded in doing so, the capital market would then provide them with an accurate measure of the true competitive cost of capital. See Robert J. Gelhaus and Gary D. Wilson, "An Earnings-Price Approach to Fair Rate of Return in Regulated Industries," *Stanford Law Rev.* (January 1968), XX: 287–317.

[71] In the foregoing example, once market value per share was reduced to book value—that is, to $50—because r was set at k, here assumed to be 5%, there would no longer be any inconsistency, provided, of course, the commission had correctly estimated k at 5%. Return per share would be $2.50, and this would be 5% of both market and book value.

[72] See note 69.

[73] If the cost of debt capital to a company is 5% and the cost of equity capital is 10%, and it raises $100 by borrowing, this will add $5 a year to its costs; if it raises it by issuing new stock, it will add not $10 but, with the corporation income tax rate at 48%, $19.23 a year to what it must recover in rates—$9.23 for the Internal Revenue Service, $10 for the new stockholders.

[74] Actually the cost of debt capital would likewise rise, reflecting growing risk to bond holders as well, as a larger and larger share of company income was pledged to them. The Grand Inquisitor's observation in *The Gondoliers*,

"When every one is somebodee,
Then no one's anybody!"

clearly applies to bondholders: when everyone

trading on equity has the effect of reducing the average cost of capital, even apart from the tax advantage. Some commissions, in consequence, have based their allowances for rate of return not on the actual capital structure of the regulated company but on their conception of a preferable one, with a lower inferred composite cost.[75]

Should the Rate Be Adjusted for Changes in Prices? What allowance, if any, should be made for changes in the purchasing power of the investor's dollar, measured in terms of its changing ability either to buy consumer goods and services or to replace capital equipment? In particular, should the owners of the business be offered some sort of protection against inflation, whether by introducing some reflection of (presumably rising) replacement costs in the rate base and/or in allowable depreciation expenses, or in a higher rate of return? On grounds of fairness? Of economic efficiency? *Ought* or *need* the same protections be offered to existing shareholders as to future suppliers of capital? If to stockholders, why not also to creditors? We consider these questions at length in Chapter 4.

The Standard of Comparable Earnings. During the early 1960s, when price/earnings ratios ran around 5 to 6%, manufacturing corporations were earning 10 to 13% on their book equity.[76] *Ought* or *need* public utility

---

who supplies capital is at the head of the line in his claim on income, no one is at the head of the line—there is no line. See the considerably more complex argument of Modigliani and Miller, "The Cost of Capital, Corporation Finance and the Theory of Investment," *Amer. Econ. Rev.* (June 1958), XLVIII: 261–297, and "Some Estimates of the Cost of Capital," *Amer. Econ. Rev.* (June 1966), LVI: 338–343, 364–367; the comments on the former article by Joseph R. Rose and David Durand and the Modigliani-Miller reply, *ibid.* (September 1959), XLIX: 638–669; Haim Ben-Shahar, "The Capital Structure and the Cost of Capital: A Suggested Exposition," *Jour. of Finance* (September 1968), XXIII: 639–653.

[75] See C. F. Phillips, Jr., *op. cit.*, 169–171, 280–283; Troxel, in Shepherd and Gies, *op. cit.*, 166–168.

"On oral argument, Respondents' counsel stated:

'. . . I think the Commission's function here is to examine a debt policy that we follow . . . but unless you find that we have abused our discretion or have been imprudent, I don't believe you should disturb it. . . .'

"We agree that this Commission is not the manager of Respondents' business. It is neither our obligation or duty to dictate the business policies and practices to be followed by management. On the other hand, we have the statutory responsibility for the establishment and maintenance of just and reasonable rates. . . . If we are to discharge this responsibility . . . we must be free to examine fully all matters affecting the future level of rates. . . . We are not limited to acting in situations in which we have first found abuse, imprudence or indiscretion on the part of management in the past. . . .

"At the 10-percent return on equity sought by respondents herein, each dollar of equity financing requires nearly five times as much gross revenue as a dollar of debt financing. Thus, the rate payer is penalized if more of the financing is by equity than is required. . . .

"We find, therefore, that a continuation by respondents of their past policies with respect to capital structure will not be conducive to the raising of future required capital in a reasonably economical fashion. . . .

"Accordingly, in fixing the rate of return to be allowed, we shall take into account this 'additional' and extraordinary amount of risk insurance respondents have given its [sic] stockholders by its low debt ratio policy. . . . respondents are in a position to improve equity earnings by increasing their debt ratio. . . ." FCC, *In the Matter of American Telephone and Telegraph Company*, Docket No. 16258, Interim Decision and Order, 9 FCC 2d. 30 (1967), sec. 86, 89, 216, 220, 222.

[76] See note 66, Chapter 2. During these same years (1960–1964, inclusive), the returns on book equity of the "electric power, gas, etc." companies surveyed by the First National City Bank of New York ranged between 10.0 and 11.0%, of telephone and telegraph companies between 9.7 and 10.3% and of transportation companies between 2.3 and 5.5%, as the following table shows. All returns are after tax.

companies be permitted earnings comparable to those received by companies in nonregulated industries, under conditions of comparable risk?[77] This question involves a number of issues, conceptual and factual.

1. Is the comparable earnings standard merely another measure of the cost of capital, reflecting what public utility companies themselves or purchasers of their stocks could obtain on their dollars elsewhere? Or may it be higher: may not returns in industry generally contain some monopoly component, for example? In point of fact, the owners or purchasers of public utility and industrial common stocks might well not be able to obtain that type of rate of return if they were to go into the market and buy those securities.[78] The cost of capital, which is what a utility company must match if it is to attract funds, is what investors could obtain by buying the *securities* of other companies in the open market—not what the companies themselves earn on a dollar of additional investment.[79]
2. If "comparable earnings" exceed the cost of capital, then, would an attempt to hold public utility earnings to the lower, competitive level reduce the prices of their services excessively, relative to the prices of other goods and services?[80]

Net Returns on Net Assets

Year	Total Mfg	Electric Power, Gas, etc.	Telephone and Telegraph	Total Transportation
1947–54	15.4	9.3	7.8	...
1959	11.7	10.1	9.9	3.9
1960	10.6	10.0	9.9	2.9
1961	9.9	10.0	9.9	2.3
1962	10.9	10.4	9.5	3.9
1963	11.6	10.6	9.7	4.6
1964	12.6	11.0	10.3	5.5
1965	13.9	11.3	9.9	6.9
1966	14.2	11.5	10.4	7.4
1967	12.6	11.6	10.2	5.4
1968	13.1	11.2	9.7	4.9
No. of Companies				
1968	2,250	237	19	176

Source. First National City Bank of New York, *Monthly Economic Letter*, April issues. 1947-54 compilation from Shepherd and Gies, *op. cit.*, 103.

[77] The Supreme Court specified such a comparable earnings standard in both its *Bluefield* and *Hope* decisions. 262 U.S. 679, 692 (1923); 320 U.S. 591, 603 (1944).

[78] See for example, Calvin B. Hoover, "On the Inequality of the Rate of Profit and the Rate of Interest," *The South. Econ. Jour.* (July 1961), XXVIII: 1–12; James Tobin, "Economic Growth as an Objective of Government Policy," *Amer. Econ. Rev., Papers and Proceedings* (May 1964), LIV: 13–14. This discrepancy is suggested by the far lower earnings to market price ratios of both industrial and public utility common stocks than those companies earn on book equity. However, as we have seen, investors have been earning more than the contemporaneous earnings/price ratios. (See note 68.) Whether what they have in fact earned in this way was the same as the cost of capital—that is, the rates that they would have been *willing* to take to make their funds available—is highly uncertain.

[79] If the cost of capital is lower, any attempt of a regulatory commission, persuaded by the comparable earnings argument, to permit investors the higher return would only be self-defeating. Investors would respond to the higher earnings per share by bidding up the prices of the securities to the point at which new purchasers would earn only the old cost of capital on their investments. The only beneficiaries would be those who happened to own the stock at the time the policy change was announced or anticipated. There is no way of giving new purchasers of stock more than the cost of capital, except by changing the rules after they have made their purchases. See the same argument in another context, p. 116, Chapter 4.

[80] This is the "problem of the second best,"

3. In applying this standard, how does one select nonregulated industries of comparable risk? How *do* risks in public utilities compare with those of other industries, and to the extent they do differ how would this difference be allowed for in translating comparable earnings elsewhere into permissible rates of return here?[81]

The Problem of Rewards and Incentives. How, if at all, can rates of return be varied in order to reward, and hence to provide an incentive for efficiency and innovation? What standards of performance are available that will separate results attributable to good or bad management from those attributable to other factors? How can such rewards be related to performance, and how much in the way of rewards is required? In particular, is there any way of punishing poorly managed companies with a reduced rate of return without jeopardizing their ability to attract the very capital they may need to do a better job?

It has been urged by defenders of the comparable earnings standard and by others that public utilities be allowed returns markedly above the bare cost of capital, in order to provide them with both the financial means and the incentive to engage in risky innovation, both technological and commercial. That regulatory commissions have in fact allowed earnings well in excess of k is suggested not just by the behavior of the market prices of public utility securities but also by the apparent ease with which such companies have been able, since World War II, to raise the huge amounts of capital required to meet growing demands. It is suggested also by their aggressiveness in seeking such capital and expanding capacity, something that they would obviously have been reluctant to do if allowable returns were less than k.[82]

But this does not necessarily prove that these companies have been offered the optimum amount of incentive for undertaking risky investments.[83] The defining characteristic of such investments is that they offer a wide range of possible outcomes; those that are nevertheless economically worthwhile are so because the possibilities of very large pay-offs balance the possibilities of failure. Any restriction on aggregate earnings, by threatening to cut off the opportunities for the great successes, will therefore have some immeasurable effect of discouraging risky investments that otherwise would be made. How important this effect may be in public utility regulation is very difficult to determine, but it is probably slight. For one thing, there are mitigating or countervailing considerations, among them the slowness of regulation in

to which we have already referred. As Shepherd has observed, the problem of the second best is the core of economic validity in the comparable earnings standard. "Regulatory Constraints and Public Utility Investment," *Land Econ.* (August 1966), XLII: 353. See pp. 195–198, Chapter 7.

[81] See, for example, Shepherd, "Utility Growth and Profits Under Regulation," in Shepherd and Gies, *op. cit.*, 35–45. "if utility stocks are compared with those of non-utility corporations of comparable size, utilities which are protected from many forms of competition will be compared with the winners in other areas with no such . . . protection. . . . Somehow, in strict logic, the shadow losses of long defunct automobile companies would have to be subtracted from the profits of General Motors, after these in turn had been adjusted downward for the hypothetical competition—and then, following this trip through the looking-glass, the result would be comparable earnings. . . ."

James R. Nelson, "Reassessment of Economic Standards for the Rate of Return Under Regulation," in Harry M. Trebing and R. Hayden Howard, *Rate of Return under Regulation: New Directions and Perspectives* (Institute of Public Utilities, Michigan State University: East Lansing, 1969), 16.

[82] See Troxel and Lewis, in Shepherd and Gies, *op. cit.*, 170–175 and 237–239 and note 64, above

[83] See Thomas G. Gies, "The Need for New Concepts in Public Utility Regulation," *ibid.*, 105–107.

reducing earnings that prove *ex post* to be "excessive"—this is the familiar "regulatory lag"—and the ability of regulated companies to seek any rate increases that may be required to keep their overall rates of return at satisfactory levels, and hence to compensate for some of their failures. More important is the fact that the regulatory restriction is on total earnings, not the returns from individual investments. It would only be if the latter were so overwhelmingly large as to threaten to push the total above permissible levels that regulation might discourage it. To the extent all these offsets and qualifications are insufficient, there is no easy solution to the incentive problem. Merely permitting all regulated companies as a matter of course to earn rates in excess of the cost of capital does not supply the answer; there has to be some means of seeing to it that those supernormal returns are *earned*, some means, for example, of identifying the companies that have been unusually enterprising or efficient and offering the higher profits to them while denying them to others. We return to these institutional problems in Chapter 2 of Volume 2.

REGULATING RATE STRUCTURES

With respect to the second major aspect of public utility price regulation—the regulation of rate patterns or structures—the typical statutory or judicial injunction is that rates be not "unduly discriminatory," that differences in the rates charged various customers or classes of service be likewise "just and reasonable." At this point we need make only two general observations about the way in which most regulatory commissions have carried out this mandate. First, outside of the transportation field, they have given far less attention to this subject than to determining general rate levels and especially the rate base and rate of return.[84] The height of particular rates and the differences between them have been from the very outset a very important consideration in the regulation of railroads: the feeling of different customers and localities that they were being subjected to unfair discrimination played a vital role

[84] The managements of public utility companies have been at least equally delinquent. See the following acid comments by the Public Utilities Commission of California on the apparent lack of interest of the Pacific Telephone Company in the various individual components of its aggregate cost of service and unwillingness to supply information about them:

"Pacific adheres to a concept of setting basic telephone rates in relation to the availability of main stations and on a statewide pattern. . . . By this scheme Pacific, as in all prior rate proposals, ignores the costs of providing service and from the present record it is apparent that it isn't even interested in knowing what its costs are for any given existing service. It is content to rely on broad and loosely-made estimates first put together at the time an initial or innovative service offering is proposed, no matter how long ago such estimates may have been made. . . . That the executives of Pacific have developed no means by which the actual costs of any of Pacific's existing basic tariff offerings may be determined or measured seems incomprehensible but this record clearly establishes that such is the fact. Equally incomprehensible is the fact that Pacific does not even know, nor can it readily determine, what revenues its individual tariff offerings produce. . . . [F]or example, Pacific cannot even tell the Commission what revenues it actually receives from its charges for colored telephones without making a special 'study' of the situation."

"[I]t has been repeatedly pointed out that Pacific has not supplied actual revenue, cost or plant data in support of its tariffs. When specifically requested to do so . . . its Counsel argued in opposition to the request. . . .

"The arguments of Pacific's counsel and the comments of its witnesses make it abundantly clear that the whole subject is distasteful to Pacific. It desires, apparently, to forever rely on estimates made prior to the setting of rates on

in the passage and enforcement of the Interstate Commerce Act, from the very beginning.[85] In the other utilities, the major issue has usually revolved around the adequacy of total or net revenues; and the solution has usually been a more or less across-the-board increase or decrease of the entire structure.[86] Second, to the extent regulatory laws and commissions have considered the pattern of prices set, they have been guided by the same sort of mixture of essentially economic and political-social considerations as have influenced their determinations of the proper returns on investment.

The relative neglect of individual prices most clearly epitomizes the difference between the traditional approach to public utility price regulation and the one the economist would recommend. In this area, the commissions typically proceed only in response to specific complaints: businessmen in locality A complain that the freight rates charged them are higher than those charged their competitors; railroads point out that they are losing particular classes of business to trucks or barges and ask permission to reduce the relevant rates to meet competition; the affected trucking and navigation companies intervene to prevent the proposed reductions. Commercial customers assert that they are paying a higher price than residential users for electricity; local utility commissions complain that high rates for local service are subsidizing unduly low rates on long-distance calls; oil jobbers argue that gas distribution companies are offering uneconomically low promotional rates on home heating; the latter maintain that too large a proportion of the capacity costs of the interstate pipelines that supply them are incorporated in the demand charges that they pay and too little is imposed on the lines' direct industrial customers; and representatives of the bituminous coal industry join in these protestations, because the low-priced gas sold for use as boiler fuel for electricity generation takes business away from them. And all too often, from the economist's standpoint, the commissions resolve such controversies on bases other than economic efficiency, seeking to protect offended competitors from excessive losses of business, to preserve a "fair share" of the

---

new services as justification for continuing rate forms and relative rate levels whether or not the services are in reality today properly priced. One of its witnesses is 'hopeful' that the original estimates will so price new services that they will not be a burden on basic service. While this Commission may share or even applaud such 'hopes,' it has the duty to see to it that rates are fair and reasonable. . . ." *In the Matter of . . . the Pacific Telephone and Telegraph Company et al.*, Decision No. 74917, November 6, 1968, mimeo., 30–31, 60–61.

[85] In describing what was to become the Act to Regulate Commerce, in 1887, the Cullom Committee said: "the provisions of the bill are based upon the theory that the paramount evil chargeable against the operation of the transportation system of the United States as now conducted is unjust discrimination between persons, places, commodities, or particular descriptions of traffic." U.S. Senate, Select Committee on Interstate Commerce, 49th Cong., 1st Sess., Sen. Report 46, Part I, Washington, 1886, 215. Correspondingly, "it would be possible to write an extensive history of railroad regulation without mentioning cost of capital or rate of return." James R. Nelson, "Pricing and Resource Allocation: The Public Utility Sector," in Shepherd and Gies, *op. cit.*, 83. Since 1922, the Interstate Commerce Commission "has not found it necessary to specify a fair rate of return for the roads." Phillips, *op. cit.*, 271.

[86] See, for example, Troxel, in Shepherd and Gies, *op. cit.*, 150–151, 175–176. Regulatory commissions and courts alike have tended to leave the designing of rate structures to the discretion of managements. Even in transportation, both company managements and the Interstate Commerce Commission for much too long neglected the much-needed reconsideration of common-carrier rate structures in the light of the intensified competition of newer transport media and of private and contract carriers. See the section on "Transportation," Chapter 1, Volume 2.

market for each, to strike some equitable or politically acceptable distribution of common costs among the various classes of patrons. We will see numerous illustrations of this kind of behavior in Chapters 1 and 2 of Volume 2.

Microeconomics, in contrast, is interested first and foremost in the determination of individual prices. Its normative models also include certain notions about the appropriate relation between an industry's average prices or total revenues on the one hand and its average or total costs on the other; but that optimum is conceived to be the result or *end product* of a competitive process that operates directly and in the first instance in individual markets, in the fixing of individual prices.[87]

With respect to those individual markets, the rules of microeconomics are in principle simple and grounded in objective facts: subject to important qualifications that we shall elaborate at a later point, prices should be equated to marginal costs. In this scheme, there is no room for separate considerations of "fairness." Or, to put it another way, fairness is defined in strictly economic terms: those prices are fair that are equal to marginal costs, those unfair that are not equal.

"As in so many other policy areas, the lawyers and engineers (and increasingly the accountants)—*not* the economists—have largely dominated regulatory policy."[88] This does not mean that economists have not written at length and incisively about public utility regulation. But until recently, their analyses have been directed mainly toward the traditional issues, and organized within the framework formulated by administrative commissions and courts and by *Smyth v. Ames* in particular. Our next chapters, following

[87] These comments may seem arbitrarily to suggest that short-run equilibrium is somehow more important than long-run, and in so doing to reflect the essentially static character of traditional economic theory, or its tendency simply to assume mobility of resources sufficient to ensure the achievement of long-run equilibrium. In a dynamic world and in the presence of resource immobilities, competition sufficiently pure to hold prices constantly at short-run marginal cost may prove destructive and violently unstable; and much of the pricing in impurely competitive or oligopolistic markets can often be understood as seeking to achieve the long-run competitive result—which in a perfectly competitive market could safely be left to instantaneous inflows and outflows of labor and capital—at the possible expense of the constant equation of price with short-run marginal cost. The student of industrial organization may be as much concerned with the process that holds an industry's total profits, averaged over some period of time, at the competitive level as that its individual prices be instantaneously equated with short-term marginal cost.

The fact remains that the welfare ideal is constructed on the basis of the equation of price to marginal cost in individual markets and in the short-run. That is where the process starts. Departures from that standard must be individually justified. The mere control of overall rates of return does not in itself ensure that the pattern of individual prices is economically efficient:

"A great many *different* patterns, efficient and inefficient, within the firm may be perfectly consistent with a *given* over-all rate of return. So, whatever the rates of return may actually have been, they cannot by themselves demonstrate whether resource allocation (to and within the utilities) has been efficient." Shepherd, in Shepherd and Gies, *op. cit.*, 20. See also Nelson, *ibid.*, 66.

Moreover—and this is a point critically important with respect to the public utility industries—even long-run equilibrium price is not the same thing as a price that covers current operating expenses plus some acceptable average rate of return on investment, which is what has principally concerned regulatory commissions. On the contrary, it involves the equation of price with long-run marginal cost. Correspondingly, the investment policy that produces long-run equilibrium in the competitive ideal is one that equates with the cost of capital the rate of return on incremental investment, not the *average* rate of return on historical investment, however the latter is valued. We shall explore these similarities and differences in the ensuing chapters.

[88] Shepherd, "Conclusion," in Shepherd and Gies, *op. cit.*, 266.

the lead of some of the recent economic literature[89] and accepting the implied invitation of the *Hope Natural Gas* decision, returns to the economic principles and attempts to apply them to the problems of public utility regulation. In so doing we will try not to neglect the traditional regulatory issues set forth in this chapter, but will instead analyze them in economic terms, while continuing, as throughout this study, to assess the limitations as well as the possible contributions of economics to their resolution.[90]

[89] See, for example, the works cited *ibid.*, 267 and throughout this chapter and those that follow.

[90] There is no intention here to exaggerate the novelty of this approach, as compared with current regulatory thinking and practice. On the contrary, the traditional approaches that we have been describing in this chapter have certainly been modified in recent years. Regulated companies and commissions alike have been paying increasing attention to the design of economically efficient rate structures; and, in this task and in others, as we have already observed, they have made dramatically increasing use of the tools and perspectives of the economist. This book is in a sense a survey, summary, and critique of this emergent practice.

B
Efficient Regulation, Stand-alone Cost Ceilings and Price Caps

[19]

WHY REGULATE UTILITIES?*

HAROLD DEMSETZ
University of Chicago

CURRENT economic doctrine offers to its students a basic relationship between the number of firms that produce for a given market and the degree to which competitive results will prevail. Stated explicitly or suggested implicitly is the doctrine that price and output can be expected to diverge to a greater extent from their competitive levels the fewer the firms that produce the product for the market. This relationship has provided the logic that motivates much of the research devoted to studying industrial concentration, and it has given considerable support to utility regulation.[1]

In this paper, I shall argue that the asserted relationship between market concentration and competition cannot be derived from existing theoretical considerations and that it is based largely on an incorrect understanding of the concept of competition or rivalry. The strongest application of the asserted relationship is in the area of utility regulation since, if we assume scale economies in production, it can be deduced that only one firm will produce the commodity. The logical validity or falsity of the asserted relationship should reveal itself most clearly in this case.

Although public utility regulation recently has been criticized because of its ineffectiveness or because of the undesirable indirect effects it produces,[2] the basic intellectual arguments for believing that truly effective regulation is desirable have not been challenged. Even those who are inclined to reject government regulation or ownership of public utilities because they believe these alternatives are more undesirable than private monopoly, implicitly accept the intellectual arguments that underlie regulation.[3]

* The author is indebted to R. H. Coase, who was unconvinced by the natural monopoly argument long before this paper was written, and to George J. Stigler and Joel Segall for helpful comments and criticisms.

[1] Antitrust legislation and judicial decision, to the extent that they have been motivated by a concern for bigness and concentration, *per se*, have also benefited from the asserted relationship between monopoly power and industry structure.

[2] Cf., George J. Stigler and Claire Friedland, What Can Regulators Regulate? The Case of Electricity, 5 J. Law & Econ. 1 (1962); H. Averch and L. Johnson, The Firm under Regulatory Constraint, 52 Am. Econ. Rev. 1052 (1962); Armen Alchian and Reuben Kessel, Competition, Monopoly, and the Pursuit of Pecuniary Gain, in Aspects of Labor Economics 157 (1962).

[3] Thus, Milton Friedman, while stating his preference for private monopoly over public monopoly or public regulation, writes:

The economic theory of natural monopoly is exceedingly brief and, we shall see, exceedingly unclear. Current doctrine is reflected in two recent statements of the theory. Samuelson writes:

Under persisting decreasing costs for the firm, one or a few of them will so expand their q's as to become a significant part of the market for the industry's total Q. We would then end up (1) with a single monopolist who dominates the industry; (2) with a few large sellers who together dominate the industry . . . or (3) with some kind of imperfection of competition that, in either a stable way or in connection with a series of intermittent price wars, represents an important departure from the economist's model of "perfect" competition wherein no firm has any control over industry price.[4]

Alchian and Allen view the problem as follows:

If a product is produced under cost conditions such that larger rates . . . [would] mean lower average cost per unit, . . . only one firm could survive; if there were two firms, one could expand to reduce costs and selling price and thereby eliminate the other. In view of the impossibility of more than one firm's being profitable, two is too many. But if there is only one, that incumbent firm may be able to set prices above free-entry costs for a long time. Either resources are wasted because too many are in the industry, or there is just one firm, which will be able to charge monopoly prices.[5]

At this point it will be useful to state explicitly the interpretation of natural monopoly used in this paper. If, because of production scale economies, it is less costly for one firm to produce a commodity in a given market than it is for two or more firms, then one firm will survive; if left unregulated, that firm will set price and output at monopoly levels; the price-output decision of that firm will be determined by profit maximizing behavior constrained only by the market demand for the commodity.

The theory of natural monopoly is deficient for it fails to reveal the logical steps that carry it from scale economies in production to monopoly price in the market place. To see this most clearly, let us consider the contracting process from its beginning.

Why must rivals share the market? Rival sellers can offer to enter into contracts with buyers. In this bidding competition, the rival who offers buyers the most favorable terms will obtain their patronage; there is no clear or necessary reason for *bidding* rivals to share in the *production* of

---

However, monopoly may also arise because it is technically efficient to have a single producer or enterprise. . . . When technical conditions make a monopoly the natural outcome of competitive market forces, there are only three alternatives that seem available: private monopoly, public monopoly, or public regulation.

Capitalism and Freedom 28 (1962).

[4] Paul A. Samuelson, Economics 461 (6th rev. ed. 1964).

[5] Armen Alchian and William R. Allen, University Economics 412 (1st ed. 1964).

the goods and, therefore, there is no clear reason for competition in bidding to result in an increase in per-unit *production* costs.

Why must the unregulated market outcome be monopoly price? The competitiveness of the bidding process depends very much on such things as the number of bidders, but there is no clear or necessary reason for *production* scale economies to decrease the number of *bidders*. Let prospective buyers call for bids to service their demands. Scale economies in servicing their demands in no way imply that there will be one bidder only. There can be many bidders and the bid that wins will be the lowest. The existence of scale economies in the production of the service is irrelevant to a determination of the number of rival bidders. If the number of bidders is large or if, for other reasons, collusion among them is impractical, the contracted price can be very close to per-unit production cost.[6]

The determinants of competition in market negotiations differ from and should not be confused with the determinants of the number of firms from which production will issue after contractual negotiations have been completed. The theory of natural monopoly is clearly unclear. Economies of scale in production imply that the bids submitted will offer increasing quantities at lower per-unit costs, but production scale economies imply nothing obvious about how competitive these prices will be. If one bidder can do the job at less cost than two or more, because each would then have a smaller output rate, then the bidder with the lowest bid price for the entire job will be awarded the contract, whether the good be cement, electricity, stamp vending machines, or whatever, but the lowest bid price need not be a monopoly price.[7]

The criticism made here of the theory of natural monopoly can be understood best by constructing an example that is free from irrelevant complications, such as durability of distributions systems, uncertainty, and irrational behavior, all of which may or may not justify the use of regulatory commissions but none of which is relevant to the theory of natural monopoly; for this theory depends on one belief only—price and output will be at monopoly levels if, due to scale economies, only one firm succeeds in producing the product.

Assume that owners of automobiles are required to own and display

[6] I shall not consider in this paper the problem of marginal cost pricing and the various devices, such as multi-part tariffs, that can be used to approximate marginal cost pricing.

[7] The competitive concept employed here is not new to economics although it has long been neglected. An early statement of the concept, which was known as "competition *for* the field" in distinction to "competition *within* the field" is given by Edwin Chadwick, Results of Different Principles of Legislation and Administration in Europe; of Competition for the Field, as compared with the Competition within the Field of Service, 22 J. Royal Statistical Soc'y. 381 (1859).

new license plates each year. The production of license plates is subject to scale economies.

The theory of natural monopoly asserts that under these conditions the owners of automobiles will purchase plates from one firm only and that firm, in the absence of regulation, will charge a monopoly price, a price that is constrained only by the demand for and the cost of producing license plates. The logic of the example does dictate that license plates will be purchased from one firm because this will allow that firm to offer the plates at a price based on the lowest possible per-unit cost. But why should that price be a monopoly price?

There can be many bidders for the annual contract. Each will submit a bid based on the assumption that if its bid is lowest it will sell to all residents, if it is not lowest it sells to none. Under these conditions there will exist enough independently acting bidders to assure that the winning price will differ insignificantly from the per-unit cost of producing license plates.

If only one firm submits the lowest price, the process ends, but if two or more firms submit the lowest price, one is selected according to some random selection device or one is allowed to sell or give his contracts to the other. There is no monopoly price although there may be rent to some factors if their supply is positively sloped. There is no regulation of firms in the industry. The price is determined in the bidding market. The only role played by the government or by a consumers' buying cooperative is some random device to select the winning bidder if more than one bidder bids the lowest price.

There are only two important assumptions: (1) The inputs required to enter production must be available to many potential bidders at prices determined in open markets. This lends credibility to numerous rival bids. (2) The cost of colluding by bidding rivals must be prohibitively high. The reader will recognize that these requirements are no different than those required to avoid monopoly price in any market, whether production in that market is or is not subject to scale economies.

Moreover, if we are willing to consider the possibility that collusion or merger of all potential bidding rivals is a reasonable prospect, then we must examine the other side of the coin. Why should collusion or merger of *buyers* be prohibitively costly if an infinite or large number of bidding rivals can collude successfully? If we allow buyers access to the same technology of collusion, the market will be characterized by bilateral negotiations between organized buyers and organized sellers. While the outcome of such negotiations is somewhat uncertain with respect to wealth distribution, there is no reason to expect inefficiency.

Just what is the supply elasticity of bidders and what are the costs of colluding are questions to be answered empirically since they cannot be deduced from production scale economies. There exist more than one firm in every public utility industry and many firms exist in some public utility industries. And this is true even though licensing restrictions have been severe; the assertion that the supply of potential *bidders* in any market would be very inelastic if licensing restrictions could be abolished would seem difficult to defend when producing competitors exist in nearby markets. The presence of active rivalry is clearly indicated in public utility history. In fact, producing competitors, not to mention unsuccessful bidders, were so plentiful that one begins to doubt that scale economies characterized the utility industry at the time when regulation replaced market competition. Complaints were common that the streets were too frequently in a state of disrepair for the purpose of accommodating competing companies. Behling writes:

> There is scarcely a city in the country that has not experienced competition in one or more of the utility industries. Six electric light companies were organized in the one year of 1887 in New York City. Forty-five electric light enterprises had the legal right to operate in Chicago in 1907. Prior to 1895, Duluth, Minnesota, was served by five electric lighting companies, and Scranton, Pennsylvania, had four in 1906 . . . . During the latter part of the nineteenth century, competition was the usual situation in the gas industry in this country. Before 1884, six competing companies were operating in New York City . . . . Competition was common and especially persistent in the telephone industry. According to a special report of the Census in 1902, out of 1051 incorporated cities in the United States with a population of more than 4,000 persons, 1002 were provided with telephone facilities. The independent companies had a monopoly in 137 of the cities, the Bell interests had exclusive control over communication by telephone in 414 cities, while the remaining 451, almost half, were receiving duplicated service. Baltimore, Chicago, Cleveland, Columbus, Detroit, Kansas City, Minneapolis, Philadelphia, Pittsburgh, and St. Louis, among the larger cities, had at least two telephone services in 1905.[8]

It would seem that the number of potential bidding rivals and the cost of their colluding in the public utility industries are likely to be at least as great as in several other industries for which we find that unregulated markets work tolerably well.

The natural monopoly theory provides no logical basis for monopoly prices. The theory is illogical. Moreover, for the general case of public utility industries, there seems no clear evidence that the cost of colluding is significantly lower than it is for industries for which unregulated market competition seems to work. To the extent that utility regulation is based on the fear of monopoly price, *merely because one firm will serve each market*, it is not based on any deducible economic theorem.

The important point that needs stressing is that *we have no theory that*

[8] Burton N. Behling, Competition and Monopoly in Public Utility Industries 19-20 (1938).

allows us to deduce from the observable degree of concentration in a particular market whether or not price and output are competitive. We have as yet no general theory of collusion and certainly not one that allows us to associate observed concentration in a particular market with successful collusion.[9]

It is possible to make some statements about collusion that reveal the nature of the forces at work. These statements are largely intuitive and cannot be pursued in detail here. But they may be useful in imparting to the reader a notion of what is meant by a theory of collusion. Let us suppose that there are no special costs to competing. That is, we assume that sellers do not need to keep track of the prices or other activities of their competitors. Secondly, assume that there are some costs of colluding that must be borne by members of a bidders' cartel. This condition is approximated least well where the government subsidizes the cost of colluding—for example, the U.S. Department of Agriculture. Finally, assume that there are no legal barriers to entry.

Under these conditions, new bidding rivals will be paid to join the collusion. In return for joining they will receive a pro rata share of monopoly profits. As more rivals appear the pro rata share must fall. The cartel will continue paying new rivals to join until the pro rata share falls to the cost of colluding. That is, until the cartel members receive a competitive rate of return for remaining in the cartel. The next rival bidder can refuse to join the cartel; instead he can enter the market at a price below the cartel price (as can any present member of the cartel who chooses to break away). If there is some friction in the system, this rival will choose this course of action in preference to joining the cartel, for if he joins the cartel he receives a competitive rate of return; whereas if he competes outside the cartel by selling at a price below that of the cartel he receives an above-competitive rate of return for some short-run period. Under the assumed conditions the cartel must eventually fail and price and output can be competitive even though only a few firms actually produce the product. Moreover, the essential ingredient to its eventual failure is only that the private per-firm cost of colluding exceeds the private per-firm cost of competing.

Under what conditions will the cost of colluding exceed the cost of competing? How will these costs be affected by allowing coercive tactics? What about buyer cartels? What factors affect how long is "eventually"? Such questions remain to be answered by a theory of collusion. Until such questions are answered, public policy prescriptions must be suspect. A market in which many firms produce may be competitive or it may be collusive; the large number of firms merely reflects production scale diseconomies; large numbers do not necessarily reflect high or low collusion costs. A market in

9 However, see George J. Stigler, A Theory of Oligopoly, 72 J. Pol. Econ. 44 (1964).

which few firms produce may be competitive or it may be collusive; the small number of firms merely relects production scale economies; fewness does not necessarily reflect high or low collusion costs. Thus, an economist may view the many retailers who sell on "fair trade" terms with suspicion and he may marvel at the ability of large numbers of workers to form effective unions, and, yet, he may look with admiration at the performance of the few firms who sell airplanes, cameras, or automobiles.

The subject of monopoly price is necessarily permeated with the subject of negotiating or contracting costs. A world in which negotiating costs are zero is a world in which no monopolistic inefficiencies will be present, simply because buyers and sellers both can profit from negotiations that result in a reduction and elimination of inefficiencies. In such a world it will be bargaining skills and not market structures that determine the distribution of wealth. If a monopolistic structure exists on one side of the market, the other side of the market will be organized to offset any power implied by the monopolistic structure. The organization of the other side of the market can be undertaken by members of that side or by rivals of the monopolistic structure that prevails on the first side. The co-existence of monopoly *power* and monopoly *structure* is possible only if the costs of negotiating are differentially positive, being lower for one set of sellers (or buyers) than it is for rival sellers (or buyers). If one set of sellers (or buyers) can organize those on the other side of the market more cheaply than can rivals, then price may be raised (or lowered) to the extent of the existing differential advantage in negotiating costs; this extent generally will be less than the simple monopoly price. In some cases the differential advantage in negotiating costs may be so great that price will settle at the monopoly (monopsony) level. This surely cannot be the general case, but the likelihood of it surely increases as the costs imposed on potential rivals increase; legally restricting entry is one way of raising the differential disadvantages to rivals; the economic meaning of restricting entry *is* increasing the cost of potential rivals of negotiating with and organizing buyers (or sellers).

The public policy question is which groups of market participants, *if any*, are to receive governmentally sponsored advantages and disadvantages, not only in the subsidization or taxation of production but, also, in the creation of advantages or disadvantages in conducting negotiations.

At this juncture, it should be emphasized that I have argued, not that regulatory commissions are undesirable, but that economic theory does not, at present, provide a justification for commissions insofar as they are based on the belief that observed concentration and monopoly price bear any necessary relationship.

Indeed, in utility industries, regulation has often been sought because of the inconvenience of competition. The history of regulation is often written in terms of the desire to prohibit "excessive" duplication of utility distribution systems and the desire to prohibit the capture of *windfall* gains by utility companies. Neither of these aspects of the utility business are necessarily related to scale economies. Let us first consider the problem of excessive duplication of facilities.

Duplication of Facilities. Communities and not individuals own or control most of the ground and air rights-of-way used by public utility distribution systems. The problem of excessive duplication of distribution systems is attributable to the failure of communities to set a proper price on the use of these scarce resources. The right to use publicly owned thoroughfares is the right to use a scarce resource. The absence of a price for the use of these resources, a price high enough to reflect the opportunity costs of such alternative uses as the servicing of uninterrupted traffic and unmarred views, will lead to their overutilization. The setting of an appropriate fee for the use of these resources would reduce the degree of duplication to optimal levels.

Consider that portion of the ground controlled by an individual and under which a *utility's* distribution system runs. Confront that individual with the option of service at a lower price from a company that is a rival to the present seller. The individual will take into consideration the cost to him of running a trench through his garden and the benefit to him of receiving the service at lower cost. There is no need for excessive duplication. Indeed, there is no need for any duplication of facilities if he selects the new service, provided that one of two conditions holds. If the *individual* owns that part of the distribution system running under his ground he could tie it in to whatever trunk line serves him best; alternatively, once the new company wins his patronage, a rational solution to the use of that part of the distribution system would be for the utility company owning it to sell it to the utility company now serving the buyer.

There may be good reasons for using community property rather than private property to house the main trunk lines of some utility distribution systems. The placement of such systems under or over streets, alleyways, and sidewalks, resources already publicly owned (a fact taken as datum here), may be less costly than routing them through private property. The failure of communities to charge fees for the use of public property, fees that tend to prevent excessive use of this property, can be explained in three ways.

(1) There was a failure to understand the prerequisities for efficient resource use. Some public officer must be given the incentives to act as a rational conservator of resources when these resources are scarce.

(2) The disruption of thoroughfares was not, in fact, costly enough to bother about.

(3) The setting of fees to curtail excessive use of thoroughfares by utility companies was too costly to be practical.

The first two explanations, if true, give no support to an argument for regulating utility companies. The third explanation may give support to some sort of regulation, for it asserts that the economic effects that are produced by the placing of distribution systems are such that it is too costly to economize through the use of a price system. The costs of taking account of these effects through some regulatory process must be compared with the benefits of realigning resource use, and if the benefits are worth the costs some regulation may be desirable. Note clearly: scale economies in serving a market are not at issue. To see this, imagine that electrical distribution systems are thin lines of a special conducting paint. The placing of such systems causes no difficulties. They are sprayed over either public or private property. Nonetheless, suppose that the use of each system is subject to scale economies. Clearly, the desire to regulate cannot now be justified by such problems as traffic disruption, even though scale economies are present. "Excess" duplication is a problem of externalities and not of scale economies.

Let us suppose that it is desirable to employ some sort of regulation because it is too costly to use the price system to take account of the disruptive effects of placing distribution systems. Regulation comes in all sizes and shapes, and it is by no means clear what type of regulation would be most desirable.

A franchise system that allows only a limited number of utility companies to serve a market area was employed frequently. A franchise system that awarded the franchise to that company which seemed to offer the best price-quality package would be one that allowed market competition between bidding rivals to determine that package. The restraint of the market would be substituted for that of the regulatory commission.

An alternative arrangement would be public ownership of the distribution system. This would involve the collection of competing bids for installing the distribution system. The system could then be installed by the bidder offering to do the specified job at the lowest price. This is the same process used by communities to build highways and it employs rival bidding and not commissions to determine that price. The community could then allow its distribution system to be used by that utility company offering to provide specified utility services at lowest cost to residents. Again the market is substituted for the regulatory commission. Public ownership of streets may make public ownership of distribution systems seem desirable, but this does not mean that the use of regulatory commissions is desirable.

The Problem of Windfalls. We must now consider a last difficulty that has sometimes been marshalled to support the regulation of utilities. This argument is based on the fact that events in life are uncertain. The application of this observation to the utility business goes like this. After a buyer enters into an agreement with a utility company for supplying utility service, there may be changes in technology and prices that make the agreed upon price obsolete. In such cases, it is asserted, the price should be changed to reflect the current cost of providing utility services. The regulation by commission of prices on the basis of current costs is needed in the utilities industries because of the durability of original investments in plant and distribution systems. This durability prohibits the use of recontracting in the market place as a method for bringing about appropriate changes in price.

Problems of uncertainty create a potential for positive or negative windfalls. If market negotiations have misjudged the development of a better technology and if there is some cost to reawarding contracts to other producers once they are agreed upon, then an unexpected improvement in the technology used by those who are awarded the contracts may generate a price that is higher than per-unit cost, but higher by an amount no greater than the cost of reawarding contracts. In such cases, the firms now holding the contracts may collect a positive windfall for a short-run period. Or, if input prices increase by more than is expected, these same firms may suffer from a negative windfall. But the same thing is true of all markets. If a customer buys eggs today for consumption tomorrow, he will enjoy a positive windfall if the price of eggs is higher tomorrow and a negative windfall if the price is lower. The difference in the two cases is that, where long-term contracts are desirable, the windfalls may continue for longer periods. In such cases it *may* be desirable to employ a cost-plus regulatory scheme or to enter a clause that reserves the right, for some fee, to renegotiate the contract.

The problem faced here is what is the best way to cope with uncertainty. Long-term contracts for the supply of commodities are concluded satisfactorily in the market place without the aid of regulation. These contracts may be between retailers and appliance producers, or between the air lines and aircraft companies, all of whom may use durable production facilities. The rental of office space for ninety-nine years is fraught with uncertainty. I presume that the parties to a contract hire experts to provide relevant guesses on these matters and that the contract concluded resolves these issues in a way that is satisfactory to both parties. Penalties for reopening negotiations at a later date can be included in the contract. I presume that buyers and sellers who agree to contract with each other have handled the problem of uncertainty in a mutually satisfactory way. The correct way to view the problem is one of selecting the best type of contract. A producer may say, "if you agree to buy from me for twenty-five years, I can use facilities that are expected to produce the service at lower costs; if you contract five years, I will not invest much in tooling-up, and, hence, I will need a higher price to cover higher per-unit costs; of course, the longer-run contract allows more time for the unexpected, so let us include an escape clause of some kind." The buyer and seller must then agree on a suitable contract; durability of equipment and longer-term commitments can be sacrificed at the cost of higher per-unit costs, but there is no reason to expect that the concluded contract will be biased as to outcome or nonoptimal in other respects.

Cost-plus rate regulation is one way of coping with these problems, but it has great uncertainties of its own. Will the commission be effective? Does a well defined cost-plus arrangement create an inappropriate system of incentives to guide the firm in its investment and operating policies? Do the continual uncertainties associated with the meaning of cost-plus lead to otherwise avoidable difficulties in formulating investment plans? Rate regulation by commissions rather than by market rivalry may be more appropriate for utility industries than for other industries, but the truth of this assertion cannot be established deductively from existing economic theory. We do not know whether regulation handles the uncertainty-rent problem better or worse than the market.

The problem of coping with windfalls must be distinguished from the problem of *forecastable* rents. Suppose that it is known that buyers will incur considerable recontracting cost if they decide to change sellers after they are part way through an awarded contract. It would appear that the seller who wins the initial contract will be able to collect a rent as large as this recontracting cost. But this is not true if this recontracting cost is forecastable, that is, if it is not a windfall. The bidding for the initial contract will take account of the forecastable rent, so that if the bidding is competitive the rent will be forfeited by the lower bid prices to which it gives rise.

To what degree should legislation and regulation replace the market in the utilities or in other industries and what forms should such legislation take? It is not the objective of this paper to provide answers to such questions. My purpose has been to question the conventional economic arguments for the existing legislation and regulation. An expanded role for government can be defended on the empirical grounds of a documented general superiority of public administration in these industries or by a philosophical preference for mild socialism. But I do not see how a defense can be based on the formal arguments considered here; these arguments do not allow us to deduce from their assumptions either the monopoly problem or the administrative superiority of regulation.

In the case of utility industries, resort to the rivalry of the market place would relieve companies of the discomforts of commission regulation. But it would also relieve them of the comfort of legally protected market areas. It is my belief that the rivalry of the open market place disciplines more effectively than do the regulatory processes of the commission. If the managements of utility companies doubt this belief, I suggest that they re-examine the history of their industry to discover just who it was that provided most of the force behind the regulatory movement.

[20]

A regulatory adjustment process for optimal pricing by multiproduct monopoly firms

Ingo Vogelsang
University of Bonn and M.I.T. Energy Laboratory

and

Jörg Finsinger
University of Bonn and International Institute of Management, Berlin

This paper describes an incentive mechanism that is shown to enforce the use of Ramsey prices by multiproduct monopolies. The constraint given is simple. It limits information requirements on the regulatory agency to bookkeeping data of the firm. Its implementation could be easily controlled by outside courts or auditors. The process, therefore, makes use of invisible hand properties shifting the workload of welfare optimization from the regulatory agency to the regulated firm.

1. Introduction

■ Following a survey by Baumol and Bradford (1970) of the by now classical literature on second-best pricing for public enterprises, a series of articles has focused on this topic. Conditions for prices to achieve a constrained welfare maximum are well known.[1] Welfare maximizing firms should inflate all demand elasticities for their products by a common factor and otherwise behave like an unconstrained monopolist (Drèze and Marchand, 1975). However, there remains the task of translating this rule into an incentive scheme for the firms so that it becomes operational for the firm's management and the regulators. This question has been raised but left open by Bawa and Sibley (1975) within the scheme of rate-of-return regulation.

If regulators had to decide on efficient price structures, they would have to know demand elasticities and cost functions within some range of the current prevailing prices and current costs. In general, the firm's staff and managers will know price elasticities and cost functions for their products better than do regulators. Hence, the firm's management may be in a superior position to

---

We owe thanks to various readers of a previous version. Truman Bewley, Peter Diamond, Jonathan Goodman, Ray Hartman, Martin Hellwig, Roger Sherman, Christian von Weizsäcker and an anonymous referee will find that their suggestions have left traces in this paper.

[1] They have been named after Ramsey, who first (1927) derived them as the solution to an optimal taxation problem.

calculate and implement welfare maximizing prices. But why should they? We see three possible reasons for them to do so. First, they may hold a professional[2] or humanitarian interest in pursuing a welfare-maximizing strategy. This cannot generally be expected from managers, and may even be an undesirable feature of somebody running an enterprise. Second, the survival of the firm may be in danger because of potential competition by newcomers. Welfare-maximizing prices can then be a limit-pricing strategy in the sense that they are best sustainable.[3] The empirical significance of this hypothesis remains largely unexplored. Third, the regulatory agency could try to force the firm to convey the necessary information or to compute welfare-maximizing prices. But without duplicating company management and staff, how could the regulators evaluate the information they receive? Even the firm is not sure of its demands and costs. Discrepancies between *ex post* figures and projections previously filed with a regulatory agency are not necessarily evidence of cheating. In the light of these problems it would be useful if we could specify a well-defined rule that motivates firms to charge economically efficient prices.

As a first step in this directon we suggest a simple incentive mechanism which leads the firm's management to improve the price structure step by step and which, under certain conditions, results in an optimum. This is described in Section 2 after we outline the concept of constrained welfare maximization used throughout in this paper. We then give the proof for our main proposition and the economic rationale behind it. After considering how our algorithm differs from conventional regulation of price structures, we examine the two complications which our rule may have to face. One is that the firm tries to undermine the short-term-oriented rule by using a long-term strategy. The other is that the firm does not face decreasing ray average costs. In Section 3 we address the policy issues that might follow from our results.

2. The model

■ **Characterization of budget-constrained welfare maximization.** We consider a regulated private or public enterprise in a natural monopoly setting.

Assumption 1 (objective of the regulatory agency): The firm's social objective as pursued by the regulatory agency is the maximization of welfare subject to a budget constraint:

$$\max W(p)$$
$$\text{subject to } \Pi(p) \geq 0.$$

$\Pi(p)$ is the firm's profit function

$$\Pi(p) = x(p)p - C(x(p))$$

and $C(x)$ is the cost function.

Assumption 2 (welfare function): Welfare is supposed to be given by consumers' surplus $W(p)$ with the following properties:

(a) $W(p)$ is continuously differentiable and convex[4]

[2] A professional interest in finding optimal price structures and in proving that they can be implemented may be assumed at the Electricité de France under the leadership of Boiteux, who first solved the problem of constrained welfare optimization for public firms.

[3] For this see Baumol, Bailey, and Willig (1977), or Panzar and Willig (1977).

[4] The convexity assumption (a) actually follows from the assumed absence of income effects by applying a revealed preference argument. This we owe to C.C. von Weizsäcker. It is given in the Appendix.

(b) grad $W(p) = -x(p)$, where $p = (p^1, \ldots p^n)$ denotes the price vector corresponding to the demand vector $x(p)$ for the n commodities produced by the firm.

It is Assumption 2(b) which characterizes $W(p)$ as consumers' surplus. This is restrictive insofar as income effects have to be insignificant. They could, in fact, play a major role, if a substantial part of the economy were regulated in the suggested way.[5] Then, however, regulation as a market-oriented policy becomes questionable. Profits of the regulated firm have been eliminated from the welfare function because in the limit they will be shown to vanish. Also, welfare effects on commodities not supplied by the regulated firm are neglected. As long as the firm's input-output decisions do not substantially affect prices on other markets, such welfare effects will be small.[6]

The nontrivial first order condition for an optimum with $\Pi(p) \geq 0$ is

Condition 1:

$$\left(p - \frac{\partial C}{\partial x}\right)\frac{\partial x}{\partial p} = -\lambda x,$$

where $0 \leq \lambda \leq 1$ and

$$\frac{\partial x}{\partial p} = \begin{pmatrix} \frac{\partial x^1}{\partial p^1} & \cdots & \frac{\partial x^1}{\partial p^n} \\ \vdots & \ddots & \vdots \\ \frac{\partial x^n}{\partial p^1} & & \frac{\partial x^n}{\partial p^n} \end{pmatrix}.$$

Condition 1 is the generalized Ramsey formula. It is implied by the optimal taxation result in Diamond and Mirrlees (1971, p. 262).[7] An unconstrained profit-maximizing monopolist in equilibrium would satisfy Condition 1 with $\lambda = 1$, but at a constrained second-best solution λ will be just high enough to allow the firm to break even. Geometrically, as seen in Figure 1, Condition 1 means that at the optimum,[8] the normal to the surface $\{p \mid \Pi(p) = 0\}$ and the demand vector x are collinear. This result is plausible once we recall that the normal to the isowelfare surfaces $\{p \mid W(p) = c\}$ is $-x$ (Assumption 2(b)). Hence, at the optimum the isowelfare surface is tangent to the zero profit surface.

□ The regulatory algorithm.

Assumption 3 (the firm and its markets): (a) We suppose a regulated private or public multiproduct enterprise whose objective is to maximize profits in each consecutive period j, $j \in N$, $N = \{0,1,2, \ldots, \infty\}$. It faces demand and cost functions which do not change over time. There are no intertemporal cost effects. The firm management is assumed to know these functions.

(b) The inverse demand function $p(x)$ shall be continuous and nonnegative for all $x \in R^n_+$ and $\lim_{r\to\infty} p(rx) \to 0$, $r \in R_+$. This is compatible with the assumed welfare function $W(p)$.

---

[5] The degree of approximation of more general welfare measures by consumer's surplus is given by Willig (1976).

[6] See Finsinger (1978).

[7] Diamond and Mirrlees use a much less restrictive framework. See also Baumol and Bradford (1970).

[8] For simplicity corner solutions meaning zero prices are ignored here and throughout.

FIGURE 1

NECESSARY OPTIMALITY CONDITION 1

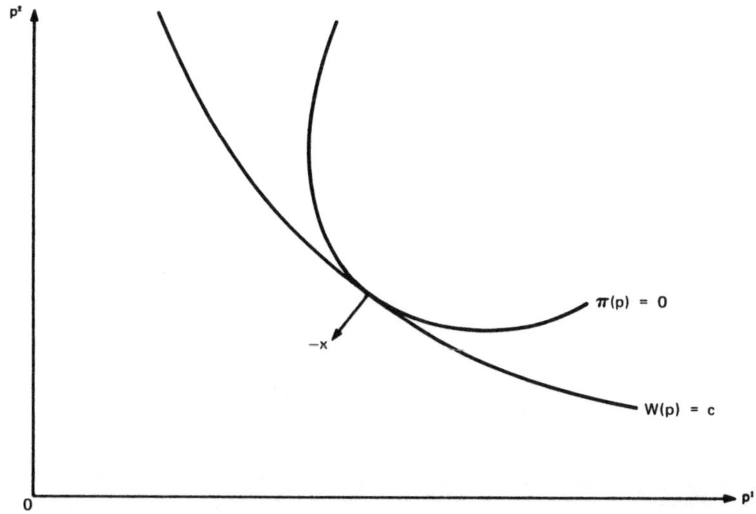

(c) The profit function $\Pi(p)$ shall have the following properties: (i) $\Pi(p)$ is continuously differentiable; (ii) In all neighborhoods of p with $\Pi(p) = 0$, there exists $p+$ with $\Pi(p+) > 0$; (iii) $\{p \mid \Pi(p) \geq 0\}$ is a compact set.
(d) The cost function $C(x)$ exhibits decreasing ray average costs:

$$\forall r \in R \quad \text{with} \quad r \geq 1 \quad C(rx) \leq r(C(x)).$$

Assumption 4 (regulatory constraint): (a) The regulatory agency knows only total costs, prices, and quantities which have been realized by the firm in the last period. The firm is required to serve all demand at current prices. Hence the data observed by the regulatory agency at time j is p_j, resulting in

$$x_j = x(p_j), \qquad C(x_j), \qquad \text{and} \qquad \Pi(p_j),$$

where p_j is the price vector at time j.
(b) The regulatory agency defines the set of feasible prices for each consecutive period $j + 1, j \in N$, by

$$R_j = \{p \mid x_j p - C(x_j) \leq 0\}.$$

Assumption 4(b) means that in period $j + 1$ the firm may ask for prices which at best would produce no profit, if applied to the quantities sold in period j.

In Figure 2 the shaded area corresponds to R_j. The firm is allowed to maximize profit constrained by R_j. Indeed, the convergence to the optimal point requires just that.[9] Hence we assume that the management of the firm will try to maximize $\Pi(p)$, subject to R_j. R_j has been constructed by moving the tangent hyperplane R at p_j into the direction of the largest welfare increase grad $W(p_j) = -x_j$. Now, assume the firm chooses the price vector p_{j+1} in period $j + 1$. In terms of welfare the firm cannot do worse than choose some point on the boundary of R_j. Then Figure 2 suggests that $W(p_{j+1}) \geq W(p_j)$. R_j can therefore

[9] See the last of the subsections for a qualification.

FIGURE 2

REGULATORY CONSTRAINT R_j

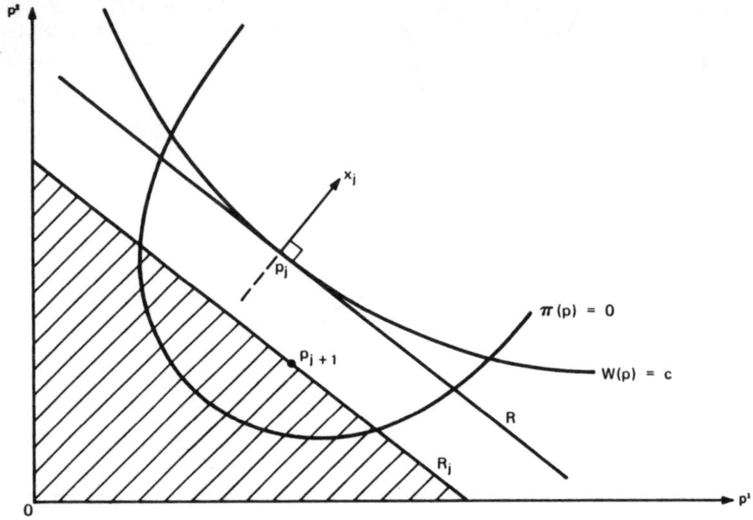

be interpreted as a linear approximation of a minimum welfare constraint. The firm thus solves a problem quite similar to the dual of constrained welfare maximization. There welfare is the objective and profit the constraint. Here profit is the objective and welfare the constraint.

The procedure can be repeated at the end of period $j + 1$ if $\Pi(p_{j+1})$ is nonnegative. It gives rise to an iterative process, which is described by the flow chart in Figure 3. To illustrate the process, assume that there is no regulation in period 0 and that the firm therefore behaves as an unconstrained monopolist.

FIGURE 3

FLOW CHART I

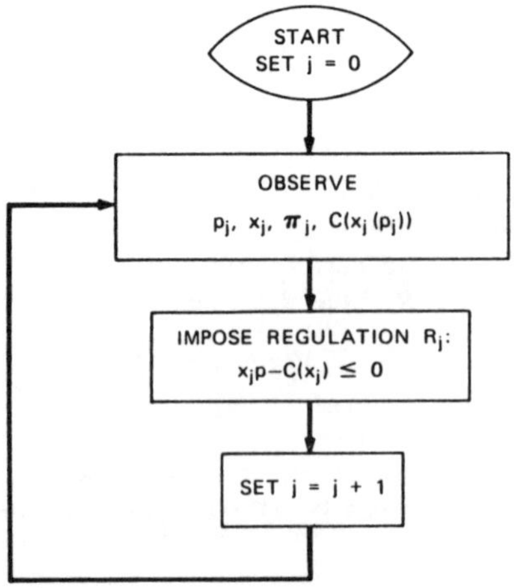

It will thus show profits Π_0 resulting from prices p_0, quantities x_0, and costs C_0. Now price regulation R_0 is imposed. This restricts pricing possibilities of the firm to an area in price space lying southwest of a hyperplane, which is defined by two properties. It is perpendicular to the demand vector x_0, and it goes through the point at which all prices have been reduced by the firm's overall profit margin of period 0. Now, under constraint R_0 the firm can maximize profits in period 1 resulting in a new set of prices p_1, quantities x_1, and costs C_1. Then profits Π_1 give rise to the regulatory agency's setting the constraint R_1 in the same manner as before. The process then goes on in an action-response manner from period to period.

The process can only work as we have described if the firm can always find a constrained price vector which yields nonnegative profit Π_j. This condition depends on the nature of the firm's cost function. If the firm is a natural monopoly by conventional standards, it is fulfilled. This means that its cost function exhibits decreasing ray average costs, i.e., $\forall r \geq 1$, $C(rx) \leq rC(x)$. Decreasing ray average costs represent the natural extension of decreasing average costs to the multiproduct firm.[10] In a local context they are equivalent with the unprofitability of marginal cost prices. In precisely this situation Ramsey prices are relevant, for they maximize welfare under the constraint of the financial viability of the firm.

Our aim was to arrive at a mechanism that sets a limit on the firm's ability to influence its price level but at the same time gives it enough degrees of freedom in maximizing profits via the price structure. The method employed has some similarity with the construction of a price index. According to our suggestion, the firm should have the freedom to choose prices in such a way that a Laspeyres price index for its products would not exceed a constrained level. The constraint R_j reduces the allowed price level for the firm's products compared to the base period j by at least the firm's profit margin of that period. This can be verified by considering that R_j implies:

$$0 = x_j p_j - C(x_j) - \Pi_j \geqq x_j p - C(x_j).$$

Thus

$$1 - \frac{\Pi_j}{x_j p_j} \geqq \frac{x_j p}{x_j p_j}.$$

Within the price level defined by this Laspeyres index the relative prices are allowed to vary. In the following period we therefore expect to get new quantities giving a new base for the index. The result is a monotonically decreasing Laspeyres chain index.

The proposed algorithm makes explicit use of a regulatory lag. In the literature the benefits of such a lag have been stressed with respect to lowering production costs. It has been shown that a lag can help to reduce factor distortion caused by regulation. If a breakeven constraint is imposed, a lag may induce a profit-maximizing firm to produce at a cost-minimizing point (Bailey, 1973). This result is also implied by our procedure. The breakeven constraint prevents a factor distortion of the Averch-Johnson kind to occur, because there is no asymmetric treatment of capital and the other factors of production. During the lag period of the process the firm is allowed to benefit from reducing its

[10] See Baumol, Bailey, and Willig (1977), Panzar and Willig (1977), or Baumol (1977) for a discussion of the concept with the view of sustainability of public utility prices.

costs *and* changing its price *structure vis-à-vis* a maximum price *level*. Obeying R_j, it will move into a profit-increasing direction. In this direction, surplus must increase. At worst this additional surplus goes entirely to the firm. But in the next period the new regulatory constraint, R_{j+1}, absorbs the additional profit and hands it over to the consumers. Thus the firm always moves into the right direction both for itself and the public at large.

Our proposition is that the process described in Figure 3 will converge to a constrained welfare maximum.

☐ **Convergence of the regulatory algorithm.**

Proposition 1: Under Assumptions 2 to 4 $W(p_j)$ converges to a point W^* with the following property: there exists $\bar{p}$ such that $W(\bar{p}) = W^*$, $\Pi(\bar{p}) = 0$, and at $\bar{p}$ the necessary optimality Condition 1 holds.

Remark: Although the sequence $W(p_j)$ converges, the sequence of the p_j need not converge. There may be many p with $W^* = W(p)$ and $\Pi(p) = 0$, between which p_j may oscillate.

Proof: Step 1: We show that $\Pi_j \geq 0 \; \forall j \in N$. Without loss of generality $\Pi_0 \geq 0$.[11] We denote the inverse demand function by $p(x)$. $\forall j \in N$ with $\Pi_j \geq 0$, there exists $r \geq 1$ such that $p(rx_j)$ exactly meets the regulatory constraint, i.e., $p(rx_j)x_j - C(x_j) = 0$. This is so, because Assumption 3(b) implies that $p(rx_j)x_j$ is a continuous function of r and approaches 0 as r gets large. Hence the intermediate value theorem is applicable. Now, we have $p(rx_j)rx_j - C(rx_j) \geq p(rx_j)rx_j - rC(x_j) = 0$. Clearly, $\Pi_{j+1} \geq p(rx_j)rx_j - C(rx_j)$ and thus $\Pi_{j+1} \geq 0$. By induction $\Pi_j \geq 0$ holds for all $j \in N$.

Step 2: We show that $W(p_j)$ converges. By step 1 $\Pi_j \geq 0 \; \forall j \in N$. Figure 2 suggests that welfare increases at each step. Indeed, we have

$$W(p_{j+1}) \geq W(p_j) + \Pi_j.$$

To see this, note that the convexity of $W(p)$ implies

$$W(p_{j+1}) \geq W(p_j) + \text{grad } W(p_j)(p_{j+1} - p_j).$$

But grad $W(p_j) = -x(p_j)$ and also the regulatory constraint R_j can be written as

$$R_j = \{p \,|\, x_j p - C_j \leq 0\} = \{p \,|\, x_j(p_j - p) \geq \Pi_j\}.$$

Hence

$$W(p_{j+1}) \geq W(p_j) + \Pi_j.$$

At each step welfare increases by at least the amount of the previous profit. Thus, $\{W(p_j)\}_{j=1}^{\infty}$ is a monotonically increasing sequence. It is bounded by the constrained welfare optimum. Because of the continuity of $W(p)$ and the compactness of $\{p \,|\, \Pi(p) \geq 0\}$ such an optimum must exist. Hence, the limit $W^* = \lim_{j\to\infty} W(p_j)$ exists. It is clear that there are points $\bar{p}$ with $W(\bar{p}) = W^*$ and $\Pi(\bar{p}) = 0$ because $0 \leq \lim \Pi_j \leq \lim (W_{j+1} - W_j) = 0$. If there is only one such point, then $p_j \to \bar{p}$. Otherwise, there exists a subsequence p_{j_K} converging to one of the $\bar{p}$, because the p_j lie in the compact set $\{p \,|\, \Pi(p) \geq 0\}$.

[11] By not constraining the firm in the first period the regulatory agency can always induce the firm to start the process with profits.

Step 3: We show that at such a $\bar{p}$ the necessary Condition 1 holds. For every period j the firm has to solve the problem

$$\max \Pi_j(p_j) = p_j x_j - C_j \qquad \text{subject to} \qquad p_j x_{j-1} - C_{j-1} \leq 0.$$

The necessary condition for this constrained profit maximization is

$$\text{grad } \Pi(p_j) = \lambda_j x_{j-1}, \quad \lambda_j \geq 0,$$

where λ_j is the shadow value giving the marginal profit increase resulting from a marginal relaxation of the constraint R_j. λ_j in general differs from λ in Condition 1. Quantities x_{j-1} are market demands at prices p_{j-1}. At any limit point $\bar{p}$ we have grad $\Pi(\bar{p}) = \bar{\lambda}\bar{x}$, where $\bar{x}$ are market demands at $\bar{p}$ and $\bar{\lambda}$ is stationary. Now, also $\Pi(\bar{p}) = 0$. Together with Assumption 2 this means that at $\bar{p}$ the three surfaces R, $\{p \mid W(p), = W(\bar{p})\}$, and the breakeven constraint of the welfare-maximizing problem, $\{p \mid \Pi(p) = 0\}$, must be tangent to each other. This completes the proof.

We want to give an intuitively more appealing explanation to Proposition 1. First, why with decreasing ray average cost can the firm always generate nonnegative profit under constraint R_j? The constraint would allow the firm to break even at quantities x_j of the previous period. This is not in general feasible for the firm, for the demanded quantities change with prices. But it can always exactly fulfill the constraint with some multiple $r \geq 1$ of x_j. Along this ray average costs are decreasing, while average prices called for by the constraint are allowed to stay constant. Hence, there always exists some $r \geq 1$ and corresponding prices fulfilling R_j which enable the firm to make nonnegative profits. Thus, decreasing ray average costs prevent the constraint from overshooting.

Second, why does welfare increase in each period by at least the profit of the last period? Here a revealed preference argument helps. The constraint R_j has been set in such a way that the sum of all consumers in period j could acquire the quantities they bought in period $j - 1$ at just Π_{j-1} less than what they actually paid during period $j - 1$. If, however, in period j they choose to buy $x_j \neq x_{j-1}$, then in terms of consumers' surplus $W(p)$ they must be at least as well off with x_j as with x_{j-1}.

Third, why does the necessary optimum Condition 1 hold at a point $\bar{p}$ of convergence of the algorithm? $\bar{p}$ lies on the zero-profit surface. Otherwise, profit could be increased which contradicts the limit property of $W(\bar{p})$. The constraint $\bar{R}$ at $\bar{p}$ is tangent to the welfare surface $\{p \mid W(p) = W(\bar{p})\}$. The necessary Condition 1 means that $\bar{R}$ is tangent to the zero-profit surface. Suppose this were not so. Then, as demonstrated in Figure 4, $\bar{R}$ intersects the set $\{p \mid \Pi(p) \geq 0\}$. The firm now is allowed to charge any price to the southwest of $\bar{R}$. Prices in the shaded area will yield positive profit owing to Property (2) of Assumption 3(d). Hence, welfare could be increased, which contradicts the limit property of $W(\bar{p})$.

Corollary: At each step of the algorithm, the welfare indicator $S(p) = W(p) + \Pi(p)$ weakly increases. $S(p)$ can be interpreted as the sum of the consumers' and producers' surplus.

Proof: From $W(p_j) \geq W(p_{j-1}) + \Pi_{j-1}$ and from $\Pi_j \geq 0 \ \forall j \in N$ we obtain

$$W(p_j) + \Pi_j \geq W(p_{j-1}) + \Pi_{j-1} \ Q.E.D.$$

FIGURE 4

LIMIT BEHAVIOR OF THE REGULATORY PROCESS

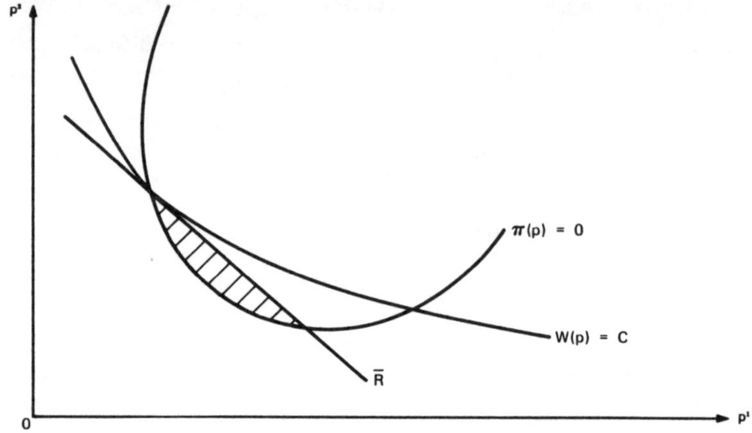

This Corollary shows that under Assumptions 2 to 4 constrained welfare optimization never decreases total surplus $S(p)$ over the unregulated situation, in particular in comparison to the unconstrained profit-maximizing monopolist. In case of increasing ray average cost this result will not necessarily hold.

□ **Characterization of the point of convergence.** Proposition 1 establishes the convergence of the regulatory process to a welfare level $W^* = W(\bar{p})$ such that at $\bar{p}$ the first-order optimality Condition 1 holds. Of course, there may be many points p fulfilling Condition 1. Some of these points represent constrained local welfare maxima. But $\bar{p}$ need not be such a maximum. Fortunately, our process does not choose $\bar{p}$ at random among the points fulfilling Condition 1. In fact, we can be highly certain that $\bar{p}$ is a constrained local welfare maximum. First, we know from Step 2 of the proof of Proposition 1 that in each period the algorithm increases welfare by at least the amount of the previous profit. Second, $W^* = W(\bar{p})$ never is a local minimum. The only type of situation where $W^* = W(\bar{p})$ is not a constrained local maximum, is shown in Figure 5. There $\bar{p}$ fulfills the tangency Condition 1. But the constrained local welfare maximum is at p^*. Without formally introducing probability arguments, we can see: The algorithm would only by "extreme mischief" (measure zero) arrive at such a point. Additionally, this point may be called unstable. A small change in the environmental conditions $x(\ )$ and $C(\ )$ will cause the firm (and the regulatory agency to induce the firm) to move into a welfare-increasing direction between $\{p \mid W(p) = c\}$, and $\{p \mid \Pi(p) = 0\}$ (cf. Figure 5).

□ **How this algorithm differs from conventional regulation of price structures.** Historically, public utility regulation in the United States has tended to lead to price structures which become rigid and/or are characterized by cross subsidization. These phenomena can be attributed to political and judicial influences on price structures. This observation has led economists to try to convince

FIGURE 5

NONFULFILLMENT OF THE SECOND ORDER CONDITION

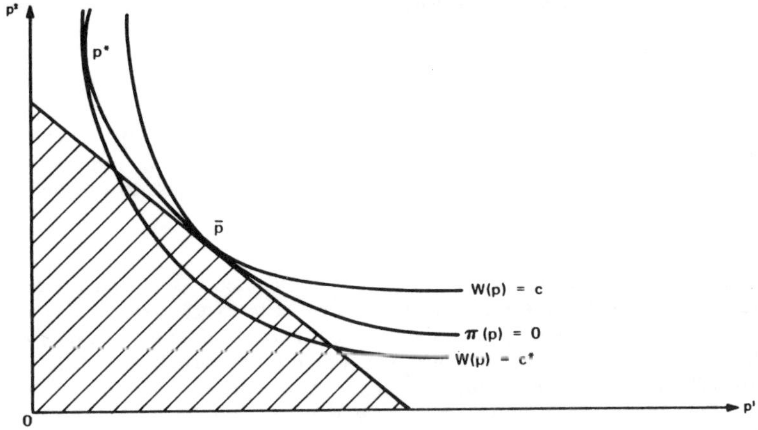

regulators that such a policy has undesirable efficiency consequences. They have therefore tediously demonstrated the positive effect of explicitly considering demand elasticities. Against this background our paper seems ironic, as it frankly asks regulators to forget what they learned from economists whenever conditions are sufficiently stable.[12]

The fair rate of return on capital and the balanced budget rule are "easily" implementable regulatory measures to constrain price levels. So far, there has been no comparable indicator for efficient price structures. The strength of the algorithm described above lies in the incentives it gives to the regulated firm to find the efficient price structure itself. The firm's management may, for instance, use peak load pricing or two-part pricing techniques. The management may split demand into demand components at different time periods and may introduce license fees. For such tariffs a necessary optimality condition analogous to Condition 1 can be derived. With two-part tariffs, for instance, x contains not only the demand x_i for good i, but also the demand $\hat{x}_i$ for licensing/subscription to good i. Similarly, p contains not only the prices p_i for good i, but also the license fee $\hat{p}_i$ for good i.

Within the limits of bookkeeping and auditing, the information requirements with respect to the regulatory agency are low. The agency is supposed to have some general knowledge about the structure of the regulated industry, especially whether it produces at decreasing ray average costs. Furthermore, it has to know what has actually happened in the past, but not the full possibility set of the firm. This contrasts for instance with the problem of finding the optimal rate of return in the Averch-Johnson model (Klevorick, 1971). Even with some knowledge of demand elasticities and costs in the neighborhood of the *status quo* of the firm, a

[12] We owe the basis of this point to an anonymous referee. The sustainability argument can lead to the same kind of policy conclusion. Indeed, in Germany peak load pricing some decades ago was introduced by high-cost electric utilities threatened by competitive pressure and takeovers.

regulatory agency can hardly hope to do better than approximate first-order conditions. To the best of our knowledge, all previous efforts to implement constrained welfare optimal prices have therefore taken the first-order conditions to be sufficient. Compared with this, our procedure ensures that $W(\bar{p})$ is no local minimum and that the point reached by the procedure is preferred to the *status quo*. Only in a small class of cases, to which we give little empirical significance, will the process stop short of a local welfare maximum.

The agency in our model has little discretionary power. It is, however, obliged to control the quality of the firm's output because the firm may want to reduce costs through hidden quality deterioration. This, of course, is a standard regulatory issue.

□ **Some qualifications and extensions.** *Myopic management behavior.* So far we have assumed that the firm maximizes profit in every period j subject to constraint R_{j-1}. However, such myopic profit maximization may deviate from the long-run interest of the management, which is to maximize the discounted flow of future profits. Does the algorithm converge in this case?

The convergence of the algorithm depends on the simple inequality $W(p_{j+1}) \geq W(p_j) + \Pi_j$. From this inequality it can be seen that the convergence is not affected as long as $\Pi_j \geq 0$ for all j. The process, however, could converge to a suboptimal point, if the firm keeps profits sufficiently low. But this would mean that in total it foregoes profits which would be allowed and feasible. It can thus only be inferred that the convergence rate may be slower in earlier periods and faster in later periods compared to the rate corresponding to the myopic profit maximization case. Management may want to produce losses for some periods in order to recoup higher profits later. With decreasing ray average costs losses are an indication of either strategic behavior or mismanagement. Thus, if losses occur, the regulatory agency can either fire the management[13] or keep the previous regulatory constraint until profits turn up.

If profits occur, the regulatory constraint for the next period becomes more binding and therefore narrows the firm's discretion for the future. Eventually, the firm will be forced by its profits to follow the convergence path. The higher the discount rate employed by the firm, the more it will want to make higher profits early. Thus, a high discount rate may speed up the process.

Nondecreasing ray average costs. Assumption 3(d), which postulates decreasing ray average cost may be violated even in case of a natural monopoly.[14] Therefore, the procedure described above should be adapted to the regulation of monopoly firms with nondecreasing ray average costs. As is illustrated in Figures 6 and 7 for the simple case of a one-product firm, there can be a striking difference in applying the algorithm for a decreasing or nondecreasing (ray) average cost firm. With decreasing (ray) average cost profits always stay nonnegative, while with increasing (ray) average costs losses may be inevitable. For a one-product firm profits and losses will follow each other in a hog cycle manner. If, furthermore, the average cost curve is absolutely steeper than the demand curve the process will explode.

[13] In the context of U.S. regulation the agency can threaten to withdraw the firm's license.

[14] Panzar and Willig (1977) show that subadditivity of the cost function does not imply decreasing ray average cost.

FIGURE 6

CONVERGENCE OF THE FLOW CHART I PROCESS WITH DECREASING AVERAGE COST

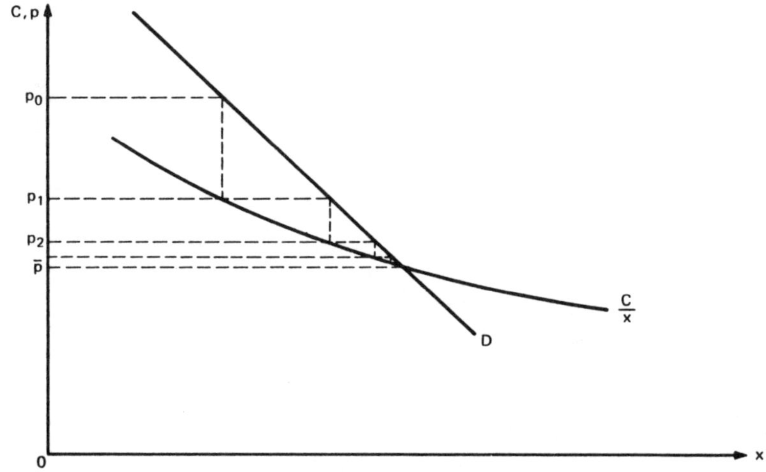

Thus, to preserve the incentive structure of the algorithm and to limit the informational requirements of the agency to bookkeeping data, we insert a second loop into the algorithm. Loop II deals with the case where the regulatory constraint was too strong. At each iteration in loop II in Flow Chart II the regulatory constraint is relaxed until nonnegative profit is again possible.

Proposition 2: Under the Assumptions 2, 3(a)–(c), and 4(a), the algorithm described in Figure 8 below converges as in Proposition 1.

FIGURE 7

CONVERGENCE OF THE FLOW CHART I PROCESS WITH INCREASING AVERAGE COST

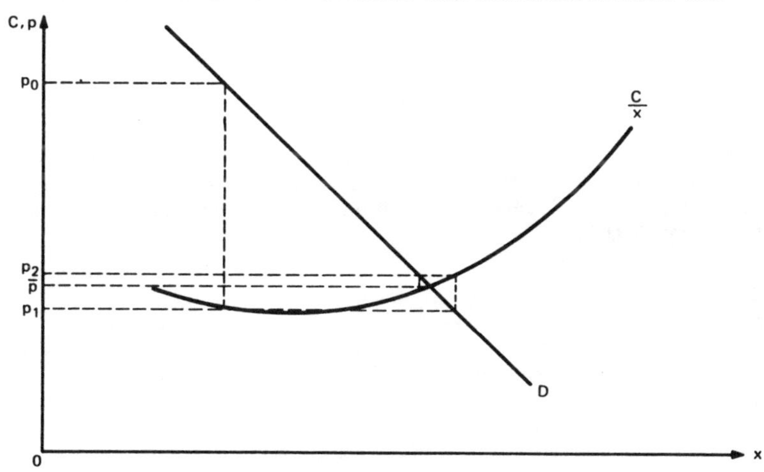

FIGURE 8

FLOW CHART II*

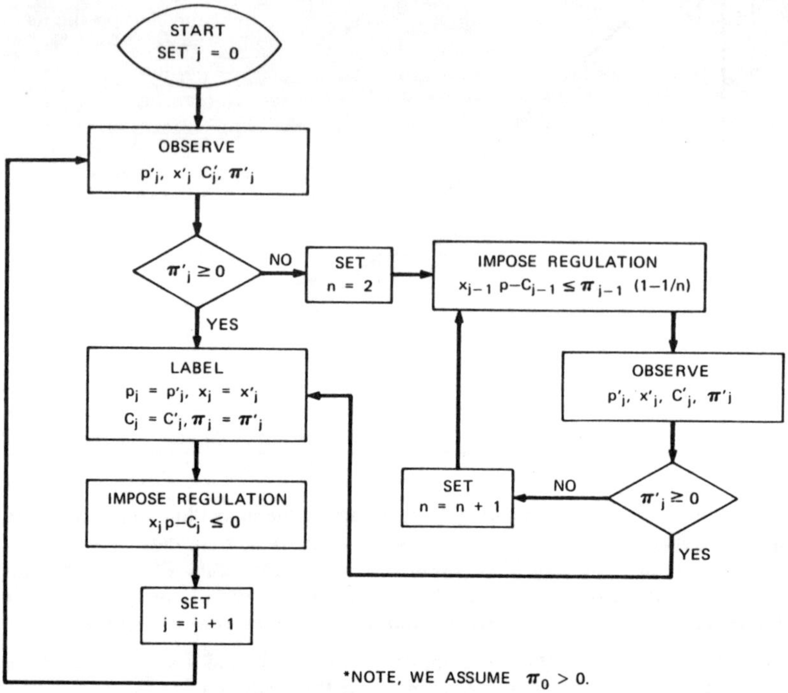

*NOTE, WE ASSUME $\pi_0 > 0$.

Proof: Step 1: We show that loop II is finite. We have $\Pi_{j-1} = 0$ implies $\Pi'_j \geq 0$. Hence, $\Pi'_j < 0$ implies $\Pi_{j-1} > 0$. But if $\Pi_{j-1} > 0$, then there exists a neighborhood of p_{j-1} such that for all $p \in U_\epsilon(p_{j-1})$, $\Pi(p) \geq 0$. Hence, there exists $n \in N$ such that $\Pi'_j \geq 0$.

Step 2: Coming out of loop II we have $x_{j-1}p_j - C(x_{j-1}) \leq x_{j-1}p_{j-1} - C(x_{j-1})$ by construction of the constraint. Therefore, $x_{j-1}(p_j - p_{j-1}) \leq 0$. This means that at prices p_j consumers could have bought x_{j-1} cheaper than at prices p_{j-1}. They, however, decided to buy x_j. Hence welfare must have increased: $W(p_j) \geq W(p_{j-1})$. This means that $\{W(p_j)\}j = {}^{\infty}_{1}$ is a monotonically increasing sequence. From here on the proof follows steps 2 and 3 of the proof of Proposition 1. *Q.E.D.*

The case of nondecreasing ray average cost is less straightforward than that of decreasing ray average cost. Although our previous arguments carry over, the number of periods necessary to come close to the optimum may increase considerably due to loop II. Current profit is no longer a lower bound for next period's welfare increase. Furthermore, strategic firm behavior producing high losses to relax the constraint may be attractive. On the other hand, it can be hoped that the fear of competitive entry into profitable submarkets—cream skimming—will in this case limit the firm's discretion.

3. Conclusion

■ The process described rests on some general principles, which are not dependent on their regulatory application. As an equilibrium, letting the firm maximize profits subject to a constraint on the welfare level of consumers generates an optimum. Convexity of the welfare function permits substitution of the tangent hyperplane for the indifference surface. Decreasing ray average costs or the mechanism of Figure 8 prevent overshooting. Hence we can converge to a local optimum by raising the allowed welfare level in each step.

The regulatory algorithm can be interpreted as an incentive pricing mechanism in the sense of Cross (1970). The regulated firm constrained by R_j is encouraged to exploit both the potential for cost decreases and the consumers' willingness to pay. The firm converts these into profits. But both these advantages are turned over to the consumers in the next period.

Our process does not differ substantially from the regulatory procedure which has traditionally been used in the United States. Here the rate level is set by applying a rate of return constraint on past cost and quantity data of the regulated monopoly firm. In theory, regulated firms are free then to adjust the rate structure subject to the proof that they stay within the overall rate of return constraint again based on past data. In practice, however, they meet many obstacles in doing so. As a policy recommendation, this paper suggests that once the rate *level* has been established the actual freedom of the firms to alter their rate *structure* on profit-maximizing grounds should be increased.[15] Basically, the argument used for this recommendation is similar to the one in favor of a regulatory lag.

Enforcement of the regulatory constraint R_j developed in this paper could be supervised by auditing. Hence, its application could be prescribed to regulatory agencies by law. Once they have accepted the philosophy behind this approach regulatory agencies could go back to using their beloved concept of historic costs.

Appendix

■ Let the direct utility function of an individual be given by $U(x,p,M) = \hat{U}(x) - px + M$, where M represents income (wealth) and $U(x)$ represents the willingness to pay for x. We want to show the convexity of the corresponding indirect utility function $V(p,M) = U(x(p),p,M)$, i.e., $\forall 0 \leq \lambda \leq 1$

$$V(\lambda p_1 + (1-\lambda)p_2,M) \leq \lambda V(p_1,M) + (1-\lambda)V(p_2,M). \tag{A1}$$

First, observe that

$$U(\bar{x},p_1,M) \leq U(x(p_1),p_1,M) \tag{A2}$$

and

$$U(\bar{x},p_2,M) \leq U(x(p_2),p_2,M) \tag{A3}$$

for any $\bar{x}$ and in particular for $\bar{x} = x(\lambda p_1 + (1-\lambda)p_2)$. Multiply (A2) and (A3) by λ and $(1-\lambda)$, respectively. Then, addition yields

$$\hat{U}(\bar{x}) - (\lambda p_1 + (1-\lambda)p_2)\bar{x} + M \leq \lambda[\hat{U}(x(p_1)) - p_1x(p_1)] + (1-\lambda)[\hat{U}(x(p_2)) - p_2x(p_2)] + M.$$

[15] We are currently working on the problem of introducing a rate of return constraint into the process. In this case an Averch-Johnson bias may occur for $s > i$.

Rewriting this inequality in terms of $V(p,M)$ yields (A1). Since $W(p)$ is the sum of the individual indirect utility functions $V(p,M)$, $W(p)$ must be convex.

References

BAUMOL, W.J. "On the Proper Cost Tests for Natural Monopoly in a Multiproduct Industry." *The American Economic Review*, Vol. 67 (1977), pp. 809–822.

——— AND BRADFORD, D.P. "Optimal Departures from Marginal Cost Pricing. *The American Economic Review*, Vol. 60 (1970), pp. 265–283.

———, BAILEY, E.E., AND WILLIG, R.D. "Weak Invisible Hand Theorems on the Sustainability of Multiproduct Monopoly." *The American Economic Review*, Vol. 67, No. 3 (1977), pp. 350–365.

BAILEY, E.E. *Economic Theory of Regulatory Constraint*. Lexington, Mass.: D.C. Heath, 1973.

BAWA, V.S. AND SIBLEY, D.S. "Dynamic Behavior of a Firm Subject to Stochastic Regulatory Review." Bell Laboratories Economic Discussion Paper No. 38, September 1975.

CROSS, J.G. "Incentive Pricing and Utility Regulation." *Quarterly Journal of Economics*, Vol. 84 (1970), pp. 236–253.

DIAMOND, P.A. AND MIRRLEES, J.A. "Optimal Taxation and Public Production II: Tax Rules." *The American Economic Review*, Vol. 61 (1971), pp. 261–278.

DRÈZE, J.H. AND MARCHAND, M.G. "Pricing, Spending, and Gambling Rules for Nonprofit Organizations." CORE Discussion Paper No. 7514, 1975.

FAULHABER, G.R. "Cross-Subsidization: Pricing in Public Enterprises." *The American Economic Review*, Vol. 65 (1975), pp. 966–977.

FINSINGER, J. "Social Surplus, Piecemeal Policy, and Partial Analysis." DP 78-52, International Institute of Management, Berlin, 1978.

KLEVORICK, A.K. "The Optimal Fair Rate of Return." *The Bell Journal of Economics and Management Science*, Vol. 2, No. 1 (Spring 1971), pp. 122–153.

PANZAR, J.C. AND WILLIG, R.D. "Free Entry and the Sustainability of Natural Monopoly." *The Bell Journal of Economics*, Vol. 8, No. 1 (Spring 1977), pp. 1–22.

RAMSEY, F. "A Contribution to the Theory of Taxation." *Economic Journal*, Vol. 37 (1927), pp. 4–61.

WILLIG, R.D. "Consumer's Surplus without Apology." *The American Economic Review*, Vol. 66 (1976), pp. 589–597.

[21]

Productivity Incentive Clauses and Rate Adjustment for Inflation

By WILLIAM J. BAUMOL*

THIS article describes a new procedure designed to deal with three critical regulatory problems related to inflation and productive efficiency:

Problem 1. Incentives for Maximum Efficiency and Growth of Productivity. Rate of return regulation seeks a structure of rates for the regulated firm which prevent it from earning excessive profits. But pursuit of this commendable objective can easily degenerate into a cost-plus arrangement which effectively precludes rewards for increases in efficiency and imposes no penalties for inefficiency. The productivity incentive clause which will be described here provides an appropriate reward for outstanding performance and a comparable penalty for performance that is below standard.

Problem 2. Provision of the Opportunity to Earn Adequate Revenues. In an inflationary period regulatory lag characteristically prevents readjustment of rates with rapidity sufficient to make up for the increases in cost that are beyond the control of the regulated firm. As a result, its real earnings are eroded and it is thereby prevented from earning returns adequate to attract the capital needed for maintenance, modernization, and the expansion required to keep up with demand. In the long run, the public must bear the burden of inadequate capacity and inefficient and obsolete plant. The productivity incentive clause described here does *not* automatically grant the regulated firm price increases that compensate fully for its rising costs, as fuel adjustment clauses are intended to do. But it does give the regulated firm the *opportunity* to earn an adequate rate of return on its capital. Such a return is *automatically* provided to it if, and only if, its productivity rises at a sufficient rate.

A successful approach to the regulatory problem of enabling utility companies to earn adequate revenues in an era of rapid inflation while avoiding the disincentives to efficiency inherent in cost-plus arrangements and at the same time continuous or unduly frequent regulatory hearings has long been sought but has seemingly eluded utility regulators. This article proposes a new approach to the problem and demonstrates why its prospects for success are optimal. The kind of productivity incentive clause which the author proposes is not to be regarded as a replacement for regulation but as a new and effective tool to be placed in the hands of regulators.

Problem 3. Frequency of Regulatory Hearings. Because of the earnings problems caused by the combination of general inflation and regulatory lag, the frequency of rate cases brought before regulatory agencies characteristically increases significantly during a period of inflation. The agencies' facilities are often clogged as a result, and the regulatory lags exacerbated. The productivity incentive clause reduces this problem by providing for adjustment in earnings opportunities which occur automatically (but *do not provide* automatic increases in prices which equal the rises in the costs of the regulated firm). These automatic arrangements continue unmodified, without regulatory intervention, for as brief or as long a period as regulators select.

*Arthur Okun joined the author in devising the basic proposal described here. Work underlying this article has been supported by the American Telephone and Telegraph Company. This concept has been analyzed more deeply in an excellent paper by P. B. Linhart and F. W. Sinden, "Productivity Incentives under Rate Regulation," Bell Laboratories Economic Discussion Paper, 1982.

William J. Baumol is professor of economics at Princeton University and New York University. He has also served as chairman to the council of economic advisors to the governor of New Jersey and as president of the American Economic Association and the Association of Environmental and Resource Economists. **Dr. Baumol** received a Bachelor of Social Science degree from the College of the City of New York and a PhD degree from the London University (LSE) and is the author of about a dozen books and numerous professional articles.

The productivity incentive clause works through a *sharing* of any productivity gains by the regulated firm and its customers. The more rapidly the firm increases productivity, the greater the benefits it will enjoy, but the greater, simultaneously, will be the benefits that accrue to the general public.

This process does not impose upon the regulator the difficult task of monitoring and measuring the firm's productivity. Rather, it works essentially in two steps: Price adjustments are permitted automatically, but at a rate slower than the rate of increase in the prices of the inputs of the regulated firm. The firm can then protect its earnings only by improvements in efficiency sufficient to offset the remainder of the increase in its input prices. If, for example, input prices rise at 15 per cent per year and the regulated firm's rates are permitted to rise 12 per cent per annum, then its profits will not be eroded if its productivity rises at least 3 per cent each year, on the average. Of course, if productivity goes up even more rapidly, it is appropriate for the firm to reap a reward for its superior performance. That is what will occur under a productivity incentive clause.

It should be noted that in this process the regulatory agency does not forgo any of its control over the rate-setting process. By selecting the formula for adjustment of the prices of the regulated firm, the regulatory agency determines how productivity gains will be shared by the regulated firm and the general public. In periodic reviews, the agency can change the terms of this division by changing the values of the parameters in the productivity incentive formula.

What is accomplished by the clause is an extension to the regulated firm of the rewards and penalties offered by a free market to a competitive enterprise. A competitive enterprise prospers only if superior performance puts it ahead of its rivals, and market pressures assure the sharing of those gains with the general public as increasing productivity is reflected in market prices. Similarly, in a free market, a firm whose productivity performance is not up to the standard set by its rivals will suffer the losses that its poor accomplishments merit. A productivity incentive clause extends such an arrangement to regulated industries. The hallmark of the era of deregulation is recognition of the benefits such market pressures offer to the general public. The public interest will surely be served if analogous incentives are introduced into the regulatory arena.

Addressing the Problems

The inflationary period of the 1970s brought with it a special set of problems for the regulated industries. Regulators were overwhelmed with requests for rate increases to permit the regulated firms to keep abreast of their rising costs. The figure accompanying this article shows the remarkable correspondence between the rate of inflation and the frequency of intrastate regulatory rate awards in the operating companies of the Bell telephone system.

RATE ORDERS FOLLOW INFLATION

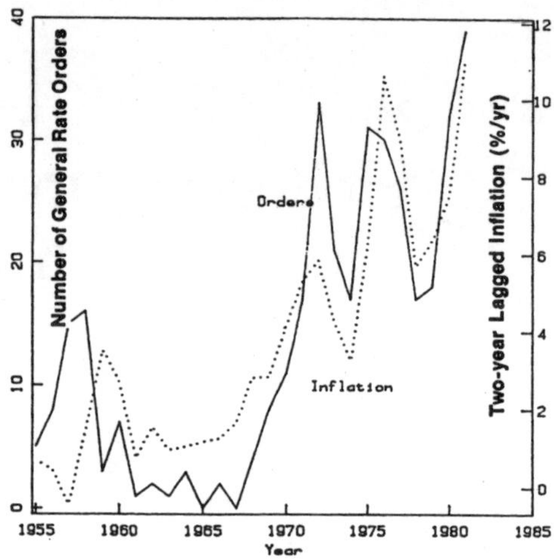

Note: The solid line represents the annual number of general rate awards to Bell system companies. (Left vertical axis gives scale: source is American Telephone and Telegraph Company internal records) The dotted line depicts percentage annual changes in the consumer price index, lagged two years–the appropriate average interval between the time a rate increase requirement becomes apparent and the award granted. (Right vertical axis gives scale.) The 1981 plotted points include partial projections. The correlation coefficient of the two curves is 0.84.

Earnings Erosion — Predictably, the resulting regulatory burden served, together with political pressures, to erode the real earnings permitted to regulated firms; that is, the value of their earnings after correction for the effects of inflation upon the purchasing power of the dollar. This was no benefit to consumers; because the earnings of the regulated firm were reduced below those of unregulated enterprises of comparable risk in other industries, the utilities found it difficult to obtain funds from the competitive market for capital. This inhibited the utilities' expenditures on maintenance, modernization, and expansion which, in the long run, must inevitably reduce the quantity or quality of service these enterprises are able to supply and ultimately deprives the customers of lower prices from increased efficiency.

In these circumstances, it has become increasingly urgent that something be done to ease the burden upon the regulatory process and to offer the regulated firms the opportunity to achieve a level of earnings necessary to compete effectively in the market for funds.

Incentives for Efficiency — The provision of inducements for efficiency is a problem which has long plagued the regulated industries, even in the era before the onset of rapid inflation. In seeking to prevent regulated firms from earning excessive profits, regulators have with good reasons relied heavily upon a ceiling over the rate of return earned by the enterprise. Those ceilings have rarely been enforced with absolute and mechanical rigor. The regulated firms have sometimes been permitted to earn more than the "fair rate of return" at least for limited periods. Frequently, these firms' rates have also prevented them from earning enough to bring them the fair rate of return. But if the rate of return ceiling had been imposed inflexibly and mechanistically it would have approximated a cost-plus contract with little penalty for inefficiency and certainly no reward for extraordinary contributions to efficiency.

This is in marked contrast to what happens in an unregulated competitive market. There, in a process which economists have examined thoroughly, an innovation which increases efficiency gives a competitive edge to the firm which institutes it first. Because it becomes relatively more efficient as compared to its rivals, it can obtain larger earnings which accrue to it until these competitors find substitute avenues of efficiency improvement with which they can respond to the innovation. In this way, the benefits of the innovation are shared by the innovating firm and the general public. At first, before its rivals succeed in catching up, the bulk of the benefits go to the innovating firm and serve as its reward for its contribution to efficiency. But once its rivals overtake it, the benefits of the innovation are passed on to consumers in the form of reduced prices. That, of course, is the social goal of the process. Note also that this same process imposes heavy penalties upon firms whose efficiency performance is persistently inferior, for they are threatened with low returns and even losses and eventual insolvency. Under rate of return regulation, these penalties for inefficiency as well as the rewards for superior efficiency are seriously attenuated.

A New Approach

This article describes a new approach which simultaneously addresses itself to all of the problems that have just been described. This new instrument of regulation will be referred to as a *productivity incentive clause*. It will be shown that it reduces the burden of inflation upon the regulatory process without in any way weakening the regulator's ability to exercise his rate-setting powers. In addition, it makes it *possible* for the regulated firm to earn adequate revenues *without* in any way *guaranteeing* such an earnings level. Finally, the productivity incentive clause, as its name suggests, provides the inducements needed to assure the outlay of maximal productivity-increasing effort by the regulated firm.

A productivity incentive clause is a regulatory mechanism which adjusts rates automatically during the interval of time between two adjacent reviews of rates by the regulatory agency. But while the rate adjustments are automatic, they do not automatically make up for all of the price increases of the regulated firm's inputs or for any resulting rise in its costs. Rather, the clause offers the regulated firm the chance to earn the fair rate of return by means of sufficient improvements in productivity to offset an appropriate portion of any rise in the prices of inputs. It will be shown that this clause can be designed in such a way that it will motivate the company to devote the socially optimal amount of investment and effort to productivity improvement. As a result, in the long run the company will be led to provide its services at the lowest possible cost to its customers as the efficiency gains are passed along to them.

Regulatory Lag, Inflation, and Incentives for Efficiency

During the past decade, when productivity growth in most of U. S. industry slowed significantly and even disappeared, the telecommunications industry has virtually been alone in terms of continued significant productivity growth.[1]

It is important for our purpose to understand the incentive structure to which such past productivity growth in the public utilities can be attributed because, as will be shown next, that incentive structure, too, has been threatened by inflation. Accordingly, the adoption of a supplementary incentive structure such as that proposed here is likely to prove absolutely critical for the future productivity performance of telecommunications and other regulated industries.

More specifically, economic analysts have concluded that in the past, before the advent of inflation, a major financial incentive for efficiency in public utilities has been provided by regulatory lag whose delays permitted the regulated firm to retain for some period any increased earnings made possible by increases in its efficiency. Whenever cost reductions were achieved, the firm was able, for a limited period, to increase its earnings on capital above its normal rate of return. The firm was able to retain such benefits until the next regulatory review of rates when the gains were normally passed on to consumers. This was a fairly common scenario until the end of the 1960s.

However, this mechanism works effectively only if the rate of productivity increase exceeds the rate of inflation. Where the reverse is true the company will normally earn less than the cost of capital in the period between two adjacent rate reviews. For when rates are fixed, as they normally are between rate reviews, and with productivity growth insufficient to offset rising input prices, costs will rise and net earnings will fall. If the rates were set initially so as to yield a return equal to the cost of capital, net revenues will soon prove inadequate to satisfy this standard. Of course, under these circumstances a strong incentive for cost reduction will still be present — the greater the success of the regulated firm in increasing is productivity, the more it will reduce the losses imposed upon it by the combination of inflation and regulatory lag. However, under this state of affairs, the company will lack the resources needed to invest in cost-reducing research and innovation. Research and innovation are not the only requisites for productivity growth. Maintenance, replacement, and expansion of capital stock are also

[1]See, e.g., *"Accounting for Slower Economic Growth,"* by Edward F. Denison, The Brookings Institution, Washington, D. C., 1979.

clearly essential. But a company which earns inadequate returns will lack both the resources and motivation to devote adequate resources to maintenance, replacement, and expansion. Economic pressures must, in the long run, induce resources away from unprofitable lines of activities. And failure to provide adequate maintenance and replacement outlays must certainly impede productivity growth.

Under these circumstances, regulatory lag can no longer serve as a satisfactory mechanism to provide incentives for productivity growth; moreover, the regulated firm then has no choice but to try to shorten regulatory lag, requesting rate reviews with increased frequency in order to maintain its solvency.

One way in which this problem has been approached has been through the adoption of fuel adjustment clauses which more or less automatically pass on to consumers in the form of higher prices the increases in costs that result from increased fuel prices. While the resulting adjustments can be rapid and can be instituted without heavy regulatory costs, the fuel adjustment clause has proved unsatisfactory in a number of ways.

First, it has done nothing about rising prices of inputs other than fuel. But rising wages, prices of raw materials, and the like can all cause financial problems for the regulated firm if the prices for its products do not reflect cost increases promptly and adequately. Thus, fuel adjustment clauses have failed to adjust public utility rates appropriately for changes in the firm's input prices. This does not necessarily imply that a fuel adjustment clause yields rate increases which are invariably inadequate. They may conceivably even prove excessive. It is only asserted at this point that these clauses lead to rate adjustments whose magnitudes may well be inappropriate.

A second deficiency of the fuel adjustment clauses which may be even more serious is that they provide no motivation for efficiency of operation on the part of the regulated firm. On the contrary, they may well contribute to inefficiency. In the last analysis, this is so because such a clause is analogous to a cost-plus contract, in which the regulated firm is, in effect, guaranteed to recoup any increase in expenditures on the one input covered, no matter how wasteful it may be.

Any cost-plus contract is an invitation to inefficiency because it insulates the supplier from any of the costs of its own wasteful behavior. But a cost-plus contract applied to just one input alone is, if anything, even more damaging to the public interest. Applied to fuel, it encourages wasteful use of energy, which is presumably the input whose use the social interest most urgently requires us to discourage. In particular, it encourages substitution of fuel for other inputs — e.g., the use of automatic machinery with large fuel requirements to save upon labor — even when the other inputs can do the job more efficiently.

Clearly, this absence of incentives for productivity improvement is inconsistent with the long-run public interest and a mechanism to improve matters is obviously required. The productivity incentive clause, which will be described next, has been designed to serve just this purpose.

Concepts of Productivity Incentive Clauses

A productivity incentive clause is any pricing formula which permits the firm and the general public to *share* the benefits of a productivity increasing innovation, where an innovation is defined in its most general sense as *any* change in the operating practices of the firm in question. The purpose of such sharing of benefits is clear. The innovating firm must reap some of the benefits because otherwise it will have neither the motivation to provide the effort nor the funds required to institute it. The consuming public should reap the remainder of the benefits since, presumably, consumer benefit is the end purpose of economic activity and constitutes the regulator's central concern.

In any productivity incentive clause the regulator can choose the value of the parameters which determine how the incremental benefits of increased productivity will be shared; that is, what proportion will go to the innovating firm and what proportion will accrue to the general public. In making such a choice it is tempting to reduce the share that is assigned to the firm and to increase that reserved for consumers. But such a move is easily carried to excess. By reducing the share of the gains the firm can expect, the firm's incentive to invest in productivity stimulating innovation will be reduced and the amount to be divided will be decreased correspondingly. In the extreme case, if the reward to the firm is limited sufficiently, there will be little or no productivity gain and, hence, no benefit to consumers.

There are various mechanisms for the sharing of productivity benefits. One of the most obvious, and one that occurs in practice, is an intertemporal sharing, with the benefits of an innovation first flowing exclusively to the innovator for some limited period and then, gradually or suddenly, being transferred to consumers. The patent system is a prime example of such a productivity incentive clause. Under its terms, innovating firms reap the benefits of their contribution for seventeen years, with the public deriving all the benefits thereafter. But even where no patent is issued and the innovating firm decides instead to attempt to rely on secrecy or speed to beat its competitors at the innovation game, an intertemporal sharing of benefits between the firm and the public can be expected to result. The innovating firm will gather the benefits for that period before its rivals are able to penetrate its secret or until they are able to come up with substitutes of their own. But once competitors are able to catch up, product prices will be driven down to match the productivity gain permitted by the innovation and thereafter all the benefits will go to the general public.

Intertemporal sharing is not the only way in which a productivity incentive clause can operate. For example, instead it may be preferred to share the gains, say fifty-fifty, from the initial date of the innovation for the indefinite future. As will be seen presently, the form of productivity incentive clause offered here employs yet a third sharing mechanism.

Before concluding the discussion of productivity incentive clauses in general, two other properties must be considered: their relationship to inflation, and the means that can be used to make it easy to administer them and for the regulatory agency to monitor their use.

So far nothing that has been said about productivity incentive clauses relates them to the issue of inflation and regulatory lag. The connection, however, is straightforward. A numerical example will make the relationship clear.

Suppose input prices happen to be rising at an annual rate of 10 per cent and that in the past the regulated firm has achieved a rate of growth of productivity averaging 3 per cent. Obviously, given adequate incentives, the firm can be expected to continue to make up for a substantial proportion of the rise in its input prices, but it is all but impossible for its productivity increases to offset the entire 10 per cent cost increase. To provide a feasible target for the company, regulation must adjust the regulated firm's rates to offset that portion of its rise in input costs which the firm cannot reasonably be expected to offset by means of productivity increases. In our example, if the regulatory agency were to institute an automatic rate adjustment mechanism for, say, a three-year period, increasing rates by enough to make up for an appropriate *portion* of the input inflation effect, it will then be left up to the firm to make up the rest through its own effort. If the firm's future productivity record turns out not to live up to the standards that can be expected from its past performance, then the company will suffer the financial consequences. But if by vigorous innovative effort the firm outdoes what was expected of it, then both the company and the public will profit.

In our example such an arrangement might involve the adoption of an automatic rate adjustment procedure which, so long as input prices were to continue to rise at 10 per cent per year, would raise rates not by 10 per cent but by 7 per cent, leaving the remainder to be made up by productivity improvements which in the past had saved 3 per cent per year. Under this arrangement, a 7 per cent rise would *not* occur automatically in each of the three years of the program. Rather, if in its second year the rate of input price inflation were to fall to 8 per cent, the automatic adjustment in the firm's rates would fall to 5 per cent, again relying on a 3 per cent productivity growth rate to compensate for the remainder.

The productivity incentive clause that has just been described is intended to illustrate the logic of the issue, though it is not precisely the same as the type of clause subsequently recommended in this article. The example was provided primarily to show why an automatic *partial* inflation adjustment must underly any effective productivity incentive clause. For without it, if the company is faced with an impossible task in which there is no prospect that its productivity growth will make up for inflation, the productivity program simply will not work because earnings will be inadequate, and so the requisite financing will not be available. Moreover, the partial price adjustment must be made *automatic* so that the regulated firm is on notice that it will suffer losses if its productivity performance turns out to be inadequate, and that it will be eligible for a financial reward if its productivity performance is commendable. An automatic rate adjustment without recourse means that the firm cannot turn to the regulator for help if its own performance is poor, and that the fruits of its efforts will not be taken away prematurely (before the end of the three-year period in our illustration) if the firm's productivity performance is outstanding.

Why, then, may one not wish to adopt a productivity incentive clause of the sort described in the illustration? There is, in fact, a good deal to be said in favor of such an arrangement, and the adoption of such a clause would undoubtedly have very desirable effects. Nevertheless, it does suffer from three shortcomings.

1) It requires data on the company's past productivity performance. But measurement of productivity is not a matter which is altogether straightforward. There are many alternative formulas for the measurement of productivity[2] and the selection and use of such a formula may well embroil the regulatory agency in precisely the sort of protracted hearings and administrative complications whose elimination is one of our prime objectives. This problem is by no means insuperable, but it is a problem, nevertheless.
2) The second issue raised by our illustrative productivity incentive clause arises from its reliance upon data about the prices of the inputs of the regulated firm. The problem here is that the rate of increase of these prices, overall, is not reported in any index compiled routinely by a disinterested agency. Rather, such an input price index for the regulated firm would have to be compiled de novo, specially for administration of the productivity incentive clause. This, too, will undoubtedly complicate the regulatory process and constitute a subject for contention.
3) Moreover, since the firm's input prices are to some degree subject to the company's influence (in the process of wage bargaining for example), it is not desirable to base automatic rate adjustments on the behavior of variables that are affected by company behavior. For such an arrangement reduces the incentive for the company to resist increases in input prices. The company will presumably resist rises in these prices in any event, but there is no special virtue in the adoption of a procedure which even offers the appearance of sapping that motivation.

Accordingly, we turn next to a productivity incentive clause which avoids *all three* of these problems: first,

[2]See, e.g., "Improving Productivity Measurement," by Albert Rees, *American Economic Review*, Vol. 70, May, 1980, pp. 340-342.

the need to measure continually the productivity of the regulated firm; second, reliance upon an index of the firm's input prices; and, third, the firm's ability to influence those figures.

Structure of the Productivity Incentive Clause

To examine in a systematic way the logic of the productivity incentive clause, we begin by asking what rate of price increase is necessary for the firm just to earn at a rate equal to its cost of capital; i.e., for the firm to break absolutely even. The resulting break-even formula is clearly *not* the clause we are seeking, but it will constitute the foundation upon which our analysis can be based.

Suppose that the company's input prices are increasing at some (perhaps varying) annual rate, I (per cent per year).

Suppose, also, that its productivity (defined as quantity of output per unit of input) is increasing at a (perhaps varying) rate, E (per cent per year). Then, just to break even — i.e., just to earn enough to pay the cost of its capital — the company's percentage rate of price increase must satisfy:

(1) $$\Delta P/P = I - E$$

This break-even formula is offered only as a basis for comparison, as already indicated. It is not usable as a productivity incentive clause because it permits the company to earn its cost of capital no matter how satisfactory or unsatisfactory its performance may be. Thus, it provides no incentives for the firm to buy from lower-cost suppliers, to bargain for favorable contracts with unions, or to devote effort to improvement in productivity. A productivity incentive formula should, of course, provide all of these sorts of incentives and should, in addition, be as immune as possible from manipulation by the firm or even charges of manipulation.

The first step towards transformation of the break-even formula (1) into a productivity incentive clause is replacement in the formula of I, the inflation rate of the company's input prices, and E, the actual productivity growth rate, by substitute *target* rates based on information beyond the control of the company.

Thus, I, the actual growth rate of the company's input prices, can be replaced by a number, call it i, indicating the regulator's expectation about the rate of growth of input prices. Similarly, E, the current rate of growth in the company's productivity, can be replaced by a target rate, e, for the prospective rate of growth of the company's productivity.

Once set by the commission, these figures can no longer be changed by the company's actions. We now obtain the modified price adjustment formula:

(2) $$\Delta P/P = i - e$$

The reasons this new formula *can* serve as a first approximation to a productivity increase clause merit brief discussion.

a. Under the modified formula (2), if the company does manage to find a cheaper source of inputs or to strike a better bargain with the unions, it will keep the resulting gains because that year's adjustment in its rates will be based not on its own costs, but on the target input cost index i. Any reduction in the rate of growth of the actual price of its own inputs will not result in an immediate reduction in its rates, and so the company will have every motivation to bargain as hard as it can with the suppliers of its inputs.

b. Similarly, if the company's actual productivity gains exceed the target rate, e, the firm will pocket the resulting *incremental* benefits. For the permitted rate of price adjustment, $\Delta P/P$, is tied not to the company's actual productivity performance, E, but to the target performance rate, e. If the firm's actual performance is better than e, it will obtain the difference as a reward for its successful efforts. But if the firm's performance falls short of e, it will bear the entire incremental penalty.

It is clear then, that the formula we are discussing passes the *incremental* benefits of productivity improvements on to the firm, thereby offering it the required incentives. But what may not be quite so clear is how the consuming public gains in the process. The answer lies in the choice of the target values, i and e. These targets must be selected so as to satisfy the second major requirement of efficiency growth: They must give the firm the *opportunity* to earn an amount sufficient to cover its cost of capital, so that it can compete effectively for funds on the nation's capital markets. But it should be clear that if the productivity incentive clause elicits an increased rate of growth in the firm's productivity, then the target productivity growth can be set so as to reduce correspondingly the rate of growth of the company's rates. In other words, such a program benefits the consumer by decreasing $\Delta P/P$, the minimum rate of growth in the firm's rates necessary to permit it to earn adequate revenues. Under this arrangement, then, the share of benefits flowing to the consuming public is assured by the commission's choice of values of the target variables i and e that take into account the likely incentive effects upon the company's productivity. The company can then benefit if it is able to outperform the adopted targets, keeping for itself any incremental benefits from such a level of performance.

One last step is now required to bring us to the sort of productivity incentive clause advocated in this article. So far, the numbers i and e have been described as if they were fixed magnitudes chosen once and for all by the regulatory commission, or as if they were subject to revision only at occasional regulatory reviews. But while such a procedure does provide the desired incentives, it subjects both the consuming public and the company to unnecessary and unavoidable risks from changes in the rate of inflation or productivity growth beyond the company's control.

Suppose, for example, that the regulatory agency were to foresee an 11 per cent rate of inflation for the next three years and therefore were to adopt a target value i = 0.11. If in fact, because of a change in monetary or fiscal policy or developments outside the U. S., the actual rate of inflation were to fall to 8 per cent, in the second year between regulatory reviews, the company would benefit from a windfall at the consumers' expense. The reverse would be true if the actual rate of inflation were to shoot upward to 13 per cent, say, because of a renewed oil crisis. Then the company would suffer a windfall loss as a result of events which it could not control.

The same danger arises from a fixed productivity target. It is a well-documented fact that the economy's rate of productivity growth varies in a predictable pattern over the course of a business cycle. It slows down as a recession begins because sales fall more rapidly than input use can be decreased, and excess plant capacity results, adversely affecting productivity. The reverse happens when the growth of the economy increases. Thus, with the onset of a recession the growth rate of productivity achievable by the firm is very likely to fall below the target rate, e, and the opposite will happen when prosperity resumes. Windfall losses will then result in the first case, and windfall gains in the second if a fixed number, e, is adopted as the commission's productivity target for the company.

Such risks are avoidable, at least in part, and therefore constitute an unnecessary cost which must ultimately be borne by consumers. One can reduce such risks by adopting instead of fixed target values, i and e, variable targets which we will represent by i(t) and e(t), where those numbers are based on data for related industries or for the economy as a whole. For example, the inflation rate standard i(t) can be determined each year by that year's rate of growth of the consumer price index, or an index of input prices, say, in related industry, or in a variety of other ways. The point is that substitution of such a variable inflation index, i(t), for a fixed inflation target eliminates the corresponding source of windfall gains and losses. If the economy's inflation rate falls from 10 per cent to 8 per cent, i(t) will automatically decline correspondingly. The opposite will happen if there is an unanticipated rise in the inflation rate. The same sort of correction can be undertaken for the productivity growth figure by adoption of a variable target e(t) based on national data or data for other industries or other similar figures, thereby taking into account productivity-affecting developments outside of the regulated firm's control. Thus, we end up with our final incentive clause formula:

$$\Delta P/P = i(t) - e(t) \tag{3}$$

under which the profit or loss which accrues to a company is largely dependent on the success of the company's actions, and is not affected critically by outside events.

Regulatory Review of the Formula

It is important to reemphasize that no formula such as that which has just been described can be permitted to supersede the work of the regulator. It is merely a regulatory tool which can facilitate the execution of his task of adjustment of rates to changing circumstances. No commission should or can be expected, after adoption of such a rule, to leave the task of rate adjustment entirely to the formula forever thereafter. Rather, an essential part of the program described in this article is a process of monitoring of the performance of the formula by the regulatory agency, which should be expected to subject it to a formal review process from time to time. A general rate case would, for example, constitute an appropriate occasion for such a review.

It may even be considered desirable to adopt, in advance, a set of criteria which can be used to trigger such a review. For example, if the rate of growth of a company's productivity were to fall below some preselected level, or if its rate of return were to exceed some other critical level, a review of the formula might be required automatically.

Indeed, if the triggering criteria are chosen appropriately, they can themselves improve the incentive mechanism for productivity improvement by the company. By providing a closer replication of the system of temporary rewards and penalties offered on free competitive markets they can lead to an approximation of the optimal level of investment by the company in productivity improving innovation.

Concluding Comments

This article has proposed a productivity incentive mechanism which simultaneously adjusts public utility rates to take account of inflation in a way that reduces the frequency of regulatory hearings and the resulting costs and delays, and also provides the incentives for a firm to invest in productivity growth that will benefit both itself and its customers.

The formula proposed here for the productivity incentive clause is designed so that in the short run the firm bears all the incremental risks of disappointing performance in its productivity stimulation program, and it is simultaneously offered all of the *incremental* benefits of extraordinary and unanticipated productivity performance. This is so because, as has been pointed out, the company will earn a return greater than the cost of capital only to the extent that its actual productivity performance exceeds the target rate, e(t), and it will fail to earn its cost of capital to the extent its productivity performance falls short of that rate. Thus, if a project intended to increase productivity happens to fail, the company will bear the full cost.

Consequently, the firm will be led by the formula to adopt any productivity enhancing measure whose expected incremental benefits exceed the incremental cost. This is precisely what the public interest requires.

In the long run, it is the general public which will benefit. To the extent that the program succeeds in stimulating productivity growth, this will be reflected in the profits of the firm. If these run persistently high, that will presumably be adjusted for in the periodic rate reviews. The value of e(t), the productivity growth target can then be adjusted upward, cutting company returns back to the cost of capital, and reducing the rate of increase in subscriber rates even further behind the rate of inflation in input prices. Such adjustments will pass along to customers the long-run benefits of the program. The efficacy of the process will, of course, be affected by the rules which define when reviews are triggered; e.g., the values of (maximum and minimum) rates of return which will be deemed to require a rate review.

The proposed program represents no giveaway to the firm nor does it guarantee adequate earnings. But it does permit the firm the opportunity to obtain adequate earnings, which it will receive, automatically, if its productivity performance merits them.

In the last analysis, it is the consumers and the general public who will benefit from the productivity incentive program. Because this program induces more rapid productivity growth and leads the firm to resist rises in input prices more strongly, consumers will obtain gains in the form of lower rates.

This can, obviously, make a contribution in the battle against inflation. More important in the long run, it will also help to enhance the economy's overall productivity growth. The standing of the U. S. economy in the international marketplace and the future standard of living of the country's inhabitants depend on nothing so much as the course of its productivity. We can ill afford to neglect any opportunity to help in this vital arena.

A Forecast for Electric Utility Automated Distribution Systems

Thanks to recent improvements in equipment reliability and cost reductions, electric utilities are now "showing a rapidly growing interest" in automated distribution systems, according to a recently released market report. Automated distribution systems employing computer-based technology are used to automate peak-load distribution, including residential and commercial end use nodes. ADS capabilities range from remote customer load control and meter reading to operational control of distribution substations.

The market study — by Frost & Sullivan, Inc., and entitled "Electric Utility Automated Distribution Systems" — refers to ADS technology as "the preferred, if not the exclusive," solution to the problems that utilities face. Because these problems are of a general nature and affect almost all utilities, especially meeting peak-load demand, the ADS market is projected to soar — from a paltry $18 million in 1981 to $364 million in 1985, $1.9 billion by 1990, and $2.7 billion in 1995. Already some eight different ADS technologies and six major manufacturers are vying for position in this market arena.

Signal transmission used to transmit control instructions in an ADS implementation may be via frequency modulation (FM) radio, ripple, power line carrier, telephone, or a combination of these media. Of the 150 ADS projects examined in the Frost & Sullivan study, unidirectional FM radio systems account for nearly half of all the installations, followed by power line carrier having a bidirectional signaling capability.

Of the five major ADS application areas — load management, distribution automation, time-of-use rate control, remote meter reading, and special services — load management is the most widely used, accounting for some two-thirds of all the projects. Not so long ago, electric utilities were interested *only* in load management. But now, these other applications are also "gaining attention." Declining costs are the major factor. FM systems and unidirectional power line control systems, now the least expensive technologies, average less than $90 per installed point. Unidirectional ripple systems average $120 per point, telephone systems $200, again, unidirectional. Bidirectional systems are much more costly, averaging as much as $325 per point. However, by middecade, costs are expected to come down to $200 per point.

[22]

Stephen C. Littlechild (1983), *Regulation of British Telecommunications' Profitability*

1.1 Alternative schemes have been proposed for regulating British Telecommunications' (BT) profitability. The task of the present study was:

(a) to prepare a practicable scheme for the Output-Related Profits Levy (ORPL) suggested by Professor Walters,

(b) to evaluate the ORPL and the Maximum Rate of Return (MRR) scheme proposed by the Inter-Departmental Working Group, and

(c) to consider possible variants and make recommendations as appropriate.

1.2 The principal conclusions are as follows.

(1) The ORPL and MRR schemes both have merits but also serious disadvantages. Neither can be recommended.

(2) A Profit Ceiling scheme would overcome some of these dis-advantages but would not provide adequate protection against BT's monopoly power.

(3) A Local Tariff Reduction scheme is recommended as the best way to achieve the desired ends.

(4) It would not be desirable to superimpose a profit ceiling on such a Local Tariff Reduction scheme.

(5) The success of any form of regulation depends upon increasing competition. There are further significant possibilities for encouraging competition in telecommunications.

1.3 Section 2 describes the background to this study. Professor Walters pointed out the objections to the original proposal to impose a maximum rate of return on BT, and proposed an alternative scheme for taxing BT at a lower rate if it increased its output above an agreed norm. The Inter-Departmental Working Group recommended a revised maximum rate of return scheme, involving customer rebates and a degree of flexibility in the maximum return. As just noted, this study was commissioned to evaluate these two schemes and to consider possible variants.

1.4 Section 3 summarises the salient features of the current Telecommunications Bill.

1.5 Section 4 sets out the conditions for effective regulation.

(a) The main purpose of regulation is to protect domestic and small business subscribers against BT's dominant market position. Improving efficiency is a means to that end. Prevention of excessive profits to shareholders is *not* a relevant consideration, since expected profits will be reflected in the price of BT's shares at flotation, so shareholders will not earn an excessive return on their investment.

(b) Competition is by far the most effective means of protection against monopoly. Vigilance against anti-competitive practices is also important. Profit regulation is merely a 'stop-gap' until sufficient competition develops.

(c) There is always a danger that regulatory authorities will be 'captured' by incumbent suppliers and influenced against allowing new entry. A non-discretionary scheme is less vulnerable in this respect. US experience in airlines and telecommunications shows how over-zealous regulation has restricted competition, to the detriment of consumers.

1.6 Section 5 sets out five criteria for evaluating the various profit regulation schemes: (1) Protection against Monopoly, (2) Efficiency and Innovation, (3) Burden of Regulation, (4) Promotion of Competition, (5) Proceeds (of flotation) and Prospects (for BT).

1.7 Section 6 examines the consequences of not imposing any explicit constraints on profits (beyond the provision in the Bill for a sufficient return on capital and references to the Monopolies and Mergers Commission (MMC). This would not seem to provide adequate protection against monopoly in the short-term, but would score highly on all other criteria.

1.8 Sections 7 and 8 set out and evaluate the Working Group's MRR scheme. It would be perceived as providing protection against monopoly, and BT's prospects would be safe but dull. However, there are disincentives to efficiency and innovation, the burden of regulation would be heavy, and new entry could be prejudiced.

1.9 Sections 9 and 10 set out and evaluate the Output Related Profits Levy. It provides a positive incentive for BT to increase output and reduce prices. The incentives to efficiency are not impaired. However, the precise effects on prices are uncertain, competitors may be disadvantaged, a levy could prejudice investment and innovation, and the burden of operating the scheme could be greater than is immediately apparent. The novelty of the scheme would mean lower proceeds on sale or delaying privatisation.

1.10 Section 11 is an interim comparative evaluation of the two schemes plus the 'no explicit constraints' scheme. It is difficult to rank the MRR and ORPL schemes overall. However, with respect to all criteria except protection against monopoly, both schemes are significantly worse than the absence of constraints. Moreover, it is not certain that either MRR or ORPL provides an adequate protection in the longer run. In both cases, the 'cure' seems to be worse than the 'disease'.

1.11 Section 12 analyses a Profit Ceiling scheme. This would constrain unacceptably high total profits, but would not focus precisely upon the monopoly services of greatest concern. Provided the ceiling were set sufficiently high, there would be no significant disadvantages on the other criteria. However, a low ceiling would involve many of the serious defects of traditional rate of return regulation.

1.12 Section 13 explores a Local Tariff Reduction scheme, by which BT would be required to set tariffs such that a Local Tariff Index increased by less than retail prices in general (the RPI – X per cent formula). This index would comprise rentals and prices of local calls (including call-boxes). BT's licence would contain conditions to prevent anti-competitive price discrimination. The scheme would focus precisely upon the domestic and small business subscribers whom it is desired to protect. The scheme scores highly on all criteria.

1.13 Section 14 contains a final evaluation of all the schemes examined; as reflected in the accompanying table of rankings. MRR and ORPL are ranked lowest on most critera. 'No explicit constraints' ranks first on four criteria but last on protection against monopoly. A Profit Ceiling ranks between 'no explicit constraints' and the two earlier schemes. Local Tariff Reduction scores highly on all criteria. It is significantly better than all other schemes with respect to protection against monopoly, and roughly as good as 'no explicit constraints' with respect to the other criteria. Local Tariff reduction is clearly the recommended scheme.

1.14 Superimposing a high profit ceiling on the local tariff reduction scheme is not recommended: a high ceiling would be unnecessary, and a low ceiling would introduce the undesirable burdens and disincentives of traditional regulation.

1.15 Section 14 also includes recommendations for measures to strengthen the effectiveness of regulation. These concern the 'sufficient return on capital' obligation in Clause 3, the provision of public subsidy for uneconomic services, and the criteria to be used by the MMC in modifying licences. Several possibilities for stimulating competition are discussed. Most important, it is recommended that new entry be encouraged by requiring unrestricted resale of BT circuits for voice, and negotiating access to international switching by Mercury and other potential competitors.

1.16 Appendix 1 develops a theoretical model of a profit-maximising firm subject to an output-related profits levy. Appendix 2 discusses the advantages and difficulties of constructing a practicable scheme for such a levy.

Final Ranking of Schemes for Regulating BT's Profitability

	No Explicit Constraints	Working Group MRR	ORPL	Profit Ceiling	Local Tariff Reduction
Protection against Monopoly	5	3	2	4	1
Efficiency and Innovation	1=	4=	4=	3	1=
Burden of Regulation	1	5	4	3	2
Promotion of Competition	1	5	4	2=	2=
Proceeds and Prospects	1=	4	5	3	1=

2. Background to this study

2.1 The Government has announced its intention to convert BT into a public limited company and to sell 51 per cent of its shares following the next General Election. BT currently holds a dominant market position in many areas of telecommunications, and it was widely believed that this would continue to be the case for many of its services even after liberalisation of entry. The question therefore arose as to whether and how the exercise of BT's market power should be controlled. A committee of officials proposed a maximum rate of return for BT as a whole.

2.2 Professor Walters expressed concern that a maximum rate of return had many of the characteristics of a 100 per cent tax rate. It would have undesirable consequences for cost control and enterprise. Research on rate of return regulation in the USA had shown that it resulted in waste of investment and a costly bureaucracy. Professor Walters proposed as an alternative an output-related profits levy. The greater the expansion in output over the year, the lower the rate at which the levy on profits would be charged. This would encourage BT to expand output and lower prices, rather than restrict output and raise prices.

2.3 An Inter-Departmental Working Group convened by DoI economists examined these and other options. It was unable to recommend the output-related profits levy, but accepted many of the criticisms of rate of return control expressed by Professor Walters and tried where possible to mitigate the adverse consequences. The Working Group recommended that an overall rate of return on capital employed should be determined for those of BT's activities which are subject to licence. If BT exceeded the maximum, more than half the excess (but less than 100 per cent) should be rebated to consumers. To prevent a recurrence, the Director General of Telecommunications (DGT) should have power to limit the general level of tariffs in any regulated activity where excess profits were made. The DGT would also have power to vary the rate of return by up to 10 per cent in return for improved performance.

2.4 After some debate on the merits of the two schemes, it was agreed to commission the present study.

3. The Telecommunications Bill

3.1 In order to understand the context in which various schemes of profit regulation are being proposed, it will be helpful to provide a brief summary of the salient points of the Telecommunications Bill ordered to be printed 17 November 1982. At the time of writing, this Bill is just beginning the 'Committee Stage' between the second and third reading.

3.2 The purpose of the Bill, according to its Long Title is:

> 'To provide for the appointment of a Director General of Telecommunications and to confer functions on the Director General so appointed; to abolish the exclusive privilege with respect to telecommunications conferred on British Telecommunications by section 12 of the British Telecommunications Act 1981 and to make new provision with respect to the provision of telecommunication services; to make provision, in substitution for the Telegraph Acts 1863 to 1916, for the matters there dealt with and related matters; to provide for the vesting of all property, rights and liabilities of British Telecommunications in a company nominated by the Secretary of State and the subsequent dissolution of British Telecommunications; to make provision with respect to the finances of that company; to amend the Wireless Telegraphy Acts 1949 to 1967 and to make further provision for facilitating enforcement of those Acts; and for connected purposes.'

3.3 Clause 1 empowers the Secretary of State to appoint the DGT, who in turn may appoint the staff of the Office of Telecommunications (OFTEL). It is expected that the staff of OFTEL will number about 50.

3.4 Clause 2 abolishes BT's exclusive privilege to run telecommunications systems.

3.5 Clause 3 provides guidelines for the Secretary of State and DGT, the first part of which may usefully be reproduced in full.

> '(1) In exercising the functions assigned to them by this Part the Secretary of State and the Director shall take into account all matters which appear to them in the particular circumstances to be relevant and, among other things, shall have regard to—

(a) the need to secure so far as practicable the provision throughout the United Kingdom of such telecommunication services as satisfy all reasonable demands for them including, in particular, public call box services, emergency services and services in rural areas;

(b) the need for persons supplying telecommunication services to achieve a return on capital employed sufficient to enable them to finance the supply of such services as are mentioned in paragraph (a) above and the development and use of new techniques;

(c) the desirability of promoting the interests of consumers, purchasers and other uses of telecommunication services and telecommunication apparatus in the United Kingdom in respect of the prices charged for them and in respect of their quality and the variety of services and apparatus supplied;

(d) the desirability of maintaining and promoting effective competition between persons supplying telecommunication services or telecommunication apparatus in the United Kingdom; and

(e) the desirability of maintaining and promoting competitive activity in markets outside the United Kingdom on the part of persons supplying telecommunication services, and persons producing and supplying telecommunication apparatus, in the United Kingdom.'

3.6 Clauses 4 to 7 require all operators of telecommunication systems (with certain exceptions) to be licensed. A licence may be granted by the Secretary of State after consultation with the DGT, or by the DGT with the consent of the Secretary of State.

3.7 Clause 8 makes provision for such licences to include certain conditions, including payment of fees, and obligations to provide services.

3.8 Clause 10 empowers the DGT to modify the licence conditions after making public his intentions and if the licensees concerned do not object. Clause 11 empowers the DGT to refer the question whether licences should be amended to the Monopolies and Mergers Commission (MMC) to which up to 3 additional members may be appointed by the Secretary of State for the purpose of considering such references.

3.9 Clause 12 requires the MMC to report on the matters referred to them and Clause 13 obliges the DGT to modify licence conditions to remedy any adverse effects identified by the MMC.

3.10 Clause 15 enables the DGT, after giving notice to the person concerned, to issue orders to secure compliance with the conditions of licences and Clause 16 allows the person concerned to question the validity of the DGT's orders in the courts.

3.11 Clause 22 empowers the Secretary of State to designate systems whose licences oblige the licensee to provide services as public telecommunication systems. Clauses 26 to 28 provide for compulsory purchase of land by public telecommunication operators for such systems. Clause 42 empowers local authorities to pay subsidies to public telecommunication operators for the provision or maintenance of telecommunication facilities (e.g. public call offices) which benefit their area.

3.12 Clause 44 places further duties on the DGT to monitor and collect information on telecommunications and to provide advice and information to the Secretary of State or the Director General of Fair Trading.

3.13 Clause 48 enables the DGT to exercise certain functions relating to telecommunications which are at present the responsibility of the Director General of Fair Trading, notably with respect to monopoly situations and anti-competitive practices.

3.14 Clause 49 provides for the Secretary of State to give general directions indicating (a) considerations to which the DGT should have particular regard in determining the order of priority in which matters are brought under review, and (b) considerations to which he should have particular regard in determining whether to exercise his functions. Such directions shall be published unless disclosure is against the commercial interests of any person.

3.15 Clause 50 gives the DGT powers to seek information and Clause 51 requires the DGT to report annually to the Secretary of State and for his reports to be laid before Parliament.

3.16 It is estimated that the costs of the DGT and his staff, plus the additional costs of the MMC and the Secretary of State, will be about £1.5 million a year. There will also be income from licence fees which will be set to cover the cost of issuing, monitoring and amending licences (at present estimated at £1 million). The total net expenditure on the regulatory arrangements is estimated at £0.5 million a year.

4. The conditions for effective regulation

4.1 Various reasons have been put forward for the current policy of liberalisation and privatisation in telecommunications. In moving the second reading of the Telecommunications Bill, Mr. Jenkin said that for BT to become a major force in the world telecommunications market, as he wanted, it needed the financial freedom which a nationalised industry did not and never could have. The Bill ends the situation in which BT licensed its competitors and gives licensing power to the Secretary of State. Elsewhere, hopes have been expressed that new competitors, and even the threat of entry, will induce greater efficiency on the part of BT, reduce prices, make available a wider range of products and services to consumers, stimulate innovation, and so on.

4.2 At the same time, Mr. Jenkin argued that telecommunications could not be a free-for-all, and the Government's approach had been coloured by the inevitable market dominance of BT for many years ahead. This view is reflected in the new regulatory system described in Section 3 above, and also in the search for a suitable scheme of profit control to be embodied in the licence issued to BT.

4.3 This section is concerned with the conditions for effective regulation. It explores in more detail (a) the main purpose which regulation is intended to achieve, (b) the means available for achieving this purpose and the contribution which a profit control scheme for BT can make, and (c) the problems which regulation and control themselves induce.

(a) *Purposes of regulation*

4.4 The Government's policy of liberalisation means that BT will no longer enjoy its exclusive privilege in any part of its business except switched international services. There will be competition in the running of public systems (from Mercury and the cellular radio companies), in the supply of services (from these two sources and suppliers of value-added network services (VANS), and in the supply of apparatus. Competitive pressures will initially be strongest in the field of VANS and apparatus. Competition may also build up fairly quickly in the supply of telecommunication services, especially in large cities. Nevertheless, for some time to come, BT may be expected to dominate the supply of telephone services to domestic and small business subscribers, especially those not in major cities. International services are also an area of significant monopoly power, but it would appear that most concern is felt for domestic and small business subscribers.

4.5 In those sectors which BT continues to dominate, where competition cannot be relied upon to exercise effective control, it is widely feared that BT will have the ability to earn monopoly profits, tolerate inefficiencies and use its monopoly power to prevent, restrict or distort competition, both in the market sectors it dominates and in other areas. For example, it is felt that BT would have the ability to earn excessive profits by overcharging domestic subscribers; it would then have a discretionary fund which it could use either to pay excessive dividends to shareholders and excessive wages to its workforce, or to engage in selective price-cutting of trunk services or extension telephones, thereby under-cutting its competitors and driving them out of business. BT could also use its market power to engage in other anti-competitive practices, such as requiring anyone who wanted to rent an exchange line to purchase from BT all the apparatus connected to that line, even though BT's prices might be higher than those of its competitors, or offering 'loyalty discounts' for not dealing with competitors such as Mercury.

4.6 From the point of view of public policy, the primary purpose of regulation is to protect the consumer. This primary purpose should be distinguished from the secondary purposes. Inefficiency and high costs, and the ability to earn excess profits and pay high wages, are of significance insofar as they lead to higher prices for the consumer. The consumer's prime concern is with the range and quality of the goods and services he is offered, and the terms on which these goods and services are offered, rather than with the reasons lying behind it all. The means should not be confused with the ends: regulation considers bringing pressure to bear on profits, wages, costs and efficiency as a means of reducing prices and improving other aspects of performance. Similarly, constraints are imposed on certain forms of market conduct, not in order to penalise BT or favour its rivals, but as a means of fostering competitive market forces which, in turn, are expected to protect the consumer and provide telecommunication services on ever-improving terms.

4.7 One misconception should be dealt with here, concerning 'excess profits' and the payment of 'excessive dividends' to shareholders. Regulation of profits is frequently advocated, not on the grounds that prices or costs are too high, but because the owners of a company are 'making too much money'. The profits are thought to be 'undeserved', and the owners 'undeserving'. But when a company's shares are first traded on the Stock Exchange, the share price adjusts to reflect the market's expectations about future profits, dividends and growth. New investors do *not* enjoy any 'excess' profits; they earn no higher return on their investment than could be earned on comparable shares elsewhere in the market.

4.8 In the case of BT, the share price established in the stock market upon flotation will reflect the market's expectations about BT's performance *and* about the regulatory environment in which it will operate. The share price will be higher or lower, depending on whether regulation is expected to be light or severe. But anticipated severity of regulation will not reduce the return to the shareholders of BT. It *will* reduce the wealth of the present owners of BT, *viz*. the taxpayers of this country. Conversely, regulation 'with a light rein' will *not* generate abnormally high returns on shareholders' investments, though it *will* increase the proceeds of flotation, which may be used to reduce taxes or borrowing, or to finance desired investments elsewhere.

4.9 On the other hand, *unanticipated* changes in regulation will generate windfall gains and losses. Thus, shareholders will gain if a harsh regulatory regime is relaxed after flotation, though they would not have gained if a relaxed regime were instituted from the outset. For this reason, it may be politically difficult to relax a harsh regime, even when changes in circumstances justify it.

4.10 There is an important consequence for the cost of capital. If BT is perceived as a growth stock, its shares will stand at a higher price. The cost to BT of raising additional capital will thereby be reduced. If, on the other hand, BT is perceived as a reliable utility but one which is unlikely to grow, or likely to be constrained, then its shares will stand at a lower price. Raising additional capital will be more costly. Thus, the regulatory climate does not determine investors' returns, but it does affect BT's cost of capital and, ultimately, the costs of providing telecommunication services in Britain.

(b) *The Means of Achieving this Purpose*

4.11 Competition is indisputably the most effective means — perhaps ultimately the *only* effective means — of protecting consumers against monopoly power. Regulation is essentially a means of preventing the worst excesses of monopoly; it is not a substitute for competition. It is a means of 'holding the fort' until competition arrives. Consequently, the main focus of attention has to be on securing the most promising conditions for competition to emerge, and protecting competition from abuse. It is important to ensure that regulation in general, and the profit control scheme for BT in particular, do not prejudice the achievement of this overall strategy.

4.12 The willingness of competitors to enter the UK telecommunications market depends in part upon technological and market conditions, but it also depends upon government policy with respect to entry. Put another way, control of BT's monopoly power does not depend solely upon the terms of BT's licence, but depends crucially upon the policy with respect to the granting of licences to others. The policy of the present government is to encourage competition. It must be acknowledged that certain decisions will have the effect of limiting competition for BT (and Mercury) — that Mercury should be the only other public telephone system for the time being, that there should be only one other mobile radio telephone company in addition to the consortium of which BT is a member, that switching of interactive services between cable TV networks should be done by BT or Mercury.

4.13 There is still scope for further competition, however. Mercury would like to obtain unrestricted access to US networks through an arrangement with a US-based carrier such as MCI. This could probably be negotiated, and perhaps similar arrangements could be made with a few other countries too. Within the UK, there is immediate scope for further competition from unrestricted resale of private circuits for voice telephony, which is at present forbidden. We return to these possibilities later. The point to establish here is that it *is* possible to introduce further competition as a means of limiting BT's monopoly power, and that licensing new entry is likely to be more effective than imposing profit regulations within BT's licence. As Mr. Jenkin pointed out in his speech, the more competition there is, the less need there would be for regulation.

4.14 The protection of emerging competition will require a vigilant policy with respect to anti-competitive practices (such as price discrimination, predatory pricing, tie-in sales, loyalty discounts, etc.). BT's rivals and consumers are all vulnerable to its dominant position. Present legislation already provides for the MMC to investigate whether anti-competitive practices are against the public interest. Given BT's abnormally dominant position it would be possible and desirable to include provisions in the licence to provide additional protection e.g. by explicitly prohibiting price discrimination or requiring publication of prices.

4.15 Turning now to the possibility of a profit regulation scheme embodied in BT's licence, the body of this Report examines and evaluates several schemes put forward. They variously focus on profits, efficiency, performance, output, prices and so on. Only one general point will be made at this stage. As far as possible, the scheme should focus on the precise area of concern. That is, it should focus on the price and quality of service provided to domestic and small business subscribers, especially those not in major cities. Clause 3 of the Bill refers explicitly to securing the provision of public call box services, emergency services and services in rural areas. It is here assumed that BT's licence will include explicit conditions to this effect, but we shall need to consider the prices charged for these services and the possibility of explicit subsidy.

(c) *Effects of Regulation*
4.16 It is obviously important to evaluate the alternative schemes for controlling BT in the light of the way they will *actually* work, rather than the way one might *like* them to work. That is, it is necessary to look beyond the formal provisions of each scheme to ask whether there would be any unintended adverse consequences, which may well have effect over the longer run rather than immediately.

4.17 Consider how regulation in general, and any profit control scheme in particular, will be implemented. Clause 3 of the Bill (paragraph 3.5 above) sets out five formal guidelines for the Secretary of State and the DGT (and the MMC). But how are these guidelines to be interpreted? How are conflicts between the different objectives to be resolved (e.g. between sufficient rate of return on capital and consumers' interests with respect to price)? Both the Secretary of State and the DGT will be subject to conflicting pressures from BT itself; from its competitors, suppliers, employees and customers (both present and potential); and from the general public, MP's and 'the media'. It seems likely that the Secretary of State and the DGT, having different decisions to take and having different conditions of accountability, will attach different weights to each kind of pressure and hence arrive at different interpretations of the public interest. The MMC is in yet a different position.

4.18 BT and other incumbent suppliers will attempt to secure maximum advantage from regulation. Firstly, with respect to the DGT's decisions, they may find it commercially advantageous to modify their policies with respect to pricing, output, investment, accounting, finance, innovation, etc. Constraints on prices or profits, or the imposition of taxes, may lead them to choose different technology, to contract or expand particular services, and so on. Secondly, these firms will wish to influence the judgements and decisions made by the DGT, e.g. with respect to profit and cost forecasts, the implementation of profit controls, and subsequent modifications to the licence. Thirdly, incumbent firms will try to influence the decisions of the Secretary of State against licensing new independent entry. Finally, they will argue for maintaining, modifying or abolishing the whole regulatory framework embodied in the Telecommunications Bill, depending upon whether they feel that, on balance, it protects them from competition or unduly constrains their growth.

4.19 It is impossible to predict precisely how each alternative profit control scheme would work. However, it seems plausible that the more discretion for the DGT which the scheme allows or requires, the more the DGT will need to rely on industry sources for information and advice (if his decisions are not to appear unreasonable), hence the more weight is likely to be attached to incumbent suppliers rather than to new entrants — in short, the more likely the DGT is to be 'captured' by the industry he is supposed to be regulating. Broadly speaking, then, a discretionary scheme is likely to favour BT (including its employees) at the expense of competition and consumers.

4.20 It is most important to take account of the effects of regulation on potential as well as existing suppliers. High prices and profits, poor performance, inefficiency, excessive wages — all these represent inducements for more efficient competitors to enter. Controls on profits, prices and performance, insofar as they are effective, diminish these inducements. Thus, against any short-term benefits to consumers of a profit-control scheme must be set the longer-term disadvantages of a reduction in the degree of competition.

4.21 Alternative profit control schemes must be examined, not in isolation, but in the context of the other means available for dealing with the problem of monopoly power. In particular, it is important to consider how the scheme will affect both the incentives of new competitors to enter and the response of regulatory authorities (Secretary of State, DGT and MMC) to such applications for entry. One must attempt to minimise the danger that a scheme for controlling profit will prejudice the future development of competition, which as noted earlier is the most effective means of tackling the monopoly problem.

4.22 US experience of regulation is not encouraging, and suggests that regulation should not be too ambitious. Profit can stem from superior performance, monopoly power or sheer good luck. An effective public policy needs to distinguish between these sources, so as to discourage the exploitation of monopoly without discouraging efficiency and innovation. In the USA, regulators have been given ample powers to extract and analyse information, and considerable discretion in approving tariff structures and rates of return. The end-result has not been a reduction in monopoly power — in general, quite the opposite has happened. At the same time, investment has been distorted and efficiency and innovation discouraged. Pressures have recently mounted to relax or abandon regulation, notably in airlines and telecommunications. Where further competition has been allowed to replace regulation, the result has invariably been lower prices and the introduction of new and improved services.

5. Criteria for evaluating alternative profit regulation schemes

5.1 The criteria to be used in evaluating the alternative regulatory schemes are the five objectives set out in Clause 3 of the Telecommunications Bill (see paragraph 3.5 above) together with the four additional objectives specified in the terms of reference. For ease of analysis it will be convenient to group these nine objectives under the following five headings, of which the first has been identified as the prime purpose of regulation.

(1) *Protection against Monopoly*
This includes preventing the use of a dominant market position to exploit consumers, particularly with respect to prices, quality, quantity and variety of services and apparatus supplied.

(2) *Efficiency and Innovation*
This includes encouraging efficient and innovative telephone systems. Efficiency includes the effective utilisation of manpower, capital and other resources; and the extent, timing and location of investment. Innovation includes the ability to earn a sufficient return on capital to finance the development and use of new techniques.

(3) *Burden of Regulation*
This includes the extent and nature of the information required to implement the regulatory scheme, the feasiblity and costs of obtaining it, the number of areas of debate or conflict concerning the implementation of regulation, and the extent of discretion involved.

(4) *Promotion of Competition*
This includes the desirability of promoting and maintaining effective competion in the UK and promoting competitive activity in the UK by UK suppliers. It also includes the danger of 'capture' by incumbent suppliers, issues of equity and efficiency *vis à vis* BT and its competitors, possible interactions between the regulatory scheme and the licensing of new entry, and the ease with which regulation can be phased out (without disturbing competition) as and when circumstances permit.

(5) *Proceeds and Prospects*
This includes ensuring the maximisation of net proceeds from sale and facilitating the successful operation of BT plc as a commercial organisation after flotation. It also includes the perceived complexity or unfamiliarity of regulatory arrangements, the ease with which regulation can be phased in, the predictability of regulation, and the prospects for the longer-term evolution of the regulatory scheme.

5.2 It is assumed that BT's licence will require it to satisfy all reasonable demands for public call box services, emergency services and services in rural areas, as specified in Clause 3 of the Bill. Hence these considerations are not dealt with explicitly in comparing alternative regulatory schemes, but reference is later made to the pricing and financing of these services.

5.3 It is perhaps worth noting that the comparisons to be made in this Report are between alternative regulatory schemes, not between regulation and nationalisation. At the time when a choice had to be made whether or not to privatise BT, it was certainly relevant to compare BT's expected performance as a nationalised industry with BT's expected performance as a private industry subject to some form of regulation. For example, it would have been relevant to ask whether regulation would dampen a privatised BT's pursuit of efficiency to the extent that efficiency would be no higher than under nationalisation. But the decision on privatisation has now been made, and the comparison with nationalisation is irrelevant to the choices to be made in the immediate future. The relevant question now is whether a privatised BT is likely to be more efficient operating under regulatory scheme A or B, regardless of how either outcome compares to the outcome under nationalisation.

5.4. The five criteria are to be used to evaluate the various alternative schemes that have been put forward for regulating BT's profitability. These schemes would be written into the terms of BT's licence. All the schemes operate within the regulatory framework set out in the Telecommunications Bill summarised in section 3 above. It is assumed that BT will be privatised after the passage of the Bill, though this may take time. It is also assumed that government policy will encourage competition, though this may take time to develop. Nevertheless, the conclusions of the analysis seem robust to these two assumptions: a different scheme would not be recommended if either privatisation or further competition were delayed.

5.5 The analysis of the Working Group's Maximum Rate of Return scheme is considerably longer than the analysis of other schemes. This happens to be the most convenient place to introduce most of the arguments, and it would be tedious to repeat essentially the same analysis wherever it applied. For brevity, reference is made back to the original argument. Consequently, the length of treatment is by no means an indicator of the deficiencies of any scheme.

6. The consequences of no explicit constraints on profits

6.1 The suggestion has sometimes been made that BT's licence should contain no explicit constraints on profits, prices or rates of return. This does not mean the abandonment of regulation. The licensing framework embodied in the Telecommunications Bill would still be in effect. The DGT would have the duty under Clause 3 to ensure that BT earned a sufficient rate of return to finance the provision of services and development of new techniques. He would also be able to make references to the MMC — for example, in the event that prices seemed to exploit monopoly power, or achieved profits seemed undesirably high, or there were evidence of anti-competitive practices. The MMC could then propose a variety of remedies, including modification of the licence. But there would be no explicit profit constraints specified in the initial licence.

6.2 One argument for this approach stresses the increasingly competitive environment in which BT will operate, the heavy burden of regulation, the advantage of comparability with other large firms, and the undesirability of prejudging the extent of BT's monopoly power and subsequent conduct. An alternative argument emphasises the need to promote competition and the danger that profit regulation will distort investment decisions and restrict entry.

6.3 It will be useful to evaluate this 'No Explicit Constraints' proposal against the five criteria established in the previous section, partly because it is a practicable option with a measure of support, and partly because it constitutes a benchmark against which to evaluate other schemes intended to improve upon it.

(a) *Protection against Monopoly*

6.4 What kind of pricing policy would a privatised BT adopt in the absence of explicit constraints? Presumably the interests of its shareholders will be an important objective — measured, perhaps, by the stock market value of the company. A commercial yardstick will be applied, and no doubt present policies will be re-examined and modified accordingly.

6.5 A large number of empirical studies conducted by BT suggests that UK demand for telephone calls is price inelastic. Current elasticity estimates range from 0.1 for local calls to 0.84 for cheap rate calls to the USA. The demand for rental seems also to be inelastic.

6.6 One scenario for the future is that BT would aggressively seek profit by increasing prices for each service until demands became elastic. In this case, BT's dominant position would indeed be exploited. However, there are a number of reasons why this scenario is implausible.

6.7 First, even if the demand for telecommunications as a whole remains inelastic, liberalisation and new entry could substantially increase the elasticity of demand for BT's own services. As noted in paragraph 4.13 this could well be the case for apparatus, trunk calls on major routes, private circuits, and even local calls between businesses in large cities. BT would still set its prices where its own demands were elastic, but the resulting prices need not be significantly higher than at present, and could be lower.

6.8 Second, it is not clear how far it would be commercially advantageous for BT to raise rentals. Some 'rebalancing' of tariffs would undoubtedly take place. But low rentals also serve to increase the size and attractiveness of the network, thereby increasing profit from calls. It is necessary to consider the total price of telephone service.

6.9 Third, BT may fear the threat of renationalisation if it 'oversteps the mark', or more likely the threat of referral to the MMC. How significant is this latter threat? BT will certainly wish to avoid the imposition of rebates, price control, divestment of parts of its business, or profit regulation, all of which are reasonably within the MMC's power to recommend under the Fair Trading Act.

6.10 BT's subscribers and customers, for their part, might feel the protection is not particularly adequate. Consider the hurdles which have to be overcome before an effective remedy is secured. The DGT may not wish to refer; he may need to take time accumulating evidence; the MMC investigation may be prolonged; the MMC may conclude that prices charged are not against the public interest; proposed remedies may not appear to alleviate the problem; the Secretary of State or the DGT may be reluctant to enforce the proposed remedies; there may be delay in enforcement; BT may not be deterred from acting similarly in future, and so on. On this view, BT may have very little to lose from exploiting its monopoly power.

6.11 There is merit in both points of view. It seems unlikely that BT will risk alienating public opinion in the immediate future. On the other hand, experience suggests that the MMC is not a particularly swift or effective mechanism for combating the market power of a dominant supplier, although a more streamlined scheme could be designed with a clear understanding as to the specific conditions under which the DGT could make a reference. For the immediate future, as noted earlier, BT's market power does seem particularly acute in the case of rentals and local calls.

(b) *Efficiency and Innovation*
6.12 As a commercial organisation, BT may be expected to seek efficiency in the use of manpower and other resources. This may take some time to achieve, however: it is not so long since the telephone system was run as a department of the Civil Service. BT is so large and dominant that it will not be subject to all the normal stock market pressures, such as the threat of takeover. Despite this, the drive to maintain sales and market share in the face of increasing competition should ensure a continuing improvement in efficiency.

6.13 In the absence of special taxes or controls on prices and profits, and again with the threat of future competition in a rapidly developing industry, the incentive to innovate should be as strong as in any other large commercial organisation and the requisite finance should be available.

(c) *Burden of Regulation*
6.14 The DGT will need to monitor the situation to decide whether and when a reference to the MMC might be called for. In the event of a reference, BT will need to provide substantial information: the burden of this is not negligible but has generally not been found unacceptable. Apart from this, it is conceivable that BT's annual accounts, coupled with the policy of 'keeping eyes and ears open' and investigation of complaints, would be sufficient for purposes of monitoring. The DGT will need to exercise discretion whether to make a reference, but thereafter responsibility is out of his hands.

(d) *Promotion of Competition*
6.15 Since the DGT's involvement is minimal, so too is the likelihood of capture. There is an obligation in the Bill to ensure that BT earns a sufficient rate of return, which implies a degree of protection, but otherwise the DGT will be free to monitor and discipline possible predatory pricing on BT's part and to recommend new entry. The problem of phasing out obsolete regulation does not arise.

(e) *Proceeds and Prospects*
6.16 BT would still enjoy a degree of regulatory protection; apart from this, its future prospects would be largely in its own hands. There would not be additional discretion which a politically appointed DGT could exercise against BT. Phasing in of regulation would present no problem beyond that of privatisation itself. Though its verdicts on mergers are unpredictable, and we do not yet know what line it would take on BT's licence modifications, nonetheless the MMC is regarded by the City and investors as a reasonably known quantity. However, there will be a question in investor's minds as to whether the government might demand a much more severe regulatory regime and this uncertainty will conceivably influence the proceeds of flotation. Nevertheless, this factor seems relatively insignificant compared to some of the other schemes discussed later.

6.17 To summarise, there would be a number of significant advantages in imposing no explicit constraints on BT's profits. Efficiency and innovation would not be discouraged, the burden of regulation would be negligible, and BT's prospects would be good. The regulatory framework does impose limitations on the development of competition, but the absence of explicit constraints minimises the danger of 'capture'. Competition can probably be relied upon to provide protection for consumers over an increasing range of services. Nevertheless, it may be felt that, in the first few years of privatisation, there is inadequate protection for domestic and small business subscribers. The task is to find a scheme which provides this protection without excessive sacrifices on the other criteria.

7. The Working Group's maximum rate of return scheme

7.1 In its report on rate of return regulation in telecommunications, the Working Group noted that the policy of liberalisation would increasingly expose BT's network services and the attachments area to competition. Nevertheless, BT would retain a monopoly in substantial areas of the business. Some control over profits seemed necessary in order to prevent excessive returns on investment and discriminatory pricing through cross-subsidisation. The Group recognised the various criticisms that could be levelled against maximum rate of return schemes, and they wished to overcome these as far as possible by limiting the scope of regulation to those areas where BT had market power, and introducing flexibility into the operation of the maximum.

7.2 The Group envisaged that the following provisions would give effect to their recommendations:

(1) BT's licence would specify the overall rate of return on capital employed that would be the trigger for regulatory action. Rates of return would be separately specified for the local, trunk and international businesses;
(2) the licence would also set out the proportion of excess profits to be returned to customers and how the rebate would be made;
(3) the Director General of Telecommunications (DGT) would have the power, if BT made excess profits, to limit the general level of tariffs in any regulated activity where excess profits were made;
(4) the DGT would be able to vary in any year the rates of return specified in BT's licence by not more than ten per cent of the specified rate of return for improvements in quality of service or other measures of efficiency agreed and achieved;
(5) while BT's performance and the conditions of its licence should be subject to review at five yearly intervals, the DGT should be able, on his own initiative, to propose an earlier review of BT's performance not less than two years after a previous review;
(6) BT should be required to provide the DGT with sufficient information for the regulation of profits to be carried out within a current cost accounting framework as soon as is feasible.

Subsequent amplifications of the Group's report enable the following details of the scheme to be filled in.

7.3 The scheme would ideally apply only to those areas of BT's operations where BT has significant market power. In practice, it is assumed to include the proposed operating divisions to be known as Local Areas, National Network Services and BT International. It would not include BT Enterprises or Martlesham Enterprises.

7.4 The maximum rate of return is to be specified on a current cost accounting basis, not on an historic cost basis. It is calculated on profits after depreciation (including supplementary depreciation to take account of replacement cost) but before interest.

7.5 The level of the maximum rate of return is not specified in the Group's report. It 'would be determined taking into account such factors as returns in competitive markets experiencing equivalent conditions of risk and the cost of capital'. It is essentially the same as the minimum rate of return embodied in Clause 3 of the Telecommunications Bill, which refers to 'the need for persons supplying telecommunication services to achieve a return on capital employed sufficient to enable them to finance the supply of such services and the development and use of new techniques'. Although in practice the maximum might be set a little higher to take account of the expected variability of the cost of capital over a period of years. The final paragraph of the Group's report gives an illustration using 6 per cent rate of return for the business overall. BT's current profit target is 6.5 per cent. It seems that 5 to 7 per cent (in real terms) is the level of magnitude envisaged for the maximum rate of return. The appropriate level may change over time, and indeed the Group recommends that the terms of the license be reviewed every 5 years.

7.6 The levels of the separate rates of return for local, trunk and international businesses are not specified. They will not be identical at first, because the services currently differ so much in profitability, but it is hoped that the same rate of return may be specified for each activity in due course. The Group's illustration involves a maximum rate of return of 1 per cent on local, 5 per cent on trunk and 15 per cent on international services. These numbers are purely illustrative, but it seems that the local rate will be significantly below the overall rate and the international rate will be significantly above.

7.7 The rebate of excess profits is to be returned to customers; it is not a tax or levy payable to the Exchequer. The operation of the rebate scheme will be monitored by OFTEL, not by the Inland Revenue. The rebate will be an allowable expense for purposes of Corporation Tax.

7.8 The level of the rebate is not specified in the Group's report but it is envisaged that the bulk of excess profits be rebated on a sliding scale, so that the percentage rebate varies with the level of excess profits. A subsequent numerical example embodies a sliding scale rising from a 52.5 per cent rebate on excess profits (when the 5 per cent maximum rate of return was only just exceeded) to a maximum rebate of 75 per cent of excess profits (when the total rate of return was greater than 11 per cent).

7.9 The Group's report does not specify precisely how the rebate is to be made. The report notes that 'unless paid directly to those who had been overcharged, regular rebates would be a further distortion of BT's revenues', so that it is envisaged that excess profits will be rebated on the same services as they occur. No conclusion was reached as to whether each customer gets the same rebate or whether the rebate is proportional to usage during the year just ended.

7.10 The Group recommended that the DGT would be empowered to seek changes in tariffs sufficient to prevent a recurrence of excess profits. He would thus have discretion as to whether or not to require a change in tariff. It is true that Clause 15 of the Bill gives the DGT discretion in the *enforcement* of all licence conditions, but exceeding the overall rate of return would not seem to be a *breach* of a licence condition, hence a greater degree of discretion seems to be envisaged here.

7.11 It is further recommended that it would be for BT to determine the specific changes in tariffs and to provide evidence that the proposed changes would suffice. The adequacy of a proposed tariff is therefore to be evaluated in the light of expected future conditions (e.g. of demand and cost), rather than with reference to past output.

7.12 No time limit for implementing tariff changes is specified. A limit of one year is intended if possible, two years if necessary. The Group's illustration suggests that action on international tariffs could be expected to remove the source of the excess profits over a two year period, but notes that as tariff reductions may take some time to be negotiated and introduced, particularly on international services, a further rebate on excess profits might be necessary in the subsequent year.

7.13 If BT does not reach its overall maximum, its tariff policy would be subject only to the normal provisions of competition policy. That is, BT would not be subject to rebates and enforced tariff reductions if it is not exceeding the specified overall maximum rate of return. Exceeding the maximum rate of return on individual services will not lead to rebates or tariff reductions if the overall rate of return constraint is not exceeded. These individual service maxima are used merely to indicate where rebates should be made. They may also facilitate the analysis of possible anti-competitive practices.

7.14 The operation of the 10 per cent flexibility element is described as follows in a subsequent DoI summary paper:

> 'If the overall maximum rate of return was fixed at, say, 6 per cent per annum on a CCA basis, the Director General could at the beginning of year one agree with BT that the maximum could be increased to 6.6 per cent if BT improved its performance by achieving, say, all of the following targets: reducing the average waiting time for a telephone line, reducing the number of dialling failures, reducing the average length of service call on domestic subscribers and reducing the costs attributable to each unit of output. These targets are illustrations only. Each performance target would have a weight so that achievement of all but one of the performance targets might allow BT to earn a maximum of say 6.4 per cent (instead of 6.6 per cent), failure to achieve two would yield say 6.3 per cent and so on.
>
> Similarly, a reduction in efficiency, say, a lengthening during year two compared with year one of the average time taken to install an exchange line, an increase in the rate of dialling failures or increased costs per unit of output would lead to a *reduction* in the maximum permitted rate of return equivalent to the increase in the maximum rate permitted when BT met its performance targets. It will be necesary for the Director General to negotiate precise performance targets before the start of each year together with methods of measurement and the weights to be attached to each target'.

8. Analysis of the Working Group's maximum rate of return scheme

8.1 It will be helpful to make a brief comparison between the Working Group's maximum rate of return (MRR) scheme and the approach adopted in the USA. (1) In the USA it is required to determine total revenue requirements (the general level of the tariff) by determining allowable expenses, the capital rate base and the appropriate rate of return. In the MRR scheme this will not be necessary as long as the achieved rate of return is below the overall maximum, but it will be necessary once the maximum is breached. (2) In both cases there is secondary concern for the structure of tariff; this is exercised in the MRR scheme via the specification of separate rates of return for each of three services which are to be used in determining rebates and tariff reductions. (3) The MRR scheme is applied annually, with no control on tariffs as long as the maximum overall rate is not exceeded. The US scheme involves hearings only when proposed new tariffs are filed, and 'escalator' clauses are increasingly being used to cope with inflation. (4) The MRR scheme involves rebates and tariff reductions in the event that the overall maximum rate is exceeded. The US scheme involves no such 'clawback' and no automatic tariff reduction: the company lives with the (favourable or unfavourable) consequences of the tariff decision until a new tariff is filed and accepted.

8.2 In some respects, the UK scheme emphasises *ex post* rather than *ex ante* control. However, my own impression is that the philosophies of the two schemes are very similar. Indeed, the MRR scheme seems rather *more* severe than the US approach (at least, as regards formal procedures), if the overall maximum is frequently breached. This seems likely to be the case unless the maximum return is set sufficiently above the minimum, to allow for forecasting error.

8.3 The theory and effects of regulation have been thoroughly studied in the USA, hence we can be more confident about the analysis of the MRR scheme than the ORPL scheme. It must be acknowledged, however, that much of the evidence has necessarily been drawn from industries other than telecommunications, since unregulated telecommunication systems have not been available for comparison.* It has also been argued that regulation works more satisfactorily in other countries (e.g. Canada).

8.4 Studies of regulation typically assume that the decision makers in any organisation (including directors, managers and other employees) have a variety of goals which they seek to achieve, subject to the constraints of limited resource availabilities, the possibly conflicting aims of their colleagues, and the nature of the environment in which the organisation operates. In a privately owned company, the actions of the decision makers are likely to be oriented towards the maximisation of the stock market value of the company, at least insofar as the shareholders (and potential take-over bidders) are able to exercise control. The regulation of profit reduces the incentive to adopt such wealth-maximising policies. Decision makers are likely to adopt policies which provide other kinds of reward, because the opportunity cost of doing so is less. That is, because profits are regulated, the adoption of another policy involves less sacrifice of profits than it otherwise would have done. As noted above, however, BT plc will be only 51 per cent privately owned, hence the effects of profit regulation may be less marked than in the USA.

(a) *Protection against Monopoly*

8.5 As regards pricing policy, a pioneering study of regulation in the US electric power industry compared prices and profits in states where electric utilities were regulated against states where prices and profits were not regulated. It found no significant effect of regulation on the level of prices, on relative prices for different types of user, or on company profits. Later evidence suggests that rates were slightly lower for regulated companies. One study estimates that regulated utilities charged about 5 per cent less than the wealth-maximising price.

8.6 Prior to the adoption of regulation, electric utilities in many cities were subject to active competition. It turns out that state regulation was promoted by the companies themselves in order to limit this competition. On this view, regulation should have led to an increase rather than decrease in prices and profits. Further evidence confirms this:

> 'The test results indicate that in 1912 electric utilities in early-regulated states had 46 per cent lower prices, 23 per cent higher output, and 38

*US evidence quoted in this section is taken by Louis De Alessi 'The Economics of Property Rights: A Review of the Evidence', *Research in Law and Economics*, vol. 2, 1980.

per cent lower gross profits than utilities in later-regulated states. By 1917, following the establishment of regulation in early-regulated states, the latter exhibited higher prices, lower output, and higher profits.'

Thus, prices were slightly lower in regulated than unregulated states, but significantly higher than if competition had been allowed to continue. The effect of regulation on price levels evidently depends crucially upon the extent to which competition is potentially viable and upon the policy adopted by the regulator with respect to entry.

8.7 There is some evidence that regulation tends to favour larger rather than smaller users i.e. industrial and commercial rather than residential users. This is consistent with the theory: the consumers with more wealth at stake have greater incentive to bring pressure to bear on the regulators.

8.8 Turning to the present proposal, the above theory and evidence suggest that applying the Working Group's MRR scheme would tend to lower the general level of prices of BT's monopoly services and increase output there, compared to a situation in which no explicit constraints were imposed. However, lower prices would only be expected in the long run if the MRR scheme did not at the same time tend to restrict the emergence of new competition (see paragraphs 8.39–42 below).

8.9 The MRR scheme seems to cover a much broader area than the area of concern with respect to monopoly. The MRR scheme covers the whole of the regulated business, whereas it is primarily local services (rentals and local calls) where concern has been expressed.

8.10 Insofar as larger users would exert more influence on the DGT, one would expect the main price reductions to be felt on such services as business rentals and private circuits (where, in any case, there is a growing element of competition).

8.11 There might be somewhat less incentive for BT to relate tariffs closely to costs. There would be less advantage in relating telephone call charges to the route characteristics and to time-of-day load patterns. Simpler, more uniform tariffs would be preferred. Cross-subsidisation would effectively become cheaper. Of course, BT's tariffs need not in any case be related closely to cost in monopoly services.

8.12 In this latter connection, it might be noted that the proposal to establish separate maximum rates of return for different services would, as intended, be likely to restrain rather than hasten the rate at which BT eliminates cross-subsidisation between local, trunk and international services — at least, if the separate rates are set at anything like the 1 per cent, 5 per cent and 15 per cent levels in the Working Group's illustration. The allocation of joint costs would need to be controlled to ensure that local service prices were held down.

(b) *Efficiency and Innovation*

8.13 A maximum rate of return constraint would undoubtedly reduce pressure on costs and efficiency. Since BT will almost always be earning profits sufficient to trigger intervention by the DGT, at least 50 per cent of any cost saving will have to be rebated to consumers, and continuing cost reductions will have to be matched 100 per cent by tariff reduction unrelated to commercial pressures. There is bound to be difficulty in convincing members of the organisation of the need for improvement. BT would be more receptive to increased wage demands, and less concerned to obtain the lowest possible input prices. Greater weight would be attached to a 'cosy relationship' with employees, suppliers and major customers. The 'cost-plus' syndrome would tend to prevail.

8.14 To overcome this problem the MRR scheme involves a 10 per cent flexibility element to encourage efficiency. A higher return is allowed for meeting performance targets specified in advance. However, it is not clear how these should be set and weighted, and there must be a danger that the DGT and BT will impose the standards they think reasonable to achieve, rather than the combination of price and performance which customers prefer. Whether 10 per cent is the right order of magnitude is not at all clear — will it be ignored as insignificant, or will it dominate BT's policy?

8.15 A typical investment decision involves weighing up a large capital expenditure now against a stream of prospective receipts in the future. If a maximum rate of return constraint is actually operative, it will reduce the magnitude of the stream of receipts. The extent and timing of this reduction cannot be precisely predicted at the time of investment. Nevertheless, an investment appears less profitable and more risky as a result of rate of return regulation. This cannot increase the attractiveness of investment; the crucial question is whether, or to what extent, investment is actually reduced as a result of regulation.

8.16 The typical defence of rate of return regulation on this score is that, if the maximum rate of return is set above the cost of capital, the lower return should not deter any desirable investment. If the cost of capital is 5 per cent, a project promising 15 per cent return should still be accepted even if a maximum return of 7 per cent is imposed. Whether this provides adequate allowance for risk is another matter. A project promising 15 per cent if successful and zero if unsuccessful could well be transformed from an attractive to an unattractive prospect by a 7 per cent maximum return.

8.17 It so happens that risk is a particularly important factor in modern telecommunications. Certainly the market as a whole is expanding rapidly, and is expected to continue to do so. Against this, the rapid development of new technology, the history of 'teething troubles' in introducing it, the emergence of new competitors within

Britain and the growing internationalisation of the market — all these factors mean that the risks associated with investment in telecommunications are very real ones for an individual firm such as BT. There must be a danger that severe limitations on profits will reduce investment and thereby jeopardise innovation.

8.18 Empirical evidence on this matter is difficult to come by and to evaluate. Regulatory agencies often take other actions to compensate the firm and encourage it to invest. For example, the risks of investment may be reduced by limitations on entry. Thus, the adverse consequences of regulation may show up in the form of higher prices and less appropriate technology, rather than in quantitatively lower investment.

8.19 One other consequence of regulation has proved easier to measure. If the maximum rate of return constraint is binding — that is, if the firm could otherwise earn a higher return — and if this maximum rate is higher than the firm's cost of capital, then profits can be increased by using more capital, thereby increasing the asset base on which the maximum rate is computed. This proposition is known as the Averch-Johnson over-capitalisation hypothesis.

8.20 Examples of over-capitalisation include choosing more capital-intensive methods of production despite higher total (operating plus capital) costs; buying equipment when leasing it would have been the commercial decision; providing higher quality or longer-lasting capital equipment than would otherwise be appropriate; engineering to higher standards, with larger margins for safety, uncertainty and growth, etc. Capital investments might be made in unprofitable activities in order to be able to increase profits (and prices) in other parts of the business. It is conceivable that equipment could be bought merely in order to lease it out, a device reputedly used by some companies to avoid Corporation Tax. Accounting policies could also be distorted — for example, by unnecessary capitalisation of expenses; reduced depreciation rates; the transfer of assets from unregulated to regulated sectors of the business; and various other forms of 'creative accounting'.

8.21 The evidence of over-capitalisation in the US power industry is claimed to be strong. One estimate is that actual production costs exceeded efficient production costs by about 12 per cent in 1962.

8.22 The Working Group expressed scepticism about the extent of Averch-Johnson effects in UK telecommunications. 'There is little immediate danger of BT providing excessive quality of service, of expanding output too far or over-investing in order to inflate the assets on which the allowable rate of return is calculated.' Against the first point, the claim made by MCI when attempting to enter the US long distance market was precisely that ATT's quality of service was too high, and that many consumers would prefer lower quality at a lower price. A similar argument might be made against BT. Second, it is certainly true that BT's access to capital has been severely limited in recent years, and one of the purposes of privatisation is to remedy this. But the rate of return constraint is to be imposed for the 25 year duration of the licence, well beyond the immediate situation of shortage. Finally, it is true that the over-capitalisation induced by rate of return constraints may work in the opposite direction to the risks of under-investment induced by these same rate of return constraints, as discussed in paragraphs 8.15 to 8.17 above. But there is no reason to suppose the two forces will precisely cancel out. We cannot say whether the *net* effect of rate of return constraints will be more or less capital investment, but we *can* predict that the *pattern* (and hence the quality) of investment will be distorted by regulation.

8.23 Research and development expenditure provides one measure of innovation. It is an admittedly weak measure insofar as it reflects at best a desire to innovate rather than success in doing so. One would expect regulation to discourage Research and Development (R&D). Evidence on this general point is apparently not available, but there is some evidence that more severe regulation deters R&D expenditure compared to less severe regulation. Specifically, in states in the USA which use historic cost depreciation and do not allow R&D to be capitalised, electric utilities undertake significantly less R&D expenditure than comparable utilities in states with a weaker regulatory climate.

8.24 The results discussed so far depend on the assumption that the maximum rate of return is set above the cost of capital. During the last few years, the allowed rate of return in several US regulated industries has been held *below* the cost of capital. This was perhaps inadvertent at first but the pressure of public opinion has prevented an increase in the allowed rate. Under these circumstances one would expect regulated firms to avoid new investment and contract their capital base. It is already reported that US electric utilities are questioning the 'obligation to serve' under such conditions, with a view to withdrawing as far as legally possible from the provision of uneconomic services. Whether or not the DGT and MMC are as sensitive to public opinion as US regulatory commissions is open to question, nonetheless errors in forecasting and lags in adjustment must be expected (see also paragraphs 8.33–8.35 below).

(c) *Burden of Regulation*

8.25 In order to carry out his allotted task, the DGT will have to determine which of BT's total expenses and revenues are appropriately allocated to the regulated sector; which operating costs are allowable in calculating rate of return; in particular, whether accounting policy (especially with respect to depreciation) is appropriate. The use of current cost accounting would require him to approve the current value of assets. Furthermore, the DGT would have to carry out these calculations for each of the three services (local, trunk, international) taken separately. This would require him to approve the allocation of joint costs and revenues.

8.26 The DGT will need to calculate whether an excess rate of return has been earned overall and, if so, which particular services are responsible. He will need to specify or approve how the rebate is to be allocated to the different services, and monitor the repayment. He will then have to discuss with BT the question of reducing tariffs, and approve the proposals which BT puts forward. This will entail, *inter alia*, taking a view as to the likely (and justifiable) movement of costs and demand over the next year. The implementation of agreed tariff reduction has also to be monitored. This could well be a more or less continual process of involvement.

8.27 Since an element of flexibility is envisaged, the DGT has to decide each year whether BT's performance has been unsatisfactory, satisfactory or more than satisfactory. BT will be judged in the light of performance criteria laid down at the beginning of the year, but the setting and weighting of these criteria has to be done for the next year. This presumably requires taking a view as to the costs and desirability of particular improvements in performance and likely short-term and longer-run effects on BT; no doubt attention must also be paid to public opinion, and the views of employees, suppliers and major customers. These views will often conflict: e.g. New York utilities accused of poor performance have pressed for *increases* in rates to finance improvements.

8.28 This is a formidable list of tasks. It is, of course, in addition to the DGT's duties of issuing, monitoring and modifying licences, making references to the MMC concerning licence modifications, enforcing design standards on equipment, approving compulsory purchase of land, providing advice and information to the Secretary of State and Director General of Fair Trading, exercising certain of the latter's functions, and taking over some of the responsibilities of the Post Office Users' National Council.

8.29 The volume of information required to be provided by BT, checked and analysed by OFTEL, and debated between them, would be very considerable. The Bill estimates that the costs of OFTEL will be about £1.5 million per year, of which about £1 million will be met by income from licence fees set to cover the cost of issuing, monitoring and amending of licences. Presumably most of this will be accounted for by BT. For its part BT will incur substantial expenses in dealing with OFTEL. One would not expect the lengthy Court cases characteristic of US regulation, where costs in the hundreds of millions of dollars are not unheard of. Nevertheless, BT's expenses will undoubtedly be no lower than those of OFTEL — and, in BT's view, could be higher by tenfold. These expenses will be passed on to consumers. If, instead, these expenses are not allowable for rate of return purposes, the proceeds of sale will be reduced. In either case, they will not be absorbed by BT's shareholders.

8.30 Any regulatory scheme must take into account the adequacy of the information available, and the consequences of basing a regulatory framework upon 'information' which, by its very nature, can be little more than opinion or value judgement. MRR is relatively vulnerable here.

8.31 The limitations of BT's accounting system are often referred to. Their precise extent is difficult to assess. It should be possible to obtain those aggregate data of a kind which are subsequently recorded in the Annual Accounts *viz.* turnover, operating expenses, capital expenditure, depreciation etc. Whether such data are available for separate services is less clear: the accounts of BT International are separate but the division between local and trunk services could cause difficulties. Available, too, should be performance data which could be used in exercising flexibility on rate of return. Asset revaluations will initially cause problems.

8.32 As to predictions about the future, BT has a number of sophisticated demand forecasting models, and has accumulated substantial evidence concerning elasticities of demand for major services with respect to prices, incomes, gross domestic product, etc. Forecasting of costs and the forward planning of cash flows are in process at present — one would hope such crucial management planning and control services would soon become operational, but for some years their reliability and suitability for regulatory control will be open to question. There is always the question how far 'official' plans reflect true beliefs and intentions, and rate of return regulation provides an incentive to keep the two distinct.

8.33 Quite apart from the adequacy of BT's information system is the question of how reliable estimates about the future can ever be. Of course, every business has to make forecasts as best it can, and act accordingly, but it also needs to preserve the flexibility to change its plans in the light of changing predictions about the future. There is surely no doubt that a regulatory framework restricts this flexibility: BT has not merely to perceive and analyse changing conditions and revise its plans accordingly, it has to persuade the DGT of the need for change as well.

8.34 The level of the maximum rate of return is a case in point. Given the uncertainty about future costs, demand, technology and competition, to what extent is it possible to say that a particular level of return is or is not adequate to stimulate the 'correct' level of investment or innovation? If BT considers that conditions have changed, making the current maximum too low, how long will it take to persuade DGT and MMC of this? A two year lag in modifying the licence would seem to be a minimum.

8.35 This raises the question of how the DGT will form a judgement on the various matters of fact and prediction. How far will he attempt to secure an independent source of expertise at OFTEL (e.g. on demand forecasting)? rather than largely rely upon BT's view? It is a difficult choice. Taking the first route, and rejecting BT's experience, puts him in an exposed position if his judgement turns out wrong. Taking the latter, safer, route rather puts him in BT's hands.

8.36 Finally, it must be noted that a number of decisions to be made by the DGT do not rest upon data at all, but upon value judgements. The allocation of joint costs is a notable example. It is well known that there is no solution, even in principle, to this problem. In US regulation, no one pretends that 'separations procedures' are anything other than a device for distributing benefits between different types of customers. This is typically done in the way likely to provoke least effective opposition. The DGT does not have to set tariffs, of course, but the MRR scheme does envisage that he will calculate rates of return for each service area (which requires allocating joint costs), and that rebates will be distributed in the light of these rates.

(d) *Promotion of Competition*

8.36 To what extent is the operation of MRR likely to encourage or discourage competition? Powers are taken elsewhere in the Bill to enable the DGT to refer to the MMC such anti-competitive practices as predatory pricing and full-line forcing. The main question here is whether maximum rate of return regulation is likely to limit or distort competition in any way. The emphasis in this section will be on possible restrictions on BT's competitors; the next section considers possible restrictions on BT itself as part of the evaluation of BT's prospects.

8.37 At first sight, regulation of BT's prices and profits is hardly likely to affect BT's competitors adversely, or to limit their desire and ability to compete. There are two potential dangers, however.

8.39 If BT sets prices for certain services which are below cost, or which generate an artificially low return on capital, this distorts the information conveyed to potential competitors and, more important, deters them from entering. Local telephone services are a case in point. The Working Group illustration involved an initial 1 per cent maximum return on local services. If this were enforced, a potential competitor with a prospect of operating at costs lower than BT's would be deterred from entry, unless he could beat BT's costs *minus* the cost of capital.

8.40 Second, OFTEL and the DGT may be 'captured' by BT and induced to advise against new entry. This could happen without deliberate design on BT's part, and without awareness by OFTEL and the DGT of what is happening. The root of the difficulty lies in the DGT's dependence on BT.

8.41 Consider how the DGT will obtain the information he needs to implement the regulatory scheme (see paragraph 8.35 above). To operate OFTEL, a staff of 50 and a budget of £1.5 million is envisaged. BT has a staff of 250,000 and a turnover of nearly £6,000 million. Surely the DGT could not sustain a serious challenge to BT with respect to information or forecasting nor could he justify a contrary view on the return on capital necessary to finance the supply of services?

8.42 In the light of the potentially serious consequences of 'getting it wrong', would the DGT *wish* to challenge BT? Once the DGT had accepted a particular forecast, and taken policy decisions based on it, surely he could not stand aside and see whether the forecast proved correct. Or he might be tempted to sweeten the pill of a low maximum return on capital by reducing the risks to BT. If the MMC decides that a particular return on capital is the appropriate level, there is an obligation on the DGT to ensure that BT achieves this level. This could involve recommending restrictions on the entry or growth of competitors.

8.43 Though BT is the major supplier of telecommunication services in the UK, it is no longer the only one. Other existing competitors will have a voice, and may protest at discriminatory treatment. Potential competitors are less easily represented. The possibility of capture by present incumbents, at the expense of future entrants, is relatively high insofar as MRR involves continual interaction and negotiation between BT and the DGT.

8.44 It is worth emphasising that present employees of BT would stand to gain from limitations on competition. Monopoly profits facilitate a larger wage bill and a quieter life. One would therefore expect the trade unions to join with BT in urging the DGT not to advise new entry.

8.45 To summarise, the DGT will find himself subject to severe pressures from within the industry. The greater his involvement in the details of profit regulation, the more pressure he will be under and the greater the danger of 'capture', albeit unconsciously. The most serious consequence of capture is not the short-term increase in profits, but the long-term restrictions on entry and potential competition, and the likelihood that regulation will become steadily more entrenched rather than gradually phased out.

(e) *Proceeds and Prospects*

8.46 The transition from a nationalised industry to a private one will be traumatic for BT, whatever the regulatory framework. One argument for maximum rate of return regulation is that it could help to ease this transition, insofar as it provides the regime most similar to that of nationalisation.

8.47 The concept of rate of return regulation is also familiar to potential investors and to the City. There will, of course, be concern as to the precise method of regulation, and the rates envisaged. Nevertheless, a maximum rate of return scheme is thought to be predictable in operation and not, in itself, likely to deter investors.

8.48 The success of the initial flotation, and more specifically the revenue derived from it, will depend inversely upon the perceived severity of the regulatory scheme. The maximum rate of return scheme proposed by the Working Group, together with their illustrative numbers, looks rather severe: fairly low maximum rate of return, immediate 50 per cent rebates of excess profits, tariff reductions to eliminate future excess profits, directions as to the particular services on which these rebates and price reductions are to apply, flexibility in maximum rate which may be exercised downwards as well as upwards, and profits and performance subject to annual review.

8.49 On the other hand, it was argued earlier that such an unfavourable outcome is unlikely to be the longer-term result of rate of return regulation. The more scope there is for 'capturing' the DGT, the more likelihood that BT will do the capturing. All the US experience points in this direction. In this event, the longer-term prospects for BT are rather more favourable than the formal appearance of the regulatory scheme suggests.

8.50 This protection is bought at a price, however. There are the risks of uninformed regulatory decisions (notably with respect to the allowed return on capital); the burdens of MRR regulation measured in terms of expense, time and reduced flexibility of response; and the constant subjection to scrutiny (which is likely to be reflected in the interest taken by the media).

9. An output-related profits levy

9.1 As an alternative to the Working Group's rate of return scheme, Professor Walters put forward the idea of an output-related profits levy (ORPL). The objective was to encourage BT to keep prices down, expand output and reduce costs. The levy would have graduated rates, all less than 100 per cent, which varied according to the extent to which BT expanded output during the year.

9.2 More precisely,

(1) BT's licence would specify a 'norm' rate of growth of output over the first 5 year period, and a base rate at which a levy would be applied to total profit in each year if the norm rate of output growth were actually achieved in that year;
(2) the licence would also specify a schedule of rates at which the levy would be applied if achieved growth of output departed from the norm rate, with lower rates of levy the greater the achieved growth of output and higher rates of levy the lower the achieved growth of output;
(3) at the end of the first 5 year period, the DGT would specify the norm rate of growth for the next 5 year period, and so on;
(4) there would be no controls on prices or outputs in the licence.

After discussion with Professor Walters, we may fill in the following further details of this scheme.

9.3 As in the case of the Working Group's scheme, the ORPL is intended to apply only to those activities in which BT has a degree of market power.

9.4 BT is liable for Corporation Tax but does not currently pay it. As with many manufacturing companies, the one hundred per cent depreciation allowances on plant and machinery outweigh current net income. BT's 1981/82 Accounts (p.29) state that no liability for Corporation Tax is expected 'within the foreseeable future', although BT currently estimates that it might become liable within 3 to 5 years. In these circumstances, an ORPL based on varying the rate of Corporation Tax would have no immediate effect. The ORPL is therefore assumed to be charged (in principle) in addition to Corporation Tax; it would be an allowable expense for Corporation Tax purposes (it was not considered appropriate that ORPL should *replace* Corporation Tax). ORPL would be assessed by the DGT, not by Inland Revenue. It would be payable by BT direct to the Treasury, not rebated to customers.

9.5 Whether ORPL would apply to profits calculated on an historic cost or current cost basis is not clear. Illustrations of the working of the scheme have been prepared on a CCA basis, with the levy applying to profit after interest on loan capital and on the pensions fund liability.

9.6 The criteria for setting the norm rate of growth have not been specified. It seems to be intended that it should reflect both achieved growth rates during the previous five year period and likely market conditions in the future. Since BT's output grew at an average rate of approximately 7 per cent per annum over the period 1977–82, this is perhaps the order of magnitude that might be envisaged for the norm in the first 5 year period of the licence. BT would no doubt be consulted in setting the norm rate, but in the event of disagreement the DGT's view would presumably prevail.

9.7 As regards the calibration of ORPL, Professor Walters gave a simple numerical example involving a standard levy of 50 per cent at a norm growth rate of 5 per cent, with the levy falling to 40 per cent if 7 per cent output growth is achieved and rising to 60 per cent if only 3 per cent output growth is achieved. Other illustrations involve a standard levy of 52.5 per cent on a 7 per cent norm growth rate, with the levy falling in three steps to 30 per cent if the growth rate exceeds 11 per cent, and rising in three steps to 75 per cent if the growth rate is less than 3 per cent. Higher levies would not be envisaged, but lower levies could be considered, while bearing in mind that the standard levy would need to be sufficiently far above zero to allow scope for reduction on above-norm output rates, otherwise the incentive to expand would be missing.

9.8 Since BT produces a great number of different services, it is not immediately obvious how output and growth are to be defined. Two alternative methods have been proposed.

(1) The first method involves defining (an index of) output in any year as BT's total sales revenue divided by a price index of its services. To illustrate, BT's accounts report turnover in 1982

of £5,708.1 million and tariff index 359.0, hence the output index for 1982 is defined as 5,708 ÷ 359.0 = 15.9. The output index for 1981 is similarly calculated as 4,554.2 ÷ 299.6 = 15.2. The rate of output growth from 1981 to 1982 is thus 15.9 ÷ 15.2 = 1.046, or 4.6 per cent. BT's tariff index referred to here is a linked Laspeyres index, with prices weighted by the previous year's revenue. It is produced in a similar way to the Retail Price Index. There is a considerable degree of disaggregation e.g. trunk calls are classified by time of day, duration, distance, operator or direct dial, etc., giving about 40 types of trunk call. New services are generally included as they become significant; some services are not yet incorporated e.g. Prestel. Price changes during the year are reflected in a revenue-weighted average price. The compilation of this tariff index takes about 3 weeks each year. If this approach were adopted, it would be necessary to construct a modified tariff index for regulated services only. This would exclude the services produced by BT enterprises, and other services where competition was thought to be adequate.

(2) The alternative method is to define an index of output directly by specifying weights to be attached to physical outputs (e.g. number of business rentals, trunk calls, international telex messages, private circuits, etc.). This possibility is discussed later; for the present we assume the tariff index method is used to define output growth.

Depending upon the method adopted, the specific tariff index or the output weights to be used would be specified in the licence rather than left to the discretion of the DGT.

9.9 It is not envisaged that ORPL be applied to the different services produced by BT. If it were thought appropriate to encourage increases in output for those services where BT's market power is greatest, it would be necessary to utilise a weighted output index (method 2), and to allocate high weights to the services it was thought advantageous to expand. This possibility is also discussed in paragraphs 10.14 and 10.15. In principle it would also be possible to adjust the weights in the tariff index; this possibility has not been explored.

9.10 As originally formulated it was envisaged that the norm rate of growth would be applied in each year to the output actually achieved in the previous year. This offers the possibility of manipulation (paragraphs 10.6 and 10.9 below). To avoid this, BT could instead be judged against the cumulative target output (at the norm rate) in each year. This variation, which is preferred by Professor Walters, is considered but there has not been time to analyse it in detail.

10. Analysis of the output-related profits levy

10.1 The output related profits levy is a novel proposal, which does not appear to have been utilised or even examined before. Econòmists have often referred to the possibility of subsidising a monopolist to increase output, possibly coupled with an increased profits tax, but they do not seem to have discovered this particular scheme, let alone analysed its likely effects. There must therefore be a considerable degree of uncertainty as to how the ORPL scheme will operate in practice, and there is bound to be some hesitancy to adopt it for that reason alone.

10.2 It may be worth noting that ORPT has similiarities to the wage-inflation tax proposed by Professor Layard. His proposal is that firms should be taxed on that part of their wage-bill which corresponds to the growth of wages above a specified norm, with the tax proceeds being handed back to the firms in a rebate proportional to their total wage-bill. It is suggested that this will lower the demand for labour at high wages and raise the demand at low wages. In effect, the tax tips the demand curve for labour, making it more realistic and therby reducing the monopoly power of the unions. The wage inflation tax has attracted some support but has not yet, of course, been put into practice. It has also been suggested to me that the new regime for local authority finance has similar characteristics.

10.3 Appendix 1 to this Report contains a formal economic analysis of the ORPL scheme under very simplified assumptions designed to facilitate the analysis. The principle conclusions from this analysis are sùmmarised in the following paragraphs. It should be noted, however, that the model examined in the Appendix assumes a profit-maximising producer of a single output. BT has not pursued the sole aim of profit-maximisation while under public ownership, and there is some doubt as to how far this objective will be its sole aim under private ownership. In addition, BT produces a large number of different but related services. Consequently, the theoretical findings from the Appendix will need to be assessed in the light of BT's likely situation. This is done after summarising the theoretical results.

10.4 An elementary result in economic theory is that a profit-maximising producer of a single product will expand output as long as the marginal (or incremental) revenue exceeds the marginal cost. Marginal revenue consists of the price received on the incremental unit less the reduction in revenue on all intra-marginal units if the selling price has to be reduced in order to sell one more unit. Thus, up to a certain point it is worth accepting a reduction in 'existing' profits in order to gain the profit on an additional sale, and the optimum output is where these two considerations just balance out, so that the net change in total profit is zero.

10.5 A flat-rate profits tax has no effect on output (since the output that maximises total profit also maximises a constant fraction of it). ORPL, in contrast, offers the firm a lower tax rate if output is expanded. The firm may thus make a lower pre-tax profit but a higher post-tax proft. Output will therefore be expanded beyond the profit-maximising level as long as the reduction in pre-tax profit is more than offset by the increase in post-tax profit. Price will be correspondingly reduced.

10.6 There is, however, a third consideration. Other things being equal, an expansion in this period's output will reduce the rate of growth achieved in the next period, and will therefore *increase* the tax rate in the next period. This reduces the profitability of expansion and could, in principle, make contraction of output temporarily profitable (see below). However, if ORPL were related to target output instead of previously achieved output, this consideration would seem not to apply.

10.7 ORPL may be thought of as 'stretching' the elasticity of demand. The firm sets its price 'as if' it were faced with a more elastic demand than actually exists.

10.8 It has been suggested that ORPL will only be effective where demand is elastic. The model analysed in the Appendix does not enable us to assess this claim, since the profit-maximising model assumes that all demands are elastic at optimum output. What it does show, somewhat surprisingly, is that an opposite result holds within the realms of elastic demand. That is, the proportional change in price and output will be greater the less elastic is demand.

10.9 ORPL related to previously achieved output will encourage expansion of output provided that the firm's profits are not growing faster than the discount rate; in the latter eventuality output will be decreased. This suggests that output will be expanded at the peak of a boom, during the ensuing decline, and in the trough of a slump, but output may be contracted during the upward part of the cycle. Conceivably, ORPL will tend to accentuate rather than dampen the impact of the business cycle on BT's output, but it may merely 'shift' it slightly. The analysis is not clear on this point.

10.10 This last analysis does seem to depend rather strongly on the assumption that the firm knows what part of the business cycle it is on, hence can calculate accurately whether expansion or contraction of output is called for. If a firm is uncertain about future profits, it may well decide to give more weight to the 'bird in hand' of lower taxes now, since the danger of higher taxes next period may not in fact materialise. Bearing in mind also the alternative of basing ORPL on target output, the danger of deliberate contraction should not be stressed.

(a) *Protection against Monopoly*

10.11 ORPL is specifically designed to counteract monopoly power, by providing an incentive for BT to increase output and lower price. As noted above (paragraph 10.3), it is not clear how far the simple profit-maximisation model will apply to BT plc. The best guess seems to be that, since BT will undoubtedly be concerned about profit, it will respond to ORPL in a similar way to that predicted by the profit-maximising assumption — that is, by reducing price and increasing output — though probably not to the same extent. There is inevitably considerable doubt concerning the precise nature of the response.

10.12 There are other important reservations. Will the DGT be able to set the norm growth rate and calibrate the tax in an adequate way? The growth rate which BT would otherwise achieve cannot be observed; it has to be conjectured, and the most informed source is BT itself. If the norm were set too low, it is conceivable that BT would merely operate at about the same price and output rates as it would have done in the absence of the tax.

10.13 If aggregate output is defined by means of an overall revenue-weighted tariff index, there is no particular inducement to expand those services where it has most monopoly power. The theoretical result that the relative changes in output and price are greater when elasticity is lower suggests that the monopoly services *may* be expanded, but without analysing such a model in detail one cannot be sure that BT would *choose* to expand these services. It is also possible that BT would find it profitable to expand some services and contract others.

10.14 If, instead, an aggregate quantity index is defined as a weighted average of the output of various services, it would be possible to attach greater weights to the monopoly services, or to the ones with lowest elasticity. This would encourage especially large increases in output for those services whose outputs are likely to have been most restricted. The device could also be used to influence the pattern of cross-subsidisation.

10.15 However, several problems arise: (1) It is not clear what criteria should be used for setting these weights. Weights proportional to unit profits, which reflect elasticities of demand, may be indicated, along the lines of the 'Ramsey pricing' approach. (2) It may be difficult to ascertain or calculate the 'appropriate' weights, particularly if elasticities and cross-elasticities are explicitly involved. (3) Distortions may arise through aggregation. (4) The DGT may find it necessary or desirable to encourage the output of services other than the monopoly ones (e.g. in response to pressure from large rather than small users). (5) Given the uncertainty about elasticities, future demand and BT's objectives, it is not clear *ex ante* what effect these weights will have, or what would constitute 'low', 'reasonable' or 'high' rates. The weights might be adjusted over time, in the light of experience, but this involves greater reliance on discretionary power, and it is not clear how far past experience provides a reliable guide to the future.

(b) *Efficiency and Innovation*

10.16 Any levy on profits is likely to have some disincentive effect. The precise level at which ORPL will operate will depend upon the calibration of the tax and the response of BT. If the norm growth rate is typically exceeded, the effective tax rate could well be between 25 and 50 per cent. The lower end of this range would not be unduly onerous, but the upper end could begin to have more serious consequences, as described in paragraph 8.13 for the MRR scheme.

10.17 Insofar as ORPL generates higher output and faster growth, it is likely to stimulate investment. BT may find it advantageous to expand services using underutilised equipment e.g. via peak-load pricing, but this increased utilisation eventually increases the attractiveness of that kind of investment.

10.18 The incentive to reduce costs is increased insofar as cost reductions enable prices to be reduced, output increased and the levy thereby reduced. The effect is thus felt on operating rather than capital costs, but the latter are the more significant for BT.

10.19 Would the provision or expansion of new services be discouraged insofar as they would not show up in the quantity index until it was redefined? This does not seem a serious objection: BT would know in advance which new services it intended to introduce, and arrangements could doubtless be made to incorporate them. If the tariff index approach were used, one could simply omit revenue as well as price of new services until it was convenient to incorporate them.

10.20 The imposition of a levy on profits reduces the attractiveness of any investment project, for the reasons given earlier in the discussion of the rate of return scheme (paragraphs 8.15–8.17). This might be particularly serious for BT insofar as R&D, innovation and investment in new technology are relatively risky and are usually financed to a greater degree from retained earnings.

10.21 ORPL would probably make BT more vulnerable to business cycle fluctuations. The demand for telecommunications is widely believed to be very dependent upon gross domestic product and the level of service sector activity, and there is empirical evidence to support this. Such factors are largely outside BT's control. An unexpected downturn in demand would reduce BT's output and profits, and simultaneously increase its levy rate. The cycle of after-levy profits would thereby be accentuated. BT's vulnerability to wrong forecasts would be greater if a 'cumulative target' were set (paragraph 9.10).

10.22 Against this, it might be argued that BT would have the incentive to respond constructively by cutting prices and expanding despite the slump. This is true, but BT has a similar incentive to expand at all times; the relevant question is whether BT has a greater incentive to expand in the slump than at other times. The theoretical analysis does not suggest that it would.

10.23 The likely increased vulnerability to the business cycle would lower the quality of BT's earnings stream. This would increase the difficulty of self-finance. It would also make BT a more risky investment, thereby increasing BT's cost of capital. Both these factors would tend to deter investment and innovation, though the magnitude of this effect would be difficult to asses.

10.24 Since Clause 3 of the Bill refers explicitly to achieving a sufficient return on capital, this would need to be taken into account in calibrating the ORPL and, if necessary, modifying it. This could alleviate some of the problems related to investment.

(c) *Burden of Regulation*
10.25 Implementing ORPL would require annual information on turnover, profits, tariff index or outputs of specified services. The problems of calculating profit are the same as for the rate of return scheme, except that the rate of return itself it not required to be calculated. Clause 3 of the Bill requires the Secretary of State and the DGT to bear in mind the need for BT to achieve a sufficient return on capital, but this would not necessarily require detailed annual calculations. Turnover, tariffs and output are relatively straightforward to obtain, though it should be borne in mind that an element of sampling and judgement is inevitably involved.

10.26 The DGT would have the task of periodically revising the growth norm. As noted earlier, the criteria for doing this are by no means clear: is the DGT supposed to estimate at what rate BT would grow in the absence of any regulation, or is he supposed to decide what growth rate would be desirable? In either case, how is the appropriate number to be obtained?

10.27 The licence is supposed to specify output weights (unless the tariff index approach were adopted). This would probably require measurement of profits and elasticities if it were not to be done in an entirely arbitrary way. Some judgement would also need to be made of BT's likely response to these weights. These are not the DGT's responsibility initially, and the MMC would be responsible for recommending modifications, but in practice the DGT would probably have to deal with this problem.

(d) *Promotion of Competition*
10.28 There is a danger that BT may be encouraged to set price below cost for some services in order to expand output. This could distort the allocation of resources, and deter the entry of competitors. In fact, lower prices make entry less attractive, even if they are not below cost. There is thus a potential conflict between the aim of expanding output and the desirability of encouraging competition and preventing anti-competitive practices such as predatory pricing.

10.29 The DGT might be perceived by BT's competitors as unfairly committed to expanding the output (hence the market share?) of BT at the expense of themselves. Potential entrants might feel at an even greater disadvantage.

10.30 There is a similar danger of BT 'capturing' the DGT as with the rate of return scheme. The level of the norm growth rate is so crucial to BT's viability and success that BT could scarcely avoid pressing its case strongly. The DGT is in a very difficult position: a low norm will not constitute any protection against monopoly, but a high norm will jeopardise competition.

10.31 There would be pressure to revise the norm levels more frequently than 5 yearly, as market prospects fluctuated. The DGT would again depend on BT for information. As before, he would find it hard to justify a contrary view to BT with respect to future growth. Once he had committed himself to a norm rate of growth, there would be an obligation to ensure that BT was not prevented from achieving it by actions on his part. For example, the licensing of a new competitor without due consultation could be argued by BT to justify a resetting of the norm.

10.32 The sudden removal of ORPL could disturb the market, depending upon the effect that ORPL had had — but this would be difficult to assess before terminating it. The alternative would be to wind down the scheme slowly, by gradually reducing the standard levy, but a low standard rate tends to destroy the effectiveness of the whole scheme.

(e) *Proceeds and Prospects*

10.33 BT would be subject to a substantial levy that its competitors would not have to bear. This would eventually be perceived by BT as inequitable, especially as competition began to develop, and would distort the allocation of resources between BT and its competitors. BT would be at a particular disadvantage with respect to investment out of retained earnings.

10.34 ORPL is likely to increase BT's vulnerability to the business cycle, and to developments in the market which are unforeseen or outside BT's control. This increased risk will adversely affect BT's credit rating and cost of capital.

10.35 Financial advisers have emphasised that uncertainty about the operation and effects of the ORPL scheme would either reduce the share price at flotation or necessitate a substantial delay before privatisation was envisaged. In this connection, it is not so much the actual effects of ORPL as the City's *beliefs* about the likely effects that are crucial.

10.36 BT could attempt to secure some protection against risk, and some compensation for the levy payments, by seeking limitations on new competition. The DGT might feel obliged to support such requests. This is unlikely to be adequate compensation for BT in the long term, unless a reduction in the rate of levy can be ensured.

11. An interim evaluation

11.1 Having examined each scheme separately in some detail, we now attempt to summarise and compare them, again on the basis of the five criteria identified earlier.

(a) *Protection against Monopoly*
11.2 There are reasonable prospects for competition in several areas of telecommunications, notably heavy density trunk routes and services for larger businesses. BT is likely to retain a dominant position in local services for some years to come. Despite the possibility of reference to the MMC, the absence of explicit constraints on prices or rates of return is unlikely to be perceived as adequately controlling this monopoly power in the short-term. However, insofar as ORPL facilitated a pro-competitive stance by the DGT, and did not deter entry by lower prices, this scheme could be effective in the long run.

11.3 The Working Group's maximum rate of return scheme tackles the problem of monopoly pricing by rebates and tariff reduction. There is some evidence from the US electric power industry that rate of return regulation leads to lower prices — provided that the alternative would be an unregulated monopoly. However, there is also evidence that the introduction of rate of return regulation in this industry was associated with the development and protection of monopoly positions, and in fact led to *higher* prices than previously existed.

11.4 The Working Group scheme covers a much broader area than the area of monopoly concern. The specificiation of separate rates of return recognises the variations in monopoly power between services. However, there is a danger that the specification of separate rates of return will perpetuate cross-subsidation unnecessarily. Expansion by BT and new entry by competitors may also be discouraged in the low-return services.

11.5 Professor Walter's ORPL tackles the problem of monopoly pricing by providing an incentive to increase output (hence, to lower prices). Given the lack of previous experience with this scheme, it is difficult to predict the likely magnitude of BT's response. On average, output is likely to be higher than the norm growth rate. However, BT is bound to be influential in the setting of this norm. Consequently, one cannot be entirely confident that prices would be lower than in the absence of ORPL.

11.6 The simpler form of ORPL, based on a tariff index, makes no specific reference to variations in monopoly power. In principle, the problem could be tackled by attaching weights to each type of output, but this is liable to be complex and arbitrary, leaving wide scope for political and other pressures to influence the outcome. With ORPL, as with MRR, lower prices may discourage new entry.

11.7 Assessing the extent to which each of these schemes provides protection against monopoly power is probably the most difficult task of all, since it is not clear that either scheme would work 'as intended'. In the short term, ORPL might be slightly superior to maximum rate of return regulation, which in turn would be more effective than the absence of regulation. But bearing in mind the increasing danger of regulatory 'capture' and the disincentive to new entry, one cannot by any means be confident that either of the first two schemes provides adequate protection against monopoly in the longer term.

(b) *Efficiency and Innovation*
11.8 BT will become 51 per cent privately owned over the next few years. One would not expect it immediately to become as efficient as a comparably large organisation already in the private sector, but it will gradually respond to the normal commercial incentives to eliminate inefficiency and take a realistic approach to wage negotiations. With no explicit constraints on profit, these incentives are not blunted. The same applies to investment and innovation.

11.9 Rate of return schemes have a very poor track record on efficiency. If, as seems likely, the maximum rate of return constraint is almost always binding, there are likely to be severe disincentive effects and a relaxed approach to wage bargaining. The discretionary 10 per cent flexibility on rate of return is an attempt to compensate for this failure but one cannot be confident either that it would provide a significant stimulus to BT or that the stimulus would be in the direction preferred by consumers.

11.10 ORPL lies somewhere in between the other two schemes: a profit levy effectively in the 25 to 50 per cent range does provide some disincentive. This might be slightly offset by the inducement to lower operating costs in order to increase output and reduce the levy.

11.11 If the maximum rate of return constraint is effective, it will reduce the profitability and attractiveness of investment, and also reduce the availability of funds (from both internal and external sources) with which to finance the investment. Innovation is likely to be reduced. There is also evidence from the USA of 'over-capitalisation'. The precise pattern of distortions due to MRR is difficult to predict, but the quality of investment is likely to be reduced, leading to higher overall costs and less effective provision of services.

11.12 Insofar as ORPL stimulates higher output, investment will also be stimulated. There is some incentive to innovate in order to exceed the norm growth rate. However, the levy could severely reduce the availability of internal finance. The pro-cyclical effect of ORPL (whereby a higher proportional levy is likely to be extracted in precisely those years when there is a downturn in market conditions) increases the degree of risk. The lower quality of BT's earning stream will increase the costs of external finance. The net effect is likely to reduce BT's ability to invest and innovate.

11.13 Both rate of return and ORPL are unsatisfactory with respect to investment and innovation; they could both be expected to lead to pressure on the DGT to provide protection against competition in order to compensate for lower profits by reduced risk. Taking this sub-heading as a whole, it is difficult to decide a ranking between MRR and ORPL. The absence of constraints involves no disincentive effects, and is clearly preferable to both.

(c) *Burden of Regulation*
11.14 With no explicit constraints, the burden of regulation is negligible. There are moderate costs to an MMC investigation, but this would presumably be at infrequent intervals. The DGT would need to monitor BT's performance in order to decide *when* to refer, but this need not require continual and detailed investigation. The DGT would not require extensive information from BT. Information on possible anti-competitive practices would need to be collected, but this would be true under any scheme; consumers and competitors who believed themselves adversely affected could be relied upon to identify problem situations.

11.15 The Working Group scheme involves the annual collection and appraising of a great deal of information, notably on revenues, operating costs, and rates of return by individual service. Important judgements have to be made by DGT concerning the allocation of costs, the distribution of rebates and the reduction in tariffs. The MMC has to consider the appropriate level of the overall maximum rate of return and the desirable maxima on individual services. Monitoring BT will be a continual task, since the maximum return constraint is likely to be binding in most years. This will be costly, time-consuming and potentially restrictive. The DGT will be heavily dependent upon BT for information and advice, and is unlikely to be able to sustain a credible view which is inconsistent with BT's.

11.16 ORPL requires the DGT to obtain similar information on revenue, operating costs and profits as does MRR. A tariff index could be made available without significant difficulty, so too could the outputs of each service. The determination of weights to be attached to such outputs is likely to be a complex and arbitrary procedure, initially embodied in the licence. The DGT will need to revise the norm growth rate, in which respect he will inevitably be heavily dependent on BT for forecasts. It is intended that weights and norms should be revised at infrequent (say 5 year) intervals, in which case the annual burden would be rather low, but it seems likely that there will be great pressure to revise these parameters more frequently insofar as conditions change unexpectedly; here the MMC and the DGT will need to exercise substantial discretion.

11.17 On balance, the burden of regulation seems very heavy under the Working Group scheme, nearly as heavy under ORPL, and negligible in the absence of explicit constraints on profits.

(d) *Promotion of Competition*
11.18 Control over entry rests with the Secretary of State. However, the alternative schemes may affect the incentives of new firms to enter and also the advice given by the DGT to The Secretary of State. The absence of constraints does not reduce the incentives represented by high profits and prices in monopoly areas, nor does it encourage the DGT to advise against entry, except insofar as the Bill requires a sufficient return on capital.

11.19 If rate of return regulation merely limited BT's profits, competitors would more likely be favoured than harmed. However, insofar as prices in monopoly areas are reduced, and even held below cost, this will deter new entry and expansion by existing competitors. Furthermore, the history of regulation in the USA shows that the regulatory agency is very susceptible to capture by the dominant supplier. The DGT will be obliged to ensure that market conditions do not prevent BT earning the specified rate of return, and there will be pressure to reduce market risks to compensate for reduced profitability. The DGT's advice to the Secretary of State on the desirability of new entry is likely to favour BT (and indeed all incumbent operators) at the expense of potential competitors.

11.20 ORPL is subject to similar limitations. The DGT will have substantial power to influence BT's growth and market share, and it is not clear how this power will be used. There is a danger that the DGT will become committed to increasing BT's output at the expense of existing and potential competitors; whether or not this is true, potential competitors might *feel* at a disadvantage, and be deterred from entry.

11.21 If BT does manage to 'capture' the DGT, there is a strong possibility that regulation will become steadily more entrenched, and less likely to fade away as competition increases. Both schemes are thus potentially inimical to competition. ORPL is perhaps less vulnerable insofar as BT's prospects are less favourable under it, hence BT is more likely to press for the abandonment of the scheme.

(e) *Proceeds and Prospects*
11.22 'No explicit constraints' offers BT excellent prospects, and this would be reflected in the proceeds of sale. BT's success will ultimately depend upon its own ability (within the licensing framework), and it should have no reason to fear this outcome. BT would be subject to reference to the MMC, just as any other large firm. There is a danger that consumers, politicians and public opinion might take a more critical view, and eventually insist on the imposition of a more severe regulatory scheme after privatisation, but there is less scope for a hostile DGT to exercise discretion against BT.

11.23 If the Working Group scheme operates with some degree of severity, the prospects for BT do not look particularly exciting. A 'reasonable' rate of return will be earned, but limitations on profits will probably restrict growth and innovation. Employees will benefit from the reduced concern for efficiency; restrictive practices may prevail. Because of lower prices, and to the extent that the DGT and the Secretary of State are persuaded to sympathise with BT, the risks of competition may be diminished. As an investment, BT's shares will be safe but dull. Proceeds of sale will be moderate.

11.24 ORPL in principle encourages BT to grow, and places no restrictions on its pricing and investment policy. However, the operation of the levy is likely to reduce the availability of internal funds and increase the riskiness of the business; the result is likely to be lower growth and uncertain prospects. BT will be dependent on the DGT's growth norm, but even if this is acceptable the levy still has to be paid. Finally, but by no means least important, the novelty and complexity of the ORPL scheme may deter investors and their advisers. This will mean either significantly lower proceeds upon flotation or delaying privatisation for several years, neither of which is in BT's interests.

11.25 ORPL is undoubtedly the least acceptable scheme with respect to BT's prospects, both immediate and long term. Maximum rate of return would damage BT's prospects if it were operated strictly; the damage could be ameliorated to the extent that BT managed to 'capture' the DGT, but even so the prospects would not be exciting. 'No explicit constraints' offers the most attractive prospect for BT.

Conclusions
11.26 With 'no explicit constraints', the degree of direct control is small. Consequently, there are hardly any adverse consequences for efficiency, investment and innovation; the burden of regulation is negligible; competition is not jeopardised; and BT's prospects are excellent. The serious disadvantage of this scheme is that in the short run it does not seriously limit the exercise of BT's monopoly power. This alternative is likely to be perceived as insufficiently effective.

11.27 The chief merits of the Working Group's rate of return scheme are that it would be widely perceived as dealing with the important problem of controlling monopoly; prices would be lower; the scheme is familiar to investors; BT would have reasonably safe if unexciting prospects. A serious attempt has been made to overcome the acknowledged defects of US regulation; nevertheless the characteristic disadvantages of this approach remain: the disincentives to efficiency and innovation; the distortions in investment patterns; the heavy burden of regulation; the disincentive to new entry and long-term threat to competition given the likelihood of 'capture'; and the uninspiring prospects for BT.

11.28 The attraction of ORPL is that it tackles the problem of monopoly power in an imaginative way, by giving BT a positive incentive not to exercise this power; as a result, output could be higher and prices lower. This scheme has serious disadvantages, however the precise effects on prices and output are uncertain. Existing and potential competitors may be deterred. In order to put the scheme into effect, a new and substantial levy must be imposed on BT's profits. This could reduce both the incentive and ability to invest and innovate. Operating the ORPL scheme will impose a greater burden than at first apparent and there is considerable scope for capture, to the detriment of competition. The novelty and complexity of the scheme make the prospects for BT very uncertain, and it would be difficult to persuade investors otherwise. When floating a company of BT's size (£6,000 million turnover) the confidence of the City is vital.

11.29 The ranking of the schemes as discussed above is set out in the accompanying Table. This is admittedly a crude repesentation, since mere numerical ranking cannot convey the complexities of the comparisons or the 'distance' between the alternatives. Nevertheless, two broad conclusions emerge quite clearly.

Table 1: *Interim ranking of schemes for regulating BT's profitability*

	No Explicit Constraints	Working Group MRR	ORPL
Protection against Monopoly	3	2	1
Efficency and Innovation	1	2=	2=
Burden of Regulation	1	3	2
Promotion of Competition	1	3	2
Proceeds and Prospects	1	2	3

11.30 The first major conclusion is that it is extremely difficult to decide which of the MRR and OPRL schemes is better (or worse) than the other. ORPL scores slightly higher on three of the sub-headings, though there is some room for difference of opinion here, but scores significantly lower with respect to Proceeds and Prospects for BT.

11.31 The second major conclusion is that on four out of the five criteria, both MRR and ORPL are significantly worse than 'no explicit constraints'. The argument against this scheme is that it does not seem to provide protection against monopoly power. Even here it is by no means certain that either of the other two schemes provides as adequate protection in the longer run.

11.32 If attention is confined to ORPL versus the MRR scheme, the choice would be between a scheme that is largely unknown and a variant of one that is known to be unsatisfactory. Neither can be recommended. The absence of constraints is superior in almost all respects, and could be strongly recommended if it were not for the apparent short-term failure to limit monopoly power.

11.33 This conclusion suggests that an attempt be made to find an alternative scheme which preserves most of the virtues of 'no explicit constraints' while incorporating a conspicuous element of control over short-term monopoly power.

12. A profit ceiling scheme

12.1 One of the major defects of conventional rate-of-return regulation is that it makes no provision for distinguishing between the different sources of profit: superior performance, monopoly and luck. As a result, superior performance is discouraged, and monopoly power is marked by inefficiency and high costs. The Working Group attempted to meet this point by introducing the 10 per cent flexibility element, but this was a relatively minor part of the scheme, and subject to difficulties of its own, as noted earlier. The fundamental constraint still remained, that rate of return should not exceed the cost of capital.

12.2 Suppose, instead, that the maximum rate of return were set at a higher level. Fewer monopoly profits would be caught, but by the same token efficiency would less often be discouraged. We are thus led to the notion of a 'ceiling' rate of return, which should not be exceeded, but which in no sense represents a 'target' or 'desired' or 'expected' rate of return. The level of the ceiling would not be an economic decision, which can be set on a rational basis after detailed comparisons with rates earned elsewhere in businesses of comparable risk. It would be a purely political decision concerning the level which consumers, voters and ministers will find tolerable. The aim of the approach is not to identify a 'reasonable' rate of return but to identify 'unreasonable' ones.

12.3 With a ceiling scheme in operation, no regulatory action would be taken on the *general* level of prices and profits as long as the ceiling were not exceeded. However, a reference could be made to the MMC if *specific* prices or practices appeared to be anti-competitive. If the ceiling were exceeded, an immediate price reduction would be required, as a short-term remedy. If the ceiling were *persistently* exceeded, more serious investigation by the MMC would be required to ascertain the reasons for this, and to recommend longer-term remedies (e.g. raising the ceiling or imposing price or profit control, as appropriate).

12.4 There is, of course, a danger that high profits due to superior performance instead of monopoly will trigger orders to reduce prices. Against this is the general presumption that discretion is, on balance, more likely to be harmful than beneficial.

12.5 The following provisions in the licence would give effect to the foregoing philosophy. Comments on these provisions follow afterwards.

(i) BT's licence should define a ceiling rate of return on capital.
(ii) If in any year BT's achieved rate of return on capital exceeds the ceiling, prices should be reduced within 4 months so as to eliminate the profit in excess of the ceiling. Prices should not be increased until achieved rate of return falls below the ceiling.
(iii) The extent of the price reduction required should be judged by reference to output and costs in the year just completed (rather than by reference to expected output and costs in the subsequent year).
(iv) If the ceiling is exceeded three or more years in any six-year period, it would be understood that the DGT would refer BT to the MMC.
(v) Provisions (ii) to (iv) should apply separately to BT Inland Division and BT International.
(vi) Provisions (i) to (v) should apply to the first 5 years of the licence only.

12.6 It has already been emphasised that the ceiling is in no sense a 'desired' level which BT 'ought' to achieve. In particular, it is *not* 'the return on capital sufficient to finance the supply of [telecommunications services] and the development and use of new techniques' which is referred to in Clause 3 of the Bill. The level of the ceiling will require further discussion, but if a level of the order of 5 per cent (in real terms) is thought to be a 'normal' rate of return, which reflects the cost of capital, then the ceiling might be roughly twice as high, say 10 per cent. As already noted, this level is primarily a matter of political judgement, though account should be taken of the increasing burdens, disincentives and distortions as the ceiling is lowered.

12.7 Whether the ceiling would be specified using CCA or historic cost would depend upon which method of accounting a privatised BT chose to adopt. Accounting rules would need to be agreed e.g. as regards depreciation, but detailed monitoring by OFTEL would not be required unless the achieved return was close to the ceiling. If this should happen frequently, it would indicate that the ceiling was set too low.

12.8 The purpose of specifying that price reductions should be judged against past output and cost rather than against future conditions is partly to simplify and speed up the procedure, and partly to avoid the need for discretion (and persuasion). Checking that an adequate price reduction has been made is then merely a matter of arithmetic. (If inflation were severe, some adjustment would need to be made — perhaps adjusting total revenue by the RPI). The term 'price reduction' is not meant to preclude the increase of some prices (e.g. in 'rebalancing' or 'de-averaging') provided that total revenue (in terms of the previous year's actual output) falls sufficiently to bring the rate of return below the ceiling.

12.9 It would be possible to specify price reductions to eliminate only a proportion (less than 100 per cent) of the excess return, but this would be less simple and appealing, and there might not be sufficient disincentive to exceed the ceiling.

12.10 The inter-relations between BT's Local and National Network Divisions are so close that any attempt to identify separate rates of return would seem fruitless. There is a much sharper split between UK and international business. In addition, the rate of return on international services, currently 26 per cent on allocated costs, has been persistently high over many years, reflecting BT's monopoly position. This is not to suggest that all the international profits are due to monopoly — BT is in active competition with other international switching centres for the overseas business of PTT's and multinationals — but some explicit monitoring and control seems appropriate.

We now briefly appraise the profit ceiling approach against the five criteria used before.

(a) *Promotion of Competition*
12.11 A profit ceiling would prevent the emergence of high total profits. However, it would not focus explicitly on the services of greatest monopoly concern. The imposition of separate ceilings on inland and international businesses would bite most severely in the latter area, but it is plausible that these could be dealt with by allowing competition if public policy so indicated.

(b) *Efficiency and Innovation*
12.12 Provided that the ceiling were set high enough so as not to be operative most of the time, there would be little disincentive to efficiency and innovation. However, there is the '100 per cent tax' problem when the ceiling does operate.

(c) *Burden of Regulation*
12.13 The burden of regulation would depend crucially upon the level of the ceiling. As long as BT was operating below the ceiling, very little monitoring would be required; the bulk would be on the international side, especially concerning the allocation of joint costs. If the ceiling were breached, there would be problems of calculating the precise rates of return, which would necessitate calculating and agreeing the rate base and allowable expenses. For this reason, it would probably be necessary to investigate and agree the accounts even in years when the ceilings were not in question. Once allowed total revenues have been agreed, implementation of the tariff reduction is quite straightforward and requires no discretion on the part of the DGT.

(d) *Promotion of Competition*
12.14 Insofar as the ceiling lowers BT's prices, it will reduce the prospects of competition, but the disincentive effect is likely to be slight. The DGT clearly has no obligation to ensure that BT achieves the ceiling and the likelihood of capture is relatively small since the DGT may not be involved too frequently and his discretion is limited. Consequently, the ceiling scheme provides no basis for advising the Secretary of State against entry.

(e) *Proceeds and Prospects*
12.15 Prospects and proceeds are good, provided that the ceiling is not set too low and is not expected to be reduced by the MMC or modified by further constraints.

12.16 Overall, the profit ceiling scheme ranks between 'no explicit constraints' and the other two schemes. It does not seem to cope with monopoly as well as the MRR scheme, at least in the short-term, but has less of the MRR's defects on other criteria.

12.17 The level of the ceiling is absolutely crucial. If the ceiling is high, as assumed so far, the scheme will operate in a way comparable to the absence of explicit constraints on profit: the complex rate of return machine will merely have to be kept ticking over ready for use. However, if the ceiling is low, this machine will have to be used fairly frequently, and the scheme will operate like conventional rate of return regulation (or like the MRR without the flexibility element).

12.18 A political difficulty with the ceiling scheme must be noted. If the Secretary of State were to set a ceiling of, say, 10 per cent on the basis that profits above that would be unreasonable, he is open to the allegation that he therefore believes a profit of 9.9 per cent *is* reasonable. The rationale of the ceiling does *not* imply this — but this is not the way it would appear. For this reason, the Secretary of State would probably be obliged to set a low ceiling, much closer to the (claimed) cost of capital — perhaps 7 or 8 per cent. At such a level, however, the scheme would have all the defects of traditional rate of return control, and could not be recommended.

13. A local tariff reduction scheme

13.1 Rate of return control, whatever the variant, suffers from two major defects. First, it is burdensome and costly to operate, reduces the incentive to efficiency and innovation, and distorts the pattern of investment. Second, it covers the whole of the business, or a large part of it, and it does not focus explicitly on the particular services where monopoly power and public concern are greatest.

13.2 In the case of BT, (i) rate of return constraints applied to the licensed business will necessarily apply also to international services (where public concern is not strong and in certain respects there is a degree of competition already, and further competition could probably be allowed), to private circuits and to heavy density trunk routes (where it is hoped that Mercury will provide significant competition); (ii) rate of return constraints do not prevent rises in the price of certain services provided they are compensated by reductions in other prices, and there is no guarantee that the rises will not be in the services of particular concern (specifically, inland versus international, rentals versus calls, domestic versus business, local versus trunk); (iii) rate of return constraints do not prevent price rises due to increases in costs (wherever these costs occur and whatever their magnitude).

13.3 The MRR scheme attempts to cope with these problems by means of the 10 per cent discretionary flexibility and the specification of separate rates of return for particular services. We have already indicated the drawbacks of these devices. Most importantly, specifying separate rates of return does not trigger action if one is exceeded, does not influence tariff structure, depends upon the arbitrary allocation of joint costs, and provides no protection against cost increases.

13.4 An alternative approach is to focus explicitly upon tariffs which are the source of the main concern. As argued in Section 4, ultimately the only effective way of combating monopoly power is by competition. However, regulation can help to assure consumers that the situation will not 'deteriorate'. Specifically, it is possible to insert conditions in BT's licence to prevent prices of monopoly services being increased faster than the rate of inflation, or perhaps to reduce them in real terms. An additional merit of a local tariff reduction scheme is that it can focus precisely upon those services of particular concern.

13.5 When the 'Buzby Bond' was under discussion, the proposal was that BT's prices should not increase by more than RPI — X per cent, where X was a specified number. This idea could be adapted to present circumstances, by incorporating a condition in BT's licence requiring it not to increase tariffs on monopoly services by more than RPI — X per cent, i.e. to reduce these tariffs by X per cent in real terms. There are several details to be settled: to which services should tariff reduction apply? Should the guarantee apply to each service separately or to a basket of services? At what level should X be set?

13.6 As noted earlier, the services where BT has significant monopoly power which are also of public concern are essentially rentals and local calls. An estimate of the revenue associated with these services would be: residential rentals £795 million, business rentals £292 million and local calls £1,011 million, totalling £2,098 million (see 1981/2 Annual Report page 44). This represents 37 per cent of BT's total turnover, or 45 per cent of their inland revenue. To some extent this overestimates the extent of monopoly. Large businesses will be able to utilise Mercury and cellular radio to reduce their volume of local calls and number of lines from BT. It is also reported that many US residential subscribers are finding it profitable to subscribe to MCI — a break-even telephone bill of about £18 per month has been suggested.

13.7 On the other hand, Mercury will initially provide competition for trunk calls between about eight major cities, but trunk calls between smaller towns will be provided only by BT. Apparently the busiest 100 trunk routes on which BT has recently cut prices accounted for a revenue of £300 million out of £1,551 million, but there are other direct heavy density lines where costs might justify similar price reductions. To ensure that Mercury's competition is felt even more widely, it would seem appropriate to incorporate non-discrimination clauses in BT's licence (see paragraph 13.15 below). For the present it seems simpler to leave trunk calls out of any tariff reduction scheme.

13.8 Should the RPI — X per cent constraint apply separately to business rentals, residential rentals and local call charges? Or should RPI — X per cent apply to a basket of local services containing these three elements, as reflected in a specially-constructed Local Tariff Index? The advantages of separate constraints are (i) it is easier for the subscriber to understand, because the constraint applies to a 'real' price with which he is familiar; and (ii) each subscriber has a guarantee about the particular service(s) of relevance to him, because separate constraints prevent 'rebalancing' within the basket — thus, a domestic subscriber need not fear that the price of the bundle will go down but domestic rentals will be increased while business rentals fall.

13.9 The advantages of a basket of services are (i) a larger number of local services could be included which it would be tedious (and undesirable, for reasons noted below) to write into the licence individually, e.g. connection charges for business and rental subscribers, connection charges and rentals on shared lines, peak, standard and cheap rate calls, operator connected calls, directory and special services, etc. (ii) new tariff variations could be introduced without revising the licence (e.g. 'de-averaging' of tariffs or rentals by geographical area); (iii) 'rebalancing' is possible, and relative prices are not constrained to stay the same over (say) 5 years regardless of movements in relative costs; (iv) BT has more flexibility in deciding where to make the required tariff reductions.

13.10 Put rather crudely, the balance of 'political' advantage may lie with the first alternative, but the balance of the 'economic' advantage lies with the second. The 'tariff basket' is recommended here.

13.11 As to the appropriate level of X, the 'Buzby Bond' envisaged a figure of 2 per cent for BT as a whole. At that time, significant reductions in BT's costs were expected. BT's performance target has in fact been set at 5 per cent in 1981/2 and 1982/3; 2.1 and 4.8 per cent have been achieved. The Chairman's statement in the latest published accounts, after referring to the need for rebalancing of tariffs and the tendency for price increases for domestic to be higher than for business customers, states that 'Overall, we are aiming to keep the average of tariff increases, for both business and domestic customers, below the general level of price increases'. The precise figure is a matter for negotiation between BT and DoI.

13.12 To avoid public misunderstanding, it should be clear that a price reduction of X per cent in real terms is consistent with a price increase in nominal terms, unless X is greater than the rate of inflation. It would presumably be politically attractive to guarantee no increase in nominal terms, but this would require BT to take an unjustified gamble with respect to the rate of inflation.

13.13 Should performance targets be set to accompany these tariff reductions? As noted in the discussion of the Working Group's flexibility proposal, the danger is that the DGT and BT will impose on consumers their own view of what consumers ought to want. Nevertheless, it would seem sensible to ensure that quality of service did not deteriorate as a result of the tariff reduction scheme. For example, there may be a danger that BT will delay in connecting new subscribers in areas where connection costs have risen over the allowed level of connection charges, or the grade of service for local calls may be allowed to deteriorate. There are so many possible attributes of quality that it seems difficult to write these into the licence in any specific way, but a clause committing BT not to reduce quality on the monopoly routes would seem useful. The DGT would be required to monitor quality of service, paying special attention to consumer complaints, and if necessary a reference could be made to the MMC.

13.14 In any event, an automatic reference to the MMC after, say, five years seems appropriate. By that time the extent and strength of competition should have become more apparent, and it may be appropriate to extend or restrict the scope of the 'monopoly basket'; to change the value of X or to rebase the calculation; to abolish the tariff reduction scheme altogether or to impose additional constraints.

13.15 An important accompaniment of this scheme would be conditions in the licence designed to ensure (a) that BT does not deter or drive out competition by predatory pricing or some variant thereof, and (b) that any tariff reductions designed to meet competition are passed on to as many consumers as possible. The principal requirement would seem to be a condition that would prevent BT from charging different prices for calls on routes having similar cost structures, so that for example BT could not cut trunk tariffs merely on the routes actually served by Mercury. Such a non-discrimination condition could also be used to ensure that 'transit calls' also benefited: for example, if prices on the route from A to B were cut, non-discrimination could require that the price of a call from A to C which typically transited through B should not exceed the price of AB plus the price of BC. Thus, it may well be that non-discrimination would require a new set of transit routes to be charged at an intermedial rate between standard and low-cost trunk routes. The details of this should be left to BT, and not incorporated into the 'monopoly basket'. However, if BT fails to respond in these directions, and there are allegations and evidence of price discrimination, the DGT will be able to take action for breach of licence.

13.16 To aid in enforcing these licence conditions, BT should be required to publish its tarrifs. This would also facilitate competition. Normally such a requirement for a commercial firm would be inappropriate, but BT is in an abnormally dominant position, and it is in the public interest to facilitate competition as far as possible.

13.17 The following provisions would seem to give effect to the Local Tariff Reduction scheme just described:

(i) BT's licence would define a Local Tariff Index (LTI) comprising rentals, local calls and other services of particular concern (e.g. call boxes);

(ii) BT would be required to set its tariffs in such a way that the LTI did not increase faster than RPI — X per cent, where X is a number to be negotiated;

(iii) BT would be required not to allow the quality of service to deteriorate on the services contained in the LTI;

(iv) BT would be required not to discriminate anti-competitively in setting its tariffs;

(v) BT would be required to publish its tariffs;

(vi) Clauses (i) to (iii) would apply for the first 5 years of the licence only;

(vii) after the fourth year of the licence there should be an automatic reference to the MMC to consider, in all the relevant circumstances and in the light of experience to date, what if any modifications to the licence would be appropriate.

We may now evaluate this scheme against the five criteria.

(a) *Protection against Monopoly*

13.18 Tariff reduction is focused precisely on the services of monopoly concern, and consumers have a guarantee of improvement. Non-discrimination provisions and the knowledge of a licence variation reference to the MMC will provide additional protection on trunk services where competition is likely to be slow to develop. Guaranteed price reductions do reduce the incentive to new entry and perhaps expansion by existing competitors, but the DGT will not be so closely involved with BT as to recommend against granting new licences. It is most important that the X per cent tariff reduction should not be so severe that BT can use it as an excuse to argue against competition in other parts of its business.

(b) *Efficiency and Innovation*

13.19 The local tariff reduction scheme provides no disincentive to efficiency or innovation — indeed, the knowledge that a target has to be met each year may prove a spur to efficiency. Any cost reductions exceeding the agreed target are kept by the company. Since the company plan is to reduce local tariffs in real terms, there is little *additional* reduction in revenue which might hamper investment.

(c) *Burden of Regulation*

13.20 The composition and definition of the LTI will need to be agreed, but BT has already constructed and calculated several indices of this kind. (For example, the Average Residential Bill Index gives weights of 0.406 to rental, 0.261 to local calls, 0.263 to trunk calls and 0.070 to international. There are similar indices for Business and Farm Bills). Monitoring of the LTI would impose a negligible burden. If the RPI — X per cent constraint is violated the DGT will need to ascertain the reason for this and remedial action may need to be taken; but a simple tariff reduction will suffice. The DGT does not have to make any judgements or calculations with respect to capital, allocation of costs, rates of return, future movements of costs and demand, desirable performance, etc. He will need to monitor the non-discrimination clause, but he would need to do so anyway as part of his duties with respect to anti-competitive practices.

(d) *Promotion of Competition*

13.21 Lower prices reduce the incentive to new entry in local services, but the incentive to enter trunk services is not impaired. The DGT would not be more susceptible to capture as a result of this scheme, and hence would not be specially influenced to advise against the licensing of new entry. The non-discrimination and tariff publication clauses, and the knowledge of automatic reference to the MMC, give competitors a better chance of success.

(e) *Proceeds and Prospects*

13.22 The concept of local tariff reduction is consistent with the Chairman's statement quoted in paragraph 13.11 and the tariff constraint leaves BT free to increase profits by reducing costs. BT's prospects should not be impaired and proceeds of sale will be maximised. BT has recently given assurances that tariffs will not be increased, and insofar as public opinion finds the scheme familiar and an acceptable restriction on BT's monopoly power, BT's long-term prospects could be even better than if no constraint at all were imposed.

14. Final evaluation and further recommendations

14.1 In order to compare the Profit Ceiling and Local Tariff Reduction schemes against the other proposed schemes, it will be helpful to extend the table of rankings developed in paragraph 11.30.

Table 2: *Final Ranking of Schemes for Regulating BT's Profitability*

	No Explicit Constraints	Working Group MRR	ORPL	Profit Ceiling	Local Tariff Reduction
Protection against Monopoly	5	3	2	4	1
Efficiency and Innovation	1=	4=	4=	3	1=
Burden of Regulation	1	5	4	3	2
Promotion of Competition	1	5	4	2=	2=
Proceeds and Prospects	1=	4	5	3	1=

14.2 As noted earlier, the MRR and ORPL schemes have merits in providing protection against monopoly, but are subject to serious deficiencies in other respects. Imposing no explicit constraints on profits scores highest on four criteria, but fails to provide adequate short-term protection against monopoly. A profit ceiling avoids the worst disadvantages of the MRR and ORPL schemes but provides less adequate protection against monopoly.

14.3 The local tariff reduction scheme scores very highly on all criteria. It is significantly better than all other schemes with respect to immediate protection against monopoly power in the services which count, for domestic and small businesses. Performance on all other criteria is as good, or nearly as good, as in the absence of explicit constraints. It must therefore be the recommended scheme.

14.4 This is not to say that the scheme has no defects. Imposing real price reductions for five successive years on services with a turnover exceeding £2,000 million, representing nearly half BT's UK telephone business, is no small matter. It represents a greater degree of intervention than would normally be acceptable in a private sector company. Some might regard it as 'the thin end of the wedge'. It could also delay the development of competition which would benefit the very customers the scheme is designed to protect — partly because new entry would be less attractive to potential competitors, and partly because the government might see less need to authorise it. Finally, there is a danger that BT will be able to persuade the government not to licence new entry in other services as a quid pro quo for accepting local tariff reductions. However, no scheme is ideal. All the other schemes we have examined have even more severe disadvantages. Despite its defects, the local tariff reduction scheme is significantly preferable to the available alternatives.

14.5 It is worth noting that profit regulation elsewhere seems to be moving in this direction. In the USA, ineffective but time-consuming annual hearings to establish how far price increases are justified by cost increases are being replaced by 'escalator clauses' which allow automatic price increases up to the amount of some index. The crucial feature is that this index is outside the control of the regulated company (e.g. input prices in the industry or economy as a whole), so that the company has the incentive to reduce costs and keep the difference. In the UK, the MMC has recently recommended abandoning the attempt to monitor the rate of return on contraceptive sheaths achieved by LRC Products (a division of LRC International),* not least because of the difficulty of allocating joint costs between the products of monopoly concern and the rest of the business, and has instead suggested a requirement that product prices not be increased each year by more than an index of costs less 1.5 per cent; this is to last for five years. Such controls are easy to understand, relatively cheap and simple to monitor, they preserve the incentives to efficiency, and they can be focused precisely on the areas of concern so as not to restrict the operation of the business in other respects.

14.6 It might be asked whether there is any advantage to be gained from combining the profit ceiling and local tariff reduction schemes. They seem to complement each other insofar as one focuses on overall profit and the other on particular prices. Indeed, if one were to start with a ceiling scheme, there would be something to be said for adding a

*Report on the supply in the United Kingdom of contraceptive sheaths. MMC, November 1982. Cmnd. 8689.

local tariff reduction scheme to make it more effective. But the converse is not true. If one starts with a local tariff reduction scheme there is no need for a profit ceiling because tariff reductions are designed to protect precisely those services where competition is thought to be inadequate. Even if it is seldom operated, a ceiling scheme still involves the burden of allocating joint costs and calculating rates of return, while if the ceiling is set so low that it is frequently breached, all the disincentives to efficiency of traditional rate of return regulation are introduced. Thus, to impose a profit ceiling on a local tariff reduction scheme is both unnecessary and undesirable.

14.7 If it is still possible to amend the terms of the Telecommunications Bill, three modifications might be considered which would make the proposed regulatory scheme more effective.

(1) Clause 3(1)(b) of the Telecommunications Bill requires the Secretary of State and the DGT to take into account the need for suppliers of telecommunications services to achieve a sufficient return on capital. This is presumably intended to prevent the imposition of too low a maximum rate of return. However, such an obligation invites regulatory capture, and there is a danger that it may be used to restrict entry or competition in order than an incumbent achieve this 'sufficient rate of return'. Such restrictions would seriously weaken the consumer's protection against monopoly. Many of the arguments against a maximum return apply equally to a minimum return. Consideration should be given to removing or modifying this sub-clause.

(2) It is envisaged that BT's licence will require it to provide 'public call box services, emergency services and services in rural areas'. There is no question but that these services ought to be provided. However, the implicit requirement that these services should be partly financed by cross-subsidisation raises the danger that the cost of provision (which will not become apparent) may be used as another argument to restrict competition or entry (the 'cream-skimming' argument) but it is not suggested that BT is to make this argument. However, to avoid this danger, provision could be made for explicit public subsidy if an adequate case can be made out by the potential beneficiaries. Clause 42 of the Bill allows local authorities to do this, but there is no provision for the Secretary of State to do so. Admittedly, it might look odd to subsidise the highly profitable BT, but the alternative of restricted competition would be worse. Furthermore, the subsidy need not be limited to BT, hence it might be used to facilitate new entry and cheaper provision (e.g. electricity boards might lay telephone cable to remote rural areas and outlying houses).

(3) Since the MMC is to play a significant role in regulating BT, particularly with respect to modifications in the licence, it is important that a consistent and constructive approach be taken. Clause 11 of the Bill requires the MMC to report on whether any matters operate against the public interest, where this will include regard to the considerations in Clause 3. Now the MMC has come under some criticism for the unpredictability of its verdicts on mergers, especially in the last two years. The main source of concern has been the varied interpretation of the phrase 'public interest'. It would seem preferable if, in the context of licences for telecommunication operators, the MMC were required to report on whether any matters were likely adversely to affect competition. Alternatively, their criteria might be Clause 3 itself. In either case, the ambiguous phrase 'public interest' would be better omitted.

14.8 It has been argued throughout this Report that effective regulation requires increasing competitive pressure. Without it, the regulator as well as consumers are at the mercy of a dominant supplier. It may be helpful here to review some of the ways in which competition could be encouraged.

(1) The Department's provisional view that switching of interactive services between cable TV networks should be done by BT or Mercury might be modified to allow the cable companies themselves to compete with BT and Mercury; their incremental costs of providing some local telephone service might be rather low. Other potential networks should also be allowed to compete with BT and Mercury for the business. Nationalised industries and other companies owning suitable rights of way should be encouraged to participate.

(2) The extent of competition from mobile radios, cellular radio and microwave networks is limited by the amount of spectrum made available for these uses. Of course, there is an overall scarcity of suitable spectrum, and there are other uses for it, but if more could be made available for telecommunications it would enable more effective competition to take place and facilitate additional public networks besides Mercury. The interim recommendation of the Merriman Committee, that spectrum formerly used for 405 line TV be reallocated to mobile radio, is a step in the right direction.

(3) There should be positive encouragement for market entry by network operators exploiting alternative terrestrial and space technologies to those being used by BT and Mercury. An important example would be a domestic satellite network combining data and video transmission with telecommunication services.

(4) A number of large companies have extensive private networks which they are not presently allowed to make available to other interested parties (such as their dealers). Allowing shared use of private networks (among a closed user group) would provide more competition.

(5) Continuation of BT's monopoly of the first instrument will restrict competition in sales of equipment. Consideration should be given to ending this monopoly at an early date.

(6) Most important of all, unrestricted resale of BT's circuits for voice telephony would bring a significant reduction in prices of trunk calls to more closely align them with the price of private circuits. BT's licence should therefore require it to allow resale for voice. Since BT might respond by raising circuit prices, it is all the more important that Mercury and other competitors are allowed to provide circuits, and that BT should be prevented from price discriminating between routes subject to direct competition and other routes where it has a monopoly.

(7) Competition should be particularly encouraged on international business. There are international agreements which must be respected, and no doubt there are also questions of national interest to be considered. Nonetheless, the arrangements which existed when BT was a nationalised monopoly will not necessarily be appropriate after privatisation. Competition for BT is presently restricted. Mercury is able to lease circuits to other countries, but the terms and standards of these leases are effectively negotiated by BT, and Mercury is prohibited from access to public switched networks abroad i.e. it can only link with individual customers. Alternative negotiating arrangements should be explored, perhaps using OFTEL or an association of telecommunications operators (with unrestricted membership). Arrangements could probably be made for linking with switched networks in the USA and perhaps with networks in other countries, provided that UK government approval and encouragement were given. The prospect of access to international business would be a significant factor in encouraging other potential entrants into the domestic market. Finally, the logic of the argument for unrestricted resale of leased lines applies with equal force to international as to domestic markets.

14.9 The Secretary of State expressed a desire for regulation with a light rein. The present study suggests that the most effective way of achieving this is by facilitating the entry of new competitors, inserting clauses in BT's licence to extend the benefits of existing competition, and introducing a local tariff reduction scheme to protect domestic and small business subscribers until adequate competition develops.

APPENDIX 1: Theoretical analysis of an output-related profits levy

1. This appendix presents a brief technical analysis of ORPL. The aim is to increase our understanding of how ORPL is likely to work — in particular, what determines a firm's response to the imposition of such a levy.

2. Large-scale computer models of a particular organisation could be envisaged as a means of exploring the effects of ORPL — from the perspective of the firm itself or the regulator. Such a model of the Bell System has been used to explore the effects of alternative depreciation policies. However, the construction and application of such a model could take several years. For present purposes we need something that can be analysed in a matter of days.

3. The model assumes a profit-maximising producer of a single product; simple cost and demand functions involving no links over time (e.g. no capital equipment) and perfect information about the future. This is undoubtedly a crude and over-simplified model, and its significance must not be over-rated. Nevertheless, it does provide certain useful insights.

4. In particular, the model enables us to examine two fundamental propositions that have been taken for granted: (1) that ORPL will increase output, and (2) that the extent of the firm's response to ORPL will be greater the higher is elasticity of demand. The model shows that the first proposition is not necessarily true, and the second is false — in fact, the converse is true (within the context of the model).

5. Intuitively, ORPL has three main effects on the firm. If this year's output is increased (past the point of profit maximisation) then, other things being equal, there will be (i) a *reduction* in this year's pre-levy profits; (ii) a *reduction* in the rate of levy applied to this year's profits; and (iii) an *increase* in the rate of levy applied to next year's profits (because increasing output this year *ipso facto* reduces growth next year). Thus, increasing output will be profitable if the levy falls enough to yield higher after-tax profits on lower pre-tax profits, *provided* that this gain is not outweighed by the reduction in post-levy profits in the next year.

6. To make all this precise, it will be convenient to use a continuous-time model. For purposes of numerical computation and forward planning, a discrete-time multiperiod model would be preferable, but our aim here is to gain some qualitative insights.

7. Let $x(t)$ denote the level of output over time t. Let $\pi(x,t)$ denote (expected total profit as a function of output. Let $\theta(\dot{x}/x)$ be the proportion of total profit retained after the imposition of the levy.* This is an increasing function of the proportional rate of growth of output, hence $\theta'(\dot{x}/x) > 0$.

8. Assume that the firm's aim is to choose its pattern of output to maximise the (expected) present value of profits at discount rate r over a finite (but distant) horizon T. Formally, the problem is to choose the function $x(t)$ to

$$\underset{x(t)}{\text{maximise}} \int_0^T e^{-rt}\, \theta(\dot{x}/x)\, \pi(x, t)\, dt \qquad (1)$$

9. After some manipulation, the Euler optimality condition for the maximisation of (1) can be written (suppressing t for simplicity)

$$\pi'(x) + \frac{\pi}{x} \cdot \frac{\delta\,(r-g)}{h} = 0 \qquad (2)$$

where $\delta = \frac{\theta'}{\theta} \cdot \frac{\dot{x}}{x}$ is the elasticity of post-levy profit retention rate with respect to output growth, $g = \dot{\pi}/\pi$ is the rate of growth of profit and $h = \dot{x}/x$ is the rate of growth of output.

10. In the conventional tax system, in which levy rate does not vary with output growth, we have $\delta = 0$ hence $\pi'(x) = 0$. This is the familiar result that a profit-maximiser chooses output such that marginal profit is zero.

11. With ORPL, positive growth reduces the tax rate, hence $\delta > 0$. Assuming that output is growing ($h > 0$), the second term in (2) is positive or negative according to whether $(r-g)$ is positive or negative, consequently the first term $\pi'(x)$ is negative or positive according to whether $(r-g)$ is positive or negative. Now $\pi'(x)$ negative indicates an output

*A dot above any parameter indicates differentiation with respect to time, a prime will denote differentiation with respect to output or growth.

beyond the profit-maximising level, and $(r-g)$ positive means that profits are growing at a lower rate than the discount rate.

12. Thus we have *Proposition 1*: The imposition of ORPL leads to an expansion or contraction of output according to whether the growth rate of profits is less than or greater than the discount rate. Under 'normal' circumstances, when pre-levy profits are growing at a rate not exceeding the discount rate, ORPL will lead to an expansion of output as expected. But in the event that profits are growing faster than the discount rate, it is advantageous to restrict current output so as to expand future output and lower the future levy rate. Roughly speaking, it is advantageous to arrange for the lowest levy to be paid on the highest profit.

13. If we consider the effect of ORPL at different points on the 'profit cycle', the firm will be induced to (i) expand at a moderate rate at the height of the boom and the depth of the slump (when $g=0$), (ii) expand at a faster rate during the post-boom downswing (when $g<0$), and (iii) expand at a slower rate, or even contract, during the post-slump upswing. At the same time, however, there seems to be a built-in 'stabiliser'; as output growth (h) increases, the adjustment is reduced, and as output growth declines, the adjustment (h) is increased, thereby tending to offset the profit cycle effect.

14. Now suppose that total cost is directly proportional to output, so that profit may be written

$$\pi(x)=[p(x)-c]\,x \qquad (3)$$

where $p(x)$ is the inverse demand function and c is constant marginal cost. Then

$$\pi'(x)=(p-c)+x\,p'=(p-c)-\frac{p}{e} \qquad (4)$$

where $e=-p/xp'$ is the absolute price elasticity of demand. Substituting (3) and (4) into (2) and rearranging yields

$$\frac{p-c}{p}=\frac{1}{ke} \qquad (5)$$

where

$$k=1+\frac{\delta\,(r-g)}{h} \qquad (6)$$

15. ORPL evidently serves to multiply the firm's perceived price elasticity of demand by the factor k, hence—

Proposition 2: The effect of ORPL is greater (i) the greater the elasticity of the levy schedule (i.e. the greater the reduction in levy for a given output increase); (ii) the greater the discount rate (i.e. the less important it is to worry about effects on future profits); (iii) the lower the growth rate of profit; and (iv) the lower the growth rate of output.

16. Finally, consider how the effect of ORPL varies with the level of price elasticity of demand. Recall, however, that a profit-maximiser will always operate where demand is price elastic, hence one can only compare different degrees of price elasticity, rather than elastic and inelastic demands. From (5), we have the explicit expression for price

$$\frac{p}{c}=\frac{ke}{ke-1} \qquad (7)$$

Proportionate change in price after imposing ORPL is given by—

$$\frac{p-p_o}{p_o}=\left(\frac{ke}{ke-1}-\frac{e}{e-1}\right)\div\frac{e}{e-1} \qquad (8)$$

$$=\frac{1-k}{ke-1}$$

For $k>1$, that is for the 'normal' case where $g<r$, this is a decreasing function of e. Proportionate change in quantity is given approximately by

$$\frac{x-x_o}{x_o}\simeq -e.\ \frac{p-p_o}{p_o}=\frac{(k-1)}{ke-1} \qquad (9)$$

which is also a decreasing function of e. That is;

Proposition 3: the higher the elasticity of demand, the *lower* the proportionate change in both price and quantity as a result of introducing ORPL.

APPENDIX 2: On constructing a practicable scheme for ORPL

1. Because ORPL is a novel idea, which had not yet been examined, the terms of reference required a practicable scheme to be developed before evaluating it against alternative schemes. The material in Section 9, and to some extent in Section 10, specify the main practical details of a possible scheme. Section 10 and this Appendix analyse some of the properties of this scheme. The Appendix is admittedly limited to a simple and unrealistic case (unconstrained profit-maximisation with perfect knowledge), but nonetheless it provides certain cautionary insights (see paragraph 4 in Appendix 1).

2. Some numerical calculations were also carried out, extending the example mentioned in paragraph 9.5 to include the response of pricing and output policy to the imposition of ORPL. These examples were based on BT's accounts for the last six years. However, the elasticities of demand and company objectives upon which these calculations were based were purely illustrative, and it was thought that to include these examples in this Report would be misleading. There was not sufficient time to make more realistic calculations.

3. If a government were contemplating introducing a variant of ORPL, it would clearly be vital to have a reasonable idea of how the company would respond with respect to price and output. This would also be necessary in order to calibrate the levy. Ideally, a 'pilot scheme' would be run, albeit on paper.

4. The difficulties of such an undertaking should not be underestimated. At a minimum it is necessary to specify (a) the objectives of the company (b) the elasticities of demand and cost which the company is facing (and those which it *believes* it is facing, if these are different). Account must be taken of uncertainty concerning the future, the problems of motivation and the effects of decentralised decision-making. The company's response, and the means of analysis, will depend upon whether an aggregate tariff index is adopted or a disaggregated set of quantities. In either case it is necessary to consider how the pattern of output, not merely the 'total', will change.

5. Despite these difficulties, further study would be worthwhile insofar as there could well be other situations more favourable to the adoption of ORPL. Circumstances here could hardly have been more adverse: a change in company ownership and objectives, the biggest company flotation by an order of magnitude, denationalisation under political opposition, rapidly changing technology and market conditions, no effective existing tax, considerable public concern, and pressure of the parliamentary timetable. In more propitious circumstances, the conclusion might be quite different.

Printed in the UK for Her Majesty's Stationery Office
PS 3419825 Dd.8248293 C5 10/83 CCP

[23]

CONTESTABILITY: DEVELOPMENTS SINCE THE BOOK

By WILLIAM J. BAUMOL* *and* ROBERT D. WILLIG†

THE ideas encompassed in the theory of contestable markets have entered both the academic literature and the discussions of practitioners with surprising speed. At hearings before regulatory agencies in antitrust cases, terms such as "economies of scope," "sustainable prices" and "contestable markets" are interjected casually as though long usage has made their connotations familiar to everyone. This is in part attributable to the steady stream of papers, published and about to be published by authors offering careful theoretical extensions and critiques, empirical and interpretative applications, as well as heated reactions to contestability theory.

The central focus of this paper is a summary of substantive developments relating to contestability since the appearance of our book. We will discuss four subjects: theoretical advances provided by others, econometric studies using the multiproduct cost concepts accompanying contestability analysis, market simulation studies testing various attributes of contestability, and policy developments, covering both policy studies in the economic literature and some remarkable decisions in the regulatory and antitrust arenas, that rely explicitly on the theory of contestability.

However, before reaching these central areas in order to deal with any remaining misunderstandings we shall begin with a brief restatement of some of the things our work does not and was not intended to imply and the things we instead hope it accomplishes. Specifically, we will deny emphatically that it offers carte blanche to mindless deregulation and dismantling of antitrust safeguards. On the contrary, so far as policy is concerned, contestability theory provides guidance in ascertaining where intervention is warranted socially, and it provides a more widely applicable benchmark to guide regulatory agencies and the courts in those arenas where intervention is called for by considerations of economic welfare.

Contestability and "libertarian" ideology

Contestability theory does not, and was not intended to, lend support to those who believe (or almost seem to believe) that the unrestrained market automatically solves all economic problems and that virtually all regulation and antitrust activity constitutes a pointless and costly source of economic inefficiency. In a market that approximates perfect contestability, it is true,

* Princeton and New York Universities.

† Princeton University. The authors want to thank the Information Science and Technology Division and the Regulation and Policy Analysis Program of the National Science Foundation and the C. V. Starr Center for Applied Economics for their generous support of this research. We also wish to acknowledge with gratitude the able assistance of Daniel Schult and the useful comments of Marius Schwartz.

we believe matters can be left to take care of themselves. Small numbers of large firms, vertical and even horizontal mergers and other arrangements which have traditionally been objects of suspicion of monopolistic taint and worse, are rendered harmless and perhaps even beneficent by the presence of contestability. But that observation is no whitewash and establishes no presumption, one way or the other, about the desirability of public sector intervention in any particular market of reality. For before anyone can legitimately use the analysis to infer that virtue reigns in some economic sector and that interference is therefore unwarranted, that person must first provide evidence that the arena in question is, in fact, highly contestable. The economy of reality is composed of sectors which vary widely in the degree to which they approximate the attributes of contestability. Thus, the conclusion that *perfectly* contestable markets require no intervention claims little more than the possibility (which remains to be proven, case by case) that *some* markets in reality may automatically perform in a very acceptable manner despite the small number of firms that inhabit them.

Thus, it is simply incorrect to associate our writings on contestability with an all-pervasive laissez-faire position on the role of regulation and antitrust (for such a characterization of our position see, e.g., Shepherd (1984)). We disagree vehemently with such a view of the world. On the other hand, we reject with equal conviction the position of those who hold that mere large size of a firm means that it *must* serve the economy badly, that high concentration ratios are sufficient to justify governmental restrictions upon the structure or conduct of an industry or that a horizontal merger merits automatic condemnation if it increases concentration ratios substantially. For it is true that a high degree of contestability, where and if it does happen to hold sway, should remove the undesirable consequences which might otherwise stem from these phenomena. Thus, contestability theory supports neither extreme interventionists nor extreme noninterventionists. We believe that antitrust and regulation have valuable roles to play, and that contestability theory can help to identify and sharpen those roles and thereby benefit the public.

Objectives of contestability research

Contestability theory offers an analytic framework within which the fundamental features of demands and production technology determine the shape of industry structure and many of the characteristics of industry prices. The theory accomplishes this via a process of simplification; by stripping away through its assumptions all barriers to entry and exit, and the strategic behavior that goes along with them both in theory and in reality.

The model of perfect competition has also served an analogous simplifying role, and in so doing has provided the foundation for the most elegant and well-articulated portions of economic theory. However, because the model of perfect competition prespecifies industry structure by its very construction, it cannot serve as a useful benchmark for the study of the determinants of industrial structure. Perfect competition is a special case of perfect contestability, and perfect contestability applies with equal force to circumstances where perfect competition is impossible because economies of scale are present. Because of this fact, and because contestability theory encompasses an endogenous determination mechanism from which any industry structure may emerge (depending on circumstances), we feel that it is an extension of the competitive model appropriate for use in the theory of industrial organization.

In addition to this broad purpose in theoretical analysis, we feel that research on contestable markets has two objectives related to policy. The first is the establishment of an improved set of guidelines for appropriate government intervention in the structure and conduct of firms and industries, that is, of the rules to bc followed by the regulators and antitrust authorities in those cases in which their intervention is called for. The second objective for policy analysis is the determination of criteria distinguishing between those cases in which intervention by the public sector is warranted and those in which it is not.

With regard to the first policy objective, it is widely understood that the basic guideline for intervention should be replication of the consequences of effective market forces in those cases in which competition, actual or potential, is insufficient to do the job. That is, intervention should aim to induce or compel an industry in which monopoly power is present to perform as it would if effective competitive pressures were available. But, for such cases perfect competition is often unsuitable as a standard, particularly in circumstances common to regulatory and antitrust issues where scale economies and related attributes dictate the presence of only a small number of firms, at least some of them relatively large.

Here, as we will see from recent developments in regulatory practice that will be reviewed presently, contestability theory was, indeed, able to suggest answers where other bodies of theory did not. Moreover, it was able to eliminate curious gaps in the standard theory of policy. Perhaps the most noteworthy of these was the lack of a defensible criterion for regulatory ceilings on prices, though one would have thought that to be the first order of business for social control of firms with monopoly power. Yet, to our knowledge, neither regulators nor courts previously had available to them from the theoretical literature any defensible test to determine just when a particular price set by one of the multiproduct firms of reality was excessive. We will also see later how contestability theory determines how high is enough and will observe that regulatory agencies have begun to adopt the criterion that emerges, with explicit acknowledgement of its source.

In saying this, we do not mean to claim that the theory sheds light on the welfare economics of markets that are highly uncontestable. The theory does not even try to contribute to the analysis of behavior in such cases or to the evaluation of the social cost of any resulting departures from optimality. All the analysis pretends to say about such cases is that if they entail behavior which is deemed socially undesirable and if government undertakes to change this behavior, then it is appropriate to require the individuals to act as they would have if the threat of potential competition had constrained them effectively. If, for example, firms charge prices and earn profits that are deemed excessive, it is appropriate to offer consumers the protection that the threat of barrier free entry would have provided them.

Finally, we feel that contestability theory has helped to show that in *some* cases where regulatory or antitrust intervention was previously common, it was in fact undesirable. Contestability theory, we think, does help to clarify which arenas are the proper candidates for deregulation and cessation of other forms of intervention. But the theory neither calls for anything like universal deregulation nor for its automatic extension without careful study of the pertinent facts, case by case.

Theoretical developments

There has been an outpouring of theoretical work on contestable markets and allied subjects, as there has been recently throughout the field of industrial organization (as this very volume indicates). Our brief overview of the recent developments cannot do justice to the full range of valuable contributions and is, unfortunately, bound to miss important items. This review is organized into four topics: (i) conditions for sustainability of prices set by a monopoly incumbent; (ii) theoretical applications of contestability; (iii) the characteristics of production cost that determine market structure in contestable markets; and (iv) the relationship between strategic firm behavior and contestability.

In our book (1982), we identified one set of conditions sufficient to assure the existence of sustainable prices for a multi-output natural monopolist, and those conditions also were shown to guarantee that the Ramsey optimal prices are sustainable. Among those conditions are the stipulations that the cost function exhibit overall economies of scale and the property of trans-ray convexity. We showed that the sustainability of Ramsey prices could tolerate some deviation from these properties, such as product-specific fixed costs of bounded magnitude. Faulhaber and Levinson (1981) developed the idea of anonymously equitable prices which offered no cross-subsidies to any possible groups of consumers, and connected the properties of such prices to sustainability. Sharkey ((1981) and (1982)) and Spulber (1984) presented new sets of conditions sufficient for the sustainability of monopoly prices, and showed that the Ramsey prices need not be among them. ten Raa ((1983) and (1984)) sharpened the connections among subsidy-free, market-clearing, and sustainable prices. Mirman, Tauman and Zang (1985) further clarified these connections, established novel sets of sufficient conditions for the existence of sustainable prices, and identified conditions under which the Aumann-Shaply prices would be sustainable.

Brown and Heal provided the valuable result that where Ramsey prices are unsustainable, the government can solve the consequent policy conflict between open entry and optimal prices via a system of excise taxes and subsidies to incumbent and any entrants alike. Working in a general equilibrium context with independent demands for the outputs of the natural monopolist, they proved the existence of such a tax system, with zero net effect on government revenues, that permits Ramsey optimal consumers' prices and sustainable producers' prices.

Panzar and Postlewaite (1985) demonstrated the sustainability of Ramsey optimal non-linear prices where costs are linear, and provided counterexamples for other circumstances. In contrast to the usual results for contestable markets, Perry (1982) showed that a natural monopolist can at once earn positive profits and deter entry by commiting itself to the sale of some units of homogeneous output at prices lower than those that apply to marginal purchases.

Our second category of new theoretical work comprises applications of contestability to various issues. Quirmbach (1982) studied vertical integration by an upstream monopolist into a competitive downstream industry. While the welfare effects are, in general, ambiguous, Quirmbach showed that profitable integration would raise social welfare if the upstream market were perfectly contestable.

In their pathbreaking book, Helpman and Krugman (1985) provide a sketch of a new theory of international trade in which industries in the trading nations are perfectly contestable rather than perfectly competitive, as in conventional trade theory. This construction permits them to study the effects of increasing returns to scale in the production processes internal to firms, without the need to specify particular forms of oligopolistic and strategic behavior. Among their conclusions are the result that the sustainable factor-price-equalization equilibrium is a highly useful construct for trade analysis; that even in the presence of economies of scale comparative advantage shapes trade patterns with unequal factor rewards; and that there is a strong presumption that there will be gains from trade when national and international markets are contestable.

Recent work on properties of production costs has been stimulated by the significance they have for the character of industry structure in contestable markets. Weitzman (1983) showed that constant returns to scale must hold when demand can be met by the instantaneous accumulation of inventories created by production that is turned on and off repeatedly without additional costs. He concluded that the hit and run entry opportunities said to be a necessary part of contestability must then be inconsistent with increasing returns to scale. In reply, we pointed out that quantities of services cannot be accumulated in inventories, no matter how short their duration, and that contestability does not require the ability to start and stop production costlessly—only the ability to sell without vulnerability to incumbents' responses for a time long enough to render all production costs economically reversible.

Teece (1982) has contributed illuminating work on the sources of economies of scope, both in theory and in specific applications. Gorman (1985) has recently provided theoretical results on economies of scope where there are complementarities or anticomplementarities in marginal costs and also product specific fixed costs that may be subadditive or superadditive. Bittlingmayer (1985) has provided a theoretical analysis that builds multiservice cost functions for airlines upon the foundation of the costs of operating aircraft. He finds economies of scope among routes arising from the hub and spoke architecture of the cost efficient configuration of routes. He goes on to study the characteristics of rate structures that are sustainable and that are Ramsey optimal.

The final category of theoretical work, the relationships between contestability and strategic firm behavior, is most difficult to review succinctly because it is intertwined with the bulk of new research in industrial organization concerning strategy and oligopoly solution concepts. Perfect contestability is a theoretical benchmark that is by its very construction immune from considerations of strategic behavior by dint of its assumption of the absence of economically sunk costs and irreversible commitments necessary for entry. Nevertheless, as pointed out by our distinguished reviewers, Brock (1983) and Spence (1983), and by our constructive critic Schwartz (1985), it is worthwhile to investigate what forms of game and what models of dynamic strategic oligopoly yield outcomes consistent or inconsistent with contestability. Here, Knieps and Vogelsang (1982) and Brock and Scheinkman (1983) have contributed models of quantity sustainability in which outcomes are quite different from those in contestable markets because potential cntrants take incumbents' quantities rather than prices as given. In view of the enlightening work of Kreps and Scheinkman (1983), it is now clear that quantity-taking behavior is a reflection of precommitments to quantity-determining capacity by firms that later simultaneously announce prices.

In contrast, contestable outcomes are yielded by Nash equilibrium in a price setting game without precommitments (Mirman, Tauman, and Zang (1983)), and in a game in which supply schedules comprise the strategy sets (Grossman (1981)). We showed that contestable outcomes are a necessary feature of equilibrium in the limit as sunk costs approach zero, using a model in which incumbents' prices are sticky for at least a short period of time (Baumol, Panzar, and Willig (1983)). Maskin and Tirole (1982) analyze a model of dynamic oligopoly involving firms with fixed costs and show that the solution approaches the contestable outcome as strategic advantages fall to zero. In contrast to these results, Dasgupta and Stiglitz (1985) provide models in which incumbents' strategic advantages over a single potential entrant, no matter how small those advantages may be, permit the incumbents to earn economic profits without danger of entry. And Applebaum and Lim (1985) have contributed a model in which the degree of contestability is endogenous, determined by the incumbent's incentives to commit to quantity-determining capacity in view of demand uncertainty and the pattern of costs over time.

In short, there is a flood of exciting research activity in the area of strategic firm behavior, and one of the ways in which the various models are differentiated is the relationship between the games' solutions and the outcomes that would emerge in perfectly contestable markets. At present, that relationship seems to be highly sensitive to the fine grained structure of the models' game forms, so much so that one suspects that empirical reality embodies relationships more robust and stable than does oligopoly theory in its current tumultuous state.

Experimental market studies of contestability

The fruitful and growing body of research using experimental simulation of market behavior has produced a number of papers investigating contestability issues. This work uses human subjects (usually students), real money payoffs and experimental rules corresponding to preselected cost and other pertinent functions that permit direct calculation of the results predicted by theory and their comparison with those that are observed from the behavior of the experimental subjects.

Taking off from earlier studies on monopoly behavior, Coursey, Isaac and Smith (1984) undertook the first of the experimental studies of contestability. They sought to determine whether complete freedom of entry and exit in a market which could most cheaply be served by one firm but where at least two (potential) participants were available would yield prices closer to the competitive than the monopoly level (they call this the "weak contestable markets hypothesis") or to prices actually equal to the competitive level (the "strong contestable market hypothesis"). Participants were given money which they were required to spend in accord with a strictly decreasing and known marginal cost function, the amount spent depending on how much of the good they decided to "produce". The consumers' demand function was also given but was not known by the sellers (except by experience derived from repeated play) who kept for themselves any excess of sales revenues over costs. A participant made a sale if that person's price offer was not undercut by a rival. Both sellers were required to post their price and quantity offers privately, *and* at the same time. Any seller was permitted (but not required) to sell less than the amount the market demanded at the posted price. The authors concluded that "the . . . experiments strongly support the contestable markets hypothesis, namely, that to observe approximately competitive behavior by a single producing firm with substantially decreasing costs, it is sufficient that (a) sunk costs are zero and (b) there are two contesting firms acting non-cooperatively in the sense that there is no explicit nonprice communication between them that leads to excessive restriction of supply" (Coursey, Isaac, Luke and Smith (1984) p. 69).

Harrison (1985) reaches a rather weaker conclusion from these results and those that emerge from a replication of the experiments (Harrison and McKee (1985) (1987)). Using as test criterion an "index of monopoly effectiveness" $M = (\pi - \pi c)/(\pi m - \pi c)$, where π, πc and πm are, respectively, the total profit that emerges from an experiment, the competitive, and the monopoly profit levels. They note that four of the six experiments did attain the $M = 0$ value expected of perfect contestability after 10 periods (i.e., 10 replications of the experiment by a given set of players). However, over all replications M averaged 29 percent in the original set of experiments and 19 percent in the second set, which while not very far from a competitive result, "... is significantly positive." Thus, they conclude, "clearly, we can reject this strong form of the CMH (contestable markets hypothesis)" (p. 13) (the pages refer to the unpublished manuscript).

The Harrison McKee study also concludes from experiments using essentially the same procedure that "... the discipline of contestability does serve to mitigate the monopoly (significantly) when we compare it to an unregulated monopoly ... (but) enlightened monopoly regulation vastly outperforms contestability in terms of reducing monopoly effectiveness" (Harrison, pp. 13–14). (Here the regulator's role is simulated by the offer of a subsidy payment equal to the consumers' surplus from any output exceeding the monopoly level, as calculated from the demand curve.)

In another experiment, Coursey, Isaac, Luke and Smith (1984) evaluate the effects of sunk costs imposed equally on "incumbents" and "entrants". The sunk cost takes the form of a $2 entry permit, valid for five periods. The incumbent is one of two sellers chosen randomly and permitted to operate as a monopolist for five periods. Thereafter, the other seller is permitted to enter and post prices that compete with the incumbent, who is required to purchase an entry permit in period 5 in order to continue operation in periods 6–10. The results, according to Harrison's reanalysis, exhibit no limit pricing behavior and indicate "... that the threat of *future* entry in period six imposed virtually no discipline on the incumbent in periods 1–5" (p. 15). He also notes that the sunk costs constitute a differential incremental risk to the entrant (and hence an entry barrier) only in period 6–10. Accordingly, he considers it noteworthy that "For all eighteen periods there is a slight and statistically insignificant effect of sunk costs reducing efficiency. However, there is a significant decline in efficiency in periods 6–10 due to sunk costs" (pp. 19–20).

Finally, Harrison tested the effects of imposition in the Bertrand–Nash (or, perhaps more accurately, the Stackelberg leader–follower) assumption that entrants take the incumbents' prices to be given—a premise widely associated with contestability. This was done by letting all participants post prices simultaneously in the first period, designating the winner as the next periods' incumbent, who is then *required to post a price before anyone else does, and to announce it publicly,* with the following periods handled in the same way. Both two and three participant experiments were run. The author concludes, "... satisfaction of the Bertrand–Nash assumption is associated with a dramatic decline in (*M*)... Moreover, we find support... for a *strong form* of the (contestable market hypothesis) that claims that observed prices will converge to *and attain* competitive predictions" p. 37, italics in original).

These results would appear to offer strong support for the conclusions of contestability theory but, unfortunately, they still leave a major gap with which future research will have to deal. As Marius Schwartz, in his latest paper criticizing contestability theory, rightly observes "Harrison's experiments basically do constitute a fair test of behavior under perfect contestability: the incumbent faces a price response lag and the entrant can hit and run costlessly. The real question, however, is not whether competitive results will emerge under perfectly contestable conditions but how often such conditions are likely to exist and what happens when they do not" (Schwartz (1985) p. 20, footnote omitted). Put another way, the critical issue that remains is the determination of the circumstances under which the Bertrand–Nash assumption holds or at least is assumed by the participants to hold approximately. It is noteworthy to have it confirmed that *imposition* of Bertrand–Nash behavior leads to the results predicted by the theory. However, that result still leaves work for future statistical or experimental investigation, which Harrison and his colleagues are pursuing.

Econometric studies: multiproduct cost functions and industry structure

In the past three years there has been an outpouring of empirical studies using the cost concepts derived from the contestable markets literature (see the survey of earlier work by Bailey and Friedlaender (1982)). They provide estimates of the shapes of ray averages cost curves, of economies of scope, of the *M*-locus (the locus of points of minimum ray average costs on each ray in product-quantity space). Many such studies use the functional forms for the multiproduct cost function that were recommended in our book. The empirical studies encompass a wide range of industries, including banking, rail, truck and water transportation, insurance, hospitals and a number of others. Here we can only recapitulate briefly a sample of these studies which, predictably, show that industries differ markedly in their scale and scope attributes and in their degree of approximation to contestability.

I. Cost function estimates

Perhaps the most consistent message of the "new" multiproduct cost studies is that the results of previous work using Cobb–Douglas or CES functional forms cannot be trusted. The more general translog form used by most of the multiproduct literature contains, as special cases, the Cobb–

Douglas and CES forms. The appropriateness of these forms can be tested within the translog framework, and in all such tests reported, those forms are rejected in favor of the general translog form.[1]

A. *Banking and related activities*

Banking institutions seem a natural subject for multiproduct analysis. Gilligan, Smirlock and Marshall (1984) and Gilligan and Smirlock (1984) divide output into deposits and loans, using data on many banks provided by the Federal Reserve System. They find that there are large economies of scope "across the balance sheet." They suggest banking theory explicitly consider that fact, and that bank regulation intended to affect one output also be analyzed in multiproduct terms. They encounter decreasing ray average costs (RAC) for small banks, concluding that some small single-bank markets may indeed be subadditive. Overall scale economies are estimated to dissipate as bank size increases, and banks with deposits of $100 million or more manifest increasing RAC. Product specific dis-economies of scale also appear and the authors conclude that policy that precludes entry and encourages mergers cannot be justified by any cost savings.

Murray and White (1983) examine the investment side of British Columbian credit unions. They find significant economies of scope between mortgages and consumer lending and no economies of scope between all lending and investments. Unlike the U.S. studies, returns to scale are observed in most credit unions in the study. The authors conclude that regulation to "inhibit growth and diversification" hampers market efficiency.

Using the same output categories (mortgages, other lending, and investments) for Californian Savings and Loan data, Mester (1985) finds both overall and product specific constant returns to scale, suggesting that large assets offer no cost advantage. She also finds no advantage to a network of branches, given asset size, and absence of economies of scope between outputs. She rejects cost convexity, although finding pairwise transray convexity, and ray subadditivity along some rays.

Kellner and Mathewson (1983) provide a multiproduct analysis of the life insurance industry. They use a four-output industry model. Scale effects are rejected for the average firm while economies of scope appear in some

[1] Note that the translog form is itself unreasonable for cases involving zero output of one product since then the translog form implies that the total cost of the remaining products must be zero, no matter what their output levels. One method used to avoid this problem is recourse to a Box–Cox transformation of the outputs. (See Caves, Christensen, and Tretheway (1980) for a discussion of the translog form.) As an alternative, Friedlaender, Winston, and Kung Wang (1983) use a quadratic approximation to a hedonic function to deal with the problem. The quadratic form also offers a simple measure of economies of scale and scope as well as marginal cost.

product lines. In contrast to previous work, they find no evidence of "natural monopoly tendencies" in the cost structure.

B. *Transportation*

Bailey and Friedlaender (1982) discuss work done on the trucking and railroad industries. Network configurations are reported to offer large economies of scope in both industries. These bias upward the measures of scale effects in single product analyses. In the case of trucking, apparent scale economies disappear for large firms when multiproduct analysis is used. Thus, single product analysis of scale effects may improperly reflect scope effects.

Stimulated by the examination of the regulation of bus transport by the Interstate Commerce Commission (ICC), Tauchen, Fravel, and Gilbert (1983) examine the cost structure, taking regular travel, charter, local service and school busing as the outputs of the industry. Using data on 950 privately owned intercity bus firms in the United States, they find that economies of scale are exhausted at low output levels while economies of scope occur throughout. They point out that price and entry regulation is usually meant to deal with economies of scale which are minor here. Economies of scope can be enhanced by fostering of service cooperation among firms in terms of schedules, interlining of tickets and baggage and use of common terminals.

Friedlaender, Winston, and Kung Wang (1983) examine the American auto industry's cost surface for the individual firm. Output is divided into small cars, large cars and trucks. They find that the size of the firm has little to do with the returns to scope or to scale and that the cost function is not convex; some regions exhibit economies of scale and scope and others exhibit diseconomies. This demonstration of the variability of the industry's cost structures indicates the danger of using the neighborhood of a particular output vector as a basis for the empirical analysis of costs. Generalizations based on studies of aggregate output data are, thus, unreliable.

Caves, Christensen, *et al.* used the multiproduct framework to analyze cost attributes other than economies of scope and scale. In Caves, Christensen and Herriges (1984) they construct models of consumer reactions to peak load electricity rate structures. They also examine productivity growth in U.S. railroads employing multiproduct estimates (Caves, Christensen and Swanson (1981)). And they analyze the effects of deregulation on airline productivity—distinguishing between local service and trunk lines (Caves, Christensen and Tretheway (1983)).

C. *Telecommunications*

Much work has been done on the telecommunications industry. Its output is readily divided at least into local and long distance service, and so constitutes a classic multiproduct case. Evans and Heckman (1984) perform an empirical test of the subadditivity of the industry's costs. To avoid the need for global cost information Evans and Heckman derive a local test for subadditivity by restricting the measurement of subadditivity to a subregion of the observed data. For each year of data they calculate the cost savings offered by a single firm relative to the minimum two-firm cost. Finding all such savings to be positive, they conclude that cost was subadditive during the period 1958–1977.

On the other side, Charnes, Cooper and Sueyoshi (1985) use a goal programing/constrained regression method (derived in operations research studies) and a multiproduct framework, data set and functional form identical with those of Evans and Heckman to obtain opposite results. Basically, they drop the standard economic assumption that the firm always operates on the efficient frontier and seek to derive an envelope from observed costs. While Evans and Heckman found the savings were positive, Charnes, Cooper and Sueyoshi found the maximal savings to be negative. They question the validity of standard econometric procedures, but accept the multiproduct nature of the issue and the test of subadditivity. They stress the importance of use of methods derived from several disciplines, particularly when large issues of policy depend on the outcome.

D. *Other industries*

Cowing and Holtmann (1983) divide hospital care into five care types to analyze the efficiency of general-care hospitals in New York state. They reject the use of a single aggregated measure of output and find the economies of scope "may be at least as important as scale effects in designing more efficient hospital service." They urge policy makers to take scope effects into account when deciding on mergers and encourage future health care research to employ multioutput specifications.

Scott (1982) examines the effects of concentration on manufacturing firms. He investigates the effects of multiproduct competition, or "contact", between firms upon excess profits and resource mobility. He constructs a measure of multimarket contact and then shows that an increase in contact in markets with high sales concentration permits larger profits. However, when sales concentration is low, multiproduct contact can drive profits toward costs.

Vertical integration theory suggests that the presence of economies of scope in an industry need have no categorical implications for the scope of individual firms. Teece (1980) examines this issue and concludes that so long as the economies of scope derive from proprietary information or a specialized indivisible physical asset, a multiproduct enterprise is most efficient. He takes the energy industry as an example of this, where petroleum search and removal techniques can be applied to coal.

Mayo (1984) examines data to pursue Teece's ideas. He uses a cost relationship with coal and petroleum as the outputs. Economies of scope, presumably attributable to similarity of extraction techniques, are found. He also shows that ray average costs decline and, near the axes, declining incremental costs and transray convexity yield evidence of output specific subadditivity. This suggests that divestiture of large laterally integrated petroleum firms may increase costs.

Water supplies are generally run as monopolies in the United States, and Kim and Clark (1983) analyze this industry's cost structure with supplies to residential and nonresidential customers as outputs. Using gallons of water per day as the metric, they find overall constancy in returns to scale. But nonresidential output offers product specific economies while diseconomies appear in residential supply. By analyzing ray average costs for many output mixes, they plot the M-locus for the industry and find it to be concave to the origin. This yields a wide range for the optimal number of firms in a market. In addition, by looking at an "average" ray (79 percent residential), they find that most firms produce near the essentially flat portion of the average cost curve. They conclude that market concentration is generally unnecessary for scale economies and may hinder potential competition in water supply.

II. Tests of the contestability of industries

There have been a number of industry studies seeking to test whether the area of the economy under investigation can legitmately be classed as "contestable". Several, but not all, have yielded results that are somewhat surprising. For example, as we will see below, some studies of the airline industry conclude that the industry is less close to the model of perfect contestability than has sometimes been suggested. On the other hand, one very recent study indicates that the aluminum industry is closer to contestability than might have been expected. Froeb and Geweke (1984) describe the U.S. aluminum industry as an area in which the long term threat of entry drives profits downward. Allowing for short run effects of entry barriers, they test the long run behavior of firms from 1949 to 1972 and find it consistent with that one would expect in an imperfectly contestable market.

On the other hand, the results of some of the studies we are now discussing are less surprising. Extensive work by Davies (1986) for the Canadian Transport Commission on the liner shipping industry concludes that contestability theory may offer the most appropriate model to describe that industry since the transferability and resaleability of capital characterize oceanic shipping. The theory "accounts for the condition of entry to the industry, the cost characteristics and structure of the industry, the existence of loyalty ties (to cartels), the reported absence of supernormal profit and the pricing structure operative in the industry. No other body of theory can explain the existence of all these different phenomena in such a coherent and elegant manner." These conclusions are supported in an independent study of ocean transport by Peter Cassidy (1982).

Contestability and public policy

As has already been said, contestability theory aspires to offer two types of guidance to policy makers: first, it undertakes to provide criteria to distinguish the cases in which government intervention is desirable from those in which it is not and, second, it seeks to offer tools to the regulator that will increase the public welfare benefits of this intervention. There have recently been significant applications of contestability theory on each of these fronts. On both issues we will examine some of the recent discussions in the academic literature and devote the bulk of our attention to pertinent developments in recent regulatory and antitrust decisions.

A. *Contestability as a guide to arenas inappropriate for intervention*

Contestability theory follows the lead of Bain, Sylos-Labini and others in stressing that *potential* competitors, like currently active competitors, can effectively constrain market power, so that when the number of incumbents in a market is few or even where only one firm is present, sufficiently low barriers to entry may make antitrust and regulatory attention unnecessary. Indeed, their costs and the inefficiencies they cause may then offer little or no offsetting benefit.

Since this viewpoint thoroughly antedates contestability theory it is not surprising that it has appeared in a variety of official policies. For example, the 1982 Merger Guidelines of the U.S. Department of Justice defines market power as the ability to profit by raising (and maintaining) price above the competitive level, not referring to market share in that definition. It includes in its market definition firms whose entry would be attracted should an elevation of price be attempted. It asserts, moreover, that mergers will go unchallenged by the Department if they affect only markets subject to potential competition that is sufficiently strong. It proposes to take concentration into account only where potential competition is inadequate.

Similarly, the Federal Communications Commission has shown its awareness of the role of potential competiton. In a recent Notice of Inquiry (FCC (1985)) it adopts a market definition for the analysis of long distance telecommunications similar to that of the Department of Justice. It asserts that "... satellite carriers readily can *shift* their capacity from one area to another and terrestrial carriers can readily *expand* their service areas through new facilities, interconnection, or resale." "There may be numerous large *potential* entrants in common carrier or private systems that further check AT & T's market power to some degree." And, "The absence of entry does not show that an existing firm possess market power; existing firms may be charging competitive prices because of competition among themselves or the *threat* of *potential* entry, and thereby make entry unattractive." Thus, the FCC implies that a large market share need not confer any monopoly power.

Contestability theory makes direct appearances in a recent decision of the Federal Trade Commission (FTC (1985)).[2] The case involved the acquisition in 1982 by the Echlin Manufacturing Corporation of the automotive aftermarket divisions of the Borg Warner Corporation, including its carburetor kit activities which overlapped with some activities of Echlin. The FTC staff challenged the acquisition under Section 7 of the Clayton Act and Section 5 of the Federal Trade Commission Act on the grounds that the merger would add significantly to the concentration of this market.

However, testimony before the Administrative Law Judge indicated that the field was not beset by any significant entry barriers and that potential entry was sufficient to deprive the merged firm of any monopoly power over the assembly and sale of carburetor kits. The Commission agreed, and permitted the acquisition. In its decision the Commission asserted (explicitly citing contestability theory and other writings on potential competition):

> "An attempt to exercise market power in an industry without entry barriers would cause new competitors to enter the market. This additional supply would drive prices back to the competitive level. Indeed, the threat of new entry can be as potent a procompetitive force as its realization. As the Supreme Court has recognized, the presence of potential entrants on the fringe of a market can prevent the exercise of market power by the incumbent firms even if the potential entrants never actually enter the market. Thus, in the absence of barriers to entry, incumbent firms cannot exercise market power, regardless of the concentration in the nominal 'market,' and indeed even if that market has been 'monopolized' by a single firm" (pp. 9–10).

The decision goes on to espouse the same definition of entry barriers as that adopted (from Stigler and others) in the contestability literature "... as additional long-run costs that must be incurred by an entrant relative to the long-run costs faced by incumbent firms" (p. 12) and, again citing the contestability literature, it concludes that "if sunk costs are considered an entry barrier, it must be because they create a difference in the risk confronting the incumbent firms who have already committed their resources and potential entrants who have yet to make that decision" (p. 17). The decision finds, along with contestability analysis, that "... we cannot agree that economies of scale and declining markets necessarily create barriers to entry" (p. 18), and that "the absence of past entry, however, does not prove the existence of entry barriers because it is equally consistent with alternative explanations, such as a declining industry or competitive prices" (p. 19).

[2] It should be made clear that the authors of this paper cannot claim to be disinterested reporters, having testified in several of the cases described here.

B. *Deregulatory experience: airlines, buses and trucks*

The intellectual foundations of the deregulation of airlines, trucking, and buses included recognition of the power of potential entry. While it was clear that in many transportation markets efficiency is not inconsistent with the operation of enough active carriers to make the replacement of regulation by competition appropriate, it was also clear that on many routes efficient operation is incompatible with the presence of several carriers. Nevertheless, deregulation proceeded in the expectation that potential competition could adequately protect consumers of transportation services in such arenas.

In the initial enthusiasm with which we described contestability analysis we agreed with this assessment, and more than once cited the airline industry as a case in point, using the metaphoric argument that investments in aircraft do not incur any sunk costs because they constitute "capital on wings." Reconsideration has led us to adopt a more qualified position on this score. We now believe that transportation by trucks, barges and even buses may be more highly contestable than passenger air tranportation. Barges and trucks have business firms rather than individual consumers as their primary customers, and that facilitates the provision of service via contracts on which potential entrants can effectively bid against incumbents. Where the contracts apply to long run relationships, as they often do in transportation, even capital costs that are physically irreversible are not economically sunk in the pertinent time period. Moreover, trucks and buses do not face the heavy sunk costs involved in the construction of airports or the shortage of gates and landing slots at busy airports such as that which prevented People Express from acquiring even a single gate of its own at Denver's Stapleton International Airport, so that it was forced instead to lease gates from other carriers, catch as catch can, during a year of flying to that airport.

In fact, post-deregulation experience in the airlines industry has revealed several elements of the structure of supply that conflict significantly with the conditions necessary for the pure theory of contestability to apply without modification. While these structural elements may be transitory, they nevertheless appear to have influenced the performance of the industry in important ways since the advent of deregulation.

First, as the previously noted difficulties of People Express exemplify, there have been constraining shortages of facilities and services of air traffic control at several pivotal airports. These constrain flights in and out of the affected airports and, in addition, they also restrict the prospects of entry and expansion on routes that would otherwise interconnect efficiently with such flights. Second, technological advances, changes in the relative prices of jet fuel and equipment, and changes in the desired configurations of route networks have significantly altered the types and mix of aircraft demanded by the industry. As a result, there have been shortages in the availability of the aircraft demanded, with delivery lags frequently stretching to three years. Third, newly certificated airlines have been able to avoid the costly labor contracts that pervaded the industry before deregulation, so that their labor costs have been substantially lower than those facing the older established carriers. Recently, the older carriers and their unionized work forces have been adapting themselves to this new competitive reality with the aid of more flexible wage contracts, dual wage structures, and less costly contract settlements. Nevertheless, substantial differences in labor costs between older and newer carriers persist.

These conditions make it easy to see why the airline industry does not conform perfectly to the contestability model, even if aircraft are "capital on wings." Thus, it remains to analyze both quantitatively and qualitatively the degree to which the performance of the industry does, or can be expected to, reflect the predictions of contestability theory. This should come as no surprise since most industries can be expected to depart in some important respects from the model of perfect contestability, and it will therefore generally be necessary in applying the theory to assess the economic significance of the deviations.

Several econometric studies have confirmed the imperfection of the contestability of the airline markets (see, e.g., Call and Keeler (1984)). They have shown, for example, that there is a significant positive correlation between profits and concentration in airline markets. Thus the threat of entry does not by itself suffice to keep profits to zero, as perfect contestability would require. Moreover, when new entry does occur, established carriers do reduce their fares in response, something one would expect in a conventional oligopolistic market other than one that is perfectly contestable. Even the study of Morrison and Whinston, which concludes that potential entry does constrain price significantly, finds that the coefficient describing the influence of potential entrants does not become significant until the number of such prospective entrants exceeds three.

The econometric study by Graham, Kaplan, and Sibley (1983) permits comparison among the effects on 1981 route-by-route prices of various influences that lie outside the predictions of contestability theory. They find that prices deviate from costs an additional 10 percent on the average and other things being equal, for routes that utilize one of the major slot-constrained airports in New York, Chicago, or Washington, D.C. In contrast, prices are reduced some 22 percent relative to costs on routes where a newly certificated carrier operates. And, prices are some 18 percent lower relative to costs if four carriers fly the route rather than only one.

These results indicate the significance of the physical constraints on entry and expansion in two ways. First, the direct influence of the slot constraints on prices shows up in the data. Second, the substantial effect of the presence of new carriers, with their low labor costs, demonstrates how much lower fares would generally be if those carriers were able to expand their operations to cover more routes. Finally, the significant effect of the number of carriers on a route shows that active competition plays a role in holding price down toward cost. However, since the size of that effect is so much smaller than would be predicted by most theories of oligopoly that focus on the role of active competitors, it can be concluded that the forces of potential competition still play an important role, despite the structural conditions that impede their workings.

Similar conclusions seem to us to follow from qualitative evaluation of the behavior of the airline markets under deregulation. As we have just seen, the responsive price cuts of incumbents when faced with incursions of low priced entrants is certainly not compatible with the predicted qualitative behavior of contestable markets in the long run. However, there are other qualitative properties that are highly pertinent. In a recent study, Elizabeth Bailey (1986) sets out to examine these. She undertakes to analyze

> " . . . the consequences that have emerged under deregulation in terms of the following behavioral properties predicted by contestability theory: a variety of products will emerge, each of which will yield zero economic profit; the revenues from any subset of the products must exceed the incremental costs of those products, so that no cross-subsidy can exist; prices for each product will equal or exceed marginal costs; and an equilibrium market structure will minimize costs of the industry. Thus, if the theory has some degree of validity, more of these properties should be displayed after deregulation than before. Cross-subsidy, which was pervasive in the regulatory era, should be significantly eroded. Prices should move nearer to costs. Products capable of producing zero economic profits, but which were formerly excluded, should now appear." (pp. 2–3, footnote omitted)

Here evidence leads her to conclude that, while the performance in each respect has not been absolutely clear-cut, on balance the patterns predicted by contestability theory have indeed emerged. She writes, in summary of the consequences of deregulation of the airlines, that

> "Prices in the cheaper-to-serve long-haul and dense markets were substantially lowered (by about forty percent), whereas prices in the more expensive short-haul and thin markets went up somewhat. A diversity of price-service options arose. Individuals could select between low-service/low-price discount carriers and full-service national carriers. Even among the full-service carriers, prices were lower for customers willing to improve load factors by traveling in off-peak periods or by taking one-stop rather than non-stop flights.
>
> The encouragement to entry under air transport deregulation brought with it a variety of contributions to efficiency. One involved delivery systems. It quickly became clear that hub-and-spoke operations rather than the mostly linear systems imposed by regulation offered savings to the airlines. Hub-and-spoke systems also substantially improved service for consumers. A second efficiency contribution involved input productivity. The post-deregulation period has been characterized by pressures to reduce pay scales toward those in unregulated economic sectors, to increase productivity through changes in work rules, and to choose a more efficient fleet configuration" (p. 22).

In light of these observations and similar evidence drawn from the opening of brokerage commissions to market determination, the deregulation of trucking, and the opening of telecommunications markets to entry, Bailey concludes that performance in these areas has shown no significant inconsistencies with the predictions of contestability analysis.

In short, in terms of the airlines case we can infer that market forces through the pressures of competition, both actual and potential, have done a commendable if imperfect job in protecting consumer interests. This is suggested by a number of developments following deregulation: the decrease in real average prices; the reduction in average time spent in traveling from point to point; the falling real costs of airline operation; the erosion or disappearance of cross subsidies, with the elimination of financing of sparsely traveled routes by those that are heavily traveled, and of peak travelers by off-peak flyers, and the considerable improvements in efficiency through computerized routing and hub-and-spoke operations—approaches that had evaded both executives and the Commission during the era of regulation.

C. *Contestability theory as guide for regulation*

We come, finally, to the arena in which the viewpoint of contestability may make its main contribution—as a guide for regulation, rather than as an argument for its elimination. How does contestability theory help in this domain? After all, perfect competition has long served usefully as the ideal for government intervention to follow; that is, as the model of performance to which it should seek to make the regulated firm adhere. What does contestability analysis have to add to this? The answer is that in some circumstances, notably in the presence of substantial economies of scale and scope, the standard of perfect competition is totally inappropriate. For example, where economies of scale and scope are present society no longer is sure to benefit if firms are required to be small, as they would be under perfect competition. Similarly, a rule that price must be set equal to marginal cost is a prescription for financial disaster. Of course, Ramsey pricing theory is of considerable help here, but in some circumstances its usefulness in practice is limited, particularly where there are no reliable data on elasticities and cross elasticities of demands for the considerable number of products at issue. It is then that contestability theory can come to the rescue (and several times already has). For it can propose, for example, to offer consumers in markets with unavoidable entry barriers just the same sort of protection from excessive pricing that they would have derived from perfect freedom of entry, if such freedom had been possible. This is precisely how the stand-alone cost criterion for price ceilings, which will be described below, emerged from contestability theory and could not have been deduced from the model of perfect competition.

To see just how contestability theory can be used to guide regulation we can do no better than to follow the outlines of a remarkable decision of the Interstate Commerce Commission (1985), a decision that encompasses the foundations of its current policies toward those elements of railroad activities in which competitive pressures are judged to be inadequate (that is, in regulatory terminology, in areas in which a railroad possesses "market dominance," or its shippers are "captive").

Early in the discussion of its economic framework the decision provides a section headed "Contestable Markets." However while, as we will see presently, much is made of the logic of contestability, the decision asserts flatly and quite appropriately that the pertinent arena is *not* contestable: "the railroad industry is recognized to have barriers to entry and exit and thus is not considered contestable for captive traffic" (p. 10).

The question, then, is what is best done to control the pricing terms on which such traffic is served. The Commission adopted a set of rules which it termed "constrained market pricing." Before getting to the details of those rules it is desirable to take note of two fundamental attributes underlying the approach: rate of return-rate base regulation of overall earnings, and acceptance of differential (non uniform) pricing. On the first of these, the Commission undertakes to avoid decisions that preclude a railroad from earning in the long run what it refers to as "adequate revenues." Following long regulatory tradition, these are defined in terms of a permitted rate of return on the railroad's rate base (its total invested capital). What is new here is that the Commission adopts for this purpose most of the criteria called for by economic analysis, for example determining that "'adequate' returns are those that provide a rate of return on net investment equal to the current cost of capital (i.e., the level of return available on alternative investments)" (p. 18).

Second, the Commission recognizes that solvency of the railroads is likely to require differential pricing:

> Most importantly, railroads exhibit significant economies of scope and density. Economy of *scope* refers to the fact that the rail plant is indivisible and can produce numerous services at less cost than those services could be produced by separate rail plants for each service. Economy of *density* refers to the fact that greater use of the fixed plant results in a declining average cost. Thus, the marginal cost of rail service is less than the average cost, because the fixed plant is used in a progressively more efficient manner. The differential between marginal costs and average costs cannot be assigned directly to specific movements by any conventional accounting methodology. Hence, we refer to it as the "unattributable costs." These are the costs which must be covered through differential pricing. (pp. 7–8, footnotes omitted)

The decision goes on to point out that where unattributable costs cannot be covered by marginal cost pricing, then demand considerations as well as cost data must enter into decision making, both in order to permit adequacy of revenues and in order to achieve efficiency.

Any means of allocating these costs among shippers other than actual market demand is arbitrary and may not permit a carrier to cover all of its costs. This is because non-demand-based cost apportionment methods do not necessarily reflect the carrier's ability (or inability) to impose the assigned allocations and cover its costs. Thus, they frequently "over-assign" or "under-assign" the carrier's unattributable costs to particular services. If a carrier sought to apply the formula price to all of its traffic, it would lose that traffic for which the demand could not support the price assigned. In that event, the remaining shippers might be required to pay a larger portion of the carrier's unattributable costs because they would lose the benefit of sharing these costs with the lost traffic.

"Ramsey pricing" is a widely recognized method of differential pricing, that is, pricing in accordance with demand. Under Ramsey pricing, each price or rate contains a mark-up above the long-run marginal cost of the product or service to cover a portion of the unattributable costs. The unattributable costs are allocated among the purchasers or users in inverse relation to their demand elasticity. Thus, in a market where shippers are very sensitive to price changes (a highly elastic market), the mark-up would be smaller than in a market where shippers are less price sensitive. The sum of the mark-ups equals the unattributable costs of an efficient producer. (p. 8, footnote omitted)

Nevertheless, the Commission comments,

Ramsey pricing is based on a mathematical formula which requires both the marginal cost and the elasticity of demand to be quantified for every movement in the carrier's system. Thus, the amount of data and degree of analysis required seemed overwhelming. We concluded that while formula Ramsey pricing is useful as a theoretical guideline, it is too difficult and burdensome for universal application. In setting flat rates, that is, rates which do not vary with the volume shipped, Ramsey pricing, in principle, yields the least inefficient price structure. However, even under pure Ramsey pricing, output levels are less than they would be if rates were set at marginal costs. This results in an economic inefficiency because the value of the lost output to the shipper is greater than the value of the resources saved by reducing output. In such a situation, it may be feasible for the parties to negotiate a contract which will leave both parties better off than at the [flat] Ramsey price. Rail freight differs from financing government services (for which shippers are relatively large and few in number). Thus, the feasibility of contracting is more evident for rail freight than for these other services.

As an alternative to pure Ramsey pricing, we proposed Constrained Market Pricing. (p. 9, footnotes omitted)

The key issue to be faced by constrained market pricing is the formulation of a criterion to be used in setting a ceiling over the price to be charged for traffic over which a railroad possesses market dominance. This is an issue with which the Commission had been struggling only since 1978. Before that, curiously, the Commission had been preoccupied primarily with the setting of floors beneath rail prices, to prevent railroads from undercutting barge and truck competitors (the Commission had once described its role as that of a "a giant handicapper").

In the early 1980's, in its search for a tenable price ceiling rule, it turned initially to the tools it had designed long before in its floor setting endeavors. Here, at least for the bulk of the postwar period, it had been using an accounting concept which it called "fully allocated cost." In essence, this assigned to each part of a railroad's traffic a figure intended to approximate the incremental cost of that traffic, plus a share of the remaining (unattributable) cost proportionate to some criterion of "relative use" such as number of carloads, weight or monetary value of the commodity in question carried by the railroad. The apportionment of the unattributable costs was admittedly arbitrary, bore no necessary relation to the cost data (such as marginal costs) that an economist would consider pertinent, and allowed for no adjustments for variations in demand conditions. Even earlier than the landmark Ingot Molds Case (1967) in which the Supreme Court threw up its hands on the matter, economists had begun to argue before the ICC that the use of a fully distributed cost floor was pernicious and a source of substantial inefficiency, and that marginal or incremental costs were the only defensible cost data for use in the calculation of price floors, a view that gradually acquired acceptance among regulatory agencies, including the ICC.

It seems odd, then, that in 1978, when the Commission began its search for a rate ceiling formula (Interstate Commerce Commission (ICC) (1978)) it turned to fully allocated cost, now discredited as a cost floor, as its candidate for a viable cost ceiling. Initially, it proposed for this purpose to allocate a railroad's unattributable costs in proportion to the variable costs (as a proxy for the incremental costs) of the various portions of its traffic. Because this formula soon proved fatally restrictive, particularly in ignoring demand considerations, the Commission permitted the railroads leeway to charge prices as much as seven percent above fully allocated costs where demand conditions permitted. The courts agreed to the legitimacy of this move toward differential pricing but rejected the use of the arbitrary seven percent range of tolerance (see, e.g., ICC (1979)). The Commission made one more attempt to salvage the fully allocated cost approach to price ceilings, but this time adopted weight and distance traversed (calling it the "ton/ton-mile" method) as its basis of allocation (ICC (1980)). However, in response to careful arguments by the railroads and others, it withdrew from this approach altogether in 1981 (ICC (1981)), and early in 1983 offered constrained market pricing as its alternative.

Here, the ceiling proposed by the Commission was *stand-alone cost,* a concept it acknowledged to have derived from the contestability literature.

> "... stand-alone cost (SAC) test ... is used to compute the rate a competitor in the market-place would need to charge in serving a captive shipper or a group of shippers who benefit from sharing joint and common costs. A rate level calculated by the SAC methodology represents the theoretical maximum rate that a railroad could levy on shippers without substantial diversion of traffic to a hypothetical competing service. It is, in other words, a simulated competitive price. (The competing service could be a shipper providing service for itself or a third party

competing with the incumbent railroad for traffic. In either case, the SAC represents the minimum cost of an alternative to the service provided by the incumbent railroad.)

The theory behind SAC is best explained by the concept of 'contestable markets.' This recently developed economic theory augments the classical economic model of 'pure competition' with a model which focuses on the entry and exit from an industry as a measure of economic efficiency. The theory of contestable markets is more general than that of 'pure competition' because it does not require a large number of firms. In fact, even a monopoly can be contestable. The underlying premise is that a monopolist or oligopolist will behave efficiently and competitively where there is a threat of losing some or all of its markets to a new entrant. In other words, contestable markets have competitive characteristics which preclude monopoly pricing (p. 10).

Here it is worth reviewing the logic of the stand-alone cost ceiling a bit more closely. The first-best lesson of the perfect competition model, calling for prices to be set equal to marginal costs, has no doubt contributed to the common regulatory ethos which *equates* price to *some* measure of cost. This doctrine has been used frequently where it is completely inappropriate and without logical foundation, that is, in cases where prices should be based on demand as well as cost considerations, because of the presence of economies of scale and scope. Such arbitrary measures as fully distributed costs cannot substitute for marginal cost measures as decision rules for proper pricing, and the search for a substitute is a remnant of inappropriate reliance on the model of perfect competition for guidance in regulation.

In contrast, contestability theory suggests cost measures that are appropriate guideposts for regulated pricing—incremental and stand-alone costs. The incremental cost of a given service is, of course, the increment in the total costs of the supplying firm when that service is added to its product line. In perfectly contestable markets, the price of a product will lie somewhere between its incremental and its stand-alone cost, just where it falls in that range depending on the state of demand. One cannot legitimately infer that monopoly power is exercised from data showing that prices do not exceed stand-alone costs, and stand-alone costs constitute the proper cost-based ceilings upon prices, preventing both cross-subsidization and the exercise of monopoly power (see Faulhaber (1975) for tests of cross-subsidy and their equivalence). A simple example will show why this is so.

First, suppose that a firm supplies two services, A and B, which *share no costs* and that each costs 10 units a year to supply. The availability of effective potential competition would force revenues from each service to equal 10 units a year. For higher earnings would attract (profitable) entry, and lower revenues would drive the supplier out of business. In this case, in which common costs are absent, incremental and stand-alone costs are equal to each other and to revenues, and the competitive and contestability benchmarks yield the same results.

Next, suppose instead that of the 20 unit total costs 4 are fixed and common to A and B, while 16 are variable, 8 of the 16 being attributable to A and 8 to B. If, because of demand conditions, at most only a bit more than 8 can be garnered from consumers of A, then a firm operating and surviving in contestable markets will earn a bit less than 12 from B. These prices lie between incremental costs (8) and stand-alone costs (12), are mutually advantageous to consumers of both services, and will attract no entrants, even in the absence of any entry barriers. In contrast, should the firm attempt to raise the revenues obtained from B above the 12 unit stand-alone cost, it would lose its business to competitors willing to charge less. Similarly, the same fate would befall it in contestable markets if it priced B in a way that earned more than 8 plus the common cost of 4, less the contribution toward that common cost from service A.

Thus, the forces of idealized potential competition in perfectly contestable markets enforce cost constraints on prices, but prices remain sensitive to demands as well. Actual and potential competition are *effective* if they constrain rates in this way, and in such circumstances regulatory intervention is completely unwarranted. But if, in fact, market forces are not sufficiently strong, then there is likely to be a proper role for regulation, and the theoretical guidelines derived from the workings of contestable markets are the appropriate ones to apply. That is, prices must be constrained to lie between incremental and stand-alone costs.[3,4] This is the approach adopted by the ICC to determine maximum rates for railroad services, and the method has already withstood appeals to the Federal courts.

[3] Note that, properly applied, the SAC criterion should hold for all subsets of a firm's products and not only for its individual products. Thus, suppose a firm produces three items, A, B and C, and that a widget of limitless capacity must be used in order to produce any A, any B or any combination of the two. The cost of the widget will then not enter either A's or B's incremental cost, but it will clearly consititute part of the incremental cost of supplying them both. Then, the combined total revenue of the two items must suffice to cover the cost of the widget as well as any other incremental cost incurred individually or in common. Note also that efficiency requires that a supplier never set price below either marginal *or* per unit incremental cost, because if it is set so low it may lure away customers from a more efficient supplier, i.e., one who can supply the product at lower marginal or per unit incremental cost, and hence supply either one unit of the product or its entire amount at lower resources cost.

[4] It is easy to prove that if a firm's total earnings are exactly equal to its cost of capital, i.e., if it earns exactly zero economic profits, then if all of its revenues equal or exceed the corresponding incremental costs they are *automatically guaranteed* not to exceed their stand-alone costs and *vice versa*. That is, the passing of either test (the SAC ceiling or the incremental cost floor) automatically demonstrates that the other must also be passed by the prices at issue. To show this simply we deal with the case of two products, though the proof is perfectly general. Let

X_1, X_2 = the quantities of the outputs supplied by a firm

P_1, P_2 = the prices of the products

$C(X_1, X_2)$ = the total cost function

$C(X_1, O)$ = the stand-alone cost of product 1 and

$C(X_1, X_2) - C(X_1, O)$ = the incremental cost of product 2.

Concluding remarks

Whatever one's attitude toward contestability theory or the policy recommendations that have derived from it, it must surely be agreed that it has evoked a flood of imaginative and valuable research and writing in opposition, in extension, and in application. To see how rapidly it and associated concepts have spread one need only recall that as recently as 1970 the concept of Ramsey pricing was unknown to most economists, though the analysis, of course, had appeared in 1927. Indeed, the term "Ramsey pricing" was coined by the present authors less than a decade ago. Terms such as "economies of scope," "stand-alone cost" and "contestable markets" were coined in the 1970's as well. Yet today they are used routinely not only in professional journals, but in hearings before U.S. courts and regulatory agencies. Clearly, propagation of the substance rather than the terminology is what really counts, but this too, is being achieved.

Thus, whatever contribution the future will judge contestability theory to have made, it will surely conclude that the analysis has succeeded in stimulating thought in both the realm of academic research and policy formulation.

Princeton and New York Universities.

REFERENCES

APPLEBAUM, E. and LIM, C., "Contestable Markets Under Uncertainty, *Rand Journal of Economics*, 16, 1, Spring 1985, pp. 28–40.

BAILEY, ELIZABETH, E., "Price and Productivity Change Following Deregulation: The U.S. Experience," *Economic Journal*, March 1986 (forthcoming).

BAILEY, ELIZABETH E. and BAUMOL, WILLIAM J., "Deregulation and the Theory of Contestable Markets," *Yale Journal of Regulation*, 1984, 1, pp. 111–137.

BAILEY, E. E. and FRIEDLAENDER, A. F., "Market Structure and Multiproduct Industries," *Journal of Economic Literature*, Vol. 20, September 1982, pp. 1024–1048.

BAUMOL, W. J., PANZAR, J. C. and WILLIG, R. D., *Contestable Markets and the Theory of Industry Structure*, San Diego: 1982.

BAUMOL, W. J., PANZAR, J. C., and WILLIG, R. D., "Contestable Markets: An Uprising in the Theory of Industry Structure: Reply," *American Economic Review*, 73, June, 1983, pp. 491–496.

BITTLINGMAYER, G., "The Economics of A Simple Airline Network," mimeo, 1985.

Then, zero economic profit requires

(1) $P_1X_1 + P_2X_2 = C(X_1, X_2)$

and the incremental cost test for product 2 requires

(2) $P_2X_2 \geqslant C(X_1, X_2) - C(X_1, O)$.

Subtraction of (2) from (1) immediately yields the stand-alone cost criterion for product 1,

(3) $P_1X_1 \leqslant C(X_1, O)$.

Similarly, subtraction of (3) from (1) immediately yields (2). Q.E.D.

BROCK, W. A., "Contestable Markets and the Theory of Industry Structure: A Review Article," *Journal of Political Economy,* 91, 6, December 1983, pp. 1055–1066.

BROCK, W. A. and SCHEINKMAN, J. A., "Free Entry and the Sustainability of Natural Monopoly: Bertrand Revisited by Cournot," in Evans, D. S. (ed.), *Breaking up Bell: Essays on Industrial Organization and Regulation,* 1983.

CALL, GREGORY D. and KEELER, THEODORE E., "Airline Deregulation, Fares, and Market Behavior: Some Empirical Evidence," in *Analytical Studies in Transport Economics,* 1984.

CASSIDY, PETER A., *Australian Overseas Cargo Liner Shipping,* University of Queensland, 1982.

CAVES, D. W., CHRISTENSEN, L. R., and HERRIGES, J. A., "Modelling Alternative Residential Peak-Load Electricity Rate Structures," *Journal of Econometrics,* Vol. 24(3), 1984, pp. 249–268.

CAVES, D. W., CHRISTENSEN, L. R., and SWANSON, J. A., "Productivity Growth, Scale Economies, and Capacity Utilization in U.S. Railroads, 1955–74," *American Economic Review,* December 1981, pp. 994–1002.

CAVES, D. W., CHRISTENSEN, L. R., and TRETHEWAY, M. W., "Flexible Cost Functions for Multiproduct Firms," *Review of Economics and Statistics,* Vol. 62(3), August 1980, pp. 477–481.

CAVES, D. W., CHRISTENSEN, L. R., and TRETHEWAY, M. W., "Productivity Performance of U.S. Trunk and Local Services Airlines in the Era of Deregulation," *Economic Inquiry,* Vol. XXI, July 1983, pp. 312–324.

CHARNES, A., COOPER, W. W., and SUEYOSHI, T., "A Goal Programing/Constrained Regression Review of the Bell System Breakup," Center for Cybernetic Studies Report 513, University of Texas at Austin, May 1985.

COURSEY, D., ISAAC, R. M., and SMITH, V. L., "Natural Monopoly and Contested Markets: Some Experimental Results," *Journal of Law and Economics,* Vol. 27, April, 1984, pp. 91–113.

COURSEY, D., ISAAC, R. M., LUKE, M., and SMITH, V. L., "Market Contestability in the Presence of Sunk (Entry) Costs," *Rand Journal of Economics,* Vol. 15, Spring 1984, pp. 69–84.

COWING, T. G. and HOLTMANN, A. G., "Multiproduct Short-Run Hospital Cost Functions: Evidence and Policy Implications from Cross-Section Data," *Southern Journal of Economics,* January 1983, pp. 637–653.

DASGUPTA, P. and STIGLITZ, J. E., "Sunk Costs, Competition, and Welfare," mineo, 1985.

DAVIES, J. E., "The Theory of Contestable Markets and its Application to the Liner Shipping Industry," Canadian Transport Commission, Ottawa-Hull, 1986.

DENNY, M., FUSS, M., EVERSON, C., and WAVERMAN, L., "Estimating the Effects of Diffusion of Technological Innovations in Telecommunications: The Production Structure of Bell Canada," *Canadian Journal of Economics,* February 1981, pp. 24–43.

EVANS, D. S. and HECKMAN, J. J., "A Test for Subadditivity of the Cost Function with an Application to the Bell System," *American Economic Review,* September, 1984, pp. 615–623.

FAULHABER, G., "Cross-Subsidization: Pricing in Public Enterprise," *American Economic Review,* 65, December 1975, pp. 966–977.

FAULHABER, G. and LEVINSON, S., "Subsidy-Free Prices and Anonymous Equity," *American Economic Review,* 71, 1981, pp. 1083–1091.

FEDERAL COMMUNICATIONS COMMISSION, *Notice of Inquiry, in the Matter of Long-Run Regulation at AT & T's Basic Domestic Interstate Sources,* Washington, D.C., 1985.

FEDERAL TRADE COMMISSION, *Final Order: In the Matter of the Echlin Manufacturing Company, and Borg-Warner Corporation,* Docket Number 9157, Washington, D.C., June 28, 1985.

FRIEDLAENDER, A., WINSTON, C., and KUNG WANG, D., "Costs, Technology and Productivity in the U.S. Automobile Industry," *Bell Journal of Economics,* Spring 1983, pp. 1–20.

FROEB, L. and GEWEKE, J., "Perfect Contestability and the Postwar U.S. Aluminium Industry," Tulane University, December 1984.

GILLIGAN, T. and SMIRLOCK, M., "An Empirical Study of Joint Production and Scale Economies in Commerical Banking," *Journal of Banking and Finance,* vol. 8, 1984, pp. 67–77.

GILLIGAN, T., SMIRLOCK, M., and MARSHALL, W., "Scale and Scope Economies in the Multi-Product Banking Firm," *Journal of Monetary Economics,* Vol. 13, 1984, pp. 393–405.

GORMAN, I. E., "Conditions for Economies of Scope in the Presence of Fixed Costs," *Rand Journal of Economics,* 16, 3, Autumn 1985, pp. 431–436.

GRAHAM, D. R., KAPLAN, D. P., and SIBLEY, D. S., "Efficiency and Competition in the Airline Industry," *Bell Journal of Economics,* Spring 1983, pp. 118–138.

GROSSMAN, S. J., "Nash Equilibrium and the Industrial Organization of Markets with Large Fixed Costs," *Econometrica,* 49, 1981, pp. 1149–1172.

HARRISON, G. W., "Experimental Evaluation of the Contestable Markets Hypothesis," in E. E. Bailey (ed.) *Regulation at the Crossroads,* Cambridge, Mass., 1986.

HARRISON, G. W. and MCKEE, M., "Monopoly Behavior, Decentralized Regulation, and Contestable Markets: An Experimental Evaluation," *Rand Journal of Economics,* Spring 1985, 16, pp. 51–69.

HARRISON, G. W., MCKEE, M., and RUTSTRÜM, E. E., "Experimental Evaluation of Institutions of Monopoly Restraint," in Green, L. and Kagel, J. H. (eds.), *Advances in Behavioral Economics* (Norwood: Ablex, 1987, forthcoming).

HELPMAN, E. and KRUGMAN, P. R., *Market Structure and Foreign Trade,* 1985.

INTERSTATE COMMERCE COMMISSION, Ex Part No. 347, "Western Coal Investigation—Guidelines for Railroad Rate Structure", 43, *Federal Register,* 22151, May 22, 1978.

INTERSTATE COMMERCE COMMISSION, *Annual Volume Rates on Coal—Wyoming to Flint Creek, Arkansas,* 361, ICC 539, 1979.

INTERSTATE COMMERCE COMMISSION, Ex Parte No. 347 (Sub-No. 1), "Coal Rate Guidelines—Nationwide," 45, *Federal Register,* 80370, December 4, 1980.

INTERSTATE COMMERCE COMMISSION, Ex Parte No. 347 (Sub-No. 1), "Coal Rate Guidelines—Nationwide," December 21, 1981, unpublished.

INTERSTATE COMMERCE COMMISSION, "Coal Rate Guidelines, Nationwide," Ex Parte No. 347 (Sub-No. 1), Washington, D.C., decided August 3, 1985.

KELLNER, S. and MATHEWSON, G. F., "Entry, Size Distribution, Scale, and Scope Economies in the Life Insurance Industry," *Journal of Business,* Vol. 56, No. 1, 1983, pp. 25–44.

KIM, H. Y. and CLARK, R. M., "Estimating Multiproduct Scale Economies: An Application to Water Supplies," U.S. Environmental Protection Agency, Municipal Environment Research Laboratory, Cincinnati, Ohio, July 1983.

KNIEPS, G. and VOGELSANG, I., "The Sustainability Concept under Alternative Behavioral Assumptions," *Bell Journal of Economics,* 13, 1, Spring 1982, pp. 234–241.

KREPS, D. and SCHEINKMAN, J., "Quantity Precommitment and Bertrand Competition Yield Cournot Outcomes," *Bell Journal of Economics,* 14, 2, Auturn 1983, pp. 326–338.

MASKIN, E. and TIROLE, J., "A Theory of Dynamic Oligopoly," mineo, 1982.

MAYO, J. W., "The Technological Determinants of the U.S. Energy Industry Structure," *Review of Economics and Statistics,* January 1984, pp. 51–58.

MESTER, L. J., "A Multiproduct Cost Study of Savings and Loans," essay 1, doctoral dissertation, Princeton University, October 1985.

MIRMAN, L. J., TAUMAN, Y., and ZANG, I., "Monopoly and Sustainable Prices As a Nash Equilibrium in Contestable Markets," Mimeo, 1983.

MIRMAN, L. J., TAUMAN, Y., and ZANG, I., "Supportability, Sustainability and Subsidy-Free Prices," *Rand Journal of Economics,* 16, 1, Spring 1985, pp. 114–126.

MORRISON, S. A. and WINSTON, C., "Empirical Implications and Tests of the Contestability Hypothesis," manuscript, 1985.

MURRAY, J. D. and WHITE, R. W., "Economies of Scale and Economies of Scope in Multiproduct Financial Institutions: A Study of British Columbian Credit Unions," *Journal of Finance,* June 1983, pp. 887–901.

PANZAR, J. C. and POSTLEWAITE, A., "The Sustainability of Ramsey Optimal Non-linear Prices," mimeo, 1985.

PERRY, M.. "Sustainable Positive Profit Multiple-Price Strategies in Contestable Markets," mimeo, 1982.

QUIRMBACH, H., "Vertical Integration, Contestable Markets, and the Misfortunes of the Misshaped U," mimeo, 1982.

SCHWARZ, MARIUS, "The Nature and Scope of Contestability Theory," Georgetown University, September 1985, unpublished.

SCHWARTZ, MARIUS and REYNOLDS, ROBERT J., "Contestable Markets: A Uprising in the Theory of Industry Structure: Comment," *American Economic Review,* June 1983, 73, pp. 488–490.

SCOTT, J. T., "Multimarket Contract and Economic Performance," *Review of Economics and Statistics,* August 1982, pp. 368–375.

SHARKEY, W. W., "Existence of Sustainable Prices for Natural Monopoly Outputs," *Bell Journal of Economics,* 12, 1, Spring 1981, pp. 144–154.

SHARKEY, W. W., *The Theory of Natural Monopoly,* 1982.

SHEPHERD, W. G., "'Contestability' vs. Competition," *American Economic Review,* 74, September 1984, pp. 572–587.

SPENCE, A. M., "Contestable Markets and the Theory of Industry Structure: A Review Article," *Journal of Economic Literature,* 21, 1983, pp. 981–990.

SPULBER, D., "Scale Economies and Existence of Sustainable Monopoly Prices," *Journal of Economic Theory,* 34, 1984, pp. 149–163.

TAUCHEN, H., FRAVEL, F. D., and GILBERT, G., "Cost Structure and the Intercity Bus Industry," *Journal of Transport Economics and Policy,* January 1983, pp. 25–47.

TEECE, D. J., "Economies of Scope and the Scope of the Enterprise," *Journal of Economic Behavior and Organization,* Vol. 1, September 1980, pp. 223–247.

TEECE, D. J., "Towards an Economic Theory of the Multiproduct Firm," *Journal of Economic Behavior and Organization,* March 1982, pp. 39–63.

TEN RAA, T., "Supportability and Anonymous Equity," *Journal of Economic Theory,* 31, 1983, *pp.* 176–181.

TEN RAA, T., "Resolution of Conjectures on the Sustainability of Natural Monopoly," *Rand Journal of Economics,* 15, 1, Spring 1984, pp. 135–141.

U.S. DEPARTMENT OF JUSTICE, *Merger Guidelines,* Washington, D.C. 1982.

U.S. SUPREME COURT, American Commerical Lines, Inc., *et al.* vs. Lousiville and Nashville Railroad Co., *et al.* (Ingot Molds case), October term, 1967, pp. 571–597.

WEITZMAN, M. L., "Contestable Markets: An Uprising in the Theory of Industry Structure: Comment," *American Economic Review,* 73, June 1983, pp. 486–487.

[24]

THE REGULATION OF MULTIPRODUCT FIRMS

Part I: Theory

Jean-Jacques LAFFONT

GREMAQ, Université des Sciences Sociales de Toulouse, F-31042 Toulouse Cedex, France

Jean TIROLE*

Massachusetts Institute of Technology, Cambridge, MA 02139, USA

Received October 1988, revised version received February 1990

This paper develops a normative model of the regulation of a multiproduct firm with private information about its technology and cost-reducing activity. It first characterizes the optimal regulatory scheme and illustrates it through examples. It then derives necessary and sufficient conditions for the 'pricing-incentive dichotomy' to hold, i.e. conditions under which the cost reimbursement rule, but not pricing, is used to provide incentives. Last, the paper studies the regulation of the multiproduct firm in a general equilibrium framework both to assess the validity of the partial equilibrium approach and to formalize the notion of 'taxation by regulation'.

1. Introduction

Over the last twenty years, the policy discussion of several industries, most notably telecommunications, has emphasized multiproduct issues in the regulation of natural monopolies. The moves from cost-of-service regulation to fully-distributed-cost pricing, and, more recently, to price caps, witnessed debates about whether these moves would promote incentives, reduce prices, remove 'cross-subsidization' or affect the regulated firms' competitors. Concurrently, the theory of multiproduct cost functions and sustainability of natural monopolies developed, culminating with the book by Baumol, Panzar and Willig (1982). By and large, this theoretical literature has ignored the regulators' informational environment.[1] The purpose of this paper is to develop a normative theory of rate of return and price control for multipro-

*The authors are grateful to Frank Fisher, Paul Joskow, David Sappington, Dick Schmalensee and two anonymous referees for helpful comments, and to the Ford Foundation, the Pew Charitable Trust, the Guggenheim Foundation, the Center for Energy Policy Research at MIT, the National Science Foundation and the Ministère de l'Education Nationale for financial support.

[1] An exception is Sappington (1983), whose work we discuss in section 4.

duct firms based on an explicit informational imperfection in the regulatory process. [A note on the terminology: we will use 'cost-of-service (COS) regulation' to denote any scheme designed to make the firm break even.[2] The often used 'rate-of-return regulation' terminology is misleading, as any regulatory schemes determine some economic rate of return, and this rate of return need not be zero. We use rate-of-return regulation to refer to the optimal cost-reimbursement rule – to be distinguished from the optimal pricing rule.]

We consider a multiproduct firm with private information about its technology and engaging in a cost-reducing activity. The regulatory instruments are the firm's total cost and prices; in particular, the regulator cannot fully distribute costs to particular products, except through an arbitrary accounting procedure. The regulator chooses an optimal regulatory policy subject to his informational gap.

Our work is divided into two parts. Part I (this paper) is devoted to the theory. Part II [the companion paper – Laffont and Tirole (1990)] looks at various applications and discusses policy implications. Section 2 gives a brief taxonomy of the concepts of cross-subsidization. Section 3 considers a general model and derives the optimal rate-of-return and price regulations. It demonstrates that the regulated price of good k satisfies the equation

$$L_k = R_k + I_k,$$

where L_k is the Lerner index (price–cost margin), R_k is a Ramsey index, and I_k is the 'incentive correction for good k'.

In contrast with the Ramsey index obtained in the conventional cost-of-service regulation model (which imposes a – somewhat ad hoc[3] – budget constraint for the regulated firm), our Ramsey index can be computed from publicly available data and requires no knowledge of the firm's cost function. Applications to linear pricing of several commodities, to second-degree price discrimination for a single commodity, and to the regulation of (verifiable) quality are given.

The incentive correction, if any, reflects the regulator's desire to limit the firm's rent without destroying incentives, and, more specifically, depends on

[2]In principle, cost-of-service regulation refers to the policy that consists of maximizing a social welfare function subject to the firm's making zero profit. The theory part was developed by Boiteux (1956) and Baumol and Bradford (1970), and later substantially extended to a competitive environment [see Faulhaber (1975), Baumol et al. (1982) and Sharkey (1982)]. An excellent survey is Brown and Sibley (1985).

[3]The existence of a budget constraint and the prohibition of transfers from the government to the firm in the models of Ramsey and Boiteux are inconsistent with their assumption that the regulator is benevolent; for, with a benevolent regulator, there is no point imposing such welfare-reducing constraints. Such constraints must thus be derived from a 'political economy' approach to regulation, which leads us to the question of the formalization of the regulator's objective function in these models.

whether an increase in good k's price helps raise incentives. A fundamental theoretical question is whether the incentive and pricing issues can be disconnected ($I_k=0$) or not ($I_k \neq 0$); that is, is the optimal rate-of-return regulation (which under some assumptions turns out to be linear in the firm's performance) a sufficient instrument to promote incentives? Using familiar techniques from the theory of aggregation, section 4 gives necessary and sufficient conditions for the dichotomy between incentives and pricing to hold. It first considers the case of a single-dimensional cost-reducing activity. It then allows the firm to allocate its cost-reducing activity among the diverse (unobserved) components of the cost functions, assuming one of two functional forms: the shared fixed-cost function, in which the n goods share a joint cost and otherwise have individual subcost functions; and the shared variable-cost function, in which a cost-reducing activity affects the marginal cost of producing each good, as is the case in the peak-load pricing model. Last, sufficient conditions are given for the optimal regulatory scheme to be implementable through a menu of linear contracts.

Section 5 analyzes the validity of the partial equilibrium approach in a simple imperfect-income-taxation, general-equilibrium model. It shows that the partial equilibrium approach yields the right qualitative Ramsey, incentive, and effort corrections. The partial and general equilibrium results coincide in the absence of redistributive concerns. In the presence of redistributive concerns, the Ramsey term depends on the relative social weights of consumers in the social welfare function. In contrast, the incentive and effort corrections depend on the relative weights of the regulated firms' insiders and outsiders. Finally, section 6 summarizes the major insights of the paper.

2. Definitions of cross-subsidization

Several definitions of cross-subsidization are explicit or implicit in the theoretical and applied literatures. They are not mutually inconsistent; rather they reflect different facets of the regulatory problem. We will restrict ourselves to three notions.

(i) *Cost-side cross-subsidization.* Such cross-subsidization occurs when the firm's managers allocate investments and their time and energy inefficiently among the firm's product lines. That is, the marginal productivity of a cost-reducing activity applied to some product exceeds that for another product; one can then say that the former product subsidizes the latter. Any regulation based on aggregate cost (cost-of-service regulation – similar to a cost-plus contract – price cap regulation – similar to a fixed-price contract – and our intermediate incentive regulation) avoids cost-side cross-subsidization, as it induces managers to allocate (given levels of) investment and effort so as to minimize cost. In contrast, fully distributed cost pricing, which allocates joint costs to services in an arbitrary accounting manner, is a natural breeding ground for such cross-subsidies [see Brennan (1987)].

(ii) *Demand-side cross-subsidization.* This kind of cross-subsidization occurs when prices are distorted to favor a targeted class of consumers. For instance, telephone pricing in the United States and the United Kingdom has reflected a strong concern about the level of access charges to residential customers, and less concern about business customers. Similarly, rural consumers have often been protected from cost-justified price discrimination. Formally, what Posner (1971) has dubbed 'taxation by regulation', may correspond to a discrepancy between a good's Lerner index and the Lerner index that would emerge from a regulatory policy that maximizes the unweighted sum of consumers' surpluses.[4] (A slight variant of) this definition can be stated in the context of our model: if $L_k < R_k + I_k$, good k is demand-side cross-subsidized (cross-taxed if $L_k > R_k + I_k$).

(iii) *Contestable cross-subsidization.* The recent theoretical literature has emphasized the quite distinct notion that a given production plan and given (inflexible) prices for a regulated firm may trigger (hit and run) entry by an unregulated competitor who faces the same technology (the contestable case). Faulhaber's (1975) definition of cross-subsidization is that the regulated firm's cost of producing a subset of goods (the 'stand-alone cost') is lower than the revenue associated with this subset of goods. Baumol et al. (1982) contains a thorough investigation of when Ramsey pricing is consistent with sustainability (the absence of contestable cross-subsidization).

Although we study in part II (possibly inefficient) entry by competitors, we abstract from the concern of this literature by assuming that the market is not contestable. That is, even though other firms may produce similar or differentiated products, the technology facing the regulated firm is unique and cannot be costlessly duplicated.

3. Optimal pricing and cost-reimbursement rule

3.1. The model

Consider a regulated firm with aggregate cost function

$$C = C(\beta, e, \boldsymbol{q}), \tag{3.1}$$

where

β is a technological parameter or firm's 'type' ($C_\beta > 0$),[5]

[4]Demand-side cross subsidization may also stem from the different powers of the various interest groups, as emphasized by the political science literature. See Laffont and Tirole (1988) for a political theory of cross-subsidization.

[5]Subscripts other than those indexing goods (k, l) denote partial derivatives: $C_\beta \equiv \partial C / \partial \beta$.

e is its managers' cost-reducing effort ($C_e < 0$), and
$\boldsymbol{q} \equiv (q_1, \ldots, q_n)$ is the firm's output vector ($C_{q_k} > 0$).

The technological parameter, β, and the effort level, e, are single-dimensional. In section 4 we allow the effort to be allocated among product lines; we also give conditions under which a multidimensional parameter space (with one parameter, β_k, per product line) can be reduced to our single-dimensional representation.

We let $E(\beta, C, \boldsymbol{q})$ denote the effort required for a firm of type β to produce $\boldsymbol{q}$ at cost C:

$$C \equiv C(\beta, E(\beta, C, \boldsymbol{q}), \boldsymbol{q}). \tag{3.2}$$

The partial derivatives of this effort function with respect to its arguments are denoted E_β, E_C, and E_{q_k} ($E_\beta > 0$, $E_C < 0$, and $E_{q_k} > 0$).

The firm's objective function is

$$U = t - \psi(e), \tag{3.3}$$

where we make the *accounting* convention that cost (which is observable) is reimbursed to the firm and that the revenue, $R(\boldsymbol{q})$, generated by the sale of the production vector $\boldsymbol{q}$ is paid directly to the regulator [$R(\cdot)$ is assumed to be increasing and concave], t is a net monetary transfer from the regulator to the firm, and $\psi(e)$ is the manager's disutility of effort ($\psi' > 0$, $\psi'' > 0$, $\psi''' \geqq 0$).[6] The firm is willing to participate in the regulatory process if and only if $U \geqq 0$.

Last the utilitarian social welfare function is the sum of consumer welfare and the firm's welfare:

$$W = [V(\boldsymbol{q}) - R(\boldsymbol{q}) - (1+\lambda)(t + C(\beta, e, \boldsymbol{q}) - R(\boldsymbol{q}))] + U \tag{3.4}$$

or, using (3.3):

$$W = [V(\boldsymbol{q}) + \lambda R(\boldsymbol{q})] - (1+\lambda)(\psi(e) + C(\beta, e, \boldsymbol{q})) - \lambda U, \tag{3.5}$$

where $V(\boldsymbol{q})$ is the social value associated with the production of $\boldsymbol{q}$ (assumed increasing and concave), and $\lambda > 0$ is the shadow cost of public funds.[7]

Eq. (3.5) shows that W can be decomposed into three terms: the

[6]The technical assumption $\psi''' \geqq 0$ guarantees that the optimal incentive scheme is not stochastic.

[7]See Ballard, Shoven and Whalley (1985) and Hausman and Poterba (1987), and the references therein. For instance, Ballard et al. find λ's in the range 0.17–0.56 depending on the saving and labor supply elasticities, and the tax used to raise public funds. λ is obtained endogenously in the general equilibrium model of section 5.

generalized social value, $V+\lambda R$, which accounts for the fact that government revenue is socially valuable when public funds are costly; the total cost, $\psi+C$, of operating the firm times the shadow price of this cost; and the social cost, λU, of leaving a rent to the firm.

To derive the optimal regulation, we keep the $V(\cdot)$ and $R(\cdot)$ functions general. We will later consider two familiar special cases.

The regulator observes the firm's cost C and quantities $\boldsymbol{q}$ (or equivalently, prices $\boldsymbol{p}\equiv(p_1,\dots,p_n)$). Unless otherwise stated, he regulates the firm's n outputs. The firm has private information about (knows) its technology parameter β, which from the regulator's viewpoint is drawn from a cumulative distribution $F(\cdot)$ on $[\underline{\beta},\bar{\beta}]$ with density $f(\cdot)$. We make the standard assumption that the hazard rate, $f(\beta)/F(\beta)$, of the distribution is monotonic: $\mathrm{d}(F/f)/\mathrm{d}\beta\geqq 0$. The cost-reducing effort e is also unobservable by the regulator. $U(\beta)$ will be called the firm's (informational) rent.

3.2. The optimal regulatory allocation

The regulator maximizes the expectation over β of the social welfare function given by (3.5), over $\{\boldsymbol{q}(\beta),e(\beta),U(\beta)\}$ [which amounts to maximizing with respect to $\{\boldsymbol{q}(\beta),e(\beta),t(\beta)\}$]:

$$\underset{\beta}{\mathrm{E}}W=\int_{\underline{\beta}}^{\bar{\beta}}[V(\boldsymbol{q})+\lambda R(\boldsymbol{q})-(1+\lambda)(\psi(e)+C(\beta,e,\boldsymbol{q}))-\lambda U]f(\beta)\,\mathrm{d}\beta, \tag{3.6}$$

subject to the individual rationality and incentive constraints. Because the firm's rent is necessarily decreasing in β, and because [from (3.5)] the regulator does not wish to leave rents to the firm, the individual rationality constraint can be written:

$$U(\bar{\beta})=0. \tag{3.7}$$

The derivation of the incentive constraint is standard [see, for example, Guesnerie and Laffont (1984)]. An intuitive argument is as follows. A firm with type $\beta-\mathrm{d}\beta$ ($\mathrm{d}\beta>0$) can produce the same output vector at the same cost as a firm with type β, and therefore obtains the same revenue and transfer by reducing its effort relative to that of type β by $\mathrm{d}e=E_\beta(\beta,C(\beta,e,\boldsymbol{q}),\boldsymbol{q})\,\mathrm{d}\beta$. This implies that the gradient of the firm's rent with respect to β, $\dot{U}(\beta)\equiv\mathrm{d}U/\mathrm{d}\beta=-\psi'(e)\,\mathrm{d}e/\mathrm{d}\beta$, is given by

$$\dot{U}(\beta)=-\psi'(e)E_\beta(\beta,C(\beta,e,\boldsymbol{q}),\boldsymbol{q}). \tag{3.8}$$

Eq. (3.8) is the first-order condition of incentive compatibility for the firm; it gives the rate at which the rent of the firm must grow to elicit its information.

Taking $e(\beta)$ and $q(\beta)$ as control variables and $U(\beta)$ as a state variable, the regulator maximizes (3.6) subject to (3.7) and (3.8). Appendix A shows that under standard technological assumptions, $\mathrm{d}C/\mathrm{d}\beta \geqq 0$ and $\mathrm{d}q_k/\mathrm{d}\beta \leqq 0$, for all k, are sufficient conditions for the firm's second-order conditions to be satisfied. Whether those conditions hold for the solution to the first-order conditions must be checked in each application of our model.

The optimal regulatory policy is derived in appendix A. Here we content ourselves with its statement and intuition.

Proposition 1. The first-order conditions of the regulator's program with respect to effort, e, and output, q_k, *are*

$$\psi'(e) = -C_e - \frac{\lambda}{1+\lambda}\frac{F(\beta)}{f(\beta)}[\psi''(e)E_\beta + \psi'(e)E_{\beta C}C_e] \tag{3.9}$$

and

$$V_{q_k} + \lambda R_{q_k} = (1+\lambda)C_{q_k} + \lambda\frac{F(\beta)}{f(\beta)}\psi'(e)\frac{\mathrm{d}}{\mathrm{d}q_k}(E_\beta). \tag{3.10}$$

To understand (3.9), note that in a symmetric information (first-best) world, the marginal disutility of effort, $\psi'(e)$, should be equal to the marginal cost savings, $-C_e$. The last term in (3.9) is due to the regulator's desire to extract the firm's informational rent. The term in brackets,

$$A \equiv \psi''(e)E_\beta + \psi'(e)E_{\beta C}C_e,$$

is the derivative with respect to e of $|\dot{U}(\beta)|$. A sufficient condition for A to be positive is that $C_{ee} \geqq 0$ (there are decreasing returns in the cost-reducing technology) and that $C_{\beta e} \geqq 0$ (the marginal cost reduction is not higher for efficient types). From (3.8), A is also the increase in the rent of all firms with type in $[\underline{\beta}, \beta]$ [which have probability $F(\beta)$], when the effort of type β is increased by one. From (3.6), the social cost of the extra rent for the types in $[\underline{\beta}, \beta]$ is $\lambda F(\beta)A$. On the other hand, the distortion in effort for type β relative to the first-best level, $\psi'(e) + C_e$, has social cost, $(1+\lambda)(\psi'(e)+C_e)$, from (3.5) and occurs with probability $f(\beta)$. The tradeoff between rent extraction and efficient effort thus yields (3.9). An implication of (3.9) that we later develop is that – like in our single-product paper [Laffont and Tirole (1986)] – the regulator uses cost-reimbursement rules that are intermediate between the cost-plus contract [which induces $\psi'(e)=0$] and the fixed-price contract [which induces $\psi'(e) = -C_e$].

Of particular interest for the subsequent analysis is the 'modified Ramsey equation' (3.10). Under symmetric information, the marginal generalized social value, $\mathrm{d}(V+\lambda R)/\mathrm{d}q_k$, is equal to the marginal social cost of production, $\mathrm{d}((1+\lambda)C)/\mathrm{d}q_k$. Under asymmetric information, there may exist an incentive correction associated with the regulator's desire to extract the firm's rent. From (3.8), a unit increase in output k affects the rent by $\psi'(e)\,\mathrm{d}(E_\beta)/\mathrm{d}q_k$, where

$$\frac{\mathrm{d}}{\mathrm{d}q_k}(E_\beta)=E_{\beta C}C_{q_k}+E_{\beta q_k} \tag{3.11}$$

is a total derivative and is a measure of how output k affects the potential effort savings associated with an increase in efficiency. As in eq. (3.9), the gain in reducing $|\dot{U}|$ is proportional to the probability $F(\beta)$ that the firm is more efficient than type β, and the cost of the distortion relative to the first-best is proportional to the probability $f(\beta)$ that the firm has type β, which explains eq. (3.10).

When the incentive correction is equal to zero (see Proposition 3 below for a necessary and sufficient condition), the incentive–pricing dichotomy holds as (3.10) determines pricing as a function of marginal costs independently of informational (control) problems.

3.3. Three special cases

3.3.1. Linear pricing of several commodities

3.3.1.1. Ramsey pricing. Suppose that the social value, $V(\boldsymbol{q})$, is simply the consumers' gross surplus, $S(\boldsymbol{q})$, and that linear pricing is used. Then, the revenue function is

$$R(\boldsymbol{q})=\sum_k p_k q_k=\sum_k S_k'(\boldsymbol{q})q_k,$$

where $S_k'(\boldsymbol{q})$ is the partial derivative of S with respect to q_k. Let $q_k(\boldsymbol{p})$ be the demand functions (defined by $p_k=S_k'(\boldsymbol{q})$) and let

$$\eta_{kl}\equiv\frac{\partial q_k}{\partial p_l}\frac{p_l}{q_k} \quad\text{and}\quad \eta_k\equiv-\frac{\partial q_k}{\partial p_k}\frac{p_k}{q_k}=-\eta_{kk}$$

denote the cross and own elasticities of demand.

For this case, eq. (3.10) can be written:

$$p_k+\lambda\left(p_k+\sum_l \frac{\partial p_l}{\partial q_k}q_l\right)-(1+\lambda)C_{q_k}-\lambda\frac{F(\beta)}{f(\beta)}\psi'(e)\frac{\mathrm{d}}{\mathrm{d}q_k}(E_\beta)=0 \tag{3.12}$$

or

$$L_k=R_k+I_k, \tag{3.13}$$

where

$$L_k\equiv(p_k-C_{q_k})/p_k \tag{3.14}$$

is the Lerner index,

$$R_k\equiv-\frac{\lambda}{1+\lambda}\left(\sum_l \frac{\partial p_l}{\partial q_k}\frac{q_l}{p_k}\right) \tag{3.15}$$

is the Ramsey index, and

$$I_k\equiv\left[\frac{\lambda F(\beta)\psi'(e)}{(1+\lambda)f(\beta)p_k}\right]\frac{\mathrm{d}}{\mathrm{d}q_k}(E_\beta) \tag{3.16}$$

is (a multiple of) the incentive correction. Possibly up to the incentive correction, the pricing structure is determined by the familiar Ramsey formula. For instance, for independent demands,

$$R_k=\frac{\lambda}{1+\lambda}\frac{1}{\eta_k}.$$

As mentioned earlier, a difference with the traditional Ramsey formula is that the 'Ramsey number', $\lambda/(1+\lambda)$, is determined economy-wide and in particular does not depend on the unknown technology, in contrast with the traditional cost-of-service theory of Ramsey, Boiteux, and Baumol and Bradford.[8]

There are other familiar expressions for the Ramsey index. We can, for instance, rewrite (3.10) taking the derivatives of the social welfare function with respect to prices instead of quantities. This yields:

[8]This approach assumes that the regulator has full information and maximizes $S(\boldsymbol{q})-C(\boldsymbol{q})$ subject to the constraint $R(\boldsymbol{q})-C(\boldsymbol{q})\geqq 0$. Letting μ denote the Lagrange multiplier of the constraint, the optimization yields $L_k=\tilde{R}_k$, where $\tilde{R}_k$ is the same as R_k except that λ is replaced by the (cost- and demand-contingent) μ.

$$(1+\lambda)\sum_{l=1}^{n}(p_l-C_{q_l})\frac{\partial q_l}{\partial p_k}+\lambda q_k-\lambda\frac{F(\beta)}{f(\beta)}\psi'(e)\left(\sum_{l=1}^{n}\left(\frac{\mathrm{d}}{\mathrm{d}q_l}(E_\beta)\right)\frac{\partial q_l}{\partial p_k}\right)=0. \tag{3.17}$$

For instance, for $n=2$, it can be shown that

$$R_k=\frac{\lambda}{1+\lambda}\frac{1}{\hat{\eta}_k},\quad k=1,2,$$

where

$$\hat{\eta}_1\equiv\eta_1\left[\frac{1-\dfrac{\eta_{12}\eta_{21}}{\eta_1\eta_2}}{1+\dfrac{p_2q_2}{p_1q_1}\dfrac{\eta_{21}}{\eta_2}}\right]$$

and symmetrically for $\hat{\eta}_2$. The 'superelasticities' $\hat{\eta}_k$ were first derived by Boiteux (1956) [see Brown and Sibley (1985) for a general exposition]. Thus, with substitutes ($\eta_{kl}>0$ for $k\neq l$), the price of good k should be adjusted upwards to account for the fact that such an increase raises the revenue received on good $l\neq k$.

3.3.1.2. Peak-load pricing. The above Ramsey analysis emphasized demand interdependencies among products. Another famous third-degree, price-discrimination paradigm – the peak-load model – emphasizes cost interdependencies.

Consider a simple peak-load pricing problem with independent demands, in which the peak demand function is $q_2=D_2(p_2)$ and the off-peak demand function is $q_1=D_1(p_1)$; let $C(\beta,e,q_1,q_2)$ denote the cost function.

We obtain a generalization of the Boiteux–Steiner formula:

$$\frac{p_1-(\partial C/\partial q_1)}{p_1}=\frac{\lambda}{1+\lambda}\frac{1}{\eta_1}+I_1,$$

$$\frac{p_2-(\partial C/\partial q_2)}{p_2}=\frac{\lambda}{1+\lambda}\frac{1}{\eta_2}+I_2,$$

where

$$I_k=\frac{\lambda}{1+\lambda}\frac{F(\beta)\psi'(e)}{f(\beta)p_k}\frac{\mathrm{d}}{\mathrm{d}q_k}\left(-\frac{\partial C/\partial\beta}{\partial C/\partial e}\right),\quad k=1,2.$$

Let us consider some special cases, assuming that off-peak demand is strictly lower than capacity at the optimal policy.

(i) *Unknown capacity cost function and known marginal cost.* Let

$$C(\beta, e, q_1, q_2) = c(q_1 + q_2) + G(\beta, e, q_2).$$

Then

$$\frac{p_1 - c}{p_1} = \frac{\lambda}{1+\lambda} \frac{1}{\eta_1},$$

$$\frac{p_2 - c - (\partial G/\partial q_2)}{p_2} = \frac{\lambda}{1+\lambda} \frac{1}{\eta_2} + \frac{\lambda}{1+\lambda} \frac{F(\beta)}{f(\beta)} \frac{\psi'(e)}{p_2} \frac{\partial}{\partial q_2}\left(- \frac{\partial G/\partial \beta}{\partial G/\partial e}\right).$$

The incentive–pricing dichotomy here always holds for the off-peak good. For the peak good, it holds iff $G(\beta, e, q_2) \equiv G(\Phi(\beta, e), q_2)$, as we show in Proposition 3.

(ii) *Unknown variable cost and known capacity cost.* Let

$$C(\beta, e, q_1, q_2) = v(\beta, e, q_1 + q_2) + \mathrm{d}q_2.$$

Then the (generalized) Boiteux (1949)–Steiner (1957) formula holds for both peak and off-peak demands:

$$\frac{p_1 - (\partial v/\partial Q)}{p_1} = \frac{\lambda}{1+\lambda} \frac{1}{\eta_1} + I_1,$$

$$\frac{p_2 - ((\partial v/\partial Q) + d)}{p_2} = \frac{\lambda}{1+\lambda} \frac{1}{\eta_2} + I_2,$$

where $\partial v/\partial Q$ is the marginal variable cost and

$$I_k \equiv \frac{\lambda}{1+\lambda} \frac{F(\beta)\psi'(e)}{f(\beta) p_k} \frac{\mathrm{d}}{\mathrm{d}Q}\left(- \frac{\partial v/\partial \beta}{\partial v/\partial e}\right).$$

These two examples show that in contrast with positive-rate-of-return regulation à la Averch–Johnson [Bailey (1973)], which induces the firm to distort the pricing rule towards low peak prices (because such prices raise the demand for capacity, a familiar Averch–Johnson excess accumulation of capital), the distortions here depend on the ability of price distortions to help reduce the rents associated with asymmetric information.

3.3.2. Second-degree price discrimination

Let us now assume that the regulated firm produces a single physical good and practices non-linear pricing. To see why we can apply the general multiproduct framework to this situation, consider two types of consumers, $k=1,2$. Consumers of type k, who are in proportion α_k (such that $\alpha_1+\alpha_2=1$), have a gross surplus function $S_k(q_k)$, with $S'_2>S'_1$. Consumers of type 2 are thus the 'high-demand consumers'. The social value function is then

$$V(\boldsymbol{q})=\alpha_1 S_1(q_1)+\alpha_2 S_2(q_2).$$

The cost function can be written $C(\beta,e,Q)$, where $Q\equiv\alpha_1 q_1+\alpha_2 q_2$ is total output.

We analyze fully non-linear pricing (subsection 3.3.2.1) and two-part pricing (subsection 3.3.2.2).

3.3.2.1. Fully non-linear pricing. Let $\{T_1,q_1\}$ and $\{T_2,q_2\}$ denote the payment–quantity pairs for the two types of consumers. Incentive compatibility requires that high-demand consumers do not pretend they have low demand:

$$S_2(q_2)-T_2\geqq S_2(q_1)-T_1. \tag{3.18}$$

Furthermore, we assume that even the low-demand consumers consume the good.[9]

$$S_1(q_1)-T_1\geqq 0. \tag{3.19}$$

Because public funds are costly, (3.18) and (3.19) are binding. The revenue function can then be written:

$$R(\boldsymbol{q})=\alpha_1 T_1+\alpha_2 T_2=S_1(q_1)+\alpha_2(S_2(q_2)-S_2(q_1)). \tag{3.20}$$

Letting $p_k\equiv S'_k(q_k)$, we can now apply eq. (3.10):

$$\alpha_1 p_1+\lambda[p_1-\alpha_2 S'_2(q_1)]=\alpha_1(1+\lambda)C_Q+I \tag{3.21}$$

and

$$\alpha_2 p_2+\lambda\alpha_2 p_2=\alpha_2(1+\lambda)C_Q+I, \tag{3.22}$$

where

[9]By familiar reasoning, the other incentive-compatibility and individual-rationality constraints are not binding.

$$I \equiv \frac{\lambda F(\beta)\psi'(e)}{f(\beta)} \frac{\mathrm{d}}{\mathrm{d}Q}(E_\beta)$$

is the common incentive correction. Or,

$$R_1 = \frac{\alpha_2}{\alpha_1} \frac{\lambda}{1+\lambda} \left[\frac{S_2'(q_1) - S_1'(q_1)}{S_1'(q_1)} \right] > 0, \tag{3.23}$$

$$R_2 = 0. \tag{3.24}$$

That is to say, we obtain the familiar result that the high consumption should not be distorted, while the low consumption is lower than the one when the firm has perfect information about preferences. The shadow cost of public funds induces the regulated firm to behave somewhat like a monopolist and to distort the consumption vector.

There are several interesting extensions of the general approach. For instance, one could allow for outside competition in this second-degree price discrimination model. The possibility of bypass in general puts other constraints on the above maximization problem (for instance, high-demand consumers of long-distance services may build their own access to the long-distance carriers and bypass the local exchanges). This issue is examined in Laffont and Tirole (1989a).

3.3.2.2. Two-part tariffs. We next restrict attention to combinations of a fixed fee and a marginal price: $T(q) = A + pq$.

Let $S_i(p)$ and $S_i^n(p)$ denote the gross and net surpluses of consumers of type i for marginal price p [$\mathrm{d}S_i/\mathrm{d}p = pD_i'(p)$, $\mathrm{d}S_i^n/\mathrm{d}p = -D_i(p)$]. For a given marginal price, p, the fixed fee is optimally chosen equal to the low-demand consumers' net surplus: $A = S_1^n(p)$. Thus, the firm's revenue is

$$R(p) = S_1^n(p) + pD(p),$$

where $D(p) \equiv \alpha_1 D_1(p) + \alpha_2 D_2(p)$ is total demand at price p. It is easily checked that the Ramsey term is given by

$$R = \left(\frac{\lambda}{1+\lambda} \frac{1}{\eta} \right) \left(\frac{\alpha_2 D_2}{\alpha_1 D_1 + \alpha_2 D_2} \right), \tag{3.25}$$

where η is the elasticity of total demand [$\eta \equiv -(\mathrm{d}D/\mathrm{d}p)/(D/p)$]. In the absence of incentive correction, the marginal price should thus lie between marginal cost and the optimal linear price (which satisfies $L = [\lambda/(1+\lambda)](1/\eta)$). Its location between these two values depends on the relative demands of the two types of consumers.

3.3.3. Verifiable quality

There are dimensions of quality that can be specified in a contract and enforced. Examples are (in a procurement context) the speed or range of an airplane, and (in a regulatory context) the number of outages of an electric utility or the timeliness of trains [see Baumol (1975)].[10] Such verifiable dimensions of quality can be treated as outputs of fictitious goods, and therefore are subject to the analysis of the section. That the good 'quality' does not have a standard demand curve is not a problem, as formulas (3.9) and (3.10) are derived for general social value and revenue functions. In this subsection we give two examples of application of these formulas; the issue of unverifiable quality is tackled in Laffont and Tirole (1989b).

3.3.3.1. A procurement example. Suppose that a contractor produces q units of a single-dimensional output of quality s at cost $C(\beta, e, q, s)$. This situation is formally equivalent to the case of a two-dimensional output ($q_1 = q, q_2 = s$). In a procurement context, $R(q, s) = 0$. Let $S(q, s)$ denote the government's surplus, with partial derivatives S_q and S_s. Applying eq. (3.10) yields:

$$S_q = (1+\lambda)C_q - \lambda \frac{F(\beta)}{f(\beta)} \psi'(e) \frac{\partial}{\partial q}\left(-\frac{C_\beta}{C_e}\right) \tag{3.26}$$

and

$$S_s = (1+\lambda)C_s - \lambda \frac{F(\beta)}{f(\beta)} \psi'(e) \frac{\partial}{\partial s}\left(-\frac{C_\beta}{C_e}\right). \tag{3.27}$$

In particular, when the incentive–pricing dichotomy holds ($C = C(\Phi(\beta, e), q, s)$: see Proposition 3 below), the marginal benefits of output and quality are equal to their social marginal costs.

3.3.3.2. A regulation example. As in subsection 3.3.3.1, consider one-dimensional output q and quality s, yielding a social surplus $S(q, s)$ and produced at cost $C(\beta, e, q, s)$. In contrast with subsection 3.3.3.1, assume that

[10] Another interesting example (communicated to us by John Vickers) is the 1988 contractual agreement between the U.K. Director General of Telecommunications and British Telecom. British Telecom accepted contractual liability for fault repair and provision of new service, forcing it to compensate customers to a minimum extent of £5.00 per day if it is more than two days late in providing a line or if it takes more than two days to repair a fault (see the statement issued by the Director General of Telecommunications in July 1988 on 'The Control of British Telecom's prices'.)

the good is sold to consumers and is subject to arbitrage among them. The revenue function is then $R(q,s)=P(q,s)q$, where $P(q,s)=S_q(q,s)$ is the inverse demand function. Assuming that the incentives–pricing dichotomy holds [the incentive corrections, if any, are the same as in (3.26) and (3.27)], (3.10) yields:

$$\frac{p-C_q}{p}=\frac{\lambda}{1+\lambda}\frac{1}{\eta} \tag{3.28}$$

and

$$S_s+\lambda P_s q=(1+\lambda)C_s, \tag{3.29}$$

where η is the price elasticity of demand.

Eq. (3.28) is the classic 'Lerner index equal Ramsey index' equation. Of more interest is eq. (3.29), which states that at the optimum the marginal surplus of quality, S_s, exceeds the marginal cost of quality, C_s, if and only if the average consumer values quality more than the marginal consumer, $S_s/q>P_s$.

4. The incentive–pricing dichotomy

4.1. Necessary and sufficient conditions

Eq. (3.10) yields a simple conclusion: incentives and pricing of good k are disconnected if and only if $\mathrm{d}(E_\beta)/\mathrm{d}q_k=0$. In this case, the regulator uses only the cost reimbursement rule [implicit in (3.9)] to extract the firm's rent while preserving incentives. If $\mathrm{d}(E_\beta)/\mathrm{d}q_k>0$ (respectively, <0), the price of good k exceeds (respectively, is lower than) its symmetric information level, ceteris paribus. Proposition 2 below states that the incentive correction favors a high price (a low quantity) for good k if an increase in output k increases the marginal rate of transformation between effort and efficiency in the cost function, that is, if this increase in output makes it easier for the firm to transform exogenous cost changes into rent.

Proposition 2. Ceteris paribus, the price of good k exceeds its symmetric information level if and only if

$$\frac{\partial}{\partial q_k}\left(-\frac{C_\beta}{C_e}\right)>0.$$

Proof of Proposition 2. Differentiating (3.2) with respect to β yields:

$$0=C_\beta+C_e E_\beta.$$

Hence,

$$\frac{\mathrm{d}}{\mathrm{d}q_k}(E_\beta)=\frac{\partial}{\partial q_k}\left(-\frac{C_\beta}{C_e}\right).$$

Substituting into (3.10) shows that $V_{q_k}+\lambda R_{q_k}-(1+\lambda)C_{q_k}$ is positive if and only if

$$\frac{\partial}{\partial q_k}\left(-\frac{C_\beta}{C_e}\right)>0. \quad \text{Q.E.D.}$$

As mentioned earlier, a central issue is whether pricing should be used to promote incentives (or to extract the firm's rent). Leontieff's (1947) well-known aggregation theorem and Proposition 2 yield:

Proposition 3. The incentive–pricing dichotomy [$\mathrm{d}(E_\beta)/\mathrm{d}q_k=0$ *for all* k] *holds if and only if there exists a function* Φ *such that*

$$C=C(\Phi(\beta,e),\boldsymbol{q}). \tag{4.1}$$

Proposition 3 is both important and straightforward. If efficiency and effort can be aggregated in the cost function, changing q_k does not affect the extent to which the firm can convert exogenous productivity increases into rent, which is entirely determined by the Φ function.

At this stage it is worth comparing our approach with Sappington's (1983) early work on incentives in multiproduct firms. Sappington, along the lines of Baron and Myerson's (1982) single product contribution, shows that in general prices are distorted to limit the firm's informational rent. There are two related differences between his results and ours. First, Sappington's (like Baron and Myerson's) symmetric information benchmark is marginal cost pricing and not Ramsey pricing because of the absence of a cost of public funds. Second, and mainly, Sappington finds that pricing cannot be disconnected from incentives as long as the uncertainty parameter affects marginal costs.

For instance, suppose that

$$C=\Phi(\beta,e)\left(\sum_{k=1}^{n} q_k\right). \tag{4.2}$$

Eq. (4.2) describes a technology in which efficiency and effort determine the constant marginal cost of a common output to be distributed in n different markets. From Proposition 2, the price of good k is set at the symmetric information level in our model, while it is set above the symmetric information level in Sappington's model. This second discrepancy is due to Sappington's assumption that the firm's cost (or a garbled version of it) is not observable. Thus, the regulator cannot use cost reimbursement rules to extract rents and is forced to use price distortion as a substitute.[11] While the condition for the dichotomy is strong in our model, it leads us to view the dichotomy as a benchmark from which a case must be built that price manipulations do promote incentives.

When the incentive–pricing dichotomy does not hold, it is interesting to know whether the incentive corrections have the same signs for all goods. A sufficient condition for this is given in

Proposition 4. Suppose that there exists a function $\Gamma(q_1, \ldots, q_n)$ such that

$$C = C(\beta, e, \Gamma(\boldsymbol{q})). \tag{4.3}$$

Then the incentive correction has the same sign for all goods.

Proof of Proposition 4. For the functional form (4.3),

$$\frac{\partial}{\partial q_k}\left(-\frac{C_\beta}{C_e}\right) = \left[\frac{\partial}{\partial \Gamma}\left(-\frac{C_\beta}{C_e}\right)\right]\Gamma_{q_k}.$$

Proposition 4 follows from the fact that all the Γ_{q_k} have the same (positive) sign. Q.E.D.

An example in which Proposition 4 applies is the case of second-degree price discrimination (see subsection 3.3.2). Then there is only one good produced and the vector $\boldsymbol{q}$ is the vector of quantities of the good consumed by the various types of consumers.

4.2. *Multidimensional effort and characteristics*

In this subsection we give examples of extensions of our analysis to cost functions with multidimensional effort and characteristics.

[11]Sappington's analysis, like most of those in this paper, assumes a single-dimensional cost parameter. See Dana (1987) for an example of regulation (without cost observation) when the firm's subcosts are determined by different (although possibly correlated) parameters. See also Proposition 7, as well as the literature on regulation with multiple adverse selection parameters [Laffont, Maskin and Rochet (1987), Rochet (1986), and Lewis and Sappington (1988)].

4.2.1. Effort allocation: The shared-fixed-cost model

Our first paradigm is that of a joint fixed cost shared by several product lines, along with a variable cost for each product line (this paradigm might depict the case of switches used for several telecommunications services):

$$C=\mathscr{C}(\beta,e_0,\ldots,e_n,\boldsymbol{q})=\sum_{k=1}^{n} C^k(\beta,e_k,q_k)+C^0(\beta,e_0). \tag{4.4}$$

In (4.4), C^k is the subcost or variable cost of good k. C^0 is the fixed cost. The fixed cost and the subcosts cannot be disentangled from accounting data (an often reasonable assumption), so that only the total cost C can be contracted on. The firm's managers allocate their cost reduction activity e among the product lines and the joint activity:

$$e=\sum_{k=0}^{n} e_k, \tag{4.5}$$

so as to minimize $\mathscr{C}$ (this behavior is optimal as long as regulation is based on total cost):

$$C(\beta,e,\boldsymbol{q})=\min_{\{e_0,\ldots,e_n\}} \mathscr{C}(\beta,e_0,\ldots,e_n,\boldsymbol{q})$$

$$\text{s.t. (4.5).} \tag{4.6}$$

Let $\{e_i^*(\beta,e,\boldsymbol{q})\}_{i=0}^n$ denote the solution to (4.6).

The goal of this section is to obtain the analogs of Propositions 3 and 4 for this model. That is to say, we look for conditions on the subcost and joint cost functions so that the dichotomy holds, or at least that all incentive corrections have the same sign when the firm allocates its cost reducing activity.

Proposition 5. Assume an interior solution to program (4.6). The incentive–pricing dichotomy holds in the shared-fixed-cost model if and only if for all k

$$\sum_{l=0}^{n} \frac{\partial}{\partial e_l}\left(\frac{C^l_\beta}{C^l_{e_l}}\right)\frac{\partial e^*_l}{\partial q_k}+\frac{\partial}{\partial q_k}\left(\frac{C^k_\beta}{C^k_{e_k}}\right)=0.^{12} \tag{4.7}$$

Proof of Proposition 5. From Proposition 3, a necessary and sufficient condition for the dichotomy to hold is that $\partial(C_\beta/C_e)/\partial q_k=0$, for all k. Let $e^*_k(\beta, e, \boldsymbol{q})$ denote the optimal effort levels ($\sum_k e^*_k=e$). One has:

$$C_\beta=\sum_{k=0}^{n}\left(C^k_\beta+C^k_{e_k}\frac{\partial e^*_k}{\partial \beta}\right).$$

Furthermore, program (4.6) implies that

$$C_e=C^k_{e_k}, \quad \text{for all } k.$$

Hence,

$$C_\beta=\sum_{k=0}^{n} C^k_\beta,$$

using $\sum_k(\partial e^*_k/\partial\beta)=0$. This implies that

$$\frac{C_\beta}{C_e}=\sum_{k=0}^{n}\left(\frac{C^k_\beta}{C^k_{e_k}}\right).$$

Hence, C_β/C_e is independent of outputs if and only if (4.7) holds. Q.E.D.

Example. Adopting the convention that $q_0\equiv 1$, the following functional form,

$$C^k(\beta, e_k, q_k)=(\exp(-\mu_k e_k))r^k(\beta)z^k(q_k), \quad \text{for} \quad k=0,1,\ldots,n, \tag{4.8}$$

satisfies (4.7), because $C^k_\beta/C^k_{e_k}$ depends only on β. Hence, for the cost function described by (4.8), the incentive–pricing dichotomy holds. Another example of a functional form for which $C^k_\beta/C^k_{e_k}$ depends only on β, and thus for which the dichotomy holds, is

$$C^k(\beta, e_k, q_k)=(\beta-a_k e_k)^b z^k(q_k), \quad \text{for } k=0,1,\ldots,n.$$

[12] $\partial e^*_l/\partial q_k$, the change in effort $e^*_l(\beta, e, \boldsymbol{q})$ resulting from a unit increase in output k, is obtained by totally differentiating the $(n+1)$-equation system $\{C^l_{e_l}=C^k_{e_k}$ for all l in $\{0,\ldots,k-1,k+1,\ldots,n\}$ and $\sum_{l=0}^{n} e_l=e\}$ with respect to q_k.

Remark. A difference between the fixed effort allocation model of subsection 4.1 (which can be thought of as allocating effort in fixed proportions among the product lines and joint cost) and this flexible effort allocation model is that *the regulator may lose some power to extract rent through price distortions when the firm can allocate effort among product lines.* For example, assume that

$$C=(\exp(-\alpha_1 e))r^1(\beta)z^1(q_1)+(\exp(-\alpha_0 e))r^0(\beta), \tag{4.9}$$

with $\alpha_0+\alpha_1=1$ (so $e_0=\alpha_0 e$ and $e_1=\alpha_1 e$, where α_0 and α_1 are positive and predetermined). [This technology can be viewed as a two-product cost function in which one of the 'products' – with associated subcost the fixed cost – is produced in quantity one.] From Proposition 3, the dichotomy always fails for the cost function described in (4.9). However, from Proposition 5, it holds for the analogous cost function with flexible effort allocation:

$$C=(\exp(-e_1))r^1(\beta)z^1(q_1)+(\exp(-e_0))r^0(\beta). \tag{4.9$'$}$$

To understand why this is so, suppose for instance that $r^0(\beta)=r^0$ [β might then be the quality or price of an input and $(\exp(-e_1))$ a measure of the efficiency of the transformation of the input into the output]. The incentive correction for (4.9) (whose sign is given in Proposition 1) consists in lowering q_1 relative to the symmetric information case. This reduces $|(\mathrm{d}e/\mathrm{d}\beta)|_{\boldsymbol{q}\text{ and }C\text{ constant}}$ and thus the firm's rent. In contrast, for the technology described by (4.9′), the firm can lower e_1 without lowering e_0 when β decreases (and is indifferent to doing so at the margin), so that marginal changes in q_1 do not affect the slope of the rent function.

More generally, when do all incentive corrections have the same sign in the shared-fixed-cost model? From Proposition 4, a sufficient condition for this is that there exists a function Γ such that the solution to (4.6) can be written $C=C(\beta,e,\Gamma(\boldsymbol{q}))$.

Formally, the existence of such a Γ is equivalent to the possibility of partially aggregating capital goods in the production function of a firm that allocates labor optimally to capitals of different vintages. [That is, the outputs, q_k, correspond to the vintages of aggregated capital, $K_{1,k}$; the efforts, e_k, correspond to the labor inputs, L_k, allocated to machines of vintage k; $\beta_k=\beta$ is the analog of a vintage specific capital, $K_{2,k}$, that is not aggregated.] The necessary and sufficient condition for the partial aggregation of capital goods was developed by Fisher (1965) [see also Gorman (1968)]. Applied to our context, Theorem 5.1 in Fisher (1965) yields:

Proposition 6. A necessary and sufficient condition for the indirect cost function obtained in (4.6) *to have the form* $C(\beta,e,\Gamma(\boldsymbol{q}))$ *is that*

$$\frac{\partial^2 C^k}{\partial q_k \partial \beta} - \frac{\dfrac{\partial^2 C^k}{\partial q_k \partial e_k}\dfrac{\partial^2 C^k}{\partial e_k \partial \beta}}{\dfrac{\partial^2 C^k}{\partial e_k^2}} = 0, \quad \textit{for all } k \textit{ in } \{1,\ldots,n\} \tag{4.10}$$

and there exists a function $g(\cdot)$ *such that for all* k *in* $\{1,\ldots,n\}$,

$$\frac{\dfrac{\partial C^k}{\partial q_k}\dfrac{\partial^2 C^k}{\partial e_k^2}}{\dfrac{\partial^2 C^k}{\partial e_k \partial q_k}} = g\left(\frac{\partial C^k}{\partial e_k}\right). \tag{4.11}$$

Hence, if (4.10) *and* (4.11) *hold, all incentive corrections have the same sign.*

Example. The conditions stated in Proposition 6 are obviously very strong, but they allow us to, for instance, find classes of cost functions such that all incentive corrections have the same sign. Suppose that the subcost functions have the following multiplicative form:

$$C^k = r^k(\beta)s^k(e_k, q_k), \quad \text{for all } k \text{ in } \{1,\ldots,n\}. \tag{4.12}$$

The reader can check that conditions (4.10) and (4.11) hold if and only if

$$\frac{\partial}{\partial e_k}\left(\frac{\partial s^k}{\partial q_k}\Big/\frac{\partial s^k}{\partial e_k}\right) = 0, \quad \text{for all } k \text{ in } \{1,\ldots,n\}$$

[as is the case for instance if $s^k(e_k, q_k) = z^k(q_k)\,\mathrm{e}^{-\mu_k e_k}$].

The same techniques of partial aggregation of capital goods can be applied to the question of when a vector of cost parameters can be reduced to a single-dimensional cost parameter. To this purpose, it suffices to reverse the roles of the exogenous cost parameters and quantities in Proposition 6. More specifically, suppose that each product line is affected by a specific cost parameter:

$$C = C(\beta_0,\ldots,\beta_n, e, \boldsymbol{q}) = \min_{\{e_0,\ldots,e_n\}} \left[\sum_{k=1}^{n} C^k(\beta_k, e_k, q_k) + C^0(\beta_0, e_0)\right]$$

$$\text{s.t.} \sum_{k=0}^{n} e_k \leqq e. \tag{4.13}$$

The set of technological parameters $(\beta_0,\ldots,\beta_n)$ is now $(n+1)$-dimensional. We allow the joint distribution over $(\beta_0,\ldots,\beta_n)$ to be arbitrary. The manager knows all parameters, while the regulator knows none.

The validity of the single-parameter representation in this case depends on the possibility of partially aggregating technological parameters in the cost function. For, suppose that there is a function $\Lambda(\cdot)$ satisfying

$$C(\beta_0,\ldots,\beta_n,e,\boldsymbol{q})=\tilde{C}(\Lambda(\beta_0,\ldots,\beta_n),e,\boldsymbol{q}). \tag{4.14}$$

One then defines $\beta\equiv\Lambda(\beta_0,\ldots,\beta_n)$. The distribution over β results from the joint distribution over $(\beta_0,\ldots,\beta_n)$. All the results obtained so far in the one-dimensional case can then be applied as long as the distribution of β satisfies the monotone hazard rate property $[\mathrm{d}(F(\beta)/f(\beta))/\mathrm{d}\beta>0]$.

Thus, Fisher's (1965) Theorem 5.1 also yields:

Proposition 7. Assuming an interior solution to (4.13), *a necessary and sufficient condition for the cost function thus obtained to have the form* $\tilde{C}(\Lambda(\beta_0,\ldots,\beta_n),e,\boldsymbol{q})$ *is that*

$$\frac{\partial^2 C^k}{\partial q_k\,\partial\beta_k}\,\frac{\partial^2 C^k}{\partial e_k^2}=\frac{\partial^2 C^k}{\partial q_k\,\partial e_k}\,\frac{\partial^2 C^k}{\partial e_k\,\partial\beta_k} \tag{4.15}$$

and there exists a function $h(\cdot)$ such that for all k in $\{0,\ldots,n\}$,

$$\frac{\partial C^k}{\partial\beta_k}\,\frac{\partial^2 C^k}{\partial e_k^2}\bigg/\frac{\partial^2 C^k}{\partial e_k\,\partial\beta_k}=h\left(\frac{\partial C^k}{\partial e_k}\right). \tag{4.16}$$

Example. The subcost functions

$$C^k(\beta_k,e_k,q_k)=(\beta_k-e_k)^{\alpha_k}z^k(q_k) \tag{4.17}$$

satisfy the conditions of Proposition 7 [if an interior solution to (4.13) prevails] so that the technological parameters can be aggregated into a single-dimensional parameter.

4.2.2. Effort allocation: The shared-marginal-cost model

In several regulated industries, the same physical good is sold at different points of time (or in different geographical areas). A reduction in the marginal cost of producing one good (where a good is the physical good indexed by time, say) cannot be separated from a reduction in the marginal cost of producing other goods, in contrast with the technology considered in subsection 4.2.1.

Consider an electric utility facing time-varying demand for electricity. A fraction $x_k \in (0,1)$ of the time, the demand for electricity is q_k (which depends on the prices charged at different points of time). One has $\sum_{k=1}^{n} x_k = 1$. Without loss of generality, let us assume that $q_1 < \cdots < q_n$ (so n denotes the peak period). The firm installs capacity for each incremental output $(q_k - q_{k-1})$: q_1 units of base capacity, $(q_2 - q_1)$ units to supplement the base capacity in period 2, etc. [By convention, $q_0 = 0$.] Let $X_k \equiv \sum_{l=k}^{n} x_l$ denote the load factor of capacity of type k. The optimal exploitation policy implies that the marginal production costs (assumed constant) associated with all types of capacity satisfy: $c_1 \leqq c_2 \leqq \cdots \leqq c_n$. Let $G(q_1, q_2 - q_1, \ldots, q_n - q_{n-1})$ denote the total cost of installing the different types of capacities; we will let $G_k \equiv \partial G / \partial(q_k - q_{k-1})$ and $\tilde{c}_k \equiv c_k X_k$. The firm's cost function can be written:

$$
\begin{aligned}
C &= \mathscr{C}(\beta, e_1, \ldots, e_n, \boldsymbol{q}) \\
&= c_1(\beta, e_1) q_1 X_1 + c_2(\beta, e_2)(q_2 - q_1) X_2 + \cdots + c_n(\beta, e_n)(q_n - q_{n-1}) X_n \\
&\quad + G(q_1, q_2 - q_1, \ldots, q_n - q_{n-1}) \\
&= \sum_{k=1}^{n} \tilde{c}_k(\beta, e_k)(q_k - q_{k-1}) + G(q_1, q_2 - q_1, \ldots, q_n - q_{n-1}).
\end{aligned}
\tag{4.18}
$$

To give an example with $n = 2$, e_1 and e_2 can be thought of as the managers' efforts to supervise or improve the technology of the nuclear power division (which supplies both peak and off-peak demands) and the coal division (which supplies peak demand only). As before, we define

$$
C(\beta, e, \boldsymbol{q}) = \min \mathscr{C}(\beta, e_1, \ldots, e_n, \boldsymbol{q})
$$

$$
\text{s.t.} \sum_{k=1}^{n} e_k = e. \tag{4.19}
$$

Proposition 8. *Assume an interior solution to program* (4.19). *The incentive–pricing dichotomy holds for the shared-marginal-cost model if and only if, for all k,*

$$
\sum_{l=1}^{n} \frac{\partial}{\partial e_l} \frac{\dfrac{\partial \tilde{c}_l}{\partial \beta}}{\dfrac{\partial \tilde{c}_l}{\partial e_l}} \frac{\partial e_l^*}{\partial q_k} = 0, \tag{4.20}
$$

where the functions $\{e_l^*\}_{l=1}^n$ *are the solutions of* (4.19).

Proof of Proposition 8. The proof is essentially the same as that of Proposition 5. From (4.19), we know that $\partial(\tilde{c}_k(\beta, e_k))(q_k - q_{k-1})/\partial e_k = C_e$ for all k. Therefore

$$\frac{\partial}{\partial q_k}\left(-\frac{C_\beta}{C_e}\right) = -\sum_k \frac{\partial}{\partial q_k}\left(\frac{\partial \tilde{c}_k/\partial \beta}{\partial \tilde{c}_k/\partial e_k}\right).$$

Because of constant returns to scale, $\tilde{c}_k$ and its partial derivatives depend on q_k only through the effect of q_k on e_k^*. This, together with Proposition 2, yields (4.20). Q.E.D.

Examples. Eq. (4.20), and therefore the incentive–pricing dichotomy, holds for the marginal cost functions:

$$\tilde{c}_k(\beta, e_k) = (\beta - e_k)^{b_k} \tag{4.21}$$

and

$$\tilde{c}_k(\beta, e_k) = \beta - \log e_k. \tag{4.22}$$

[For marginal cost function (4.21),

$$\frac{\partial}{\partial e_l}\left(\frac{\partial \tilde{c}_l}{\partial \beta}\Big/\frac{\partial \tilde{c}_l}{\partial e_l}\right) = 0, \quad \text{for all } l.$$

For marginal cost function (4.22), the same term is equal to -1 for all l; the equality $\sum_{l=1}^n (\partial e_l^*/\partial q_k) = 0$ then yields (4.20).]

4.3. Linearity of cost reimbursement rules

Linear cost (or profit) sharing rules have the attractive property that they are still optimal under an additive cost disturbance or accounting error $[C \equiv C(\beta, e, \boldsymbol{q}) + \varepsilon]$ as long as the parties are risk-neutral. One may wonder whether the optimal regulatory policy can be implemented through a menu of linear cost reimbursement rules as in Laffont and Tirole (1986). Strong assumptions are needed to get exact linearity. Finding the minimal such assumptions is a difficult task, and we content ourselves with stating a sufficient condition for a menu of linear contracts to be optimal.

Proposition 9. Assume that

(i) *$C(\beta, e, \boldsymbol{q}) = G(\beta - e)H(\boldsymbol{q})$, where $G' > 0$, $G'' > 0$, and the curvature of G is 'not too high':*

$$\max_{\beta} (G''/G') \leqq \min_{\beta} \left(\frac{\mathrm{d}(F/f)}{\mathrm{d}\beta}\right) \Big/ (F/f).$$

(ii) $\psi''' \geqq 0$.

(iii) *Letting $\{e(\beta), \boldsymbol{q}(\beta)\}$ denote the solution to* (3.9) *and* (3.10),

$$\frac{\mathrm{d}}{\mathrm{d}\beta} G(\beta - e(\beta)) \geqq 0 \quad \text{and} \quad \frac{\mathrm{d}}{\mathrm{d}\beta}(q_k(\beta)) \leqq 0, \quad \text{for all } \beta.$$

Then the optimal regulatory policy can be implemented through a menu of linear contracts.

Assumption (iii) in Proposition 9 is reasonable. For the optimal policy, a firm with a higher β is likely to produce less, $\mathrm{d}q_k/\mathrm{d}\beta \leqq 0$, and to have a higher $G(\beta - e(\beta))$. [It is easy to find sufficient conditions for these to hold. Note that from Proposition 4, the dichotomy holds, so that the outputs are the solutions to $V_{q_k} + \lambda R_{q_k} = (1+\lambda)C_{q_k}$, for all k.] Assumption (ii) is technical and is much stronger than necessary. It ensures that the optimal regulatory scheme is not stochastic. Assumption (i) is strong. The proof of Proposition 9 can be found in appendix B.

5. General equilibrium analysis: Foundations of the shadow cost of public funds and taxation by regulation

5.1. Motivation

This paper has followed the partial equilibrium tradition of the regulation literature. This raises two potential issues.

First, recall that in our formulation of the social welfare function, we multiplied the firm's cost, transfer, and revenue by a factor $(1+\lambda)$ and stated that $\lambda > 0$, the shadow cost of public funds, is determined by economy-wide considerations. The factor $\lambda/(1+\lambda)$, which measures the relative social cost of transfers and real expenses, plays a crucial role in the effort correction [eq. (3.9)], in the Ramsey index [eq, (3.15)], and in the incentive correction [eq. (3.16)]. Clearly, the existence of a shadow cost of public funds and the validity of the partial equilibrium approach to incentives and pricing can be ascertained only in a general equilibrium model.

Second, the gross consumer surplus was taken to be the unweighted sum of individual gross consumer surpluses. In practice, the distribution of income is not socially optimal, and one may wonder whether regulation should be used as a substitute for a (non-existent) perfect taxation system. In more technical terms, should the Lerner index differ from the sum of the Ramsey index and the incentive correction for specific goods? That is, in the terminology of section 2, should there be demand-side cross-subsidization? Posner (1971) has argued that 'existing views of regulation do not explain well the important phenomenon of internal subsidization' (p. 28) and offers to 'modify existing views by admitting that one of the functions of regulation is to perform distributive and allocative chores usually associated with the taxing or financial branch of government' (p. 23). Examples of regulated pricing that seem to be motivated by redistributive concerns are the use of uniform rates for mail and telephone, avoiding cost-based price discrimination between rural and urban areas, or British Telecom's license agreement preventing low-usage residential customers' line rental charges from growing faster than the retail price index plus 2 percent per year.[13]

The issue of demand-side cross-subsidization closely relates to the debate on direct vs. indirect taxation in public finance about whether the responsibility for redistribution should be assumed by income taxation only, or by differential excise taxes as well. One of the main findings of this literature [Atkinson and Stiglitz (1976), Mirrlees (1976)] is that using indirect taxation to redistribute income is a less obvious policy than one might have thought. Indeed, if (i) consumers differ in their ability (or wage w earned per unit of labor), (ii) their utility function exhibits weak separability between consumption and labor [$U=U(A(q_1,\dots,q_n),L)$, where L is labor], and (iii) the government uses optimal excise taxes on goods and optimal non-linear income taxation [so taxes paid by a consumer of 'type' w have the form $\sum_{k=1}^{n}\tau_k q_k+T(wL)$], the government need not use indirect taxation. [That is, it can pick $\tau_k=\tau$ for all k; and, without loss of generality, τ can be taken to be zero from the homogeneity of the consumers' budget constraints.]

This result does not imply that taxation by regulation is socially inefficient, simply that it is not a foregone conclusion. There are several ways to reintroduce motives for demand-side cross-subsidization. First, the strong assumption of weak separability may be relaxed; however, as Atkinson and Stiglitz (1980, p. 437) note, nearly all empirical studies of demand and labor supply functions have made this assumption and are therefore of little guidance for our purpose. Second, one may assume that income is imperfectly observable because of perks, of domestic production, or of tax evasion [Deaton (1977), for instance, takes this route]. Third, consumers may differ with respect to attributes other than ability. To these three reasons listed by

[13]An alternative to the redistribution concerns explanation is the political science view that a number of instances of demand-side cross-subsidization result from interest group politics. In Laffont and Tirole (1988) we show how the agency's potential identification with consumer groups may result in uniform pricing even if the costs of serving different categories of consumers differ.

Atkinson and Stiglitz (1980, p. 440) can be added a fourth. There may exist situations in which commodity taxation can be based on information not available for income taxation, because of different arbitrage possibilities. For instance, it may be costly to make income taxation contingent on the rural or urban character of the consumer's place of residence, because of potential manipulation of fiscal address. However, the consumptions of electricity or telephone in urban and rural areas are less subject to arbitrage. So, for instance, if the distribution of the unit wage, w, profile in urban areas first-order stochastically dominates that for rural areas, one can show that, under some conditions on preferences, the prices of electricity and telephone in rural areas should be subsidized relative to those in the urban areas.

5.2. An imperfect income taxation model

We now show how foundations for the shadow cost of public funds and for taxation by regulation can be obtained in a general equilibrium framework. We follow Deaton's line of analyzing imperfect income taxation. To keep the model as simple as possible and to focus on essentials, we assume away income taxation. This situation corresponds to the extreme case in which the consumers' incomes are not observable by the government.

The model has $n+1$ goods. Good 0, the numeraire, is a privately produced good. Goods 1 through n are produced by the regulated sector and have prices $p_1,\dots,p_n$.

5.2.1. Consumers

There are m categories of consumers (one can, for instance, have in mind that there is a continuum of consumers in each category). Consumers of type i have quasi-linear preferences:

$$S^i(Q_1^i,\dots,Q_n^i)+Q_0^i,$$

where Q_0^i and $(Q_1^i,\dots,Q_n^i)$ are the consumptions of private and regulated goods. They have endowment $\bar{Q}_0^i$ of the numeraire and no endowment of the regulated goods. Their net surplus is

$$S^i(Q_1^i,\dots,Q_n^i)+\bar{Q}_0^i-\sum_{k=1}^{n} p_k Q_k^i.$$

5.2.2. Regulated firms

To remove aggregate uncertainty and simplify the exposition of the government budget balance condition, we assume that there is a continuum of regulated firms producing goods 1 through n. (Alternatively, there could be a single firm, and the government budget constraint would be interpreted in expectation.) A regulated firm is indexed by its efficiency parameter β in $[\underline{\beta},\bar{\beta}]$ and has cost function $C=C(\beta,e,\boldsymbol{q})$ in terms of numeraire. The managers of the regulated firms know their firm's β, but the government only knows the distribution $F(\beta)$ of parameters (and views all firms as ex ante identical). Each regulated firm is run by a manager with utility function $U=t-\psi(e)$, where t is the transfer from the government and $\psi(e)$ the disutility of effort, both expressed in terms of numeraire (the functions C and ψ satisfy the assumptions of section 3). For notational simplicity, we assume that the managers of regulated firms consume only the numeraire; nothing would be altered if they consumed also regulated goods. Last, recall from section 3 that the individual rationality and incentive compatibility constraints are

$$U(\bar{\beta})=0 \tag{3.7}$$

and

$$\dot{U}(\beta)=-\psi'(e)E_\beta(\beta,C(\beta,e,\boldsymbol{q}),\boldsymbol{q}). \tag{3.8}$$

5.2.3. Budget constraint

The government must balance its budget. In our framework, the revenue from regulated goods must exceed the total cost (cost plus managerial income) of running the regulated firms. Using the fact that $t(\beta)=U(\beta)+\psi(e(\beta))$, and expressing the budget constraint in terms of numeraire, we have

$$\sum_{k=1}^{n} p_k\left(\sum_{i=1}^{m} Q_k^i\right)\geqq\int_{\underline{\beta}}^{\bar{\beta}}[C(\beta,e(\beta),\boldsymbol{q}(\beta))+U(\beta)+\psi(e(\beta))]f(\beta)\,\mathrm{d}\beta. \tag{5.1}$$

5.2.4. Market clearing

The demand for regulated goods must not exceed supply:

$$\forall k=1,\ldots,n,\int_{\underline{\beta}}^{\bar{\beta}} q_k(\beta)f(\beta)\,\mathrm{d}\beta\geqq\sum_{i=1}^{m} Q_k^i. \tag{5.2}$$

5.2.5. Social welfare function

The government maximizes a weighted average of the consumers' and managers' net surpluses. Let α^i and α^0 denote the weights on consumers of type i and managers. Thus,

$$W=\sum_{i=1}^{m}\alpha^i\left[S^i(Q_1^i,\ldots,Q_n^i)+\bar{Q}_0^i-\sum_{k=1}^{n}p_kQ_k^i\right]+\alpha^0\int_{\underline{\beta}}^{\bar{\beta}}U(\beta)f(\beta)\,\mathrm{d}\beta. \qquad (5.3)$$

Let $Q_k\equiv\sum_{i=1}^m Q_k^i$, and let $p_k(Q_1,\ldots,Q_n)$ denote the inverse demand for regulated good k. The social optimum is obtained by maximizing (5.3) with respect to the control variables Q_k^i, $q_k(\beta)$, and $e(\beta)$, and the state variable $U(\beta)$ subject to constraints (3.7), (3.8), (5.1), and (5.2). Letting $\mu(\beta)$, γ, and v_k denote the multipliers associated with constraints (3.8), (5.1), and (5.2), the first-order conditions are:

$$\sum_i\alpha^i\left(-\sum_l\frac{\partial p_l}{\partial Q_k}Q_l^i\right)+\gamma\left(\sum_l\frac{\partial p_l}{\partial Q_k}Q_l+p_k\right)-v_k=0, \qquad (5.4)$$

$$-\mu(\beta)\psi'(e)\frac{\mathrm{d}}{\mathrm{d}q_k}(E_\beta)-\gamma C_{q_k}f+v_kf=0, \qquad (5.5)$$

$$-\mu(\beta)\frac{\mathrm{d}}{\mathrm{d}e}(\psi'(e)E_\beta)-\gamma(C_e+\psi'(e))=0, \qquad (5.6)$$

$$\dot{\mu}(\beta)=(\gamma-\alpha^0)f(\beta). \qquad (5.7)$$

Using the fact that $\bar{\beta}$ is a free boundary, (5.7) implies that

$$\mu(\beta)=(\gamma-\alpha^0)F(\beta). \qquad (5.8)$$

Substituting (5.5) into (5.4) yields:

$$L_k=R_k+I_k, \qquad (5.9)$$

where

$$L_k\equiv(p_k-C_{q_k})/p_k$$

is good k's Lerner index,

$$R_k\equiv-\sum_l\frac{1}{p_k}\frac{\partial p_l}{\partial Q_k}\left(\frac{\gamma Q_l-\sum_i\alpha^iQ_l^i}{\gamma}\right)$$

is its Ramsey index,

$$I_k \equiv \frac{\gamma - \alpha^0}{\gamma} \frac{F(\beta)}{f(\beta) p_k} \psi'(e) \frac{\mathrm{d}}{\mathrm{d}q_k} (E_\beta)$$

is its incentive correction, and (5.6) yields the optimal effort:

$$\psi'(e) = -C_e - \frac{\gamma - \alpha^0}{\gamma} \frac{F(\beta)}{f(\beta)} \frac{\mathrm{d}}{\mathrm{d}e} (\psi'(e) E_\beta). \tag{5.10}$$

Clearly (5.9) and (5.10) bear a strong resemblance to (3.13) and (3.9). The effort correction is still proportional to $F(\beta)/f(\beta)\ \mathrm{d}(\psi'(e)E_\beta)/\mathrm{d}e$. And the incentive correction is equal to zero if and only if the cost function is separable $[\mathrm{d}(E_\beta)/\mathrm{d}q_k = 0$ for all k or $C = C(\Phi(\beta, e), \boldsymbol{q})]$. Proposition 10 provides the exact link between partial and general equilibrium results.

Proposition 10.

(i) *Suppose that the social welfare function puts equal weight on all parties* ($\alpha^i = \alpha$ *for all* $i = 0, \ldots, m$). *Then*

- *the shadow cost of public funds expressed in terms of numeraire is given by* $\lambda = (\gamma - \alpha)/\alpha$ (*that is,* $1 + \lambda = \gamma/\alpha$),
- *the partial and general equilibrium approaches coincide* [(5.9) *and* (5.10) *coincide with* (3.13) *and* (3.9)].

(ii) *If the weights in the social welfare function differ, the partial and general equilibrium results still coincide as long as:*

- *one defines 'consumer-specific shadow costs of public funds':* $\lambda^i \equiv (\gamma - \alpha^i)/\alpha^i$ *for consumers* $i = 1, \ldots, m$ *and* $\lambda^0 \equiv (\gamma - \alpha^0)/\alpha^0$ *for managers,*
- *the shadow cost of public funds that applies to the effort eq.* (3.9) *and the incentive correction* (3.16) *is the cost* λ^0 *of public funds collected from managers, and*
- (*taxation by regulation*) *the coefficient* $[\lambda/(1+\lambda)]Q_l$ *in the Ramsey index* (3.15) *is taken equal to*

$$\left(1 - \sum_{i=1}^{m} \frac{x_l^i}{1 + \lambda^i}\right) Q_l,$$

where $x_l^i \equiv Q_l^i / Q_l$ *is consumer i's share of consumption of good* l.

The intuition for Proposition 10 is straightforward. If all parties are weighted equally, there is no redistribution concern among consumers or between consumers and managers. The partial equilibrium approach need not be amended. To understand the definition of the shadow cost of public funds, suppose that for some exogenous reason the government must collect one more unit of numeraire, which is thrown away. By definition, the loss in social welfare is equal to the multiplier, γ, of the government budget constraint. Because one unit of numeraire for any party has value α in the social welfare function, the welfare loss caused by this extra budgetary need is $1+\lambda=\gamma/\alpha$.

When weights in the social welfare function differ, under imperfect income taxation, the formulas must be amended slightly. First, when managers and consumers are weighted differently, what matters in eqs. (3.9) and (3.16) is the shadow cost of public funds collected from managers. The reason is that the reduction in the power of incentive schemes [eq. (3.9)] and the incentive correction on prices [eq. (3.16)] are two alternative ways of extracting managerial rents. Their social cost thus relates to λ^0.

Second, when consumers are weighted differently among themselves, the Ramsey index must take into account redistributive concerns (taxation by regulation). In particular, goods that are much consumed by consumers whose utility matters a lot in the social welfare function (x_k^i high, α^i high) have low Ramsey indices and therefore low prices.[14]

A special case of taxation by regulation is that of third-degree price discrimination. Suppose that the regulated firms produce a single physical good (electricity), which is consumed by city inhabitants (consumers 1) and rural inhabitants (consumers 2). Let p_1 and p_2 be the prices charged in urban and rural areas. If incomes are lower in rural areas, so that $\alpha^2>\alpha^1$, the fact that $x_1^1=x_2^2=1$ together with (5.9) yields $p_1>p_2$.

6. Conclusion

This paper developed a normative model of the regulation of a multi-product firm based on a full description of the informational constraints faced by the regulator. Let us summarize the main findings:

(a) Optimal pricing requires that each product's Lerner index be equal to the sum of a Ramsey term and an incentive correction.

(b) The Ramsey term is entirely determined by the industry demand data and the economy-wide shadow cost of public funds, and may reflect redistributive concerns. In contrast to the Ramsey–Boiteux model, the Ramsey term is independent of the firm's cost structure.

(c) The possibility of using pricing to extract the firm's informational rent may give rise to an incentive correction. The incentive correction, if any, is entirely cost-determined (is independent of the demand function) and can be analyzed by using aggregation techniques. But prices should not necessarily

[14]The reader may be surprised by the fact that λ^i is low when α^i is high. Recall, however, that the λ^i in the Ramsey index corresponds to the social *value* of raising revenue to cover the regulated firms' costs. Raising revenue from poor consumers (α^i high) yields low social welfare.

be used to promote incentives (in which case the incentive correction is equal to zero), because cost reimbursement (or profit-sharing) rules may be a sufficient instrument to do so. Indeed, we view the dichotomy between the cost reimbursement rule as an incentive device and pricing as an allocation device as a good benchmark. A strong case must be built that the cost technology is conducive to incentive corrections.

Part II [Laffont and Tirole (1990)] extends the analysis to various competitive environments and draws and discusses policy implications.

Appendix A: Proof of Proposition 1

Assuming differentiability for convenience (differentiability almost everywhere can be proved using standard techniques) we first derive the first-order condition of incentive compatibility for the firm:

$$\max_{\beta} \left[t(\hat{\beta}) - \psi(E(\beta, C(\hat{\beta}), \boldsymbol{q}(\hat{\beta})))\right]$$

yields the F.O.C. (at $\hat{\beta}=\beta$):

$$\frac{\mathrm{d}}{\mathrm{d}\beta}(t(\beta) - \psi'\left[E_C\frac{\mathrm{d}C}{\mathrm{d}\beta} + \sum_k E_{q_k}\frac{\mathrm{d}q_k}{\mathrm{d}\beta}\right] = 0.$$

The sufficient second-order condition is [see Guesnerie and Laffont (1984)]:

$$-\psi'' E_\beta\left[E_C\frac{\mathrm{d}C}{\mathrm{d}\beta} + \sum_k E_{q_k}\frac{\mathrm{d}q_k}{\mathrm{d}\beta}\right] - \psi'\left[E_{C\beta}\frac{\mathrm{d}C}{\mathrm{d}\beta} + \sum_k E_{q_k\beta}\frac{\mathrm{d}q_k}{\mathrm{d}\beta}\right] \geqq 0.$$

If $E_\beta > 0$, $E_C < 0$, and $E_{q_k} > 0$, for all k, then $\mathrm{d}C/\mathrm{d}\beta \geqq 0$ and $\mathrm{d}q_k/\mathrm{d}\beta \leqq 0$, for all k, ensure that second-order conditions are satisfied. As usual, we do not impose these inequality constraints, but check that they are satisfied by our solutions.

Letting $U(\beta)$ denote the rent of the firm, we can rewrite the first-order condition:

$$\dot{U}(\beta) = -\psi'(e)E_\beta(\beta, C(\beta, e, \boldsymbol{q}), \boldsymbol{q}) < 0. \tag{A.1}$$

Because $U(\beta)$ is decreasing, the individual rationality constraint of the firm is achieved by imposing

$$U(\bar{\beta}) \geqq 0. \tag{A.2}$$

The regulator maximizes (3.6) under (A.1) and (A.2) with respect to $e(\beta)$, $q_k(\beta)$, for all k treating U as the state variable. The Hamiltonian is:

$$H=[V(\boldsymbol{q})+\lambda R(\boldsymbol{q})-(1+\lambda)(\psi(e)+C(\beta,e,\boldsymbol{q}))-\lambda U]f(\beta)$$

$$-\mu(\beta)\psi'(e)E_\beta(\beta,C(\beta,e,\boldsymbol{q}),\boldsymbol{q}).$$

We have: $\dot{\mu}(\beta)=-\partial H/\partial U=\lambda f(\beta)$. Since $\mu(\underline{\beta})=0$, $\mu(\beta)=\lambda F(\beta)$. Substituting $\mu(\beta)$ into H, the first-order conditions $\partial H/\partial e=0$ and $\partial H/\partial q_k=0$, for all k, yield (3.9) and (3.10). Q.E.D.

Appendix B: Proof of Proposition 9

Let $\bar{C}\equiv C/H(q)$ and $I\equiv G^{-1}$ (with $I'=1/G'>0$ and $I''=-G''/G'^3<0$). Thus,

$$\beta-e=I(\bar{C}).$$

Because $\bar{C}$ is a 'sufficient statistic' for e given β, the transfer function can be made contingent on $\bar{C}$ only: $t(\bar{C})$. Linearity with respect to C is equivalent to linearity with respect to $\bar{C}$. The firm chooses $\bar{C}$ so as to maximize

$$t(\bar{C})-\psi(\beta-I(\bar{C})),$$

yielding the first-order condition:

$$\frac{\mathrm{d}t}{\mathrm{d}\bar{C}}=-\psi' I'$$

and the second-order condition (after using the first-order condition as an identity):

$$I'\frac{\mathrm{d}}{\mathrm{d}\beta}(\bar{C})\geqq 0$$

or

$$\frac{\mathrm{d}}{\mathrm{d}\beta}\left(\frac{C(\beta)}{H(\boldsymbol{q}(\beta))}\right)\geqq 0.$$

Condition (i) in Proposition 9 thus guarantees that the firm's second-order condition is satisfied.

The regulator can use a menu of linear cost-reimbursement rules if and only if the transfer function $t(\bar{C})$ is convex (the linear cost-reimbursement rules are then given by the tangents to the convex curve). But

$$\frac{\mathrm{d}^2 t}{\mathrm{d}\bar{C}^2} = -\psi''\left(\frac{\mathrm{d}\beta}{\mathrm{d}\bar{C}} - I'\right)I' - \psi' I''.$$

Using the definition of $\bar{C} \equiv G(\beta - e)$ and $I' = 1/G'$, one has:

$$\frac{\mathrm{d}\beta}{\mathrm{d}\bar{C}} - I' = \frac{\dot{e}}{(1-\dot{e})G'},$$

where $\dot{e} \equiv \mathrm{d}e/\mathrm{d}\beta$. Differentiating (3.9), and using the fact that $E_{\beta C} = 0$:

$$\dot{e} = \frac{HG'' - \dfrac{\lambda}{1+\lambda}\dfrac{\mathrm{d}(F/f)}{\mathrm{d}\beta}\psi'' + \left(\sum H_k \dot{q}_k\right)G'}{\psi'' + HG'' + \dfrac{\lambda}{1+\lambda}\dfrac{F}{f}\psi'''}.$$

Note that under our assumptions, $\dot{e} < 0$ *and hence the firm's second-order condition is satisfied*. Now, if $\psi''' \geqq 0$ and $\dot{q}_k < 0$, for all k,

$$\frac{\dot{e}}{1-\dot{e}} \leqq \frac{HG'' - \dfrac{\lambda}{1+\lambda}\dfrac{\mathrm{d}(F/f)}{\mathrm{d}\beta}\psi'' + \left(\sum H_k \dot{q}_k\right)G'}{\psi''},$$

so that, using $\mathrm{d}(F/f)/\mathrm{d}\beta \geqq 0$,

$$\frac{\mathrm{d}^2 t}{\mathrm{d}\bar{C}^2} \geqq \frac{\psi' G''}{G'^3} - \frac{HG'' - \dfrac{\lambda}{1+\lambda}\dfrac{\mathrm{d}}{\mathrm{d}\beta}\left(\dfrac{F}{f}\right)\psi''}{G'^2}.$$

Replacing ψ' using (3.9) yields, after some simplifications:

$$\frac{\mathrm{d}^2 t}{\mathrm{d}\bar{C}^2} \geqq \frac{\lambda}{1+\lambda}\left(\frac{\psi''}{G'^3}\right)\left[G'\frac{\mathrm{d}(F/f)}{\mathrm{d}\beta} - G''\frac{F}{f}\right].$$

Hence, if condition (i) in Proposition 7 holds, $\mathrm{d}^2 t/\mathrm{d}\bar{C}^2 \geqq 0$ (recall that the hazard rate is monotonic). This implies that the regulator can use a menu of linear contracts. The slope of each incentive contract is given by the firm's first-order condition:

$$\frac{\mathrm{d}t}{\mathrm{d}\bar{C}} + \psi'(\beta - I(\bar{C}))I'(\bar{C}) = 0;$$

it suffices to invert the equilibrium function $\bar{C}=\bar{C}(\beta)$ into $\beta=\beta(\bar{C})$ and eliminate β in the previous equation. Q.E.D.

References

Atkinson, A. and J. Stiglitz, 1976, The design of tax structure: Direct and indirect taxation, Journal of Public Economics 6, 55–75.

Atkinson, A. and J. Stiglitz, 1980, Lectures on public economics (McGraw-Hill, New York, NY).

Bailey, E., 1973, Economic theory of regulatory constraint (Lexington Books, Lexington, MA).

Ballard, C., J. Shoven and J. Whalley, 1985, General equilibrium computations of the marginal welfare costs of taxes in the United States, American Economic Review 75, 128–138.

Baron, D. and R. Myerson, 1982, Regulating a monopolist with unknown costs, Econometrica 50, 911–930.

Baumol, W., 1975, Payment by performance in rail passenger transportation: An innovation in Amtrak's operations, Bell Journal of Economics 6, 281–298.

Baumol, W. and D. Bradford, 1970, Optimal departures from marginal cost pricing, American Economic Review 60, 265–283.

Baumol, W., J. Panzar and R. Willig, 1982, Contestable markets and the theory of industry structure (Harcourt, Brace, Jovanovich, New York).

Boiteux, M., 1949, La tarification des demandes en pointes: Application de la théorie de la vente au coût marginal, Revue Genérale de l'Electricité 58, 321–340.

Boiteux, M., 1956, Sur la gestion des monopoles publics astreints à l'equilibre budgétaire, Econometrica 24, 22–40.

Brennan, T., 1987, Cross subsidization and discrimination by regulated monopolists, EAG DP no. 87–2, US Department of Justice.

Brown, S. and D. Sibley, 1985, The theory of public utility pricing (Cambridge University Press, New York, NY).

Dana, J., 1987, The organization and scope of monitored agents: Regulating multiproduct industries, Mimeo. (MIT).

Deaton, A., 1977, Equity, efficiency and the structure of indirect taxation, Journal of Public Economics 8, 299–312.

Faulhaber, G., 1975, Cross-subsidization: Pricing in public enterprises, American Economic Review 75, 966–977.

Fisher, F., 1965, Embodied technical change and the existence of an aggregate capital stock, Review of Economic Studies 35, 263–288.

Gorman, W., 1968, Reviewing the quantities of fixed factors, Chapter 5 in: J.N. Wolfe, ed., Value, capital and growth: Essays in honor of Sir John Hicks (Edinburgh University Press, Edinburgh).

Guesnerie, R. and J.-J. Laffont, 1984, A complete solution to a class of principal-agent problems with an application to the control of a self-managed firm, Journal of Public Economics 25, 329–369.

Hausman, J. and J. Poterba, 1987, Household behavior and the tax reform act of 1986, Journal of Economic Perspectives 1, 101–119.

Laffont, J.-J. and J. Tirole, 1986, Using cost observation to regulate firms, Journal of Political Economy 94, 614–641.

Laffont, J.-J. and J. Tirole, 1988, The politics of government decision making: A theory of regulatory capture, Quarterly Journal of Economics, forthcoming.

Laffont, J.-J. and J. Tirole, 1989a, Optimal bypass and creamskimming, American Economic Review, forthcoming.

Laffont, J.-J. and J. Tirole, 1989b, Provision of quality and power of incentive schemes in regulated industries, to appear in Proceedings of a Conference in Honor of Jacques Drèze.

Laffont, J.-J. and J. Tirole, 1990, The regulation of multiproduct firms, Part II: Applications to competitive environments and policy analysis, Journal of Public Economics (this issue).

Laffont, J.-J., E. Maskin and J.-C. Rochet, 1987, Optimal nonlinear pricing: The case of buyers with several characteristics, in: T. Groves, R. Radner and S. Reiter, eds., Information, incentives and economic mechanisms: In Honor of L. Hurwicz (University of Minnesota Press).

Leontieff, W., 1947, Introduction to a theory of the internal structure of functional relationships, Econometrica 15, 361–373.

Lewis, T. and D. Sappington, 1988, Regulating with unknown demand and cost functions, Rand Journal of Economics, forthcoming.

Mirrlees, J., 1976, Optimal tax theory: A synthesis, Journal of Public Economics 6, 327–358.

Posner, R., 1971, Taxation by regulation, Bell Journal of Economics 2, 22–50.

Ramsey, F., 1927, A contribution to the theory of taxation, Economic Journal 37, 47–61.

Rochet, J.-C., 1986, Monopoly regulation with a two-dimensional uncertainty, Journal of Mathematical Economics, forthcoming.

Sappington, D., 1983, Optimal regulation of a multiproduct monopoly with unknown technological capabilities, Bell Journal of Economics 14, 453–463.

Sharkey, W., 1982, The theory of natural monopoly (Cambridge University Press, New York, NY).

Steiner, P., 1957, Peak loads and efficient pricing, Quarterly Journal of Economics 71, 585–610.

Journal of Public Economics 43 (1990) 37–66. North-Holland

THE REGULATION OF MULTIPRODUCT FIRMS

Part II: Applications to Competitive Environments and Policy Analysis

Jean-Jacques LAFFONT

GREMAQ, Université des Sciences Sociales de Toulouse, F-31042 Toulouse Cedex, France

Jean TIROLE*

Massachusetts Institute of Technology, Cambridge, MA 02139, USA

Received October 1988, revised version received February 1990

This paper extends our companion paper [Part I – Laffont and Tirole (1990)] on the regulation of the rate of return and prices of a multiproduct firm in two directions. First, it studies optimal pricing by a regulated firm competing with regulated or unregulated rivals, with or without market power or other distorted pricing. It then focuses on the access pricing problem and its potential foreclosure effects. Second, it shows how optimal pricing can be decentralized to the regulated firm in the absence of cost and demand information.

1. Introduction

Our companion paper [Part I – Laffont and Tirole (1990)] developed a normative model of a multiproduct regulated firm, which we briefly review. Consider a regulated firm with cost function $C=C(\beta,e,\boldsymbol{q})$, that depends on the vector of outputs $\boldsymbol{q}=(q_1,\ldots,q_n)$, a technological parameter β that is private information to the firm, and the firm's managers' cost-reducing activity e. Regulatory contracts are contingent on observables: cost and prices (or outputs). Let $V(\boldsymbol{q})$ be the social value of output vector $\boldsymbol{q}$, $R(\boldsymbol{q})$ the revenue associated with the sale of these outputs, and λ the shadow cost of public funds. Under some assumptions, the optimal cost reimbursement rule is linear in the firm's cost. Of particular interest for this paper is the optimal pricing rule: maximizing social welfare over the output of good k yields for all $k\in\{1,\ldots,n\}$:

$$V_{q_k}+\lambda R_{q_k}=(1+\lambda)C_{q_k}+I_k. \tag{1.1}$$

*The authors are grateful to Frank Fisher, Paul Joskow, David Sappington, Dick Schmalensee and two anonymous referees for helpful comments, and to the Ford Foundation, the Pew Charitable Trust, the Guggenheim Foundation, the Center for Energy Policy Research at MIT, the National Science Foundation and the Ministère de l'Education Nationale for financial support.

0047–2727/90/$03.50

Alternatively, maximizing social welfare with respect to prices yields:

$$\sum_l (V_{q_l} + \lambda R_{q_l} - (1+\lambda)C_{q_l}) \frac{\partial q_l}{\partial p_k} = \tilde{I}_k. \tag{1.2}$$

The term I_k (or $\tilde{I}_k$) is an 'incentive correction' that depends only on the cost functional. It is equal to zero if the regulator and the firm have symmetric information about the firm's technology. If the firm has private information about its technology, the incentive correction is equal to zero if and only if the cost function is separable in outputs and asymmetric information parameters: $C = C(\Phi(\beta, e), \boldsymbol{q})$, in which case the 'incentive–pricing dichotomy' is said to hold. Our companion paper supplied conditions under which the incentive–pricing dichotomy holds when the firm chooses both the cost-reducing activity and its allocation among product lines. It also provided a general equilibrium analysis endogenizing the shadow cost of public funds.

Most of this paper aims to analyze pricing in greater detail and assumes that the cost function is separable in order to abstract from incentive issues. Alternatively, if the incentive–pricing dichotomy fails to hold, one can add the incentive correction to the formulas derived in this paper.

When $V(\boldsymbol{q})$ is equal to the gross consumer surplus [$V(\boldsymbol{q}) = S(\boldsymbol{q})$ with $S_{q_k} = p_k$, the price of good k], when demands are independent and when $R(\boldsymbol{q}) = \sum_{k=1}^{n} p_k q_k$, (1.2) takes the familiar form (assuming $\tilde{I}_k = 0$):

$$L_k \equiv \frac{p_k - C_{q_k}}{p_k} = R_k \equiv \frac{\lambda}{1+\lambda} \frac{1}{\eta_k}, \tag{1.3}$$

where L_k is good k's Lerner index, and η_k is its demand elasticity. Unlike in the traditional Ramsey–Boiteux model, the coefficient $(\lambda/(1+\lambda))$ in the Ramsey index R_k is determined economy-wide and can be obtained from available data. When goods are substitutes or complements, the Lerner index must lie above or below the Ramsey term narrowly restricted to the good's own elasticity of demand.

But (1.1) and (1.2) are very general as $V(\cdot)$ and $R(\cdot)$ are left unspecified. Our companion paper, for example, applied them to the problems of second-degree price discrimination and of incentives to provide verifiable quality. Section 2 of the present paper applies them to various competitive environments in which the regulated firm (a) faces a regulated competitor, (b) faces an unregulated firm with or without market power, and (c) faces a subsidized competitive fringe. Because the derivations involve straightforward applications of formula (1.1), we ignore the computational details to focus on the results and their intuition.

Section 3 pursues the investigation of pricing in a competitive environment by studying the issue of access pricing. In several industries (telecommunications, railroads, energy) a regulated firm must supply an input (local access, trackage services, transportation of energy) to a competitor in order for the latter to be able to compete in the product market. The regulation of access has two dimensions. First, putting aside incentive issues, one must analyze the optimal access price to be charged to the competitor; a key to the understanding of this pricing problem is to view the intermediate good supplied to the competitor and the final good of the regulated firm as substitutes. The pricing of the intermediate good then follows standard Ramsey principles. Second, there is the incentive issue of whether the regulated firm can gain by foreclosing the market for the final good through an excessive access price. We argue that the difficulty in eliciting the appropriate access price from the regulated firm depends on the technology. If the regulated firm and its competitor have identical requirements of the intermediate good to produce their final outputs, the firm cannot claim that the production of the intermediate good is costly without making a case against its own final output. The regulator can detect anticompetitive access pricing by comparing a high access price and a high final output of the regulated firm. Suppose, in contrast, that the regulated firm must produce a distinct intermediate good for its competitor (or must add to its existing capacity at a privately known cost to supply its competitor); the regulated firm then has an incentive to charge an excessive access price to restrict competition and increase its informational rent on the final good market. Section 3 analyzes the effect of such foreclosure on the power of the regulated firm's incentive scheme and on welfare and compares the access pricing problem with the bypass problem.

Section 4 analyzes whether the optimal prices can be obtained by decentralizing price decisions to the regulated firm. That is to say, can an economist implement the socially optimal prices without resorting to information held by a regulatory agency (or, to put it still differently, can one do without agency discretion?). Section 4 first shows that the optimal prices can be obtained if the economist knows the demand function, even if the cost function is known by the regulated firm only. Then it proceeds to the construction of an algorithm based on historically-known data (prices and output), which thus requires no information about cost or demand. The firm's price changes are taxed and the firm retains a fraction of its profits. Under some conditions, the prices charged by the firm converge to the socially optimal ones, and furthermore the mechanism has good incentive properties. The section concludes by showing how to modify the price tax in the presence of technological progress and inflation.

2. Pricing and competition

This section obtains the Ramsey index for some competitive variants of the third-degree price discrimination model: regulated competition, unregulated competitive fringe, and unregulated competition with distorted pricing. The following analysis is simple and often will only state the results; yet it contains some pitfalls. Its general goal is to explain how to compute elasticities correctly. To simplify, we will assume that the demands for the regulated firm's n products are independent, and that a competitor produces a good $(n+1)$ that is an imperfect substitute for good n. Thus, the consumer gross surplus can be written:

$$S(\boldsymbol{q}, q_{n+1}) = \sum_{k=1}^{n-1} S^k(q_k) + \tilde{S}(q_n, q_{n+1}).$$

The competitor produces with cost function $C^{n+1}(q_{n+1})$. [We abstract from possible incentive issues for the competitor. The absence of uncertainty about the competitor also implies that the regulator cannot learn from the quantities traded information he does not infer from the regulated firm's choice of prices, which he could do if the two firm's technologies were correlated.]

Before proceeding, we should discuss the social value of a unit profit of the competitor. We will assume that \$1 of the competitor's profit has social value $\$(1+\lambda)$ if the competitor is regulated, and \$1 if it is not. The assumption in the regulated competitor case is easy to justify: any dollar in its revenue reduces the cost of regulation by one dollar and thus reduces the deadweight loss of distortionary taxation by $(1+\lambda)$ dollars. In contrast, the assumption in the unregulated firm's casc depicts only a particular situation, in which none of the profits is redistributed to the government. If a fraction τ of the competitor's profit were captured by the government (through a profit tax, say), the social value of the competitor's unit of profit would be $\$(1+\lambda\tau)$. Thus, we are in a sense restricting attention to the polar cases $\tau=1$ and $\tau=0$, but it is straightforward to extend our formulae to general social values of the competitor's profit (we will do so in section 3 on access pricing).

We also will use the following notation for revenues and elasticities: $R_k = p_k q_k$ is the revenue attached to good k; $\eta_{kl} = (\partial q_k/\partial p_l)/(q_k/p_l)$ is the elasticity of good k relative to the price of good l. Finally, $\eta_k = -\eta_{kk}$ is the own elasticity of demand of good k.

We start with the case in which the competitor is regulated.

2.1. Regulated competition

Suppose that good $(n+1)$ is produced by another regulated firm. For instance, electricity and local gas distribution are both regulated at the state level in the United States and are substitutes for heating and cooking. The competitor's revenue value has then social value $\lambda p_{n+1}q_{n+1} = \lambda q_{n+1}(\partial \tilde{S}/\partial q_{n+1})$. Hence, $V(\boldsymbol{q}) = S(\boldsymbol{q}, q_{n+1}) + \lambda p_{n+1}q_{n+1} - C^{n+1}(q_{n+1})$. Then the nth Ramsey index for the multiproduct firm is given by a superelasticity formula:[1]

$$R_n = \frac{\lambda}{(1+\lambda)\eta_n}\left[\frac{1+\dfrac{p_{n+1}q_{n+1}}{p_n q_n}\dfrac{\eta_{n+1,n}}{\eta_{n+1}}}{1-\dfrac{\eta_{n,n+1}\eta_{n+1,n}}{\eta_n\eta_{n+1}}}\right]. \tag{2.1}$$

That is, aside from the incentive correction (which here is equal to zero from our technological assumption), the price of good n should be regulated as if the two firms were merged (see subsection 3.3.1.2 of our companion paper). A regulated firm must be induced to internalize the loss in another regulated firm's revenue due to its pricing behavior. This conclusion is very natural, yet it does not hold in the traditional cost-of-service model.[2,3] The conclusion is more subtle than it appears as it hinges on the shadow price of public funds being firm independent.

2.2. Unregulated competitive fringe

We now suppose that the competitor is *unregulated*. We maintain the assumption that goods n and $n+1$ are substitutes (one may think of the competition between AT&T and unregulated long-distance carriers or

[1]To derive such a superelasticity formula, social welfare must be maximized with respect to prices. In section 3 we give an example of a similar derivation.

[2]In the COS model, even if the definition of social surplus is modified to include the externality on the competitor (by adding the term $\mu_{n+1}p_{n+1}q_{n+1}$, where μ_{n+1} is the shadow cost of the competitor's budget constraint), there is no reason why a formula of the type (2.1) should hold (as the shadow price of the multiproduct firm's budget constraint, μ, in general differs from μ_{n+1}). See Brauetigam (1984). The correct superelasticity is obtained in the COS model only in Boiteux's (1956) second case of a single budget constraint for the public sector (as opposed to the individual budget constraints of the traditional COS model) or in Brauetigam's (1984) 'viable industry Ramsey optimum', in which the regulator can impose lump-sum transfers among the regulated firms.

[3]Brauetigam (1979) considers a model of an increasing returns-to-scale firm facing constant-returns-to-scale competitors. In the 'totally regulated second best', the increasing-returns firm is regulated in a Ramsey–Boiteux fashion, and the competitors are taxed. However, the taxes do not enter the social welfare function, as the shadow cost of public funds is assumed equal to 0. The conclusion thus differs from (2.1). The Ramsey–Boiteux firm in Brauetigam is instructed to behave as if there were no competition [in our notation: $R_n = \lambda/(1+\lambda)\eta_n$]. See also footnote 2.

between the railway and road freight. The case of complements – e.g. public transportation and private accommodation – can be treated analogously). We assume that the regulated and the unregulated firms compete in prices and we consider both the sequential and simultaneous timing. In the sequential timing, the regulator is able to choose a regulatory scheme and induce price-setting by the regulated firm before the unregulated competitor chooses its price. In the other timing, the two decisions are simultaneous, so the regulator loses his commitment power. Needless to say, conclusions that are insensitive to the timing are more attractive.

In the social welfare function, the competitor's revenue now has no weight, as it cancels with the consumers' expenditure on good $n+1$:

$$V(\boldsymbol{q})=\sum_{k=1}^{n-1} S^k(q_k)+\tilde{S}(q_n,q_{n+1})-C^{n+1}(q_{n+1}).$$

Suppose that the fringe is a price-taker ($p_{n+1}=\partial\tilde{S}/\partial q_{n+1}=\mathrm{d}C^{n+1}/\mathrm{d}q_{n+1}$), and consider first the simultaneous timing. The optimal regulatory policy then yields:

$$L_n=\frac{\lambda}{1+\lambda}\frac{1}{\eta_n}. \tag{2.2}$$

That is, the regulated firm should 'ignore' the competitive fringe [i.e. not internalize the effect of its pricing, unlike in (2.1)].[4]

When the regulator is a Stackelberg leader (sequential timing), p_n has an effect on p_{n+1}. We let

$$\varepsilon\equiv\frac{\mathrm{d}p_{n+1}}{\mathrm{d}p_n}\bigg/\frac{p_{n+1}}{p_n}$$

denote the elasticity of the fringe's price reaction. Let us define the 'generalized or net elasticity of demand for good n' (which takes into account the fringe's reaction):

$$\tilde{\eta}_n\equiv-\left(\frac{\partial q_n}{\partial p_n}+\frac{\partial q_n}{\partial p_{n+1}}\frac{\mathrm{d}p_{n+1}}{\mathrm{d}p_n}\right)\bigg/\frac{q_n}{p_n}=\eta_n-\eta_{n,n+1}\varepsilon.$$

For strategic complements ($\varepsilon>0$) and demand substitutes ($\eta_{n,n+1}>0$), $\tilde{\eta}_n<\eta_n$. The optimal regulatory policy for the sequential timing yields:

[4]This result was first obtained by Brauetigam (1979) in a Ramsey–Boiteux framework.

$$L_n = \frac{\lambda}{1+\lambda}\frac{1}{\tilde{\eta}_n}. \tag{2.3}$$

That is, the price of good n is higher under sequential timing, because a high p_n induces the fringe to raise its price, which increases the regulated firm's revenue.

A useful conclusion is that both cases can be summarized in a single recommendation. The relevant elasticity of demand is the net elasticity of demand, which may or may not coincide with the ordinary elasticity of demand. This result is useful because it, together with the price tax analysis of section 4 below, implies that the optimal price decision can be delegated to the firm. That is, the regulator need not know the exact game firms are playing (sequential or simultaneous), as long as the regulated firm knows it. The regulated firm will automatically adopt the net elasticity as the correct measure of a change in price on its demand.[5]

2.3. *Unregulated competition with distorted pricing*

Subsection 2.2 assumed that the producer of good $n+1$ charges the social marginal cost. In practice, his price may be distorted because of either market power or subsidies.

2.3.1. *Competitor with market power*

Suppose that the competitor equates marginal revenue and marginal cost:

$$q_{n+1} + p_{n+1}\frac{\partial q_{n+1}}{\partial p_{n+1}} = \frac{\mathrm{d}C^{n+1}}{\mathrm{d}q_{n+1}}\frac{\partial q_{n+1}}{\partial p_{n+1}}.$$

Under simultaneous competition, the optimal Lerner index for good n is:

$$L_n = \frac{\lambda}{(1+\lambda)\eta_n} + \frac{(p_{n+1}q_{n+1})\eta_{n+1,n}}{(p_n q_n)(1+\lambda)\eta_n\eta_{n+1}}. \tag{2.4}$$

Eq. (2.4) implies that, if goods n and $n+1$ are substitutes, the price of good n should exceed the level corresponding to the ordinary elasticity of demand. This conclusion is not surprising. A standard result is that the demand for a monopolized product should be encouraged by a commodity subsidy. Here, reducing the demand for good n has a similar effect as a (missing)

[5]The knowledge of the timing of the game may however help the regulator to better initialize the historical scheme and thus obtain faster convergence toward optimal prices.

commodity subsidy on good $n+1$, in that both encourage consumption of good $n+1$.[6]

Under sequential competition, the optimal Lerner index for good n is:

$$L_n = \frac{\dfrac{\lambda}{(1+\lambda)\eta_n} + \dfrac{(p_{n+1}q_{n+1})(\eta_{n+1,n} - \eta_{n+1}\varepsilon)}{(p_n q_n)(1+\lambda)\eta_n\eta_{n+1}}}{1 - \dfrac{\eta_{n,n+1}\varepsilon}{\eta_n}}. \tag{2.5}$$

Eq. (2.5) unveils two new and straightforward effects that correspond to the terms in ε. By raising p_n, the regulated firm induces the competitor to raise p_{n+1}, which induces a further distortion in the consumption of good $n+1$; this effect shows up in the numerator of (2.5). But the increase in p_{n+1} also raises the regulated firm's revenue, which has a social value;[7] this explains the new term in the denominator.

2.3.2. Subsidized competition

It may happen that the unregulated competitor's pricing is distorted by subsidies. For instance, it is often asserted that railroads face 'unfair competition' from subsidized competitors (barges which may not pay for the use of facilities and trucks which may not pay for congestion costs or highway maintenance); and that subway tokens should be subsidized to account for the fact that charging congestion and pollution costs on city drives is too costly.

Let us assume that the competitor is a price-taker and that the subsidy in question is the absence of payment of some social cost (pollution, congestion cost). The modified consumer gross surplus function is thus $\sum_{k=1}^{n-1} S^k(q_k) + \tilde{S}(q_n, q_{n+1}) - \tau_{n+1}q_{n+1}$, where τ_{n+1} is the implicit subsidy on good $n+1$. The competitor produces until p_{n+1} equals his private marginal cost dC^{n+1}/dq_{n+1}. The optimal Lerner index for good n in the simultaneous mode is given by

$$L_n = \frac{\lambda}{(1+\lambda)\eta_n} - \frac{(\tau_{n+1}q_{n+1})\eta_{n+1,n}}{(p_n q_n)(1+\lambda)\eta_n}. \tag{2.6}$$

Thus, the price of good n is lowered to reduce the demand for, and hence the negative externality created by, good $n+1$.

In the sequential mode, the formula is the same as (2.6), except that the

[6] Note that our framework implies that commodity subsidies are an imperfect instrument because of the existence of a shadow cost of public funds.

[7] As long as the previous effect is not so powerful that it induces the regulated firm to charge below marginal cost (an unlikely occurrence).

elasticities must be replaced by the net elasticities [which include the elasticity $\varepsilon = (dp_{n+1}/dp_n)/(p_{n+1}/p_n)$ of reaction of the competitive fringe]:

$$\tilde{\eta}_n = \eta_n - \eta_{n,n+1}\varepsilon$$

and

$$\tilde{\eta}_{n+1,n} = \eta_{n+1,n} - \eta_{n+1}\varepsilon.$$

Assuming that (2.6) yields pricing above marginal cost (which is not guaranteed), the fringe's reaction lowers the net elasticity of demand for good n, and thus calls for a higher price p_n. Furthermore, the fringe's reaction to an increase in p_n reduces demand for the subsidized good $n+1$, a socially useful effect. Hence, the two effects have the same sign, so that the sequential timing calls for a higher price p_n than the simultaneous timing.

3. Access pricing

We now analyze a variant of the unregulated competitive fringe of subsection 2.2 to study the pricing of an input by a regulated multiproduct firm to a firm producing a good that competes with another product of the regulated firm. Such 'access pricing' is a common issue and has been the subject of much legal and regulatory activity lately. For instance, before the divestiture, AT&T, a regulated firm, had monopoly over the local exchange and competed with a couple of unregulated companies on the long-distance market; the rivals needed access to AT&T's local network to supply toll calls. A railroad may have a monopoly position from A to B, and compete with trucks or another railroad from B to C; to carry freight from A to C, the competitors need access to the segment AB. In the energy field, British Gas's rivals need access to British Gas's distribution network to compete for gas customers. Similarly, the U.S. Public Utility Regulatory Policy Act of 1978 requires electric utilities to purchase power from 'qualified' independent suppliers. As discussed in the Introduction, the regulation of access has two components: pricing (studied in subsection 3.1) and incentives (studied in subsection 3.2). First, leaving incentives aside, there is a pure problem of optimal pricing of access, which must deal with the complex interaction of input and output markets as well as the fiscal treatment of the fringe's profit. To abstract from the incentive issue, subsection 3.1 assumes that the dichotomy holds (so that prices are not used to provide incentives) and derives the optimal pricing rule. Second, it may be difficult to induce the regulated firm to reveal information about the cost of giving access because competition on the final product market may lower its rent. Subsection 3.2 illustrates this idea through a simple example in which the regulated firm has private information about the cost of given access and that of producing a final good.

3.1. Access and pricing

Suppose that one unit of good 1, an intermediate good produced by the regulated firm, is consumed to produce each unit of good n (produced by the regulated firm) or of good $n+1$ (produced by the fringe). Total production of good 1 is thus q_n+q_{n+1}. Letting p_1 denote the transfer price, the fringe's cost is $C^{n+1}(q_{n+1})+p_1q_{n+1}$, while the regulated firm's cost is $C(\Phi(\beta,e),q_n+q_{n+1},q_2,\dots,q_n)$.

We will assume that the fringe's profit has social value $(1+\tilde{\lambda})$ per unit where $0\leqq\tilde{\lambda}\leqq\lambda$. As discussed in section 2, $\tilde{\lambda}$ might for instance be equal to $\lambda\tau$ if a fraction τ of the fringe's profit is recouped by the government through profit taxation.

We will also assume that $\mathrm{d}^2C^{n+1}/\mathrm{d}q_{n+1}^2\geqq 0$ (the fringe has convex costs). The fringe's price is determined by the prices p_1 and p_n by:

$$p_{n+1}=\frac{\mathrm{d}C^{n+1}}{\mathrm{d}q_{n+1}}(q_{n+1}(p_n,p_{n+1}))+p_1.$$

Weighting the fringe's profit by $(1+\tilde{\lambda})$, the social welfare function is:

$$\begin{aligned}W={}&S^2(q_2(p_2))+\cdots+S^{n-1}(q_{n-1}(p_{n-1}))+\tilde{S}(q_n(p_n,p_{n+1}),q_{n+1}(p_n,p_{n+1}))\\&+\lambda\sum_{k=2}^{n-1}p_kq_k(p_k)+\lambda p_nq_n(p_n,p_{n+1})-\lambda U\\&-(1+\lambda)(\psi(e)+C(\Phi(\beta,e),q_n(p_n,p_{n+1})\\&+q_{n+1}(p_n,p_{n+1}),q_2(p_2),\dots,q_n(p_n,p_{n+1}))\\&+\lambda q_{n+1}(p_n,p_{n+1})\left(p_{n+1}-\frac{(\lambda-\tilde{\lambda})}{\lambda}\frac{\mathrm{d}C^{n+1}}{\mathrm{d}q_{n+1}}(q_{n+1}(p_n,p_{n+1}))\right)\\&-(1+\tilde{\lambda})C^{n+1}(q_{n+1}(p_n,p_{n+1})),\end{aligned}\tag{3.1}$$

where U is the regulated firm's rent (see our companion paper).

Maximizing with respect to p_k, $k=2,\dots,n-1$, we obtain the usual Ramsey formula for goods 2 through $n-1$:

$$L_k = \frac{\lambda}{1+\lambda}\frac{1}{\eta_k}, \quad k=2,\dots,n-1. \tag{3.2}$$

Maximizing with respect to p_n and p_{n+1} yields:

$$\begin{aligned}
& p_n\frac{\partial q_n}{\partial p_n} + p_{n+1}\frac{\partial q_{n+1}}{\partial p_n} + \lambda q_n + \lambda p_n\frac{\partial q_n}{\partial p_n} \\
& -(1+\lambda)\left[\frac{\partial C}{\partial q_1}\left(\frac{\partial q_n}{\partial p_n}+\frac{\partial q_{n+1}}{\partial p_n}\right)+\frac{\partial C}{\partial q_n}\frac{\partial q_n}{\partial p_n}\right] \\
& +\lambda\frac{\partial q_{n+1}}{\partial p_n}\left(p_{n+1}-\frac{(\lambda-\tilde{\lambda})}{\lambda}\frac{\mathrm{d}C^{n+1}}{\mathrm{d}q_{n+1}}(q_{n+1})\right) \\
& -\lambda q_{n+1}\left(1-\frac{\lambda-\tilde{\lambda}}{\lambda}\right)\frac{\mathrm{d}^2C^{n+1}}{\mathrm{d}q_{n+1}^2}(q_{n+1})\frac{\partial q_{n+1}}{\partial p_{n+1}} \\
& -(1+\tilde{\lambda})\frac{\mathrm{d}C^{n+1}}{\mathrm{d}q_{n+1}}\frac{\partial q_{n+1}}{\partial p_{n+1}} = 0,
\end{aligned} \tag{3.3}$$

$$\begin{aligned}
& p_n\frac{\partial q_n}{\partial p_{n+1}} + p_{n+1}\frac{\partial q_{n+1}}{\partial p_{n+1}} + \lambda p_n\frac{\partial q_n}{\partial p_{n+1}} \\
& -(1+\lambda)\left[\frac{\partial C}{\partial q_1}\left(\frac{\partial q_n}{\partial p_{n+1}}+\frac{\partial q_{n+1}}{\partial p_{n+1}}\right)+\frac{\partial C}{\partial q_n}\frac{\partial q_n}{\partial p_{n+1}}\right] \\
& +\lambda\frac{\partial q_{n+1}}{\partial p_{n+1}}\left(p_{n+1}-\frac{(\lambda-\tilde{\lambda})}{\lambda}\frac{\mathrm{d}C^{n+1}}{\mathrm{d}q_{n+1}}(q_{n+1})\right) \\
& +\lambda q_{n+1}\left(1-\frac{(\lambda-\tilde{\lambda})}{\lambda}\frac{\mathrm{d}^2C^{n+1}}{\mathrm{d}q_{n+1}^2}(q_{n+1})\frac{\partial q_{n+1}}{\partial p_{n+1}}\right) \\
& -(1+\tilde{\lambda})\frac{\mathrm{d}C^{n+1}}{\mathrm{d}q_{n+1}}\frac{\partial q_{n+1}}{\partial p_{n+1}} = 0.
\end{aligned} \tag{3.4}$$

Algebraic manipulations yield:

$$L_n \equiv \frac{p_n - \left(\dfrac{\partial C}{\partial q_1} + \dfrac{\partial C}{\partial q_n}\right)}{p_n} = \frac{\lambda}{1+\lambda} \frac{1}{\hat{\eta}_n}, \tag{3.5}$$

where

$$\hat{\eta}_n \equiv \eta_n \frac{\left(1 - \dfrac{\eta_{n,n+1}\eta_{n+1,n}}{\eta_n \eta_{n+1}}\right)}{\left(1 + \dfrac{R_{n+1}}{R_n} \dfrac{\eta_{n+1,n}}{\eta_{n+1}}\right)} < \eta_n \tag{3.6}$$

is good n's superelasticity, and

$$L_1 \equiv \frac{p_1 - \dfrac{\partial C}{\partial q_1}}{p_1} = \frac{\lambda}{1+\lambda} \frac{1}{\hat{\eta}_1}, \tag{3.7}$$

where

$$\hat{\eta}_1 \equiv \eta_1 \frac{1}{\dfrac{R_{n+1}\eta_n \eta_1 + R_n \eta_{n,n+1}\eta_1}{R_1(\eta_n \eta_{n+1} - \eta_{n,n+1}\eta_{n+1,n})} + \dfrac{\lambda - \tilde{\lambda}}{\lambda}\left(1 - \dfrac{\mathrm{d}p_{n+1}}{\mathrm{d}p_1}\right)} \tag{3.8}$$

and

$$\frac{\mathrm{d}p_{n+1}}{\mathrm{d}p_1} = \frac{1}{1 - \dfrac{\partial q_{n+1}}{\partial p_{n+1}} \dfrac{\mathrm{d}^2 C^{n+1}}{\mathrm{d}q_{n+1}^2}} \in (0, 1]. \tag{3.9}$$

The key to understanding eqs. (3.5) and (3.7) is to view goods 1 and n as substitutes. An increase in p_n raises the demand for good $n+1$, which in turn raises the demand for the access good by an equal amount. It is therefore not surprising that the Lerner index for good n is given by a familiar superelasticity formula. Eq. (3.6) reflects the fact that a unit decrease in q_{n+1} implies a unit decrease in q_1 and thus a loss of revenue for the regulated firm.

Of particular interest is eq. (3.7) which determines the access price p_1. Note first that $\hat{\eta}_1 > 0$, so that the price of the 'access good' must exceed its marginal cost. Observing an external transfer price in excess of the internal transfer price is no evidence that the regulated firm has too much incentive to weaken competition, as this pricing formula must hold even when the regulator has full information about, and therefore perfectly controls, the firm.

An interesting case is that of a fringe operating under *constant returns to scale*, $\mathrm{d}^2C^{n+1}/\mathrm{d}q_{n+1}^2=0$. Then $\mathrm{d}p_{n+1}/\mathrm{d}p_1=1$ and (3.8) can be written as a superelasticity formula:

$$\hat{\eta}_1=\eta_1\frac{1-\dfrac{\eta_{n,n+1}\eta_{n+1,n}}{\eta_n\eta_{n+1}}}{1+\dfrac{R_n}{R_{n+1}}\dfrac{\eta_{n,n+1}}{\eta_n}}<\eta_1. \tag{3.10}$$

Because of constant marginal cost the fringe makes no profit and therefore the social value of its profit ($\tilde{\lambda}$) is irrelevant. Good 1 can just be treated as a substitute for good n and its pricing is given by the usual Ramsey rule. Note in particular that the access price exceeds not only the marginal cost of providing access, but also the 'myopic' Ramsey price $\lambda/(1+\lambda)\eta_1$ associated with good 1's elasticity of demand.

When the marginal cost of the fringe is not constant, $\mathrm{d}p_{n+1}/\mathrm{d}p_1<1$; as long as $\tilde{\lambda}<\lambda$ (the government is unable to recoup 100 percent of the fringe's profits), the second term in the denominator of (3.8) introduces a downward distortion in $\hat{\eta}_1$ and thus an upward correction in the access price. Because the taxation of the fringe's profit is imperfect, its profits have less social value, which justifies an increase in the access charge.

3.2. Access and incentives

Subsection 3.1 studied pricing independently of incentives, as is legitimate under the dichotomy property. Another interesting issue is whether the firm has an incentive to reveal a cost parameter that determines the transfer price to its rival.[8] We should realize that the combination of two features of our presumed cost function in subsection 3.1, while quite realistic in some situations, understates the difficulty in eliciting information about optimal access prices in other situations. First, the technological uncertainty is one-dimensional. Second, the regulated firm and the fringe have identical requirements of the intermediate good to produce their substitute products (one unit each in this model). Thus, the regulated firm cannot claim that the production of the intermediate good is costly in order to hurt the fringe without making a case against the production of its own good, n. In other words, the regulator can call the firm's bluff of a high price for the intermediate good by imposing a low output for good n.

Suppose that one relaxes these two features. Suppose first that the fringe

[8] In particular one would like to know whether the optimal incentive scheme is 'separating' [$\Phi(\beta,e(\beta))$ is strictly increasing in β] or exhibits some 'pooling' [$\Phi(\beta,e(\beta))$ is constant over some interval]. This issue is linked with the firm's second-order condition [see Guesnerie and Laffont (1984)]. The optimal incentive scheme is separating if $-\psi''[E_C\dot{C}+\sum_k E_{q_k}\dot{q}_k]E_\beta-\psi'[E_{\beta C}\dot{C}+E_{\beta q}\dot{q}]>0$. A general study of this condition is outside the scope of this paper.

uses more of the intermediate good than the regulated firm. For instance, the intermediate good might be the access to the regulated firm's network, which the regulated firm already has. [A (European) example is that of country A wanting to sell electricity to country C and needing transportation of electricity through country B who is already a supplier of country C. Typically, the electricity company in country B has private information about the cost of adding transportation capacity and reoptimizing its network when giving access to country A's electric utility; a similar case is that of country A's company's needing access to country B's network to sell electricity to country B's industrial customers.] Second, suppose that the regulated firm's private information about technology is two-dimensional: one component indexes the subcost of giving access, the other component indexes the subcost of producing the firm's final good(s), and the two components are independent. Then the regulated firm can claim to have a high cost of giving access without necessarily producing a low output on the final product market(s). The high access price squeezes out the fringe, and allows the regulated firm to enjoy a high information rent on its second technological parameter. Unfortunately, multidimensional uncertainty models are hard to solve, and we will content ourselves with a highly stylized example to illustrate the idea.

A two-dimensional example

Let the regulated firms and the fringe produce the same final output. There are Q customers with unit demands and reservation price r per unit, so total output is Q. The regulated firm's cost is

$$C=(\beta_0-e_0)x+(\beta-e)q+K,$$

where K is a fixed cost, β_0 and β are two independent adverse-selection parameters, and $x=1$ if access is given to the fringe and $x=0$ otherwise. The disutility of effort is $\psi(e_0+e)$. If the fringe is given access, it can produce any amount at constant unit cost, $c<r$. We assume that β_0 can take only two values: β_0^{L} (low) or β_0^{H} (high), while β is drawn from the distribution $F(\beta)$ on $[\underline{\beta},\bar{\beta}]$ with density $f(\beta)$ [with the usual properties that $f(\beta)>0$ and $\mathrm{d}(F/f)/\mathrm{d}\beta\geqq 0$ for all β].

We assume that β_0^{H} is very large ('infinite') so that all outputs should be produced by the regulated firm when $\beta_0=\beta_0^{\mathrm{H}}$; and that when $\beta_0=\beta_0^{\mathrm{L}}$ it would be optimal to let the fringe supply the entire market if the regulator had full information about the adverse-selection parameters (that is, c and β_0^{L} are sufficiently small; see below).

(a) *Full information.* First, consider the case in which the regulator knows β_0 and β. If $\beta_0=\beta_0^{\mathrm{L}}$, the regulator gives access to the fringe at price $r-c$ per unit of output, and requires effort $e_0=\hat{e}$ such that $\psi'(\hat{e})=1$ (marginal disutility of effort equals marginal cost reduction). The firm receives an income equal to $\psi(\hat{e})$. Social welfare is

$$W^{L}=(1+\lambda)\{(r-c)Q-[\beta_0^{L}-\hat{e}+K+\psi(\hat{e})]\}.$$

If $\beta_0=\beta_0^{H}$, no access is granted to the fringe. The regulator requires effort $e=e^*$ such that $\psi'(e^*)=Q$ (marginal disutility of effort equals marginal cost reduction) and gives $\psi(e^*)$ to the firm. Social welfare is

$$W^{H}(\beta)=(1+\lambda)\{rQ-[(\beta-e^*)Q+K+\psi(e^*)]\}.$$

We assume that $W^{L}>W^{H}(\underline{\beta})$ so that it is always optimal to use the fringe if $\beta_0=\beta_0^{L}$.

(b) *Asymmetric information.* Under asymmetric information the regulator must elicit the information about cost. The appendix shows that:

(i) No access is given to the fringe when $\beta_0=\beta_0^{H}$.

(ii) There exists $\beta^*\in[\underline{\beta},\bar{\beta}]$ [independent of $\alpha=\text{Prob}(\beta_0=\beta_0^{H})$] such that when $\beta_0=\beta_0^{L}$, types in $[\underline{\beta},\beta^*]$ do not give access (i.e. might as well claim that $\beta_0=\beta_0^{H}$) and types in $(\beta^*,\bar{\beta}]$ give access and do not produce the final output. The later types receive a lump-sum transfer to allow access giving them rent equal to the rent of type β^* under the no-access policy (then even type $\bar{\beta}$ gets a strictly positive rent when $\beta_0=\beta_0^{L}$). There is *less access than under full information* ($\beta^*>\underline{\beta}$) unless the cost differential between the regulated firm and the fringe is so high that there is the same amount of access ($\beta^*=\underline{\beta}$).

Asymmetric information makes the use of the regulated firm's intermediate good more costly than under complete information. Consequently, *less* access is given. This result can be contrasted with that for the bypass problem. In Laffont and Tirole (1989) it was shown that asymmetric information about the regulated firm led to *more* bypass. The apparent conflict between these two conclusions (asymmetric information yields less competition in one case and more in the other) is easily resolved: in both cases, incentives issues raise the cost of the regulated firm's goods. In the access pricing problem, the good is an input for a competitor while it is a final good in the bypass problem.

(iii) *The regulated firm's slope of the incentive scheme and rent are lower than under full information* when $\beta_0=\beta_0^{H}$. There is thus a spillover between the two revelation problems. To discourage the regulated firm from refusing access to the fringe when it is optimal to grant it, the regulator lowers the rents in the no-access policy and to this purpose lowers the incentives. One can actually show the stronger result that the regulated firm's rent in the no-access policy decreases with the probability that access is feasible (i.e. with the probability that $\beta_0 = \beta_0^L$).

(iv) *The effect of an increased possibility of access on the regulated firm's rent is ambiguous.* While we have already noted that types β close to $\bar{\beta}$ gain when the probability $(1-\alpha)$ that access is feasible is positive rather than 0, the rent of types β in $[\underline{\beta}, \beta^*]$ decreases with $(1-\alpha)$.

4. Policy implications

The purpose of a normative approach to regulation is to specify optimal rate-of-return and pricing decisions as functions of the cost and demand environment, including the distribution of uncertainty and the informational constraints faced by the regulator. In contrast, considerable weight is given in the policy arena to rules that are 'simple'. We define a rule as being simple if it can be prescribed by an economist lacking a detailed knowledge of cost and demand functions, and if it is nevertheless comprehensive enough to be readily applicable by (i.e. to leave little discretion to) regulators. This concern for simplicity stems from the possibility that the regulatory hierarchy (administrative agency and its oversight structure) does not use its information efficiently. On the one hand, a regulator may be put off by – or may not have the incentive to devote time to – the application of complex regulatory rules. On the other hand, while a regulatory agency is unlikely to be as well informed as the regulated firm about the technology (and possibly demand), it still has a substantial informational edge over its oversight structure (Congress, courts, etc.). This second asymmetry of information raises the possibility of collusion between the agency and the regulated firm. Simple rules, which by definition remove agency discretion, give less scope to collusion than complex rules relying on an intimate knowledge of the likely distribution of the cost and demand parameters that the oversight structure is unlikely to possess; that is, simple rules are immune to the threat of regulatory capture by the industry (or other interest groups).

Thus, under an inefficient regulatory hierarchy (that is, a hierarchy which, for either of the above two reasons, is unable to implement the optimal incentive scheme conditional on its finest information structure), a normative theory that ignores this imperfection (like the one presented in this paper) is ultimately judged by whether its optimal allocation can be approximately implemented through simple rules.

The purpose of this section is first to briefly discuss the informational requirements of the two existing policy mechanisms: cost-of-service (COS) and price capping (PC); and second to propose an alternative mechanism based on our normative analysis.

4.1. COS and PC regulations

The economist's benchmark for 'efficient pricing' is marginal cost. For instance, the 1967 White Paper recommended that the prices of U.K. public enterprises reflect long-run marginal costs (with potential adjustments towards short-run marginal costs for low capicity levels). Marginal cost pricing is not only theoretically unsatisfactory [see eq. (1.1)], it is also impractical and incomplete: impractical because regulators have little knowledge of marginal costs; incomplete because it does not specify the cost reimbursement or rate-of-return rule that settles the tradeoff between incentives and rent extraction.

A much more influential paradigm is that of cost-of-service rate making. A naive description of this rule (corresponding to the theoretical Ramsey–Boiteux model) is that the regulator sets prices so that the revenue meets the firm's cost. To be applied stricto sensu, COS ratemaking would require a formidable knowledge of the cost and demand functions from regulators. In practice, cost estimates are based on the firm's previous performance, creating notorious incentive problems: the firm has little incentive for cost control and innovation as such policies feed back into lower allowed prices and revenue in the future. The approximate cost-plus character of COS rate making has been rightly decried by many academic economists.[9]

In principle, PC regulation attempts to regulate prices, but not cost or rate-of-return (in this latter respect, it resembles a 'fixed-price contract'). It imposes ceilings on the firm's rates, either on individual goods or on a weighted average of a basket of goods. For instance, the 1984 regulatory reform in Great Britain required that British Telecom's weighted average rate of change of prices of certain services do not increase at a rate of more than the inflation rate minus 3 percent ('RPI − 3'), where the 3 percent term reflects an estimated annual average productivity growth. Because it in principle offers much more scope for incentives,[10] PC regulation has been accepted as an improvement over COS regulation.

PC regulation also has serious drawbacks [Joskow and Schmalensee (1986)]. First, its fixed-price nature makes no attempt at capturing the regulated firm's rent.[11] This neglect is socially very costly when the shadow cost of public funds is high. Second, a 'fundamental shortcoming of price-cap

[9]For sharp criticisms of this scheme and its fully distributed cost variant, see, for example, the comments (in particular Schmalensee's) on the matter of Policy and Rules Concerning Rates for Dominant Carriers before the U.S. Federal Communications Commission (CC Docket 87-313), as well as Joskow and Schmalensee (1986).

[10]However, it is recognized that at the regulatory review (in 1988 for British Telecom) the regulators are likely to adjust prices to reflect past performance (cost, profit), so that PC regulation may be closer to COS regulation than it might appear.

[11]At least in the absence of regulatory review: see footnote 10. Regulatory reviews lead to some capture of rent, but at the expense of discouraging cost control and innovation.

regulation is the danger that the values of the price caps will be set at inappropriate levels' [Baumol and Willig (1987, pp. 11–12)]. On the one hand, the appropriate levels must be related to some formal approach. On the other hand, like COS rate making, PC regulation requires information about cost and demand that regulators are unlikely to possess. In the presence of considerable uncertainty about its correct levels (assuming the latter is determined by a theory), a price cap may be chosen so high that it is not binding for the firm; in this case, the monopoly price falls below the cap, a clear perversion of the regulatory process. Or the cap may be binding (lower than the monopoly level), in which case it can still be chosen too high or too low. Last, there is no guarantee that the firm is viable at the caps chosen by the regulator.

To summarize, COS and (the more attractive) PC regulations are informationally demanding with respect to both price and rate-of-return setting, yet they have normative drawbacks.

4.2. Implementation of the optimal regulatory scheme: An introduction

In this subsection and the next we offer several rules that allow the decentralization of the pricing decisions to the regulated firm. We emphasize the informational requirements and the amount of agency discretion for each of these rules.

We will assume that the incentives–pricing dichotomy holds. The optimal prices are then given by

$$V_{q_k} + \lambda R_{q_k} = (1+\lambda) C_{q_k}, \quad \text{for all } k, \tag{4.1}$$

which is obtained by maximizing the social welfare function, $V(\boldsymbol{q}) + \lambda R(\boldsymbol{q}) - (1+\lambda)C$, with respect to outputs. An equivalent expression is obtained by taking the derivative of the social welfare function with respect to prices:

$$\sum_l (V_{q_l} + \lambda R_{q_l} - (1+\lambda) C_{q_l}) \frac{\partial q_l}{\partial p_k} = 0, \quad \text{for all } k. \tag{4.2}$$

We start with a rule that requires perfect knowledge of the demand functions and no knowledge of the cost function.

Price-setting

Suppose that the regulated firm receives benefit

$$B(\boldsymbol{q}) \equiv \frac{V(\boldsymbol{q}) + \lambda R(\boldsymbol{q})}{1+\lambda} \tag{4.3}$$

(from our accounting convention, the government receives $R(\boldsymbol{q})$ and pays $B(\boldsymbol{q})$ to the firm). Its profit is then $\pi(\boldsymbol{q}) = B(\boldsymbol{q}) - C(\boldsymbol{q})$.

Rate-of-return setting

To control the rate of return, the regulator uses linear rate-of-return rules. The firm's bonus or income is then

$$t = a + b\pi, \tag{4.4}$$

where a is a fixed fee and b belongs to $[0, 1]$ ($b=0$ corresponds to a cost-plus contract and $b=1$ to a fixed-price contract). Optimally, the regulator offers a menu of such contracts from which the firm chooses one. Alternatively, the firm can be asked to announce its expected profit, π^e, and is then paid

$$t = \tilde{a}(\pi^e) + \tilde{b}(\pi^e)(\pi - \pi^e), \tag{4.5}$$

where $\pi - \pi^e$ is the excess profit (or loss). Incentive compatibility requires that both $\tilde{a}$ and $\tilde{b}$ increase with π^e.[12]

This rate-of-return setting is inspired by Proposition 9 of our companion paper, which establishes that under some circumstances, optimal cost reimbursement or profit-sharing rules are linear in the firm's performance (cost or profit). Now optimal rules are certainly not always linear, but from a policy viewpoint, Proposition 9 tells us that the simple linear rules may not be too off-track as approximations to the optimal scheme. The coefficient b in $[0, 1]$ reflects the tradeoff between rent extraction (which requires $b=0$) and incentives (which require $b=1$). Ideally, the regulator ought to offer a menu

[12]The profit of the entire firm is subject to the rate-of-return setting in order to avoid 'cost-side cross subsidization'. Thus, if the firm produces unregulated goods $k=n+1,\ldots,m$, these goods should not be treated separately. Rather, their costs and revenues should be included in the definition of π.

Because of rapid technological change (in particular in the telecommunications industry) or of legal limitations on the scope of regulation, regulatory agencies continually face a dilemma between allowing and prohibiting entry by regulated firms into new markets. Prohibition has obvious drawbacks in terms of product diversity offered to consumers. Assuming that immediate regulation of new products is infeasible, it still may be preferable to let the regulated firm enter and charge a monopoly price on a new market, which it would do under our regulatory scheme. Of course, the theory of industrial organization tells us that a monopoly may introduce too many or too few products. Furthermore, it might be the case that expansion into new markets leads to a loss of control by the regulator concerning the optimal cost reimbursement rule. These points are well worth further investigation.

of linear contracts, including one with $b=1$ and several with $0<b<1$. While it is possible to further characterize the optimal menu of contracts without knowledge of the exact distribution of uncertainty, we realize that our rate-of-return prescription is informationally demanding, as its details depend on the regulator's formulating a subjective distribution about the technological parameter; so is any prescription aiming to promote incentives (as it seems that only a cost-plus contract can abstract from the question of whether the firm will remain viable or, conversely, enjoy an excessive rent if the regulator errs in estimating the distribution of uncertainty).

It should be noted that the prices selected by the firm are optimal given the cost structure even if the profit-sharing schemes are the 'wrong' ones: while the optimal choice of effort for the firm depends on b, its optimal choice of prices or outputs is obtained by maximizing $B(\boldsymbol{q})-C(\boldsymbol{q})$ and is thus independent of b. Clearly, this maximization yields the socially optimal outputs given in (4.1).

It is worth emphasizing the reason why the optimal prices can be obtained without regulator's information about cost unlike in the traditional Ramsey–Boiteux approach to cost-of-service pricing: λ is an economy-wide shadow cost of public funds, while the shadow cost of the firm's budget constraint in the Ramsey–Boiteux model depends on the cost function.

Finally, let us note that the price-setting rule implicit in (4.2) requires the knowledge of the demand functions. The regulator, who observes revenues $R(\boldsymbol{q})$ and production levels $\boldsymbol{q}$, must also know the consumer's gross surplus function in order to base its reward scheme on $B(\boldsymbol{q})$.

We next describe a related pricing rule that does not formally require knowledge of the demand side, but requires estimates of the quantities to be produced by the regulated firm. Knowing these quantities even approximately is of course informationally demanding, and the main interest of this rule is to offer a useful introduction to the historical scheme described in subsection 4.3 and to indicate the domain of validity of this historical scheme.

Price-setting

The regulator forms a *rough* estimate of the demand, $\bar{q}_k$, for each of the firm's products at the optimal prices. $\bar{q}_k$ can result from survey data. Or, as will be shown in subsection 4.3, it can be obtained from historical data, a policy more in line with the simplicity – i.e. absence of discretion – requirement. The regulator imposes a price tax on good k equal to $p_k\bar{q}_k/(1+\lambda)$. He otherwise gives entire price freedom to the firm. The firm maximizes its profit, π, like a monopolist, subject to the price tax. Thus,

$$\pi=\max_{p}\left\{\sum_{k=1}^{n} p_k D_k(p)-C(\Phi(\beta,e),D(p))-\sum_{k=1}^{n}\frac{p_k\bar{q}_k}{1+\lambda}\right\},\tag{4.6}$$

where $p\equiv(p_1,\ldots,p_n)$ and $D(p)\equiv[D_1(p),\ldots,D_n(p)]$.

Rate-of-return setting
As above.

Suppose that $V(q)=S(q)$, the consumers' gross surplus. Then $V_{p_k}=\sum_l p_l\,\partial D_l/\partial p_k$ and $R_{p_k}=\sum_l p_l(\partial D_l/\partial p_k)+q_k$. Eq. (4.2) then yields the following socially optimal prices:

$$\sum_l\left[(1+\lambda)(p_l-C_{q_l})\frac{\partial D_l}{\partial p_k}+\lambda q_k\right]=0,\quad \text{for all } k.\tag{4.7}$$

The firm's privately optimal prices are obtained by the maximization in (4.6):

$$\sum_l(p_l-C_{q_l})\frac{\partial D_l}{\partial p_k}+\left[D_k-\frac{\bar{q}_k}{1+\lambda}\right]=0.\tag{4.8}$$

If $\bar{q}_k\simeq D_k$, then (4.8) coincides with eq. (4.7), and the pricing structure is socially optimal.

In practice, the regulator is likely to make substantial errors in estimating demand, and thus the optimal $\bar{q}_k$ (see subsection 4.3 for the use of historical data to reduce errors). Yet the errors in pricing[13] are likely to be lower than those resulting from COS or PC regulations, which, besides relying on a theoretically less satisfactory approach, compound errors in cost *and* demand estimations.

When is the price tax scheme appropriate? As we noted, the reliance on the price tax scheme depends not only on a good estimate of optimal outputs (which we will analyze in subsection 4.3), but also on the social value $V(q)$ of the vector of outputs being equal to the gross surplus function $S(q)$.

$V(q)$ is equal to $S(q)$ when either the firm has no competitor (and does not exert externalities such as polluting its environment) or faces a competitive

[13]For instance, if demands are independent, if good k's elasticity of demand is equal to 2, and if $\lambda=1/2$, the optimal price of good k [given by (4.7)] is 20 percent above its marginal cost. However, eq. (4.8) yields a price 11 percent (respectively 30 percent) above marginal cost if the regulator overestimates (respectively underestimates) $\bar{q}_k$ by 20 percent.

fringe whose profit is untaxed and who is not subsidized. We have supplied a number of instances in which the two differ. In the case of a regulated competitor (subsection 2.1), $V(\boldsymbol{q})=S(\boldsymbol{q})+\lambda p_{n+1}q_{n+1}$. Similarly, when a fraction, τ, of an unregulated fringe's profit, π_{n+1}, is taxed, $V(\boldsymbol{q})=S(\boldsymbol{q})+\lambda\tau\pi_{n+1}$ (see, for example, section 3). Or, when the competition is subsidized (subsection 2.3), $V(\boldsymbol{q})=S(\boldsymbol{q})-\tau_{n+1}q_{n+1}$. Last, when the competitor has market power, $V(\boldsymbol{q})$ differs from $S(\boldsymbol{q})$ in a more complex way (see subsection 2.3). In such situations the price tax will not yield the optimal prices. When the revenue of the competitor is socially valuable (regulated competition, taxed unregulated fringe) and goods are substitutes, prices must be adjusted upwards from the values that result from the price tax. When the regulated firm faces a subsidized fringe, its prices must be adjusted downwards.

There is of course another reason why the price tax scheme is not appropriate. If the incentives–pricing dichotomy does not hold, prices obtained by the use of a price tax must be adjusted for incentive purposes.

We view the unit price tax, $\bar{q}_k/(1+\lambda)$, as a benchmark from which adjustments must be made. The regulator can raise λ when an upward adjustment is needed, and conversely for a downward adjustment.

Quality issues A concern with PC regulation is that the firm might evade a binding price cap by an unverifiable cut in product quality. Indeed, Vickers and Yarrow (1988, p. 228), using Oftel's quality-of-service indicators, note the 'British Telecom's quality of service has not deteriorated since privatization, but that it had not improved much either. Given the rate of advance of telecommunications technology, this record is poor.'[14] A similar problem may arise for our price tax regulation. To simplify notation, consider the shared-fixed-cost model of subsection 4.2 of our companion paper and independent demands. Under a price tax regulation, the regulated firm maximizes, for each k:

$$\max_{(p_k,s_k)}\left\{p_kD_k(p_k,s_k)-\frac{p_k\bar{q}_k}{1+\lambda}-C^k(\beta,e_k,D_k(p_k,s_k),s_k)\right\} \tag{4.9}$$

over the price p_k and the quality of service s_k. Like a pure monopoly [Spence (1975)], the firm chooses a quality that is higher or lower than the socially optimal level, depending on whether the marginal consumer values quality more or less then the average consumer.[15] So, in general, the regulated firm can under- or oversupply quality.

[14]Some dimensions of quality subsequently became the objects of monetary incentives. See footnote 10 of our companion paper.

[15]Note that, unlike Spence, we do not have to add the qualifier 'for a given price', as the regulated firm's price is optimal given the quality.

Remark. There is a case in which the firm clearly undersupplies quality under our scheme (and under price caps). Suppose that price reductions and quality increases are perfect substitutes for both the consumers and the firm $(D_k(p_k, s_k) \equiv \tilde{D}_k(p_k - s_k)$ and $C^k(\beta, e_k, D_k(p_k, s_k), s_k) \equiv \tilde{C}^k(\beta, e_k, \tilde{D}_k(p_k - s_k)) + s_k\tilde{D}_k(p_k - s_k))$. The program (4.9) then yields the monopoly outcome. The firm has an incentive to drive p_k to 0 to escape the price tax, and to choose a quality level equal to minus the monopoly price[16] if such a low level of quality is feasible and unverifiable by the regulatory agency. Furthermore, the allocation (including the firm's profit) is the same as under a price cap.[17] All this is not surprising. If the regulator cannot monitor quality and if quality is a perfect substitute for price, everything is as if the price itself were not regulated. Such goods naturally fall under the heading of unregulated goods. Any attempt at regulating pricing seems to require quality control, or at least an imperfect substitutability between price and quality.

4.3. Using historical data to construct the price tax

An alternative to basing the price tax on good k on a rough estimate of $\bar{q}_k$ is to use past quantity observations, if such exist. But the regulator must be careful not to offer perverse incentives to a foresighted firm. To simplify notation, let us assume in the whole subsection that there is a single product, and that the incentives–pricing dichotomy holds. One scheme based on historical data consists in taxing *price changes*. More precisely, let

$$T(p_t, p_{t-1}, q_{t-1}) \equiv \frac{(p_t - p_{t-1})q_{t-1}}{(1+\lambda)(1-\delta)} \tag{4.10}$$

be the tax levied on the firm at date t, where $q_{t-1} = D(p_{t-1})$ is the date-$(t-1)$ sale. Faced with this price tax, the firm maximizes

$$\sum_{t=0}^{\infty} \delta^t \{b_t[p_t D(p_t) - T(p_t, p_{t-1}, D(p_{t-1})) - C(\Phi(\beta, e_t), D(p_t))] - \psi(e_t)\}, \tag{4.11}$$

where δ denotes the discount factor and b_t is the slope of the firm's incentive scheme at date t.

The normative analysis implies that the incentive scheme should be time invariant (as is easily seen). So let us complete our tax-on-price-changes

[16] Which maximizes $\{p_k\tilde{D}_k(p_k) - \tilde{C}_k(\beta, e_k, \tilde{D}_k(p_k), s_k)\}$.

[17] Under a price cap, $\bar{p}_k$, the profit attributable to good k is obtained by maximizing $\pi_k = p_k D_k(p_k, s_k) - C^k(\beta, e_k, D_k(p_k, s_k), s_k)$ subject to $p_k \leqq \bar{p}_k$. The two cases yield a generalized price, $p_k - s_k$, equal to the monopoly generalized price and a profit, π_k, equal to the monopoly profit.

scheme by a time-invariant rate-of-return rule; in particular, let $b_t = b$ for all t. The first-order condition with respect to p_t in (4.11) yields:

$$(p_t - C_q)D'(p_t) + D(p_t) - \frac{D(p_{t-1})}{(1+\lambda)(1-\delta)} - \frac{\delta((p_{t+1}-p_t)D'(p_t) - D(p_t))}{(1+\lambda)(1-\delta)} = 0. \tag{4.12}$$

In the steady state, $p_{t-1} = p_t = p_{t+1}$, and hence

$$(p - C_q)D' + \frac{\lambda D}{1+\lambda} = 0, \tag{4.13}$$

which is the socially optimal pricing policy.

Actually the price tax schemes based on survey data and on historical data may be used jointly. For new products in particular, the survey data may be used to initiate the price yax (i.e. to yield a $\bar{q}_0$), and to let the price tax be later determined by (4.10). This procedure may yield faster convergence than a price tax initiated by the monopoly output.

The dynamic behavior of price p_t is given by (4.12), the initial price p_{-1}, and demand $q_{-1} = D(p_{-1})$ at data (-1) and the transversality condition. Let us make the following assumption:

Assumption A. $D(p) = \alpha - \gamma p$; $C = (\beta - e)q$; $\psi(e) = e^2/2$.

Given a slope b of the incentive scheme, the date-t effort is given by $\psi'(e_t) = bq_t$ or $e_t = b(\alpha - \gamma p_t)$. Substituting e_t into (4.12) yields a second-order linear difference equation in the price.

Proposition 1. Under Assumption A, the optimal price is given by

$$p_t = p^* + (p_{-1} - p^*)r^{t-1},$$

where p^* is the steady state solution given by (4.6) (i.e., the socially optimal price) and

$$r \equiv \left[1 + \lambda(1-\delta) - \frac{\gamma b}{2}(1+\lambda)(1-\delta) \right.$$

$$\left. - \sqrt{\left[1 + \lambda(1-\delta) - \frac{\gamma b}{2}(1+\lambda)(1-\delta)^2 \right] - \delta} \right] \Big/ \delta.$$

[*A sufficient condition for r to be less than* 1 *is that* $(1-\delta)(1+\lambda)<1$. *So for* $\lambda=0.3$, $\delta>0.23$ *is sufficient for* $r<1$.]

The proof of Proposition 1 is available upon request from the authors. We conclude that the delegated price converges in a non-oscillatory way toward the socially optimal price.

Technological progress

Our mechanism is tailored to a stationary environment. To be more realistic, it ought to be adapted to changing technological environments.[18] An obvious difficulty in doing this is that the optimal policy may involve time variations in the slope of the incentive scheme. Because the optimal output increases as cost decreases and because technological progress may interact with the marginal productivity of effort in the cost function in subtle ways, the effort to be required from managers, and thus the slope of the incentive scheme, changes over time, in contrast to the stationary case. While a general analysis can be conducted, we will content ourselves with a simple case in which a straightforward extension of (4.10) can be obtained. Let us assume a single product supplied at cost:

$$C_t(\beta, e_t, q_t)=\alpha^t c q_t+\Phi(\beta, e), \quad \text{where } 0<\alpha<1. \tag{4.14}$$

The cost function in (4.14) exhibits not only the dichotomy property (the optimal relationship between price and marginal cost is unaffected by incentives considerations) but also a separability between pricing and effort decisions (the optimal price is independent of the effort level and conversely) because the incentive problem concerns only the fixed cost. It is easily verified [see eqs. (3.9) and (3.10) of our companion paper] that (i) the optimal effort and slope of the incentive scheme is time-independent; and (ii) the optimal price is given by the Ramsey formula:

$$\frac{p_t-\alpha^t c}{p_t}=\frac{\lambda}{(1+\lambda)\eta_t}, \tag{4.15}$$

where η_t is the elasticity of demand at date t.

We further assume that the demand function has constant elasticity:

$$q_t=D(p_t)=\mathrm{d}p_t^{-\eta}, \quad \text{where } \eta>1. \tag{4.16}$$

[18]That technological progress ought to be reflected in regulatory design is apparent in the British Telecom 'RPI – 3 percent' rule, which indexes the price caps to the retail price index and to an anticipated rate of technological progress equal to 3 percent.

Suppose that the regulator imposes a price tax,

$$T(p_t, p_{t-1}, q_{t-1}) = (xp_t - yp_{t-1})q_{t-1}, \tag{4.17}$$

where x and y are to be determined, and gives an incentive scheme leaving a bonus, $a + b(p_t q_t - C_t - T_t)$, at date t to the firm, where a and b are two positive constants. The firm then maximizes

$$\sum_{t=0}^{\infty} \delta^t [a + b[p_t q_t - \alpha^t c q_t - \Phi(\beta, e_t) - (xp_t - yp_{t-1})q_{t-1}] - \psi(e_t)]. \tag{4.18}$$

Let x and y be given by

$$x = \frac{1}{(1+\lambda)(\alpha^{-1/\eta} - \delta\alpha)} \tag{4.19}$$

and

$$y = \alpha x. \tag{4.20}$$

We leave it to the reader to check that in the 'steady state' the firm charges the optimal prices given by eq. (4.15).

Formulae (4.17) thus generalizes (4.10) to account for technological progress. It is worth noting that the price tax is based not on the change in price, $p_t - p_{t-1}$, but on the *corrected change in price*, $p_t - \alpha p_{t-1}$.

Like in the absence of technological progress the steady-state price is optimal even if the slope b of the incentive scheme is not chosen optimally. However, we should note that the price tax becomes informationally more demanding in the presence of technological progress. While (4.10) does not require any information about cost and demand functions (beyond the fact that they are stationary), (4.17) makes use of the rate of technological progress and of the elasticity of demand. While assuming knowledge of these two data is much weaker than assuming knowledge of the demand and cost functions, the algorithm based on historical data is no longer simple in that it leaves discretion to the regulator.

Inflation. Correcting for inflation is a simple matter. The formulae derived above are expressed in real prices. Let X be equal to one plus the rate of inflation. Thus, if p_t denotes the real price and $\tilde{p}_t$ the nominal price, $\tilde{p}_t = X^t p_t$. Formula (4.17) gives the price tax in real terms. The nominal price tax $\tilde{T}$ is thus

$$\tilde{T} = X^t T = X^t (xp_t - yp_{t-1})q_{t-1} = (x\tilde{p}_t - yX\tilde{p}_{t-1})q_{t-1}.$$

We thus conclude that the price tax must be based on the corrected difference, $\tilde{p}_t-(\alpha X)\tilde{p}_{t-1}$, as one would expect.

In practice, it often makes sense to index regulatory schemes not on the overall rate of inflation, but on the rate of inflation of a basket of key inputs of the firm (e.g. fuel for electric utilities), as is done in 'automatic rate adjustment mechanisms'. The derivation of the appropriate price tax follows the lines of the one for technological progress and overall inflation and is left to the reader.

Comparison with the literature

Our mechanism using historical data bears some resemblance to those of Finsinger and Vogelsang (1979, 1981, 1982) and Tam (1981).[19] We briefly review these mechanisms in the single-good context.

Finsinger and Volgelsang offer to give regulated firms a bonus:

$$B_t=a+\pi_t-\pi_{t-1}+(p_{t-1}-p_t)q_{t-1}, \tag{4.21}$$

where $\pi_t\equiv p_tq_t-C(q_t)$ and a is a constant. Finsinger and Vogelsang's major insight was that this scheme, which depends only on historically observable data (profit, quantity, and price), yields Ramsey prices in the long run. However, as Sappington (1980) pointed out [see also Gravelle (1985)] this scheme has perverse incentive properties. If the cost function, C, depends on a cost-reducing activity, this cost-reducing activity is vastly undersupplied. This can be seen intuitively from (4.21); in a steady state $\pi_t=\pi_{t-1}$ and the firm does not gain from reducing its cost.

Tam (1981) proposed the following bonus:

$$\tilde{B}_t=a+b[\pi_t-p_tq_{t-1}]. \tag{4.22}$$

Tam showed that if the firm behaves myopically (i.e. maximizes its current bonus instead of the present discounted value of the bonus), the firm's price converges to marginal cost in the long run. One drawback of this mechanism is that the long-run steady state is marginal cost rather than Ramsey pricing. Another, and more important one, is that when the firm does not behave myopically there is no convergence to marginal cost pricing [Finsinger and Vogelsang (1985)].

The link between our mechanism and those of Finsinger–Vogelsang and Tam is that they all are negative price incentive schemes. The firm is penalized for increases in its current price. Our mechanism can be seen as combining the positive aspects of the two other schemes. Like Finsinger and

[19]For discussions of the properties of these mechanisms, see the 1985 *Quarterly Journal of Economics* papers by Finsinger and Vogelsang, Gravelle and Tam.

Vogelsang's, it is based on a taxation of price changes rather than of price levels. Like Tam's, it lets the firm retain (at least part of) its long-term profit and thus has desirable incentive properties. Finsinger and Vogelsang introduced rewards based on changes in profits to obtain convergence to Ramsey prices. The fact that under optimal regulation Ramsey prices depend on the economy-wide shadow cost of public funds allows us to finely compute the tax on price changes and base rewards on profit levels rather than on changes of profit levels.

Last, Vogelsang (1989a, b) designs a subsidy mechanism very much in the spirit of (4.10). The mechanism differs much from ours[20] in terms of prices it implements, but by making the firm residual claimant for its cost savings, it has good incentive properties.

Appendix: Access pricing and incentives

This appendix proves the results listed in subsection 3.2. From the revelation principle, we know that the regulator can restrict attention to mechanisms in which the firm announces its parameters truthfully.

If $\beta_0=\beta_0^{\mathrm{H}}$, the firm is a monopolist, as giving access to the fringe is too expensive. Let $e^*(\beta)$ be the effort to type β and $U^*(\beta)=\int_{\beta}^{\bar{\beta}}\psi'(e^*(\tilde{\beta}))\,\mathrm{d}\tilde{\beta}$ its rent.

If $\beta_0=\beta_0^{\mathrm{L}}$, the regulator has two options: either to give access to the fringe and let the fringe supply total output, or not to give access.[21] By incentive compatibility, it is easily seen that for types $\beta\in[\underline{\beta},\beta^*]$ no access is given, and for types $\beta\in(\beta^*,\bar{\beta}]$ access is given [this is because lower-cost types enjoy a higher rent under the no-access policy, while all types enjoy the same rent under the access policy]. To induce types $\beta\in(\beta^*,\bar{\beta}]$ to give access (i.e. not to announce β_0^{H}), the regulator must give a lump-sum transfer, $p=U^*(\beta^*)$, beyond the compensation for the effort, $e_0=\hat{e}$, when giving access.

Letting $\alpha=\mathrm{Prob}(\beta_1=\beta_1^{\mathrm{H}})$, the social welfare is thus:

[20]Letting $\lambda_g>1$ denote the government's transfer cost (to use Vogelsang's notation), Vogelsang suggests giving a subsidy,

$$S_t=S_{t-1}+\left(\frac{q_{t-1}}{\lambda_g-1}\right)(p_{t-1}-p_t),$$

to the firm (so that the firm's total income at date t is $p_tq_t-C_t+S_t$). This formula differs from (4.10) in (a) the coefficient of the price tax, and (b) its autoregressive character.

[21]The policy of giving access and sharing the market of the final good is dominated. If access is given to the fringe, choosing $q=0$ is optimal because, first, the fringe has lower marginal cost and, second, $q=0$ allows the regulator to perfectly control e_0.

$$W=\max\left\{\alpha\int_{\underline{\beta}}^{\bar{\beta}}[(1+\lambda)(rQ-(\beta-e^*(\beta))Q-F-\psi(e^*(\beta)))-\lambda U^*(\beta)]f(\beta)\,\mathrm{d}\beta\right.$$

$$+(1-\alpha)\left[\int_{\underline{\beta}}^{\beta^*}[(1+\lambda)(rQ-(\beta-e^*(\beta))Q-F-\psi(e^*(\beta))-\lambda U^*(\beta)]f(\beta)\,\mathrm{d}\beta\right.$$

$$\left.\left.+\int_{\beta^*}^{\bar{\beta}}[(1+\lambda)((r-c)Q-\beta_0^{\mathrm{L}}+\hat{e}-F-\psi(\hat{e}))-\lambda U^*(\beta^*)]f(\beta)\,\mathrm{d}\beta\right]\right\}, \tag{A.1}$$

subject to $U^*(\bar{\beta})=0$ and $\dot{U}^*(\beta)=-\psi'(e^*(\beta))$. Integrating by parts and optimizing yields:

$$\psi'(e^*(\beta))=Q-\frac{\lambda}{1+\lambda}\frac{F(\beta)}{f(\beta)}\psi''(e^*(\beta)),\quad \text{for } \beta\leqq\beta^*, \tag{A.2}$$

$$\psi'(e^*(\beta))=Q-\frac{\lambda}{1+\lambda}\frac{F(\beta)+\dfrac{1-\alpha}{\alpha}}{f(\beta)}\psi''(e^*(\beta)),\quad \text{for } \beta>\beta^*. \tag{A.3}$$

The interpretation of these equations is as follows. (A.2) is the version of eq. (3.9) of our companion paper for this model. Because types under β^* do not give access whatever β_0, the trade-off between bringing marginal benefit and marginal disutility closer together (lowering $Q-\psi'$) and leaving more rent to better types is resolved in the classic way. In contrast, types above β^* give access when $\beta_0=\beta_0^{\mathrm{L}}$. An increase in $e^*(\beta)$ for such types not only raises the rent of more efficient types, but also with probability $(1-\alpha)$ raises the rent of types in $[\beta^*,\bar{\beta}]$ who also get the lump-sum transfer, $U^*(\beta^*)$, for giving access. This results in lower incentives than those predicted by eq. (A.2).

We now optimize with respect to β^*. Assuming an interior solution:

$$\lambda(1-F(\beta^*))\psi'(e^*(\beta^*))$$

$$=(1+\lambda)f(\beta^*)[(\beta^*-e^*(\beta^*))Q+\psi(e^*(\beta^*))-cQ-\beta_0^{\mathrm{L}}-\psi(\hat{e})+\hat{e}], \tag{A.4}$$

where $e^*(\beta^*)$ denotes the value in the no-access policy [eq. (A.2)]. The assumption that $W^{\mathrm{L}}>W^{\mathrm{H}}(\underline{\beta})$ and the fact that $e^*(\beta^*)\leqq e^*$ imply that the right-hand side of (A.4) is positive. (A.4) expresses the equality between the marginal benefit of increasing access [by raising β^* by $\mathrm{d}\beta^*$, one lowers the rent of types in $[\beta^*,\bar{\beta}]$ when no access is given by $\psi'(e^*(\beta^*))\,\mathrm{d}\beta^*$]; and the marginal cost of production associated with more access. Note that β^* is independent of α.

The possibility of using linear contracts when F/f is increasing and no access is granted follows the usual lines.

References

Baumol, W. and R. Willig, 1987, Price caps: A rational means to protect telecommunications consumers and competition, Statement before the Federal Communications Commission, Docket 87-313.

Boiteux, M., 1956, Sur la gestion des monopoles publics astreints à l'equilibre budgetaire, Econometrica 24, 22–40.

Brauetigam, R., 1979, Optimal pricing with intermodal competition, American Economic Review 69, 38–49.

Brauetigam, R., 1984, Socially optimal pricing with rivalry and economies of scale, Rand Journal of Economics 15, 127–134.

FCC, Policy and rules concerning rates for dominant carriers, CC Docket 87–313.

Finsinger, J. and I. Vogelsang, 1979, Regulatory adjustment process for optimal pricing by multiproduct monopoly firms, Bell Journal of Economics 10, 157–171.

Finsinger, J. and I. Vogelsang, 1981, Alternative institutional frameworks for prize-incentive mechanisms: Some comments, Kyklos 34, 388–404.

Finsinger, J. and I. Vogelsang, 1982, Performance indices for public enterprise, in: L.P. Jones, ed., Public enterprise in less-developed countries (Cambridge University Press, Cambridge).

Finsinger, J. and I. Vogelsang, 1985, Strategic management behavior under reward structures in a planned economy, Quarterly Journal of Economics 100, 263–270.

Gravelle, H., 1985, Reward structures in a planned economy: Some difficulties, Quarterly Journal of Economics 100, 271–278.

Guesnerie, R. and J.-J. Laffont, 1984, A complete solution to a class of principal-agent problems with an application to the control of a self-managed firm, Journal of Public Economics 25, 329–369.

Joskow, P. and R. Schmalensee, 1986, Incentive regulation for electric utilities, Yale Journal on Regulation 4, 1–49.

Laffont, J.-J. and J. Tirole, 1989, Bypass and creamskimming, American Economic Review, forthcoming.

Laffont, J.-J. and J. Tirole, 1990, The regulation of multiproduct firms, Part I: Theory, Journal of Public Economics (this issue).

Sappington, D., 1980, Strategic firm behavior under a dynamic regulatory adjustment process, Bell Journal of Economics 11, 360–372.

Sappington, D., 1983, Optimal regulation of a multiproduct monopoly with unknown technological capabilities, Bell Journal of Economics 14, 453–463.

Spence, M., 1975, Monopoly, quality, and regulation, Bell Journal of Economics 6, 417–429.

Tam, M., 1981, Reward structures in a planned economy: The problem of incentives and efficient allocation of resources, Quarterly Journal of Economics 96, 111–128.

Vickers, J. and G. Yarrow, 1988, Privatization, and economic analysis (MIT Press, Cambridge, MA).

Vogelsang, I., 1989a, Public enterprise in monopolistic and oligopolistic industries, forthcoming in: J. Lesourne and H. Sonnenschein, eds., Fundamentals of pure and applied economics (Harwood, London).

Vogelsang, I., 1989b, Two-part tariffs as regulatory constraints, Journal of Public Economics, forthcoming.

C
Pricing of Bottleneck Inputs

[25]

The Theory of Network Access Pricing

Robert D. Willig

This paper presents a theoretical normative analysis of prices of access to a network. While the immediate motivation for the study is the bevy of presently pending policy issues concerning the telephone network,[1] the analysis will clarify the principles of pricing the services of other networks as well. For example, with few modifications, applications would be appropriate to the postal system and to computer networks.

There are two basic features of networks that create special pricing problems and issues. First, the value to an individual of access to a network depends on the size and composition of the group that also has access.[2] For example, telephone service is more valuable the more of one's friends and associates are subscribers so that they can be conveniently reached by telephone. This effect, termed network externalities, causes private decisions about whether or not to purchase network access to have ramifications for others who are not parties to those decisions. As such, it may be in the public interest for prices of network access to be lower than they would otherwise be, with the difference reflecting the value to others of individuals' purchases of access.

The second basic feature of networks that creates special pricing problems is the technological feasibility of interconnection. Firms other than the one operating the network could, if they had technical access to the network (that is, if they were interconnected), offer services to consumers with network access.[3] These (called network services) might be perfect or close substitutes for those sold by the network operator. The financial success of such a competitive offering may or may not be in the public interest, and, either way, it may or may not be in the financial interest of the network operator. In any case, the profitability of such competing network services will depend critically on the structure and levels of prices for the technical network access necessary for interconnection.

Thus, network externalities and interconnection are basic features of networks that create special complexities in the analyses of prices for network access — both that of final consumers and that of vendors of network services (henceforth called technical network access). These complexities, their interactions, and the consequent lessons for public interest network access prices are the focus of this paper.

The next section describes the abstract stylized network to which the subsequent analyses will pertain. The third section develops a theory of network externalities that is cast within the framework of the standard theory of consumer welfare. Much care is taken to show that network externalities need not be viewed as metaphysical phenomena and that, instead, they can be measured with observable demand data organized as the incremental consumers' surplus in network services. In the fourth section, characterizations of first best network access prices are derived, and it is shown that it is plausible that they are significantly below marginal production costs due to the network externality effects. Consequently, first best prices can be expected to yield financial losses that may not be feasible. Hence, profit constrained welfare optimal (Ramsey) network prices are characterized. These, too, are affected by network externalities, and they have the additional property of being demand as well as cost differentiated.

The fifth section discusses technical network access prices from the viewpoint of public interest desiderata concerning incentives for competitive entry. It is shown that the Ramsey optimal network prices are consistent with these desiderata only if the technical network access prices are differentiated by final use and if each is set equal to the unit contribution to network profit of the final use. Finally, in the concluding section, relationships between such prices and some (abstract) institutional mechanisms are discussed.

The Stylized Network

For the sake of clarity, the analyses will be conducted in the context of a highly simplified and stylized network that is just complex enough to represent the features at issue. As pictured in Figure 1, the network links those consumers who are equipped with the good or service called network access. Each local switching center is the termination point of lines to all the connected consumers in a local area. Flows along the network from one consumer to another within the same local area traverse the access lines of the two consumers, which are temporarily interconnected for the duration of the flow by means of facilities in the local switching center. Such flows will be termed local network services, or local usage. Other, nonlocal network services, or just network services, are flows between more distant consumers. These are switched at local switching centers from consumers' access lines to transmission facilities that interconnect the various local switching centers. In Figure 1, the junctions between transmission facilities and local switching centers are symbolized as squares.

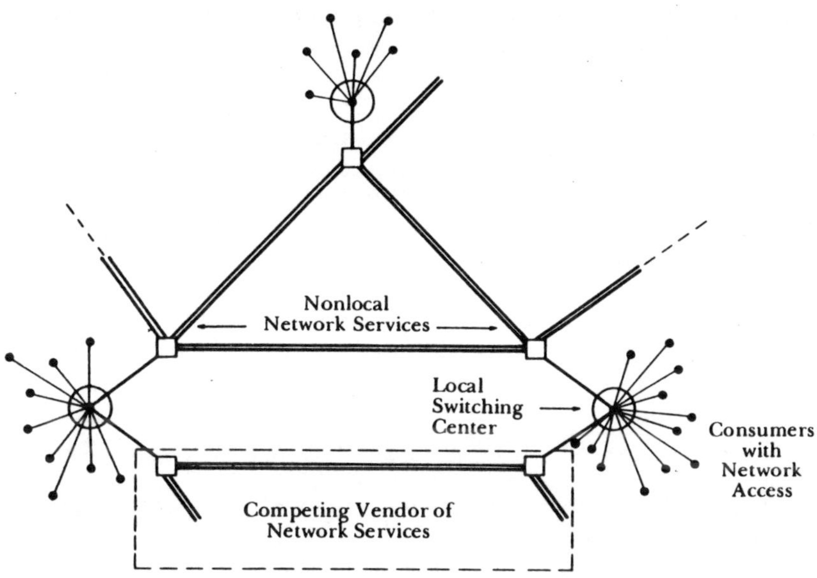

Figure 1. ***The Network***

In this abstract physical model, it is clear that local usage serves as an input needed for the production of network services. And, as depicted in the figure, it is technologically feasible for a competing vendor of network services to construct its own junction and transmission facilities, while purchasing technical access and local usage from the network. The network services thereby produced need not be identical to those offered by the network operator, and, even if identical, they need not incur the same production costs. For example, the network operator may enjoy economies of scope from the integration and coordination of network access, local usage, and network services. Such economies of scope would be unavailable to a competing vendor of only network services. On the other hand, the latter may be able to employ a newer and less costly transmission system than that embodied in the sunk plant of the network.

For present purposes, let the cost of efficient operation of the network be represented as

$$C(N, S^L, S^T)\,. \tag{1}$$

Here, N is the vector whose i^{th} component, N_i, is the number of consumers of type i with access to the network. Consumers in different local areas or with different locations within the same area are of different types as long as their connections to the network incur different costs. Also, consumer types may be distinguished by such demand related factors as business or residential status. Here, too, S^L is the vector whose j^{th} component, S^L_j, is the amount of the jth local network service produced. Similarly, S^T is the vector of the quantities produced of nonlocal network services (T = transmission). It will often be convenient to combine the vectors S^L and S^T into the single vector S. Throughout, network services that cause different costs must be segregated into different categories. The categories may be distinguished by such factors as various dimensions of quality, time of day, distance, special handling, and nature of end-point areas. However, it is also possible that categories will be distinguished by purchaser characteristics.

Each of the variable elements of the network's output is captured in a component of the vectors N and S, and each can, in principle, have a distinct price. The vector E represents the prices of consumer access to the network, and the vectors P, P^L, and P^T represent the prices of all, local, and nonlocal network services, respectively. It need not be assumed that the prices, P, are borne by the party that initiates the network service. Rather, as a matter of terminology, the prices will be borne by the purchaser, who is assumed to have the power of decision over the purchase. The notation precludes neither the possibility that some prices of distinct categories are identical, nor the possibility that some prices are zero.

The next section develops some new theory of the behavior and welfare of consumers who may purchase network access. This theory is essential for a careful analysis of the public interest pricing of network access and network service.

Network Externalities and Incremental Consumers' Surplus

It is certainly intuitively plausible that the value to a consumer of network access be sensitive to the size and composition of the group that also has access. As such, a consumer's decision on whether or not to purchase access would depend on the group with access.[4] More important for present purposes, the welfare of a consumer committed to purchasing access in the relevant situations would be increased if the population of network subscribers were to grow more favorable. The aims of this section are to explain and then formalize these intuitive notions in a manner that enables the size of the effects to be assessed by means of observable market behavior. In particular, it will be argued and then shown that the magnitude of network externalities can be estimated with a recently developed consumers' surplus tool called incremental surplus.

Roughly speaking, a consumer's surplus for a particular service is the value to the consumer of the total number of units purchased, over and above the money paid for those units. Such surplus would be positive, even at relatively high prices, as long as the consumer would continue to buy some, albeit less, of the service if its price were to rise. Each unit purchased contributes to the surplus an amount equal to the difference between the highest price the consumer would pay for it (the reservation price) and the price the consumer actually must pay. Consequently, consumer's surplus can be measured as the area between the demand curve, which depicts the schedule of reservation prices, and the horizontal drawn at the market price.

Consumer's surplus in a particular service can be validly interpreted as the value to the consumer of the opportunity to purchase all he wants of the service at the going price, *vis-à-vis* the comparison scenario in which the service were unavailable, or its price were so high that none of it would be demanded. Rather loosely, then, for heuristic purposes, we could express this relationship as: (consumer's surplus in the service) = (real income at market prices) − (real income in comparison scenario). The following rearrangement will provide an analytic handle on network externalities: (real income at market prices) = (real income in comparison scenario) + (consumer's surplus in the service).

From this viewpoint, consider a change in the economic environment of the consumer that would have no effect on him in the comparison scenario, but that might have an impact when the service is available at the going price. For such a change, (change in real income at market prices) = (change in consumer's surplus in the service). This heuristic relationship suggests that the effect, in dollar terms, of a change in the external circumstances of a consumer can be measured as the resulting incremental consumer's surplus in a purchased service. The crucial stipulation is that the change would have no impact on the consumer in the comparison scenario in which the service were not purchased at all.

This requirement can be plausibly assumed in a variety of circumstances. For example, a change in the quality of a good or service would certainly have no direct effect on an individual who did not consume the good or service.[5] Also, there are public goods (such as highways) which are "asymptotic complements" to certain private goods (such as automobile and motorcycle services) in that the one would be valueless to a consumer without the other.[6] Consequently, the change in the real income of a consumer caused by a change in product quality and by a change in the level of a public good can be measured by the associated incremental consumer's surplus in, respectively, the good with changing quality and in the good which is an asymptotic complement to the public good.

In the context of a network, a change in the population of subscribers with access to the network would have no direct effect on a consumer utilizing no network services, because it is only through network services that a consumer has access to other subscribers. This observation would seem to indicate that incremental surplus in network services can be used to measure the effects on others of an individual's decision as to whether or not to purchase access. Such effects on others are exactly what have been termed network externalities.

Here, however, there are two intrinsic complications that do not necessarily arise in other contexts. First, although only one consumer is the purchaser of a unit of a network service, the service is a flow between two consumers, and it may benefit both. As such, while it is self-evident that changes in the population of subscribers would have no effect on a consumer with no *usage* of network services, such changes may nonetheless affect a consumer who *purchases* no network services, but who is a recipient of network flows purchased by others. Thus, incoming flows must be explicitly analyzed. The treatment of this complication is deferred until later in this section; in the interim, it is assumed that incoming flows have no value to the recipient.

The second complication arises from the fact that there are many distinct network services. As such, it can only be asserted that changes in network size would fail to affect an individual consuming none of these diverse services. (This contrasts sharply with changes in the quality of a product which would fail to affect an individual consuming none of that one product.) Consequently, it is the incremental surplus in the totality of network services that must be used to measure network externalities. If the demands for the different network services were independent of one another's prices, then this would be just the sum of the incremental surpluses in each of the services. Otherwise, however, some care (explained in the next subsection) must be exercised in forming the correct sum.

Figure 2 displays a representative component of the incremental consumer's surplus used to measure network externalities. Each of the curves is a demand curve of a particular consumer for the ith network service, as a function of its price P_i. The inner curve gives the consumer's demands for the service for a given population of network subscribers. If that population were larger, the consumer's demands at all prices would expand to those along the outer curve. The concomitant increase in the value to the consumer of the availability of the service at price P_i is given by the shaded area — the incremental consumer's surplus. It is the sum of areas of this form, over all network services, that measures the benefit to the consumer of the expansion of the network. Of course, the reverse also holds. That is, the loss to the consumer from a shinkage of the network would be measured by the incremental surplus areas eliminated by the contractions in the demand curves of the network services.

Thus far, the discussion has been limited to the effect on one consumer of changes in the population of network subscribers. Yet, such changes can simultaneously affect all of those who remain connected to the network. Fortunately, a straightforward extension of the analysis can be made to measure the total effect of network externalities.

Demand curves of individuals can be summed, horizontally, to form the market demand curve which gives total market demand as a function of price. The consumers' surplus area under the market demand curve is the sum of the individual consumer's surplus areas. The incremental consumers' surplus associated with the market demand curve is, likewise, the total of those of all consumers. It follows that the sum of the effects on individuals' real incomes of an expansion or a contraction of the network can be measured by inframarginal consumers' aggregate incremental surplus in network services.[7]

This discussion has indicated, in heuristic terms, how network externalities can be measured with consumers' surplus tools. The use of these tools involves intuitive manipulations of data on observable market demand behavior. As such, it must be recognized that network externalities need not be considered metaphysical phenomena; instead, they are quantifiable and amenable to scientific analysis.

Furthermore, the analytic representation of network externalities as incremental consumers' surplus enables qualitative insights into their sources and qualitative assessments of their importance. For example, a change in the population of network subscribers that did not affect demand for network services at market prices, and at all

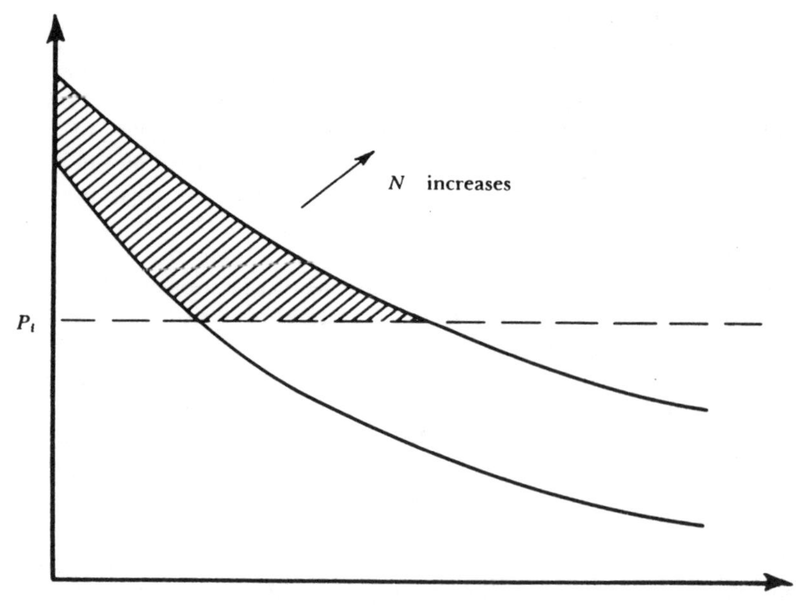

Figure 2. ***Incremental Consumer's Surplus***

higher prices, would yield no incremental surplus and would therefore cause no network externalities. In contrast, sensitivity of inframarginal consumers' demand for network services to the size of the network, at market prices, would indicate the existence of network externalities. Yet, the inverse does not hold, because it is plausible that demand for network services would be relatively sensitive to composition of the group with access at high prices and be relatively insensitive at low prices. This would occur if consumers were willing to redirect their relatively low value network flows, while, at higher prices, the remaining high value flows were less flexibly directed to particular recipients. In any case, the more sensitive to network size and composition are inframarginal consumers' demands for network services, the more important are network externalities.

With this heuristic groundwork in place, it is now necessary to give a careful treatment of the theory. Only a formal development can eliminate remaining feelings that network externalities are metaphysical. Only the formal framework will enable more general consideration, in a later section, of incoming flows. And only the use of the accepted theoretical paradigm will enable the determination, in the fourth section, of the implications of network externalities for optimal network access pricing.

Consumer Theory and Network Externalities

In this section, the standard theory of the welfare of an individual consumer is extended to allow for network externalities.[8] A principal maintained assumption is that incoming flows have no value to the recipient. The relaxation of this assumption is the subject of the next section.

The consumer is assumed to have preferences that are representable by the utility function

$$U(s,\bar{x},N), \tag{2}$$

where s is the vector of purchased network services, $\bar{x}$ is the vector of all other goods and services consumed, and N is the vector of the numbers of consumers of different types (as in the previous section) who have access to the network. The utility function is assumed to be regular in that it is continuously differentiable in all arguments, and it is nondecreasing and strictly quasi-concave jointly in s and $\bar{x}$. The consumer has income m and faces the vectors of prices p and $\bar{p}$ for the goods and services in the vectors s and $\bar{x}$, respectively. The consumer also faces a price of E for network access, without which the vector s of purchased network services must be zero.

The critical presumption that will permit network externalities to be linked to observable demand behavior is that utility is insensitive to changes in N when s is zero. Thus,

$$\frac{\partial U(o,\bar{x},N)}{\partial N_i} = 0, \qquad \text{for all } i, \bar{x}, \text{ and } N. \tag{3}$$

An associated condition that will also be assumed throughout is that network services are inessential in that there are levels of other goods and services great enough to compensate the consumer for the absence of any network services.[9] This condition is needed to impute economic meaning to equation (3) because, otherwise, the consumer would be unconsolably injured by the absence of network services, and no changes would be of consequence to him in that state.

It is hypothesized that the consumer chooses his purchases in accord with his own preferences and within the limits of his income. Consequently, if he were to purchase network access, he would choose his other purchases, s and $\bar{x}$, to maximize utility (U). That is,

$$\underset{s,\bar{x}}{\text{maximize}}\ U(s,\bar{x},N), \text{ subject to } p \cdot s + \bar{p}\,\bar{x} = m - E\ . \tag{4}$$

Let $s(p,\bar{p},m-E,N)$ and $\bar{x}(p,\bar{p},m-E,N)$ denote the choices of s and $\bar{x}$ that maximize utility, subject to the budget constraint, as in equation (4). These are conditional demand functions that give the consumer's optimal purchases of s and $\bar{x}$, as functions of prices, disposable income, and the population of network subscribers, all conditional on the consumer purchasing access to the network. Correspondingly,

$$\ell(p,\bar{p},m-E,N) \tag{5}$$

is the conditional indirect utility function that gives the optimal level of utility, from equation (4), as a function of the parameters facing the consumer, conditional on the purchase of network access.

The analogue of equation (4) that is conditional on the consumer not purchasing network access is:

$$\underset{\bar{x}}{\text{maximize}}\; U(o,\bar{x}), \text{ subject to } \bar{p} \cdot \bar{x} = m\ . \tag{6}$$

The associated indirect utility function that gives the optimized level of utility in equation (6) is denoted by $\hat{\ell}(\bar{p},m)$. Note that N does not appear as an argument of utility here, due to the assumption in equation (3).

This simple theory predicts that the consumer will purchase access if his optimized utility conditional on such purchase exceeds the maximal utility he can obtain without it, that is, if

$$\ell(p,\bar{p},m-E,N) > \hat{\ell}(\bar{p},m). \tag{7}$$

Then, the consumer's unconditional indirect utility function which takes endogenous account of the access decision is

$$\ell^*(p,\bar{p},E,m,N) = \max \left\{\ell(p,\bar{p},m-E,N),\ \hat{\ell}(\bar{p},m)\right\} \tag{8}$$

Now, it is clear that N is of no concern to a consumer who is not purchasing network access, so that attention can be limited to the case in which $\ell^* = \ell(p,\bar{p},m-E,N)$. Here, network externalities can appear through the effect of N on indirect utility, ℓ . However, in this form, the effect would be in terms of units of utility, which are essentially arbitrary.

Thus, it is most useful to transform ℓ into the ordinally equivalent indirect utility function that is scaled in terms of real income, relative to some base. This is the income compensation function,

$$\mu(p^o,\bar{p}^o,N^o\,|\,p,\bar{p},N,m), \tag{9}$$

defined to be the income necessary for the consumer, when facing the exogenous parameters $(p^o,\bar{p}^o,N^o)$, to reach the same level of utility attainable with income m and parameters $(p,\bar{p},N)$. Formally, this definition is:[10]

$$\ell(p^o\bar{p}^o,N^o,\mu(p^o,\bar{p}^o,N^o\,|\,p,\bar{p},N,m)\,) = \ell(p,\bar{p},N,m). \tag{10}$$

Hence, equation (9) is the real income of the consumer in the situation summarized by $(p,\bar{p},N,m)$, relative to the base defined by the parameters $(p^o,\bar{p}^o,N^o)$. Of course, if the parameters are the same in the two situations, then real and nominal income coincide; that is,

$$\mu(p^o,\bar{p}^o;N^o\,|p^o,\bar{p}^o,N^o,m) = m. \tag{11}$$

Otherwise, real and nominal incomes differ by an adjustment for the effects on the consumer of the changes in parameters. In particular,

$$\mu(p^o,\bar{p}^o,N^o\,|p^o,\bar{p}^o,N',m-E)-\mu(p^o,\bar{p}^o,N^o\,|p^o,\bar{p}^o,N^o,m-E) = \mu(p^o,\bar{p}^o,N^o\,|p^o,\bar{p}^o,N',m-E) - (m-E) \tag{12}$$

is the change in real income caused by the change in the population of network subscribers from N^o to N'.

In other words, equation (12) formally represents the network externality effect on the consumer, in dollars of real income. It is this representation that can be linked to incremental consumer's surplus. The linkage is effected through the fundamental differential equation of welfare economics,[11] which here takes the form

$$\frac{\partial\mu(p,\bar{p},N\,|p',\bar{p}',N',m')}{\partial p_i} = s_i(p,\bar{p},N,\mu(p,\bar{p},N\,|p',\bar{p}',N',m')\,). \tag{13}$$

This equation can be interpreted as saying that, to the first order, the increase in μ from an increase in the price of the ith service is just that price increase multiplied by the number of units of the ith service that is demanded. The relevant level of demand is found along the compensated demand curve, because the income argument of s_i, in equation (13), holds μ instead of the consumer's actual income.

To study the effect of N on real income, equation (13) can be differentiated with respect to N_j, the jth component of N. Suppressing the arguments of μ, and substituting $\partial^2\mu/\partial N_j\partial p_i$ for $\partial^2\mu/\partial p_i\partial N_j$, the result of this operation is:

$$\frac{\partial^2\mu}{\partial N_j\partial p_i} = \frac{\partial s_i(p,\bar{p},N,\mu)}{\partial N_j} + \frac{\partial s_i(p,\bar{p},N,\mu)}{\partial m}\,\frac{\partial\mu}{\partial N_j}. \tag{14}$$

These relationships, for all of the network services, comprise a system of differential equations which could, in principle, be solved for $\partial\mu/\partial N_j$ if a boundary condition were stipulated. The requisite boundary condition is

$$\lim_{p\to\infty}\ \frac{\partial\mu(p,\bar{p},N\,|p',\bar{p}',N',m')}{\partial N_j} = 0\,, \tag{15}$$

which is the dual equivalent of equation (3), given that network services are inessential.[12] Here, the notation $p\to\infty$ is shorthand for $p_i\to\infty$, for all i.

Equation (15) has the intuitive interpretation that μ must be unaffected by N when p is so large that no network services can be afforded.[13]

The clearest solution to the system given by equations (14) and (15) obtains in the case in which there are no income effects on the demands for network services. Then, $\partial s_i/\partial m = 0$, and equation (14) becomes

$$\frac{\partial^2 \mu}{\partial N_j \partial p_i} = \frac{\partial s_i(p,\bar{p},N,m)}{\partial N_j}, \tag{16}$$

and integration of equation (16) for all services, between p and p'', yields

$$\frac{\partial \mu}{\partial N_j}(p'',\bar{p},N\,|\,p',\bar{p}',N',m') - \frac{\partial \mu}{\partial N_j}(p,\bar{p},N\,|\,p',\bar{p}',N',m') = \oint_{\Gamma(p,p'')} \sum_i \frac{\partial s_i(q,\bar{p},N,m)}{\partial N_j}\, dq_i\,, \tag{17}$$

where $\Gamma(p,p'')$ is any smooth path between p and p''. Now, taking the limit of equation (17) as p''_∞ , invoking the boundary condition in equation (15), and letting $\Gamma(p,\infty)$ denote the limit of $\Gamma(p,p'')$ as $p'' \rightarrow \infty$ results in

$$\frac{\partial \mu}{\partial N_j}(p,\bar{p},N\,|\,p',\bar{p}',N',m') = -\oint_{\Gamma(p,\infty)} \sum_i \frac{\partial s_i(q,\bar{p},N,m)}{\partial N_j}\, dq_i\,. \tag{18}$$

This is the solution to the system comprised of equations (14) and (15), when $\partial s_i/\partial m = 0$. It can be immediately applied to the representation of network externalities that is defined in equation (12) through these relationships:

$$\mu(p^o,\bar{p}^o,N^o\,|\,p^o,\bar{p}^o,N',m-E) - (m-E) = \mu(p^o,\bar{p}^o,\ N^o\,|\,p^o,\bar{p}^o,N',m-E) - \mu(p^o,\bar{p}^o,N'\,|\,p^o,\bar{p}^o,N',m-E) =$$

$$-\oint_{\Lambda(N^o,N')} \sum_j \frac{\partial \mu(p^o,\bar{p}^o,N\,|\,p^o,\bar{p}^o,N',m-E)}{\partial N_j}\, dN_j\,, \tag{19}$$

where $\Lambda(N^o,N')$ is a smooth path from N^o to N'. Substituting the equalities in equation (18), reversing the order of integration between N_j and q_i, and utilizing the fundamental theorem of calculus yield

$$\mu(p^o,\bar{p}^o,N^o \mid p^o,\bar{p}^o,N',m-E) - (m-E) = \oint_{\Gamma(p,\infty)} \sum_i [s_i(q,\bar{p}^o,N',m-E) - s_i(q,\bar{p}^o,N^o,m-E)]\, dq_i. \qquad (20)$$

Equation (20) is a precise version of the incremental consumer's surplus representation of network externalities that was introduced in an earlier section. The left-hand side of equation (20) is the change in the consumer's real income, base (p^o, $\bar{p}^o$,N^o), caused by the change in the population of network subscribers from N^o to N'. The right-hand side is the difference between the total consumer's surplus in network services with network population N' and that with network population N^o. Each total consumer's surplus is a line integral calculated over any smooth path, Γ (p,∞), that runs from the vector of market prices, p, outward so that each component price, p_i, increases without bound.

Perhaps the most natural such path is the rectangular one that unboundedly increases each price, in turn, from its market level. Along this path, when the ith price is increased, the $(i-1)^{th}$, $(i-2)^{th}$, and so forth, have already been increased without bound, and the $(i+1)^{th}$, $(i+2)^{th}$, and so forth, are still at their market levels. Then, the total incremental surplus that appears in equation (20) is the sum of areas like that depicted in Figure 2. However, it must be recognized that the relevant demand curves for the ith network service are defined in terms of the levels of other prices that obtain on the segment of the path along which the ith price is increased.

Furthermore, it must be recognized that the relevant demand curves in equation (20) are those conditional on the consumer purchasing network access. By hypothesis, these are the demand curves in force at the market prices. Yet, it may well be the case that somewhere along the path $\Gamma(p,\infty)$ the consumer would choose to leave the network if he actually faced those prices for network services. Consequently, at such a point, unconditional demands would discontinuously drop to zero and thereby diverge from conditional demands. Nonetheless, the derivation of equation (20) shows that it is the conditional demand curves that yield the incremental consumer's surplus measurement of network externalities.

Finally, it must be recognized that the above derivation of equation

(20) rests upon the unrealistic assumption of no income effects on the demands for network services. And, in fact, equation (20) does not precisely hold absent this condition. However, it can be shown that equation (20) holds as a tight approximation in a broad range of realistic circumstances.

The demonstration of this fact proceeds from the explicit solution[14] of equations (11), (13), (14), and (15) in the case that all the network services exhibit the same constant income elasticity of demand, η:

$$\mu(p^o,\bar{p}^o,N^o|p',\bar{p}^o,N',m) = m \left[1 + \frac{(1-\eta)\Delta A}{m} \right]^{1/1-\eta}, \tag{21}$$

where

$$\Delta A = \oint_{\Gamma(p',\infty)} \sum_i s_i(q,\bar{p}^o,N',m)\,dq_i - \oint_{\Gamma(p^o,\infty)} \sum_i s_i(q,\bar{p}^o,N^o,m)\,dq_i. \tag{22}$$

Here, ΔA is the change in total consumer's surplus in network services that is caused by the change in network population from N^o to N', and by the change in prices from p^o to p'. Note that equation (20) is the specialization of equation (21) that obtains when $\eta=0, p'=p^o$, and m is replaced by the disposable income $m-E$. A Taylor Series expansion of the right-hand side of equation (21), together with numerical analysis of the remainder term,[15] shows that

$$\mu(p^o,\bar{p}^o,N^o|p',\bar{p}^o,N',m) \approx m+\Delta A\ . \tag{23}$$

provided that $\eta(\Delta A)^2/m$ is small. This condition will hold as long as the income elasticity of demand is in the usual range and the surplus changes at issue are only a small portion of disposable income.

The specialization of equation (23) when only N is varying is this restatement of equation (20) as an approximation:

$$\mu(p^o,\bar{p}^o,N^o|p^o,\bar{p}^o,N',m-E) - (m-E) \approx \Delta A\ . \tag{24}$$

Finally, equation (24) will hold with nonconstant income elasticities of demand, for a monotone path $\Gamma(p^o,\infty)$, as long as $\eta(\Delta A)^2/(m-E)$ is small in absolute value for all values of η equal to the income elasticity of any of the network services at any of the relevant points.[16]

Hence, with the exercise of considerable care, it has been shown that the standard theory of consumer welfare can be extended to incorporate network externalities. Within this framework, it has been demonstrated that the real income of a network subscriber can be affected by changes in the population that can be reached via the network. Moreover, the actual change in real income can be closely approximated by the incremental consumer's surplus in network services that is caused by an expansion or a contraction of the network.

Network Externalities with Valued Incoming Flows

The preceding analysis maintained the unrealistic assumption that incoming network flows have no value to the recipient consumer. However, it is intuitively clear that if they do have such value, then the linkage between network externalities and incremental surplus may be considerably complicated. The aims of this section are to expose and elucidate some of these complications, and to determine the requisite modifications of the preceding results.

Let $\bar{s}$ denote the vector whose i^{th} component, $\bar{s}_i$, is the quantity of incoming network flows of type i. The consumer's utility function is now

$$U(s,\bar{x},\bar{s},N), \tag{25}$$

instead of that in equation (2) which explicitly rules out any effect of $\bar{s}$. Clearly, if $\bar{s}$ were invariant to changes in s, $\bar{x}$, N, and prices, then the analysis that was based on equation (2) would apply without alteration.

There is another and far more interesting case in which the previous analysis is left unchanged by valued incoming flows.[17] Suppose that the quantity of each type of incoming network flow is a function of only the quantities of network services and other goods purchased by the consumer. That is,

$$\bar{s}_i = \bar{s}_i\ (s,\bar{x}). \tag{26}$$

This specification does permit $\bar{s}_i$ to vary with N and with prices, but only through their effects on s and on $\bar{x}$. For example, equation (26) would be satisfied if all incoming flows were responses to purchased outgoing ones, with some fixed response ratio. Or, the response ratio could vary with the quantity of network services, or with other purchases, $\bar{x}$.

In this case, equation (25) can be rewritten as $U(s,\bar{x},\bar{s},N) = U(s,\bar{x},\bar{s}(s,\bar{x}),N) \equiv V(s,\bar{x},N)$, where V is a new utility function that depends only on s, $\bar{x}$, and N, as required by equation (2) and the subsequent analysis. Here, the effects of s and $\bar{x}$ on V arise from two distinct sources: the direct effects from the value of consuming the purchases, and the indirect effects from the value of the induced incoming flows. Because these indirect effects fully exhaust the variability of $\bar{s}$, the analysis can proceed in terms of s, $\bar{x}$, and N alone, as in the earlier section.

This conclusion is left unchanged by the following technically minor, but economically meaningful, generalization of equation (26); if

$$\partial U(s,\bar{x},\bar{s},N)/\partial\bar{s}_t \neq 0,$$

then

$$\bar{s}_t = \bar{s}_t(s,\bar{x}) \,. \tag{27}$$

In this extension, categories of incoming flows that have no value to the consumer are not required to bear the special relationship to the consumer's purchases that is stipulated in equation (26).

In summary, network externalities can be measured by the incremental consumer's surplus in network services if the variability in all valued incoming flows is internalized by the consumer. For, in this case, the demands for network services will fully reflect the value of the thereby induced incoming flows. And the effects of the size of the network on the consumer will be fully reflected in its effects on the consumer's demands for network services.

This does seem to be a plausible scenario, to the extent that valued incoming flows arise in the context of ongoing relationships between others and the consumer.[18] However, the restrictiveness of equation (27) is most clear in the limiting case of $s=0$. Here, for equation (27) to hold, there must be no valued incoming flows, or the remaining variability in valued incoming flows must be internalized through the purchase of $\bar{x}$. In particular, valued components of $\bar{s}$ may not vary with the population of network subscribers. But if any valued incoming flows remain when $s=0$, then surely they would be eliminated if their purchasers left the network. Hence, an implication of equation (27) is that there be no valued incoming flows when $s=0$.

To relax this restriction, equation (27) can be generalized as follows: If

$$\partial U/\partial\bar{s}_t \neq 0,$$

then

$$\bar{s}_i = \bar{s}_i(s, \bar{x}, N) \; . \qquad (28)$$

Then, as before, equation (25) can be rewritten:

$$U(s, \bar{x}, \bar{s}, N) = U(s, \bar{x}, \bar{s}(s, \bar{x}, N), N) \equiv V(s, \bar{x}, N) \; . \qquad (29)$$

But here, even though $\partial U / \partial N_i = 0$ when $s = 0$, at such a point $\partial V / \partial N_i = \Sigma_j (\partial U / \partial \bar{s}_j) \cdot (\partial \bar{s}_j / \partial N_i)$, which is not necessarily zero. Thus, equation (3) may fail to hold, and, consequently, the analysis of the preceding section must be modified. In particular, the boundary condition in equation (15) must be replaced with an arbitrary one. As a result, equation (24) becomes

$$\mu(p^o, \bar{p}^o, N^o \,|\, p^o, \bar{p}^o, N', m) \approx m + \Delta A +$$

$$\lim_{p' \to \infty} \left[\mu(p^o, \bar{p}^o, N^o \,|\, p', \bar{p}^o, N', m) - \mu(p^o, \bar{p}^o, N^o \,|\, p', \bar{p}^o, N^o, m) \right] \; . \qquad (30)$$

Here, the new term is the change in real income that the consumer would experience due to the change from N^o to N', if the prices he faced for network services were unboundedly large and if he still had access to the network. It is this term that equation (3), or equation (15), guaranteed to be zero. But now, in view of equation (28), it captures the value of the change in incoming flows that would be caused by the change from N^o to N' were $s = 0$. As such, presuming that incoming flows are positively related to the size of the network, and assuming that the newly induced incoming flows have positive value, the new term is positive if $N' > N^o$, and it is negative if $N' < N^o$.

Hence, in this case, the positive incremental consumer's surplus in network services understates the consumer's gain in real income from an expansion of the network. And, obversely, the negative incremental consumer's surplus in network services understates the consumer's loss in real income from a contraction of the network. These understatements would be smaller, the less sensitive to network size would be the value of incoming flows were no network services purchased by the consumer.[19]

In the most general case, incoming flows would depend directly on the prices of network services, as well as on s, $\bar{x}$, and N. It greatly facilitates the analysis of this case to separate conceptually the prices of network services, p, faced by the consumer in question from those, $\bar{p}$, faced by others for their purchases of what will be the consumer's incoming flows. Then, the consumer's utility function is

$$U(s,\bar{x},\bar{s}(s,\bar{x},\bar{p},N),N) \equiv V(s,\bar{x},\bar{p},N). \tag{31}$$

To derive an expression for the effect of network externalities, $\bar{p}$ can be held fixed as a parameter, and the development based on equations (28) and (29) can be utilized. Consequently, this extension of equation (30) holds:

$$\mu(p^o,\bar{p}^o,\bar{p}^o,N^o|p^o,\bar{p}^o,\bar{p}^o,N',m) \approx m+\Delta\bar{A} +$$

$$\lim_{p'\to\infty}\left[\mu(p^o,\bar{p}^o,\bar{p}^o,N^o|p',\bar{p}^o,\bar{p}^o,N',m) - \mu(p^o,\bar{p}^o,\bar{p}^o,N^o|p',\bar{p}^o,\bar{p}^o,N^o,m)\right], \tag{32}$$

where

$$\Delta\bar{A} = \int_{\Gamma(p^o,\infty)}\sum_i [s_i(q,\bar{p}^o,\bar{p}^o,N',m) - s_i(q,\bar{p}^o,\bar{p}^o,N^o,m)]dq_i\ . \tag{33}$$

The interpretation of equation (32) is the same as that given for equation (30), with one exception. The incremental surplus, $\Delta\bar{A}$, is defined in equation (33) in terms of demand functions for network services that include $\bar{p}$ among their arguments. In view of equation (31), this is sensible because $\bar{p}$ affects $\bar{s}$, which may well itself affect demands for outgoing flows. However, in the incremental surplus calculation given by equation (33), $\bar{p}$ remains fixed at the level $\bar{p}^o$, while the prices p move along the path $\Gamma(p^o,\infty)$. Consequently, the demand curves which define the relevant incremental consumer's surplus pertain to situations in which the prices faced by the purchasers of the consumer's incoming flows are numerically different from the prices paid by the consumer for his outgoing flows. Such situations are, in most cases of practical interest, strictly hypothetical and unobserved.

Thus, there is a considerable loss in analytic power concomitant with the extension of equation (29) to the completely general formulation of equation (31). Nonetheless, even equation (31) permits the economically meaningful decomposition of network externality effects given by equation (32). The first portion is the change in value of the hypothetically purchased network services caused by the change in the population of network subscribers. The second portion is the change in values of incoming flows, if the consumer were purchasing no network services.

The first portion of equation (32), $\Delta\tilde{A}$, can differ from the observable incremental surplus, ΔA, because the general formulation allows for uninternalized values of incoming flows at all levels of s. Here, with $\bar{p}=p$, each consumer is injured by increases in network service prices not only because they make his own purchases more expensive, but also because they cause the loss in the uninternalized values of discouraged incoming flows. Then, such uninternalized values would argue for subsidization of the prices of network services. The counterargument would question the rationale for social or network-wide subsidization of flows from one consumer to another, when that same subsidization, if appropriate, could be effected by the very recipients of the valued incoming flows.

This counterargument seems to be compelling. And, in the vocabulary developed in this section, it suggests the plausibility of assuming that the variability in valued incoming flows is internalized by network subscribers. Consequently, the normative study of network prices below is based on equation (29), the model of consumer welfare that incorporates this assumption, rather than on the more general model in equation (31).

The Gradient of the Indirect Utility Function

Necessary ingredients of the normative analysis of network access prices are measures of the effects on consumers' utilities of changes in the prices of network access and network services. This section sketches the derivation from the preceding theory of the gradient of consumers' indirect utility functions.

Consider a consumer, h, who is an inframarginal network subscriber and whose behavior is described by the model inherent in equation (29). His indirect utility function, $\ell^h(p,\bar{p},E,N,m^h)$, is the maximum level of his utility that he can achieve by choices of s^h and $\bar{x}^h$ that remain within his budget. The Lagrangian of his utility maximization program is:

$$\mathcal{L}\equiv U^h(s^h,\bar{x}^h,\tilde{s}^h(s^h,\bar{x}^h,N),N)+\lambda[m^h-E^h-p\cdot s^h-\bar{p}\cdot\bar{x}^h], \tag{34}$$

where E^h is the component of E that pertains to consumer h. Then, by the envelope theorem, the derivatives of ℓ^h are equal to the derivatives of $\mathscr{L}$, evaluated at the levels of the decision variables that are optimal for $\mathscr{L}$.

Hence, the marginal utility of income is given by

$$\partial\ell^h/\partial m^h = \lambda\ , \tag{35}$$

and

$$\partial\ell^h/\partial E^h = -\lambda = -\partial\ell^h/\partial m^h\ , \tag{36}$$

$$\partial\ell^h/\partial p_i = -\lambda s_i^h = -(\partial\ell^h/\partial m^h)\, s_i^h, \tag{37}$$

where s_i^h is the consumer's demand for the ith network service.

Moreover, it can be shown that in a broad range of cases,[20] the marginal network externality effect is given by:

$$(\partial\ell^h/\partial N_j)/(\partial\ell^h/\partial m^h) = \oint_{\Gamma(p,\infty)} \sum_i \frac{\partial s_i^h(q,\bar{p},E,N,m^h)}{\partial N_j}\, dq_i$$
$$+ \lim_{p'\to\infty} \left[\frac{\partial\ell^h(p',\bar{p},E,N,m^h)}{\partial N_j} \bigg/ \frac{\partial\ell^h(p',\bar{p},E,N,m^h)}{\partial m^h}\right] \tag{38}$$

The divisions by the marginal utility of income transform the terms into units of real income. Thus, equation (38) is exactly the marginal version of equation (30), which represents the network externality effect of a noninfinitesimal change in N. Hence, the discussions of equation (30) pertain to equation (38) as well.

The above results apply to a consumer who is a network subscriber. A consumer, k, who chooses not to join the network is described by the indirect utility function $\ell^k(\bar{p},m^k)$. This depends on only $\bar{p}$ and m^k because the parameters of the network are of no concern to a consumer without network access.

Public Interest Network Access Pricing

This section is devoted to the study of prices for network access that are in the public interest. Unavoidably, because of the interrelationships of the network system, the study must deal with the prices of network services as well. The normative stance underlying the analysis is a social decision maker's social preference ordering that respects individuals' preferences and that reflects the Pareto principle. As such, the public interest objective function takes the form of a Bergson-Samuelson social welfare function whose arguments are the levels of each individual's utility: $W[\ell^1, \ell^2, \ldots]$.

To keep the focus sharply on the effects of the intrinsic properties of a network, various other complications that might be important in particular applications are assumed away. Thus, below, assumptions are made on the social welfare function that preclude concerns about the distribution of income. Furthermore, possible interactions are ignored between the network prices and prices and quantities in other sectors of the economy. Analysis of potential and actual entry of competing vendors of network services is deferred until the next major section.

The following subsection studies the "first best" network prices that are optimal for social welfare. The next section characterizes the Ramsey network prices that are optimal under a constraint on the size of the profit or loss from the operation of the network.

First Best Network Prices

The first best network prices are chosen to maximize

$$W[\ell^h(p,\bar{p},E,N,m^h+\alpha^h\Pi),\ \ell^k(\bar{p},m^k+\alpha^k\Pi)]\ . \tag{39}$$

Here, the arguments of W are the utility levels of all consumers. The expression in equation (39) is an abbreviation in that it includes the utility of only some representative network subscriber, h, and the utility of only some representative individual, k, who is not a subscriber. The constants α^h and α^k denote the shares of the network's profit, Π, that accrue to consumers h and k, respectively. These shares sum to one over all consumers. Network profit is defined to be the revenues from the sale of network access and network services, minus the cost of network operation defined in equation (1):

$$\Pi = p\cdot S + E\cdot N - C(N,S)\ . \tag{40}$$

Here, S is the vector of total quantities purchased and produced of network services, so that

$$S = \sum_h s^h\ . \tag{41}$$

Necessary conditions for equation (39) to be maximized by choices of p and E are that its partial derivatives with respect to every component of p and E be equated to zero. These necessary conditions will be analyzed by utilizing the results derived earlier to provide economically meaningful characterizations of the first best prices.

Mechanical differentiation of equation (39) yields[21]

$$\frac{\partial W}{\partial p_i} = \sum_h \frac{\partial W}{\partial \ell^h}\left[\frac{\partial \ell^h}{\partial p_i} + \sum_j \frac{\partial \ell^h}{\partial N_j}\frac{\partial N_j}{\partial p_i} + \alpha^h \frac{\partial \ell^h}{\partial m^h}\frac{\partial \Pi}{\partial p_i}\right] + \sum_k \frac{\partial W}{\partial \ell^k}\frac{\partial \ell^k}{\partial m^k}\alpha^k \frac{\partial \Pi}{\partial p_i}, \tag{42}$$

$$\frac{\partial W}{\partial E_i} = \sum_h \frac{\partial W}{\partial \ell^h}\left[\frac{\partial \ell^h}{\partial E_i} + \sum_j \frac{\partial \ell^h}{\partial N_j}\frac{\partial N_j}{\partial E_i} + \alpha^h \frac{\partial \ell^h}{\partial m^h}\frac{\partial \Pi}{\partial E_i}\right] + \sum_k \frac{\partial W}{\partial \ell^k}\frac{\partial \ell^k}{\partial m^k}\alpha^k \frac{\partial \Pi}{\partial E_i}. \tag{43}$$

The term $(\partial W/\partial \ell^h)(\partial \ell^h/\partial m^h)$ that appears in equations (42) and (43) is the rate of change of social welfare with respect to the income of consumer h. If these rates of change were different for the incomes of two different consumers, then the social decision maker would find it preferable to effect an income transfer between them. Consequently, the assumption that the distribution of income is of no concern to the social decision maker implies that the rate of change of social welfare with respect to the income of any consumer is the same. That is, for all h and k,

$$\frac{\partial W}{\partial \ell^h}\frac{\partial \ell^h}{\partial m^h} = \frac{\partial W}{\partial \ell^k}\frac{\partial \ell^k}{\partial m^k} = w . \tag{44}$$

Making use of equation (44) and the fact that the shares of Π sum to one, equations (42) and (43) become

$$\frac{1}{w}\frac{\partial W}{\partial p_i} = \sum_h \left(1 \Big/ \frac{\partial \ell^h}{\partial m^h}\right)\left[\frac{\partial \ell^h}{\partial p_i} + \sum_j \frac{\partial \ell^h}{\partial N_j}\frac{\partial N_j}{\partial p_i}\right] + \frac{\partial \Pi}{\partial p_i}; \tag{45}$$

$$\frac{1}{w}\frac{\partial W}{\partial E_i} = \sum_h \left(1 \Big/ \frac{\partial \ell^h}{\partial m^h}\right)\left[\frac{\partial \ell^h}{\partial E_i} + \sum_j \frac{\partial \ell^h}{\partial N_j}\frac{\partial N_j}{\partial E_i}\right] + \frac{\partial \Pi}{\partial E_i}. \tag{46}$$

Recall from equation (36) that $\partial\ell^h/\partial E_i = -\partial\ell^h/\partial m^h$ if price E_i pertains to consumer *h*, and that it is zero otherwise. Consequently,

$$\sum_h \left(1\Big/\left(\frac{\partial\ell^h}{\partial m^h}\right)\left(\frac{\partial\ell^h}{\partial E_i}\right)\right) = -N_i ,$$

where N_i is the number of consumers who purchase network access at the price E_i. Substituting this relationship, equation (37), and equation (41) into equations (45) and (46), and rearranging, yields

$$\frac{1}{w}\frac{\partial W}{\partial p_i} = \sum_j \frac{\partial N_j}{\partial p_i}\sum_h \frac{\partial\ell^h}{\partial N_j}\Big/\frac{\partial\ell^h}{\partial m_j} - S_i + \frac{\partial\Pi}{\partial p_i} \tag{47}$$

and

$$\frac{1}{w}\frac{\partial W}{\partial E_i} = \sum_j \frac{\partial N_j}{\partial E_i}\sum_h \frac{\partial\ell^h}{\partial N_j}\Big/\frac{\partial\ell^h}{\partial m^h} - N_i + \frac{\partial\Pi}{\partial E_i} \tag{48}$$

Mechanical differentiation of equation (40) gives

$$\frac{\partial\Pi}{\partial p_i} = S_i + \sum_j \frac{\partial S_j}{\partial p_i}\left(p_j - \frac{\partial C}{\partial S_j}\right) + \sum_j \frac{\partial N_j}{\partial p_i}\left(E_j - \frac{\partial C}{\partial N_j}\right) ; \tag{49}$$

$$\frac{\partial\Pi}{\partial E_i} = N_i + \sum_j \frac{\partial S_j}{\partial E_i}\left(p_j - \frac{\partial C}{\partial S_j}\right) + \sum_j \frac{\partial N_j}{\partial E_i}\left(E_j - \frac{\partial C}{\partial N_j}\right) . \tag{50}$$

Substitution of equations (49) and (50) into equations (47) and (48), together with rearrangement, yields these useful expressions:

$$\frac{1}{w}\frac{\partial W}{\partial p_i} = \sum_j \frac{\partial S_j}{\partial p_i}\left(p_j - \frac{\partial C}{\partial S_j}\right) + \sum_j \frac{\partial N_j}{\partial p_i}\left(E_j - \frac{\partial C}{\partial N_j} + \sum_h \frac{\partial\ell^h}{\partial N_j}\Big/\frac{\partial\ell^h}{\partial m^h}\right) ; \tag{51}$$

$$\frac{1}{w}\frac{\partial W}{\partial E_i} = \sum_j \frac{\partial S_j}{\partial E_i}\left(p_j - \frac{\partial C}{\partial S_j}\right) + \sum_j \frac{\partial N_j}{\partial E_i}\left(E_j - \frac{\partial C}{\partial N_j} + \sum_h \frac{\partial\ell^h}{\partial N_j}\Big/\frac{\partial\ell^h}{\partial m^h}\right) . \tag{52}$$

The necessary conditions for p and E to maximize W are that the expressions in equations (51) and (52) equal zero, for all components i. The solution to this system of equations is now easy to state:[22]

$$p_j = \frac{\partial C}{\partial S_j}; \tag{53}$$

$$E_j = \frac{\partial C}{\partial N_j} - \sum_h \frac{\partial \ell^h}{\partial N_j} \bigg/ \frac{\partial \ell^h}{\partial m^h} \quad . \tag{54}$$

These are the conditions that characterize the first best network prices. Not unexpectedly, optimal prices for network services are equal to the associated marginal costs of production.

In contrast, each optimal network access price is below the associated marginal production cost by an amount equal to

$$\sum_h \frac{\partial \ell^h}{\partial N_j} \bigg/ \frac{\partial \ell^h}{\partial m^h} \quad . \tag{55}$$

This term is the marginal network externality effect on the total real income of all individuals. Thus, it can be said that first best network access prices are equal to the associated marginal social costs, and that these are the marginal production costs less the marginal network externalities.

The expression in equation (55) makes it clear that the marginal network externality effects that are relevant for pricing are potentially spread over all consumers with network access. In contrast, the effects of potential uninternalized values of incoming flows discussed earlier were concentrated on one consumer. For this reason, it was argued that such values were indeed likely to be privately internalized. And, obversely, it is because network externalities are likely to be diffuse that network access prices appropriately correct for them.

The marginal network externality term in equation (55) can be related to observables by summing the equality in equation (38) over all network subscribers, h. Thus, by ignoring the limit term in equation (38), it follows that equation (55) is not less than

$$\int_{\Gamma(p,\infty)} \sum_i \frac{\partial S_i(q,\bar{p},E,N,M)}{\partial N_j} \, dq_i \, . \tag{56}$$

Here, $S_i(q,\bar{p},E,N,M)$ is the aggregate demand function for the ith network service, and M represents the entire distribution of disposable income. So equation (56) is the rate of change with respect to N_j of the aggregate consumers' surplus in all network services. And this observable quantity provides a lower bound on the amount by which the marginal production cost exceeds the first best network access price.[23]

A heuristic argument based on the model in equation (27) can help to build intuition on the quantitative importance of equation (56). Consider the discrete analogue of the latter, which is the change in aggregate inframarginal consumers' surplus in network services caused by the departure of one marginal consumer from the network. This would be the aggregate surplus in purchased flows to the marginal consumer, if demand for flows to others were unaffected by his departure. Let β be the ratio, at all prices, between the quantity of network flows to the marginal consumer and the quantity of network services demanded by him. Equation (56) is then β times the consumer's surplus in network services of the marginal consumer. And, because he is marginal, this surplus is exactly E_j.[24] Consequently, in this case, equation (56) is equal to βE_j, and equation (54) yields this expression for the first best network access price:

$$E_j = \frac{1}{1+\beta} \frac{\partial C}{\partial N_j}. \tag{57}$$

If there were no flows to the marginal consumer at any prices equal to or above market levels, then $\beta=0$, no one would care about departure from the network, and the optimal level of E_j would be marginal production cost. If, instead, every flow demanded by the marginal consumer were matched by an incoming flow purchased by others, then β would be one, and the optimal level of E_j would be one-half the marginal production cost. It is conceivable that β would be greater than one, with the consequent first best E_j less than one-half of marginal production cost.

Hence, the previously derived relationships between network externalities and observable demand data make it clear that first best network access prices can plausibly be significantly below marginal production costs. The combination of these relationships with the results derived in this section provides a framework for applying demand and cost information to the determination of first best network prices.

Ramsey Optimal Network Prices

With the first best prices of network access below marginal production cost, the question inevitably arises as to their financial impact. The answer depends, in part, on the returns to scale properties of the network technology. If it were to exhibit constant returns to the scale of both network services and the population of subscribers, then total cost would be exactly covered by the revenues obtained from prices equal to marginal production costs. In this case, the first best prices would cause negative profit. The losses would be still greater in the more plausible case of increasing returns to scale because, here, even prices equal to marginal production costs leave a deficit.[25]

If the network is to be self-supporting, or if the available funds for subsidization are limited, the first best network prices may not be financially feasible. And, in view of equations (53) and (54), such a financial problem is more likely, the more significant are the network externalities that drive the optimal network access prices below marginal production costs. Consequently, for most applications, the relevant normative viewpoint imposes the constraint on prices that they yield a profit of no less than some predetermined figure, Π^o. Then, what are called Ramsey optimal network prices, or just Ramsey network prices,[26] maximize the social welfare function in equation (39) subject to the profit constraint.

The Kuhn-Tucker necessary conditions for p and E to be optimal for this program are:

$$\frac{\partial W}{\partial p_i} + \gamma \frac{\partial \Pi}{\partial p_i} = 0\,, \quad \frac{\partial W}{\partial E_i} + \gamma \frac{\partial \Pi}{\partial E_i} = 0\,; \tag{58}$$

$$\gamma[\Pi - \Pi^o] = 0\,, \; \gamma \geqslant 0\,, \text{ and } \Pi \geqslant \Pi^o\,, \tag{59}$$

where i ranges over all components of p and E, and where γ is the Lagrange multiplier on the constraint. If the first best prices satisfy the profit constraint, then they are also Ramsey optimal, and $\gamma=0$ at the optimum. If, however, due to network externalities or to economies of scale, the first best prices yield a level of profit below the feasible floor, Π^o, then the profit constraint is binding, γ is positive, and the Ramsey prices deviate from social marginal costs.

The Ramsey optimal network prices are characterized by these combinations and rearrangements of equations (58), (51), (52), (49), and (50):

$$\sum_j \frac{\partial S_j}{\partial p_i}\left(p_j - \frac{\partial C}{\partial S_j}\right) +$$

$$\sum_j \frac{\partial N_j}{\partial p_i}\left[E_j - \frac{\partial C}{\partial N_j} + \left(\frac{1}{1+\gamma/w}\right)\sum_h \frac{\partial \ell^h}{\partial N_j}\Big/\frac{\partial \ell^h}{\partial m^h}\right]$$

$$= -\left(\frac{1}{1+w/\gamma}\right) S_i \;; \tag{60}$$

$$\sum_j \frac{\partial S_j}{\partial E_i}\left(p_j - \frac{\partial C}{\partial S_j}\right) +$$

$$\sum_j \frac{\partial N_j}{\partial E_i}\left[E_j - \frac{\partial C}{\partial N_j} + \left(\frac{1}{1+\gamma/w}\right)\sum_h \frac{\partial \ell^h}{\partial N_j}\Big/\frac{\partial \ell^h}{\partial m^h}\right]$$

$$= -\left(\frac{1}{1+w/\gamma}\right) N_i \;. \tag{61}$$

Here, the terms $\partial S_j/\partial p_i$, $\partial N_j/\partial p_i$, $\partial S_j/\partial E_i$, and $\partial N_j/\partial p_i$ are price derivatives of market demand functions for network services and for network access.

The qualitative lessons of equations (60) and (61) are clearest when all cross-elasticities of demand are small enough to be ignored. Then equations (60) and (61) can be rearranged into this inverse elasticity rule, suitably modified to account for network externalities:

$$\left[\frac{p_j - \partial C/\partial S_j}{p_j}\right]\left(-\frac{\partial S_j}{\partial p_j}\frac{p_j}{S_j}\right) = \frac{1}{1+w/\gamma} =$$

$$\left[\frac{E_i - \partial C/\partial N_i + \left(\frac{1}{1+\gamma/w}\right)\sum_h \frac{\partial \ell^h}{\partial N_i}\Big/\frac{\partial \ell^h}{\partial m^h}}{E_i}\right]\left(-\frac{\partial N_i}{\partial E_i}\frac{E_i}{N_i}\right), \tag{62}$$

for all i and j. This rule can be interpreted to say that across all the network services and all the categories of network access, the proportional deviations between the Ramsey prices and the associated marginal social costs are inversely proportional to the associated own price elasticities of demand. Because all such demand elasticities are positive (as defined in equation [62]), all the Ramsey optimal network prices are above the associated marginal social costs when the profit constraint is binding. And the less sensitive to its own price is the demand for a network service or the demand for a category of access, the larger is the ratio between the Ramsey optimal price and the marginal social cost.

The marginal social cost of a network service is just the marginal cost of production. But the marginal social cost of a category of network access is the marginal production cost, less the marginal network externality term of equation (55) adjusted for the profit constraint. This adjustment is made by multiplying by the factor $(1/(1+\gamma/w))$. It is equal to one for a nonbinding profit constraint, and it shrinks slowly from that level as prices are constrained away from their first best values.[27] Hence, due to network externalities, the marginal social cost of network access can be substantially less than production marginal cost. Thus, although the Ramsey network access prices are above the corresponding marginal social costs, they may nonetheless fall below the marginal production costs of access.

The principal lessons are the same in the general case with cross-elasticities of demand. In fact, equations (60) and (61) are the standard general optimality conditions for Ramsey prices,[28] with one important exception. For the determination of optimal network access prices, the role usually played by marginal production costs is here played instead by the marginal social costs, which are smaller by the adjusted marginal network externalities.

It is important to reemphasize that the Ramsey optimal prices for network services generally deviate from marginal production costs to differing degrees that depend upon the characteristics of demands. While this is not the case for first best prices, such prices would cause negative profits, given constant or increasing returns to scale, due to network externalities. Thus, it can be concluded that the special properties of networks generally force optimal prices of network services to be demand as well as cost differentiated. The implications of this fact for technical network access prices are discussed in the next section, after characterizations of desirable structures of such prices are developed.

Technical Network Access Prices

As discussed in the first two sections, a typical feature of networks is the technological feasibility of interconnection with competing vendors of network services. To produce its services, such a firm must purchase the use of access lines, and/or associated switching facilities, that interconnect its transmission equipment with the local switching centers of the network. And it must purchase local network services as variable inputs for its production of nonlocal network services. The subject of this section is the public interest pricing of such purchases of technical network access.

It is assumed that the network services potentially or actually offered by competing vendors are identical to those offered by the network.[29] A potential entrant's cost of producing the categories of network services in the set A, at the same levels given by the corresponding components of S^T, is denoted as $C^e(S^T_A)$. Here, e stands for entrant. This cost is additional to the costs of purchasing the requisite technical inputs from the network.

The cost to the network of providing the access facilities needed by an entrant is denoted as c_e, and the corresponding price faced by an entrant is a_e. The vector of local network services that an entrant requires to produce S^T_A is denoted by S^{Le}_A. Then, for example, $C(N, S^L + S^{Le}_A, S^T_B) + c_e$ is the total cost incurred by the network to provide access for the subscriber population N and for an entrant, to produce local network services of S^L for consumers and S^{Le}_A for the entrant which itself produces S^T_A, and to produce the vector of nonlocal network services S^T_B. Finally, a_i is the price charged by the network to an entrant for the local network services that the entrant uses to itself produce a unit of the ith nonlocal network service. The vector of these prices is denoted by a^T, and the vector of its components that pertain to the subset of services A is denoted by a^T_A.

This notation allows two dimensions of price discrimination to be represented. First, the prices of local network services to consumers, p^L, may be different than the prices of those same services to firms that utilize them as inputs for the production of nonlocal network services. Second, the price to such a firm of a unit of local usage may depend upon the use to which it is put — the particular nonlocal service that it is utilized to produce.

A study by John Panzar [1979] in an analogous framework shows that the first of these dimensions of price discrimination can be essential for the sustainability of Ramsey optimal prices. Furthermore, it may enable prices to be set that all consumers would prefer to any prices that could be achieved absent such discrimination. Moreover, it can make the difference between a financially viable network and one that would be unable to cover its costs. For these reasons, and because such price discrimination between consumers and competing vendors of network services appears to be practically feasible,[30] the analysis will proceed under the presumption that this kind of price discrimination may be practiced.

In general, price discrimination is feasible only if the seller can, without expensive information collection, distinguish the customers who face the higher prices from those who face the lower ones. The second precondition is that the purchasers who face the lower prices be unable to resell the good or service to the higher price group, and thereby arbitrage away the price differentials. These two necessary conditions seem to hold in the case of sale of local network services at different prices to final consumers and to producers of other network services. However, the satisfaction of the conditions seems far more problematical in the case of the aforementioned second dimension of discrimination based on final use.

On the one hand, the network can, no doubt, inexpensively monitor the time, date, and one of the end points of the services into whose production the purchased local network services are an input. On the other hand, monitoring other characteristics of these nonlocal services, such as destination, may be impossible without direct and detailed examination of the operations or records of the customer firms. Thus, while it is clear that the prices of local network services can precisely discriminate among some characteristics of their final uses, it may be more difficult to differentiate prices according to others. In view of this potential difficulty, the analysis will assume that precise discrimination is feasible and provide a framework for assessing the importance of such precision. Mechanisms are suggested to increase the precision of price differentiation in cases when monitoring is difficult.

The analysis of technical access prices rests on the fundamental desiderata that they yield profit incentives for the entry of firms that would lower total industry costs and that they discourage socially undesirable entry.[31] These desiderata can be applied to the potential entry of firms that would supply all the nonlocal services offered by the network, or just some subset of those services.

First, a firm that faced technical network access prices a^T and a_e, and that incurred costs of producing S^T equal to $C^e(S^T)$, would experience a profit incentive to market the full quantities of nonlocal services, S^T, if and only if

$$p^T S^T - C^e(S^T) - a^T S^T - a_e > 0 . \tag{63}$$

This inequality is the condition that the market prices, p^T, provide revenues in excess of the entrant's total costs — production costs plus the technical network access fees that it would be required to pay. The desiderata are that this profit incentive occur if and only if total social cost would be lowered by such entry:

$$C(N,S^L,S^T) > C^e(S^T) + C(N,S^L+S^{Le},0) + c_e \ . \tag{64}$$

The left-hand side of equation (64) is the industry cost with all production effected by the network, while the right-hand side is the total industry cost with the entrant producing S^T and with the network providing access for the population N of consumers and for the entrant, local services S^L for consumers, and the local services S^{Le} used by the entrant as inputs.

The desiderata dictate that a^T and a_e be chosen so that equation (63) holds for each $C^e(S^T)$ if and only if equation(64) holds. Algebra shows that this requirement is equivalent to the following relationship:

$$p^TS^T - (a^TS^T+a_e) = C(N,S^L,S^T) - C(N,S^L+S^{Le},0) - c_e \ . \tag{65}$$

The interpretation is that the difference between the revenues obtained by the network from its sale of S^T to consumers and that it would obtain from the technical access charges levied on the entrant is equated to the difference between the levels of costs incurred by the network in the two situations. Hence, the technical access prices that satisfy the desiderata would leave the profit of the network unchanged if an entrant replaced its production of S^T.

Analogous desiderata can also be applied to potential entrants that would produce the subset of S^T denoted by $S^T_{A_j}$. These desiderata are

$$p^T_{A_j} S^T_{A_j} - C^e\left(S^T_{A_j}\right) - a^T_{A_j} S^T_{A_j} - a_e > 0 \tag{66}$$

if and only if

$$C\left(N,S^L,S^T\right) > C^e\left(S^T_{A_j}\right) + C\left(N,S^L+S^{Le}_{A_j},S^T-S^T_{A_j}\right) + c_e \ . \tag{67}$$

As before, equation (66) is the condition that an entrant marketing $S^T{}_{A_j}$ be profitable, and equation (67) is the condition that industry costs would be lowered by such entry. The requirement that equation (67) hold if and only if equation (66) holds is equivalent to:

$$p^T_{A_j} S^T_{A_j} - \left(a^T_{A_j} S^T_{A_j} + a_e\right) = C\left(N,S^L,S^T\right) - C\left(N,S^L+S^{Le}_{A_j},S^T-S^T_{A_j}\right) - c_e \ . \tag{68}$$

In analogy to equation (65), equation (68) says that the profit of the network would be unchanged if an entrant replaced its production of the subset of its services, $S^T{}_{A_j}$.

Now, consider a partition of the nonlocal network services into disjoint subsets of services, A_i, which have production processes that are incrementally separable from one another in the following sense:

$$C\left(N,S^L,S^T\right)-C\left(N,S^L+S^{Le},0\right)=$$

$$\sum_i\left[C\left(N,S^L,S^T\right)-C\left(N,S^L+S^{Le}_{A_i},S^T-S^T_{A_i}\right)\right] \quad . \qquad (69)$$

The left-hand side is the incremental cost to the network of providing S^T, exclusive of the local services used as inputs into the production of S^T. This exclusion follows from the fact that both $C(N,S^L,S^T)$ and $C(N,S^L+S^{Le},0)$ incorporate the costs of these input local services; the former does so implicitly because the costs are incurred on behalf of the network's own production of S^T, while the latter incorporates them explicitly because here they are incurred for services sold to an entrant producing S^T. The right side of equation (69) is the sum of the incremental costs to the network of providing each subset of network services, S^T_{Ai}, with each increment again exclusive of local services used as inputs. Hence, equation (69) stipulates that the incremental costs of the subsets of services sum to the incremental cost of the entire set.

This condition would not obtain if two or more of the subsets of services shared some common production facilities. In this case, none of the incremental costs of the subsets taken one at a time would include the cost of the common facilities. But, since the incremental cost of the entire set would include the common cost, this increment would exceed the sum of the incremental costs of the subsets, in violation of equation (69). It is critical to note, however, that the increments of equation (69) hold constant the population of network subscribers, the local services that they purchase, and the local services required as inputs for the production of S^T. Consequently, the common facilities that would cause equation (69) to be violated must be additional to those utilized to produce local services and consumers' access.

Hence, there are bound to be subsets of services with common transmission facilities that would cause equation (69) to be an inequality rather than an equality. The implications of this for technical access prices will be studied below. However, it is also plausible that there be some partition of subsets, perhaps on the basis of geography, which are incrementally separable in production in the sense of equation (69).

If there is at least one such collection of subsets, then application of the desiderata to them implies that $a_e=c_e$. This can be seen by summing equation (68) over the subsets in the partition, subtracting equation (65) from the sum, and invoking equation (69). Thus, the desiderata require that the network charge each potential entrant a fee for its hookup to the network that is equal to the cost thereby incurred.

When the requirement that $a_e = c_e$ is combined with equation (65), and with equation (68) for each subset in an incrementally cost separable partition, the following implications of the desiderata emerge:

$$a^T S^T = \left\{ C\left(N, S^L + S^{Le}, 0\right) - C\left(N, S^L, 0\right)\right\} + \left\{ p^T S^T - \left[C\left(N, S^L, S^T\right) - C\left(N, S^L, 0\right)\right]\right\} \quad ; \tag{70}$$

$$a^T_{A_i} S^T_{A_i} = \left\{ C\left(N, S^L + S^{Le}_{A_i}, S^T - S^T_{A_i}\right) - C\left(N, S^L, S^T - S^T_{A_i}\right)\right\} + \left\{ p^T_{A_i} S^T_{A_i} - \left[C\left(N, S^L, S^T\right) - C\left(N, S^L, S^T - S^T_{A_i}\right)\right]\right\} . \tag{71}$$

In both equations (70) and (71), the charges levied on an entrant for its input local services are equated to the sum of two portions. The first portion is the incremental cost to the network of providing the input local services. The second is the difference between the revenues the network earned on the network services lost to the entrant and the incremental costs those lost services caused. Equation (70) shows that the desiderata require this equality to hold over the full set of nonlocal network services, and equation (71) shows that it must hold for each subset of an incrementally cost separable partition.

The implications of equation (71) are clearest when the subset A_i contains only network service i. Then, rearrangement gives

$$a^T_i = C^{Le}_i + \left(p^T_i - C^T_i\right) \quad , \tag{72}$$

where C^{Le}_i is the average incremental cost of the input local services, and C^T_i is the average incremental cost to the network of the ith nonlocal service. Thus, the technical usage price a^T_i exceeds the associated average incremental cost by the unit contribution to network profit from the displaced network service.

The representation given by equation (72) exposes the potential conflicts that can occur, absent precise price differentiation, between

Ramsey pricing of network services and technical access prices that satisfy the desiderata. Suppose that a_i^T must equal a_j^T due to exhorbitant costs of effecting the monitoring needed to distinguish the ith final use from the jth. Suppose, too, that the average incremental costs of the input local services are the same for the two final uses, so that $C_i^{Le} = C_j^{Le} = C^{Le}$. Then, equation (72) shows that the desiderata would be satisfied only if the unit contributions from network services i and j were equal. Of course, this will generally not be true for the Ramsey optimal levels of the network service prices.

For simplicity, consider the inverse elasticity rule version of the Ramsey characterization. Then, for each nonlocal network service, the Ramsey prices satisfy this condition:

$$\frac{\left(p_i^T - \dfrac{\partial C}{\partial S_i^T}\right)}{p_i^T} \epsilon_i = \alpha \ ,$$

where ϵ_i is the price elasticity of demand for the service, and α is a constant. The corresponding unit contributions are

$$p_i^T - C_i^T + p_i^T \left[1 - \delta_i \left(1 - \frac{\alpha}{\epsilon_i}\right)\right] \ , \tag{73}$$

where δ_i, the degree of scale economies in service i, is equal to the ratio of the average incremental cost to the marginal cost of that service. This same relationship can also be expressed as

$$p_i^T - C_i^T = \frac{\partial C}{\partial S_i^T}\left(\frac{1}{1-\alpha/\epsilon_i} - \delta_i\right) \tag{74}$$

Thus, the Ramsey optimal levels of the unit contributions are smaller for services with smaller marginal costs, with larger price elasticities of demand, and with larger degrees of scale economies. And such welfare efficient variations in unit contributions are inconsistent with the desiderata when technical access prices cannot be precisely differentiated. One way to resolve such conflicts is to give up on the Ramsey variations in unit contributions from the nonlocal network services whose input local service prices cannot be suitably differentiated. The welfare losses from this approach would be larger, the greater were the variation in the corresponding levels of the right-hand side of equation (74), and the larger were the elasticities of demand for the affected services.

Another approach is to differentiate the input local service charges in a manner that is less precise, but that requires less costly monitoring. For example, even if final uses i and j could not be feasibly distinguished, it might still be feasible to monitor the firm's total revenues obtained from the sale of those services. Then, total charges for input local services could be levied according to the formula

$$\left(S_i^T+S_j^T\right) C^{Le} + r \left(p_i^T S_i^T + p_j^T S_j^T\right) .$$

This mechanism combines a nondifferentiated unit price for the input local services with a proportional levy on revenues. It is equivalent to setting $a_i^T = C^{Le} + rp_i^T$ and $a_j^T = C^{Le} + rp_j^T$. Generally, this pair of input local service prices would be imperfectly differentiated by final use. Nonetheless, equations (73) and (72) show that it is consistent with both the desiderata and Ramsey optimality in the special case in which services i and j have the same elasticities of demand and the same degrees of scale economies, albeit different marginal costs.

In general, the less precisely the technical access prices can be differentiated by final use, the more serious will be the welfare losses from the requisite compromises between the desiderata and the Ramsey pricing. The lesson from the above example is that more complex payment mechanisms may be socially desirable when precisely differentiated rates are infeasible.

Thus far, the treatment of specific technical access prices has rested on an incrementally cost separable partition of the nonlocal network services. Unfortunately, the implications of the desiderata are less clear for the input local service prices associated with the individual members of one of the subsets in such a partition. For specificity, suppose that the subset of services A is part of such a partition, so that the desiderata imply that equation (71) holds for A. Suppose, further, that A is comprised of services 1 and 2 that are not incrementally cost separable because their production involves a common transmission facility. Thus

$$C\left(N,S^L,S^T\right) - C\left(N,S^L,S^T-S_A^T\right) > \left[C\left(N,S^L,S^T\right) - C\left(N,S^L,S^T-S_1^T\right)\right] + \left[C\left(N,S^L,S^T\right) - C\left(N,S^L,S^T-S_2^T\right)\right] . \qquad (75)$$

However, it will be assumed that the local service inputs for these nonlocal services are incrementally cost separable.

Then it follows from equation (75) that for equation (71) to be satisfied for the subset A, at least one of these relationships must hold:

$$a_1^T < C_1^{Le} + \left(p_1^T - C_1^T\right) \text{ , } a_2^T < C_2^{Le} + \left(p_2^T - C_2^T\right) . \tag{76}$$

Thus, given that the desiderata are fulfilled over the subset A, they cannot be satisfied for both of the individual services that comprise A. While the desiderata give the strong guidance embodied in equation (71) for $a_1^T S_1^T + a_2^T S_2^T$, they are as yet silent in this case on the individual levels of a_1^T and a_2^T.

A persuasive case can be made for avoiding

$$a_j^T > C_j^{Le} + \left(p_j^T - C_j^T\right) . \tag{77}$$

Such a high level of an input local service price could exclude from the market an entrant with costs below the incremental costs of the network, to the detriment of consumers. And, even if the network would find it advantageous to encourage such an entrant, once its potential were clear, a technical access price such as that in equation (77) might discourage the technological or marketing efforts needed to expose the potential.

Technical access prices such as those in equation (76) can yield incentives for entry by firms with costs above the network's incremental costs. This possibility cannot be eliminated for all services, simultaneously, given that some of them share common transmission facilities. The lesson is that responsive flexibility in technical access pricing is required for the preservation of industry cost efficiency. The network may have to realign its prices for input local services in response to potential entrants in order to deter entry that would raise total industry costs.

However, the theory has suggested limits on such responsively flexible prices. First, for every subset of nonlocal network services, the analogue of equation (77) should be avoided. That is, the technical access charges over any subset should not exceed the sum of the network's incremental costs of providing the input local services and the contribution to the network's profit obtained from that subset of nonlocal services. Second, this inequality should instead be an equality, as in equation (71), for any subset that is part of an incrementally cost separable partition. Third, the same equality should hold, as in equation (70), for the entire set of nonlocal network services. Finally, charges for technical hookup to the network should be equal to the associated costs.

It should be noted that a network operator who were to experience some gain from additional profits and who were not rate of return regulated would have private incentives to set technical access prices that fulfilled the desiderata. It is not surprising that incentives exist to deter industry cost raising entry. However, incentives also exist to encourage the entry of firms with costs below the network's incremental costs. The lost contribution to network profits from the sale of nonlocal network services can be recovered from technical access charges that satisfy the above guidelines. And total profit can be increased if the entrant charges consumers lower prices for its nonlocal network services than the network was able to with its higher costs.

However, if the network were rate of return regulated and experienced the Averch-Johnson effect, it would have incentives to deter socially beneficial entry. In its comparison of an entrant's costs with its own incremental costs, the network would have a profit incentive to utilize a shadow price for its capital below its actual market cost of capital. Thus, the network would impute private incremental costs to its nonlocal services below the social incremental costs. Consequently, it would gain by deterring socially desirable entrants that have costs between the private and social incremental costs of the network. And it would have incentives to set technical access prices above the levels given by equations (70) and (71).

There is one institutional framework that may promote the vitality of competition in nonlocal services without necessarily causing baneful side effects. This involves separating the network, at least as far as its financial flows and records, into two divisions. The local division would sell network access and local services to consumers, but it would stay out of markets for nonlocal network services. However, it would sell technical network access services to the other, nonlocal network division and to any firms who cared to enter the markets for nonlocal services. It would be required to offer its technical network access services to the nonlocal division and to the potential competitors of that division on the same terms. The nonlocal division and its potential competitors would utilize their purchases of technical network services to produce and sell nonlocal network services.[32]

It is fruitful to explore the forms taken in this framework by the technical network access prices and their guidelines that were analyzed above. Here, it is the local division that levies the final use differentiated technical network access prices a_e and a^T. The nonlocal division sees these charges as part of its costs. Then, this rearrangement of equation (70),

$$p^T S^T = C\left(N,S^L,S^T\right) - C\left(N,S^L+S^{Le},0\right) - c_e + a^T S^T + a_e \ , \quad (78)$$

can be interpreted to say that the revenues of the nonlocal division are just sufficient to cover its costs. For the interpretation to hold, its costs must be defined as the networkwide incremental costs of S^T, exclusive of input local services, plus the charges incurred for the purchase of the requisite technical services from the local division. Furthermore, the generalization of the undesirable condition in equation (77) can be rearranged as follows:

$$p^T_{A_i} S^T_{A_i} < C\left(N,S^L,S^T\right) - C\left(N,S^L+S^{Le}_{A_i},S^T-S^T_{A_i}\right) + a^T_{A_i} S^T_{A_i} \ .$$

In this framework its interpretation is a familiar one — that revenues from services A_i fail to cover the division's incremental costs of producing A_i. Such a case is essentially one of cross-subsidization, the dangers of which are well understood.[33]

Finally, if all the network prices together yield revenues that just cover total costs, then equation (78) is equivalent to

$$a_e + N\cdot E + p^L S^L + a^T S^T = C\left(N,S^L+S^{Le},0\right) + c_e \ . \quad (79)$$

This says that the revenues earned by the local division are equal to the costs of providing network access and local network services for consumers and for the nonlocal division. In particular, the revenues from the sale of technical network services exactly compensate for the relatively low level of revenues obtained from network access prices that reflect network externalities.

It is important to note that the costs imputed to the two network divisions in equations (78) and (79) need not correspond closely to accounting notions of costs. In particular, $C(N,S^L+S^{Le},0)$ are the costs that would be efficiently incurred if no nonlocal services were produced by the network. Hence, if the network were actually producing such services, then this cost figure would be a hypothetical one. Also, the incremental costs in equation (78) are calculated from this same hypothetical base.

However, the imputed costs in equations (78) and (79) of the two divisions do sum to the total cost of network operations, $C(N,S^L,S^T)$. And if the production costs of the network were separable, with

$$C\left(N,S^{L},S^{T}\right)=C\left(N,S^{L}+S^{Le},0\right)+T\left(S^{T}\right), \tag{80}$$

then the imputed division costs might well be directly accountable. In fact, equation (80) would be likely to hold only if the production processes of the divisions were physically separable. In this case, the divisions could actually be separate organizational, financial, and legal entities.

In contrast, economies of scope between nonlocal and local network services and the concomitant physical or human capital utilized jointly by the divisions would imply that equation (80) does not hold. In this case, splitting total network costs between the divisions would require economic and engineering analyses in addition to mechanizable accounting procedures. This effort would be more important, and more difficult, the more significant were the economies of scope and the jointly utilized factors of production. Nonetheless, equations (78) and (79) provide a firm conceptual basis for the task. And the fact that equation (80) would obviate the task suggests that the boundary between local and nonlocal services, and the boundary between divisions, be drawn in a manner that minimizes the capital that straddles it.

Conclusion

Whether or not the network is thought to have two divisions, it is now evident that the economics of network access and local network services are quite different from, and yet inextricably related to, the economics of nonlocal network services. Network externalities are an intrinsic characteristic of networks, and they cause public interest prices of consumer access to be low relative to the associated physical costs. The consequent revenue shortfalls must burden all other network services. Yet, the value of those services to their consumers is enhanced by the size of the population of subscribers enabled by the low access prices. It is these countervailing effects that the optimal network access prices balance.

Interconnection of competing vendors of nonlocal network services is often technologically feasible. Technical network access prices best serve the public interest if they render profitable entry that lowers industry costs and, simultaneously, render unprofitable any entry that is cost increasing. Prices for technical network services that fulfill these desiderata must exceed the costs caused by the purchased services. The reason is that the prices the network charges the consumers of its local and nonlocal services generally reflect contributions to the costs of the network access that make the network services possible and valuable. Hence, the prices charged potential entrants for technical network services must reflect these same contributions, on as close to a service-by-service basis as possible.

When such technical access fees are also viewed as internal transfer prices between local and nonlocal divisions of the network, it becomes clear that they afford equal opportunities to the nonlocal division and to its potential competitors in nonlocal services. At the same time, it is these fees that complete the coverage of the vital costs of subscribers' network access.

Notes

1. See Leland Johnson [1978] for an excellent overview.
2. This effect has been noted and analyzed from a variety of insightful viewpoints. For example, see Roland Artle and Christian Avernous [1973], Jeffrey Rohlfs [1974], Lyn Squire [1973], and Roger Klein and Robert Willig [1977].
3. The clearest example is provided in the telephone industry by the specialized common carrier firms that offer communications services through their own long distance microwave links that are interconnected at both ends with the local facilities of Bell System and independent operating companies. Analogously, the Mailgram service is produced by Western Union through the interconnection of its electronic links with the delivery system of the U.S.Postal Service. Also, much surface freight transportation is accomplished through the interconnection of rail networks owned by different firms and through the interconnection of rail networks with truck routes.
4. See Rohlfs [1974].
5. See Robert Willig [1978] for the development of methods to measure the welfare effect of quality changes by means of incremental consumer's surplus.
6. See D. F. Bradford and Gregory Hildebrandt [1977] for the development of this case.
7. In this measurement, one must not confuse two conceptually distinct effects of network size on market demand for network services. First, as subscribers join or leave the network, their own demands for network services will augment or be subtracted from market demands. Second, the demands of inframarginal consumers, those whose network access remains unchanged, may be affected by network size. It is only the latter effect that should be included in the incremental surplus calculation of network externalities.
8. See Hal Varian [1978] for a complete treatment of the standard theory. The analogous theory of firms, in a form amenable to analyzing network externalities that affect them, is available in Willig [1978]. Essentially, all results derived below for consumers hold for firms as well. Throughout, for the sake of relative simplicity, many possibly important features of reality are assumed away. These include consumers' uncertainties about prices and about their own income and demands, dynamic effects, non-

recurring charges for joining the network, and the availability of less convenient and less costly alternative modes of access to the network.

9. See Willig [1978; 1973] for more detailed expositions and tests of this type of condition.
10. The definitive and most general treatment of this function, when only prices and income are at issue, is due to Leonid Hurwicz and Hirofumi Uzawa [1971]. The extension to such variables as product quality or N is developed in Willig [1978].
11. See Hurwicz and Uzawa [1971] or Varian [1978] for formal developments and proofs.
12. See Willig [1978] for the proof of this assertion in a different, but mathematically equivalent, context.
13. The inessentiality condition assures that μ remains bounded as p increases without bound.
14. This solution is derived by straightforward, but tedious, application of the methods developed in Willig [1976b].
15. These approximation techniques are the same ones utilized in Willig [1976a].
16. This follows from the results reported in Willig [1979].
17. The investigation of this case was stimulated by some unpublished work by Rohlfs on what he termed "caller-called externalities" in the context of the telephone network.
18. Rohlfs argues that this is the case in telephone communications.
19. How to link the magnitudes of these understatements to observable demand data must here remain an intriguing unsolved problem.
20. The precise condition is that p and N be separable from m^h in the function ℓ^h. This condition is satisfied when all network services have equal and constant income elasticities of demand. It is also satisfied in many other cases described in Willig [1978].
21. Note that, for analytic convenience, it is assumed that all functions are differentiable. In particular, the discreteness of the set of potential network subscribers is ignored.
22. The solution is guaranteed to be unique if the Jacobian of the demand mapping from (p,E) to (S,N) is everywhere nonsingular.
23. Of course, equations (55) and (56) are equal if all variability in valued incoming flows is internalized, as in equation (27).
24. This follows from equation (27) because in this model a consumer's entire value of network access is captured by his surplus in network services. If this value were not equal to the price of network access, the consumer would not be a marginal subscriber.
25. See John Panzar and Willig [1977] and William Baumol [1975].
26. This normative viewpoint was first applied by Frank Ramsey [1927] to the determination of optimal taxes. See Baumol and Bradford [1970] for a history and survey of this approach to pricing, and Willig and Elizabeth Bailey [1977] for an application to the prices of telephone services.
27. For example, the numbers calculated in Willig and Bailey [1979] for long distance telephone services and for postal services would imply in both cases that this adjustment factor were greater than .8.
28. For example, see Peter Diamond and James Mirrlees [1971].
29. This strong assumption is made in the interest of brevity. It can be weakened in a straightforward manner to accommodate quality differ-

ences that are equivalent in consumers' views to differences in "full prices." See Willig [1978].

30. For example, in the telephone network, the ENFIA tariffs for local services purchased by competing carriers are higher than the rates faced by final consumers. In the rail network, "joint rates" that apply to interlined freight are typically lower than the rates that apply to local movements along the same route.
31. These desiderata would be unimpeachable in a "first best" context. However, the results of Ronald Braeutigam [1979] imply that if an incumbent is subjected to a binding profit constraint, and if potential entrants are not, then social welfare is not necessarily served by industry cost minimization. Instead, it may be socially preferable for some outputs to be produced by the incumbent at higher costs than would be incurred by the entrant. The reason for this is that, on the margin, the incumbent's profits are more socially valuable than the entrant's due to the incumbent's profit constraint. However, in our context this effect does not arise because, as will be seen, the desiderata require technical access prices to protect the incumbent's profits. As such, the social values of profits do not play a role, and the desiderata are hence consistent with the Ramsey as well as the first best point of view.
32. Panzar [1979] discusses the same institutional framework in an analogous context.
33. See Gerald Faulhaber [1975].

References

Artle, Roland, and Christian Avernous. 1973. "The Telephone System as a Public Good: Static and Dynamic Aspects." *Bell Journal of Economics and Management Science* 4 (Spring): 89–100.

Baumol, William. 1975. "Scale Economies, Average Cost and the Profitability of Marginal Cost Pricing." In *Essays in Urban Economics and Public Finance in Honor of William S. Vickrey,* edited by Ronald Grieson. Lexington: D. C. Heath.

Baumol, William, and David Bradford. 1970. "Optimal Departures from Marginal Cost Pricing." *American Economic Review* 60 (June): 265–283.

Bradford, David, and Gregory Hildebrandt. 1977. "Observable Preferences for Public Goods." *Journal of Public Economics* 8 (October): 111–32.

Braeutigam, Ronald. 1979. "Optimal Pricing with Intermodal Competition." *American Economic Review* 69 (March): 38–49.

Diamond, Peter, and James Mirrlees. 1971. "Optimal Taxation and Public Production II: Tax Rules." *American Economic Review* 61 (June): 261–78.

Faulhaber, Gerald. 1975. "Cross-Subsidization: Pricing in Public Enterprise." *American Economic Review* 65 (December): 966–77.

Hurwicz, Leonid, and Hirofumi Uzawa. 1971. "On the Integrability of Demand Functions." In *Preferences, Utility, and Demand,* edited by J. S. Chipman et al. New York: Harcourt Brace. Pp. 114–48.

Johnson, Leland. 1978. "Boundaries to Monopoly and Regulation in Modern Telecommunications." In *Communications for Tomorrow,* edited by Glen O. Robinson. New York: Praeger.

Klein, Roger, and Robert Willig. 1977. "Network Externalities and Optimal Telecommunications Pricing: A Preliminary Sketch." In *Proceedings of Fifth Annual Telecommunications Policy Research Conference.* Volume 2, pp. 475–505.

Panzar, John. 1979. "Sustainability, Efficiency, and Vertical Integration." Bell Laboratories Economics Discussion Paper.

Panzar, John, and Robert Willig. 1977. "Economies of Scale in Multi-Output Production." *Quarterly Journal of Economics* 91 (August): 481–94.

Ramsey, Frank. 1927. "A Contribution to the Theory of Taxation." *Economic Journal* 37: 47–61.

Rohlfs, Jeffrey. 1974. "A Theory of Interdependent Demand for Telecommunications." *Bell Journal of Economics and Management Science* 5 (Spring): 16–37.

Squire, Lyn. 1973. "Some Aspects of Optimal Pricing for Telecommunications." *Bell Journal of Economics and Management Science* 4 (Autumn): 515–25.

Varian, Hal. 1978. *Microeconomic Analysis.* New York: W. W. Norton.

Willig, Robert. 1973. "Welfare Analysis of Policies Affecting Prices and Products." Memorandum no. 153, Center for Research in Economic Growth, Stanford University.

———. 1976a. "Consumer's Surplus Without Apology." *American Economic Review* 66 (September): 589–97.

———. 1976b. "Integrability Implications for Locally Constant Demand Elasticities." *Journal of Economic Theory* 12 (June): 391–401.

———. 1978. "Incremental Consumer's Surplus and Hedonic Price Adjustment." *Journal of Economic Theory* 17 (April): 227–53.

———. 1979. "Consumer's Surplus Without Apology: Reply." *American Economic Review* 69 (June): 469–74.

——— and Elizabeth Bailey. 1977. "Ramsey Optimal Pricing of Long Distance Telephone Services." In *Pricing in Regulated Industries: Theory and Application,* edited by J. T. Wenders. Denver: Mountain States Telephone and Telegraph Co. Pp. 68–97.

———. 1979. "The Economic Gradient Method." *American Economic Review* 69 (May): 96–101.

[26]

Having Your Cake: How to Preserve Universal-Service Cross Subsidies While Facilitating Competitive Entry

William J. Baumol[†]

Differential pricing for access to bottleneck inputs such as local telephone facilities or electricity transmission facilities is shown to solve the old dilemma of deregulation: facilitating competitive entry without destroying cross subsidies indispensable for "universal service" programs. If bottleneck facilities are inputs to two services, one of which subsidizes the other, entrants that provide the subsidized service must receive the same subsidy in the access price as consumers receive when they purchase those services. Rivals in the supply of the other service must contribute an equivalent subsidy through paying a higher access price. Differential access pricing allows efficient competitors to find it equally profitable to supply either service because any motive for "cream skimming" disappears. Such differential pricing, coupled with access pricing consistent with the Efficient Component Pricing Rule, is shown to be necessary for economic efficiency.

† Director, C.V. Starr Center for Applied Economics, New York University; and senior research economist and professor emeritus, Princeton University. I am grateful to the C.V. Starr Center for its support of this work. I am exceedingly indebted to Scott Bohannon of Sidley & Austin for his invaluable contribution in finding appropriate references to the legal literature and related matters. I must also thank the editors of this Journal for their very helpful suggestions and, as always, Sue Anne Batey Blackman, who deserves much credit and bears none of the guilt.

Introduction

Regulators have long suffered from an apparently irreconcilable dilemma. Their own understandable predilections, supplemented by powerful political pressures, have led them to impose a set of cross subsidies on the prices of the firms they regulate. Cross subsidies systematically favor particular groups of customers, such as household customers or isolated farmers, at the expense of other groups, such as business customers or those near supply sources, by forcing the latter group to subsidize the former.[1] At the same time, however, regulators have also sought to stimulate entry and competition in regulated industries. For example, the Telecommunications Act of 1996[2] requires a monopoly local telephone service provider to lease parts of its network to its competitors at cost-based rates, thereby allowing entrant firms to offer service without incurring the tremendous expense of building a duplicative network before beginning service. The dilemma is that the twin goals of imposing cross subsidies and promoting competition are ordinarily incompatible. Effective competition tends to eliminate the source of cross subsidies by driving down the prices of items that yield particularly large profits.

A number of misguided expedients have been adopted in an effort to reconcile these two conflicting objectives. Most notably, some regulators have taken actions that severely handicap incumbent firms in some portions of the regulated market while impeding entrant firms in other parts. The result is the creation of a cartel in which each firm is assigned its own monopolized terrain.[3] Of course, this gives the *appearance* of

1 For example, suppose it costs Bell Atlantic only $10 to provide most customers in New Jersey with local telephone service. Suppose further that the cost of service for some rural customers is considerably higher, say $50, and that the average cost of statewide service is $15. Rather than setting local rates near $10 for the majority of customers and $50 for the more costly rural customers, regulators may require Bell Atlantic to charge approximately $15 for all of its customers. The low-cost customers are then said to be cross-subsidizing the rural customers.

2 Pub. L. No. 104-104, 110 Stat. 56 (codified in scattered sections of 47 U.S.C.).

3 For example, it can be argued that in the U.K., telephone rates were set by regulation in a way that favored entrants in dealing with large business firms but handicapped entrants in sales to

competition but ultimately helps only to protect cross subsidies from the eroding effects of true competition.

In this Article, I propose a regime of *non-uniform* and competitively neutral pricing of access to bottleneck services owned by an incumbent monopoly. By "bottleneck" services, I refer to services that are indispensable to both the incumbent and its competitors in the production or delivery of the final product. I will show that the proposed arrangement is *competitively neutral*, meaning that it does not favor either the incumbent or the entrants in the final-product market. Moreover, I will prove that the arrangement is the only access pricing rule that can achieve neutrality in the presence of cross subsidy and price discrimination in final-product sales. Lastly, I will argue that all affected parties can gain from this arrangement, since it offers full access to efficient suppliers in each and every pertinent market. Both incumbents and entrants will gain by having access to all markets. The public will gain because competition will pervade the industry. Finally, regulators will gain because their apparently inconsistent goals will be reconciled: Pervasive competition will coexist with the cross subsidies they deem to be in the social interest.

This Article is divided into two parts. Part I provides relevant background information on bottleneck pricing issues. It discusses the importance of bottleneck pricing for regulatory policy, the parity-pricing formula for competitively neutral access to a single product market, and previous approaches to bottleneck pricing. Part II shows how parity pricing can be adapted to ensure competitive neutrality in a multi-product industry with cross-subsidies or differential pricing. It demonstrates that competitive neutrality requires differential access pricing that precisely replicates the price-cost differences among the final products for which the bottleneck facility is an input.

households. *See* ELI NOAM, TELECOMMUNICATIONS IN EUROPE 110-13 (1992); JOHN VICKERS & GEORGE YARROW, PRIVATIZATION: AN ECONOMIC ANALYSIS 229-30, 238-39 (1988). In the United States, some electricity cogenerators were not permitted to compete for customers with the utilities, but the utilities were forced to buy electricity from the cogenerators at prices set by regulatory formula. *See* MICHAEL E. SMALL, A GUIDE TO FERC REGULATION AND RATEMAKING OF ELECTRIC UTILITIES AND OTHER POWER SUPPLIERS 148-51 (3d ed. 1994).

I. Background: The Bottleneck Pricing Issues[4]

A. *Current Importance of the Issue for Privatization and Facilitation of Competitive Entry*

How to price bottleneck services is an issue that is being debated vigorously before courts and regulatory agencies throughout the industrial and industrializing world, with the formulas presented in this Article often being the focus of these litigative proceedings.[5] In the United States, the issue of pricing is at the forefront of discussion of means to facilitate competitive entry into activities that have traditionally been run by franchised monopolies.[6]

Bottleneck pricing is now a pivotal issue in at least three industries: telecommunications,[7] electric power,[8] and rail transportation.[9] In telecommunications, the equipment of the monopolist local telephone company become bottleneck facilities. Entrants are not able to operate without them, and the facilities are available from only one owner. In response, the government has required current monopoly providers of local telephone services to rent their facilities to entrants who desire to use them.[10] This allows entrants to avoid having to build expensive plants and equipment of their own, making entry a practical possibility. While this solution *seems* to solve the entry barrier problem, the regulating government agency must also specify the *price* at which the facilities will be offered to entrants. If the owner of the facilities is permitted to charge any price, it can protect itself from entry by setting the price at such an exorbitant level that no entrant can afford to pay it. In State Commission

4 For references to the current literature on the issue, the reader may want to consult William J. Baumol et al., *Parity Pricing and Its Critics: A Necessary Condition for Efficiency in the Provision of Bottleneck Services to Competitors*, 14 YALE J. ON REG. 145 (1997).

5 *See, e.g.*, Telecom Corp. v. Clear Communications, Ltd. [1995] 1 N.Z.L.R. 385; St. Louis Southwestern Ry.—Intertrackage Rights Over Mo. Pac. R.R.—Kan. City to St. Louis, 8 I.C.C.2d 80 (1991); Alternative Regulatory Frameworks for Local Exch. Carriers, 33 C.P.U.C.2d 43 (1989).

6 *See, e.g.*, Implementation of the Local Competition Provisions in the Telecommunications Act of 1996, 11 F.C.C.R. 15,499, ¶¶ 3-5, at 15,505-06 (1996) (presenting this issue as one that the Telecommunications Act of 1996 seeks to address) [hereinafter *Local Competition Order*].

7 *See id.* ¶¶ 625-766, at 15,814-83.

8 *See* Inquiry Concerning the Commission's Pricing Policy for Transmission Services Provided by Public Utilities Under the Federal Power Act, 59 Fed. Reg. 55,031, 55,033-35 (1994); WILLIAM J. BAUMOL & J. GREGORY SIDAK, TRANSMISSION PRICING AND STRANDED COSTS IN THE ELECTRIC POWER INDUSTRY 115-58 (1995) (discussing the efficient pricing of electric transmission facilities and past pricing decisions by the Federal Energy Regulatory Commission).

9 *See, e.g.*, FMC Wyo. Corp. v. Union Pac. R.R., S.T.B. Fin., No. 33467, 1997 WL 768315 (S.T.B. Dec. 12, 1997); Central Power & Light Co. v. Southern Pac. Transp. Co., No. 41242, 1997 WL 299703 (S.T.B. Apr. 28, 1997).

10 *See* 47 U.S.C. § 251(c)(3) (Supp. II 1996); *Local Competition Order*, *supra* note 6, ¶¶ 342-365, at 15,671-83.

arbitrations and in proceedings before the Federal Communications Commission, carriers such as Bell Atlantic, GTE, and AT&T have advocated various cost standards, including both book (or historic) costs and forward-looking cost standards such as the Efficient Component Pricing Rule and Total Service Long-Run Incremental Cost.[11]

In electricity, the issue has been raised by the inauguration of competition in power *generation.* Today, and increasingly so in the near future, the established electric utility firms in the United States will face the competition of rival generators of electricity.[12] However, before electricity can be sold as a final product, it must be transported to customers. The large capacity and high cost of electricity transmission facilities make rivalry in electricity *transmission* (as distinguished from generation) impractical. Transmission facilities are often owned by electric utilities; these companies and their competitors in generation must use the same facilities to transport electricity from generating stations to customers. Thus, the transmission facilities are bottleneck inputs to the supply of the final product—delivered electric power—and the pricing issue is clearly analogous to the setting of a fee for use of a telecommunications facility as a bottleneck input.

The rail transportation case will bring out the issue most clearly.[13] Consider two railroads, *A* and *B*, which want to compete in serving cities *C* and *D*. The cities are separated by high mountains with a single pass, through which railroad *A* owns tracks and in which there is no room for a second set of tracks. Railroad *B* therefore rents permission to traverse (or trackage rights over) that portion of *A*'s route. The mountain pass is clearly a bottleneck input to the transportation of freight between the two cities. In these circumstances, the question is what is the efficient price that railroad *A* should charge its potential rival, *B*, for use of the tracks? Too high a price will patently exclude competition, while too low a price will entail a competition-distorting subsidy from the pass-owning railroad to the

11 *See, e.g.*, AT&T Communications, Inc. v. Bellsouth Telecomms., Inc., 20 F. Supp. 2d 1097 (E.D. Ky. 1998); Southwestern Bell Tel. Co. v. AT&T Communications Inc., No. A97-CA-132-SS, 1998 WL 657717 (S.D. Tex. Aug. 31, 1998); GTE South Inc. v. Morrison, 6 F. Supp. 2d 517 (E.D. Va. 1998).

12 *See, e.g.*, Promoting Wholesale Competition Through Open Access Non-Discriminatory Transmission Servs. by Public Utils., 61 Fed. Reg. 21,540 (1996) (discussing several Federal Energy Regulatory Commission proceedings initiated to facilitate a more competitive electric industry); Ralph Cavanagh, *California Scores with New Electricity Choices*, SACRAMENTO BUS. J. (Aug. 11, 1997) <http://www.amcity.com/sacramento/stories/081197/editorial5.html>.

13 The simple example provided in the text has been litigated on numerous occasions. The most famous case, *United States v. Terminal Railroad Ass'n*, 224 U.S. 383 (1912), established the essential facilities doctrine in antitrust law. There, a group of railroads that jointly owned a bottleneck railroad terminal in St. Louis were denying their competitors access to the terminal. The Supreme Court found that this practice violated Section 1 of the Sherman Antitrust Act because it denied access to a facility essential for their competitors to compete. Today, railroad mergers continue to concern agencies such as the Surface Transportation Board. *See, e.g.*, *Central Power & Light Co.*, 1997 WL.

entrant.

The bottleneck pricing issue has arisen similarly in Australia,[14] the United Kingdom,[15] Hong Kong,[16] and the European Union.[17] Indeed, it appears wherever privatization initially leaves an industry in the hands of a monopoly or, at the very least, a large firm that possesses substantial market power. The issue of pricing is also likely to become an international matter of great urgency in the near future as a result of the Telecommunications Agreement of 1997, under which approximately seventy countries agreed to open their telecommunications markets to foreign competition.[18] If international competition is to become a reality, obstacles that impede entry by foreign rivals must be removed or reduced.

B. *Parity Pricing (ECPR): The Rule for Efficient Pricing of Bottleneck Services*

The most discussed solution to the problem of determining an efficient price for a bottleneck service is based on a result I call the Level-Playing-Field Theorem. This theorem tells us that only by using certain formulas (equations (1a) or (1b) below) can we *neutrally* price a monopoly-owned bottleneck service required by both the bottleneck owner and its final-product competitors. This rule is called the Efficient Component Pricing Rule (ECPR) or the *parity pricing* formula. The term "parity price" refers to the price at which a competitor neither receives nor gives up a competitive advantage to the owner of a bottleneck service for using that service. According to the theory, a level playing field, and hence efficiency in the competition between the bottleneck owner and its

14 To resolve the issue, the Australian Competition & Consumer Commission chose to use Total Service Long-Run Incremental Cost, the standard advocated by many potential entrants, over the Efficient Component Pricing Rule. *See* AUSTRALIAN COMPETITION & CONSUMER COMM'N, ACCESS PRICING PRINCIPLES (1997).

15 OFTEL, the telecommunications regulatory agency in the U.K., has embraced long-run incremental cost principles for pricing of bottleneck facilities owned by dominant carriers such as British Telecommunications. *See* OFFICE OF TELECOMM., OFTEL'S SUBMISSION TO THE MONOPOLIES AND MERGERS COMMISSION INQUIRY INTO THE PRICES OF CALLS TO MOBILE PHONES ¶ 3.2 (1998) ("OFTEL believes that the most appropriate and economically efficient basis for assessment of charges for a bottleneck service is that derived from forward looking Long Run Incremental Costs (LRIC).").

16 *See* 1 INTERNATIONAL TELECOMM. UNION, GENERAL TRENDS IN TELECOMMUNICATIONS REFORM 1998, at 96 (1998).

17 *See* Directive 97/51/EC of the European Parliament and of the Council of 6 October 1997 Amending Council Directives 90/387/EEC and 92/44/EEC for the Purpose of Adaptation to a Competitive Environment in Telecommunications, 1997 O.J. (L 295) 23; Council Directive 92/44/EEC of 5 June 1992 on the Application of Open Network Provision to Leased Lines, 1992 O.J. (L 165) 27; Directive 97/33/EC of the European Parliament and of the Council of 30 June 1997 on Interconnection in Telecommunications with Regard to Ensuring Universal Service and Interoperability Through Application of the Principles of Open Network Provision (ONP), 1997 O.J. (L 199) 32.

18 *See* World Trade Organization: Agreement on Telecommunications Services (Fourth Protocol on General Agreement on Trade in Services), 36 I.L.M. 354, 366 (1997).

competitors, can only arise if the bottleneck service in question is priced as follows:[19]

Bottleneck service price per unit = Bottleneck owner's final product price minus the incremental cost to the owner of all final-product inputs, other than bottleneck service, (1a)

or, in convenient symbols:

$$P_b = P_{bf} - IC_{br} \qquad (1b)$$

where the subscript f refers to *final* product, so that P_{bf} is the price of the bottleneck owner's final product, and r refers to the *remaining* inputs (other than the bottleneck input) that enter into the incremental cost of the final product.

Exhibit 1, below, demonstrates that at any other price for the bottleneck service, a competitor's minimum viable final product price will not be equal to the bottleneck owner's price plus (or minus) the competitor's cost advantage (or disadvantage) in supplying the inputs other than the bottleneck service needed for the final product. In other words, at any other bottleneck service price, one of the suppliers will be unable to achieve the final product price advantage to which its own efficiency entitles it.

19 As I have previously written and emphasized, this pricing rule is necessary but not sufficient for economic efficiency or protection of the public interest. In addition to equations (1a) or (1b), these goals require either effective competition or regulation in the final-product markets to ensure that the final-product prices yield no monopoly profits and no other efficiency-undermining distortions. For a summary of the discussion and references, see Baumol et al., *supra* note 4, at 147-48. It should be noted that the pertinent output increment for which the cost is calculated is the volume of business that is expected to be lost to competitors. I am grateful to Robert Graniere of the National Regulatory Research Institute for discussion related to this point.

EXHIBIT 1
The Level-Playing-Field Theorem:
Derivation of the Competitive Neutrality Formula for Access Pricing[20]

To derive competitive-neutrality formula (1), we define a **level playing field** in the pricing of access to require the following:

Suppose a firm's incremental cost (IC) per unit of output of supplying the non-bottleneck components of the final product is X dollars less than that of a bottleneck-owning competitor (or the reverse). Then, this more efficient firm should just be able (without losing money) to price the final product by X dollars less than the price charged by its less efficient competitor.

More formally, we have as the definition of a level playing field:

bottleneck owner final-product price – minimum competitor final-product price = IC of owner-supplied remaining inputs – IC of competitor-supplied remaining inputs. (2)

But we know that the competitor's minimum (financially-viable) price is:

minimum competitor final-product price = price of bottleneck service + IC of competitor-supplied remaining inputs. (3)

Adding these two equations we immediately obtain the **competitive neutrality formula**:

the only price of bottleneck service that provides a level playing field = bottleneck owner final-product price – IC of owner-supplied remaining inputs. (4)

Competitive neutrality formula (4) is clearly the same as formula (1), so that any bottleneck service price that violates equation (4) or its equivalent (1) must tilt the playing field, favoring either the bottleneck owner at the expense of its competitors or the reverse.

It should be noted that the rule is not very difficult to carry out in practice or for the regulator to monitor. Nowadays in regulatory arenas, estimates of incremental costs are provided fairly routinely and appear to be determinable to a reasonable degree of approximation without

20 This formula was originally contributed by Robert Willig, with the current author participating in dissemination and adaptation to particular regulatory and analytic issues. For an early description of the analysis, see Robert D. Willig, *The Theory of Network Access Pricing*, *in* ISSUES IN PUBLIC UTILITY REGULATION 109 (Harry M. Trebbing ed., 1979).

enormous cost or effort. For example, telecommunications regulatory agencies in the United States (and possibly other countries as well) can use a number of off-the-shelf models such as the HAI Model, the Benchmark Cost Proxy Model, and the Hybrid Cost Proxy Model, to calculate universal service subsidies or incremental cost of telecommunications network components.[21] In addition, most of the state regulatory commissions have conducted a number of incremental cost studies over the past two years to determine unbundled network element prices.[22] Thus, if the rule is correct, to calculate the efficient price of a bottleneck service, one merely needs to observe the final-product price currently charged by the owner of the bottleneck facility and subtract from it the pertinent incremental cost.

C. *Previous Approaches to the Pricing of Bottleneck Services*

It is not possible to offer a general characterization of the methods previously used to determine the prices charged for bottleneck services. These prices were often arrived at by informal negotiation between the owner of the facility and its users. As far as I know, there were no generally accepted regulatory rules, but where the issue of pricing did arise, its resolution was based on what was deemed to be the pertinent cost, which generally meant the "fully allocated cost." The fully allocated cost of any product or activity may be described as the cost directly attributable to the item in question (in practice, an approximation to its incremental cost) plus some share of the firm's remaining costs. These remaining *common costs* range from the salary of the company president to the cost of a railroad track's construction and maintenance, which is attributable in common to the various commodities carried over the given route. Since no unique allocation standard is possible for costs that inseparably serve several purposes simultaneously, the share of common cost assigned to a particular product or activity was determined on the basis of an arbitrarily selected accounting criterion. The result was frequent litigation over the cost calculations.

21 *See* Federal-State Joint Bd. on Universal Serv., 12 F.C.C.R. 18,514 (1997) (analyzing a variety of models that use forward-looking cost methods for calculating universal service support). Many parties have submitted extensive comments and reply comments on how those models should be refined. *See id.* The FCC has recently released its guidelines on telecommunications cost modeling. *See* Federal-State Joint Bd. on Universal Serv., 1998 WL 751153 (F.C.C. Oct. 28, 1998)

22 *See, e.g.*, Petitions by AT&T Communications, Inc., MCI Telecomm. Corp. and MCI Metro Access Transmission Servs., Inc., for Arbitration of Certain Terms and Conditions of a Proposed Agreement with GTE Florida, Inc. Concerning Interconnection and Resale Under the Telecomm. Act of 1996, No. 970847-TP, 1997 WL 41243, at *63-*64 (Fla Pub. Serv. Comm'n May 21, 1997); AT&T Communications, Inc., No. P-140, Sub 50, 1996 WL 769763, at *30-*34 (N.C. Util. Comm'n Dec. 23, 1996), *aff'd*, No. P-140, Sub 50, 1997 WL 233035 (N.C. Utils. Comm'n Apr. 11, 1997).

A simple example will bring out most clearly the contrast between such procedures and parity pricing, using a rough characterization of earlier practice. I refer again to my railroad case, in which railroads *A* and *B* compete in serving cities *C* and *D*.[23] Railroad *A* owns the only tracks that can fit in the pass through the high mountains that separate the cities. Therefore, the mountain pass is clearly a bottleneck input to the transportation of freight between the two cities. Suppose railroad *A*'s incremental cost of carrying a carload of lumber between the two cities is $1,000, with $10 of this amount attributable to wear and tear of track when a carload of lumber crosses the pass. Railroad *A* has been charging shippers $1,500 per carload for this traffic and using the $500 surplus over the incremental cost of lumber transport for the entire route to cover costs common to lumber and other types of freight—costs such as track maintenance and replacement. The railroad earns no more than competitive profit overall.

Under these circumstances, the ECPR price for the right of railroad *B* to send a carload of lumber over the mountain pass is, by formula (1), the $1500 price charged by *A* for transport over the route, minus the $990 incremental cost of the non-bottleneck portion of the shipment ($990 = $1000 total IC minus the $10 bottleneck IC). Thus, the parity price is $510, which equals $1500 minus $990. However, at least until very recently, the regulators would have calculated the fee quite differently. For example, since the $10 incremental cost of *B*'s traversal is only one percent of the total incremental cost of the route, they can be expected to have reasoned that railroad *A* is entitled only to one percent of the contribution to common costs that flows from *B*'s shipment between the two cities, making the regulatory fee $15 rather than the $510 price required by the parity principle.

We see that the two prices can be dramatically different because one is based on a regulatory concept of equity and the other (the ECPR price) is based on the requirements of economic efficiency. At first glance it may appear that the far higher ECPR price is unfair because it extracts so high a fee for traversal of a small portion of the route. However, as Exhibit 1 implicitly demonstrates, the fee set at this level allows one to say that both railroads are paying the same price for traversal of the mountain pass. The lower, more traditional fee is therefore not only a subsidy to the other railroad that can permit it to take business away from a more efficient competitor; it also treats the two railroads differently, permitting railroad *B* to rent use of the mountain-pass tracks at a cost far lower than what it costs railroad *A* to provide the tracks.

---

23 *See supra* note 13 and accompanying text.

II. The Differential-Pricing Issue for Bottleneck Services

We come at last to the central issue of this Article: How can regulators permit competition in regulated industries without making it impossible to retain the cross subsidies that commonly serve as the instruments of universal service? Regulators seek to maintain cross subsidies in deregulated industries. However, universal service often makes this difficult, since it requires very low prices to impecunious consumers or consumers whose location makes them extremely costly to serve. These prices often fail to cover the costs of serving these customers, who are expected to refrain from purchasing the regulated service if the price of the service is not subsidized. But where such cross subsidies exist, competition will be driven to engage in "cream skimming." Competitors will focus on the more lucrative products of the regulated firm, which are the products that provide the revenues that finance the cross subsidies. Thus it may appear, at first glance, that competition is incompatible with the cross subsidies of universal service. This Part will show that competition and cross subsidies can, in fact, be made to coexist.

It should be noted here that cross subsidies may have a defensible social purpose. For example, an increase in the number of subscribers to telephone service increases the value of telecommunications facilities to retailing firms. Since these indirect benefits ("positive externalities" in the jargon of economics) accrue to the firms rather than to the subscribers who pay for the service they receive, both equity and efficiency can call for some subsidy from business subscribers to household subscribers. As another example, it may well be agreed that impecunious elderly persons should be ensured access to telephone service or to electric power, and that this requires that such services be provided to them at prices that do not cover the pertinent costs. But it may only be politically feasible to provide the funding for such low prices from the buyers of other services of the firm in question. Other reasonable grounds for the preservation of cross subsidies, both economic and sociological, can readily be suggested. There is nothing new in the observation that cross subsidies can sometimes be justifiable. Rather, the novel point is that such desirable cross subsidies can be made sustainable, despite the presence of competition, by appropriate access pricing rules.

An extension of the Level-Playing-Field Theorem demonstrates that it is possible to make competition and cross subsidies compatible. The Theorem shows that where there is cross subsidy or price discrimination of any sort in final product prices, then any *uniform* price for access to a bottleneck service cannot be competitively neutral. Such a uniform price *must* tilt the playing field by favoring some of the rival suppliers of final products at the expense of the others.

Yale Journal on Regulation Vol. 16:1, 1999

This observation is pertinent because, in practice, bottleneck inputs are rarely used only to produce a single product. A railroad bridge that all competitors along a given route must use can carry coal and wheat and many other products. A local telecommunications loop carries business and household telephone messages, data and voice messages, and messages from California and Connecticut. The question, then, is whether the price of a homogeneous bottleneck service should be fixed and independent of the final product in whose production it is used, or should *differential pricing* of the bottleneck service be permitted or even required, depending on the pricing of the final product for which it is employed. Here, I will argue that:

a) If there is discrimination in the bottleneck owner's prices of the final products, I and J, for which the bottleneck input is used, so that the difference between the bottleneck owner's prices for I and J is not equal to the difference between the incremental costs for I and J (that is, $P_{fbi} - P_{fbj}$ is not equal to $IC_{rbi} - IC_{rbj}$), then uniform pricing of the bottleneck service will either force the bottleneck owner to end its discriminatory pricing of the final product, or the market must, in effect, be transformed into a cartel in which different suppliers specialize in the supply of different products and do not compete with one another.

b) On the other hand, if there is differential pricing of the bottleneck service, so that the competitive neutrality formulas (1) are satisfied for *each* product for which the bottleneck service is required, then the differential pricing of the final product can be preserved, and effective competition can continue in the market for each of the final products. Specifically, such a differential pricing arrangement will be the only viable solution in a regulated market in which the regulator seeks to preserve effective competition and to impose some cross subsidy that is deemed to serve the public interest or to be required by political pressures

A. *Interfirm Discrimination Through Uniformity Of Access Price*

The analysis is straightforward. I will show that if differential prices are charged for final products that use the bottleneck service but the bottleneck service is priced uniformly in all uses, the playing field cannot be level. To show this, suppose that the bottleneck input is used to produce (at least) two final products, I and J, that are sold by the bottleneck owner at prices that are discriminatory in the sense that the price for product I

minus the incremental cost for product I is greater than the price for product J minus the incremental cost for product J:

$$P_{fbi} - IC_{rbi} > P_{fbj} - IC_{rbj} \qquad (5)$$

where the subscript r, again, refers to the cost of the *remaining* (non-bottleneck) inputs, assuming for simplicity that the incremental cost of bottleneck use is the same for both products. If the price of the bottleneck service, P_b, is set at the average (perhaps weighted) of the difference between the final price and the incremental cost ($P_f - IC_r$) for the two products, then the price of bottleneck service is greater than the price for product J minus the incremental cost for J:

$$P_b > P_{fbj} - IC_{rbj} \qquad (6)$$

So, if a competitor, C, has the same cost for the remaining inputs (that is, $IC_{rbj} = IC_{rcj}$), then

$$P_{fbj} < P_b + IC_{rcj} = min\ P_{fcj} \qquad (7)$$

meaning that a competitor who is just as efficient as the bottleneck owner in supplying product J will be unable, without losing money on sales of J, to charge a final-product price, P_{fcj}, that is as low as that of the bottleneck owner. Clearly, the playing field for sale of J will not be level, and the competitor will find itself unable to compete in the product-J market, even though it is an equally efficient producer of J. Of course, the problem is that the uniform price of the bottleneck service must exceed the competitively-neutral price for that input when it is used to produce output J. The competitor will be saddled with what amounts to an excessive discriminatory price for the bottleneck service that handicaps or prevents its competition with the bottleneck owner in the supply of product J.

The same reasoning shows that the uniform averaged competitively-neutral price for the bottleneck service will render the bottleneck service owner's price for product I greater than the competitor's minimum price for product I,

$$P_{fbi} > min\ P_{fci} \qquad (8)$$

if the bottleneck owner and the competitor are equally efficient in supplying product I. Thus, the averaged uniform price for the bottleneck service must tilt the playing field in the competitor's favor in the supply of product I.

More generally, we have the Uniform Access-Price Theorem: If the final-product prices for two goods that use a bottleneck service as an input are discriminatory in the sense of (5), then no uniform bottleneck-service price can satisfy the competitive neutrality requirement (4) for every final product, so that for those products for which it is not satisfied one of the suppliers of those products must be handicapped in a discriminatory manner.

The implications are clear. The competitor will be forced to supply those products in which the net yield to the bottleneck owner, $P_{fb} - IC_{rb}$, is greatest. This is another way of saying that the competitor will have no option but to engage in cream skimming.

There are two possible scenarios for the sequel:

a) The bottleneck owner will reduce its price for final-product *I*, and (particularly if it is losing money on *J*, meaning that a cross subsidy is involved) it may be forced to raise its price for final product *J* until the two sides of inequality (5) are made equal to one another. Then the discrimination in final-product prices will have been ended by competition—the expected sequel to cream-skimming competition.

b) Alternatively, either regulatory fiat or self-interest or some other exogenous force may keep the final-product prices of *I* and *J* at their discriminatory level. Then the bottleneck owner will find itself the sole supplier of product *J*, while the other firm (if there are only two firms) will become the sole supplier of *I*. In that case, the result will be, in effect, the establishment of a cartel in which each firm finds itself assigned an exclusive territory that is immune from direct competition. Some truncated competitive force will remain in the market, since each firm will have to keep the price of its final product below the level that will make entry into that field by the other firm financially feasible. But up to that limit each firm will be shielded from the constraint of effective competition. There will be more than one firm in the industry, but there will be no real competition.

B. *Consequences of Differential Competitively-Neutral Prices for Bottleneck Services*

As an alternative, the regulator can impose strict compliance with competitive neutrality for a bottleneck service, final product by final product. By now, it should be evident that this requires the price charged by the bottleneck owner to vary with the use to which the bottleneck service is put by a competitor. It may require a bottleneck service fee of X dollars per minute when the bottleneck is used to carry calls from business customers and Y dollars per minute if it transmits calls from households. Competitive-neutrality formula (4) tells us, *ceteris paribus*, that the bottleneck service price must vary from one bottleneck use to another precisely by the amount that the corresponding final product prices vary. For example, given two final products with equal incremental costs for which the price of one product is 0.2 dollars more than the other, the competitively-neutral prices of bottleneck service for the two uses must also differ by exactly 0.2 dollars. Several consequences follow from such a pricing arrangement.

1. Bottleneck-Owner Indifference Among Suppliers

With these access prices, the bottleneck owner will be *indifferent*, so far as profits are concerned, between use of its facilities by itself and use of those facilities by its competitors. The competitive neutrality pricing formula guarantees that the bottleneck owner will obtain exactly the same profit whichever of the two courses is taken. For with price set in accord with formula (4), the sale of I by a rival will yield bottleneck price:

$$P_{bi} = P_{fbi} - IC_{rbi} = R \qquad (9)$$

where R is defined as the cost of providing a unit of bottleneck service for product I *plus* the profit the bottleneck owner would obtain from its own sale of a unit of I.

Thus, for each product I, the price charged by the bottleneck owner to competitors for bottleneck services will give the owner exactly the same profit as if it had used the services to supply product I itself. This result is well known in the literature on parity (ECPR) pricing.[24]

2. Access Prices for Cross-Subsidized Products

The second implication of differential and competitively-neutral pricing is more surprising: It follows from (9) that if final-product J is the recipient of a cross subsidy and is therefore priced below incremental cost (its profit yield to the bottleneck owner is negative), then the competitively-neutral price for bottleneck service to be used in the production of J *must also be less than the incremental cost* of supplying the bottleneck service for the purpose!

24 *See, e.g.*, Baumol et al., *supra* note 4, at 146.

Though this result may seem bizarre at first, its logic is straightforward. Cross subsidy by the bottleneck owner means that in order for rivals to compete effectively with the bottleneck owner, replication of this cross subsidy must be available to them in some way. If the bottleneck owner sells product *J* to consumers at a price below cost, then it must provide its rivals with bottleneck service at a price that does not cover cost as well. In other words, if product *J* is the recipient of a cross subsidy when sold by the bottleneck proprietor, then competitive neutrality requires that the same cross subsidy be made available to rival suppliers of *J* through access pricing. Otherwise, rivals that have no other source of cross subsidy will not be able to compete in the supply of *J* because of their inability to match the bottleneck owner's final-product price of *J*. In these circumstances, if the bottleneck service price covers the entire incremental cost of providing the service for output *J* production, the playing field cannot be level.

3. Open Competition in all Industry Products

Differential and competitively-neutral prices offer entrants and other rivals of the bottleneck owner the prospect that they will be able to compete in every market in which the bottleneck owner offers products. Thus, unless their entry or survival is threatened by the inefficiency of their *own* operations, they will not find themselves excluded from any branch of the regulated industry.

4. Cream Skimming Prevention—Competitor Indifference Among the Different Products That Are Supplied with the Aid of the Bottleneck

The fourth consequence of differential and competitively-neutral prices is that they eliminate any incentive for cream skimming by competitors. The differential bottleneck service price is adjusted so that when a final product price is relatively high, the bottleneck service price for use in making that product will be elevated by exactly the same amount, other things being equal. Consequently, the competitor will have no incentive to favor high-priced products over low-priced products.

5. Preservation of Cross Subsidies Despite Effective Competition

The final implication of differential and competitively-neutral pricing should now be obvious. In contrast to what is normally expected, such a pricing arrangement is consistent with continued competition in each and every one of the bottleneck owner's products, along with preservation of any and all cross subsidies in the bottleneck owner's final-product prices. Thus, these access prices enable the regulator to have it both ways. They enable competition to survive and even to permeate every branch of the regulated industry. They also permit retention of the cross-subsidies characteristically favored by regulators. Regulators can now require impoverished families, or isolated farmers and other customers whom it is especially costly to serve, to be granted subsidized prices. They can also demand that prices favor household over business customers. In short, differential and competitively-neutral pricing promotes universal service by means of cross subsidy without precluding the forces of competition that otherwise undermine universal service.

Conclusion

It is this last feature of differentiated, competitively-neutral pricing that may make it most attractive to regulators in practice and that may be most relevant for practice. It reconciles the goal of promoting competition with the objective of helping particular classes of customers. Moreover, it opens the regulated fields to entrants and permits them and other rivals to compete in every product market on the basis of relative efficiency. The public can benefit from the pervasive competition that it makes possible. Even the bottleneck owner has something to gain from the arrangement. Although the owner will end up facing rivals in the sale of every one of its products, it will not find itself effectively excluded from any of those markets by distorted prices. Furthermore, its legitimate profits will be protected through the competitively-neutral character of the bottleneck prices. It has been proven here that in an industry that is characterized by differential final-product prices and cross subsidy, as most regulated industries are in reality,[25] any uniform access price for bottleneck services cannot be competitively neutral. Productive efficiency is necessarily undermined when less efficient firms are allowed to undercut suppliers that are more efficient in their use of resources. Despite its advantages, differential competitive neutrality has rarely been considered as an option by either practitioners or analysts. This option should not be overlooked. Although it may prove to have shortcomings that have not yet been recognized, it merits careful consideration at the very least.

25 *See* W. KIP VISCUSI ET AL., ECONOMICS OF REGULATION AND ANTITRUST 532 (2d ed. 1995).

Name Index

The International Library of Critical Writings in Economics

1. Multinational Corporations
   Mark Casson
2. The Economics of Innovation
   Christopher Freeman
3. Entrepreneurship
   Mark Casson
4. International Investment
   Peter J. Buckley
5. Game Theory in Economics
   Ariel Rubinstein
6. The History of Economic Thought
   Mark Blaug
7. Monetary Theory
   Thomas Mayer
8. Joint Production of Commodities
   Neri Salvadori and Ian Steedman
9. Industrial Organization
   Oliver E. Williamson
10. Growth Theory (Volumes I, II and III)
    R.Becker and E. Burmeister
11. Microeconomics: Theoretical and Applied (Volumes I, II and III)
    Robert E. Kuenne
12. The Economics of Health (Volumes I and II)
    A.J. Culyer
13. Recent Developments in Macroeconomics (Volumes I, II and III)
    Edmund S. Phelps
14. Urban and Regional Economics
    Paul C. Cheshire and Alan W. Evans
15. Modern Public Finance (Volumes I and II)
    A.B. Atkinson
16. Exchange Rate Economics (Volumes I and II)
    Ronald MacDonald and Mark P. Taylor

17. The Economic Value of Education: Studies in the Economics of Education
Mark Blaug

18. Development Economics (Volumes I, II, III and IV)
Deepak Lal

19. The New Classical Macroeconomics (Volumes I, II and Ill)
Kevin D. Hoover

20. The Economics of the Environment
Wallace E. Oates

21. Post Keynesian Theory of Growth and Distribution
Carlo Panico and Neri Salvadori

22. Dynamic Labor Demand and Adjustment Costs
Giorgio Galeazzi and Daniel S. Hamermesh

23. The Philosophy and Methodology of Economics (Volumes I, II and III)
Bruce J. Caldwell

24. Public Choice Theory (Volumes I, II and III)
Charles K. Rowley

25. Evolutionary Economics
Ulrich Witt

26. Economics and Psychology
Shlomo Maital and Sharone L. Maital

27. Social Choice Theory (Volumes I, II and Ill)
Charles K. Rowley

28. Non-Linear Dynamics in Economic Theory
Marc Jarsulic

29. Recent Developments in Experimental Economics (Volumes I and II)
John D. Hey and Graham Loomes

30. Monopoly and Competition Policy (Volumes I and II)
F.M. Scherer

31. The Economics of Technical Change
Edwin Mansfield and Elizabeth Mansfield

32. The Economics of Exhaustible Resources
Geoffrey Heal

33. The Economics of Institutions
Geoffrey M. Hodgson

34. The Economics of Transport (Volumes I and II)
Herbert Mohring

35. Implicit Contract Theory
Sherwin Rosen

36. Foundations of Analytical Marxism (Volumes I and II)
John E. Roemer

37. The Economics of Product Differentiation (Volumes I and II)
Jacques-François Thisse and George Norman

38. Economic Growth in Theory and Practice: A Kaldorian Perspective
John E. King

39. Markets and Socialism
Alec Nove and Ian D. Thatcher

40. Recent Developments in the Economics of Education
Elchanan Cohn and Geraint Johnes

41. The Theory of Inflation
Michael Parkin

42. The Economics of Location (Volumes I, II and III)
Melvin L. Greenhut and George Norman

43. Financial Intermediaries
Mervyn K. Lewis

44. The Political Economy of Privatization and Deregulation
Elizabeth E. Bailey and Janet Rothenberg Pack

45. Gender and Economics
Jane Humphries

46. Macroeconomics and Imperfect Competition
Jean-Pascal Bénassy

47. Labor Economics (Volumes I, II, III and IV)
Orley C. Ashenfelter and Kevin F. Hallock

48. The Economics of Altruism
Stefano Zamagni

49. The Economic Analysis of Rent Seeking
Robert D. Tollison and Roger D. Congleton

50. Economics and Biology
Geoffrey M. Hodgson

51. The Economics of Ageing
John Creedy

52. Fiscal and Monetary Policy (Volumes I and II)
Thomas Mayer and Steven M. Sheffrin

53. The Economics of Information (Volumes I and II)
David K. Levine and Steven A. Lippman

54. Transaction Cost Economics (Volumes I and II)
Oliver E. Williamson and Scott E. Masten

55. Agricultural Economics
George H. Peters

56. International Debt (Volumes I and II)
Graham Bird and P. Nicholas Snowden

57. Economics and Discrimination (Volumes I and II)
William A. Darity, Jr

58. Business Cycle Theory
Finn E. Kydland

59. International Trade (Volumes I and II)
J. Peter Neary

60. The Money Supply in the Economic Process
Marco Musella and Carlo Panico

61. Small Firms and Economic Growth (Volumes I and II)
Zoltan J. Acs

62. Producer Cooperatives and Labor-Managed Systems (Volumes I and II)
David L. Prychitko and Jaroslav Vanek

63. Ethics and Economics (Volumes I and II)
Alan P. Hamlin

64. The Economics of the Family
Nancy Folbre

65. The Economics of Training (Volumes I and II)
Orley C. Ashenfelter and Robert J. LaLonde

66. Chaos Theory in Economics: Methods, Models and Evidence
W. Davis Dechert

67. General Equilibrium Theory (Volumes I, II and III)
Gérard Debreu

68. Economic Growth: Theory and Evidence (Volumes I and II)
Gene M. Grossman

69. Long Wave Theory
Christopher Freeman

70. The Economics of Communication and Information
Donald M. Lamberton

71. The Foundations of Public Finance (Volumes I and II)
Peter Jackson

72. The Theory of the Firm
Mark Casson

73. The Economics of Uncertainty (Volumes I and II)
John D. Hey

74. The Economics of Global Warming
Tom Tietenberg

75. The Development of Ecological Economics
Robert Costanza, Charles Perrings and Cutler Cleveland

76. Economic Growth in the Long Run: A History of Empirical Evidence (Volumes I, II and III)
Bart van Ark

77. The Economics of Productivity (Volumes I and II)
Edward N. Wolff

78. The Economics of Population: Key Modern Writings (Volumes I and II)
Julian L. Simon

79. Political Business Cycles
Bruno S. Frey

80. Cultural Economics: The Arts, the Heritage and the Media Industries (Volumes I and II)
Ruth Towse

81. Law and Economics (Volumes I, II and III)
Richard A. Posner and Francesco Parisi

82. Independent Central Banks and Economic Performance
Sylvester Eijffinger

83. Culture, Social Norms and Economics (Volumes I and II)
Mark Casson

84. Industrial Policy and Competitive Advantage (Volumes I, II and III)
David B. Audretsch

85. The Economics of Housing (Volumes I and II)
John M. Quigley

86. Economic Demography (Volumes I and II)
T. Paul Schultz

87. Trade and the Environment: Economic, Legal and Policy Perspectives
Alan M. Rugman and John J. Kirton with Julie A. Soloway

88. The Economics of Fiscal Federalism and Local Finance
Wallace E. Oates

89. Price Theory and its Applications
Bernard Saffran and F.M. Scherer

90. Women in the Labor Market (Volumes I and II)
Marianne A. Ferber

91. Market Process Theories (Volumes I and II)
Peter Boettke and David Prychitko

92. Input–Output Analysis (Volumes I, II and III)
Heinz Kurz, Erik Dietzenbacher and Christian Lager

93. Mathematical Economics (Volumes I, II and III)
Graciela Chichilnisky

94. The Foundations of Regulatory Economics (Volumes I, II and III)
Robert B. Ekelund, Jr.

95. The Economics of Marketing
Martin Carter, Mark Casson and Vivek Suneja

96. Service Industries in the Global Economy (Volumes I and II)
J.R. Bryson and P.W. Daniels

97. Economic Justice (Volumes I and II)
Giorgio Brosio and Harold M. Hochman

98. Foreign Exchange Intervention: Objectives and Effectiveness
Sylvester C.W. Eijffinger

99. Economic Anthropology
Stephen Gudeman

100. Consumer Theory
Kelvin Lancaster

101. The Economics of Famine
Jean Drèze

102. Microeconomic Theories of Imperfect Competition
Jean J. Gabszewicz and Jacques-François Thisse

103. The Economics of Executive Compensation (Volumes I and II)
Kevin F. Hallock and Kevin J. Murphy

104. The Foundations of Long Wave Theory (Volumes I and II)
Francisco Louçã and Jan Reijnders

105. The Economics of Commodity Markets
David Greenaway and C.W. Morgan

106. Corporate Governance (Volumes I, II, III and IV)
Kevin Keasey, Steve Thompson and Mike Wright

107. Economic Welfare: Concepts and Measurement (Volumes I and II)
John Creedy

108. Economic Forecasting
Terence C. Mills

109. Recent Developments in Game Theory
Eric S. Maskin

110. The Economics of Increasing Returns
Geoffrey Heal

111. The Economics of Corruption and Illegal Markets (Volumes I, II and III)
Gianluca Fiorentini and Stefano Zamagni

112. The Economics of Price Discrimination
George Norman

113. The Economic Theory of Auctions (Volumes I and II)
Paul Klemperer

114. The Economics of Regional Policy
Harvey W. Armstrong and Jim Taylor

115. Economic Integration and International Trade
Carsten Kowalczyk

116. The Political Economy of Science, Technology and Innovation
Ben Martin and Paul Nightingale

117. The Economics of Science and Innovation (Volumes I and II)
Paula E. Stephan and David B. Audretsch

118. Innovation, Evolution of Industry and Economic Growth (Volumes I, II and III)
David B. Audretsch and Steven Klepper

119. The Economics of Energy (Volumes I and II)
Paul Stevens

120. Privatisation in Developing Countries (Volumes I and II)
Paul Cook and Colin Kirkpatrick

121. The Economics of Tourism (Volumes I and II)
Clem Tisdell

122. The Economics of Unemployment (Volumes I, II, III and IV)
P.N. Junankar

123. Privatisation and Corporate Performance
David Parker

124. Income Distribution (Volumes I, II and III)
Michael Sattinger

125. International Finance (Volumes I and II)
Robert Z. Aliber

126. Welfare Economics (Volumes I, II and III)
William J. Baumol and Charles A. Wilson

127. The Theory of Trade Policy Reform
Carsten Kowalczyk

Future titles will include:

The Economics of Defence
Keith Hartley and Todd Sandler

Economic Theory and the Welfare State
Nicholas Barr

The Economics of Property Rights
Svetozar Pejovich

The Economics of Politics
Dennis C. Mueller

The Economics of Sport
Andrew Zimbalist

The Political Economy of Development
Amitava Krishna Dutt

The Regulation and Supervision of Banks
Maximilian J.B. Hall

Public Procurement
Sue Arrowsmith and Keith Hartley

The Economics of Advertising
Kyle Bagwell

Forms of Capitalism: Comparative Institutional Analyses
Ugo Pagano and Ernesto Screpanti

The Economics of Business Strategy
John Kay

The Economics of Crime
Isaac Ehrlich

The Economics of Organisation and Bureaucracy
Peter Jackson

Realism and Economics: Studies in Ontology
Tony Lawson

The International Economic Institutions of the Twentieth Century
David Greenaway and Robert C. Hine

The Economics of Structural Change
Harald Hagemann, Michael Landesmann and Roberto Scazzieri

The Economics of the Mass Media
Glenn Withers

Alternative Theories of the Firm
Richard Langlois, Paul Robertson and Tony F. Yu

International Financial Integration
Sylvester C.W. Eijffinger

The Economics of Budget Deficits
Charles Rowley

The Economics of Intellectual Property
Ruth Towse and R.W. Holzhauer

Path Dependence
Paul David

The Economics of Contracts
Lars A. Stole

New Developments in Exchange Rate Economics
Lucio Sarno and Mark P. Taylor

The Political Economy of Monetary Union
Paul De Grauwe

New Institutional Economics
Claude Ménard

The Economics of Barter and Countertrade
Bernard Yeung and Rolf Mirus

Comparative Law and Economics
Gerrit de Geest and Roger Van Den Bergh

Cost-Benefit Analysis
Arnold C. Harberger and Glenn P. Jenkins

The Economics of Migration
Klaus F. Zimmermann and Thomas Bauer

The Economics of Networks
Michael Katz and Carl Shapiro

The Economics of Technology Transfer
Sanjaya Lall

Regulation, Economics and the Law
Anthony I. Ogus

The Economics of Labor Unions
Alison Booth

The Economics of Poverty and Inequality
Frank A. Cowell

The Economics of Business Strategy
John Kay

The Economics of Free Trade
Robert W. Staiger

Forecasting Financial Markets
Terence C. Mills